HANDBOOK OF SUSTAINABILITY-DRIVEN BUSINESS STRATEGIES IN PRACTICE

For Vesna and Cristina G., with love — Stefan
For Ferran and Sofia, with love — Cristina
For Christine, Joëlle, Valérie, François, and Peter, with thanks for great
collaborations over the years — Adam

Handbook of Sustainability-Driven Business Strategies in Practice

Edited by

Stefan Markovic

Associate Professor, Department of Marketing, Copenhagen Business School, Denmark

Cristina Sancha

Associate Professor, Department of Operations, Innovation and Data Sciences, ESADE Business School, Universitat Ramon Llull, Spain

Adam Lindgreen

Professor, Copenhagen Business School, Denmark and Extraordinary Professor, Gordon Institute of Business Science, University of Pretoria, South Africa

Edward Elgar
PUBLISHING

Cheltenham, UK • Northampton, MA, USA

Published by
Edward Elgar Publishing Limited
The Lypiatts
15 Lansdown Road
Cheltenham
Glos GL50 2JA
UK

Edward Elgar Publishing, Inc.
William Pratt House
9 Dewey Court
Northampton
Massachusetts 01060
USA

Paperback edition 2023

A catalogue record for this book
is available from the British Library

Library of Congress Control Number: 2021949003

This book is available electronically in the **Elgar**online
Business subject collection
http://dx.doi.org/10.4337/9781789908350

ISBN 978 1 78990 834 3 (cased)
ISBN 978 1 78990 835 0 (eBook)
ISBN 978 1 0353 1687 8 (paperback)

Printed and bound by CPI Group (UK) Ltd, Croydon, CR0 4YY

Contents

Figures

Tables

Appendices

About the editors

Stefan Markovic

Dr. Stefan Markovic holds a Ph.D. in Management Sciences (*cum laude*), a Master of Research in Management Sciences, and a Bachelor and Master in Business Administration from ESADE Business School, Universitat Ramon Llull, Spain. He is currently an Associate Professor in the Department of Marketing at Copenhagen Business School (CBS), Denmark. In addition, he is the Chair of the Marketing Ethics Research Cluster, a Co-Chair of the Advances in Branding Research Cluster, and a member of the Consumer Research Cluster at CBS.

Apart from his involvement at CBS, Markovic is also the National Representative of Denmark, the Chair of the Special Interest Group on Branding, and an Executive Committee Member at the European Marketing Academy (EMAC). Moreover, he is Co-Editor-in-Chief of *Business Ethics, the Environment & Responsibility* (formerly, *Business Ethics: A European Review*) and Associate Editor for Interdisciplinary Research with *Industrial Marketing Management*. Markovic is a member of the Editorial Advisory Boards of *European Business Review* and *Industrial Marketing Management*, as well as an ad hoc reviewer for many top-tier international academic journals (e.g., *Journal of Business Ethics*, *Journal of Business Research*, *IEEE Transactions on Engineering Management*, *Technovation*) and renowned international academic conferences (e.g., European Marketing Academy Conference, American Marketing Association Conference).

Markovic's research addresses various intersections among brand management, marketing, innovation, business ethics, corporate social responsibility, and sustainability. He has published in well-established international academic journals, including *Journal of Business Ethics*, *Journal of Business Research*, *Journal of Brand Management*, *Industrial Marketing Management*, *Technological Forecasting and Social Change*, and *IEEE Transactions on Engineering Management*. With his doctoral thesis, entitled "21st-Century Brands: An Innovation Opportunity and an Ethical Challenge," Markovic won third prize in the 2017 International Doctoral Thesis Competition held by the European Doctoral Association in Management and Business Administration (EDAMBA).

Cristina Sancha

Dr. Cristina Sancha holds a Ph.D. in Management Sciences (*cum laude*), a Master of Research in Management Sciences, and a Bachelor and Master in Business Administration from ESADE Business School, Universitat Ramon Llull, Spain. She also holds a Master in Teaching Mathematics from Universitat Politècnica de Catalunya (UPC), Spain. During her Ph.D. studies, she visited Hong Kong Polytechnic University.

Sancha has been a lecturer at Universitat Pompeu Fabra (2015), a Rosalind Franklin Fellow at Groningen University (2016), and a lecturer and researcher at Grupo Planeta Formación y

Universidades (2016–2019), where she also held the positions of Academic Director of the Operations and Systems Management Area and Vice-Dean of Faculty, Research and Quality. She has been a visiting scholar at Universidad de las Américas (2018). Since 2019, she has been a lecturer in the Department of Operations, Innovation and Data Sciences at ESADE Business School, and she serves as the Academic Director of the Master of Science in Global Strategic Management.

Sancha's research interests center around the concepts of sustainable operations and supply chain management. In her doctoral dissertation, she investigated the mechanisms that help extend sustainability upstream in supply chains, their antecedents, and performance outcomes. Her research has been published in international academic journals, including *Industrial Marketing Management, Journal of Cleaner Production, Supply Chain Management: An International Journal, International Journal of Production Economics, Journal of Purchasing & Supply Management*, and *International Journal of Production Research*. She frequently attends and presents her work at the European Operations Management Association, Academy of Management, and Productions and Management Society. She is a member of BuNeD and an affiliated member of MERC (Copenhagen Business School).

Adam Lindgreen

After studies in chemistry (Copenhagen University), engineering (the Engineering Academy of Denmark), and physics (Copenhagen University), Professor Adam Lindgreen completed an MSc in food science and technology at the Technical University of Denmark. He also finished an MBA at the University of Leicester. He received his Ph.D. in marketing from Cranfield University. His first appointments were with the Catholic University of Louvain (2000–2001) and Eindhoven University of Technology (2002–2007). Subsequently, he served as Professor of Marketing at Hull University's Business School (2007–2010); University of Birmingham's Business School (2010), where he also was the research director in the Department of Marketing; and University of Cardiff's Business School (2011–2016). Under his leadership, the Department of Marketing and Strategy at Cardiff Business School ranked first among all marketing departments in Australia, Canada, New Zealand, the United Kingdom, and the United States, based on the hg indices of senior faculty. Since 2016, Lindgreen has been Professor of Marketing at Copenhagen Business School, where he also heads the Department of Marketing. Since 2018, he also has been Extraordinary Professor with University of Pretoria's Gordon Institute of Business Science.

As a Visiting Professor, Lindgreen has worked with various institutions including Georgia State University, HEC Paris, and Melbourne University. His publications have appeared in *Business Horizons, California Management Review, Entrepreneurship and Regional Development, Industrial Marketing Management, International Journal of Management Reviews, Journal of Advertising, Journal of Business Ethics, European Journal of Marketing, Journal of Business and Industrial Marketing, Journal of Marketing Management, Journal of the Academy of Marketing Science, Journal of Product Innovation Management, Journal of World Business, Organization Studies, Psychology & Marketing*, and *Supply Chain Management: An International Journal*, among others. His scores of books in business and economics include *A Stakeholder Approach to Corporate Social Responsibility* (with Kotler, Vanhamme, and Maon), *Managing Market Relationships, Memorable Customer Experiences* (with Vanhamme and Beverland), *Not All Claps and Cheers* (with Maon, Vanhamme, Angell, and Memery), *Public Value* (with Koenig-Lewis, Kitchener, Brewer, Moore, and Meynhardt), and *Sustainable Value Chain Management* (with Maon, Vanhamme, and Sen).

The recipient of the "Outstanding Article 2005" award from *Industrial Marketing Management* and the runner-up for the same award in 2016, he serves on the board of several scientific journals; he is Co-Editor-in-Chief of *Industrial Marketing Management*. His research interests include business and industrial marketing management, corporate social responsibility, and sustainability. He has received the Dean's Award for Excellence in Executive Teaching. Furthermore, he has served as an examiner (for dissertations, modules, and programs) at a wide variety of institutions around the world. Lindgreen is a member of the International Scientific Advisory Panel of the New Zealand Food Safety Science and Research Centre (a partnership among government, industry organizations, and research institutions), as well as of the Chartered Association of Business Schools' Academic Journal Guide (AJG) Scientific Committee in the field of marketing.

Beyond these academic contributions to marketing, Lindgreen has discovered and excavated settlements from the Stone Age in Denmark, including the only major kitchen midden – Sparregård – in the south-east of Denmark; because of its importance, the kitchen midden was later excavated by the National Museum and then protected as a historical monument for future generations. He is also an avid genealogist, having traced his family back to 1390 and published widely including eight books and numerous articles in scientific journals (*Personalhistorisk Tidsskrift*, *The Genealogist*, and *Slægt & Data*) related to methodological issues in genealogy, accounts of population development, and particular family lineages.

About the contributors

Pilar Acosta

Pilar Acosta is *maître de conférences* at the Management, Innovation and Entrepreneurship Department at École Polytechnique, France, and adjunct researcher at the School of Business and Economic Sciences at Universidad Icesi, in Cali, Colombia. She earned her Ph.D. at ESCP Europe and Université Paris 1-Panthéon Sorbonne. Her work has been published in international journals such as *Organization Studies* and *Journal of Business Ethics*, in book chapters, and in proceedings of international conferences. Her research focuses on the evolution of corporate social responsibility and sustainability-related practices in developing countries.

Armando Agulini

Armando Agulini is a junior researcher in the field of humanistic management studies, preparing to start a Ph.D. Since earning a Master's in Digital Marketing and Communications from LUMSA University, he has collaborated with various researchers to study sustainable development, organizational behavior in new business paradigms, flourishing and teal organizations, and corporate social responsibility.

Michael Antioco

Michael Antioco is Professor of Marketing at Edhec Business School, where he also is Dean. He holds a Ph.D. in Marketing & Innovation Studies from Eindhoven University of Technology. The broad area of his quantitative research is customer understanding, with a particular focus on formulating practical recommendations for decision-making, product innovation, and marketing communications. He mainly carries out his research in the skincare and luxury sectors. Professor Antioco's publications have appeared in *Journal of the Academy of Marketing Science*, *International Journal of Research in Marketing*, *Decision Support Systems*, and *Journal of Product Innovation Management*, among others.

Melek Akin Ateş

Melek Akın Ateş received her doctoral degree in Purchasing and Supply Management from Rotterdam School of Management, Erasmus University (the Netherlands) in 2014. She is currently an Assistant Professor at Sabanci Business School, Sabanci University (Turkey). Her main research areas are strategic purchasing, buyer–supplier relationships, sustainable supply chain management, and supplier involvement in innovation generation. She was awarded the Best Student Paper Prize at the Decision Sciences Conference in 2011 and Chris Voss Highly Commended Award at the EurOMA/P&OM World Conference in 2012, and she was a finalist for the Chan Hahn Best Paper Award at the Academy of Management Conference in 2014. She received the *JPSM* Best Reviewer Award in 2017. Her work has appeared in *Journal of Purchasing & Supply Management, International Journal of Operations and Production Management*, and *International Journal of Production Research.*

Nüfer Yasin Ateş

Nüfer Yasin Ateş is Assistant Professor of Strategy and Organization at Sabanci Business School, Sabanci University, Turkey. He received his Ph.D. from the Erasmus Research Institute of Management, Erasmus University Rotterdam (the Netherlands). His research revolves around behavioral strategy topics at the intersection of strategic management and organizational psychology, including organizational change, corporate entrepreneurship, and strategy processes, with a special focus on top and middle managers. He actively advances quantitative research methods. His research has appeared in *Strategic Management Journal, Journal of Management*, and *Strategic Organization*.

Selena Aureli

Selena Aureli is Associate Professor of Financial Reporting and Analysis at Bologna University (Italy). Her research interests are in financial and sustainability reporting, managerial accounting, networks, and tourism. Her latest article, pertaining to the transposition of the EU non-financial directive, was published in *Journal of Accounting, Economics, and Law: A Convivium*. She teaches accounting to graduate and undergraduate students and has extensive experience in collaborative research, in conjunction with other universities and industry actors. She was formerly enrolled at the University of Urbino and has had visiting appointments at Tampere University in Finland, Higher School of Economics of Moscow, and Technological University Dublin in Ireland.

David M. Boje

David M. Boje is what Foucault calls a "specific intellectual," an international scholar confronting and deconstructing the regimes of truth with his own storytelling paradigm. His research focuses on ethics, socially responsible capitalism, and sustainability, using a storytelling science perspective. His most recent books are *True Storytelling* (with Larsen and Bruun) and *Doing Conversational Storytelling Interviewing for Your Dissertation* (with Rosile). He created the field of "antenarrative" research, which analyzes antecedents to Western narratives and indigenous living stories. In addition to his books, Boje has published more than 120 articles in leading journals such as *Administrative Science Quarterly, Academy of Management Journal, Academy of Management Review, Organization Studies, Academy of Management Annals, Management Science, Management International Review, Journal of Business Ethics*, and *Human Relations*.

Federico Caniato

Federico Caniato is Full Professor in the School of Management of Politecnico di Milano and Director of the Master in Supply Chain and Purchasing Management. His research interests are in the fields of supply chain and purchasing management, and in recent years he has focused on sustainability and supply chain finance. He has coordinated and participated in international research projects such as the International Manufacturing Strategy Survey and International Purchasing Survey. His publications appear in various operations and supply chain management journals.

Rosalía Cascón-Pereira

Rosalía Cascón-Pereira is Senior Lecturer of HRM and OB at University Rovira I Virgili, in Tarragona (Spain). She holds a B.Sc. in Business Administration from URV (2000), a B.Sc. in Psychology from University of Barcelona (2006), a MBS in human resource management from University of Limerick (2003), a Master's in Social Cognitive Therapy from University of Barcelona (2015), and a Ph.D. in Economics and Business at URV (2006). Her research focuses on social identity in its multiple manifestations: professional, cultural, chronically ill, ethical consumer, and expatriate. She also researches emotions, meanings, and healthcare management. Her articles have been published in *British Journal of Management*, *Journal of Consumer Culture*, *Journal of Pain*, *Business Research Quarterly*, *Social Science and Medicine*, *Thinking Skills and Creativity*, *Gaceta Sanitaria*, *Journal of Vocational Education and Training*, and *Journal of Geography in Higher Education*, among others.

Siriwan Chaisurayakarn

Siriwan Chaisurayakarn is a lecturer in the Faculty of Management Sciences, Kasetsart University, Sriracha Campus. She teaches logistics in the Bachelor of Business Administration (BBA) Logistics Management Program and was Program Leader from 2017–2019. She currently sits on the Program's Curriculum and Faculty's BBA Special Programs Committees. She received her doctoral degree from Hull University in 2015; her thesis, exploring green and logistics service quality of Thai logistics service providers, received the Chartered Institute of Logistics & Transport's James Cooper Memorial Cup PhD Award. Her research interests include customer service, logistics performance, and sustainable logistics; her article on improving layout design and process flows to reduce waste in business processes was selected by the 21st Symposium on TQM-Best Practices in Thailand as a TQM-progressive learner case. She reviews for several journals including *Journal of IEEE Transactions on Engineering Management* and *Songklanakarin Journal of Science and Technology*.

David Coldwell

David Coldwell (B.Sc. [Soc] London, B.A. [Economics], M.A., D. Litt et Phil, FCIPD, FRSA) is Professor of Management and Human Resources Management at the School of Business Sciences, University of the Witwatersrand, Johannesburg. He worked as Professor of Management at the University of Natal, Head of School of Management at the University of KwaZulu-Natal, and Visiting Professor at the Open University in England. He has also worked as a researcher for the CSIR (Council for Scientific and Industrial Research) and research consultant for the Chamber of Mines Research Organization. He is an accredited researcher at the National Research Foundation and contributes to books and encyclopedias, as well as national and international peer-reviewed journals such as *Journal of Business Ethics*, *Journal for the Theory of Social Behavior*, and *Entropy*. He is Associate Editor (Middle East & Africa) for *Personnel Review* and Director of the Strategic Foresight Research Group, an international collaborative research group of Witwatersrand University.

Susana Costa e Silva

Susana Costa e Silva is Associate Professor at Universidade Católica Portuguesa, where she is also a researcher. She is a Visiting Professor at University of Saint Joseph (Macao/China). She holds a Ph.D. in Marketing from the University College of Dublin (Ireland). Her research interests include international marketing, internationalization processes, social and cause-related marketing, and digital consumer behavior. Her contributions have been published in *International Marketing Review, International Business Review, European Journal of International Management, Journal of Retailing and Consumer Services*, and *Journal of Global Marketing*, among other. She also has authored several international books and book chapters. She is the national representative of Portugal in the EMAC (European Marketing Academy Conference) and an active member of EIBA (European International Business Academy).

Mara Del Baldo

Mara Del Baldo is Associate Professor of Business Administration at the University of Urbino (Italy), Department of Economics, Society and Politics. She is a member of the European Council for Small Business, the Centre for Social and Environmental Accounting Research, the SPES Institute (Leuven), the European Business Ethics Network Italia, and the academic advisory committee in the Global Corporate Governance Institute. She serves as a board member and a reviewer for several scientific journals. Her main research interests include entrepreneurship and small businesses management; corporate social responsibility, sustainability and entrepreneurial business ethics; social and environmental accounting and accountability; integrated reporting and accounting; and gender. She publishes in various Italian and foreign journals, as well as national and international conferences proceedings and books. She offers lectures and invited seminars for many Italian and foreign universities.

Rasmus Downes-Rasmussen

Rasmus Downes-Rasmussen is currently executive chef in Comwell's flagship Hotel Copenhagen Portside and has been one of the driving forces and implementers of its sustainability strategy, as part of Comwell's sustainability steering group and chairperson of its head chefs. He is an award-winning chef who has been working in Food & Beverage management for over 20 years. Among other awards, he was crowned 2010 world champion chef by the International Association of Conference Centres. He has completed management courses at Copenhagen Business School, Copenhagen Hospitality College, and Cornell University and is a regular guest lecturer at Roskilde University and Copenhagen Hospitality College. He is associated with a number of industry networks, including a hotel partnership against food waste, Organic Denmark, and Chaîne des Rôtisseurs.

Andreas Dutzi

Andreas Dutzi is Professor for Business Administration, Accounting and Corporate Governance at the University of Siegen. He previously was Professor for Accounting and Management of Family Firms at Witten Institute of Family Business (Witten/Herdecke University). Dutzi studied business administration at the University of Mannheim and Trinity College Dublin (Ireland). He earned a doctorate (Dr. rer.pol.) at Johann Wolfgang Goethe-University Frankfurt am Main and worked at the Central Audit Department at Schitag Ernst & Young, Stuttgart. Beyond his academic efforts, he supports entrepreneurs and distressed firms. Dutzi is member of several academic associations, including the European Accounting Association, European Academy of Management, Schmalenbach Society for the Advancement of Research in Business Economics and Business Practice, and International Association for Accounting Education & Research. He is ad hoc reviewer for various academic journals and conferences.

David B. Grant

David B. Grant is Dean of Research and Societal Impact and Professor of Supply Chain Management & Social Responsibility, Hanken School of Economics, Helsinki, and Bua Luang ASEAN Chair Professor, Thammasat University, Bangkok. He received his Ph.D. from Edinburgh University in 2003; his thesis, investigating customer service, satisfaction, and quality in UK food processing logistics, received the Chartered Institute of Logistics & Transport's James Cooper Memorial Cup PhD Award. His research interests include customer service, satisfaction, and quality; retail logistics; reverse and sustainable logistics; and humanitarian and societal logistics. He has more than 250 publications, and his co-authored books *Sustainable Logistics and Supply Chain Management* and *Fashion Logistics* are in their second editions. He was ranked fifth in Economics, Business and Management and first in Industrial Economics and Logistics in a 2019 academic study that identified the top ten professors in Finland in terms of research impact and productivity.

Ilia Gugenishvili

Ilia Gugenishvili holds an M.Sc. degree from the University of Stavanger (Norway) and currently is a doctoral candidate in international marketing at the Åbo Akademi University, Turku (Finland). His research interests include mobile applications, engagement, consumer behavior, culture, and cross-cultural psychology. In particular, he is interested in how social norms can be used to support charities. He has published conference proceedings with the Association of Marketing Theory and Practice and International Telecommunications Society, as well as an article in *International Journal of E-Services and Mobile Applications*.

Sreyaa Guha

Sreyaa Guha is a Ph.D. candidate and Adjunct Professor at IE Business School, IE University (Spain). She received her undergraduate degree in Electrical Engineering from WBUT and MBA from University of Calcutta (India). She completed a master's degree in Research in Management Science from IE University in 2017. She is a core Member of the Risk, Uncertainty and Decisions Group at IE Business School and was a visiting scholar at McDonough School of Business, Georgetown University (USA). She teaches data analytics for decision-making at graduate and post-graduate levels, and her research focuses on decision-making under uncertainty and social interactions. She designs behavioral experiments and uses multivariate and machine learning-based analyses.

David Harness

David Harness is Senior Lecturer in Marketing at University of Hull's Business School. He has more than 24 years' experience in higher education teaching, academic management, and leadership, including heading a subject group and serving as post-graduate director, in which role he achieved substantial growth in student numbers. He has delivered practitioner-oriented lessons to national and global organizations pertaining to customer care, relationship management, end-stage customer management, and corporate social responsibility.

Roberto Hernandez-Chea

Roberto Hernandez-Chea concluded his doctoral degree in Management and Organization at the Department of Food and Resource Economics, University of Copenhagen (Denmark), in 2017. His postdoctoral research at the International Institute for Industrial Environmental Economics, Lund University (Sweden) pertained to "Sustainable Business Models and Intellectual Property," as part of the Intellectual Property Strategies and Sustainable Business Models for Sustainability Transitions research project. He has an interdisciplinary research background in the fields of sustainable business, sustainability, innovation management, social entrepreneurship, and intellectual property. He works as an environmental specialist to support and accelerate the sustainability agenda in the private sector.

Ana Beatriz Hernández-Lara

Ana Beatriz Hernández-Lara is an Associate Professor and Director of the Department of Business Management at Rovira i Virgili University (Spain). She obtained her Ph.D. from Pablo de Olavide University (Spain) in 2007 by studying the influence of corporate governance on innovation. Her research lines relate to corporate governance, innovation, tourism, and e-learning. She currently participates in research groups and projects in the field of social and organizational studies. Her research has been published in journals such as *Computers in Human Behavior*, *Behaviour and Information Technology*, *Management Decision*, and *Current Issues in Tourism*.

Oriol Iglesias

Oriol Iglesias is an Associate Professor and Head of the Marketing Department at ESADE Business School. Previously he was Director of the ESADE Brand Institute and Chair of the Research Group on Brand Management. He is a member of the Scientific Committee of the Global Brand Conference and the Scientific Committee of the Special Interest Group on Brand, Identity, and Corporate Reputation of the Academy of Marketing. He is a member of the editorial board of *Journal of Brand Management* and editorial review board of *Journal of Product & Brand Management*. He has been a member of the Executive Committee of the

European Marketing Academy. He has published articles in *California Management Review*, *Journal of Business Ethics*, *Industrial Marketing Management*, *Journal of Business Research*, and *European Journal of Marketing*. He also is a member of the Medinge Group, an international think tank focused on conscientious brands.

Nicholas Ind

Nicholas Ind is Professor at Kristiania University College, Oslo, and Visiting Professor at ESADE Business School and Edinburgh Napier University. He has a Ph.D. in Media Philosophy (*magna cum laude*) from the European Graduate School (Switzerland). He is a member of the advisory board for *Corporate Reputation Review*, editorial board of *Journal of Brand Management*, and editorial review board of *Journal of Product & Brand Management*. The author of 13 books, published in nine languages, he also has published articles in *Journal of Brand Management*, *California Management Review*, *Business Horizons*, *European Business Review*, and *Industrial Marketing Management*. He is a founding member of the Medinge Group, an international think tank focused on conscientious brands.

Thomas E. Johnsen

Thomas E. Johnsen (M.Sc., Ph.D.) is Professor of Purchasing and Supply Management at Audencia Business School (France) and Visiting Professor at Copenhagen Business School (Denmark). He previously was Gianluca Spina Professor of Supply Chain Management at Politecnico di Milano (Italy) and has held positions at the University of Bath (UK), Jönköping International Business School (Sweden), and University of Southern Denmark. He is Associate Editor of the *Journal of Purchasing & Supply Management*. His book (with Howard and Miemczyk) *Purchasing and Supply Chain Management: A Sustainability Perspective* is now in its second edition.

Slobodan Kacanski

Slobodan Kacanski obtained his doctoral degree in Social Sciences from Roskilde University (Denmark) in 2017. He is currently Associate Professor in Accounting at Roskilde University and a member of the Melbourne-based Consortium of Experts in Social Network Analysis. In addition, he is a member of the European Accounting Association and the Danish Audit Research Network. In developing his research profile, his focus has been on understanding social and organizational aspects of accounting; his interest in social networks and accounting contributes to accounting literature by revealing complex, dynamic relationships among accounting, auditing, and corporate governance. He has published articles in renowned international journals, including *Corporate Governance* and *European Accounting Review*.

Nikolina Koporcic

Nikolina Koporcic earned her Ph.D. in Economics and Business Administration in 2017, at Åbo Akademi University in Turku (Finland). She is currently senior researcher at Laurea University of Applied Sciences (Finland). Prior to that, she served as an Assistant Professor of Marketing at Nottingham University Business School (UK). Her research pertains to corporate branding, entrepreneurship, business-to-business relationships, and networks. In particular, she is studying the importance of Interactive Network Branding for small firms in business markets. In addition to academic articles published in *Industrial Marketing Management*, *Journal of Business and Industrial Marketing*, *IMP Journal*, and *Econviews*, Koporcic has published two books.

Polina Landgraf

Polina Landgraf is a doctoral candidate in Marketing at IE Business School, IE University (Spain). As a behavioral scientist, she studies individual behaviors and uses inventive combinations of experiments and unique, large-scale field data sets to generate insights about human interactions with technology (use of algorithms, data privacy, crowdfunding) and consumption under macro-level pressures (terrorist attacks, viral pandemics, political elections). She has presented her work at international conferences, including Association for Consumer Research, INFORMS, and EMAC, and her work has been published in renowned academic journals, including *Industrial Marketing Management*. She also holds a degree of Candidate of Economic Science from St. Petersburg State University (Russia), and she has been a visiting scholar at multiple internationally acclaimed institutions.

Verónica León-Bravo

Verónica León-Bravo obtained her Ph.D. from the Department of Management, Economics and Industrial Engineering in Politecnico di Milano. She is currently Assistant Professor at the School of Management in Politecnico di Milano. She holds an M.Sc. from Ecole des Mines de Nantes (France) in Management of Logistics and Production Systems, as well as a B.Sc. from Universidad San Francisco de Quito (Ecuador) in Industrial Engineering. Her research focuses on sustainability in supply chains, including the food industry sector. Her research has been published in several supply chain management and sustainability journals.

Joan Llonch Andreu

Joan Llonch Andreu is Associate Professor of Marketing in the Business Department of the Autonomous University of Barcelona (Spain). He holds a Ph.D. in Economics and Business Administration and an MBA from IMD in Lausanne (Switzerland). He is the author of various books, chapters, and papers, published in both national and international academic journals, such as *European Management Journal*, *International Journal of Market Research*, *Higher Education*, *International Journal of Contemporary Hospitality Management*, *Journal of Fashion Marketing and Management*, *Transformations in Business & Economics*, *Spanish Journal of Marketing*, and *International Journal of Business Environment*. His research interests are in strategic marketing, international marketing, marketing communications, and marketing on the Internet. He is a member of the editorial review board of *Journal of Product & Brand Management* and serves as an ad hoc reviewer for different academic journals.

Rosa Lombardi

Rosa Lombardi is Associate Professor in Business Administration & Business Plan at Sapienza University of Rome (Italy). She earned her Ph.D. in Business Administration at University of Cassino and Southern Lazio. Her research interests and scientific publications pertain to financial and non-financial information, sustainability accounting, intellectual capital, management accounting, smart technologies, corruption prevention, and entrepreneurial universities. She serves as Editor-in-Chief for *International Journal of Digital Culture & Electronic Tourism*, as well as an associate/guest editor, editorial board member, and reviewer for various international journals (e.g., *Meditari Accountancy Research*, *Management Decision*, *Business Strategy & Environment*, *CSR&EM*, *International Journal of Applied Decision Sciences*). She is board member of the Società Italiana di Ragioneria e di Economia Aziendale and serves as the research group coordinator for "Smart Technologies, Digitalization & Intellectual Capital." She has won several awards (e.g., EMERALD/EMRBI Award for Emerging Researchers; Best Paper Award SOItmC&RTU).

Pilar López Belbeze

Pilar López Belbeze is Associate Professor of Marketing in the Business Department of the Autonomous University of Barcelona (Spain). Her main research focus involves consumer behavior, neuromarketing research, leisure, and sustainable consumption. Her articles have appeared in *European Marketing Journal*, *European Management Journal*, *Journal of Product & Brand Management*, and *International Journal of Contemporary Hospitality Management*, among others. She is researcher in the European Research Project H2020 (Invent Culture). A member of the Executive Committee of the Spanish Association of Academic and Professional Marketing (AEMARK), she also served as the Executive Committee Organizer of the XXX International Congress of AEMARK 2018. She provides reviews for different academic conferences and journals.

Joana César Machado

Joana César Machado is an Assistant Professor at Católica Porto Business School, Universidade Católica Portuguesa, as well as Visiting Professor at the Faculty of Engineering of the University of Porto and Burgundy School of Business, Dijon. She holds a Ph.D. in Marketing from ISCTE, University Institute of Lisbon. Her research interests include brand identity, brand gender, social media branding, and consumer behavior. She is a member of CEGE, the research center of Católica Porto Business School, and Chair of the scientific committee of the Academy of Marketing's Brand, Corporate Identity and Reputation Special Interest Group. She is a member of the editorial board of *Journal of Product & Brand Management*. Her previous work has been published in several international journals, and she is the co-author of several books, including *O Livro da Marca* (*The Brand Book*), on branding in Portugal.

Tahereh Maghsoudi

Tahereh Maghsoudi is a doctoral student in Business and Management in Universitat Rovira i Virgili. She won a Marie Skłodowska-Curie grant from the European Union's Horizon 2020 research and innovation program. Maghsoudi's research spans interactions among healthcare, human resource management, sustainability, and psychological capital. She has published several articles in international academic journals, such as *Sustainability Journal, Labour & Industry: A Journal of the Social and Economic Relations of Work, International Journal of Business Innovation and Research, International Journal of Human Resource Development and Management*, and *International Journal of Entrepreneurial Venturing.*

Maral Mahdad

Maral Mahdad is a senior researcher and lecturer of innovation and entrepreneurship at Wageningen University and Research (WUR) in the Department of Business Management and Organization (BMO). She formerly was a postdoctoral fellow of Innovation Management in the Department of Food and Resource Economics, University of Copenhagen. Her research activities focus on innovation management, open innovation, university–industry collaborations, and innovation in entrepreneurial ecosystems. She has published several peer-reviewed articles on these topics in renowned journals such as *Journal of Business Research, Industry and Innovation*, and *International Journal of Innovation Sciences*. She is on the academic board of the World Open Innovation Conference and acts as an assistant program chair.

François Maon

François Maon is Professor at IESEG School of Management. He received his Ph.D. from the Catholic University of Louvain. He has published in *California Management Review, International Journal of Management Review, Organization Studies*, and *Journal of Business Ethics*, among others.

Toloue Miandar

Toloue Miandar is Assistant Professor at the Department of Management of University of Bologna. Prior to this position she held two postdoctoral research fellow positions in the Department of Economics and Management of University of Padova and at the Politecnico di Milano School of Management. She received a doctoral degree in Economic Sociology and Labour Studies from University of Milan in 2017. Her research interests involve corporate social responsibility, corporate sustainability, supply chain sustainability, and organizational behavior. She has published in international academic journals such as *Journal of Business Ethics.*

Milena Micevski

Milena Micevski is an Associate Professor at the Department of Marketing at Copenhagen Business School (CBS), Denmark. Micevski's research lies within the areas of business-to-business sales management, retail and service frontline employee management, the role of stereotyping, identification, ethics and emotions in consumer decision-making processes. She also conducts research related to corporate responsibility and sustainability. Micevski's work has appeared in internationally renowned journals, such as *Journal of Business Ethics, Journal of International Marketing, Journal of Travel Research, Industrial*

Marketing Management, International Marketing Review, and *Journal of Business Research.* She serves as an associate editor for *Business Ethics, the Environment & Responsibility.*

Andrew Ngawenja Mzembe

Andrew Ngawenja Mzembe is a Senior Lecturer in Sustainable Business at the Academy of Hotel and Facility Management, Breda University of Applied Sciences (the Netherlands). He is also a Senior Research Associate at the University of Johannesburg's School of Tourism and Hospitality in South Africa. Some of his research work has appeared in international journals and edited books.

Giorgia Nigri

Giorgia Nigri is a practitioner and active researcher in the field of economics. She has worked for Italy's export credit agency since 2013 and is a certified benefit impact manager. She participates with various alumni associations as a business consultant and collaborates with researchers in several other disciplines through academic networks. Nigri completed her Ph.D. at LUMSA University, her MBA at the Luiss Guido Carli Business School, and her undergraduate studies at John Cabot University and University of Wales. Her research interests lie in the areas of sustainability, sustainable development, and corporate social responsibility, with particular attention to new, hybrid forms of business such as benefit corporations and social purpose companies.

Inês Padilha Campelos

Inês Padilha Campelos is a junior brand manager at Sogrape Vinhos, S.A., a Portuguese company operating in the wine industry. She holds a B.Sc. in Marketing from Instituto Superior de Contabilidade e Administração do Porto and an MsC in management from Católica Porto Business School, Universidade Católica Portuguesa. Her research interests include cause-related marketing, brand management, and consumer behavior in business-to-consumer markets.

Yuqian Qiu

Yuqian Qiu is a doctoral candidate in Management Sciences at ESADE Business School (Spain). She holds a Master's of Research degree from ESADE Business School and a Master's of Science degree from University of Manchester (UK). She has been a visiting scholar at Copenhagen Business School (Denmark). Qiu's work has appeared in *Industrial Marketing Management,* and she is an ad hoc reviewer for international journals including *Journal of Business Ethics, Journal of Business Research,* and *Business Ethics: A European Review.* Before pursuing a career in academia, she gained research and management experience in the energy sector in China, responsible for conducting preliminary research into investment feasibility and human resources management. Her research interests cover areas such as brand management, corporate social responsibility, co-creation, and innovation.

Mohammad B. Rana

Mohammad B. Rana is Associate Professor of International Business and Strategy at Aalborg University Business School (Denmark). He holds a Ph.D. in International Business from Aalborg University, an M.Sc. from the University of Stirling (UK), and an MBA from University of Rajshahi, Bangladesh. His research focuses on the international management strategies of multinational corporations in emerging markets, using an institutionalist perspective. His findings have contributed insights into multinationals' strategies related to internationalization, capabilities, legitimation, and sustainable strategic management; business models and their impacts on and relationships with global value chains, climate change, the circular economy, and capability development; and firms' innovation, technology adoption, and digital strategies and sustainable adaptation. He has received research grants from the Danish International Development Agency and European Commission. He has published in internationally acclaimed books and journals, including *Global Strategy Journal*, *International Business Review*, *Journal of International Management*, *Technovation*, and *Advances in International Management*.

Miguel Saiz García

Miguel Saiz García is an industrial engineer from Tecnun, University of Navarra. He also is a lecturer at ESADE, EAE Business School, and Tecnocampus Mataró. He holds an MBA from ESADE Business School and is certified as a Project Management Professional by the Project Management Institute. His extensive experience in R&D project management comes from working for Grupo Antolin, Bosch, and Lear Corporation, for clients such as VW, Seat, Audi, Ford, Chrysler, Honda, and GM. He is the founder of weOptimize (project management consulting and Microsoft Partner) and a member of the Internet Computing Systems Optimization research group at Universitat Oberta de Catalunya, where he also is a doctoral candidate. In addition to speaking at prestigious international conferences, he has published in *International Transactions in Operational Research*.

Marija Sarafinovska

Marija Sarafinovska is currently a doctoral fellow in the Department of Marketing in Copenhagen Business School (Denmark). She has obtained an M.Sc. degree in Accounting, Strategy, and Control from Copenhagen Business School as well. She has worked for renowned companies such as Novo Nordisk and Reckitt Benckiser Nordic, where she performed various roles including reporting, forecasting, performing analyses, and communicating about pre-launches and product innovations. Her work has been published in *Industrial Marketing Management*. Her research interests include brand management, innovation, corporate social responsibility (CSR), and ethics, with a focus on the relationships of innovation and CSR and of co-creation and CSR. She teaches brand management and supervises theses on such topics.

Julian Schröter

Julian Schröter holds a Ph.D. and a master's degree from the University of Siegen. His research area is unstructured data analysis with neural networks. He has worked as an IT consultant and data analyst.

Sophia Schwoy

Sophia Schwoy holds a master's degree in Accounting, Auditing and Taxation and is currently a doctoral candidate at the chair of Business Administration, Accounting and Corporate Governance at the University of Siegen. Her research interest lies in the area of corporate social responsibility (CSR) and sustainability, and her doctoral thesis examines individual-level drivers for CSR performance and greenwashing. Schwoy is a member of the European Academy of Management and ad hoc reviewer for several conferences. Prior to her academic career, she worked in the Audit Department of PricewaterhouseCoopers GmbH, with a special focus on financial institutions.

Natalia Semenova

Natalia Semenova is Associate Professor of Accounting at the School of Business and Economics, Linnaeus University (Sweden). She previously held positions at Umeå University (Sweden). Semenova received her Dr.Sc. degree in Accounting from Åbo Akademi University (Finland). Her research interests are sustainability accounting, performance measurement, corporate valuation, active ownership, and stakeholder governance, and her research into companies and industries features both quantitative and qualitative empirical approaches. Her research has been published in *Journal of Applied Accounting Research*, *Journal of Business Ethics*, *Nordic Journal of Business*, and *Sustainable Development*. Her research has been awarded by the Sustainable Investment Forum in Finland.

Sarah Shaw

Sarah Shaw is a Senior Lecturer, Researcher, and Programme Director in Logistics and Supply Chain Management at Hull University Business School (UK). Her research interests include green/sustainable logistics, closed-loop supply chains, performance measurement/reporting, and agrisupply chains and food security. Her business experience includes a variety of senior supply chain management roles: operations, transport, reverse logistics, and customer service management. She has been instrumental in leading changes and transformational projects across supply chain. She won Leader of the Year, the UK Women in Logistics Awards 2017, for her work with the Chartered Institute of Logistics & Transport to encourage young people to work in the logistics sector. She leads various multidisciplinary research projects and has published in a variety of scientific journals.

Alex Nikolai Shenin

Alex Nikolai Shenin is Portfolio and Innovation Lead at Unilever in Finland. He obtained a master's in Economics, specializing in supply chain management and social responsibility, from Hanken School of Economics, Helsinki, in 2015. His master's thesis investigated environmental management in the Finnish logistics sector and was presented at the Chartered Institute of Logistics & Transport's 20th Annual Logistics Research Network (LRN) Conference in 2015 at the University of Derby.

Kristian J. Sund

Kristian J. Sund is Professor of Strategic Management at Roskilde University (Denmark). His research focuses on business model innovation, uncertainty, and management education and has recently appeared in outlets such as *MIT Sloan Management Review*, *Technological Forecasting and Social Changes*, and *Studies in Higher Education*. He is co-editor of the *New Horizons in Managerial and Organizational Cognition* book series. Sund holds a doctorate in Management and Licentiate (M.Sc.) in Economics from the University of Lausanne, as well as an M.A. from the Ecole Polytechnique Fédérale de Lausanne, where he also completed his postdoc research.

Valérie Swaen

Valérie Swaen is Professor at Louvain School of Management, Catholic University of Louvain, from which she also received her Ph.D. She has published in *International Journal of Human Resources*, *Journal of Business Ethics*, *Journal of Management*, *Journal of Management Studies*, *Journal of Organizational Behavior*, and *Marketing Letters*, among others.

Ilona Szőcs

Ilona Szőcs is Assistant Professor in the Department of Marketing and International Business at the University of Vienna (Austria). She holds a Ph.D. in International Marketing Management from Vienna University of Economics and Business (WU). Her research interests include corporate responsibility, sustainability and culture, and consumer research, particularly at the intersection of brand preferences and consumer stereotypes. Her work has appeared in internationally renowned journals such as the *Journal of the Academy of Marketing Science*, *Journal of World Business*, *Journal of Cleaner Production*, and *Electronic Commerce Research and Applications*, as well as in books, such as the *SAGE Handbook of Contemporary Cross-Cultural Management*, *Handbook on Ethics and Marketing*, and *The New Role of Regional Management*. She is co-editor of a book entitled *Rethinking Business Responsibility in a Global Context: Challenges to Corporate Social Responsibility, Sustainability and Ethics* (CSR, Sustainability, Ethics & Governance Series).

Minh Thai

Minh Thai is senior researcher in the Upscaling Innovation at International Water Management Institute (Ghana) and project leader in the Feed the Future Innovation Lab for Small Scale Irrigation. She formerly was Assistant Professor of Innovation Systems in the Department of Food and Resource Economics at University of Copenhagen. She leads innovation scaling research to develop systemic approaches to scale agricultural water management and farmer-led irrigation that can enhance sustainable and resilient food systems. In more than

25 years working in development and academia in Asia, Africa, and Europe, her research addresses institutional innovation, innovation systems, and innovation scaling in agriculture, agri-business, and food systems, using action research approaches to enhance developmental impacts.

Karin Tollin

Karin Tollin earned her Doctor of Economics from University of Stockholm (Sweden), in 1990. Since 1995, she has been employed as Associate Professor of Marketing at Copenhagen Business School. Her field of lecturing and research deals with the association among marketing, strategy, and innovation. This specialization has resulted in the design and leadership of two master's programs and courses focused on marketing's role and contribution to change and innovation processes in firms. Tollin's research sits at the intersection of marketing management, innovation, and corporate sustainability. She has published in international anthologies and academic journals, including *European Journal of Marketing*, *Journal of Strategic Marketing*, and *Journal of Business Ethics*.

Jan-Åke Törnroos

Jan-Åke Törnroos earned his Ph.D. in Economics and Business Administration in 1991 at Åbo Akademi University (ÅAU) (Finland). He is currently an Emeritus Professor at ÅAU. He has been Professor of Corporate Geography at Hanken School of Economics (Finland) and Professor of International Marketing at ÅAU. Törnroos also acted as the Dean of the School of Business & Economics at ÅAU during 2006–2015. His research focuses on three themes: international marketing and internationalization; business marketing from a network perspective; and process methods, time, and qualitative research. His research has been published in international peer-reviewed journals such as *Industrial Marketing Management*, *Journal of Business Research*, *European Journal of Marketing*, *Time & Society*, and *Scandinavian Journal of Management*.

Remi van der Sloot

Remi van der Sloot graduated with an M.Sc. from Eindhoven University of Technology. He is now Purchasing Unit Manager at DAF Trucks NV, in the Netherlands.

Robert Venter

Robert Venter received a Ph.D. in entrepreneurship from the University of the Witwatersrand in Johannesburg, South Africa. He is currently a Senior Lecturer in the School of Business Sciences and Sessional Lecturer in the Graduate School of Business at the University of the Witwatersrand. In addition, he is Co-Director of the international collaborative Strategic Foresight Research Group, based at the University of the Witwatersrand. His research interests include developmental entrepreneurship, social entrepreneurship, and entrepreneurial education, as well the ethics of entrepreneurship, with a particular focus on the intersections of economic inclusivity, sustainability, and entrepreneurial behavior. His research appears in journals such as *Development Southern Africa*, *Journal of Social Entrepreneurship*, and *Journal* of *International Education in Business*, as well as in edited books, such as *Entrepreneurship and Society* (2014), and *Sustainable Entrepreneurship* (2019). He is co-editor of three books for Oxford University Press: *Entrepreneurship Theory in Practice*, *Labour Relations in South Africa*, and *Project Management in Perspective*.

Francisco Villegas Pinuer

Francisco Villegas Pinuer is a doctoral researcher in entrepreneurship and management at the Autonomous University of Barcelona. He has authored book chapters and papers published in international academic journals, such as *Kybernetes*, *Revista Brasileira de Gestão de Negócios*, *Revista Internacional Administración & Finanzas*, and *Revista de Administração de Empresas*. His research interests are environmental sustainability, the circular economy, entrepreneurship, and management. In addition, Villegas serves as a reviewer for different academic journals.

Duane Windsor

Duane Windsor received a doctoral degree from Harvard University. He is currently the Lynette S. Autrey Professor of Management in the Jesse H. Jones Graduate School of Business at Rice University. He was editor of *Business & Society* (2007–2014) and an associate editor of the *Encyclopedia of Business Ethics and Society* (first and second editions). His research interests include corporate social responsibility, stakeholder theory, environmental sustainability, and anti-corruption reform. His articles have appeared in various international academic journals including *Academy of Management Journal*, *Asia Pacific Business Review*, *Business & Society*, *Business Ethics Quarterly*, *Critical Sociology*, *Journal of Business Ethics*, *Journal of Business Research*, *Journal of International Management*, *Journal of Management Studies*, *Philosophy of Management*, and *Public Administration Review*.

Eshari Withanage

Eshari Withanage is a doctoral candidate with the chair of Business Administration, Accounting and Corporate Governance, at the University of Siegen. She holds a master's degree in Business Administration (University of Wales–United Kingdom) and bachelor's degree specializing in Finance (University of Colombo–Sri Lanka). She is an Associated Charted Management Accountant (United Kingdom) and Chartered Global Management Accountant (United States). Her research interest refers to corporate social responsibility in emerging market contexts. She has corporate and managerial experience with several global and multinational firms.

Preface

Sustainability can be defined as the "ability of an organization to favorably drive its actions towards concerns and welfare of people, planet and profits in a way that the company will be able to empower itself to meet its own and its customers' current and future requirements successfully" (Gupta et al., 2013, p. 288). The operationalization of sustainability in practice tends to rely on the triple bottom line (Elkington, 1998), which encompasses environmental, social, and economic dimensions of corporate performance. Environmental sustainability refers to the use of energy and other resources, which create a footprint that companies leave behind as a result of their operations. Social sustainability exists if firms support the preservation and creation of skills and capabilities among current and future generations, promote health, and foster equal and democratic treatment within and outside their boundaries (McKenzie, 2004). Economic sustainability implies that in conducting their operations, firms obtain cost reductions or positive financial results. Thus, according to a triple bottom line approach, sustainable performance depends on environmental, social, and economic performance.

The conservation and management of resources, along with the quest for social and economic development, have been on global agendas for several decades. During conferences and summits, from the United Nations Conference on the Human Environment in 1972 in Stockholm to the United Nations Conference on Sustainable Development (Rio+20) in Brazil, world leaders and participants from the private and nonprofit sectors gather to discuss sustainability-related issues, including social equity and environmental protection. These gatherings strongly emphasize the role of companies in sustainable development efforts: they have substantial influence on environmental and social priorities, including reducing CO_2 emissions and ensuring workers' well-being.

Considering this influence, the definition of sustainability strategies should reflect a top-down approach, starting with the commitment of the top managers and boards that define the corporate strategy, to guarantee sufficient resources to achieve sustainability goals (Gimenez and Tachizawa, 2012; Large and Gimenez, 2011; Reuter et al., 2010). Once a firm's sustainability agenda is defined, governance bodies and corporate boards often rely on functional areas and departments to deploy it (Chams and García-Blandón, 2019; Gomes Teixeira and Canciglieri, 2019). Extant literature also highlights the central roles of functional areas and departments, such as marketing (Chabowski et al., 2011), innovation and entrepreneurship (Nidumolu et al., 2009), operations and information systems (Kettinger et al., 1994; Longoni et al., 2014), finance and accounting (Scholtens, 2006), and human resources (Daily and Huang, 2001). For example, recognizing greater sustainability awareness among consumers, marketing departments seek to position their organizations' product and service offerings as sustainable, by communicating their benefits for the environment or their contribution to the development of society (Markovic et al., 2018; Polonsky, 2011). Innovation and entrepreneurship departments have worked to develop new products and services that feature sustainable, eco-friendly processes and components (Iglesias et al., 2020; Markovic and Bagherzadeh, 2018). From an operations or information systems point of view, requiring clean transportation services, demanding that suppliers meet sustainable principles, implementing environmental and social certifications, and performing sustainable data management represent examples of practices implemented to fulfill sustainability goals (Gimenez et al., 2012; Sancha et al., 2016). Finance and accounting departments seek ethical investments or redeploy capital to sustainable activities, while still trying to guarantee the financial and economic sustainability of the company. Finally, human resources departments increasingly develop inclusive recruitment criteria and work–life balance policies, to ensure fairness and employee well-being (Stofkova and Sukalova, 2020). Thus, each department contributes to the implementation of sustainability strategies. But it also is critical to ensure their coordination and integration.

The motivation for this book accordingly stems from the need for a holistic approach to sustainability strategy implementation efforts. This anthology aims to provide a comprehensive view of the development and deployment of sustainability-driven business strategies across functional areas and departments. Sustainability may be a top priority for organizations and a key strategy in corporate agendas (Deloitte, 2013), but the effective deployment of any business strategy demands consistent, aligned, functional strategies (Hayes and Wheelwright, 1984). In particular, a sustainability strategy must encompass environmental, social, and economic dimensions. Instead though, most research focuses on individual dimensions (e.g., Osburg and Schmidpeter, 2013; Rosenberg, 2015) or else the implementation of sustainability-driven business strategies in specific sectors (e.g., Filho et al. 2018; Fletcher, 2014). By explicitly distinguishing the roles of each functional area or department in the development and deployment of sustainability strategies, we can gain a better understanding of the features and tools needed to develop and implement a sustainability-driven business strategy in an organization. Beyond the academic contributions, we thus seek to provide practical guidelines for managers interested in implementing sustainability-driven business strategies.

In support of this effort, we organize the 31 chapters in this book into eight themes:

● Part 1: Defining a sustainability-driven business strategy
● Part 2: Sustainability-driven business strategies in marketing
● Part 3: Sustainability-driven business strategies in innovation and entrepreneurship
● Part 4: Sustainability-driven business strategies in operations and information systems
● Part 5: Sustainability-driven business strategies in finance and accounting
● Part 6: Sustainability-driven business strategies in human resources
● Part 7: Sustainability-driven business strategies across functional areas in an organization
● Part 8: Case studies on sustainability-driven business strategies

PART 1: DEFINING A SUSTAINABILITY-DRIVEN BUSINESS STRATEGY

François Maon, Adam Lindgreen, and Valérie Swaen start us off by "Developing a sustainability strategic agenda," with the recognition that organizations communicate with stakeholders about societal issues in conflicting ways, which in turn makes it difficult for them to prioritize different societal issues within their corporate social responsibility (CSR) programs. Therefore, the authors propose a conceptual framework of the processes by which CSR issues emerge and become integrated into organizational goals. With a basis in systems thinking, CSR, and organizational interpretation theories, this opening chapter clarifies the relevant influence of top managers' perceptions on CSR strategic agendas.

Pilar Acosta also recognizes that sustainability is a central priority for businesses, so she asks about "Corporate foundations as vehicles for sustainable development: how do corporate foundations work with parent companies to achieve sustainability?" If a company establishes a corporate foundation to help it achieve sustainability, the resulting hybrid organization integrates a business logic with a philanthropic approach. In turn, various actors can define the sustainability strategy. This chapter notes three roles of corporate foundations and three types of work for actors on both the business and corporate foundation sides.

The development of such strategies also might rely on materiality analyses that identify relevant sustainability features. Yet companies lack guidelines for structured approaches to materiality analyses of sustainability, which limits their contributions to developing and managing sustainability activities and even may lead to flawed analyses. To establish "Materiality analysis as the basis for sustainability strategies and reporting – a systematic review of approaches and recommendations for practice," Sophia Schwoy and Andreas Dutzi review studies that describe practical approaches, which consist of two categories: studies that define material topics for specific firms and those that suggest adaptable assessments for firms to apply to their own case. The resulting critical analysis provides insights for how companies should evaluate available models and then conduct their own materiality assessments.

Another distinct approach might take a storytelling science view, involving abduction, induction, and deduction to perform self-correcting, ongoing considerations of what is true and how to deconstruct the regimes of truth embraced by various stakeholders. In applying this perspective, David M. Boje and Mohammad B. Rana offer a conceptual overview of sustainability-driven business modeling (SBM) by exploring differences across sustainability strategies and their links to other business modeling elements. That is, by "Defining a sustainably-driven business modeling strategy with a 'storytelling science' approach," they establish how SBM and storytelling about socially responsible capitalism can reveal socially and ecologically sustainable actions, beyond what benefits specific stakeholders; clarify both methodological and philosophical perspectives; and specify drivers, enablers, and barriers to SBM strategy implementation efforts.

PART 2: SUSTAINABILITY-DRIVEN BUSINESS STRATEGIES IN MARKETING

To address pressures on companies to act responsibly, Ilona Szőcs and Milena Micevski note the strategic impact of corporate responsibility (CR) on consumer reactions to companies or brands. In "Corporate responsibility as an effective marketing practice for improving consumers' brand evaluations – critical overview, new insights, and future directions," they consider effective responsible business practices and their potential variation across brands or CR domains. In turn, they establish the importance of juxtaposing corporate engagement domains while also considering them in relation to multiple brand characteristics (e.g., environmental and social domains according to brands' relational and performance features).

But even as companies incorporate sustainability into their communications, Nicholas Ind and Oriol Iglesias caution that communicating effectively and then keeping those promises remains challenging—as well as critical to enable stakeholders to distinguish what is real. They call on companies to make authentic commitments that reflect not just their own organizational beliefs but also their stakeholders' needs, in "Promises, promises: how to showcase the authenticity of sustainability claims through digitalization." In particular, they propose that digitalization can structure and provide verification of sustainability claims, monitor processes, and even share relevant stories, as exemplified by firms such as illy Coffee and Tony's Chocolonely. Ultimately, the meaning of sustainability claims must be co-created by companies and stakeholders together.

Nikolina Koporcic and Jan-Åke Törnroos focus specifically on small and medium-sized enterprises (SMEs) with a business network and sustainability perspective on their branding strategies. With their conceptual contributions in "Interactive network branding: towards a sustainability-driven strategy of small and medium-sized enterprises" they seek to clarify SMEs' uses of interactive network branding (INB) as a sustainability-driven strategy. In addition to providing a foundation for further research, this chapter identifies strategic implications of INB.

Cause-related marketing (CrM) can signal CSR too, while also providing benefits for the company, the cause, and consumers. Inês Padilha Campelos, Susana Costa e Silva, and Joana César Machado build on findings that show brand–cause fit determines CrM success by investigating influences on the relationship between brand–cause fit and consumer responses to CrM. With a qualitative case strategy, they thus seek to answer the question, "How does brand-cause fit influence the success of CrM campaigns?" The findings, based on five CrM campaigns, identify mitigating influences of consumer–cause involvement and corporate image on the impact of brand–cause fit on purchase intentions. However, they find that positive corporate images, track records of CrM initiatives, consumer–cause engagement, and cause relevance all can increase consumer trust and CrM success.

PART 3: SUSTAINABILITY-DRIVEN BUSINESS STRATEGIES IN INNOVATION AND ENTREPRENEURSHIP

The business model concept arguably can help firms and managers develop a holistic, dynamic view of their way of doing business, which in turn might help them make relevant adaptations. For example, Stefan Markovic and Karin Tollin note how some firms are pursuing business model innovation (BMI) or business model innovation for sustainability (BMIfS). In "Business model innovation for sustainability: the intersections among business models, innovation, and sustainability," they review prior research that applies business model concepts to innovation and sustainability efforts and thereby determine the ongoing need to explore BMI practices, especially with regard to BMIfS, further.

Sustainable entrepreneurial ecosystems are another emerging approach, so in "Social challenges within sustainable entrepreneurial ecosystems," Roberto Hernandez-Chea, Maral Mahdad, and Minh Thai undertake an empirical analysis of how stakeholders collaborate in such ecosystems, the challenges they face, and opportunities for improvements. In particular, they identify social uncertainty as a cause of challenges related to green technology transfer and product development, and they further assert that such social uncertainty results from contextual factors, perceptions, and behaviors. The result is inefficient collaborations. By outlining some strategies for countering social uncertainty, their chapter provides recommendations for ensuring continuous, successful collaborations that can lead to sustainable business strategies.

The SDG Action Manager is a web-based, impact management solution designed to help businesses pursue sustainable development goals (SDGs) by granting them access to ideas and methods for managing and improving their sustainability performance. According to the analysis that Giorgia Nigri, Armando Agulini, and Mara Del Baldo provide in "The UN Global Compact SDG Action Manager: how benefit corporations and purpose-driven businesses are driving the change," whereas a profit- and shareholder-centric economic mindset harms both the environment and society, hybrid organizational designs can combine profit and non profit sectors (e.g., benefit corporations, B Corps, social purpose companies) and support practices that underlie teal and flourishing enterprises. Integrating the SDG Action Manager with benefit impact assessments can produce such transformations.

PART 4: SUSTAINABILITY-DRIVEN BUSINESS STRATEGIES IN OPERATIONS AND INFORMATION SYSTEMS

Emphasizing environmental sustainability in particular, Francisco Villegas Pinuer, Joan Llonch Andreu, and Pilar López Belbeze take a supply chain perspective and gather empirical data from managers of SMEs in different sectors, located in Spain and Chile. The findings they report in "SMEs, environmental sustainability and waste management: a comparative empirical study Spain and Chile" indicate some clear differences in the current status and implementation of environmental regulations and waste management systems across nations. These variations have notable implications for SMEs' knowledge, as well as their access to sufficient quality, recycled raw materials. Thus, the authors call for enhanced environmental regulations that target tangible aspects of supply chains.

Also focused on supply chains, David B. Grant, Sarah Shaw, Siriwan Chaisurayakarn, and Alex Nikolai Shenin consider how Environmental Management Systems (EMS) might be applied to meet sustainability challenges. By comparing the "Adoption of Environmental Management Systems: Perspectives from UK, Finland and Thailand," across studies that refer to logistics and supply chain actors in all three countries, they identify some common facilitators and barriers to EMS adoption. Although the ISO 14001 and Eco-Management Audit Scheme are the most popular EMS, their application is inconsistent, and practitioners frequently acknowledge their lack of understanding of EMS overall. Some practitioners develop their own systems; others offer no reports. Encouraging EMS adoption requires financial support, reduced waste, and operational efficiency, as well as overcoming primary barriers, such as the lack of standard measures or government mandates, and supply chain complexity. Without a standard system for reporting environmental supply chain performance, normative theory has diverged substantially from practice.

Extending their supply chain view to multi-tier supply networks, Thomas E. Johnsen, Federico Caniato, and Toloue Miandar consider how companies might encourage sustainability throughout supply networks and highlight a key role of purchasing and supply management (PSM). Five cases from the Italian luxury fashion and food industries reveal various diffusion strategies, which support "The role of purchasing in the diffusion of sustainability in supply networks." But the cases also vary widely in the level of sustainability maturity, such that some companies express positive intentions but nothing more. The authors suggest leveraging PSM, in combination with CSR and sustainability functions, to enhance sustainability diffusion.

Food supply chains in particular must be sustainable, but according to "Sustainability assessment in the food supply chain," limited research provides measures or assessments of sustainability across the different stages of this supply chain. Verónica León-Bravo and Federico Caniato therefore investigate companies' tactics for doing so, with particular attention to what factors might encourage them to consider sustainability through different supply chain stages. With 12 cases sourced from the fresh fruit and vegetables supply chain in Italy, they identify substantial heterogeneity in the way companies respond to various stakeholder pressures at different stages. They detail three particularly influential factors: company size, measure complexity, and extent of vertical integration.

Sreyaa Guha and Polina Landgraf present several questions that underlie their efforts in "Sustainable data management," related to the role of sustainability in data-driven economies and the options for organizations to adopt sustainable data management practices but still use them to pursue novel business opportunities. Following an analytical summary of data management thinking, the authors discuss what leads to (un)sustainable data management. In turn, they propose a CURLS (Constraints, Utility, Risks, Liability, and Span) framework for developing sustainability-driven data management strategies, then apply CURLS to a data analytics case study. The framework and example reveal several actionable guidelines for sustainable data management efforts.

PART 5: SUSTAINABILITY-DRIVEN BUSINESS STRATEGIES IN FINANCE AND ACCOUNTING

Andreas Dutzi, Julian Schröter, and Eshari Withanage have a key question: "Do CSR reports impact firms' stock returns? A pilot study analysis." To answer it, they seek to determine shareholders' sensitivity to firms' communications about sustainability activities. With a pilot study, involving 39 of the top 50 companies from *Fortune*'s 500 list for 2015, they find that the share prices of 26 firms change significantly when they start reporting their CSR. The detailed findings can inform firm managers wondering whether they should disclose CSR information; investors who want insight for their investment decisions; analysts developing their assessments and advice; regulators considering whether to mandate CSR disclosures; and any other stakeholders interested in firm accountability.

A different form of reporting, private social reporting, refers to dialogues between Nordic institutional investors and the companies in which they invest. With a discourse analytic method, Natalia Semenova performs "An analysis of business actions in private social reporting" to learn about strategic efforts to manage social issues by drawing on private reports that describe successful dialogues about human and labor rights. The private reports largely focus on social risk, social norms, the dialogue process, and social actions. Private reporting also appears relevant for helping investee companies improve their sustainability policies, as well as their management systems and transparency.

Then in "How environment, social and governance scores impact company financial performance indicators: evidence from Denmark," Slobodan Kacanski investigates how the constituent components of ESG scores influence financial performance indicators, among a sample of companies listed on the Danish stock market during 2010–2018. In this empirical study, involving a panel data regression with fixed effects, he measures the effects of an aggregated ESG score and its components on return on assets (ROA) and Tobin's Q. Each of the scores indicates positive impacts on Tobin's Q but not ROA, implying the distinct directions of the effects of the separate components on these commonly used financial performance indicators.

Using an internal audit function (IAF) can help boards of directors achieve broad corporate objectives and governance; in "The role of the internal audit function in fostering sustainability reporting," Mara Del Baldo, Selena Aureli, and Rosa Lombardi investigate if an IAF can also encourage sustainability reporting and sustainability strategies. With a case study methodology, they apply institutional theory and learn that the IAF in the case firm functioned as an internal key agent that initiated and then managed the internal process toward sustainability reporting. Rather than acting as an inspector, it worked more like a consultant or educator, sharing technical advice and hosting sustainability meetings within the company.

PART 6: SUSTAINABILITY-DRIVEN BUSINESS STRATEGIES IN HUMAN RESOURCES

The integrative literature review of sustainability-driven human resource management (HRM) offered by Rosalía Cascón-Pereira, Tahereh Maghsoudi, and Ana Beatriz Hernández-Lara to start this section critically addresses what the concept means, its impacts, and which human resource practices lead to social sustainability. They differentiate this notion from related concepts (e.g., green HRM, CSR, strategic HRM) and consider its influence on social indicators of sustainability. Thus, the chapter "Sustainability-driven HRM: The WHAT, the WHAT FOR, and the HOW" provides a roadmap for practitioners to aim toward sustainability and for researchers to advance the conceptualization.

Andrew Ngawenja Mzembe also considers the influences of HRM on sustainability agendas, using the hotel industry as his study context. Interviews with 18 human resource managers (specialists) and employees of 12 hotels in the Netherlands reveal "The role of human resource management function in the institutionalisation of sustainability: the case study of the Dutch hotel industry." The professionals take on five roles, consistent with existing HRM models: coach, facilitator, architect, leader, and custodian of sustainability. Their propensity to perform each role in turn depends on the organizational context, including the relative position and sophistication of the HRM function within a hotel's decision-making structure, as well as stage of advancement of the hotel's sustainability agenda.

Whereas the previous chapter suggests how managers can advance sustainability, this chapter notes the potential for toxic leader responses to demands for sustainable policies. In "Profits with purpose: corporate and entrepreneurial toxic leadership and threats to organizational sustainability," David Coldwell and Robert Venter identify how toxic leadership manifests in large, macro organizations, as well as in smaller, micro organizations that have not yet been fully established. Then they propose an exploratory balanced leadership model that suggests ways to combine profit- and purpose-oriented organizational leadership strategically, in ways that can encourage long-term sustainability.

PART 7: SUSTAINABILITY-DRIVEN BUSINESS STRATEGIES ACROSS FUNCTIONAL AREAS IN AN ORGANIZATION

This section contains chapters that move across internal organizational boundaries, such as by considering "Cross-functional integration in sustainability-driven business practice." According to Duane Windsor, such cross-functional integration is a management task, such that managers and employees design and implement the integration, and it is critical for achieving sustainability. Focusing on the environmental dimension, he seeks to define the current state of knowledge pertaining to sustainability integration across human resources, production, and operations and supply chain management. This effort establishes a conceptual framework that could be extended to include further business dimensions and functions, as illustrated by the cases of Walmart and REI.

To find sustainable suppliers, identify risky suppliers, and help suppliers develop their sustainability, the purchasing function needs to embrace broader corporate goals and functions. On the basis of this claim, Melek Akın Ateş and Nüfer Yasin Ateş call for "Strategic alignment of purchasing for sustainability: a multi-level framework." The multi-level framework they propose spans vertical alignment (top management team with purchasing function), horizontal alignment (purchasing function and other functions), and internal alignment (among individual members of the purchasing function). By integrating a tool from strategy literature, they also analyze the distinct levels of purchasing alignment for sustainability with a case study.

From the perspective of supplier organizations, product sustainability might offer a means to differentiate their offerings. Therefore, Adam Lindgreen, Michael Antioco, David Harness, and Remi van der Sloot detail how suppliers should determine their customers' perceptions of the environmental and social dimensions of sustainability, such that they can promote more relevant factors. A focus group study involving members of a leading supplier of magnetic resonance imaging (MRI) scanning equipment reveals five social aspects (which consist of 11 indicators) that are relevant to buyers. Then the authors conduct customer perception interviews with key decision makers in seven types of hospitals and an imaging center that would be involved in MRI scanning equipment purchases. As they report in "Purchasing and marketing of social and environmental sustainability in high-tech medical equipment," environmental and social sustainability dimensions appear personally relevant, but from a professional view, they are secondary to cost, performance, and the easy integration of the equipment into the physical infrastructure. Still, citing the product's environmental and social benefits can enhance differentiation and perceptions of the product offering among decision makers.

PART 8: CASE STUDIES ON SUSTAINABILITY-DRIVEN BUSINESS STRATEGIES

This final section presents five detailed case studies that reflect on various sustainability-driven business strategies. First, in detailing "Ecoalf: a brand with a conscience," Nicholas Ind details how this Spanish fashion brand, founded in Madrid in 2012, has collaborated with partners to develop recycled fabrics from plastic bottles, used car tires, and fishing nets. He also highlights the company's clear activist stance, reflecting Ecoalf's stakeholder-based philosophy, in which interdependence among actors is a given, and transparency is a persistent goal.

Second, Kristian J. Sund and Rasmus Downes-Rasmussen describe how Comwell Hotels first defined its sustainability strategy in 2016, leading within just a few years to its recognition as the most sustainable Danish hotel brand, according to the Sustainable Brand Index. With "Sustainability as strategy: the case of Comwell Hotels," they explain how a chain of traditional conference hotels embraced sustainable development, which produced some meaningful lessons. They note that implementing a sustainability strategy demands revisions to the mindsets and behaviors of all participating actors, and then a constant focus over time. Rather than a one-time goal, Comwell Hotels regards sustainability as a journey and a strategic initiative, with profound effects on HRM. It must be initiated and championed by top management, but it also must be driven by employees.

Third, Song Saa Private Island seeks to combine luxury tourism with environmental conservation. In "Boat trip adventure changing the lives of thousands: the story of Song Saa Private Island," Ilia Gugenishvili and Nikolina Koporcic describe how the resort consistently has embraced environmental, economic, and socio-cultural sustainability, in pursuit of its goals to protect the planet, end poverty, and provide equal opportunities. Supported by the nonprofit Song Saa Foundation, it only constructs buildings with eco-friendly and low impact materials; provides education to both tourists and locals; recycles water and waste; produces organic food; purchases local products, such as ceramics, arts, décor, and food; and further gives back to the local community through educational and medical care initiatives.

Fourth, in describing "Doing business the sustainable 'Novo Nordisk Way'," Marija Sarafinovska and Yuqian Qiu propose that the Danish pharmaceutical firm is radically altering diabetes, obesity, and hemophilia care, as well as practices for hormone replacement and growth hormone therapy. Using secondary data, they gain insights into the Novo Nordisk Way as a decision-making philosophy that embraces the triple bottom line of environmental, social, and economic sustainability. It also identifies various stakeholders that require responsible consideration: customers, employees, communities, suppliers, and investors. For Novo Nordisk, successful solutions benefit the health and well-being of people living with chronic diseases, help prevent disease, and widen access to affordable health care worldwide.

Fifth, Miguel Saiz García outlines an initiative in the chemical industry to adopt green technologies, including new steam generation processes that rely on boilers burning recycled wood chips instead of fuel derivatives. The chapter, "Sustainability in the chemical industry through an industrial spin-off: the case of Apricot," thus summarizes a circular economy that reuses waste material, avoids the costs to transport and dispose of tons of wooden material, and converts the waste into a source of energy that is carbon neutral. Beyond the benefits for the environment, this approach is likely to create local jobs and even could develop into an autonomous business that serves multiple actors in chemical industries.

CLOSING REMARKS

We extend a special thanks to Edward Elgar and its staff, which has been most helpful throughout the entire process. Equally, we warmly thank the contributors who submitted their manuscripts for consideration for this book. They have exhibited the worthy desire to share their knowledge and experience with the book's readers—and a willingness to put forward their views for possible challenge by their peers. There is still a lot we do not know about sustainability and how it drives business strategies. We are hopeful that the chapters in this book fill some of the knowledge gaps that readers, practitioners, and academics still suffer—and that they also stimulate further thought and action pertaining to sustainability-driven business strategies.

Stefan Markovic, Copenhagen, Denmark
Cristina Sancha, Barcelona, Spain
Adam Lindgreen, Copenhagen, Denmark, and Pretoria, South Africa

REFERENCES

Chabowski, B.R., Mean, J.A., Gonzalez-Padron, T.L. (2011), "The structure of sustainability research in marketing, 1958-2008: a basis for future research opportunities", *Journal of the Academy of Marketing Science*, Vol. 39, No. 1, pp. 55–70.

Chams, N., García-Blandón, J. (2019), "Sustainable or not sustainable? The role of board of directors", *Journal of Cleaner Production*, Vol. 226, pp. 1067–1081.

Daily, B.F., Huang, S. (2001), "Achieving sustainability through attention to human resource factors in environmental management", *International Journal of Operations and Production Management*, Vol. 21, No. 12, pp. 1539–1552.

Deloitte (2013). *CFO Insights Sustainability: Why CFOs Are Driving Savings and Strategy*, Deloitte University Press.

Elkington, J. (1998), *Cannibals with Forks: The Triple Bottom Line of the 21st Century*, New Society Publishers.

Filho, W.L., Marans, R.W., Callewaert, J. (2018), *Handbook of Sustainability and Social Science Research*, Springer.

Fletcher, K. (2014), *Handbook of Sustainability and Fashion*, Routledge.

Gimenez, C., Sierra, V., Rodon, J. (2012), "Sustainable operations: their impact on the triple bottom line", *International Journal of Production Economics*, Vol. 140, pp. 149–159.

Gimenez, C., Tachizawa, E. (2012), "Extending sustainability to suppliers: a systematic literature review", *Supply Chain Management: An International Journal*, Vol. 17, No. 5, pp. 531–543.

Gomes Teixeira, G., Canciglieri Jr., O. (2019), "How to make strategic planning for corporate sustainability?", *Journal of Cleaner Production*, Vol. 230, pp. 1421–1431.

Gupta, S., Czinkota, M., Melewar, T.C. (2013), "Embedding knowledge and value of a brand into sustainability for differentiation", *Journal of World Business*, Vol. 48, No. 3, pp. 287–296.

Hayes, R.H., Weelwright, S.C. (1984), *Restoring our Competitive Edge: Competing through Manufacturing*, John Wiley.

Iglesias, O., Markovic, S., Bagherzadeh, M., Singh, J.J. (2020), "Co-creation: a key link between corporate social responsibility, customer trust, and customer loyalty", *Journal of Business Ethics*, Vol. 163, No. 1, pp. 151–166.

Kettinger, W.J., Grover, V., Guha, S., Segars, A.H. (1994), "Strategic information systems revisited: a study in sustainability and performance", *MIS Quarterly*, Vol. 18, No. 1, pp. 31–58.

Large, R.O., Gimenez, C. (2011), "Drivers of green supply management performance: evidence from Germany", *Journal of Purchasing and Supply Management*, Vol. 17, No. 3, pp. 176–184.

Longoni, A., Golini, R., Cagliano, R. (2014), "The role of new forms of work organization in developing sustainability strategies in operations", *International Journal of Production Economics*, Vol. 147, No. A, pp. 147–160.

Markovic, S., Bagherzadeh, M. (2018), "How does breadth of external stakeholder co-creation influence innovation performance? Analyzing the mediating roles of knowledge sharing and product innovation", *Journal of Business Research*, Vol. 88, pp. 173–186.

Markovic, S., Iglesias, O., Singh, J.J., Sierra, V. (2018), "How does the perceived ethicality of corporate services brands influence loyalty and positive word-of-mouth? Analyzing the roles of empathy, affective commitment, and perceived quality", *Journal of Business Ethics*, Vol. 148, No. 4, pp. 721–740.

McKenzie, S. (2004), *Social Sustainability: Towards Some Definitions.* Hawke Research Institute, University of South Australia, Magill.

Nidumolu, R., Prahalad, C.K., Rangaswami, M.R. (2009), "Why sustainability is now the key driver of innovation", *Harvard Business Review*, September.

Osburg, T., Schmidpeter, R. (2013), *Social Innovation: Solutions of a Sustainable Future (CSR, Sustainability, Ethics and Governance)*, Springer.

Polonsky, M.J. (2011), "Transformative green marketing: impediments and opportunities", *Journal of Business Research,* Vol. 64, No. 12, pp. 1311–1319.

Reuter, C., Foerstl, K., Hartmann, E., Blome, C. (2010), "Sustainable global supplier management: the role of dynamic capabilities in achieving competitive advantage", *Journal of Supply Chain Management*, Vol. 46, No. 2, pp. 45–63.

Rosenberg, M. (2015), *Strategy and Sustainability: A Hardnosed and Clear-eyed Approach to Environmental Sustainability for business*, IESE Business Collection.

Sancha, C., Gimenez, C., Sierra, V. (2016), "Achieving a socially responsible supply chain through assessment and collaboration", *Journal of Cleaner Production*, Vol. 112, pp. 1934–1947.

Scholtens, B. (2006), "Finance as a driver of corporate social responsibility", *Journal of Business Ethics*, Vol. 68, No. 1, pp. 19–33.

Stofkvoa, Z. and Sukalova, V. (2020), "Sustainable development of human resources in globalization period", *Sustainability*, Vol. 12, No. 18, pp. 76–81.

'Addressing the grand challenges of our time will require collaborative efforts across organizational and disciplinary boundaries. Sustainability is arguably one of the major challenges that has received attention for quite some time but for which progress is also hampered due to limited perspectives on both problems and solutions. Luckily, this book offers a step in the right direction as it not only bridges sustainability and business strategies—in itself a major factor for actually achieving change—but it also does so by drawing on different disciplines. By offering a basis for comparing and contrasting different domains and perspectives, this book helps to better understand the complexity of the underlying problem and thereby also contributes to research and practice.'
Marcel Bogers, Eindhoven University of Technology, the Netherlands

'I strongly recommend the Handbook of Sustainability-Driven Strategies in Practice as an essential reading for all stakeholders in the sustainability ecosystem, wishing to make concrete and practical efforts in driving sustainable business in the real world. The challenge in sustainability is always moving beyond rhetoric to actual practice and implementation, and this Handbook can provide useful tips and strategies to push for more progress and make our world a better place.'
Dima Jamali, University of Sharjah, United Arab Emirates

'Sustainability is high on the corporate and public agenda but developing and implementing strategies for sustainability often remains challenging. In this edited volume, Markovic, Sancha, and Lindgreen bring together a rich collection of chapters examining sustainability-driven business strategies from a holistic perspective. Considering sustainability strategies across the main functional business areas, the different chapters offer an inspiring set of ideas and experiences that can guide both research and practice on this important theme.'
Frank de Bakker, IESEG School of Management, France

'Sustainability has quickly become a key business imperative in contemporary markets. Stefan Markovic, Cristina Sancha, and Adam Lindgreen have edited a timely Handbook that covers the perspectives of versatile business domains and functions in a comprehensive manner, and offers rich insight for developing and researching sustainability-driven business strategies. This book is useful for anyone seeking to understand how businesses can realize opportunities for differentiation, renewal, and enhanced value creation through sustainability.'
Elina Jaakkola, University of Turku, Finland

'Professors Markovic, Sancha, and Lindgreen have compiled in a single Handbook a great set of actionable ideas on how to design and deploy sustainability strategies across a variety of organizations, industries, and countries. What is most appealing is that the Handbook moves beyond corporate strategy and takes the reader to how corporate strategies get applied across each of the key functional areas such as marketing, finance, and HR, with a closing section discussing specific cases to further illustrate sustainability-driven business strategies in action.'
Ruth V. Aguilera, Northeastern University, US

'Sustainability is today's leading business imperative. For the sake of our planet and humanity, businesses must find effective, profitable ways to assure a future for our natural environment, while providing safe, meaningful work that allows employees to live and prosper. Sustainability efforts cannot simply address pieces of business—they must permeate all operations. This book offers a comprehensive approach to sustainability, addressing all functional areas, including marketing, human resources, operations, accounting, finance, and more. It also covers all facets of sustainability, including people, planet, and profit. This thorough coverage is followed by several practical case studies to demonstrate sustainability efforts in action. This book offers business practitioners and academics a comprehensive approach to meaningful, viable sustainability efforts.'
Debra Z. Basil, University of Lethbridge, Canada

'This well-structured Handbook *edited by Stefan Markovic, Cristina Sancha, and Adam Lindgreen is an important step forward in our understanding of sustainability-driven business strategies. Sustainability is one of the most critical issues of the 21st century for businesses and societies. The* Handbook *begins with definitional materials and ends with selected case studies. The sections in between address sustainability in various functions of business: marketing, innovation and entrepreneurship, operations and information systems, finance and accounting, human resources, and also cross-functional integration. Both researchers and practitioners will find lots of new insights and recommendations concerning sustainability-driven business strategies.'*
Duane Windsor, Rice University, US

'*Addressing sustainability issues is one of the key mission of enterprises in the coming decades. This book provides insights and tools to assist managers to develop and execute business strategies in key functions of organizations, including marketing, innovation, operations, finance, and human resources management. The* Handbook of Sustainability-Driven Strategies in Practice *offers not only information, but also inspiration for everyone who wants to gain insights into sustainability practices.'*
Christina Wong, The Hong Kong Polytechnic University, Hong Kong

'*Sustainability has become a strategic imperative of today's businesses. Accompanied by a cast of international academics, Professors Markovic, Sancha and Lindgreen lead you on a comprehensive journey through the essential areas of management, brilliantly addressing the strategic role of sustainability. This content oriented to practice together with the case studies that illustrate previous concepts, make the* Handbook of Sustainability-Driven Strategies in Practice *a reference and inspiration resource for all those who want to understand the strategic role of sustainability.'*
Leopoldo Gutierrez, University of Granada, Spain

PART 1

DEFINING
A SUSTAINABILITY-DRIVEN
BUSINESS STRATEGY

1. Developing a sustainability strategic agenda

François Maon, Adam Lindgreen and Valérie Swaen

INTRODUCTION

Environmental excellence and the well-being of people within and outside the organization increasingly represent issues that organizations must integrate into the core of their business strategy and practices. Beyond the traditional objectives of supplying services and goods, organizations encounter increasing pressures to address and respond to the societal issues arising from their activities. Managers face virtually constant demands from various groups to devote resources to corporate social responsibility (CSR) and sustainability (in the following: CSR) policies and initiatives (Pinkston & Carroll 1994). These pressures arise not only from nongovernmental organizations (Doh & Guay 2004), shareholder activists (O'Rourke 2003), business customers (Roberts 2003), socially responsible investors (Aslaksen & Synnestvedt 2003), union federations (Egels-Zandén & Hyllman 2006), and communities (Waddock & Boyle 1995), but also from general societal trends, such as growing attention to ethical consumerism (Harrison et al. 2006) and institutional expectations (Waddock et al. 2002). Even industry peers and competitors can pressure organizations to make socially responsible decisions (Berry and Rondinelli, 1998).

Furthermore, perceived unethical or unsustainable corporate practices might "alienate the organization from the rest of society, resulting in reduced reputation, increased costs, and decreasing shareholder value through erosion of its license to operate" (Hill 2001, p. 32). In contrast, demonstrating responsible behavior can create substantial benefits through the development of positive attitudes toward the organization (McWilliams & Siegel 2001; Sen et al. 2006; Turban & Greening 1996) and its products (Brown & Dacin 1997; Sen & Bhattacharya 2001), as well as the development of competitive advantages (Porter & Kramer 2006) and valuable organizational capabilities (Sharma & Vredenburg 1998). Therefore, more and more organizations are developing CSR strategic agendas and implementing CSR-related initiatives. A CSR strategic agenda must establish the main CSR directions for the organization, the method by and extent to which CSR principles will be integrated in its structures and culture, and the plan of actions associated with CSR strategic choices.

However, CSR-related issues conveyed by internal and external stakeholders are often varied and conflicting. Organizations thus have trouble identifying the range of relevant societal issues they must address, as well as the priority with which they should do so. The development and implementation of integrated CSR strategic agendas by organizations therefore becomes a process of change that occurs through managerial understanding and sense making (Cramer et al. 2006). Each organization must develop its own meaning of CSR to clarify the motivation that underlies its commitments and identify the stakeholders and issues that represent key priorities (Maignan et al. 2006). During such a definition stage, the essential interactions with various stakeholder groups (Ilmolaa & Kuusi 2006) require significant resources and appropriate organizational and managerial capabilities.

Furthermore, organizations can represent interpretation systems (Daft & Weick 1984), such that constructing a CSR strategic agenda results from the translation of events and issues into shared understanding and conceptual schemes among upper managers. These managers, with their personal characteristics, then become key drivers of the design and implementation of CSR-related initiatives. In turn, the central objectives of this research are to contribute to a better understanding of the organizational processes associated with considering and developing a CSR strategic agenda, as well as to recognize the role of managerial perceptions for these processes.

The remainder of this theoretical chapter is structured as follows: First, we highlight the importance of processes to identify CSR issues as a basis for developing coherent CSR initiatives. Second, we emphasize the relevance of a systems-thinking perspective for the design and development of a CSR strategic agenda. In particular, we regard the organization as both a stakeholder system and an interpretation system. Third, we highlight the importance of managers' perceptions and personal characteristics during the process of recognizing and prioritizing the CSR issues that the organization faces. Fourth, on this basis, we suggest a model in which we conceptualize the development of a CSR strategic agenda with a systems-thinking perspective that emphasizes the role of upper managers. Fifth, we discuss the usefulness of the model through its application in a pharmaceutical company that is developing a CSR strategic agenda. Finally, we note some limitations of our work and discuss potential avenues for further research.

CONCEPTUAL FRAMEWORK: UNDERSTANDING THE DEVELOPMENT OF A CSR STRATEGIC AGENDA

Identifying CSR Issues as a Basis for Developing a CSR Strategic Agenda

As a rich but still undefined concept, CSR encompasses a broad range of concerns (Carroll 1999; de Bakker et al. 2005; Garriga & Melé 2004; Secchi 2007). According to the European Commission (2001, p. 6), CSR is "a concept whereby organizations integrate social and environmental concerns in their business operations and in their interactions with their stakeholders on a voluntary basis." Thus, it includes concerns and issues related to human rights, people's well-being at work, environmental impacts, business ethics, community investments, governance, and the marketplace (e.g., Maignan & Ralston 2002).

Yet, CSR cannot mean the same thing to everyone, because CSR issues "vary by business, by size, by sector and even by geographic region" (Business for Social Responsibility 2003). In addition, complex CSR issues involve multifaceted networks of stakeholders whose conceptions of responsible organizations vary across both groups and individuals (Zyglidopoulos 2002). Stakeholders' CSR expectations may be inconsistent (Dawkins & Lewis 2003) and inexorably evolve over time (Polonsky & Jevons 2006). A responsible initiative today may become a potentially harmful action in the future (Polonsky & Rosenberger 2001).

As a result, any organization trying to embrace CSR must recognize that "the subject can easily be interpreted as including almost everyone and everything" (WBCSD 2001). Identifying appropriate CSR issues therefore entails a tricky task. To respond to societal expectations and allocate resources, organizations must first identify relevant CSR issues so that they can develop their CSR strategic agenda. Thereafter, CSR issues and related organizational practices demand constant reassessments. Thus, the task of management is to under-stand the past, current, and future operating environments of the organization (Renfro 1993). A systems perspective provides a relevant foundation for such tasks.

Adopting a Systems Perspective to Developing a CSR Strategic Agenda

Systems thinking involves seeing the world not as discretely compartmentalized units but rather as a network of overlapping and interrelated elements (Reich 1992), that is, "seeing interrelationships rather than things, ... seeing patterns of change rather than static snapshots" (Senge 1990, p. 68). Systems thinking focuses on recognizing the interconnections among the various parts of a system and then synthesizing them into a cohesive view of the whole (Anderson & Johnson 1997).

From a systems viewpoint, organizations are open social systems that must cope with environmental and organizational uncertainty, as well as develop characteristics and perform processes that enable them to adapt to the opportunities, threats, and constraints that constitute the environment and society (Tushman & Nadler 1978). Because they are influenced by exter-nal forces and environmental conditions, organizations cannot control their own behaviors entirely (Cummings & Worley 2004). Adopting an open social system perspective, we assert that organizations should be regarded as specific systems of stakeholders (Vos 2003) and of interpretations (Daft & Weick 1984). Furthermore, similar to Gregory and Midgley (2003), we regard systems thinking as a necessary perspective that enables an organization to comprehend and respond to rising concerns about CSR issues at local, regional, and international levels.

Organizations as stakeholders' systems

From a systems viewpoint, the open system of stakeholders that constitutes an organization operates "within the larger system of the host society that provides the necessary legal and market infrastructures for the firm's activities" (Clarkson 1994, p. 21).

Furthermore, according to stakeholder theory, organizations have a moral duty to take stakeholders' concerns into consideration (Evan & Freeman 1988), which means addressing the concerns of "any individual or group who can affect or is affected by the actions, decisions, policies, practices, or goals of an organization" (Gatewood & Carroll 1991, p. 673; adapted from Freeman 1984). Stakeholder groups that convey their societal expectations to organi-zations may include owners and investors, customers, suppliers, managers and employees, competitors, the local community, government, and the media. Such groups often form coali-tions that "have more influence than a stakeholder alone" (Vos 2003, p. 142). Consequently, organizations need a reliable mechanism to identify the relevant coalitions and related issues and then define the clear limits of the stakeholder system that it represents.

Critical systems thinking can help resolve the managerial problem of identifying stake-holder coalitions and issues (Achterkamp & Vos 2007; Vos 2003). On the basis of critical systems heuristics (see Ulrich, 1983, 1988) and considering a case of specific innovation projects (rather than focusing on organizations as a whole), Achterkamp and Vos (2007) propose a four-phase method—initiation, development/performance, implementation, and maintenance—for identifying stakeholders according to their level and timing of involvement with regard to a particular project.

We apply this method to the problem of identifying CSR stakeholders. Thus, each key CSR issue the organization faces represents a project to manage. For example, an innovation project might try to adapt existing procedures by modifying suppliers' auditing practices to address human rights issues; another project could develop new processes linked to a particular CSR issue, such as developing innovative solutions to reduce carbon dioxide emissions; or projects could pertain to the cultural evolution as the organization attempts to design long-term education programs to sensitize workers to sustainability issues. The CSR strategic agenda that results from such an approach would regroup different projects according to whether they appear decisive and coherent with corporate goals.

However, to develop a consistent CSR strategic agenda, organizations must recall that CSR does not simply entail various, disconnected issues. Rather, it pertains to doing some good by developing several interconnected initiatives that help manage the relationships that are central to the future success of the organization and resolve any dilemmas among the competing interests of stakeholders (Werther & Chandler 2006). Consequently, projects that constitute the CSR strategic agenda must achieve moving equilibrium and help build mutually beneficial relationships with key stakeholders; no part of the system can persist if it lacks equilibrium with other parts. The interrelationships among CSR issues and their related projects therefore must be recognized to enable the organization to design a constructive and coherent CSR strategic agenda. Furthermore, this perspective demands a sound understanding of each key issue, as well as an organizational mindset that appreciates the complexities of the environment.

Organizations as interpretation systems

To identify the key coalitions of stakeholders, the decisive CSR issues, and their interrelationships, organizations should develop information processing mechanisms they may use to detect events, trends, and developments that are relevant to their activities. To "know" the environment, they must develop internal scanning processes that "identify emerging issues, situations, and potential pitfalls that may affect [their] future" (Albright 2004, p. 40). Environmental data then require interpretation (Daft & Weick 1984) to translate them into knowledge and understanding before the organization can determine whether and how to respond to a potentially critical CSR issue. Ashmos et al. (1998) note that such decision making requires knowledge of which stakeholders possess information that can help resolve a specific issue and which groups should participate in the decision-making process.

Identifying these key issues and coalitions of stakeholders requires managers to listen to, look for, and show consideration for stakeholders' limits (Bowen & Heath 2005). Organizational mechanisms for apprehending the environment, processing information, and setting goals cannot be divorced from the individuals who possess these capabilities (Daft & Weick 1984). In this sense, the organization's interpretation of environmental data and subsequent decisions depend on how managers perceive the interdependencies among stakeholder systems. When managers share interpretations, they create an overriding organizational interpretation.

Central Influence of Managers' Perceptions in Developing a CSR Strategic Agenda

Managers interpret the signals sent by the environment (Hegarty & Tihanyi 1999) and determine the resulting organizational responses (Child 1972; Mitchell et al. 1997); that is, their interpretations form the basis for organizational decisions. Managerial perceptions thus might be considered "the substratum that business decisions feed upon" (Santos & Garcia 2006, p. 752). In this substratum, managers' personal characteristics play key roles in defining corporate strategic orientations. To interpret stakeholders' expectations of their organization, managers "must wade into the ocean of events that surround the organization and actively try to make sense of them" (Daft & Weick 1984, p. 286).

Yet, managers, as humans, perceive their environment both uniquely and imperfectly. Because they are subject to various inevitable biases, their perceptions provide only a flawed reflection of the environment. In particular, managers interpret selective information through the filter of their own values (Rokeach 1973) and cognitive predispositions. Furthermore, their bounded rationality limits their ability to apprehend the full complexity of the business world (Simon 1957), restricting their perceptions to the phenomena that appear in the limited field of their vision. In turn, managers' perceptions "may diverge significantly when witnessing the same event" (Santos & Garcia 2006, p. 753), and no manager can fully comprehend the complex systems that characterize organizational activities.

Previous studies illustrate that relevant managerial interpretations of the environment can contribute to the success of an organization by improving performance (Downey & Slocum 1975; Hegarty & Tihanyi 1999; Miller 1993). Misinterpretation, however, leads to performance deterioration and crises (Milliken 1990).

The role of upper management perceptions

Previous research confirms that personal characteristics and backgrounds influence people's level of social involvement (e.g., Borkowski & Ugras 1992; Burton & Hegarty 1999).

Because CSR corporate commitments are extensively "maintained, nurtured and advanced by the people who manage them" (Quazi 2003, p. 822), individual drivers such as beliefs, values, demographics, educational and cultural backgrounds, and personal attributes play significant roles in shaping managers' perceptions about societal issues and CSR strategic agendas (e.g., Campbell et al. 1999; Deshpande 1997; Hemingway & Maclagan 2004; Menon & Menon 1997; Quazi 2003; Thomas & Simerly 1994). For example, women tend to demonstrate a higher CSR orientation (Burton & Hegarty 1999); more risk-averse managers are less inclined to invest in enviropreneurial marketing strategies (Campbell et al. 1999); and managers with more experience demonstrate a superior ability to develop and implement relevant policies to meet stakeholders' needs (Thomas & Simerly 1994). Thus, managers and their personal characteristics dictate the strategy toward and modes of corporate responses to environmental expectations and demands (Wood 1991).

Acknowledging the central influence of managers' perceptions and interpretations when designing strategic agendas, Thomas and Simerly (1994) show that upper managers play an especially decisive role in articulating the strategic posture of the organization. The key influence of upper versus middle managers mirrors Bedeian's (2002) claims that middle management reflects top managers' values, knowledge bases, and understanding, because they usually get promoted on the basis of their persistent support of top management perspectives. Further research confirms that upper managers—who are responsible for overseeing and guiding the organization to success through their strategic, long-term decisions—exert the central influence on the development and implementation of an organization's CSR orientation (e.g., Banerjee 2001; Maxwell et al. 1997; Waldman et al. 2006).

Because of the role played by upper managers in defining the organization's CSR orientation, the CSR strategic agenda must be subject to diverse subjective perceptions that determine its ultimate form. Convergence among such diverse perceptions is critical as a means to organize and design the policies of an organization (Weick 1979); moreover, it enables the organization to "interpret as a system" (Daft & Weick 1984, p. 285). Coherence among managers' perceptions thus establishes the organization's interpretation of CSR issues and affects its responsiveness to those issues. This coherence further depends on the organization's interpretative frame, which results from its unique features and culture (Bowen & Heath 2005).

UNDERSTANDING THE DEVELOPMENT OF A CSR STRATEGIC AGENDA: A DUAL LOOP MODEL

The preceding theoretical background leads us to suggest a comprehensive conceptual framework for understanding how CSR strategic agendas are developed and implemented by organizations (see Figure 1.1).

Our descriptive model consists of two sequential loops, interconnected by two central elements: (1) managerial perceptions of CSR issues and their importance and (2) the resulting convergence of these managerial perceptions into an organizational interpretation, leveraged by existing organizational attributes and features. In large organizations, convergence often requires an established CSR committee or department (e.g., Beadle & Donnelly 2004; Walker 2005), composed of key managers who debate and prioritize CSR issues. Such committees usually deal with and evaluate the relevance of CSR issues for the business and culture of the organization, orient the CSR strategic agenda, and coordinate CSR initiatives within the various components of the organizational system.

The first loop of our model, the *stakeholder dialogue loop*, refers to the process of interaction between the organization and its stakeholders. Through this process, stakeholders can express their views about CSR issues through a structured exchange (Stoll-Kleemann & Welp, 2006) on a continuous (or at least regular) basis. Such dialogue influences managers' perceptions of the external environment and generates greater awareness of the CSR issues at stake. Feedback during the stakeholder dialogue process eventually influences managers' personal perceptions of CSR issues and their relevance for the organization. In this sense, an organization can obtain no more important information than feedback from its environment (Krippendorf & Eleey 1986). The constructive nature of stakeholder dialogue and feedback depends, however, on the resources initially invested in the process.

The second loop of our model, the *CSR integration loop*, addresses the development and implementation of key CSR initiatives. Specifically, upper managers provide their perceptions of CSR issues, which become the organizational interpretation, which in turn serves as the basis for the CSR strategic agenda. From a strategic planning perspective, upper managers typically assess the organization's internal CSR strengths and weaknesses, evaluate alternative strategies, and then develop action plans. Implementing CSR initiatives and perceptions about the fulfillment of strategic objectives eventually influences upper managers' perceptions of the various CSR issues and their importance.

Finally, perceived stakeholder feedback combines with the perceptual outcomes of CSR-related initiatives and influences managers' perceptions of CSR issues and their importance, percolated through the filter of their personal values, beliefs, and characteristics. This process induces a better understanding of current issues and the identification of new CSR issues. It also demands recurrent adaptations to the organization's CSR strategic agenda. Our model further highlights the need to establish efficient procedures to initiate CSR strategic agenda development. This issue is especially critical in organizations that lack any structured CSR policies or systematic CSR-related scanning processes; for these organizations, managers' awareness, knowledge, and perceptions likely are severely restricted or, at the very least, tacit and unshared.

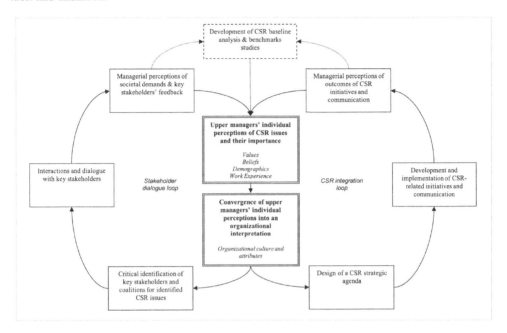

Figure 1.1   A dual loop model for understanding the development of a CSR strategic agenda

EMPIRICAL USEFULNESS OF THE SUGGESTED MODEL

To assess the usefulness of the suggested model, we develop a partnership with a large, autonomous subsidiary of a multinational pharmaceutical company. The subsidiary already had implemented some CSR-related initiatives but without a clear vision or any coherence or coordination among the different initiatives.

Action research undertaken during a four-month period (January–April 2007) pursues the following objectives: to (1) assess the status of CSR within the company; (2) raise CSR awareness among upper managers; and (3) propose guidelines for developing an integrated and structured CSR orientation. To reach these objectives and initiate the process of CSR-oriented thinking within the organization, we apply the suggested model by collecting various sources of information about the company's CSR initiatives, upper managers' perceptions of CSR and relevant issues, and organizing different meetings with upper managers about CSR.

First, 13 upper managers (from 12 distinct functional departments) received a generic questionnaire to provide their pre-diagnosis of CSR. To select the appropriate managers, we considered their work experience, function within the organization, and membership in distinct departments. This pre-diagnosis questionnaire provides a review CSR practices by articulating 120 items in nine sections: (1) well-being at work and social responsibility toward staff; (2) company's involvement in the community; (3) top management's dedication to CSR principles; (4) workers' education and training with respect to CSR issues; (5) company's organization and structure; (6) CSR-related normative aspects and commitments; (7) CSR-related procedures and documentation; (8) CSR performance indicators; and (9) crisis and nonconformity management. In the next step, we interviewed these 13 upper managers to determine their conception of CSR practices and highlight CSR dimensions and concerns that they considered missing from the pre-diagnosis questionnaire. With this first data collection, we outline the organization's perception of performance with regard to common CSR aspects and, more important, gain an overview of the different managers' opinions about CSR issues.

Managers' perceptions about the CSR concept depend on their functional orientation and field of managerial knowledge. The CSR issues identified as critical for the company tend to demonstrate this function bias and vary according to the upper manager interviewed. This result is coherent with prior literature in the broader strategic management field; that is, managers perceive the elements of a situation that relates more specifically to the activities and goals of their own department (Dearborn & Simon 1958).

Upper managers whose function tends to be externally oriented—such as marketing and external relations—consider the CSR concept from an instrumental and self-protective perspective, with a focus on image and reputation:

> I essentially look at the CSR concept in a commercial way. What I think is interesting is the corporate image. What matters to me is first and foremost that the corporate reputation is good and that we don't have any trouble with clients, and that we don't find us represented as ruffians in the press. (Marketing manager)

Managers in production and financial functions instead associate the concept of CSR with normative and regulatory requirements, as well as with the impact of noncompliance or negligent behaviors on the company:

> For me, it [the CSR concept] is primary linked to compliance with norms legislations. Since we operate in a highly regulated environment, we must be considered as an organization that respects the rules. Afterwards, we should consider whether we go further. In all cases, potential deficiencies must not affect our core business. (Finance manager)

By contrast, upper managers from departments that deal with functional issues more clearly linked to CSR concerns—such as human resources or the environment, health, and safety departments—demonstrate more consideration for the impact of organizational activities on the social and ecological environment, both within and outside the organization, and refer more systematically to the duties associated with the stakeholders of the organization:

> I think CSR can be considered as the capacity of the organization to take its responsibilities toward the various actors who intervene within the framework of organizational activities. I would say that the first actors to be taken into account are the workers, and then comes the shareholders, and what is generally defined by the general term of 'community.' The community includes people, neighbors, and the ecological environment. (Environment, health, and safety manager)

From a research and development viewpoint, the concept of CSR appears more directly apprehended into a "finality" perspective. That is, these managers consider the nature of the business activities and the products and services offered as the first vector of social responsibility for the organization:

Even if we remain an organization with commercial objectives, our CSR activities are primarily related to the development of products aimed at providing a greater well-being to the people who need them. (Research and development manager)

On the basis of this pre-diagnosis questionnaire and the subsequent interviews with upper managers, we identify two distinct categories of CSR issues that the organization must address: generic issues, which are essential to any organization in the process of developing an integrated CSR approach, and industry-specific issues. First, generic CSR issues include (1) dialogue and engagement with stakeholders and community; (2) organizational CSR culture and leadership; (3) managing environmental, health and safety concerns; and (4) employment practices. Second, six main CSR issues relate specifically to the ethical and managerial issues of the pharmaceutical industry: (1) access to medicines for needy persons; (2) specific quality management concerns; (3) clinical trials and publication of their results; (4) responsible product design; (5) responsibility in the procurement chain; and (6) promotion of products and marketing ethics.

Figure 1.2 illustrates how these two distinct categories of CSR issues articulate across the central spheres of the activities of the business organization—production, sales and marketing, and research and development—in the case of our pharmaceutical organization.

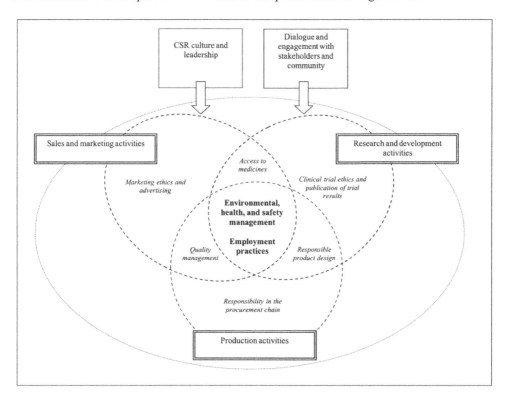

Figure 1.2   Key CSR issues in the three spheres of business activity in the case company

To assess the subsidiary organization's CSR position and perhaps highlight some best practices in the industry, we next undertake a benchmarking study of the CSR actions and policies of key players within the competitive environment. We also assess another specific organization with an excellent reputation in CSR-related matters within the broader industry.

The benchmarking study based on publicly available data (annual and sustainability reports, corporate communication, press releases, articles) highlights several areas in which the focal subsidiary might improve in terms of environmental, health, and safety management (i.e., it has no systematic policy to design environmentally friendly products; it has suffered frequent accidents or incidents, despite significant improvements in recent years); employment practices (i.e., no satisfaction survey, growing psycho-social pressures); the development of a CSR culture (i.e., absence of explicit CSR policy, and no financial and human resources dedicated specifically to CSR issues); and dialogue with external stakeholders (cf. punctual discussions generated by daily business).

During participative meetings, the interviewed managers received the findings from the pre-diagnosis, interviews, and benchmarking studies; they offer personal perceptions of these findings and arrive at a common interpretation of the identified CSR issues and their importance, which provides refinement and validation of the findings. Convergence between the managers' perceptions of key CSR issues emerged progressively through discussions and debates during the meetings. A comprehensive map of the CSR issues that the company faces finally resulted from this process, from which a CSR strategic agenda could progressively be built. In response, the subsidiary designated a CSR champion and initiated some CSR projects, including assessing external stakeholders' perceptions about its CSR posture, integrating key stakeholders into reflections about CSR issues, and designing a structured CSR external communication scheme.

According to our model (Figure 1.1), the action research led to a systematic inventory of existing CSR engagements, as well as the definition of key axes of development for a CSR strategic agenda. The outcomes of the action research further highlight how an organization can rely on diversified internal managerial perceptions and know-how to identify key CSR-related issues and establish its current CSR status. Finally, this case study enables us to suggest simple and practical recommendations in terms of internal processes that companies should develop.

1. A designated CSR facilitator should initiate CSR status analyses and supervise subsequent steps of the process.
2. Because managers reveal a function-biased understanding of the meaning of CSR in their organization, efforts to identify CSR issues thoroughly require the combination and convergence of different managerial perspectives to establish a comprehensive basis for developing the CSR strategic agenda. This requirement in turn demands that the organization identify key upper managers within the distinct functional departments of the organization who have significant know-how about organizational features and culture. All key functional departments should be represented to leverage the comprehensive examination of potential CSR issues faced by the organization.
3. Because CSR issues vary from one industry to the other, the company's CSR positioning must be benchmarked continuously within the sector of industry activities, with a simultaneous, continuous search for best practices in generic CSR issues, even outside that sector of activities. The relative strengths and weaknesses of an organization with respect

   to CSR generic and industry-specific issues should be evaluated through a simple rating process, such as below average performance, average performance, and upper average performance.

4. Meetings pertaining to CSR issues that involve managers from different functional areas should be organized to reach progressive convergence among managers' perceptions of CSR issues priority and to develop a commonly shared CSR strategic agenda.

5. Not only should a CSR champion be designated within the organization, but a CSR committee should take charge of developing a structured CSR strategic agenda on the basis of the awareness and potential strategic lines provided by the simple CSR mapping process developed in the previous steps.

DISCUSSION AND CONCLUSION

Most organizations confront environments that continue to grow more complex, unpredictable, and multifaceted. Because stakeholders convey "a variety of conflicting values and interests" (Lozano, 1996, p. 233), organizations face serious challenges in their efforts to identify and prioritize the range of societal issues they should address. In particular, developing a CSR strategic agenda can be a challenging task.

   In this context, we offer three main contributions. First, we provide a better understanding of the processes and rationales that underlie the development of a CSR strategic agenda. By integrating systems thinking, CSR, and organizational interpretation theories, we offer the first comprehensive conceptual framework to highlight how CSR issues emerge, get prioritized, and become integrated into organizational goals. Moreover, the systemic nature of the continuous process we imagine requires organizations to design structured dialogue with their stakeholders and efficient monitoring systems if they want to implement CSR strategic objectives. In accordance with Hebel and Davis (2005, p. 526), our framework emphasizes that at all points during the development process toward a CSR orientation, "the requirements of the various stakeholders involved must be accounted for, matched or adapted according to need in order to achieve the required development." Furthermore, we specify that organizations must find ways to scan their environments regularly to identify potential key CSR issues, as well as societal and business demands.

   Second, we note the critical role of upper managers and their perceptions during the development of a structured CSR-related agenda. Together, these elements contribute to an innovative perspective into the development of CSR strategic agendas by contemporary organizations.

   Third, findings from the action research portion of our study confirm that existing managerial knowledge within an organization constitutes a strong basis for initiating a CSR strategic agenda. Specifically, our findings highlight how different perceptions about CSR by various managers from various departments must complement one another if the company hopes to identify its CSR status comprehensively. Our findings further emphasize that CSR issues systematically consist of two distinct groups pertaining to generic and industry-specific CSR concerns.

   However, our article is not exempt from limitations. First, our conceptual framework requires further empirical support, perhaps with specific case studies that could provide relevant insights. Second, by emphasizing the central role of upper managers' perceptions, we may limit potential constructive inputs from the organization's main stakeholders. However, our study conceives of CSR development primarily as an organizational, strategic, or moral option, initiated by the organization and the people who manage it. This organization may be subject to multiple constraints and pressures from multiple actors, but its chief constraints involve its own resources and capabilities. Thus, although our intent certainly is not to underestimate the power and influence of key stakeholders, our conceptual framework focuses on reaffirming the role of the subjective human factor in the dynamic processes of responding to the environment and developing CSR initiatives.

Any successful process to develop organizational strategic initiatives and policies must rely on a comprehensive understanding of the issues that the organization faces. This proscription is not specific to the case of CSR. However, for CSR in particular, organizations benefit when they achieve a cohesive definition of the issues they must consider (Jaques 2006). Developing CSR involves a long, continuous process, and establishing a solid foundation for the coherent agenda represents a prerequisite for any constructive initiative. We hope our chapter contributes to such ends for organizations.

ACKNOWLEDGMENTS

The authors contributed equally. They thank Benoît Gailly and Nadine Fraselle for helping to collect data; they also thank the case organization. This chapter was first published as Maon, F., Lindgreen, A., and Swaen, V. (2008), "Thinking of the organization as a system: the role of managerial perceptions in developing a CSR strategic agenda," *Systems Research and Behavioural Science*, Vol. 25, No. 3, pp. 413–426.

REFERENCES

Achterkamp, M. C., and Vos, J. F. 2007. Critically identifying stakeholders: evaluating boundary critique as a vehicle for stakeholder identification. *Systems Research and Behavioral Science*, 24(1): 3–14.

Albright, K. S. 2004. Environmental scanning: radar for success. *The Information Management Journal*, 38(3): 38–45.

Anderson, V., and Johnson, L. 1997. *Systems thinking basics: from concepts to causal loops.* Waltham, MA: Pegasus Press.

Ashmos, D. P., Duchon, D., and McDaniel, R. R. 1998. Participation in strategic decision making—the role of organizational predisposition and issue interpretation. *Decision Science*, 29(1): 25–51.

Aslaksen, I., and Synnestvedt, T. 2003. Ethical investment and the incentives for corporate environmental protection and social responsibility. *Corporate Social Responsibility and Environmental Management*, 10(4): 212–223.

Banerjee S. B. 2001. Managerial perceptions of corporate environmentalism: interpretations from industry and strategic implications for organizations. *Journal of Management Studies*, 38(4): 489–513.

Beadle, R., and Donnelly, N. 2004. Linking reports to action at British American Tobacco. *Corporate Responsibility Management*, 1(1): 30–33.

Bedeian, A. G. 2002. The dean's disease: how the darker side of power manifests itself in the office of the dean. *Academy of Management Learning and Education*, 1(2): 164–173.

Berry, M. A., and Rondinelli, D. A. 1998. Proactive corporate environment management: a new industrial revolution. *Academy of Management Executive*, 12(2): 38–50.

Bowen, S. A, and Heath, R. L. 2005. Issue management, systems, and rhetoric: exploring the distinction between ethical and legal guidelines at Enron. *Journal of Public Affairs*, 5(2): 84–98.

Brown, T., and Dacin, P. 1997. The company and the product: corporate associations and consumer product responses. *Journal of Marketing*, 61: 68–84.

Borkowski, S. C., and Ugras, Y. J. 1998. Business students and ethics: a meta-analysis. *Journal of Business Ethics*, 17(11): 1117–1127.

Burton, B. K., and Hegarty, W. H. 1999. Some determinants of student corporate social responsibility orientation. *Business and Society*, 38: 188–205.

Business for Social Responsibility. 2003. Overview of corporate social responsibility, *BSR Issue Brief*, available at http://www.bsr.org/insight/issue-brief-details.cfm?DocumentID=48809.

Campbell, L., Gulas, C. S., and Gruca, T. S. 1999. Corporate giving behaviour and decision maker social consciousness. Journal of Business Ethics, 19(4), 375–83.

Carroll, A. B. 1999. CSR: evolution of a definitional construct. *Business and Society*, 38(3), 268–295.

Child, J. 1972. Organizational structure, environment and performance: the role of strategic choice. *Sociology*, 6(1): 1–22.

Clarkson, M. 1994. A risk based model of stakeholder theory. Proceedings of the Second Toronto Conference on Stakeholder Theory. Toronto, CA: Centre for Corporate Social Performance & Ethics, University of Toronto.

Cramer, J. M., van der Heijden, A. J. W., and Jonker, J. 2006. Corporate social responsibility: making sense through thinking and acting. *Business Ethics: A European Review*, 15(4): 380–389.

Cummings, T., and Worley, C. 2004. *Organization development and change*, 8th ed. Cincinnati, OH: South-Western College Publishing.

Daft, R., and Weick, K. 1984. Toward a model of organizations as interpretation systems. *Academy of Management Review*, 9(2): 284–295.

Dawkins, D., and Lewis, S. 2003. CSR in stakeholder expectations and their implication for company strategy. *Journal of Business Ethics*, 44(2/3): 185–193.

Dearborn, D. and Simon. H. 1958. Selective perception: a note on the department identifications of executives. *Sociometry*, 2(2): 140–144.

De Bakker, F., Groenewegen, P., and Den Hond, F. 2005. A bibliometric analysis of 30 years of research and theory on corporate social responsibility and corporate social performance. *Business and Society*, 44(3): 283–317.

Deshpande, S. P. 1997. Managers' perception of proper ethical conduct: the effect of sex, age and level of education. *Journal of Business Ethics*, 16(1): 79–85.

Doh, J. P., and Guay, T. R. 2004. Globalization and corporate social responsibility: how non-governmental organizations influence labor and environmental codes of conduct. *Management International Review*, 44 (2): 7–30.

Downey, H. K., and Slocum, J. W. Jr. 1975. Uncertainty: measures, research, and sources of variation. *Academy of Management Journal*, 18(3): 562–578.

Egels-Zandén, N., and Hyllman, P. 2006. Exploring the effects of union–NGO relationships on corporate responsibility: the case of the Swedish clean clothes campaign, *Journal of Business Ethics*, 64(3): 303–316.

European Commission. 2001. Promoting a European framework for corporate social responsibility. Green Paper, Luxembourg: Office for Official Publications of the European Communities.

Evan, W., and Freeman, R. E. 1988. A stakeholder theory of the modern corporation: Kantian capitalism. In: Beauchamp, T., and Bowie, N. (Eds.). *Ethical Theory and Business*, 3rd ed. Englewood Cliffs, NJ: Prentice-Hall, 101–105.

Freeman, R. E. 1984. *Strategic management: a stakeholder approach*. Boston, MA: Pitman.

Garriga, E., and Melé, D. 2004. Corporate social responsibility theories: mapping the territory. *Journal of Business Ethics*, 53 (1–2): 51–71.

Gatewood, D., and Carroll, A. B. 1991. Assessment of ethical performance of organization members: a conceptual framework. *Academy of Management Review*, 16(4): 667–690.

Gregory, W., and Midgley, G. 2003. Systems thinking for social responsibility. *Systems Research and Behavioral Science*, 20(2): 103–105.

Harrison, R., Newholm, T. and Shaw, D. 2006. *The ethical consumer*. London, UK: Sage.

Hebel, M., and Davis, C. 2005. Determining value in organizations: myths, norms, facts and values. *Systems Research and Behavioral Science*, 22(6): 525–536.

Hegarty, W. H., and Tihanyi, L. 1999. Surviving the transition: Central European bank executives' view of environmental changes: a metamorphosis model of convergence and reorientation. *Journal of World Business*, 34(4): 409–422.

Hemingway, C. A., and Maclagan, P. W. 2004. Managers' personal values as drivers of corporate social responsibility. *Journal of Business Ethics*, 50(1): 33–44.

Hill, J. 2001. Thinking about a more sustainable business: an indicators approach. *Corporate Environmental Strategy*, 8(1): 30–38.

Ilmolaa, I., and Kuusi, O. 2006. Filters of weak signals hinder foresight: monitoring weak signals efficiently in corporate decision-making. *Futures*, 38(8): 908–924.

Jaques, T. 2006. Issue definition: the neglected foundation of effective issue management. *Journal of Public Affairs*, 4(2): 191–200.

Krippendorf, K., and Eleey, M. I. 1986. Monitoring a group's symbolic environment. *Public Relations Review*, 12(1): 13–36.

Lozano, J. M. 1996. Ethics and management: a controversial issue. *Journal of Business Ethics*, 15(2): 227–236.

Maignan, I., and Ralston, D. 2002. Corporate social responsibility in Europe and the U.S.: insights from businesses' self-presentations. *Journal of International Business Studies*, 33: 497–514.

Maignan, I., Ferrell, O. C., and Ferrell, L. 2006. A stakeholder model for implementing social responsibility in marketing. *European Journal of Marketing*, 39(9–10): 956–976.

Maxwell, J., Rothenberg, S., Briscoe, F., and Marcus, A. 1997. Green schemes: corporate environmental strategies and their implementation. *California Management Review*, 39(3): 118–134.

McWilliams, A., and Siegel, D. 2001. Corporate social responsibility: a theory of the firm perspective. *Academy of Management Review*, 26(1): 117–227.

Menon, A., and Menon, A. 1997. Enviropreneurial marketing strategy: the emergence of corporate environmentalism as market strategy. *Journal of Marketing*, 61(1): 51–67.

Miller, K. D. 1993. Industry and country effects on managers' perception of environmental uncertainties. *Journal of International Business Studies*, 24(4): 693–714.

Milliken, F. J. 1990. Perceiving and interpreting environmental change: an examination of college administrators' interpretation of changing demographics. *Academy of Management Journal*, 33(1): 42–63.

Mitchell, R. K., Agle, B. R., and Wood, D. J. 1997. Toward a theory of stakeholder identification and salience: defining the principle of who and what really counts. *Academy of Management Review*, 22(4): 853–886.

O'Rourke, A. 2003. A new politics of engagement: shareholder activism for corporate social responsibility. *Business Strategy and the Environment*, 12: 227–239.

Pinkston, T. S., and Carroll, A. B. 1994. Corporate citizenship perspectives and foreign direct investment in the U.S. *Journal of Business Ethics*, 13(3): 157–169.

Polonsky, M., and Jevons, C. 2006. Understanding issue complexity when building a socially responsible brand. *European Business Review*, 18(5): 340–349.

Polonsky, M., and Rosenberger, P. 2001. Re-evaluating to green marketing: an integrated approach. *Business Horizons*, 44(5): 21–30.

Porter, M. E. and Kramer, M. R. 2006. Strategy and society: the link between competitive advantage and corporate social responsibility. Harvard Business Review, 84(12): 78–92.

Quazi, A. M. 2003. Identifying the determinants of corporate managers' perceived social obligations. *Management Decision*, 41(9): 822–831.

Reich, R. 1992. *The work of nations: preparing ourselves for 21st century capitalism*. New York: Vintage.

Renfro, W. 1993. *Issues management in strategic planning*. Westport, CT: Quorum Books.

Roberts, S. 2003. Supply chain specific? Understanding the patchy success of ethical sourcing initiatives. *Journal of Business Ethics*, 44(2/3): 159–170.

Rokeach, M. 1973. *The nature of human values*. New York: Free Press.

Santos, M. V., and Garcia, M. T. 2006. Managers' opinions: reality or fiction: a narrative approach. *Management Decision*, 44(6): 752–770.

Secchi, D. 2007. Utilitarian, managerial and relational theories of corporate social responsibility. *International Journal of Management Reviews*, 9(4): 347–373.

Sen, S., and Bhattacharya, C. B. 2001. Does doing good always lead to doing better? Consumer reactions to corporate social responsibility. *Journal of Marketing Research*, 38(2): 225–243.

Sen, S., Bhattacharya, C. B., and Korshun D. 2006. The role of corporate social responsibility in strengthening multiple stakeholder relationships: a field experiment. *Academy of Marketing Science Journal*, 34(2): 158–166.

Senge, P. 1990. *The fifth discipline: the art and practice of the learning organization.* New York: Doubleday.

Simon, H. 1957. *Administrative behaviour.* New York: Free Press.

Sharma, S., and Vredenburg, H. 1998. Proactive corporate environmental strategy and the development of competitively valuable organizational capabilities. *Strategic Management Journal*, 19: 739–753

Stoll-Kleemann, S., and Welp, M. 2006. Towards a more effective and democratic natural resources management. In Stoll-Kleemann, S., and Welp, M. (Eds.). *Stakeholder Dialogues in Natural Resources Management.* Heidelberg: Springer-Verlag, 17–40.

Thomas, A., and Simerly, R. 1994. The chief executive officer and corporate social performance: an interdisciplinary examination. *Journal of Business Ethics*, 13(12): 959–968.

Turban, D. B., and Greening, D. W. 1996. Corporate social performance and organizational attractiveness to prospective employees. *Academy of Management Journal*, 40: 658–672.

Tushman, M., and Nadler, D. 1978. Information processing as an integrating concept in organizational design. *Academy of Management Review*, 3(3): 613–624.

Ulrich, W. 1983. *Critical heuristics of social planning. A new approach to practical philosophy.* Bern: Haupt, 1994 reprint edition, Chichester: Wiley.

Ulrich, W. 1988. Systems thinking, systems practice, and practical philosophy: a program of research. *Systems Practice*, 1(2): 137–163.

Vos, J. 2003. Corporate social responsibility and the identification of stakeholders. *Corporate Social Responsibility and Environmental Management*, 10(3), 141–52.

Waddock, S. A., and Boyle, M-E. 1995. The dynamics of change in corporate community relations. *California Management Review*, 37: 125–140.

Waddock, S. A., Bodwell, C., and Graves, S. 2002. Responsibility: the new business imperative. *Academy of Management Executive*, 16(2): 132–148.

Waldman, D. A., Sully de Luque, M., Washburn, N., and House R. J. 2006. Cultural and leadership predictors of corporate social responsibility values of top management: a GLOBE study of 15 countries. *Journal of International Business Studies*, 37(6): 823–837.

Walker, E-J. 2005. Transitioning from charity to community investment at Marks & Spencer. *Corporate Responsibility Management*, 1(6): 26–29.

WBCSD. 2001. Corporate social responsibility—narrowing the focus. *WBCSD News*, available at http://www.wbcsd.org.

Weick, K. 1979. *The social psychology of organizing.* Reading, MA: Addison-Wesley.

Werther, W., and Chandler, D. 2006. Strategic corporate social responsibility: stakeholders in a global environment. Thousand Oaks, CA: Sage Publications.

Wood, D. J. 1991. Corporate social performance revisited. *Academy of Management Review*, 16(4), 691–718.

Zyglidopoulos, S. 2002. The social and environmental responsibilities of multinationals: evidence from the Brent Spar case. *Journal of Business Ethics*, 36(1/2): 141–151.

2. Corporate foundations as vehicles for sustainable development: how do corporate foundations work with parent companies to achieve sustainability?

Pilar Acosta

INTRODUCTION

The business–society interface has historically taken multiple forms and denominations that currently remain and coexist (Acosta & Pérezts, 2019). One of these entities is the corporate foundation, which has grown in number in several regions of the world (Corporate Citizenship, 2014; Roza et al., 2019) alongside the expansion of Corporate Social Responsibility (CSR), sustainability-related strategies, and changes in public funding for areas including the arts, culture, and education.

Although there is no universal definition of the corporate foundation and understanding varies depending on the institutional context, in a broader sense, they are legally separated organizations created by corporate actors (for-profit entities) with a public benefit purpose (Roza et al., 2019).

Corporate foundations are usually established as vehicles of corporate philanthropy to advance social causes that are not necessarily linked to the core business of the founding company. In developing regions, corporate foundations have traditionally worked with communities located in the territories of operation, or on the social problems of other groups, such as employees or disadvantaged communities. At a global level, they tend to focus on grant-making, donate locally, and support a variety of causes (see Roza et al., 2019, for a comparison of corporate foundations across institutional settings).

In Europe, there has been an increase in the number of foundations since the 1980s; nevertheless, the number of corporate foundations remains small. Corporate foundations offer grants in areas poorly financed by the state or they implement corporate volunteering programs. They can also help communicate the CSR commitments of the parent company (Gehringer & von Schnurbein, 2019) thereby enhancing the company's reputation. In Latin America, early corporate foundations appeared under the influence of the Catholic Church, who pushed local elites to become involved in social welfare. At the turn of the last century, in the context of limited state intervention and the increasing international influence of CSR, the numbers of corporate foundations rose (Rey-García et al., 2019).

Over the last few decades, changes in the conception of the business–society relationship have pushed companies to reconceptualize social and environmental problems as business issues. The development of CSR and corporate sustainability concepts alongside changes in publicly funded programs fostered the private sector's direct involvement in the creation of prosperous societies. In this context, there has been a shift toward the stronger alignment of corporate foundations with the core business of the founding corporation in several regions of the world such as Europe, Latin America, and the United States (Roza et al., 2019).

Indeed, corporate philanthropy has gained momentum on a global scale (Gautier & Pache, 2015) and calls for more strategic philanthropy (Porter & Kramer, 2002) have increased. In both developed and developing countries, corporate foundations are increasingly understood as strategic arms of the organization that fulfills philanthropic activities. Although corporate foundations remain tools of broader CSR strategies, there is a global trend toward the integration of corporate foundations with parent companies.

Companies may obtain several benefits from this integration such as an enhanced reputation, gathering social insights, increased expertise and knowledge (Westhues & Einwiller, 2006), and increased employee satisfaction (Bethmann & von Schnurbein, 2019). However, the integration process is not easy, particularly because the competencies and priorities of companies and corporate foundations differ. CSR or sustainability departments and corporate foundations may perform redundant tasks.

In multiple cases, business objectives may clash with the role of corporate foundations and their central activities. Companies may also fall into the trap of using corporate foundations as vehicles for enhancing their public reputation without reflecting on their activities' long-term social impacts. In the nonprofit literature, there is even a dispute over companies' influence in philanthropy (Roza et al., 2019). If a corporate foundation is not focused on its social mission this can also jeopardize its particular tax regime (if applicable) (Bethmann & von Schnurbein, 2019).

A study by the Charities Aid Foundation (2007) identified that the integration of CSRs has had an impact on certain corporate foundations. In some cases, the rationale for the foundation's existence has disappeared. In other cases, the foundation has become a component of CSR. In either case, the social purpose of the foundation might be at risk.

Research on corporate foundations is scarce although it has increased in recent years. Few studies focusing on corporate foundations depict how tensions between corporate control and freedom play out in practice (Renz et al., 2019; Bethmann & von Schnurbein, 2019). In this context, this chapter reflects on the role of corporate foundations and their links with sustainability-CSR departments.

We share preliminary insights from an ongoing study of relationships between corporate foundations and CSR-sustainability-related departments in Latin America, particularly in Colombia. We conducted interviews with both parent companies and corporate foundations. Our research question was *how do corporate foundations contribute to achieving corporate sustainability while ensuring an appropriate balance between advancing the interests of the parent company and delivering social welfare?*

Our starting point conceived of the corporate foundation as a hybrid vehicle for the practice of corporate sustainability to characterize the types of relationships between corporate foundations and parent companies. Corporate foundations navigate two types of logic as organizations that use private means for public ends. We conceive of them as hybrid organizations where both business and philanthropic logic are at play (Battilana & Lee, 2014; Roza ct al., 2019). Given our goal was understanding how corporate foundations make their activities acceptable to corporate actors while contributing to corporate sustainability, we drew on the institutional work literature (Lawrence & Suddaby, 2006). This literature focuses on how actors implement practices in daily life to build, elaborate, or contain institutions. This literature is of particular interest because it permitted us to study the work actors perform during the process of hybrid organizing; for example, the activities, structures, processes, and meanings which actors use to make sense of and combine both business and philanthropic logic (Battilana & Lee, 2014).

This chapter is structured as follows. First, we define corporate foundations and discuss their hybrid nature. Next, we present the methodology. Third, we describe our findings divided into two sections. We begin by describing the three types of relationships between corporate foundations and sustainability departments, namely (i) corporate foundations as internal experts dedicated to the company's sustainability objectives; (ii) corporate foundations as internal experts that accompany the sustainability objectives of the company; (iii) corporate foundations as external actors with no links to the sustainability objectives of the company. We then move on to depict the types of work performed during the process of delivering social welfare and contributing to corporate sustainability. We conclude our chapter with a discussion of the results.

THEORETICAL BACKGROUND

Corporate philanthropy is broadly defined as the provision of private goods for public aims. There is still a debate about whether corporate philanthropy is an altruistic or a for-profit activity. In a literature review on this issue, Gautier & Pache (2015) identified three rationales for corporate philanthropy: an expression of a company's strategy for achieving the common good, a long-term community investment, or a commercial tool deployed to promote cause-related marketing.

Corporate philanthropy may include voluntary financial contributions, in-kind donations, or corporate volunteering (Roza et al., 2019). Businesses may choose to channel their philanthropic activities in-house or create a corporate foundation to make a greater social impact. Therefore, corporate foundations are a vehicle of corporate philanthropy.

Questions about the appropriateness of corporate philanthropy remain the source of some debate. For some, philanthropic activities contradict the profit-making motive of businesses. Meanwhile, others argue that philanthropy has potential positive benefits for a company (Roza et al., 2019).

In either case, corporate foundations have increasingly emerged as vehicles that channel corporate philanthropy. However, what exactly are corporate foundations and how are they involved in corporate sustainability?

Corporate Foundations

The definition of corporate foundations may change depending on the institutional context. Social origins theory (Salamon & Anheier, 1998) distinguishes cross-national variations in the nonprofit sector according to two variables: government social welfare spending and the scale of the nonprofit sector. For instance, Rey-García et al., 2019, report that in Latin America the lack of evidence on the sector and the specificities of the institutional setting make it difficult to adopt an existing definition. They propose a definition that includes regional traits.

Our empirical sample was located in the Latin American region; therefore, we used this definition and combined it with the one proposed by Roza et al. (2019). We define corporate foundations as (1) separate legal entities from parent companies; (2) public benefit objectives,

(3) established, funded, governed, and controlled to some degree by private businesses, state-owned enterprises, and standalone firms or business groups.

According to the definition above it is clear that corporate foundations have a relationship with parent companies that govern them to some degree. The parent company is to some extent the resource provider, mainly through donations, dividends, or endowments.

Our definition also considers corporate foundations as hybrid organizations that straddle business logic and nonprofit logic (Smith, 2010; Roza et al., 2019). Institutional logics are defined as taken-for-granted beliefs and practices that guide actors' behavior in fields of activity (Friedland & Alford, 1991). Hybridity occurs when organizations have to navigate competing and sometimes conflicting demands because they are positioned between the business sector and civil society. For instance, Cemex is a global player in the construction materials business and has a corporate foundation in Colombia that works on poverty reduction through social programs for vulnerable communities located in the company's zones of influence. The company's sustainability webpage[1] includes the corporate foundation. In 2020, the foundation developed training programs and built schools among other activities, but also focused on programs related to the core business such as *Bloqueras Solidarias*,[2] a solution created for families to build their houses with concrete blocks that they produce themselves. Cemex provides training in the production of concrete blocks, machinery, and raw materials.

Over the last few decades, the numbers of corporate foundations have increased in several regions and their rise has been concomitant with the expansion of CSR. Although no studies are focusing on this link, corporate foundations can be an effective tool for creating shared value (Bethmann & von Schnurbein, 2019). Indeed, in recent years there have been calls for greater investment in strategic philanthropy (Porter & Kramer, 2002). Following this, corporate foundations have faced increasing demands to comply with business objectives. In the next section, we discuss corporate foundations as hybrid organizations.

Corporate Foundations as Hybrid Organizations

Existing knowledge of corporate foundations has identified their diversity. However, corporate foundations present a peculiarity that distinguishes them from other organizations engaged in social action, since their activities are located at an intermediate, hybrid point, between the public and private spheres. On the one hand, they may serve the business logic of the founding company by leveraging the company's approach to sustainability. On the other hand, their traditional identity makes them more attuned to social issues.

Most corporate foundations are moving away from a purely philanthropic logic, toward work agreements with the founding company. "One thing that was apparent is that many corporate foundations across the globe are in a state of flux. A number commented on a blurring of lines as the business becomes more involved in social issues" (Corporate Citizenship, 2014, p. 7).

This trend has also been noted in Europe by Gehringer & von Schnurbein (2019) and in the case of Latin America by Rey-García et al. (2019):

> during the last 30 years, a reconceptualization of civil society and a new understanding of the roles of the state, market, and civil society play unfolded. A role for NGOs and other civil society organizations, including foundations, emerged, and competition for funding led them to become increasingly entrepreneurial. Societal expectations of local and foreign firms also evolved as the pressure to

behave responsibly and commit themselves to community development and environmental sustainability increased. (Rey-García et al., 2019, p.185)

Thus, for some corporate foundations, one of the biggest challenges they face is the (re)definition of their role and their integration into their resource company's approach to sustainability. This means not only thinking about what sustainability means for the company but defining how the corporate foundation, which in many cases was created for purely philanthropic and charitable purposes, must (or not) uphold the company's social and environmental responsibilities. Inevitably, this generates political tensions about the jurisdictions of each entity and involves reflecting on the identities, roles, and activities of each organization.

The literature points to the benefits corporate foundations provide for companies in terms of CSR or sustainability-related programs. Westhues and Einwiller (2006) describe corporate foundations as sensors of societal needs, knowledge generators, and facilitators of access to external contacts and organizations that improve a company's reputation.

However, because corporate foundations are increasingly tied to CSR, their activities should be linked to what corporate leaders consider appropriate. In other words, the orientation of corporate leadership has an impact on the governance (i.e., the systems and processes providing the overall direction, control, and accountability) of corporate foundations (Renz et al., 2019).

In extreme cases, parent companies may decide that a foundation is not an appropriate vehicle for achieving philanthropic goals, which increases tensions in corporate foundations, particularly those without endowments. Corporate foundations are thus to a certain extent forced to find a balance between their existing programs and addressing their parent company's sustainability activities.

In this chapter, we investigate these tensions to understand how corporate foundations respond to the challenges in the shift toward this new role and how they contribute to their parent company's achievement of their sustainability objectives.

To grasp the state of flux of corporate foundations' nature and purpose, we conceptualize them as hybrid entities that integrate the logic of philanthropy and business to a greater or lesser extent. Corporate foundations are agents of social change that are structurally related to the company's corporate sustainability. Figure 2.1 depicts the main dimensions of the relationship between corporate foundations and their parent companies (Battilana & Lee, 2014; Renz et al., 2019). Table 2.1 describes the dimensions involved in this relationship.

To understand how actors navigate hybridity (i.e., perform work in the dimensions of hybridity) we consulted the institutional work literature. This literature has been useful for understanding how CSR has been hybridized to combine and adapt to different CSR approaches (Acquier et al., 2018), and how CSR becomes strategic (Gond et al., 2018). In this chapter, we use the institutional work approach to understand how different groups of actors (actors from CSR or sustainability departments in parent companies and actors in corporate foundations) interact through institutional work (Acosta et al., 2019). Using an institutional work framework, we investigate how both groups interact in response to corporate sustainability and social welfare challenges.

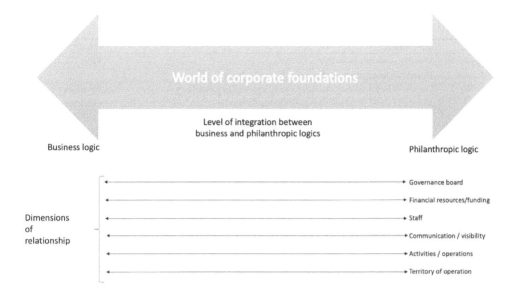

Figure 2.1   *Dimensions of the relationship between corporate foundations and parent company, developed based on Battilana and Lee (2014) and Renz et al. (2019)*

Table 2.1   *Dimensions of the relationship between corporate foundations and their parent companies*

Dimension	Description
Governance/board	Refers to the process of direction, control, and accountability
	Board composition
Financial resources/funding	Includes sources of income
	Includes in-kind services (e.g., human resources processes, legal advice, IT services, offices, etc.)
Staff	Refers to staff expertise, payroll, and recruitment
Communication/visibility	Refers to brand similarity and communication processes
Activities/operations	Refers to the activities, programs, and links to parent company CSR or sustainability programs
Territory of operation	Location of operations

METHODOLOGY

We share preliminary insights from an ongoing study of corporate foundations. We focused on Colombia. The country stands out in the region due to the number, seniority, and significance of corporate foundations (Rey-García et al., 2019).

We used a qualitative approach based on interviews and observation. We conducted 12 semi-structured interviews in Colombian organizations with members of the parent company and their corporate foundation. We also observed two meetings where members of corporate foundations discussed their new roles and challenges when meeting the demands of the social and corporate worlds. Table 2.2 summarizes the interview sources.

Table 2.2   *Data sources–interviews*

Company	Interviewees	Industry
Company 1	Director – corporate foundation	Paper
	Director social development department – parent company	
Company 2	Director of both corporate affairs department and corporate foundation	Beverages
Company 3	Director of both CSR department and corporate foundation	Construction materials
Company 4	Director – corporate foundation	Energy
	Director – CSR department parent company	
Company 5	Director of partnerships – corporate foundation	Food
	Director of sustainability department – parent company	
Company 6	Director – corporate foundation	Food
	Director of sustainability department – parent company	
Company 7	Director – corporate foundation	Utilities
	Director of sustainability department – parent company	

Interviews explored the organization's history and sustainability strategy, the purpose of both entities, the synergies between them, as well as areas of tension. All interviews were recorded and transcribed.

We conducted a three-step analysis. During the first phase, we conducted a line-by-line analysis of each interview to extract answers to the different questions and topics of the interview. Second, we grouped these first-order activities into second-order themes (Gioia et al., 2013) that corresponded to the patterns of tensions, challenges, and roles of corporate foundations. We also identified the best practices for managing such tensions. We identified three types of relationships between corporate foundations and sustainability departments. These ideal types captured the roles that corporate foundations play in relation to the achievement of CSR or sustainability objectives. We understand sustainability includes a wide range of economic, social, and ecological goals (Baumgartner & Ebner, 2010).

During the third phase, we focused on the actors' work performance. We conducted a second round of coding the tensions and challenges identified during the first phase of analysis. We identified specific practices in each dimension of the relationship (see Figure 2.1 and Table 2.1). Following an iteration between data and insights from prior research on institutional work, we grouped specific challenges and tensions in each dimension according to the best practices for managing them. For instance, when corporate foundations faced the risk of mission drift due to the expectation of short-term results, we identified the best practices for managing this challenge: constructing boundaries, establishing spaces for dialog, and training employees. We then grouped these practices into types of institutional work. We identified three types of institutional work: deliberative political work, material work, and educational work.

FINDINGS

The sample included a range of relationships between corporate foundations and corporate sustainability departments. As noted by Rey-García et al. (2019), Colombian corporate foundations have followed an idiosyncratic path compared with other Latin American countries. In this section, we present two sets of findings: the roles of corporate foundations in parent companies' achievement of their sustainability strategy and the different types of institutional work involved in the relationship between corporate foundations and parent companies when implementing their sustainability strategy.

Roles of Corporate Foundations to Achieve Corporate Sustainability of Parent Companies

Following the conceptualization of corporate foundations as hybrid organizations, we classified them into groups according to a combination of the two logics across relationship dimensions. In the first group, corporate foundations were identified as internal structures of expertise dedicated to the company's sustainability. In the second group, corporate foundations were also structures of expertise, but their role was to accompany (and not dedicate themselves to) the company when implementing its sustainability strategy. In the third group, the corporate foundation was disconnected from the parent company and its sustainability objectives.

Corporate Foundations as Internal Experts Dedicated to the Company's Sustainability

This first type of relationship integrates the corporate foundation into the company's existing areas or departments. The corporate foundation resembles a business unit that depends on one area of the company, although they are legally separate entities. These types of corporate foundations are closer to business logic. The corporate foundation is an expert for the company and is usually responsible for the company's actions toward communities, helping the business to maintain its license to operate and improve its reputation.

For example, this was the case with Company 2. A couple of years ago, the corporate foundation joined the corporate affairs area. The corporate foundation is in charge of working on large projects related to the company's sustainability and is in charge of relationships with external stakeholders such as communities when social issues are at stake. Some examples include responsible consumption issues, distribution in remote or rural areas, or working with suppliers to improve their organization:

> The foundation was not completely misaligned but did nothing with the core business of the company. Although the corporate foundation worked with small distributors, they were not necessarily from our network. I had some projects related [to the core business], but there was no alignment between the company's CSR and sustainability approaches with the corporate foundation's programs. What we did was completely align them. The corporate foundation became the sustainability and social responsibility arm of the company. (Company 2)

The corporate foundation is responsible for the actions of the company vis-à-vis communities and helps achieve sustainability objectives using their expertise in social issues.

> The foundation was recently created with the objective not only of having a business unit responsible for social actions. The purpose of creating the foundation was to improve efficiency in the processes involved in the social license to operate. (Company 3)

Owing to this close alignment, the foundation's management processes follow a business logic, managed with indicators, responding to an efficiency model:

[The corporate foundation] operates under the assumption that it is responsible for its costs, efficiency, and impact. Before, it was not like that, the board of directors was not very focused on whether someone was over budget or if costs were reasonable or not, people were a little irresponsible when handling money because we paid more or less what we wanted. There was no business logic within the foundation. (Company 2)

The corporate foundation helps improve the company reputation in operational areas:

All CSR programs are developed throughout the foundation. The purpose of the existence of the social foundation is to execute not only CSR actions, but also to improve our social license to operate. We have extractive activities and use of non-renewable natural resources, within our environmental licenses there is a chapter of social license to operate. (Company 4)

Corporate Foundations as Internal Experts Accompanying the Company's Sustainability

In this configuration, the foundation is an autonomous entity with projects that accompany the company, and other projects of its own that may or may not be related to the core business of the company. This type of business foundation would be located at the center of the continuum, sharing the two logics (see Figure 2.1).

This was the case for most of the corporate foundations in our sample. These corporate foundations have progressively developed activities that are closer to the parent company's sustainability strategy. For instance, in the case of Company 1, the foundation was originally focused on giving scholarships to employees' children. Today the corporate foundation has education or housing programs for communities that are related in some way to the company's core business.

Although differences exist between corporate foundations that fulfill this role, in general, corporate foundations work closely with parent companies to achieve a corporate sustainability strategy:

The corporate foundation has a philanthropic purpose, improving the quality of education, but there is also a relationship with the company. If there is an issue of the company where the foundation needs to go, we support them. (Company 4)

In this model, the corporate foundation serves as an expert closer to the social world and provides social intelligence (Rossetti, in Fundación Promigas and Fundación DIS, 2012). The corporate foundation "has to be that think-tank that helps to analyze long-term processes" (Company 7) or "the social knowledge brain" (Company 6).

The development of reports, studies, or informal meetings between the two organizations facilitates this role:

Every year we do a reading of the context, its economic, social, and cultural characteristics [...] we do this analysis to include the social aspect in the decision-making processes of the company. The foundation has to be the company's social think-tank. Companies should have think-tanks monitoring the territory and alerting them when necessary so the company can take strategic decisions. (Company 6)

Thus, the corporate foundation acts as a structure that detects and explores new trends and social conditions, helping the company to anticipate and reduce risk.

Both actors from the parent company and the corporate foundation recognize the key role of corporate foundations as articulators of the company's and communities' needs. More and more foundations are seen: "as hinge entities between the company giving them birth and the community that [receives] CSR actions" (Company 3).

This role of articulator inevitably leads to improving the reputation of the company, without compromising the social role of the foundation:

> Today my role is to maintain the reputation of the company. However, our social contribution is not to develop communities so we can sell more products. We have to do our job in a way that our communities are sustained, to maintain their traditions, their ancestral knowledge … I am not thinking about selling them products, I am thinking about how to recover their knowledge, how they learn, who listens to them. That is different but it obviously enhances reputation and management. (Company 7)

> We are not generating public goods for the company; we are contributing to the creation of public goods for communities. We want communities in good conditions. This generates good conditions for the company to be competitive and sustainable. The company has also worked very well with its programs, creates employment and is a generator of well-being in the areas where it is located. I believe that the foundation has played an important role in bringing conditions to vulnerable communities. (Company 1)

Corporate Foundations as External Actors with no Direct Links to the Company's Sustainability

A third group is those foundations not articulated with the founding company. These tend to have a portfolio of projects not related to a parent company's core business. They operate far from the value chain of the founding company, maintaining a philanthropic purpose as a central praxis. These foundations are closer to the end of the continuum and embrace philanthropic logic (see Figure 2.1).

Although increasingly rare, there are some corporate foundations with the same brand name that do not work in close articulation.

> The peculiarity of this foundation is an external entity to the company. The corporate foundation was born from the will of the owners to contribute to a general problem that is guaranteeing food. The foundation was born, but with the idea of not having ties with the corporation's value chain. (Company 5)

We identified the same tensions across the three types of relationships. First, there is a risk of drifting from the corporate foundation's mission. An essential difference lies in the work of each of the organizations: while the company wants to develop activities that generate social and economic well-being, the foundation will prioritize social objectives. For a corporate foundation, combining commercial and social objectives is in itself a challenge since these do not necessarily entail the same types of activities. Concentrating on one purpose can lead the foundation to neglect the other.

In extreme cases, this tension can lead to an instrumentalization of the corporate foundation. The articulating nature of foundations can add value, but at the same time, a risk of unethical work with communities can arise. The corporate foundation tries to remain autonomous to avoid solving conflicts and operational emergencies which benefits the company. Several comments from interviewees indicated the risks involved:

> The tensions began when the company wanted the foundation to solve those problems. For example, when communities block roads because the company damaged them, and the company wants the corporate foundation to fix that problem. That is not the responsibility of the corporate foundation, the company has to be responsible for its impacts. (Company 1)

Second, corporate foundations and parent companies find it difficult to balance their cultural differences, which are reflected in staff competencies and time horizons (long-term versus short-term results). The hybrid nature of corporate foundations evokes staff tensions when they are required to respond to corporate and social logics (Battilana & Dorado, 2010). Due to their training and past experiences, each individual in the organization has a disposition to work with one of these two logics. Each person in the company–corporate foundation binomial identifies to a greater or lesser extent with one of the two logics. This means that for some people it may be more difficult to understand decisions that are made based on one of the perspectives, or they may be inclined to make decisions or actions considering only one logic. As mentioned by the sustainability manager of Company 6: "we even had to rethink our capacities to understand each other. There are tensions that arise even from the language."

The time to accomplish philanthropic objectives is by nature longer, while the company operates on many occasions with a short-term perspective focused on solving urgent matters:

> The company could go on without the foundation, not at the depth communities need. The corporate foundation can take the time to think about strategies, methodologies, and design issues to deliberate with the communities. It doesn't mean that the company can't do it, it can hire professionals. Operational times are different and results too. Without the foundations, those complementary actions would disappear, and the company would lose. Foundations create positioning, reputation, commitment, and closeness to the communities. (Company 7)

Furthermore, organizing internal resources to serve multiple purposes can itself be challenging. A common tension involves securing funding, particularly for foundations without an endowment. Some foundations implement some for-profit activities to finance their social programs and others apply for grants or work with government funds.

Our results indicate that actors from both organizations manage to find a balance between the two logics (even if gray spaces still exist). How do actors from both parent companies and corporate foundations achieve such a balance between achieving corporate sustainability and social welfare? In the next section, we present three types of institutional work from actors of corporate foundations and parent companies.

Actor's Work in Balancing Corporate Sustainability and Social Welfare

We identify three types of work performed by actors: deliberative political work, material work, and educational work.

Deliberative political work

This work includes all practices involving dialogical processes that facilitate mutual understanding, deliberation, and collective learning (Scherer, 2018). In our case, we found that both company and corporate foundation actors managed hybridity through dialog spaces and cross-coordination across different hierarchical levels.

One of the practices that allowed a fluid relationship was the use of permanent dialog spaces. Two aspects are necessary for such conversations to bear fruit. On the one hand, the use of argumentation and persuasion strategies:

> We always seek agreement, and progressively reach consensus. It never was, it never has been, and it can never be, because that would damage relationships, something imposed by one of the two parties, and that is super clear. (Company 6)

On the other hand, permanent dialog spaces go hand in hand with these argumentation and discussion strategies. Spaces allow a collective definition of what sustainability means from a social point of view. Furthermore, these committees facilitate work with communities across operational territories: "the social committee is a concertation space where we define our areas of intervention" (Company 1). Defining the territorial boundaries of operations is important because it can be a source of tension. The territory is where communities and professionals from the corporate foundation and the parent company meet. Professionals from both organizations meet regularly to discuss the evolution and needs of projects.

Material work
This type of work includes practices aimed at defining structures and systems to facilitate a balance between the two logics. Once spaces for dialog are defined and functional, usually corporate foundations and companies formalize the roles of each organization and facilitate the maintenance of agreements. Doing so officially defines the corporate foundation's contribution to the parent company's sustainability objectives.

The first practice involves recording dialog. Usually, actors document discussions so everyone can have access to the guidelines defined:

> We registered dialogs, debates, and progress. At one point in the technical committee, we managed to produce a booklet documenting the whole process. We documented the process of identifying groups, subgroups, actors, interests, material issues, we have all of that documented. (Company 6)

Second, actors push for an integration of relationships into the routines and artifacts of both the company and the corporate foundation. For instance, in some cases, there is a joint planning activity to agree on budgets to work with communities. This avoids redundancies by maximizing the impact and use of resources: "the joint planning and budgeting exercise allows covering more populations. By doing so, we do not waste time and focus" (Company 1).

Education work
This type of work includes practices related to socialization, training, and enabling actors to understand the respective roles and relationships between corporate foundations and parent companies. Actors described achieving a permanent training program as one of the biggest difficulties. Actors from both organizations saw educational work as a means to develop a relationship based on supporting project implementation and not the resolution of last-minute problems within communities.

To work on this issue, the first actors socialized the logic and purpose of each organization. These factors were mentioned by some foundations as the key to success. Each actor's role was communicated at all levels of the company, always understanding that the foundation was a philanthropic endeavor with a greater purpose, with results that were only obtained in the medium and long-term.

> Employees did not know the work of the foundation. The foundation wasn't communicating about its programs or wasn't participating in commercial meetings. That has changed. Employees now visit the foundation's programs, do volunteer work, and see what the company is doing for some communities. (Company 4)

Second, formal training has been implemented to improve sensitivity to social issues and understanding each organization's processes.

> We realized that employees from the company lack knowledge about the foundation and vice versa. Employees from the foundation didn't know the processes of the company, especially forestry. We began some exchanges, both teams started to visit each other's projects in the field. (Company 1)

DISCUSSION

In this chapter, we identified a typology of corporate foundation roles that contribute to parent companies' sustainability objectives. We also uncovered how actors from both parent companies and corporate foundations work together in that direction. By doing so, our work explains the interactive nature of developing sustainability. In the following section, we present the implications of our work for the study of corporate foundations and for the implementation of sustainability.

Implications for Corporate Foundations as Vehicles of Corporate Sustainability

Traditionally, corporate foundations in Latin America and particularly in Colombia worked in education, community development, or economic and business development (Acosta & Pérezts, 2019; Rey-García et al., 2019). Today, our results indicate that these areas remain but with a focus on helping parent companies achieve their sustainability objectives.

For corporate foundations to contribute to their parent company's sustainability objectives, they have to navigate both philanthropic and business logic. The degree to which each corporate foundation combines the logics in each of the dimensions confirms the diversity of corporate foundations. Our three roles capture ideal types that contribute to sustainability strategies while each corporate foundation follows a unique path. Each model works with specific features of parent companies and sustainability actions. The corporate foundations of multinational companies work more on core business issues in a model that is closer to shared value or strategic philanthropy. However, local companies with their roots in Catholic principles and charity maintain a strong philanthropic orientation.

In our sample, most corporate foundations acted as articulators of the needs of local communities and corporate sustainability strategies. This articulation defines corporate foundations as experts at developing social intelligence about the communities where they operate. Corporate foundations build capacity in communities (i.e., education, training, and income generation) whereas companies focus on technical sustainability issues.

This role occupies a crossroads between instrumental and complementary philanthropy (Bethmann & von Schnurbein, 2019). In these models, corporate foundations have a high alignment with the core business, a high degree of independence from the complementary model, and a low degree of independence from the instrumental model. In our sample, corporate foundations worked more closely with the parent company on its sustainability issues and the benefits accrued were not necessarily spillovers but joint projects. At the same time, corporate foundations developed their own projects.

In this model, corporate philanthropy seems strategic and corporate foundations contribute to the achievement of their parent company's sustainability objectives. They develop parent company markets, increase their license to operate and, when brand names are the same, they enhance corporate reputation. This model has the advantage of reducing the corporate foundation's risk of instrumentalization by developing long-term projects that create social welfare in communities where companies operate (Von Schnurbein et al., 2016). For instance, companies may work with small suppliers to improve their technical capacities (e.g., in terms of agricultural practices) while the foundation trains communities to improve their business literacy or to safeguard their traditions.

The instrumental approach to philanthropy is the dominant model of corporate philanthropy (Bethmann & von Schnurbein, 2019). This poses ethical questions about why foundations exist and how accountable they are to the communities they serve. The corporate foundation must be careful not to repair damage (i.e., solve urgent problems related to a license to operate in communities).

The foundation's role as articulator may counteract this challenge and enable parent companies to reach their sustainability objectives, particularly social goals. Our work thus complements other typologies by focusing on the complex interaction between corporate foundations and parent companies in the development of sustainability. Further studies could further investigate combinations of different dimensions of hybridity and the resulting outcomes in terms of the type of sustainability strategy (Baumgartner & Ebner, 2010). For instance, it would be interesting to find out if a corporate foundation's role as an articulator relates to a visionary strategy, particularly when dealing with social issues.

Following the idea of social sustainability as the result of negotiations between parent companies and corporate foundations, our results show three types of work performed by these entities to achieve such an outcome.

We uncover the importance of deliberative practices for managing the tensions of hybridity resulting from different approaches to social issues. These practices encompass a series of unobtrusive influence tactics that are useful for overcoming constraints (Daudigeos, 2013). In the context of CSR, these tactics help compensate for the lack of formal power of both corporate foundations vis-à-vis parent companies and sustainability departments within parent companies (Acosta et al., 2019). By working together, corporate foundations and sustainability departments join forces to influence strategies to ensure that sustainability criteria are included in decision-making processes. For instance, in one of the cases in this study, collaboration and joint work led to the creation of a sustainability committee on the board of the parent company.

The use of deliberative politics is a necessary but not sufficient condition. Actors also work on the formalization of the relationship in existing structures and management systems and education at all levels. Once safe spaces are created, actors have some freedom to develop or change existing structures to formalize the defined relationship.

However, maintenance of boundaries is secured through education. Socialization and training facilitate work in the territories of operation where professionals from both organizations meet with communities.

Recent literature has paid attention to the role of individuals in the development of CSR or sustainability-related approaches (Gond et al., 2017). We contribute to this line of inquiry, showing how different actors from organizations with different logics perform the same practices facilitating the implementation of sustainability objectives. Recent research has shown how actors from different hierarchical positions perform similar types of work to achieve common outcomes (Acosta et al., 2019). This study also points in this direction showing how actors from heterogeneous groups, in this case, organizations with different logics, collaborate (Zietsma & Lawrence, 2010) using the same type of work to advance sustainability.

Corporate foundations may then be seen as boundary spanners (Zietsma & Lawrence, 2010) that extend the competences of parent companies (Santos & Eisenhardt, 2005) to achieve social sustainability. Boundary work helps understand the process of alignment between parent companies and some of their stakeholders (Velter et al., 2020); in this specific case, local communities.

CONCLUSION

Corporate foundations can be an important source of added value to the company. Interviewees from both companies and corporate foundations highlighted the role of the foundation vis-à-vis the company when pointing to the complexity and diversity of the social world. For the parent company, a corporate foundation offers a vehicle to achieve meaningful social impact in communities. However, the value they bring to the business has only recently caught management researchers' attention. In this chapter, we provided an overview of the roles corporate foundations play in achieving corporate sustainability strategies. We also enriched existing literature with our account of the work performed by heterogeneous actors to advance corporate sustainability strategies that combine business and philanthropic logic.

ACKNOWLEDGMENTS

The author is grateful to the interviewees and the Colombian chapter of Red America (https://www.redeamerica.org) who made this research possible.

NOTES

1.   https://www.cemexcolombia.com/sostenibilidad
2.   https://www.cemexcolombia.com/sostenibilidad/asuntos-sociales/generamos-valor-compartido/vivienda-social-e-infraestructura/bloqueras-solidarias

REFERENCES

Acosta, P., & Pérezts, M. (2019). Unearthing sedimentation dynamics in political CSR: The case of Colombia. *Journal of Business Ethics*, *155*(2), 425–444.
Acosta, P., Acquier, A., & Gond, J. P. (2019). Revisiting politics in political CSR: How coercive and deliberative dynamics operate through institutional work in a Colombian Company. *Organizational Studies*. doi:10.1177/0170840619867725.

Acquier, A., Carbone, V., & Moatti, V. (2018). Teaching the sushi chef: Hybridization work and CSR integration in a Japanese multinational company. *Journal of Business Ethics*, *148*(3), 625–645.

Battilana, J., & Dorado, S. (2010). Building sustainable hybrid organizations: The case of commercial microfinance organizations. *Academy of Management Journal*, *53*, 1419–1440,

Battilana, J., & Lee, M. (2014). Advancing research on hybrid organizing – Insights from the study of social enterprises. *The Academy of Management Annals*, *8*(1), 397–441.

Baumgartner, R. J., & Ebner, D. (2010). Corporate sustainability strategies: Sustainability profiles and maturity levels. *Sustainable Development*, *18*(2), 76–89.

Bethmann, S., & von Schnurbein, G. (2019). Effective governance of corporate foundations. In L. Roza, S. Bethmann, L. Meijs, & G. von Schnurbein (Eds.), *Handbook of corporate foundations: Corporate and civil society perspectives* (pp. 17–37). Cham, Switzerland: Springer Nature Switzerland.

Charities Aid Foundation (2007). *The changing nature of corporate responsibility – what role for corporate foundations?* Charities Aid Foundation.

Corporate Citizenship (2014). Corporate foundations a global perspective.

Daudigeos, T. (2013). In their profession's service: How staff professionals exert influence in their organization. *Journal of Management Studies*, *50*(5), 722–749.

Friedland, R., & Alford, R. R. (1991). Bringing society back in: Symbols, practices, and institutional contradictions. In W.W. Powell & P.J. DiMaggio (Eds.), *The new institutionalism in organizational analysis* (pp. 232–263). Chicago, IL: The University.

Fundación Promigas & Fundación DIS (2012). Las fundaciones empresariales en Colombia: Una mirada a su estructura y dinámicas. Bogotá: Asociación de las Fundaciones Empresariales de Colombia.

Gautier, A., & Pache, A. C. (2015). Research on corporate philanthropy: A review and assessment. *Journal of Business Ethics*, *126*(3), 343–369.

Gheringer, T., & von Schnurbein, G. (2020). Corporate foundations in Europe. In L. Roza, S. Bethmann, L. Meijs, & G. von Schnurbein (Eds.), *Handbook of corporate foundations: Corporate and civil society perspectives* (pp. 85–106). Cham, Switzerland: Springer International Publishing.

Gioia, D. A., Corley, K. G., & Hamilton, A. L. (2013). Seeking qualitative rigor in inductive research: Notes on the Gioia methodology. *Organizational Research Methods*, *16*(1), 15–31.

Gond, J. P., Cabantous, L., & Krikorian, F. (2018). How do things become strategic? 'Strategifying' corporate social responsibility. *Strategic Organization*, *16*(3), 241–272.

Gond, J. P., El Akremi, A., Swaen, V., & Babu, N. (2017). The psychological microfoundations of corporate social responsibility: A person-centric systematic review. *Journal of Organizational Behavior*, *38*(2), 225–246.

Lawrence, T. B., & Suddaby, R. (2006). Institutions and institutional work. In S. R. Clegg, C. Hardy, T. B. Lawrence, & W. R. Nord (Eds.), *Handbook of organization studies* (pp. 215–254). London: Sage.

Porter, M. E., & Kramer, M. R. (2002). The competitive advantage of corporate philanthropy. *Harvard Business Review*, *80*(12), 56–58.

Renz, D., Roza, L., & Simons, F. P. (2019). Challenges in corporate foundation governance. In L. Roza, S. Bethmann, L. Meijs, & G. von Schnurbein (Eds.), *Handbook of corporate foundations: Corporate and civil society perspectives* (pp. 17–37). Cham, Switzerland: Springer Nature Switzerland.

Rey-García, M., Layton, M. D., & Martin-Cavanna, J. (2019). Corporate foundations in Latin America. Introduction. In L. Roza, S. Bethmann, L. Meijs, & G. von Schnurbein (Eds.), *Handbook of corporate foundations: Corporate and civil society perspectives* (pp. 167–190). Cham, Switzerland: Springer Nature Switzerland.

Roza, L., Bethmann, S., Meijs, L., & von Schnurbein, G. (2019). Introduction. In L. Roza, S. Bethmann, L. Meijs, & G. von Schnurbein (Eds.), *Handbook of corporate foundations: Corporate and civil society perspectives* (pp. 1–13). Cham, Switzerland: Springer Nature Switzerland.

Salamon, L. M., & Anheier, H. K. (1998). Social origins of civil society: Explaining the nonprofit sector cross-nationally. VOLUNTAS: *International Journal of Voluntary and Nonprofit Organizations*, *9*(3), 213–248.

Santos, F. M., & Eisenhardt, K. M., 2005. Organizational boundaries and theories of organization. *Organization Science*, *16*(5), 491–508.

Scherer, A. G. (2018). Theory assessment and agenda setting in political CSR: A critical theory perspective. *International Journal of Management Reviews*, *20*(1), 1–24.

Smith, S. R. (2010). Hybridization and nonprofit organizations: The governance challenge. *Policy and Society*, *29*(3), 219–229.

Velter, M. G. E., Bitzer, V., Bocken, N. M. P., & Kemp, R. (2020). Sustainable business model innovation: The role of boundary work for multi-stakeholder alignment. *Journal of Cleaner Production*, *247*, doi:10.1016/j.jclepro.2019.119497.

Von Schnurbein, G., Seele, P., & Lock, I. (2016). Exclusive corporate philanthropy: Rethinking the nexus of CSR and corporate philanthropy. *Social Responsibility Journal*, *12*(2), 280–294.

Westhues, M., & Einwiller, S. (2006). Corporate foundations: Their role for corporate social responsibility. *Corporate Reputation Review*, *9*(2), 144–153.

Zietsma, C., & Lawrence, T. B. (2010). Institutional work in the transformation of an organizational field: The interplay of boundary work and practice work. *Administrative Science Quarterly*, *55*(2), 189–221.

3. Materiality analysis as the basis for sustainability strategies and reporting – a systematic review of approaches and recommendations for practice

Sophia Schwoy and Andreas Dutzi

INTRODUCTION

Sustainability has become a mantra for our time in many ways (Schmeltz, 2012). It is a time in which the understanding of the role and responsibility of companies has changed dramatically, a time in which companies are expected to act responsibly and tackle issues "which, in the old world economy, they would have ignored in their pursuit of profit" (Ellis, 2010, p. 9). The Brundtland Report defines the concept of sustainability as "development that meets the needs of the present without compromising the ability of future generations to meet their own needs" (WCED, 1987, p. 43). In relation to corporate activities, sustainability refers to the environmental, social, and governance (ESG) dimensions of a company's performance and operations. As such, it encompasses companies' actions to manage their ESG impacts in terms of valuable contributions to society (SASB, 2017a).

Against this background, an increasing number of companies are identifying sustainability issues as strategically important and trying to integrate them into their business strategies (Khan et al., 2016). To demonstrate their commitment and reduce information asymmetry towards stakeholders, most companies are voluntarily reporting on their sustainability engagement in sustainability reports (Calabrese et al., 2017). Moreover, an increasing number of countries around the world are gradually enacting regulations that obligate companies to report on their sustainability (Baret & Helfrich, 2019). However, due to the complexity of the topic and company-specific differences, these regulations are kept relatively broad, meaning that reporting on sustainability is required, but the concrete scope, depth, and design is left for the companies to decide. To create a transparent, truthful, and accountable report, it is essential to integrate those sustainability issues that are material for the company with respect to its individual characteristics (Arena & Azzone, 2012; GRI, 2013). A properly conducted materiality analysis, which represents a multi-purpose tool for identifying, selecting, and ranking the most significant sustainability issues of the company (Calabrese et al., 2019), is therefore crucial for prioritizing relevant sustainability information, ensuring a complete and reliable report (Hess, 2007) and thereby improving the credibility of the company's sustainable commitments (Schmeltz, 2014). However, the materiality analysis is not only important for setting up the sustainability report, but also for setting up the general sustainability strategy since companies often fail to distinguish between more and less material sustainability issues in their business strategies, thus mismanaging sustainability as a whole (Eccles et al., 2012; Grewal et al., 2016; Maniora, 2018; Porter & Kramer, 2006).

In conducting materiality analyses in practice, companies face the problem that neither regulations nor sustainability reporting frameworks provide any structured approach to performing the assessment (Calabrese et al., 2017). The analyses therefore are based on a high degree of subjectivity on the part of companies (KPMG, 2014; Zhou, 2011), which leads to higher probabilities of discrimination between material and immaterial sustainability topics. Several empirical studies analysing the quality of sustainability reports across various countries and industries have shown in this context that information about materiality is often insufficient and many companies conduct flawed materiality analyses (e.g. Guix et al., 2019; Jones et al., 2016; Lubinger et al., 2019; Rashidfarokhi et al., 2018). These inconsistencies can lead to increased stakeholder scepticism that in turn reduces the company's reputation (Ashforth & Gibbs, 1990) with regard to sustainability. Therefore, systematic approaches are required to help companies effectively handle materiality analyses that deal with the subjectivity of judgements and provide completeness by comprising all material aspects and engaging with stakeholders to ensure capturing their views, thus enhancing trust (Calabrese et al., 2017; Zhou, 2011). To tackle this issue, our chapter provides a systematic review of current studies that provide approaches or models for conducting materiality analyses. Our main purpose is to summarize and evaluate these approaches to uncover practical implications for, and offer support to, companies regarding materiality assessment.

BACKGROUND AND REVIEW METHODOLOGY

The Concept of Materiality and its Definition in Different Sustainability Reporting Standards

Before specifying the methodological details of the study, it is necessary to explain the concept of materiality in general and provide an overview of its different understandings in sustainability reporting standards. Traditionally, the principle of materiality originates from the financial accounting methodology, where it is understood as the presenting of a true and fair view of the financial information. In particular, information is material if its misstatement or omission could influence the economic decision-making of users of the financial statement (IASB, 2018). Transferred to sustainability, it means that corporations need to disclose information about their environmental and social impacts. Specifically, information is material if it affects present and future stakeholder needs (Calabrese et al., 2019; Hahn & Kühnen, 2013). Materiality in terms of sustainability thus broadens the traditional definition by addressing a wider range of information users, e.g. costumers, government, and general society (GRI, 2016), and expanding the reporting timescale (Zadek & Merme, 2003). To evaluate the relevance of sustainability topics and determine the extent to which they should be addressed in sustainability reports, companies need to conduct a comprehensive, thorough materiality analysis with explicit focus on stakeholder engagement (Bellantuono et al., 2016; Puroila & Mäkelä, 2019). The results of such materiality assessments enable companies to align their sustainability strategy and sustainability management and provide the basis for the content and extent of the sustainability reports (Taubken & Feld, 2018).

In line with this, various sustainability reporting standards define materiality as a guiding principle for determining the contents of the disclosure. However, what is problematic in this context is the fact that the standards use diverse definitions of materiality (Puroila & Mäkelä,

2019) and consequently differ in their requirements for materiality assessments. To provide a comprehensive overview, we present the definitions and materiality-assessment requirements of the most used and well-known global sustainability reporting standards (GRI, IIRC, and SASB) in Table 3.1.

Table 3.1   *Overview of materiality definitions and assessment requirements of different sustainability reporting standards*

Sustainability reporting standard	Materiality definition	Requirements for materiality assessment
GRI (Global Reporting Initiative)	Material topics are those that "reflect the organization's significant economic, environmental and social impacts; or substantively influence the assessments and decisions of stakeholders" (GRI, 2016, p.10)	The identification of material topics and their assessment should be performed using a *materiality matrix* that shows the significance of economic, environmental, & social impacts on the horizontal axis & the influence on stakeholder assessments & decisions on the vertical axis (GRI, 2016)
SASB (Sustainability Accounting Standards Board)	Material information is sustainability information that "is important to investors in making investment and voting decisions" (SASB, 2017b, p.2)	To identify material issues, the SASB provides a *materiality map* that comprises material sustainability issues within various industries (SASB, 2017a)[a]
IIRC (International Integrated Reporting Council)	A matter is material "if it could substantively affect the organization's ability to create value in the short, medium or long term" (IIRC, 2015, p.4)	To conduct materiality analyses, companies need to assess the magnitude of an issue's effect (influence on strategy, governance, performance, or prospects), as well as the likelihood of its occurrence (IIRC, 2015)

Note: [a] The materiality assessment used for developing the map generally relies on two forms of evidence: first, evidence of interest to a reasonable investor which is evaluated by means of financial risk, legal drivers, industry norms, stakeholder concerns, and innovation opportunities. Second, the potential or actual impact of the sustainability topic on the financial condition or operating performance of the company. For achieving good distinction between material and non-material issues in this context, the SASAB assesses different types of financial impact, in particular revenues and costs, assets and liabilities, and cost of capital (SASB, 2017a).

When comparing these definitions, it is striking that the standards highlight different points of view for the selection and determination of material issues. While GRI focuses on the broad stakeholder perspective, SASB clearly emphasizes the shareholder perspective, thereby sticking closer to the traditional materiality definition of the financial accounting methodology (Khan et al., 2016; Puroila & Mäkelä, 2019; Remmer & Gilbert, 2019). IIRC on the contrary chooses a combined approach by highlighting the role of hard financial factors on the one hand, but also using the term value on the other hand, which leaves open to question what makes up such value, and thus can only be determined by companies themselves and in respect of their specific business models (IIRC, 2015; Taubken & Feld, 2018). In line with these different definitions, the proposed materiality assessments also differ. GRI directs attention to the environmental, social, and economic impacts of an organization's performance, as well as stakeholder preferences, to reflect the broad and inclusive view. IIRC, however, stresses the magnitude and likelihood of the impact on value creation for several forms of capital, thereby also including the investor-focus. However, both GRI and IIRC only provide relatively superficial guidance for conducting the materiality assessment and fail to offer structured approaches. SASB goes further and provides predefined lists of material issues that have financial implications on an industry-by-industry basis (Puroila & Mäkelä, 2019). Even though, at first glance, this approach seems to overcome the shortcomings of GRI and IIRC, it cannot account for individual company characteristics, thus also failing to ensure appropriate materiality distinctions.

In summary, all standards strive to provide an appropriately narrow focus on the truly significant sustainability topics (Taubken & Feld, 2018). Sustainability reports should be improved with regard to precision, effectiveness, and relevance for corporate strategy and thus support a positive change in sustainability performance for companies (SustainAbility, 2014). However, the fact that all standards define materiality differently and fail to provide structured approaches to perform materiality assessments makes it hard for companies to conduct materiality analyses and sufficiently narrow the focus.

Review Methodology

For our review of the literature, we followed the methodology of a systematic review. While various review approaches exist, a distinction is typically made between systematic and narrative reviews (Tranfield et al., 2003). In contrast to the latter, a systematic review is characterized by its adoption of a scientific, replicable, and transparent process to minimize personal bias in the selection of research literature, thereby offering an audit trail of the author's decisions, procedures, and conclusions (Cook et al., 1997). In our systematic review, we followed the guidelines of Fink (2014) and implemented the proposed five process steps detailed below.

In our first step, we specified the research question that guided the review. As shown above, materiality plays an important role in corporate sustainability reporting as well as in sustainability management in general. However, companies struggle to conduct appropriate materiality analyses, which can lead to problems in differentiating material from immaterial sustainability topics, thereby leading to further mismanagement of sustainability (Maniora, 2018). Against this background, the objective of our review is the identification and evaluation of practical approaches for conducting materiality analyses.

The second step comprises the identification of relevant databases. To cover a wide spectrum of research and ensure valid results, we performed the review using the international databases Web of Science, EBSCO, and SpringerLink. These databases comprise more than 4000 peer-reviewed journals across various dimensions (e.g. accounting, business, finance, and management), which makes us confident that our review captures the relevant studies on sustainability management and reporting.

Third, a detailed search using the following keywords was executed: ("sustainab* report*" OR "CSR report*" OR "integrated report*") AND ("materiality" OR "creditability"). This search term includes the common synonyms for sustainability reports, employing asterisks as a truncation symbol to search for different endings and combining it with the materiality aspect. Through this procedure, the search remained relatively open so as not to miss relevant articles.

In the fourth step, we specified practical screening criteria to include or exclude articles from our systematic review. The initial search required that articles included in the review fulfil the following criteria: (a) be published in a peer-reviewed journal; (b) be in the English language; and (c) include our keywords. This search strategy resulted in a total of 613 articles. After excluding duplicates, both contributing authors, as well as one researcher who was not further involved in the project, independently screened all the articles in accordance with further inclusion and exclusion criteria. In the first screening round, we excluded all studies that did not focus on materiality in sustainability reporting, which left us with 34 articles. In the second screening step, we ensured that all studies provided models or approaches for conducting materiality analyses. This step led to the exclusion of a further 28 articles. The comparably high exclusion number here, was due to the fact that most of the studies just gave superficial remarks for improving materiality analysis, e.g. using GRI guidelines or conducting interviews, rather than providing comprehensive approaches or models for the assessment. As a last step, the references of the articles were checked for further suitable studies which led us to identify one additional article. The whole screening process (Figure 3.1) left a total of seven studies that matched the inclusion criteria and were therefore considered essential for our review (see Table 3.1A later, for details). This relatively low number of studies is justified by the fact that research on practical approaches for materiality analyses, to date, represents a less mature research stream (see also Kraus et al., 2020; Petticrew & Roberts, 2006).

Fifth, we conducted the actual review of the literature and used interpretive and explanatory synthesis. We inductively developed different categories to which each study could be assigned, based on their suggested approach for materiality analyses. Through this procedure, we systematically organized the studies' results and were able to illustrate connections and differences between the examined articles and derive evaluations of the suggested approaches. The concrete categories and syntheses are presented in detail in the section entitled "Materiality analysis in sustainability reports".

GENERAL CHARACTERISTICS OF THE INCLUDED STUDIES

The review process allowed us to identify a total of seven studies that focused specifically on developing approaches or models for determining material issues for sustainability reporting. Table 3.2 provides an overview of the studies and summarizes their general characteristics, which are further explained below.

For all the studies, the materiality definition and general considerations regarding materiality assessment of the GRI served as a basis for the development of the models. This is reasonable given that GRI is commonly perceived the most complete and best structured framework for CSR reporting (Bouten et al., 2011; Farneti & Guthrie, 2009; Lamberton, 2005) and, moreover, represents the most widely used sustainability reporting guideline worldwide (Alonso-Almeida et al., 2014). Muñoz-Torres et al. (2012) and Bellantuono et al. (2018) further extended this basis by also considering SME-related CSR literature and other sustainability guidelines.

With regard to the required steps in conducting materiality analyses covered by the proposed models, the studies differ slightly. While the models of Bellantuono et al. (2016) and Calabrese et al. (2019) provide complete guidance by comprising the stakeholder engagement process as well as the actual assessment of materiality, the studies of Ortar (2018), Hsu et al. (2013), and Calabrese et al. (2016) focus specifically on the identification and assessment of sustainability aspects. However, despite the differing coverages, the five studies have in common that they all provide models that need to be applied by the companies themselves. In contrast to this, the studies of Muñoz-Torres et al. (2012) and Bellantuono et al. (2018) offer lists of material issues that are relevant for a particular target group, thereby concentrating on supporting corporations in their identification of material sustainability aspects.

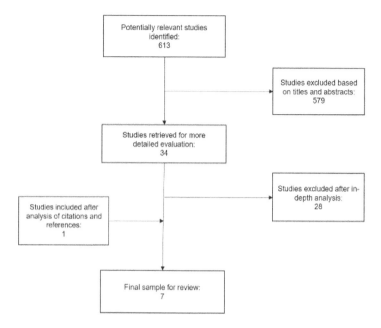

Figure 3.1   Systematic review flow diagram

Owing to their different focuses, the models propose different methods for conducting materiality analyses. The five articles that provide materiality-assessment approaches for companies all use multi-criteria decision-making techniques. Specifically, Calabrese et al. (2019) and Ortar (2018) recommend matrices methods, whereas Bellantuono et al. (2016) propose a quantitative multi-attribute group decision-making technique. To solve the problem of subjective evaluations and hierarchical structures in decision-making, Calabrese et al. (2016) suggest using a fuzzy analytic hierarchy process (AHP) method, while Hsu et al. (2013) combine an analytic network process (ANP) method with failure modes and effects analysis (FMEA). Contrary to this, both studies that offer lists of material issues for specific companies used surveys for their materiality assessment.

As a consequence of the provision of concrete materiality issues, the studies of Muñoz-Torres et al. (2012) and Bellantuono et al. (2018) have relatively small target groups, namely Spanish SMEs and agri-food companies. The approaches of the other studies can be applied by all types of companies. However, Bellantuono et al. (2016) and Calabrese et al. (2016, 2019) particularly emphasize the benefits of their models for SMEs.

Table 3.2   *Overview of the studies' general characteristics*

Study	Sustainability definition and issues considered	Steps covered in the materiality analysis	Approach/method	Target group for application
Bellantuono et al. (2016)	Based on GRI	Whole materiality analysis	Multi-attribute group decision-making	Large companies and SMEs of any sector
Calabrese et al. (2019)	Based on GRI	Whole materiality analysis	Zone matrices	Large companies and SMEs of any sector
Ortar (2018)	Based on GRI	Identification and assessment of sustainability aspects from stakeholders' viewpoint	Questionnaire-based matrices	No specific target group is mentioned
Calabrese et al. (2016)	Based on GRI	Identification and assessment of sustainability aspects	Fuzzy analytic hierarchy process	Focus on SMEs but also applicable for large companies
Hsu et al. (2013)	Based on GRI	Identification and assessment of sustainability aspects	Analytic network process combined with failure modes and effects analysis	No specific target group is mentioned
Muñoz-Torres et al. (2012)	Based on GRI and CSR literature with focus on SMEs	Identification of material sustainability aspects	Expert panel and survey	Spanish SMEs
Bellantuono et al. (2018)	Based on GRI, SAFA guidelines, Dow Jones Sustainability World Index, MSCI ESG Index, and FTSE ESG Ratings	Identification of material sustainability aspects	Survey	Agri-food companies

MATERIALITY ANALYSIS IN SUSTAINABILITY REPORTS

Examining the proposed approaches for materiality analyses reveals that the articles included in this review can be classified into two main categories: articles that identify topics that are material for specific companies, suggesting them as mandatory for their sustainability reporting; and articles that offer approaches for materiality assessments that companies can independently adapt to their individual characteristics. In this section, we therefore present the synthesis of our thematic findings in relation to these two categories. However, due to the complexity of achieving this, we introduced further subcategories to ensure a clear understanding and derive appropriate comparisons. Specifically, we present the results based on the two main steps necessary for a materiality assessment, namely the identification of relevant stakeholders and the identification and assessment of sustainability aspects. In this way, it is possible to present the review itself as a guideline for materiality analysis, comprising the provision and evaluation of possible approaches for every analysis step. Since the second step (identification and assessment of relevant sustainability aspects) represents the core element of materiality analysis, and the approaches propose different methods to achieve this, we present the results according to their suggested method. Figure 3.2 illustrates the organization of our findings' presentation and discussion.

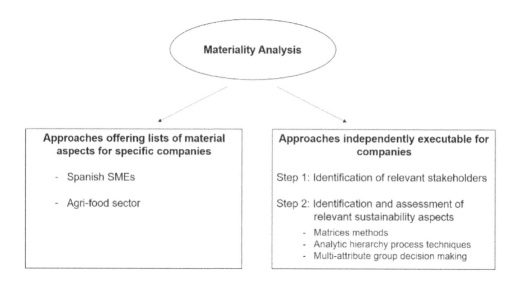

Figure 3.2   Review organization

Approaches Offering Material Topics for Specific Companies

The studies of Bellantuono et al. (2018) and Muñoz-Torres et al. (2012) provide lists of material topics for specific companies. Bellantuono et al.'s (2018) focus was on the agri-food sector and, to identify relevant sustainability topics, the authors autonomously assessed the sustainability aspects listed in the Dow Jones Sustainability World Index, FTSE4Good Index, Morgan Stanley Capital Investments ESG Index, Global Reporting Initiative sector disclosures, and Sustainability Assessment of Food and Agriculture (SAFA) systems guidelines with regard to their relevance for the agri-food sector. After comparing the lists obtained, a unique list of the resulting key topics was defined. This list served as a basis for a questionnaire in which each topic's relevance was ascertained by means of a five-point Likert scale. The questionnaire was sent to a panel of international experts, comprising 165 scholars who belonged to two subsets. The first subset comprised 43 authors of peer-reviewed papers in the field of sustainability with reference to the food sector, while the second included 122 experts from scientific board committees within the European Food Safety Authority and the Food and Agriculture Organization of the United Nations. To compare results, the questionnaire was also sent to practitioners from 30 Italian agri-food SMEs. Based on the questionnaire results of the experts (response rate of 10.3%), the authors identified a list of sustainability topics that they qualified as mandatory for any sustainability report prepared by companies in the agri-food sector. A topic was assessed as material if all experts gave it a value equal or greater than 3. The answers of the practitioners (response rate of 40%) were used to verify and exemplify the impact of the potential adoption of the proposed list of mandatory topics.

Muñoz-Torres et al.'s (2012) focus was on Spanish SMEs and they used a slightly different approach to identify relevant sustainability topics. In a first step, they conducted a thorough analysis of the various tools used for sustainability management in SMEs and identified a group of potentially relevant stakeholders in the field, as well as issues related to the socially responsible management of these stakeholders. In a questionnaire, a group of qualified experts then assessed the materiality of the issues in terms of the following parameters: financial performance; competitive position; interest groups; future regulations; and opportunity for innovation. To analyse and discuss the results, an expert panel was used. Special focus was herein paid to the issues where materiality was not agreed upon. After all doubtful issues were reclassified, the results of the panel were used to build a second questionnaire, this time for a telephone survey administered to 500 Spanish SMEs. The survey was aimed at the managers or directors of small companies that belonged to the food and agriculture, industry, construction, and services sectors. Based on the survey results, the final proposal of topics considered as material for Spanish SMEs was derived.

Discussion

> *The major advantage of both approaches is that they prevent their target companies from "overseeing" relevant topics in their sustainability reports and general sustainability management. In particular, the engagement of designated experts in the materiality analysis suggests that the proposed lists of material sustainability aspects are relatively precise and complete. This becomes even more obvious when considering that the questionnaire results of Bellantuono et al. (2018) revealed that five out of the 18 relevant sustainability topics were not considered material by the practitioners. Moreover, the approaches are time- and resource-saving since they already provide the results of the materiality analysis for companies. However, alongside these advantages, there are also weaknesses in the approaches. The most serious in this context is the fact that the target groups to which the material issues should be applied are too broad. Therefore, the risk increases that individual company characteristics that could lead to different materiality assessments are overlooked. This shortcoming is particularly pronounced in the approach of Muñoz-Torres et al. (2012) because they include completely different industries in their assessment. Bellantuono et al. (2018) focus on one specific sector, which leads to comparatively more precise results; however, there is still the chance that relevant topics have been missed (e.g. "genetically modified organisms" was excluded from the material aspects list, which is definitely a material topic for some agri-food companies). Even though the authors of both articles emphasize that companies that use the provided lists should add further topics that are material for them, it is questionable whether companies actually edit the given lists, especially when it comes to critical issues. Another problem is that the consideration of the proposed material topics is not mandatory for companies. Therefore, organizations*

still have the chance to purposely omit specific topics, thereby hiding sustainability problems from stakeholders not involved in the process.

Approaches For Companies to Independently Conduct Materiality Analyses

Step 1: Identification of relevant stakeholders

One of the fundamental steps in defining the content and relevance of communicated information in sustainability reports is stakeholder engagement (Manetti, 2011). Stakeholders are all individuals and parties that can influence, or are influenced by, the organization. Due to this interrelation, stakeholders have the right to receive information about the impacts of the company that may not be directly or easily observable to them, especially with regard to environmental and social impacts (Gray, 2001). If these disclosures are not made and companies withhold how they address environmental and social challenges, stakeholders might penalize and revoke the corporation's "license to operate", thereby creating risk and causing financial damage (Searcy & Buslovich, 2014; Ortar, 2018).

To ensure that the report reflects stakeholders' interests and the expectations of the corporation, it is important to identify all stakeholders whose participation in the materiality assessment would be useful. Bellantuono et al. (2016) and Calabrese et al. (2019) developed approaches that specifically focus on the identification of relevant stakeholders as a first step of the materiality analysis. Calabrese et al. (2019) suggest identifying two groups of stakeholders that should be categorized dependent on their influence on the organization's strategic decisions and actions. The first group (decision-makers) should comprise stakeholders with direct influence on strategic decisions, such as senior executives and middle line managers, who are able to evaluate sustainability aspects in terms of their importance to the organization. The second group (stakeholders), responsible for assessing the importance to stakeholders, should contain individuals who only have indirect influence on strategy, e.g. other employees, suppliers, clients, the local community, and other external parties. To identify the stakeholders belonging to the decision-maker group, Calabrese et al. (2019) recommend analysing the organizational chart and interviewing top managers, whereas the selection of the other stakeholders should involve stakeholder representatives that have dialogue with management. Overall, the selection criterion should rely on the stakeholders' ability to offer relevant information on sustainability topics, as well as their representativeness of stakeholder categories.

The approach of Bellantuono et al. (2016) puts the focus more on prioritizing stakeholders based on their relevance for different topics. The suggested approach also starts with identifying relevant stakeholders, but then differs from Calabrese et al. (2019) by recommending that stakeholders should be provided with a specific salience depending on the categories to which the sustainability issues belong, i.e. economic, environmental, and social. In this way, account is taken of the fact that stakeholders are not equally relevant to all sustainability topics. Taking corruption used to win competitive tender as an example, this approach makes it possible to assign a lower salience to shareholders than to customers or competitors. To determine the specific salience, the company needs to compare stakeholders pairwise regarding their importance within each category of sustainability aspects. The comparison should be expressed in terms of the dominance index, according to the fundamental scale of judgements of Saaty (1990). On the basis of the organization's characteristics, the comparisons should be carried out by entrepreneurs, top managers, or other professionals who have a comprehensive view of the organization. To check the consistency of the pairwise comparisons, Bellantuono et al. (2016)

suggest using the geometric consistency index proposed by Aguarón and Moreno-Jiménez (2003). In case of inconsistencies, the adjusting procedure presented in Wu and Xu (2012) should be followed.

Discussion

> *What is beneficial about both approaches is that they emphasize the importance of stakeholder engagement in the materiality analysis and provide guidance for identifying relevant stakeholders. However, both are lacking in terms of clearly designating whose responsibility the stakeholder selection is. In our opinion, it would make sense to assign this task to the CSR committee, or to managers of the CSR department in larger firms and to the CEO in smaller companies. Moreover, the problem of high subjectivity is still present in these approaches. When applying the proposed processes for stakeholder selection, corporations are still able to choose for themselves which stakeholders to engage. Therefore, they have the opportunity to remain in their comfort zones and involve only those stakeholders who they expect to pose minimal risk regarding different opinions and potential conflicts. However, what is positive in this context is that the approach of Bellantuono et al. (2016) helps to assign appropriate voting weights to different stakeholders (see also Calabrese et al., 2017). Even though the subjectivity problem in stakeholder selection is not solved, the approach ensures that dominant stakeholders with specific interests cannot outvote other stakeholders over all categories. Depending on the number of engaged stakeholders, companies adopting this approach must be prepared for the fact that the computational efforts for prioritizing stakeholders can be high and time-consuming.*

Step 2: Identification and assessment of relevant sustainability aspects

Approaches based on matrices methods

The step that follows the determination of relevant stakeholders is the identification and assessment of relevant sustainability aspects for the company. This is the core element of the analysis since it represents the actual evaluation of materiality. Ortar (2018) and Calabrese et al. (2019) both recommend using matrices methods for the assessment. The approach of Ortar is focused on identifying stakeholders' perceptions of relevant sustainability aspects and excludes the view of decision-makers. For this purpose, he presents a surveyed materiality matrix based on two quantitative multiple-item scales, which can be seen as an advancement of the GRI matrix. To conduct this approach, companies need to build up a questionnaire as a first step. The questionnaire is aimed at the relevant stakeholders of the company and should request the evaluation of sustainability aspects using a continuous scale from 0 to 100. The respondents should be asked to assess the importance of the issues first for themselves and second for the success of the company. This way, two positions of every surveyed person are taken into account instead of just one, as in the traditional GRI approach. To validate the questionnaire, the results need to be analysed using principle component analysis. If the results are reliable, a juxtaposition of the answers on one matrix (horizontal axis, personal importance; vertical axis, importance to company success) can be conducted in the next step. This way, the most material issues for the stakeholders are revealed in the upper right quarter of the matrix. Moreover, the matrix presents the range of answers to each question.

   Calabrese et al. (2019) propose a zone matrices method for conducting materiality analyses. This approach provides the selection of relevant sustainability aspects as a second step, after identifying relevant stakeholders (see above). The basis for potentially applicable sustainability issues is represented by the GRI sustainability aspects. The selection process itself should be carried out by the corporations' senior decision-makers, due to their experience within the company and their awareness of the organizational structures and processes. Stakeholders and decision-makers are then asked to assess the importance and adequacy of disclosure of the identified sustainability aspects. Since stakeholders may have lower levels of expertise and experience, the authors suggest engaging unbiased facilitators to guide them through the process and explain the importance of the dimensions under analysis. To ensure that no influence is exerted on the stakeholders, the company should hire external and independent professionals as facilitators who do not have an interest in the outcomes of the materiality assessment. The concrete assessment comprises an interval and an ordinal ranking. For the interval ranking, the respondents judge importance and adequacy on six-point Likert scales, while for ordinal ranking they are asked to indicate the sustainability issues in order of importance/adequacy, expressed as ordinal rankings. The approach proposed for checking internal consistency is Spearman's correlation coefficient for trend detection (Gauthier, 2001). On basis of the ranking results, the different sustainability aspects are then positioned within the following zone matrices: "materiality zone", "emerging materiality zone", and "not material zone"; and similarly, with regard to the adequacy of the sustainability communication, "adequacy zone", "improving zone", and "not adequacy zone". The threshold level for material aspects is set at 3.5 on the Likert scale. The actual positioning of the aspects within the zone matrices is derived from calculation of the weighted average values of importance and adequacy for stakeholders and decision-makers. To achieve effective multi-stakeholder contributions to the materiality analysis, the different respondents should be assigned with different relative weights according to their knowledge of the company and experience concerning the analysed GRI aspects. By comparing the positioning of each sustainability aspect in the two matrices (importance and adequacy), the alignment between the effectiveness of sustainability communication and the strategic importance of the issue can be derived and improved.

Discussion

> *The comparison of both matrices approaches reveals their individual benefits and shortcomings. Regarding the approach of Ortar (2018), its main benefit is that it strengthens the position of stakeholders in the materiality assessment. The "traditional" materiality matrix of the GRI claims that the most important issues from a sustainability point of view are placed in the upper right corner of the matrix, which means that topics that are assessed as very important by stakeholders, but not important by company decision-makers (upper left corner of the matrix), are not necessarily classified as material. By focusing on stakeholders' perceptions, Ortar (2018) ensures that critical topics cannot be outvoted. However, this benefit is weakened by the fact that all stakeholders, regardless of their topic-specific expertise, are equally weighted. Moreover, the process of identifying important stakeholders and sustainability aspects relevant for setting up the questionnaire is not explained. Contrary to this, the approach of Calabrese et al. (2019) is very*

detailed and complete. In particular, the different weighting of importance of the various stakeholders is a big advantage because it ensures an appropriate consideration of the specific know-hows, as well as an adequate handling of potential divergences among stakeholders' opinions. The main weakness we see within this concept is the fact that only the decision-makers decide which sustainability aspects should be assessed in the rankings. By including some stakeholders in this process, the risk of missing important issues could significantly be reduced.

Approaches based on AHP methods

The articles of Calabrese et al. (2016) and Hsu et al. (2013) both provide materiality analysis approaches based on AHP methods. Specifically, Calabrese et al. (2016) propose the use of a fuzzy AHP method for conducting the analysis. The AHP hierarchies are represented by the structured framework of sustainability aspects and indicators of the GRI. The problem of materiality assessment is structured in the three hierarchies (economic, environmental, and social) and the goal of each analysis is a decision about the more significant aspects and indicators relevant to the three dimensions. To begin the procedure, the decision-makers of the organization first need to assess which aspects of the GRI framework are applicable for the company and exclude all irrelevant aspects from the hierarchies. All decision-makers and other involved stakeholders then compare the relevance of the GRI aspects in pairwise comparisons regarding the economic, environmental, and social goals of the analysis using linguistic terms (equally, weakly more, moderately more, strongly more, or extremely more important). Subsequently, the linguistic judgements are converted into triangular fuzzy numbers (for the scale for conversion, see Calabrese et al., 2016), which are organized in fuzzy comparison matrices. To synthesize the different comparison matrices of the decision-makers and stakeholders in aggregated matrices, the approach of Chang (1996) is recommended. The fuzzy AHP method offered by Calabrese et al. (2013) should then be applied to each comparison matrix, thereby identifying the relative weights of the GRI aspects without the zero weights problem.

The study of Hsu et al. (2013) suggests calculating risk priority numbers for determining material issues to be included in sustainability reporting. Specifically, the authors developed an assessment framework for materiality issues' risk priority numbers based on the FMEA method. The three evaluation criteria that were identified through this procedure were occurrence (percentage of concerned stakeholders), detection (level of concern to stakeholders), and severity (impact of issues to strategic communication). Hsu et al. then used the ANP technique, which is a more general form of the AHP, to determine the relative importance of each criterion (for actual results, see Hsu et al., 2013). To conduct this approach, companies should first start by identifying their relevant stakeholders and sustainability aspects. As a basis for choosing the applicable sustainability issues, the authors suggest using the GRI aspects and adding further relevant aspects outside of the GRI framework. The selected issues should then be included in a two-part questionnaire that captures the concerns of stakeholders regarding the issues on the one hand, and the level of stakeholders' concerns or interests related to each issue on the other hand. The rating should be carried out using a five-point scale. To evaluate the results, the above explained framework needs to be applied. The risk priority of every issue is calculated as a weighted average of occurrence, detection, and severity indices and represents the ranking position of the issue. The higher the rank, the more material the sustainability issue, and the greater the importance of addressing the topic in the sustainability report.

Discussion

> A closer examination of the two approaches reveals that they overlap in their main weakness. While it is advantageous that both models allow stakeholder engagement, neither Calabrese et al. (2016) nor Hsu et al. (2013) take into account that stakeholders should be assigned with different weights of relevance depending on the evaluated aspects. Therefore, potential conflicts in stakeholder opinions cannot adequately be resolved. Moreover, the approach of Hsu et al. (2013) fails to concretely define when materiality is reached. Although the ranking shows which aspects are most relevant, it leaves open up to which risk number aspects should be considered material (see also Calabrese et al., 2017). On the positive side, however, it is important to point out that the combination of ANP and FMEA allows the handling of dependencies and interactions among decisional criteria, so that different weights of the criteria are considered (Sarkis & Sundarraj, 2002). With regard to Calabrese et al. (2016), it is advantageous that the fuzzy logic makes it possible to deal with subjectivity (Mardani et al., 2015). Moreover, the prioritization of sustainability aspects enables the identification of a threshold of completeness for the sustainability report (see also Calabrese et al., 2017).

Approaches based on multi-attribute group decision-making technique

The approach of Bellantuono et al. (2016) is based on a multi-attribute group decision-making technique. It starts with the identification of possibly relevant sustainability issues. To do so, they suggest using the broad list of aspects provided by the GRI and further adding other aspects that are specific for the company. After identification, a set of verbal labels should be developed, which will be used to assess the sustainability issues in a later step. The set should comprise around five labels so that it allows for a reliable assessment while not leaving too many selection options. Since meanings assigned to the same labels may vary among different stakeholders, a preliminary pairwise comparison procedure should be performed by each stakeholder to calibrate the set of labels. Although this leads to additional effort, it enhances the evaluation reliability. Here again the comparison should be expressed in terms of the dominance index, according to the fundamental scale of judgements of Saaty (1990) (see also proposed approach of Bellantuono et al., 2016, above, for prioritizing stakeholders), and consistency should be checked. On the basis of the developed labels, the organization and all included stakeholders then assess every sustainability aspect. The organization should consider the significance of its economic, environmental, and social impacts, while the stakeholders should perform the evaluation with regard to the influence the corresponding aspects have on their assessments and decisions. To aggregate the diverse opinions of the several assessors, Bellantuono et al. (2016) suggest using the arithmetic weighted means, wherein weights are stakeholders' salience. In the final step, the results of the assessment should be transferred to the materiality matrix as proposed by the GRI. By using a rule of thumb based on the Euclidean norm, the company can then determine which aspects are material and, therefore, necessary topics in the sustainability report.

Discussion

> What is beneficial about the approach of Bellantuono et al. (2016) is that it offers a structured and accurate procedure to assess materiality. Particularly notewor-

thy in this context is the step of calibrating the set of labels used for assessment. The authors thus reduce the risk of different understandings of the rating scale and, consequently, distortions in the assessment. Moreover, the proposed method considers different weights for stakeholders and calculates materiality thresholds by Euclidean norm, thereby ensuring an appropriate handling of potential stakeholder conflicts and a precise analysis (see also Calabrese et al., 2017). Overall, the approach is very advantageous; however, the calibration of the labels and the pairwise comparisons require significant computational effort, which some companies may not be willing to expend.

CONCLUSION AND RECOMMENDATIONS

Materiality is the driver through which companies can identify those sustainability aspects that are most relevant for them (Torelli et al., 2020). Therefore, a proper materiality analysis of sustainability aspects is essential to derive adequate sustainability strategies, successfully manage sustainability activities, and ensure the preparation of transparent, relevant, and reliable sustainability reports (Lai et al., 2017; Maniora, 2018). However, research has shown that companies struggle with three main problems in conducting materiality analyses: high subjectivity; incompleteness of the aspects; and missing or insufficient stakeholder engagement. This is primarily because current sustainability standards and frameworks do not provide any structured approach to perform this task (Calabrese et al., 2017). This review thus focuses on identifying and analysing studies that offer practical approaches for conducting materiality analyses to show companies ways of successfully determining materiality. As can be seen from the relatively low number of seven identified articles, researchers so far have focused on analysing and identifying the weaknesses of materiality analyses in sustainability reports rather than developing professional guidance for conducting them.

Summing up the above presented analyses of the assessment approaches, it can be concluded that there is no perfect solution for materiality analyses that completely eliminates the three main problems. However, this is not possible at all, since the problem of subjectivity could only be solved if companies were not to perform the analyses themselves, but were prescribed by law which materiality aspects they must consider. Against this background, the proposed approaches offer some promising ways of reducing the known problems. With regard to the approaches that provide material topics for specific companies, it can be said that they offer the best way of reducing the risk of high subjectivity, since the authors conducted the materiality analyses with expert panels for specific target groups. However, due to the fact that these approaches present "standard solutions" for a large number of companies (same industry/SMEs), they do not consider individual company characteristics and thus fail to ensure completeness. We would therefore advise companies to use approaches that they can independently conduct themselves. In particular, we evaluate the zone matrices approach of Calabrese et al. (2019) as an appropriate instrument for conducting materiality analysis. However, we suggest extending with some additional steps to eliminate the existing weaknesses and further improve it. Our recommended approach is described below.

First of all, we recommend that every firm should engage an unbiased facilitator to support the entire materiality-assessment process in order to reduce the subjectivity of decision-makers in the materiality analysis.

Step 1: Identification of relevant stakeholders

Regarding the identification of relevant stakeholders, we think it is most advantageous when the CSR committee or the manager of the CSR department (or the CEO in smaller firms), together with the unbiased facilitator, identify the relevant stakeholders that should be included in the assessment and sort them into the two main categories: "internal decision-makers"; and "stakeholders". Subsequently, every stakeholder should be provided with a specific salience, depending on the different sustainability aspect categories obtained through pairwise comparisons (as suggested by Bellantuono et al., 2016). This ensures that every stakeholder is assigned with an appropriate voting weight, and dominant stakeholders are not able to outvote other stakeholders over all categories.

Step 2: Identification and assessment of relevant sustainability aspects

1. To select the relevant sustainability aspects that will be included in the assessment, we suggest using the GRI sustainability aspects as a basis and then let the decision-makers, together with representatives of every stakeholder group, decide which aspects are relevant for the company. This way, the risk of leaving out critical aspects from the assessment is reduced.
2. The internal decision-makers and stakeholders should then assess the importance, as well as the adequacy of disclosure, of every identified sustainability aspect by using an interval and an ordinal ranking (as suggested by Calabrese et al., 2019). In this context, we recommend that the facilitator guides the stakeholders through the whole assessment and is available for any questions and uncertainties.
3. On basis of the ranking results, the different sustainability aspects can be positioned within the zone matrices "materiality zone", "emerging zone" and "not material zone", and with regard to the adequacy of disclosure "adequacy zone", "improving zone", and "not adequacy zone" (Calabrese et al., 2019). The concrete positioning of the aspects within the zone matrices is derived from the calculation of the weighted average values of importance and adequacy for decision-makers and stakeholders. These calculations should be performed on basis of the specific saliences derived for every stakeholder in Step 1.
4. The comparison of the positioning of each sustainability aspect in the two matrices (importance and adequacy) reveals the alignment between the effectiveness of sustainability communication and the strategic importance of the issue.

In our opinion, this approach is the most appropriate to ensure an adequate stakeholder engagement, significantly reduce the risk of subjectivity, and increase the probability of identifying all material aspects. By using the results as basis for specifying the content of the sustainability report, companies are able to ensure that the report represents a transparent and reliable source of sustainability information for markets and stakeholders. Although the suggested model may lead to a significant time investment, companies should accept this because a proper materiality analysis is crucial for the sustainability strategy and sustainability management as a whole.

With regard to future research avenues, we suggest that the recommended approach should be tested in large samples that comprise firms of different sizes from different industries and countries. Based on the findings, the approach can be further developed and better tailored to specific needs. It would also be interesting to investigate whether the application of the approach and the associated improvement in identifying materiality issues leads to a significant enhancement in general sustainability management and performance.

Our findings should be considered in light of various potential limitations related to the systematic review approach. One limitation might be seen in our focus on English-language literature and our choice of databases. However, English is the primary language of the international research community (Narvaez-Berthelemot & Russell, 2001) and the three selected databases comprise the major journals in the field of social science research. The focus on peer-reviewed journal articles in our database search was chosen to enhance the validity of our study, since the peer-review process is generally considered as an effective measure to validity (Hahn & Kühnen, 2013). Only one study, Ortar's (2018) working paper, identified through the analysis of citations and references had not undergone peer review. However, after checking the paper for obvious weaknesses and inconsistencies, which we could not find, we decided to include it in the study so as not to miss promising ideas. Another limitation of our review arises from the fact that it resulted in a relatively low number of suitable papers. This is mainly because we explicitly focused on studies that provide approaches for performing materiality analyses in practice. This research stream is comparatively less mature since most research in this field, at least to date, has concentrated on exploring the quality of materiality analyses carried out by companies, including the mistakes that occur in this context. Systematic reviews in less mature areas regularly lead to fewer results (Kraus et al., 2020; Petticrew & Roberts, 2006). Our study aims for reliability through the fact that both authors, as well as one researcher who was not further involved in the project, independently screened the collected material before the authors analysed and jointly synthesized the findings.

REFERENCES

Aguarón, J., & Moreno-Jiménez, J. M. (2003). The geometric consistency index: Approximated thresholds. *European Journal of Operational Research, 147*, 137–145.

Alonso-Almeida, M. d. M., Llach, J., & Marimon, F. (2014). A closer look at the "global reporting initiative" sustainability reporting as a tool to implement environmental and social policies: A worldwide sector analysis. *Corporate Social Responsibility and Environmental Management, 21*(6), 318–335.

Arena, M., & Azzone, G. (2012). A process-based operational framework for sustainability reporting in SMEs. *Journal of Small Business and Enterprise Development, 19*(4), 669–686.

Ashforth, B. E., & Gibbs, B. W. (1990). The double-edge of organizational legitimation. *Organization Science, 1*(2), 177–194.

Baret, P., & Helfrich, V. (2019). The "trilemma" of non-financial reporting and its pitfalls. *Journal of Management and Governance, 23*(2), 485–511.

Bellantuono, N., Pontrandolfo, P., & Scozzi, B. (2016). Capturing the stakeholders' view in sustainability reporting: A novel approach. *Sustainability, 8*(4), 379.

Bellantuono, N., Pontrandolfo, P., & Scozzi, B. (2018). Guiding materiality analysis for sustainability reporting: The case of agri-food sector. *International Journal of Technology, Policy and Management, 18*(4), 336–359.

Bouten, L., Everaert, P., van Liedekerke, L., Moor, L. de, & Christiaens, J. (2011). Corporate social responsibility reporting: A comprehensive picture? *Accounting Forum, 35*(3), 187–204.

Calabrese, A., Costa, R., Ghiron, N. L., & Menichini, T. (2017). Materiality analysis in sustainability reporting: A method for making it work in practice. *European Journal of Sustainable Development, 6*(3), 439–447.

Calabrese, A., Costa, R., Levialdi, N., & Menichini, T. (2016). A fuzzy analytic hierarchy process method to support materiality assessment in sustainability reporting. *Journal of Cleaner Production, 121*, 248–264.

Calabrese, A., Costa, R., Levialdi Ghiron, N., & Menichini, T. (2019). Materiality analysis in sustainability reporting: A tool for directing corporate sustainability towards emerging economic, environmental and social opportunities. *Technological and Economic Development of Economy, 25*(5), 1016–1038.

Calabrese, A., Costa, R., & Menichini, T. (2013). Using fuzzy AHP to manage intellectual capital assets: An application to the ICT service industry. *Expert Systems with Applications, 40*(9), 3747–3755.

Chang, D.-Y. (1996). Applications of the extent analysis method on fuzzy AHP. *European Journal of Operational Research, 95*, 649–655.

Cook, D. J., Mulrow, C. D., & Haynes, R. B. (1997). Systematic reviews: Synthesis of best evidence for clinical decisions. *Annals of Internal Medicine, 126*(5), 376–380.

Eccles, R. G., Krzus, M. P., Rogers, J., & Serafeim, G. (2012). The need for sector-specific materiality and sustainability reporting standards. *Journal of Applied Corporate Governance, 24*(2), 65–71.

Ellis, T. (2010). *The New Pioneers. Sustainable Business Success through Social Innovation and Social Entrepreneurship*. Chichester: Wiley.

Farneti, F., & Guthrie, J. (2009). Sustainability reporting by Australian public sector organisations: Why they report. *Accounting Forum, 33*(2), 89–98.

Fink, A. (2014). *Conducting Research Literature Reviews: From Paper to the Internet* (4th ed.). Thousand Oaks: Sage Publications.

Gauthier, T. (2001). Detecting trends using Spearman's rank correlation coefficient. *Environmental Forensics, 2*(4), 359–362.

Gray, R. (2001). Thirty years of social accounting, reporting and auditing: What (if anything) have we learnt? *Business Ethics: A European Review, 10*(1), 9–15.

Grewal, J., Serafeim, G., & Yoon, A. (2016). Shareholder activism on sustainability issues. Working Paper, Harvard University.

GRI (2013). G4, Part2: Implementation Manual. file:///C:/Users/s/AppData/Local/Temp/G4 -Sustainability-Reporting-Guidelines-Implementation-Manual-GRI-2013.pdf. Accessed 29 July 2020.

GRI (2016). GRI Standards – GRI 101: Foundation. https://www.globalreporting.org/standards/gri -standards-download-center/?g=f8b044f4-231e-4f38-b716-19c0cbbab274. Accessed 29.07.2020.

Guix, M., Font, X., & Bonilla-Priego, M. J. (2019). Materiality: Stakeholder accountability choices in hotels' sustainability reports. *International Journal of Contemporary Hospitality Management, 3*(6), 2321–2338.

Hahn, R., & Kühnen, M. (2013). Determinants of sustainability reporting: A review of results, trends, theory, and opportunities in an expanding field of research. *Journal of Cleaner Production, 59*, 5–21.

Hess, D. (2007). Social reporting and new governance regulation: The prospects of achieving corporate accountablility through transparency. *Business Ethics Quarterly, 17*(3), 453–476.

Hsu, C.-W., Lee, W.-H., & Chao, W.-C. (2013). Materiality analysis model in sustainability reporting: A case study at Lite-On Technology Corporation. *Journal of Cleaner Production, 57*, 142–151.

IASB (2018). Definition of "material". https://www.ifrs.org/news-and-events/2018/10/iasb-clarifies-its -definition-of-material/. Accessed 3 March 2020.

IIRC (2015). Materiality in [IR] - Guidance for the preparation of integrated reports. https:// integratedreporting.org/wp-content/uploads/2015/11/1315_MaterialityinIR_Doc_4a_Interactive.pdf.

Jones, P., Comfort, D., & Hillier, D. (2016). Materiality in corporate sustainability reporting within UK retailing. *Journal of Public Affairs, 16*(1), 81–90.

Khan, M., Serafeim, G., & Yoon, A. (2016). Corporate sustainability: First evidence on materiality. *The Accounting Review, 91*(6), 1697–1724.

KPMG (2014). Sustainable insights: The essentials of materiality assessment. https://assets.kpmg/ content/dam/kpmg/cn/pdf/en/2017/the-essentials-of-materiality-assessment.pdf.

Kraus, S., Breier, M., & Dasí-Rodríguez, S. (2020). The art of crafting a systematic literature review in entrepreneurship research. *International Entrepreneurship and Management Journal, 16*(1), 1023-1042.

Lai, A., Melloni, G., & Stacchezzini, R. (2017). What does materiality mean to integrated reporting preparers? An empirical exploration. *Meditari Accountancy Research, 25*(4), 533–552.

Lamberton, G. (2005). Sustainability accounting – a brief history and conceptual framework. *Accounting Forum, 29*(1), 7–26.

Lubinger, M., Frei, J., & Greiling, D. (2019). Assessing the materiality of university G4-sustainability reports. *Journal of Public Budgeting, Accounting & Financial Management, 31*(3), 361–391.

Manetti, G. (2011). The quality of stakeholder engagement in sustainability reporting: Empirical evidence and critical points. *Corporate Social Responsibility and Environmental Management, 18*(2), 110–122.

Maniora, J. (2018). Mismanagement of sustainability: What business strategy makes the difference? Empirical evidence from the USA. *Journal of Business Ethics, 152*(4), 931–947.

Mardani, A., Jusoh, A., & Zavadskas, E. K. (2015). Fuzzy multiple criteria decision-making techniques and applications – two decades review from 1994 to 2014. *Expert Systems with Applications, 42*(8), 4126–4148.

Muñoz-Torres, M. J., Fernandez-Izquierdo, M. A., Rivera-Lirio, J. M., Leon-Soriano, R., Escrig-Olmedo, E., & Ferrero-Ferrero, I. (2012). Materiality analysis for CSR reporting in Spanish SMEs. *International Journal of Management, Knowledge and Learning, 1*(2), 231–250.

Narvaez-Berthelemot, N., & Russell, J. M. (2001). World distribution of social science journals: A view from the periphery. *Scientometrics, 51*(1), 223–239.

Ortar, L. (2018). Materiality matrixes in sustainability reporting: An empirical examination. *SSRN.* https://ssrn.com/abstract=3117749 or https://dx.doi.org/10.2139/ssrn.3117749.

Petticrew, M., & Roberts, H. (2006). *Systematic Reviews in the Social Sciences: A Practical Guide.* Oxford: Blackwell Publishing.

Porter, M. E., & Kramer, M. R. (2006). Strategy and society: The link between competitive advantage and corporate social responsibility. *Harvard Business Review, 84*(12), 78–92.

Puroila, J., & Mäkelä, H. (2019). Matter of opinion – Exploring the socio-political nature of materiality disclosures in sustainability reporting. *Accounting, Auditing & Accountability Journal, 32*(4), 1043–1072.

Rashidfarokhi, A., Toivonen, S., & Viitanen, K. (2018). Sustainability reporting in the Nordic real estate companies: Empirical evidence from Finland. *International Journal of Strategic Property Management, 24*(1), 51–63.

Remmer, S., & Gilbert, D. U. (2019). Applying materiality assessment in strategic management: The implicit coating of the materiality lens. In T. Wunder (Ed.), *Rethinking Strategic Management – Sustainable Strategizing for Positive Impact* (pp. 267–291). Cham: Springer.

Saaty, T. L. (1990). How to make a decision: The Analytic Hierarchy Process. *European Journal of Operational Research, 48*, 9–26.

Sarkis, J., & Sundarraj, R. P. (2002). Hub location at Digital Equipment Corporation: A comprehensive analysis of qualitative and quantitative factors. *European Journal of Operational Research, 137*, 336–347.

SASB (2017a). SASB Conceptual Framework. https://www.sasb.org/wp-content/uploads/2019/05/SASB-Conceptual-Framework.pdf.

SASB (2017b). SASB's Approach to Materiality for the Purpose of Standards Development. http://library.sasb.org/wp-content/uploads/2017/01/ApproachMateriality-Staff-Bulletin-01192017.pdf?hsCtaTracking=9280788c-d775-4b34-8bc8-5447a06a6d38%7C2e22652a-5486-4854-b68f-73fea01a2414.

Schmeltz, L. (2012). Consumer-oriented CSR communication: Focusing on ability or morality? *Corporate Communications: An International Journal, 17*(1), 29–49.

Schmeltz, L. (2014). Introducing value-based framing as a strategy for communicating CSR. *Social Responsibility Journal, 10*(1), 184–206.

Searcy, C., & Buslovich, R. (2014). Corporate perspectives on the development and use of sustainability reports. *Journal of Business Ethics, 121*(2), 149–169.

SustainAbility (2014). See change – How transparency drives performance. https://sustainability.com/wp-content/uploads/2016/07/see_change_how_transparency_drives_performance.pdf.

Taubken, N., & Feld, T. Y. (2018). Impact measurement and the concept of materiality—new requirements and approaches for materiality assessments. *NachhaltigkeitsManagementForum | Sustainability Management Forum, 26*(1-4), 87–100.

Torelli, R., Balluchi, F., & Furlotti, K. (2020). The materiality assessment and stakeholder engagement: A content analysis of sustainability reports. *Corporate Social Responsibility and Environmental Management*, *27*(2), 470–484.

Tranfield, D., Denyer, D., & Smart, P. (2003). Towards a methodology for developing evidence-informed management knowledge by means of systematic review. *British Journal of Management*, *14*, 207–222.

WCED (1987). *Our Common Future*. Oxford: Oxford University Press.

Wu, Z., & Xu, J. (2012). A consistency and consensus based decision support model for group decision making with multiplicative preference relations. *Decision Support Systems*, *52*(3), 757–767.

Zadek, S., & Merme, M. (2003). *Redefining Materiality: Practice and Public Policy for Effective Corporate Reporting*. London: Institute of Social & Ethical Accountability.

Zhou, Y. (2011). Materiality approach in sustainability reporting: Applications, dilemmas, and challenges. *1st World Sustainability Forum*, *1*, 1–12.

APPENDIX 3.1 DETAILS OF ARTICLES INCLUDED IN THE SAMPLE

Table 3.1A   *Details of articles included in the sample*

Abstract	Materiality analysis is a multi-purpose tool for prioritising sustainability issues from the double perspective of companies and stakeholders, meaning that both parties contribute to identifying the present and emerging social and environmental risks and opportunities. The current study proposes a practical and structured approach for performing materiality analysis, integrating the well-known Global Reporting Initiative (GRI) materiality matrix and a new "adequacy matrix". The purpose of the GRI materiality matrix is to prioritize sustainability issues in terms of relevance to both companies and stakeholders. The adequacy matrix supports evaluation of the transparency and effectiveness of corporate sustainability (CS) communication. In particular, the paper aims to give indications to companies that want to prepare a sustainability report according to the GRI guidelines by planning the allocation of resources to reporting activities: the comparison between the positioning of GRI sustainability aspects in the two matrices serves in identifying the most critical issues for improving accountability. The proposed method includes a consistency test, to overcome the subjectivity, uncertainty and vagueness affecting judgements. The results provide managers with useful information for aligning CS strategic decision-making, sustainability reporting, and accountability to stakeholders. An illustrative application to a small and medium-sized (SME) company completes the paper.
Journal	*Technological and Economic Development of Economy*
Title	Materiality analysis in sustainability reporting: A tool for directing corporate sustainability towards emerging economic, environmental and social opportunities
Author and year of publication	Calabrese et al. (2019)
Abstract	By materiality analysis, companies identify material aspects, i.e., the most relevant topics that their sustainability report must address. This paper questions the excessive subjectivity that the global reporting initiative (GRI) guidelines grants to companies in identifying their own material aspects, which might elicit opportunistic behaviours. To mitigate the abuse of discretion and prevent its consequences, we present an approach to identify topics to be mandatorily considered as material, and apply it to the agri-food sector. Results are rooted in international standards and rating systems and move from evaluations of an international panel of scholars acknowledged as experts in that sector. By identifying the topics that are at the core of sustainability for the agri-food companies and suggesting them as mandatory for sustainability reporting, the paper helps reduce the chance of relevant topics being omitted, and ultimately improves reliability and comparability of sustainability reports.
Journal	*International Journal of Technology, Policy and Management*
Title	Guiding materiality analysis for sustainability reporting: The case of agri-food sector
Author and year of publication	Bellantuono et al. (2018)

Abstract

Purpose – The purpose of this article is to critically explore the concept of materiality in sustainability reporting. Materiality is a concept adopted from financial accounting practice, in which it is used to differentiate between financially influential activities and those that carry no financial risk. As sustainability reporting is a concept rooted in stakeholder theory, materiality has been adapted to include stakeholders' perspectives in the prioritization process. Today, this is a common practice in most sustainability reports and companies are required to report on their materiality processes as an integral part of the reporting outcome. Design/methodology/approach – In addition to its critical perspective on the current qualitative materiality approach, this article offers a quantitative methodology that was developed through the construction of an empirical model specifically for this purpose. The model consists of two major elements. The first is a preference survey, while the second is a juxtaposition exercise in which the survey results are graphically presented on a two-axis matrix. The model was validated using principle component analysis. Findings – The findings presented in this article indicate that an empirical quantitative method for materiality is feasible. While there is still much to explore in the field of materiality in order to broaden the applications of this model, it does provide an important contribution as a scholarly starting point. Social implications – The model proposed is this article has vast social implications mainly in the realm of sustainability reporting. As the article explains, sustainability reporting is currently in a phase of transition from a voluntary approach to a more regulated one. This transitional phase demands the exploration of alternative validated means of prioritizing the issues reported. Originality/values – The literature review conducted for this study revealed that no published research has attempted to suggest an alternative practical method of materiality decision-making. This article's unique value is that it suggests such a method and presents the methodological reasoning for doing so.

Journal   *SSRN*

Title   Materiality matrixes in sustainability reporting: An empirical examination

Author and year of   Ortar (2018)
publication

Abstract	Sustainability reporting is the process by which companies describe how they deal with their own economic, environmental, and social impacts, thus making stakeholders able to recognize the value of sustainable practices. As stressed in the Global Reporting Initiative guidelines, which act as a de facto standard for sustainability reporting, sustainable reports should take into account the stakeholders' view. In particular, engaging stakeholders is essential to carry out the materiality analysis, by which organizations can identify their own more relevant sustainability aspects. Yet, on the one hand, the existing guidelines do not provide specific indications on how to get stakeholders actually engaged; on the other hand, research on quantitative techniques to support stakeholder engagement in materiality analysis is scarce. Therefore, the purpose of this paper is the development of a quantitative structured approach based on multi-attribute group decision-making techniques to effectively and reliably support stakeholder engagement during materiality analysis in sustainability reporting. As it more strictly guides the reporting process, the proposed approach at the same time simplifies materiality analysis and makes it more reliable. Though any company can adopt the approach, small- and medium-sized enterprises (SMEs) are expected to particularly benefit from it, owing to the quite limited implementation effort that is required. With this respect, the approach has been validated on a sample of Italian SMEs belonging to different sectors.
Journal	*Sustainability*
Title	Capturing the stakeholders' view in sustainability reporting: A novel approach
Author and year of publication	Bellantuono et al. (2016)
Abstract	The purpose of materiality assessment in sustainability reporting is to identify, select and prioritize the issues that have the most significance to companies and their stakeholders. Reporting on the material aspects of sustainability provides greater transparency for the stakeholders and achieves greater accountability for the company. To date, few studies have inquired into quantitative methods to support materiality assessment in sustainability reporting, and these have not addressed the issues of subjectivity or of completeness in the reporting. To respond to this gap in the literature we propose a 'fuzzy analytic hierarchy process' method. This method facilitates sustainability reporting by means of a structured materiality analysis based on the Global Reporting Initiative Guidelines. The outcome of the proposed method is a prioritization of sustainability aspects and indicators, which offers a guide to companies in identifying the appropriate content for preparation of their reports. Each GRI aspect and indicator can be reported with a level of accuracy corresponding to its level of importance (materiality). In addition, the method allows the company managers to identify a threshold of completeness below which sustainability aspects and indicators can be reported in only summary form, as not being substantially material. The *ex-ante* choice of a level of completeness is particularly important for companies with limited resources to dedicate to reporting activities, as is typical for small and medium enterprises. As they address the reporting task, companies can use the proposed method to assess materiality, thus enhancing the credibility and accountability of the sustainability reports while containing costs in time and resources. The paper illustrates the method through a step-by-step application to a medium-sized Italian company active in the water technology sector.
Journal	*Journal of Cleaner Production*
Title	A fuzzy analytic hierarchy process method to support materiality assessment in sustainability reporting
Author and year of publication	Calabrese et al. (2016)

Abstract	An increasing number of companies involved in stakeholder engagement demonstrate social responsibility through sustainability reporting. However, a key challenge for most reporting organizations is on how to identify relevant issues for sustainability reporting and prioritize those material issues in accordance with stakeholder needs. This study utilized failure modes and effects analysis to construct a model of materiality analysis for determining material issues to be included in sustainability reporting as in the case of Lite-On Technology Corporation in Taiwan. This study employed three FMEA indices: occurrence (O), which can be determined from the percentage of concerned stakeholders; likelihood of being detected (D), which refers to the level of concern among stakeholders; and severity (S), which can be quantified from the impact of issues on the strategic communication objective. The analytic network process was then applied to determine the relative weights of the three indices. A risk priority number of materiality analysis was then calculated for each issue, which is provided by the companies to identify material issues of information disclosure in sustainability reporting. The proposed model not only helps firms systematically determine the material issues of sustainability reporting in accordance with stakeholder needs but also facilitates the effectiveness of corporate social responsibility communication.
Journal	*Journal of Cleaner Production*
Title	Materiality analysis model in sustainability reporting: A case study at Lite-On Technology Corporation
Author and year of publication	Hsu et al. (2013)
Abstract	Most corporate social responsibility (CSR) standards have not been designed to be implemented in small and medium sized enterprises (SMEs). Given that 99% of Spanish companies are SMEs, this study aims to propose a selection of basic CSR material issues that, because of their usefulness and significance, should be adapted to Spanish SMEs and their stakeholders. This study provides a CSR model for SMEs that includes the most important social, environmental, and corporate governance issues. This model, which is based on expert knowledge, is useful for integrating sustainability in the management of SMEs and enhancing the management of stakeholders.
Journal	*International Journal of Management, Knowledge and Learning*
Title	Materiality analysis for CSR reporting in Spanish SMEs
Author and year of publication	Muñoz-Torres et al. (2012)

4. Defining a sustainability-driven business modeling strategy with a "storytelling science" approach

David M. Boje and Mohammad B. Rana

INTRODUCTION

Recently, business modeling has taken a turn toward an emphasis on ecological sustainability (Bocken et al., 2019; Boons & Laasch, 2019; Dentchev et al., 2018; Hahn et al., 2014; Joyce & Paquin, 2016; Lüdeke-Freund et al., 2019a, 2019b; Nielsen et al., 2018; Vladimirova, 2019). There is a similar sustainability-driven turn toward the development of a storytelling science methodology in business storytelling (see, Boje, 2019a, 2019b, 2019c; Boje & Rosile, 2020b; Rosile et al, 2018). This chapter seeks to combine these two trends. While the ecological sustainability-driven turn tends to focus on ecological and environmental issues in business modeling from efficiency and financial logic perspectives, the sustainability-driven turn in business storytelling presents more detailed stories, explanations, arguments, and contextual concerns through a wider range of frames of logic. Both turns can potentially be grounded in a terrestrial ethics approach to business modeling (Boje & Jørgensen, 2020). The ecological and sustainability turns in business modeling can benefit from a terrestrial ethics foundation because it brings into question the premise of infinite economic growth and the assumptions of "sustainable [economic] development" modeling that fail to take account of the planet's finite natural resources. Put simply, a terrestrial ethics approach offers a whole systems view toward limiting economic growth in accordance with Earth's finite resource capacities, and not exhausting these capacities faster than natural systems can renew them. Thus, the combination of storytelling and the ecological turns will help future researchers to present the reality of terrestrial capacities from multiple perspectives and logics, covering both people's subjective perspectives (i.e. diverse cultural contexts and individual interests) and multi-contextual phenomena through the application of what Foucault (2011) calls "regimes of truth". Truth regimes include the reactions and logics of heterogeneous actors, the strategies and logics of firms, and discourses on ethics, which in turn focus on optimum use, allocation, and exploitation of resources and care and protection of the planet. Each business model has stories and discourses it accepts as true and distinguishes these from those it frames as false. A business model also offers strategies, techniques, and procedures to create or grant value added in a value chain and supply chain. At issue in this chapter is how to include various discussion on sustainability and storytelling that distinguish true and false in different ways, and to identify the storytelling techniques that can be helpful to business modelers. A terrestrial capacities approach has the potential to change the way business modelers look at many aspects of doing business, including product development, production, marketing, supply changes, value chain management, and social responsibility. In this chapter, we propose a business storytelling approach to business modeling strategizing, and explain its relevance to sustainability-driven business modeling (SBM).

In particular, we explain how SBM strategy benefits from storytelling science, and how we understand the particular SBM that can be useful for future researchers combines methods of storytelling science with SBM.

Our approach is based on a self-correcting iterative "storytelling science" paradigm that includes iterative processes of phase-by-phase testing of assumptions and propositions. For example, self-correcting involves adjusting the theory using the perspectives of multiple actors, as examined through interviews and case studies. It is expected that some of this data will confirm elements of the theory, while others will disconfirm it; disconfirmations are taken into account and the theory and propositions corrected and the story re-narrated rather than using a method such as snowball sampling that confirms initial theorizing. Each round of self-correcting tests (interviews, experiments, cases, etc.) reveals new information that enables increasing confidence in a truth that fits with the reality of the audience of confirmers and disconfirmers (Boje & Rosile, 2020a).

In the following section, we discuss conceptual, methodological, and philosophical positioning that can help researchers to explain the benefits of a storytelling approach for the illustration of complex realities in SBM.

THE CONTRIBUTIONS OF STORYTELLING SCIENCE

Storytelling is defined as the combination and interplay of diverse narratives, living stories, and their antenarrative relationships, communicated in a convincing manner (Boje, 2001, 2008, 2011). "*Antenarrative*" relationships are defined as antecedent to narratives and stories, including the not yet told, and interacting in moving-fragments that are already constituted in narratives and stories in a social setting. Antenarratives theory was initially concerned primarily with *before* narratives, and various *bets* on the future possibilities of world-making strategies (Boje, 2001, 2008, 2011). The theory later gained additional concepts that interconnected the *before* and *bets* elements with conceptualizations of the *beneath, between, becoming,* and *beyond*. Stories are frequently challenged, reinterpreted, and revised by listeners as they unfold in conversation, and thus they are dynamic and constructed socially and contextually. We therefore need to carefully link it with narratives and antenarratives considering multiple facets of it. While a full review is beyond the scope of this chapter, we can offer an introduction to relevant antenarrative concepts and how they can potentially contribute to business modeling:

- *Beneath* refers to the fore conceptions, the thoughts and ideas about sustainability, such as the presumption of unlimited economic growth that often underlies ideas of sustainable development, in contrast to sustainability modeling that presumes limits to growth.
- *Before* is the history of modeling of extraction approaches, both with and without consideration of terrestrial capacities.
- *Between* concerns infrastructures, such as how organizations are embedded in supply, productions, and management chains, which, as COVID-19 has demonstrated, are easily disrupted by a lingering pandemic.

- *Bets on the future* are strategic forecasts about how the future will unfold. In business modeling, these relate to differing temporal horizons of when Earth's capacities will renew or when rising sea levels will unleash a cascade of other tipping points (e.g., coral reefs, once bleached, do not return; ocean currents that change may take centuries to stabilize).
- *Becoming* involves what is ethical, considering what kinds of ethics are becoming more entrenched. We focus on two ethics presented by Bakhtin (1993): the bystander ethics of looking on and not intervening in unsustainable practices, and the moral answerability of reflecting on one's own obligation to act with whatever skills and resources are available.
- *Beyond* is a foregrasping which can be described as what is beyond the senses, a way of knowing that Charles Sanders Peirce calls abduction, those flashes of intuition that need inquiry and some inductive testing, so the deducing of modeling is not, as the nursery rhyme says, built on a house of straw.

A "storytelling science" approach (Boje & Rosile, 2020a) also attempts to move beyond the duality of quantitative versus qualitative approaches. Our approach to storytelling science is rooted in Charles Sanders Peirce's (1933–1937) semiotics of "abduction–induction–deduction", which we apply here to both business storytelling and business modeling strategy. According to Peirce, abduction (or hypothetic inference) begins with intelligent guesswork and intuition about how a phenomenon will present itself. Induction investigates experiences in order to confirm or refute abductive hypotheses. Deduction depends on the theorizing ability to analyze meanings of semiotic signs by deducting the less/no possibilities. Karl Popper (2008) has his own way of responding to induction, through a process he calls "trial-and-error" problem solving. Despite the difference in approach, both Peirce and Popper are concerned that without doing disconfirmation tests of one's own theories, assumptions, and adductions, one only is doing confirmation inquiry, which in turn means that the induction fallacy continues to be a problem for research. To refute or falsify one's own work is part of a self-correcting method. This involves using qualitative and quantitative methods and not treating them as *either–or*, but rather as *both–and* approaches in the process of self-correction.

We can combine quantitative induction tests with qualitative induction tests. For example, a qualimetrics approach (based on Peirce's AID (Abduction–Induction–Deduction) triad) includes quantitative financial data, quantitative data on business processes such as frequencies of a given challenge or problem, and qualitative interviews and ethnographic field notes (Bonnet et al., 2018). There is an important grounding in terrestrial ethics, which has significant implications for business modeling. A social and ecological shift in capitalism itself integrates the use of qualimetrics (the integration of financial and quantitative indicators along with qualitative field case studies) with an ecological understanding of limited planetary capacities (Savall et al., 2018). Since different natural resource contexts and institutional arrangements shape and manifest capitalism differently (Rana, 2014), this in turn informs decision-making processes and logics for firms in business modeling strategies (Rana & Nipa, 2019), and business storytelling science can help investigate and explain SBM in a comprehensive manner by taking into account the dynamics and diversity of capitalism and social systems around the world that have planetary capacity limits to growth. In sum, this approach recognizes that business storytelling is situated not only in socioeconomic practices, but also within planetary limits and multiple perspectives.

INTEGRATION OF STORYTELLING SCIENCE WITH SBM

It is time for business modeling, with its value proposition, global value chain management, etc., to no longer exceed 12 critical planetary limits that are moving business practices and societies from safe risk to increasing risk, and high risk crises (Ripple et al., 2017):

1. Climate change (increasing risk).
2. Novel entities (unknown risk, as yet un-quantified).
3. Stratospheric ozone depletion (low risk, for now, but unknown risk in the long term).
4. Atmospheric ozone loading (not yet quantified risk).
5. Ocean acidification (low risk, moving to increasing risk).
6. Biogeochemical flows (high risk).
7. Fresh water (low risk, moving to increasing risk).
8. Land system change (increasing risk).
9. Biosphere integrity (high risk).
10. Social inequality (risk of discrimination, inequality of wealth and living conditions).
11. Workplace and customer health, safety, and satisfaction (risk to employees and consumers rights, safety, and happiness).
12. Human rights, deprivation, equality, and justice (risk to social order and justice).

Business modeling is beginning to develop its value proposition logic to include ecology and society, and has the potential to address planetary limits such as these. There is now a need for a transdisciplinary approach which integrates a business modeling strategy and a business storytelling science that are both responsive and "morally answerable" (Bakhtin, 1993, p. 3) to planetary limits.

This chapter is organized around the following questions: (i) how is SBM linked to storytelling science in ecologically and socially responsible capitalism? (ii) How are the methodological and philosophical perspectives of storytelling science linked with SBM? And (iii) how do drivers, enablers, and barriers influence the development and implementation of SBM? This conceptual understanding will form the basis for specific cases and anecdotes to illuminate future studies with a storytelling perspective in strategizing SBM.

CONCEPTUAL UNDERSTANDING

SBM and Storytelling of Ecologically and Socially Responsible Capitalism

SMB and storytelling
Savall et al. (2018) provide an approach to the development of a socially responsible capitalism that is also ecologically responsible. Savall (2018) develops ways to respond to socioeconomic crises following the Spanish economist German Bernácer. Boje has worked with Savall and other colleagues in France for over 20 years to integrate storytelling science into their socioeconomic approach. For example, so-called "researcher-intervenors" collect stories from interviews, meetings, and documents in order to analyze how specific situations have developed, and better understand the reality in relation to the research question. Project teams then work on resolving problems using the AID approach. Abduction searches for theories, deduction seeks predictions, and induction searches for facts. If the facts prove elusive, the

process restarts from the beginning, following deduction, and repeating itself until the facts that "fit" are found, and leading to the process of abduction. Induction, deduction, and abduction are forms of logical reasoning that are used in every type of research (both qualitative and quantitative). Alongside observation, they create the basis of all research. Therefore, these forms of thinking are not concepts or methods or tools of data analysis; rather, they are the means of connecting and generating ideas and developing reasoning for research process.

The "socio-economic approach to management" (SEAM) developed by Henri Savall and colleagues stresses investigation through the Peircean "AID" approach and through the "qualimetrics" triadic of qualitative–quantitative–financial in order to establish a moral ontology of socially responsible capitalism. Given the focus on combining qualitative, quantitative, and financial together with a scientific SEAM intervention, there is compatibility here with storytelling science. Both focus on AID, and SEAM also emphasizes the scientific method in storytelling science, this comes through in the self-correcting phases of projects.

By "storytelling science", then, we mean ways of iteratively documenting abductive first guesses (flashes of intuition), by doing inductive tests (both qualitative and quantitative inquiries) and adjusting deduced theories in a process of ongoing self-correction. This process gradually brings us closer to the truth, and highlights the need to model and test all relevant competing regimes of truth.

Thus we have suggested that SBM can benefit from a storytelling science of self-correction by incorporating qualimetric (i.e., financial, quantitative, and qualitative field cases) in longitudinal research designs. We have stressed that such an approach is not concerned solely with confirming theories, but also involves actively attempting to include qualimetrics to disprove theories and/or challenge assumptions in order to come up with a more valid and reliable explanation.

Next, we discuss how SBM and the Storytelling of Ecologically and Socially Responsible Capitalism connect, and how they can be applied in tandem to business modeling and communication.

Application of SBM in a storytelling science paradigm
In this section, we apply our integrated storytelling science approach to the deployment of sustainability-driven business modeling and apply it to practical cases. The benefit of ecological and social sustainability-driven models is that they can utilize the storytelling method of AID cycles to find ways of doing business that do not exceed planetary carrying capacities.

We suggest that storytelling science has an important contribution to make toward business modeling by diagnosing the regimes of truths, documenting the various abductions, and engaging in inductive tests to generate deductive theories that deconstruct the fake or the fantasy from what might remain as the truth (Larsen et al., 2020; Boje & Rosile, 2020a).

At a more general level, storytelling science helps researchers to follow and organize the research process in a way that can combine multiple ontological lenses (i.e. following AID). However, storytelling can also help researchers to deconstruct or explain the complexity of a phenomenon by combining multiple perspectives, dynamics, dimensions, details, and contexts from micro to macro levels of ecologically and socially responsible capitalism by following the triadic of Peircean "AID" and "qualimetrics" to make reality concrete, sense-making and useful for strategy formulation.

For example, research on customer satisfaction with a consumer electronics product follows a relatively linear process concerned with the understanding of consumers' social, cultural, financial, and technological backgrounds and expectations. However, a study on shop floor workers' satisfaction with supplier factories involves the dynamics of multiple actors, organizational practices, and incentive structures, and is even more complex when the supplier is located in a different institutional context and linked with a global value chain in which foreign buyers from Western countries determine requirements and conditions for production. In such a case, storytelling science can help accurately assess and communicate the reality of the situation, and move SBM to the next level of analysis, seeking the truth and constructing the reality.

A business model works at the organizational and functional levels by describing the logic of how an organization creates, delivers, and captures value. This takes into consideration economic, social, and environmental rationales, concerns, and priorities (Amit & Zott, 2001). A sustainability-driven business model is specifically intended to be an innovative part of a business strategy that considers all stakeholder expectations and the future survival of humanity and the planet. Storytelling science has an important role to play in the process of socially constructing the meaning of SBM at the corporate and functional strategy level, taking into account these macro-level dynamics.

In general, a business model explains how a firm's activities work together to develop strategies and bridge strategy and implementation. It also reflects how the firm targets customers and positions its products by creating value throughout its activities – in other words, it is concerned with how a business can best meet customer needs and get paid for doing so (Richardson, 2008; Teece, 2010).

A sustainability-driven business model goes beyond this to include innovation in business modeling. This innovation delivers a way to survive, not only for the firm but also for society and the planet. The meaning of "a way" (i.e. how) and "survival" in this definition is derived from organizational design and is socially constructed. It is broadly understood that sustainability in business modeling means models should lead to coexistence, complementarity, a better future and further growth to ensure balance and stability for all stakeholders concerned in value creation, delivery, capture, consumption, and recycling processes. Innovation in business modeling therefore includes both technological and societal innovation that aims to achieve long-lasting outcomes for economic, social, and ecological survival and compatible and balanced development.

However, value creation in SBM cannot necessarily be found in the operation of one firm; rather it is created, captured, and consumed across the value chain or network of organizations and stakeholders around the globe. Business value chains and operations are not confined to one country in the interconnected global business context, and thus sustainable business modeling requires multidimensional, multi-stakeholder, and multi-contextual perspectives designed to include the expectations, interests, standards, goals, and powers of multiple actors. As a result, a storytelling method becomes the most suitable way to present this complex and multidimensional reality.

Societal discourses and ideologies, and their policy implications in relation to sustainable goals, vary widely from country to country. As a result, the dimensions of sustainability which must be addressed in business modeling and the appropriate approaches to creating, capturing, and appropriating value largely depend on the cultural context shaping consumer purchasing decisions and the institutional rules of a given context (Rana & Sørensen, 2014).

For instance, in the last decade a surge in lithium-ion battery production has led to an 85% decline in prices, making electric vehicles (EVs) and energy storage commercially viable for the first time in history. Batteries therefore hold the key to transitioning away from fossil fuel dependence, and are set to play a greater role in the coming decade that is likely to influence business modeling in different ways across different countries (see, Stevens, 2019).

Because of the institutional policies and rules in effect and the social discourses underpinning the auto industry, sustainability-driven business model innovation has been undertaken to reconfigure not only automobile technology but also the industry's entire R&D approach, cost parameters, market segments, competitiveness, process configuration, product platforms, and value chain management. Some EV companies, e.g. Tesla, have not limited their focus to battery technology and electric cars, but have expanded their attention to innovation in electrical grid technologies, batteries for "large-scale energy storage, vehicle charging infrastructure for going the distance, and supply chain management" in order to maximize their competitive advantage. Companies that have developed new business models or reconfigured existing models for sustainable vehicle production have benefited from supportive institutional arrangements in those national contexts where social discourses, business ecosystems, and incentives inspired those companies to focus on consistent innovation, for example in the USA, China, and Japan.

In contrast, some companies in other countries (e.g. Germany) could not benefit to the same extent due to the lack of supportive institutional conditions, leading to slow advancement in product, process, and technology development as well as business model innovation (Ewing, 2019). This indicates that the development of SBM is socially constructed, incorporating the expectations of multiple stakeholders and requiring a compatible institutional and ecosystem configuration. This helps to explain the variations in organizational capability development in designing SBM across different forms of capitalism.

Even in the EV industry, SBM faces challenges in creating additional customer benefits, particularly to compensate for the higher initial investment compared with conventional cars. EVs could create such benefits by enabling more comprehensive mobility solutions, thus moving from product-based to service-based business models. For example, EVs may in the future serve as energy storage in so-called "smart energy" systems, and EV firms are already generating new revenue streams from battery leasing programs, and refurbishing batteries for second-use applications. Firms across and within different national contexts pursue different business models through a process of learning, experimentation, and adaptation (see Bohnsack et al., 2014).

This research requires the adoption of storytelling techniques in order to explain the complexity and multiple realities in which the roles, actions, and institutional characteristics of multiple actors contribute to creating a certain reality.

While business modeling emphasizes a holistic system-level approach and is complementarity among different business stakeholders, the business model has emerged as a new unit of analysis explaining both novelty and efficiency centered design themes (Zott & Amit, 2008). A novelty centered business model refers to new ways of conducting economic exchanges by connecting previously unconnected parties, by linking transaction participants in new ways, or by designing new transaction mechanisms. Digital technology provides support in executing this business model, because firms require a particular type of governance in order to ensure connectivity, the flow of information, and standardization among various parties.

In contrast, an efficiency centered business model refers to the measures firms take to achieve transaction efficiency (i.e., reducing transaction costs for participants). This increase in efficiency derives from the reduction of uncertainty, complexity, or information asymmetry, as well as from reduced coordination costs and transaction risks. This stretching of the usual efficient-business model to be socially and ecologically responsible is also essential to the SEAM approach.

Both the business model and SEAM can therefore offer a competitive advantage in case it is designed to offer distinct value from the competitors and link actors consistently with appropriate coordination for making value creation, appropriation, and delivery process sustainable to attain the sustainability goals (Christensen, 2001). Casadesus-Masanell & Ricart (2010) refer to the business model as the "logic of the firm", in the way it operates and how it creates value for its stakeholders, and argue that business models are made of concrete choices as well as the consequences of these choices. They contend that business models are composed of two different sets of elements: (a) the concrete choices made by management regarding how the organization must operate; and (b) the consequences of these choices. The choices involved include compensation practices, contracts, commitments and promises, facilities, use and distribution of assets, the extent of vertical integration, and sales and marketing. Moreover, Casadesus-Masanell and Ricart (2010) argue that there are three types of choices: policy choices (e.g. a firm may choose to internalize its sales outlets rather than franchise); asset choices (e.g. the ownership of asset choices will be impacted if a firm internalizes sales and distribution outlets, as opposed to franchising or licensing); and governance choices (e.g. the structure of governance including contractual or tacit promissory relational arrangements that confer decision rights, control, and commitment over policies or resource sharing as well as the condition of information and knowledge flow). Johnson et al. (2008) argue that business models consist of four key elements: a customer value proposition, a profit formula, key resources, and key processes, which in turn include how both actors and activities should be governed and maintained.

These perspectives on business modeling focus on decision-making, strategy, and management aspects as they influence the value outcomes. SBM, however, must also include sustainable management aspects such as employee satisfaction, occupational health and safety, equality and diversity management, responsible management practices, shared value creation, and the legitimacy of the strategic activities that aim to earn acceptance from key actors (Rana & Sørensen, 2014, 2020). It is not enough, in a sustainability-driven model, to focus solely on profit and shared value creation to value chain actors, as Porter & Kramer (2011) advocate.

In this regard, resilience thinking in management and business modeling for social and ecological systems must be considered a key component in understanding sustainability and the need for preserving natural resources in the face of external challenges (Xu et al., 2015). Most studies tend to emphasize ecological aspects of resilience; however, human activities, management strategies, and resilience thinking in the modeling process can also inform sustainability in a meaningful way.

Business model innovation has seen a recent surge due to changes in research and business practices with an aim to attain sustainability. Changes to business models are recognized as a fundamental component of realizing innovations for sustainability, but this requires firms to have supportive organizational structures and dynamic capabilities (Evans et al., 2017; Teece, 2010). These are firm-specific advantages, but their realization depends on the ways in which institutional structures, market conditions, and industry ecosystems are organized, and how supportive these are of the organizational approach to SBM (Rana & Morgan, 2019).

Teece (2010) argues that the essence of a business model defines the manner by which the enterprise delivers value to customers, entices customers to pay for value, and converts those payments into profit. However, business model innovation emphasizes a system-level, holistic approach to explaining how firms do business and organize activities and strategies to create and capture value (Zott et al., 2011). SBM revolves around the processes and designs that connect social and ecological sustainability to the creation of economic value, in order to promote long-term sustainability for both organization and society at large.

The reduced centrality of profit generation in SBM poses several intriguing challenges and requirements that storytelling science should consider. These include, but are not limited to:

i. The business model must include sustainability thinking (both social and ecological) at the heart of corporate strategy and resource management.
ii. It must be commercially profitable.
iii. It has potential for long-term success, not just in the shorter term, i.e. skimming the cream.
iv. It utilizes resources for the long term and focuses on long-term orientation.
v. It must ensure value for all stakeholders and earn legitimacy.
vi. It must be open to learning and responsive to change, including the changing expectations of legitimating actors.
vii. It must ensure diversity and resiliency in its reliance on resources, people, and investments.
viii. Organizations using SBM must be less interdependent, and focus on modularity and effective governance so they can be insulated from unexpected events.
ix. It has slack resources by which innovation and adaptation can be carried out to develop creative, explorative, and risky investments that aim to attain long-term social and ecological sustainability.

An example from the apparel industry, which is among the most polluting industries in the world (Ivang & Rana, 2019), can better illuminate the complexity of SBM that requires the illustrative qualities of a storytelling perspective. Multinational apparel enterprises are rightly criticized for their ongoing damage to the planet, as well as their general failure to provide fair wages and adequate health and safety conditions for employees. In response to such criticism and in order to attain sustainability goals, Swedish company H&M has designed its business model and governance with the goal of reducing pollution and water consumption, while improving wages, workplace health and safety, and welfare conditions throughout the global value chain. At the same time, H&M has introduced a circular economy model to ensure post-consumption waste management of its apparel products. This illustrates that although H&M is addressing sustainability issues through mainstream business modeling and governance with its global supply chains, the company has also realized that post-consumption waste requires a different business model to address ecological sustainability (Rana & Tajuddin, 2021). This inspired H&M to introduce an innovative parallel business model using circular economy concepts. Such initiatives are part of SBM. Due to its focus on sustainability modeling, H&M is pushing sustainability issues along the global value chain to the fore, even in crisis situations, such as the collapse of Rana Plaza in Bangladesh that led to thousands of worker deaths in factories that supply global brands for the UK, USA, and Italy. The CEO of H&M was the first representative of a global brand to fly to Bangladesh after the incident, in order to conduct a timely inquiry and confirm that none of H&M's suppliers was impacted by the Rana Plaza collapse. Despite this, the company announced a support package for the victims and called for new transnational governance approaches for health and safety management. H&M further undertook serious new governance measures in their supply chain management in order to ensure fair wages, better health and safety conditions, reduced CO_2 emissions and water consumption, and sustainable management (Hoque & Rana, 2020). Even during the COVID-19 pandemic, when market demand dropped rapidly in Western countries and led global brands to cancel orders from suppliers in sourcing countries, H&M pledged to continue buying from suppliers as part of shared responsibility in a sustainable buyer–supplier relationship (Cosgrove, 2020)

The Capitalism turn and storytelling science

From the sustainability issues related to firms, people, and society, as illustrated in recent literatures, the question arises as to whether such issues are independent from the type of capitalism in which they emerge. Alternatively, we may also ask why sustainability issues arising in connection with firms' behavior manifest differently and with different magnitudes across different societies. The answers to these questions require studies to consider the differing perspectives on capitalism in explaining sustainability issues in connection with firms' behavior and business modeling strategies in different societies (see, for further explanation on capitalism, Wood and Allen, 2020; Rana & Morgan, 2019; Morgan et al., 2010).

Comparative capitalism literatures argue that the nature of institutional systems (e.g., state roles and policies, labor institutions, financial institutions, and skill development institutions), the interactions among these systems, and the interactions between these systems and businesses operating within them, give rise to different forms of capitalism. For example, different conditions emerge within a liberal market economy (USA and UK), a coordinated/cooperative market economy (Germany, Japan), a collaborative market economy (Denmark, Sweden), and an incoherent/fragmented market economy (Greece, several emerging economies) (Rana & Morgan, 2019; Morgan & Kristensen, 2015). Such variations in capitalism and market structure contribute to variations in income and inequality in society, in the consumption and appropriation of natural resources, and in the ways in which local and multinational firms behave toward sustainable initiatives (Wood & Allen, 2020).

Rana et al. (2018) argue that home and host country institutions and firm ownership structure, including governance, influence multinational enterprises (MNEs) subsidiaries to design local sustainability strategies. Their study demonstrates how UK-based GSK and Denmark-based Novo-Nordisk have been able to design different local strategies in collaboration with market and non-market actors in order to include locally relevant societal and economic goals in their business modeling strategies. This has in turn led to the long-term legitimacy and survival of Novo-Nordisk in Bangladeshi business systems, while GSK had to shut its pharmaceutical operation due to contrasting strategy (i.e. low level of collaboration with market and non-market actors) shaped by HQ decisions and business modeling. Thus, we can conclude that firm structure and contextual forms of capitalism shape how a firm is able to adopt sustainability in its business modeling. Storytelling science can help us to better grasp this complexity and better understand these realities.

While many firms claim to address sustainability issues through corporate social responsibility (CSR) initiatives, this may turn out to be a window-dressing strategy concerned only with improving the company's image. The particular forms of capitalism at play in multinational firms' home countries tend to inspire inclusion of sustainability in business modeling through CSR and other strategies, but firms often behave differently in foreign markets, under different structures and different forms of capitalism. This often leads to paradoxical or questionable behavior. The example of Norwegian firm Telenor may illuminate this dimension. Telenor addresses social and economic sustainability issues in its business modeling in the home region; however, the company has been implicated in misconduct in relation to environment, labor rights, and local laws in Bangladesh (Rana and Jokela, 2017). Surprisingly, the company carried out several CSR activities at the same time that it was weakening its compliance with social and legal standards; this was possible because of the weaker institutional context in Bangladesh that does not necessarily ensure sustainability standards paralleling those in Scandinavia.

SBM and strategies are thus socially constructed within contextual forms of capitalism and internal firm structures. Hence, sustainability studies that plan to use a storytelling science perspective should consider capitalism literature, particularly that relating to ecologically and socially responsible capitalism, in explaining the issues and mechanisms of sustainability and business (modeling) strategies. Narratives and antenarratives can be better reflected and explained if studies take into account the antecedents and characteristics deriving from capitalism. Storytelling method can help narrate and explain the SBM strategies of firms – particularly those which illuminate the *between* and *becoming* in a certain context in connection with the *before*, *beneath*, and *beyond*.

The communication turn in SBM and storytelling science

Storytelling is a process by which a series of events is transformed into a story or narrative and expressed to its audience. This is not a neutral process; it is a bid or attempt to reshape opinions, create shared realities and understandings, and spur action. Through storytelling, the individual actor attempts to influence the world using narratives and communication. Storytelling is therefore crucial to an organization's value and value proposition mechanism as stories express the impression that stakeholders and owners have of a company in terms of trust, quality, reliability, efficiency, and development. These views are formed in the context of specific forms of capitalism which in turn shape firms and their strategies.

It is thus important not only in business modeling but also in a company's communications – including advertisements, annual reporting, sustainability reporting, company websites, and digital media channels. By using a storytelling science approach, a company can work to develop a reality, discourse, or truth about how the company cares for the consumer, society, and the world. It should be noted that, at times, storytelling may have a tarnished image and reputation because the audience may perceive that there is no connection between what a company says or promises and what it actually does, as described in the Telenor case above. Weak institutions and fragmented capitalist systems may make firms more likely to opt for such opportunism and misrepresent reality in their reporting. Many multinational companies tell pleasant stories in their CSR and sustainability reports in order to present the image of a sustainable firm, while their actions reflect the complete opposite. This creates a negative image of the company for stakeholders. Companies wishing to engage in an honest storytelling approach should work systematically from a holistic perspective, in which micro, meso, and macro institutional factors are taken into account to explain *beneath*, *between*, *becoming*, and *beyond* factors as part of truthful communication with the public.

Methodological and Philosophical Perspectives of Storytelling Science and SBM

Storytelling science is rooted in the philosophy of pragmatism, which is particularly evident in the work of C. S. Peirce. The method, as we have described in passing, is a self-correcting AID approach. This is accomplished in phases, working out the abductions, the induction tests to use at the beginning of the research process, and the deductions made ahead of the fieldwork.

Popper was familiar with the work of C. S. Peirce in self-correcting inductions, and both proposed similar ways to test induction in relation to deduction and hypotheses (though Peirce preferred to call the later *abduction* or *retroduction*). We believe that future studies applying a storytelling science perspective in business modeling strategy can benefit from applying the following four tests:

1. Test one: Try through acts of self-reflection to dismiss, refute, or falsify the logic, methods, or precepts of a business modeling strategy. If that does not work, move on to the second test.
2. Test two: Engage other people (relevant informants) in conversations, focus groups, or interviews about the business model's value propositions, mechanisms, and consequences to see whether self-corrective induction is true or not. If this disproves the theory, method, practice, or logic, stop. If not, go on to the next test.
3. Test three: Use the laws of nature, as understood across various scientific disciplines, in order to assess the strategic assumptions and logics of the business modeling. If this does not refute the current understanding of the strategy, proceed to the final test.
4. Test four: Conduct interventions and or experiments that test the business modeling strategy's assumptions or logics using deduction.

The tests of inferences (abductive–inductive–deductive) depend on what we call the storytelling science of self-correction (Boje & Rosile, 2020b). Karl Popper was particularly concerned with not making inferences that are post-hoc. Instead, like Peirce, he preferred making antecedent predictions that could be tested and potentially refuted. Indeed, Popper (1994) was concerned that theorists did not buy into the "myth of the framework". Peirce described the relationships between his three kinds of induction as follows:

1. *Crude Induction*: This does not include acts of refutation of one's deductive theory, abductive propositions, or inductive tests (e.g. sampling cases). In assuming linearity, the beginning–middle–end structure of crude induction misses complex dynamics and often leaves out important events, histories, and characters necessary to a full understanding of how complex adaptive and living systems operate.
2. *Quantitative Induction*: What is the "actual probability" that an individual member of a population will have the same pattern of causes and effects as the population overall? Peirce advocated repeated sampling, in order to avert the inductive fallacy we now call the black swan effect. Just because all the swans sampled have been white does not mean the next sample will not include a black swan.
3. *Qualitative Induction*: There is an intermediate approach between Crude and Quantitative Induction, and a way to integrate them rather than treating them as either–or. Qualitative Induction comprises those inductions that are neither founded on experience in one mass, as Crude Induction is, nor upon a collection of numerable instances of equal evidential values, as Quantitative Induction is. Instead, Qualitative Induction is built upon a stream of experience in which the relative evidential values of different parts must be estimated according to our sense of the impressions they make on us. It is like "predictions", being antecedent (i.e. coming before in time) and investigator's knowledge of their own truth and other's truths, as the truth-making negotiations occur (and mostly never are completed). Even assuming the successful collection of innumerable cases of equal evidential value of different parts of a complex system such as a supply chain or value proposition mecha-

nism, the carrying capacities of the planet for the whole system can still only be understood by estimate. We first deduce such an estimate from an abductive assumption, making sure that the planet and social system will not be harmed, then pin down the tests, and make the deductions through a modeling approach that does not leave out parts of the system as a whole.

Drivers, Enablers, and Barriers of Implementing SBM

Researchers using storytelling science can benefit from an understanding of the forces driving and impeding the implementation of SBM. At this point in dynamic global markets, the development of SBM is primarily driven by the desire to gain a competitive advantage through corporate sustainability, particularly for large multinationals modeling. Sustainability is rarely positioned as a firm's core corporate strategy; however, it is common for firms to view sustainability as a driver in business modeling in two ways.

In the first type, firms are proactive in embracing sustainability as a core corporate strategy, and thus they design organizational structures, governance, operations, and products accordingly in compliance with sustainability goal(s); they refer, for example, to UN or national sustainability goals. However, this is not a linear approach in adopting SBM, as firms' existing business models predate the focus on sustainability. Instead of changing the entire existing business model, which is a difficult and risky proposition, firms tend to introduce a parallel sustainability-driven business model and continue the existing business model by incorporating sustainability concepts into their operational strategies as deemed suitable. The aim is to transform the entire organizational structure, business operation, management, and product marketing toward a sustainability-driven business model over a defined period of time. As highlighted above, in this case firms appear to be proactive in their strategic decision-making, trying to reconfigure their asset bases, management, governance structures, operations, and technological capabilities in order to make it happen.

These types of firms are driven by corporate visions of sustainability and sustainable strategic management, market and societal legitimacy, changes in institutional policy and consumer perception, reputation and branding, competitive advantage, welfare and responsible business attitude, etc. An example of this kind of firm is H&M, which has adopted sustainability into its existing business model along with introducing a circular economy concept modeling as a parallel approach that aims to transform the entire organizational structure, operation, and business model into a sustainability-driven approach. Within a proactive approach, firms develop their business models by keeping the mission of sustainability at the core of business plans and business model designs. Thus, they pursue sustainability as a core mission of their ventures. Many start-ups and SMEs taking advantage of institutional incentives are starting ventures under this category; for example, "Better World Fashion" sells leather fashion goods based on used leather apparels using a circular economy model as prescribed by the Ellen MacArthur Foundation (see, Ivang & Rana, 2019)

In the second type, firms are reactive to external forces related to sustainability rules, policies, customer perceptions, collaborating partners' expectations, changing practices, and market competition dynamics. Transnational or multilateral institutions (e.g., UN, EU, WHO) are increasingly forcing national institutions and MNEs to comply with sustainability goals by pressing them to develop rules and practices that fit with UN agenda. In turn, these goals impact standards and key performance indicators of production, operation, process, supply chain, products, and waste management (which involve, for example, CO_2 emissions and water consumption), human health and welfare, poverty, inequality, etc. These external pressures are forcing firms to reconfigure existing business models to earn internal, external, procedural, and product legitimacy – especially for firms involved in global operation and marketing (Rana, 2015).

Firms of this type feel pressure to adapt to sustainability issues and requirements, integrating green concepts and specific sustainability agendas into organizational structures, strategies, operations, and value propositions in order to fit with changes in institutional regulations, standards, market characteristics, and customer expectations. Firms of this type tend to reconfigure their existing business models to fit with the sustainability-driven agenda and key performance indicators as much as they can, but are unlikely to be able to address sustainability goals entirely.

In both cases, firms must have dynamic capabilities in order to sense changes and new expectations across markets, institutional fields, and business systems, seize the capabilities and resources required for changing or innovating the business model, and reconfigure the existing organizational design, strategies, operations, resource allocation, and management for innovation and change (Bocken, and Geradts, 2019). Danish firm Bestseller is a good example of this; the company has adopted sustainability issues into its existing business model and is redesigning products in order to meet the market and institutional expectations.

Organizational design, which includes the process of aligning the structure of an organization with an objective of improving efficiency and effectiveness, is one of the key foundations as well as challenges in developing and implementing SBM. This process of alignment requires firms to have supportive ownership structures. There are various forms of ownerships, such as family ownership, pension funds, business angels, bank or capital market financing, institutional investments, etc., and each form contributes to different structure and vision leading to variable efficiencies in management and governance and resource capabilities (technological, management, and financial) as well as strategizing. The owners or firms should not only be able to sense the need for change and the path toward achieving it through reconfiguration and innovation, but must also be able to implement the business model and strategies in pursuit of corporate success and the firm's legitimation. Determining where to focus on a sustainability agenda and how to operationalize this agenda is a key challenge for firms, as innovation entails high risk in terms of investment, market share, revenue, and change management.

Many organizations, particularly technology-rich firms, tend to use big-data or small-data analysis using artificial intelligence in order to understand what competitors are doing, what institutions and customers are expecting, and how these contextual facts are changing (Nielsen & Lund, 2019). The experiences and intuitive capacities of entrepreneurs or top managers play a vital role in sensing the right ideas and methods for innovating or reconfiguring organizational designs and business models.

The biggest challenge in SBM, however, is in optimizing balance and complementarity between sustainability-oriented visions and practices, and corporate revenue goals and legitimacy. Often shareholders are not ready to accept the decision to shift to SBM as it is likely to result in revenue and profit loss in the short term, even if it could be lucrative in the longer term. Foundations or pension funds that own significant shares of large firms, which are common in Denmark, are interested in long-term investment for sustainability driven-business modeling in cases that show promising market position and competitive advantage. However, this is not the case in many countries. As a result, large MNEs whose key shareholders are striving for short-term profit maximization are prevented from innovating or reconfiguring organizational structures for an SBM that may hamper immediate revenue or require high investment that affects profitability.

In such cases, larger firms tend to prefer models of corporate social responsibility that reflect a limited sustainability agenda sufficient to fulfil the local and multilateral institutional requirements and establish a positive local image and legitimacy. Cost is therefore one of the biggest challenges that many firms face in innovating or developing SBM, and this is applicable across many emerging economies where national institutions do not have necessary support systems, incentives, and consistent ecosystems to support the development of SBM (Rana & Sørensen 2020; Rana & Allen, 2018).

However, it is not only state support and consistent industry/ecosystem development that shapes how and whether firms can emphasize sustainability in business modeling, but also consumer perception. As sustainability development involves risks and high costs, though institutional rules are in place, if the consumer mindsets and perceptions are not consistently in line with sustainability, investment in sustainable product development and operation may not be seen as beneficial even where institutional supports are in place. Consumers may not be ready to pay the price or perceive the value proposition as differentiated and unique, thus leaving no impact on the competitive advantage for firms in competition. However, differences in ownership structure and governance, particularly in global firms, underpin how MNEs would configure SBM.

A comparison between two MNEs can better illuminate this argument. H&M and Inditex (owner of the Zara fashion brand), two global firms in the apparel industry, have addressed sustainability differently in their business modeling due to differences in the ownership structures of their respective retail stores and in the ways they govern suppliers. Although H&M and Zara both sell apparel, H&M primarily sells low-cost workwear while Zara primarily sells higher-priced fashions and workwear. Both firms intend to respond to the emergence of fast fashion as an industry trend in nearly 70 countries. H&M has introduced a separate circular economy model parallel to its existing business model, and has undertaken initiatives to reduce CO_2 emissions and water consumption and increase recycling of clothes. It has been very successful in this regard, due partly to the fact that it owns nearly all 4900 of its stores and thus can ensure the quick collection of used clothes. However, it does not own any of its suppliers and has developed arms-length governance relationships with nearly 800 suppliers across Asia, Africa, Europe, and Latin America. Thus, it cannot force all suppliers to comply with circular production and sustainability operations. Sourcing from distant locations has increased H&M's lead times (adding, on average, two weeks) to bring fashions to the market, making it slower in responding to fashion changes than Zara. However, this externalization of supply networks has reduced the cost of production and investment for H&M.

On the other hand, Inditex has internalized its product network, and owns most of its suppliers located in geographical proximity to its headquarters, i.e. in Turkey, Spain, Portugal, and Eastern Europe. Thus, it has an advantage in being able to bring fashions to the market faster than H&M – albeit at a higher cost and with more intensive management requirements. Thus, it is easier for Inditex to reconfigure the supply network to introduce circular production compared with H&M. However, as Inditex only owns one-third of its retail stores, its volume of used clothes collection is not as high as H&M's. This is the reason H&M introduced a separate circular business model, working with the smaller selection of suppliers who could afford to reconfigure their production and operations management, while Inditex could institute such a change internally. However, both have been very serious in responding to climate change issues in operations and business modeling.

Although many global firms are working to develop sustainability-driven business models, they cannot all implement strategies used in SBM in the same way in all countries, and neither can they offer the same value proposition in the same ways, because of the differences in regulative, normative, and cognitive institutions and markets. Thus, adaptation, capability development, and legitimation are the key factors that global firms should take into consideration in order to embrace and apply a sustainability agenda in business modeling and organizational design.

CONCLUSION

In this chapter, we have provided a conceptual overview of a SBM strategy within a storytelling science paradigm. Storytelling science uses C. S. Peirce's AID approach in iterative stages of self-correcting investigative cycles, in order to deconstruct regimes of truth about sustainability that are unjustified, or fail to account for carrying capacities. While there are always multiple versions of a given story, some may be truer and more artificial than others. We have shown that storytelling science can be a useful tool in accounting for the variations and characteristics of firms, and surrounding forms of capitalism can impact SBM. We have also proposed ways of integrating storytelling science with SBM, and described the methodological and philosophical perspectives in SBM research. Finally, we have presented an extensive discussion as to how drivers of and barriers to implementing a SBM strategy can be understood; namely, by focusing on what is socially and ecologically sustainable rather than only on what is profitable.

REFERENCES

Amit, R., & Zott, C. (2001). Value creation in e-business. *Strategic Management Journal, 22*(6-7), 493–520.

Bakhtin, M. M. (1993). *Toward a Philosophy of the Act.* Written as unpublished notebooks written between 1919–1921, first published in the USSR in 1986 with the title *K filosofii postupka*; 1993 English V. Liapunov, Trans.

Bocken, N. M. P. & Geradts, T. H. J. (2019). Barriers and drivers to sustainable business model innovation: Organization design and dynamic capabilities. *Long Range Planning.* https://doi.org/10.1016/j .lrp.2019.101950

Bocken, N., Boons, F., & Baldassarre, B. (2019). Sustainable business model experimentation by understanding ecologies of business models. *Journal of Cleaner Production, 208*, 1498–1512.

Bohnsack, R., Pinkse, J., & Kolk, A. (2014). Business models for sustainable technologies: Exploring business model evolution in the case of electric vehicles. *Research Policy, 43*(2), 284–300.

Boje, D. M. (2001). *Narrative Methods for Organizational & Communication Research.* Thousand Oaks, CA: Sage Publications.

Boje, D. M. (2008). *Storytelling Organizations.* Thousand Oaks, CA: Sage Publication.

Boje, D. M. (2011). *Storytelling and the Future of Organizations: An Antenarrative Handbook.* New York, NY: Routledge.

Boje, D. M. (2019a). *Storytelling in the Global Age: There is no Planet B.* Hackensack, NJ: World Scientific Publishing Pte. Ltd.

Boje, D. M. (2019b). *Organizational Research: Storytelling in Action.* London/NY: Routledge.

Boje, D. M. (2019c). *A Storytelling Science about Water for All Species.* Singapore/London/NY: World Scientific.

Boje, D., & Jørgensen, K. M. (2020). A 'storytelling science' approach making the eco-business modeling turn. *Journal of Business Models.*

Boje, D. M., & Rosile, G. A. (2020a). *Doing 'Storytelling Science' for Your Dissertation.* Cheltenham, UK: Edward Elgar Press.

Boje, D., & Rosile, G. A. (2020b). *How to Use Conversational Storytelling Interviews for Your Dissertation.* Cheltenham, UK: Edward Elgar Publishing.

Bonnet, M., Savall, A., Savall, H., & Zardet, V. (2018). The socio-economic approach to management: Preventing economic crises by harnessing hidden costs and creating sustainable productivity. In *The Routledge Companion to Risk, Crisis and Emergency Management* (pp. 447–463). New York, NY: Routledge.

Boons, F., & Laasch, O. (2019). Business models for sustainable development: A process perspective. *Journal of Business Models*, 7(1), 9–12.

Casadesus-Masanell, R., & Ricart, J. E. (2010). From strategy to business models and onto tactics. *Long Range Planning*, 43(2–3), 195–215.

Christensen, C. M. (2001). The past and future of competitive advantage. *MIT Sloan Management Review*, 42(2), 105–109.

Cosgrove, E. (2020). H&M pledges to accept orders in production from sales. https://www.supplychaindive.com/news/coronavirus-hm-accept-supplier-orders/575191/

Dentchev, N., Rauter, R., Jóhannsdóttir, L., Snihur, Y., Rosano, M., Baumgartner, R., Nyberg, T., Tangh, X., van Hoof, B., & Jonker, J. (2018). Embracing the variety of sustainable business models: A prolific field of research and a future research agenda. *Journal of Cleaner Production*, 194(1), 695–703.

Evans, E., Vladimirova, D., Holgado, M., Fossen, K. V., Yang, M., Silva, E. A., & Barlow, C. Y. (2017). Business model innovation for sustainability: Towards a unified perspective for creation of sustainable business models. *Business Strategy and the Environment*, 26(5), 597–608.

Ewing, J. (2019, December 31). Electric cars threaten the heart of Germany's economy. *The New York Times.* https://www.nytimes.com/2019/12/31/business/electric-cars-germany-economy.html, accessed on 6 April 2020

Foucault, M. (2011). The courage of truth: The government of self and others – Lectures at College de France 1983-1984. Edited by F. Gors, with General Editors: F. Ewald, A. Fontana, A. I. Davidson; translated by G. Burchell. H. Mills, Basingstoke, Hampshire, UK: Palgrave Macmillan.

Hahn, T., Preuss, L., Pinkse, J., & Figge, F. (2014). Cognitive frames in corporate sustainability: Managerial sensemaking with paradoxical and business case frames. *Academy of Management Review*, 39(4), 463–487.

Hoque, I., & Rana, M. B. (2020). Buyer–supplier relationships from the perspective of working environment and organisational performance: Review and research agenda, *Management Review Quarterly*, 70(1), 1–50.

Ivang, R., & Rana, M. B. (2019). Better world fashion: Circular economy and competitive advantage. In IVEY Teaching Case (pp. 1–16). [9B19A021] Ivey Publishing.

Johnson, M. W., Christensen, C. M., & Kagermann, H. (2008). Reinventing your business model. *Harvard Business Review*, 86(12), 57–68.

Joyce, A., & Paquin, R. L. (2016). The triple layered business model canvas: A tool to design more sustainable business models. *Journal of Cleaner Production*, 135, 1474–1486.

Larsen, J., Boje, D.M., & Bruun, L. (2020). *True Storytelling: Seven Principles for an Ethical and Sustainable Change-Management Strategy.* London: Routledge.

Lüdeke-Freund, F., Bohnsack, R., Breuer, H., & Massa, L. (2019a). Research on sustainable business model patterns: Status quo, methodological issues, and a research agenda. In *Sustainable Business Models* (pp. 25–60). Cham, Switzerland: Palgrave Macmillan.

Lüdeke-Freund, F., Rauter, R., Pedersen, E.R.G., & Nielsen, C. (2019b). Sustainable value creation through business models. *Journal of Business Model*, 7(1), 1–4. https://journals.aau.dk/index.php/JOBM

Morgan, G., & Kristensen, P. H. (2015). The comparative analysis of capitalism and the study of organizations. In P. S. Adler, P. du Gay, G. Morgan, & M. Reed (Eds.). *Oxford Handbook of Sociology,*

Social Theory and Organization Studies: Contemporary Currents (pp. 220–245). Oxford: Oxford University Press.

Morgan, G., Campbell, J. L., Crouch, C., Pedersen, O. K., & Whitley, R. (Eds.). (2010). *The Oxford Handbook of Comparative Institutional Analysis*. Oxford: Oxford University Press.

Nielsen, C., & Lund, M. (2019). Small data: Data strategies that most companies can profit from. *California Management Review, 62*(1). https://cmr.berkeley.edu/2019/11/small-data/

Nielsen, C., Montemari, M., Paolone, F., Massaro M., Dumay J., & Lund, M. (2018). *Business Models: A Research Overview*. London: Routledge.

Popper, K. R. (1994). *The Myth of the Framework: In Defense of Science and Rationality*. M.A. Notturno (Eds.). London/NY: Routledge.

Popper, K. R. (2008). After the open society: Selected social and political writings. In J. Shearmur, & P. N. Turner (Eds.) *Karl Popper*. Abingdon (Oxfordshire), UK/NY: Routledge.

Porter, M. E., & Kramer, M. R. (2011). Creating shared value. *Harvard Business Review, 89* (1/2), 62–77.

Rana, M. B. (2014). *Rethinking Business System Theory from the Perspective of Civil Society, Transnational Community, and Legitimacy: Strategies of European MNCs in Bangladesh* (PhD Thesis). Department of Business and Management, Aalborg University, Denmark.

Rana, M. B. (2015). Tri-space framework for understanding MNC behaviour and strategies: An institutionalism and business systems perspective. In S. T. Marinova (Eds.) *Institutional Impacts on Firm Internationalisation* (pp. 299–333). London, UK: Palgrave Macmillan.

Rana, M. B., & Allen, M. M. C. (2018). Business systems perspective on entrepreneurship. In R. Turcan, & N. Fraser (Eds.) *The Palgrave Handbook of Multidisciplinary Perspectives on Entrepreneurship* (pp. 271–291). Cham: Palgrave Macmillan.

Rana, M. B., & Jokela, P. (2017). Paradox in CSR practice: Suggesting ambidexterity capability for MNEs. In *EIBA 2017 Milan Conference*. European International Business Academy.

Rana, M. B., & Morgan, G. (2019). Twenty-five years of business systems research and lessons for international business studies. *International Business Review, 28*(3), 513–532.

Rana, M. B., & Nipa, F. S. (2019). Entrepreneurship in an institutionally distant context: Bangladeshi diaspora entrepreneurs in Denmark. In: M. Elo & I. Minto-Coy (Eds.) *Diaspora Networks in International Business* (pp. 529–555). Cham: Springer.

Rana, M. B., & Sørensen, O. J. (2014). Sentiments that affect socio-political legitimacy of TNCs in Bangladesh, India, and Pakistan: Sustainable strategic management from an institutional perspective. *Journal of Transnational Management, 19*(1), 62–106.

Rana, M. B., & Sørensen, O. J. (2020). Levels of legitimacy development in internationalization: Multinational enterprise and civil society interplay in institutional void. *Global Strategy Journal*, 1–35. https://doi.org/10.1002/gsj.1371

Rana, M. B., & Tajuddin, S. A. (2021). Circular economy and sustainability capability: The case of H&M. In M. B. Rana, & M. Allen (Eds.) *Upgrading the Global Garment Industry: Internationalization, Capabilities and Sustainability* (pp. 253–283). Edward Elgar Publishing. New Perspectives on the Modern Corporation series.

Rana, M. B., Allen, M., & Liu, J. (2018). How MNEs respond to institutional voids and why do they differ: The influence of firm factors, local partnership, and institutional contexts. In *44 European International Business Academy Conference 2018*. European International Business Academy.

Richardson, J. E. (2008). The business model: An integrative framework for strategy execution. *Strategic Change, 17*, 133–144.

Ripple, W. J., Wolf, C., Newsome, T. M., Galetti, M., Alamgir, M., Crist, E., Mahmoud, M. I., & Laurance, W. F. (2017). World scientists' warning to humanity: A second notice. *BioScience, 67*, 1026–1028

Rosile, G. A., Boje, D. M., & Claw, C. M. (2018). Ensemble leadership theory: Collectivist, relational, and heterarchical roots from indigenous contexts. *Leadership, 14*(3), 307–328.

Savall, H. (2018). Why publish this work on Germán Bernácer, the great pioneering Spanish economist, now? In *Radical Origins to Economic Crises* (pp. 3–19). Cham: Palgrave Macmillan.

Savall, H., Péron, M., Zardet, V., & Bonnet, M. (2017). *Socially Responsible Capitalism and Management*. New York, NY: Routledge.

Stevens, P. (2019, June 4). The battery decade: How energy storage could revolutionize industries in the next 10 years. *CNBC*. https://www.cnbc.com/2019/12/30/battery-developments-in-the-last-decade -created-a-seismic-shift-that-will-play-out-in-the-next-10-years.html

Teece, D. J. (2010). Business models, business strategy and innovation. *Long Range Planning*, *43*(2–3), 172–194.

Vladimirova, D. (2019). Building sustainable value propositions for multiple stakeholders: A practical tool. *Journal of Business Models*, *7*(1), 1–8.

Wood, G. T., & Allen, M. M. C. (2020). Comparing capitalisms: Debates, controversies and future directions. *Sociology*, *54*(3), 482–500.

Xu, L., Marinova, D., & Guo, X. (2015). Resilience thinking: A renewed system approach for sustaina- bility science. *Sustainability Science*, *10*, 123–138.

Zott, C., & Amit, R. (2008). The fit between product market strategy and business model: Implications for firm performance. *Strategic Management Journal*, *29*, 1–26.

Zott, C., Amit, R., & Massa, L. (2011). The business model: Recent developments and future research. *Journal of Management*, *37*(4), 1019–1042.

PART 2

SUSTAINABILITY-DRIVEN BUSINESS STRATEGIES IN MARKETING

5. Corporate responsibility as an effective marketing practice for improving consumers' brand evaluations – critical overview, new insights, and future directions

Ilona Szőcs and Milena Micevski

INTRODUCTION

In January 2020, the World Economic Forum celebrated its 50th anniversary in Davos (Switzerland) amid the global crises of climate change, environmental degradation, and social inequality. The meeting, once again, highlighted disenchantment with the dominant business model of profit and shareholder value maximization, and stressed the inability of the current form of capitalism to serve society. Soon after, coronavirus disease 2019 (COVID-19) hit the entire globe, jeopardizing the health of billions of people. Its unprecedented consequences heavily affected economies, enterprises, global supply chains, and labor markets, leading to widespread business disruptions (ILO, 2020). The pandemic has relentlessly exposed our society's weaknesses and has accentuated the interdependence between business and society.

Marked by COVID-19 as well as ongoing societal challenges, corporations are increasingly told to be responsible for their impact on our society, moving the topic to the forefront of many business and governmental debates. Corporate strategies, actions, and processes have widespread consequences and businesses are called upon to take a more accountable approach directed not only toward their shareholders, but toward all their stakeholders, including employees, communities, governments, suppliers, and customers. There is a clear demand for a more holistic business model; one that simultaneously meets expectations for quality products and services as well as for positive impact on society. International bodies, such as the European Commission, the International Organization for Standardization, and the United Nations (UN) are benchmarking businesses against the extent to which they accept responsibility for the environmental and social impacts they cause. Moreover, the UN Sustainable Development Goals (SDGs), effective as of 2016, are considered by several global organizations, including the World Business Council for Sustainable Development, the Global Reporting Initiative, and the UN's Global Compact as an appeal for business to serve society.

Broadly, the UN's World Commission on Environment and Development defined the principle of sustainable development more than 30 years ago in the 'Brundtland Report' as "development that meets the needs of the present without compromising the ability of future generations to meet their own needs" (WCED, 1987, p. 37). Named after the Commission's Chairwoman and Prime Minister of Norway, Gro Harlem Brundtland, the report urged a progressive transformation of economy and society, and developed guiding principles for sustainable development as it is generally understood today. Four primary dimensions of sustainable development have been derived from this report: safeguarding long-term ecological sustainability (i.e., the conservation of nature, such as plant and animal species), satisfying basic human needs (i.e., employment, food, energy, housing, water supply, sanitation, and health care), and promoting intragenerational as well as intergenerational equity (i.e., the current generation must meet its needs without compromising the ability of future generations to meet theirs and this social equity must be extended to equity within each generation) (Holden et al., 2014). From a corporate perspective, these dimensions have found resonance in the Triple Bottom Line (TBL) concept of corporate sustainability, coined by John Elkington in 1994 (Elkington, 1994). The TBL concept – originally aimed at provoking a deeper thinking about capitalism and its future (Elkington, 2018) – put forward a sustainability framework focusing on companies' impacts within three dimensions (economic, social, and environmental) and has been commonly applied to conceptualize various aspects related to corporate sustainability (such as economic prosperity, social justice, and environmental integrity). The environmental dimension encompasses issues such as preserving the natural environment and its resources through environmentally friendly production; the social dimension includes concerns such as health, welfare, and social justice; while the economic dimension refers to the financial bottom-line of the organization and its long-term economic prosperity. Accordingly, by committing to sustainability, business can take shared responsibility for achieving a better world.[1]

CORPORATE RESPONSIBILITY

The mounting pressure of various stakeholders challenges companies' traditional focus on maximizing shareholder wealth toward finding a balance between profitability and responsibility, marked by the concept of 'shared value' (Porter & Kramer, 2011). Over the years, the three dimensions of the TBL concept of corporate sustainability have been integrated into the concept of Corporate Responsibility (CR) and translated into a responsible approach companies have to be concerned with (i.e., economic, social, and environmental responsibility). CR is broadly defined as a firm's or a brand's commitment to maximizing long-term economic, societal, and environmental well-being through business practices, policies, and resources (Du et al., 2011). Thus, while sustainability constitutes the ultimate goal (i.e., meeting the needs of the present without compromising the ability of future generations to meet their own needs), CR represents an intermediate stage within corporate sustainability where companies aim for a balance between the TBL domains of sustainability (Kaptein & Wempe, 2002). CR is therefore part of and completes the corporate sustainability framework (van Marrewijk, 2003).

From a strategic point of view, CR is "a global mandate today" (Sen et al., 2016, p. 73) and viewed as a core part of any corporate strategy (van Doorn et al., 2017). CR offers business benefits since responsible companies get noticed and receive positive public attention. For example, TOMS is a brand known for having a business model built around its contributions to global sustainable development. The most reputable brands globally are enjoying highest standings due to their enhanced perception of CR (Reputation Institute, 2020). Moreover, several global reports rank brands according to their level of engagement in environmental and social issues. For example, the Sustainable Brand Index, Europe's largest independent brand study on sustainability, publishes sustainability perceptions by important stakeholders of over 1400 brands across a variety of industries and countries since 2011 (Sustainable Brand Index, 2020). Beyond large-scale rankings and media attention, the academic literature is abundant with proofs of the 'business case'[2] for CR. Many empirical studies show that CR can, among other things, improve companies' reputation and legitimacy, competitive advantage, employee morale, customer loyalty, relationships with stakeholders, long-term shareholder value, and reduce costs and risks (for a review, see Carroll & Shabana, 2010). Hence, the question is no longer whether companies should engage in responsible activities but rather how can companies excel in their responsible efforts (Madden et al., 2012).

CORPORATE RESPONSIBILITY AND MARKETING

In marketing, the topic of CR has become an attractive tool for business to view its responsibilities through the TBL perspective (Elkington, 1998). This perspective, comprising the environmental, social, and economic responsibilities, emphasizes the long-term nature of the benefit that business is expected to provide to society (Schwartz, 2011). The environmental and social responsibilities are primarily of consumer concern, while the more traditional economic responsibility is mainly a managerial issue (Bangsa & Schlegelmilch 2020). Several scholars argue that CR has to be part of corporate strategy (e.g., Porter & Kramer, 2011; Szőcs & Schlegelmilch, 2020). As such, it affects corporate marketing strategy, and, ultimately, different stakeholder groups (e.g., consumers, employees, investors, communities). Essentially, responsible business conduct in marketing should aim for

> the strategic creation, communication, delivery, and exchange of offerings that produce value through consumption behaviors, business practices, and the marketplace, while lowering harm to the environment and ethically and equitably increasing the quality of life (QOL) and well-being of consumers and global stakeholders, presently and for future generations. (Lunde, 2018, p. 94)

In achieving this overall goal, CR needs to play a critical role in effective corporate marketing strategies (Hildebrand et al., 2011). Corporations aim for favorable responses from their stakeholder groups toward the company and its products/brands (Sen and Bhattacharya, 2001; Balmer et al., 2007), and, if done right, CR may be viewed as a key instrument of corporate marketing in building a positive corporate identity and, consequently, long-lasting relationships with stakeholders (Hildebrand et al., 2011).

The Impact of Corporate Responsibility on Consumer Outcomes

Consumers represent a key external stakeholder group at which different marketing strategies are aimed. Their beliefs about a company can influence their reactions to the specific company's products and services (Ind et al., 2017). Therefore, managing the associations that consumers have about a company, including its responsible practices, is an important strategic task (Markovic et al., 2018).

Empirical research points to consumers' increasing willingness to adopt a 'win-win' perspective, one that acknowledges that CR initiatives can and should be strategic, serving both the needs of society and the bottom-lines of business (Ellen et al., 2006; Sen et al., 2006). Accordingly, consumers' perceptions of why a company is engaging in CR is a focal driver of their responses to it (e.g., Bolton & Mattila, 2015; Chernev & Blair, 2015; Du et al., 2007; Garretson Folse et al., 2010; Vlachos et al., 2009). Previous consumer research has found that CR can lead to more favorable consumer beliefs, attitudes, and intentions toward the company or its brands (e.g., Becker-Olsen et al., 2006; Liu et al., 2014; Nan & Heo, 2007; Szőcs et al., 2016). Positive CR beliefs held by consumers are associated with longer-term brand loyalty and advocacy behaviors as well as stronger stakeholder–company relationships (e.g., Ailawadi et al., 2014; Bolton & Mattila, 2015; Du et al., 2007), even in business-to-business markets (Homburg et al., 2013). On the product/brand level, as one of the seminal studies in this field, Brown and Dacin (1997) found that positive CR associations can enhance consumers' product evaluations, while negative CR associations can have a detrimental effect on overall product evaluations. Beyond positive attitudinal responses, the findings of extant research also show that consumers are more likely to choose products/brands they perceive to be socially responsible (e.g., Andrews et al., 2014; Du et al., 2011; Henderson & Arora, 2010; Krishna & Rajan, 2009) and are likely to buy more or pay a higher price for products from a responsible company (Trudel and Cotte, 2009). However, favorable responses to CR are dependent on brands' perceived characteristics (e.g., van Doorn et al., 2017) and consumers' affinity or support of the CR issue (Joireman et al., 2015; Koschate-Fischer et al., 2012; Öberseder et al., 2013).

THE INTERPLAY BETWEEN BRAND PERCEPTIONS AND CORPORATE RESPONSIBILITY DOMAINS: NEW INSIGHTS

The effectiveness of responsible business practices may critically vary among brands. While CR initiatives often represent an asset for the firm (e.g., in terms of enhanced consumer responses), the magnitude of the outcome of such initiatives is not uniform and dependent on brands' characteristics and positioning. For example, CR initiatives may negatively affect consumer evaluations of luxury brands (Torelli et al., 2012) as well as of brands positioned on their strength versus gentleness (Luchs et al., 2010). Moreover, consumers respond more positively to CR of standalone brands (i.e., brands with low corporate brand dominance) rather than of those being part of a dominant corporate brand (Berens et al., 2005).

Previous research shows that brand concepts (i.e., unique abstract meanings associated with brands) interact with CR information (Torelli et al., 2012). Consumers' evaluations of brand-related CR information (e.g., environmental or social initiatives of the brand) are intertwined with their prior information about the brand. Brands are thus associated with concepts, which position them in the minds of consumers. For example, Armani may be associated with high status, power, and ambition, while Jack Wolfskin may be associated with creativity and freedom. Hence, the evaluations of Armani's engagement in CR activities will likely differ from those of Jack Wolfskin. This may be due to consumers' differing expectations in terms of a specific brand's CR engagement: Based on initial brand perceptions, CR activities of the brand may be viewed as either contradictory or consistent with their expectations (cf. Shea & Hawn, 2019).

Scholarly literature examining the effects of brands' responsible engagement indicates a positive impact on building connections with consumers (Porter and Kramer, 2002) and on improving product performance perceptions (Montillaud-Joyel and Otto, 2004). At a more general company level, the link between CR associations and consumer behavior has been investigated through consumers' perceptions of corporate abilities and the relationship between the consumer and the company (Crespo & Inacio, 2019). Literature, for example, asserts that CR matters more for quality considerations than the actual purchase behaviour (Bhattacharya and Sen 2004). However, the nexus between brands' performance and CR is unclear. On the one hand, some scholars argue that perceptions of company (brand) abilities might be compromised if a company (brand) invests more of its resources in CR (Sen and Bhattacharya, 2001). On the other hand, this is not straightforward since specific characteristics of the brand can determine CR's effectiveness. For example, literature shows that weaker, less successful brands (usually characterized by low levels of awareness or market share) are more likely to benefit from CR activities than strong brands (those already enjoying high levels of awareness among consumers) (van Doorn et al., 2017). In terms of building connections with customers, brands' personality (i.e., humanlike characteristics) plays a central role (Aaker, 1997). Although brands by their very nature are impersonal, consumers are able to develop strong relationships with brands. Such brands "can take the role of the 'other' with whom the consumer identifies, especially if consumers animate, humanize or somehow personalize the brand" (Fournier, 1998, p. 346). Thus, people may relate to brands as they relate to other people (Fournier, 2009). Moreover, CR activities can further help in creating a trusting relationship with brands (Torres et al., 2012) and increase consumers' willingness to identify with and support the company and its brand(s) (Lichtenstein et al., 2004).

Next to brands' characteristics, the CR domain the brand engages in (e.g., the environmental or social) may likewise determine the effectiveness of CR. Previous research has shown that consumers' responses differ across the types of CR initiatives (Bolton & Mattila, 2015; Du et al., 2007). Responsible business practices in different domains elicit diverse reactions from consumers, for example, depending on the extent to which these domains are categorized by consumers as individual-oriented (e.g., corporate practices concerning human rights and employee relations) versus group-oriented (e.g., corporate practices concerning diversity and community; Baskentli et al., 2019). More broadly, several studies in consumer research have conceptualized CR engagement as either social, environmental, or both (for an overview see Table 5.1). These two dimensions correspond to two dimensions of the TBL perspective, and, unlike the third (economic) dimension, are primarily of consumer concern (Bangsa & Schlegelmilch 2020).

Taken collectively, there is a lack of knowledge regarding the underlying mechanisms that lead to different consumer reactions to CR (Aguinis & Glavas, 2012) and more research is needed to improve our understanding of how consumers respond to responsible business conduct. First, extant research has largely ignored CR's potential domain-specific differences in consumer responses to brands. To our best knowledge, no consumer research to date has compared the effectiveness of the environmental versus social CR. This is surprising, since previous research suggests that consumer responses to CR are sensitive to the CR domain (Baskentli et al., 2019). Second, we argue that both brand characteristics discussed above (i.e., relational and performance aspects) are equally important factors to consider simultaneously when engaging in CR activities. Previous research has investigated brand characteristics independently from each other; however, brands have multiple associations in consumers' minds and with differing combinations. Hence, brands with differing combinations of relational and performance characteristics may benefit from CR variably. Third, corporate practice is filled with examples of companies engaging in both environmental and social issues. Nestlé, for example, invests in environmental responsibility, educates consumers on decreasing their household food waste, reduces green gas emissions in their supply chains, makes donations to communities, and communicates the responsible sourcing of its ingredients.[3] Thus, while corporations often take a combined approach toward these domains, it is unclear whether and how these domains interact with brand characteristics in influencing consumers' evaluations of brands.

Table 5.1   Overview of studies on consumer responses to corporate responsibility (CR)

Author/s (year)	CR domain	Dependent variables	Findings	Method	Country of research
Baskentli et al. (2019)	environmental & social	company attitude, advocacy behaviors	When consumers' moral foundations are congruent with CSR domains, positive pro-company behaviors increase. This congruency effect is observed only in positive CSR actions but not in CSR lapses. Consumer-company identification is the underlying process driving the consumer-domain congruence effect on pro-company reactions.	experiment	USA
Brown & Dacin (1997)	social	Product evaluation	CSR associations influence the overall evaluation of the company, which in turn can affect how consumers evaluate products from the company. All else being equal, more positive evaluations should produce greater revenues for a firm.	experiments	USA
Feldman & Vasquez-Parraga (2013)	environmental & social	willingness to pay (WTP)	CSR initiatives are positively related to willingness to pay. Product quality and the company's environmental commitment contribute to consumers' utility the most. Good labor practices and the company's leadership in the industry do not affect WTP among Peruvian consumers whereas they do among American consumers.	choice-based conjoint model	USA & Peru
Ferreira & Riberio (2017)	social	purchase intentions, willingness to pay	CSR and corporate social irresponsibility (CSI) affect consumer behavior and, particularly, consumers' willingness to pay and purchase intention. The study supports both the moderation hypothesis of country of origin in the relationship between CSR and willingness to pay and between CSR and purchase intention.	first-price sealed bid auction approach	Portugal
Groza et al. (2011)	environmental	attitude toward the firm, purchase intention	Proactive (vs reactive) CSR positively impacts attitudes toward the firm and higher purchase intentions through perceived organizational motives. Consumers assign different organizational motives to a CSR initiative depending on the source of the message (internal vs external).	experiment	USA
Nan & Heo (2007)	social	attitude toward: the ad, the brand, the company	An ad with an embedded cause-related marketing (CRM) message, compared with a similar one without a CRM message, elicits more favorable consumer attitude toward the company. This is so regardless of the level of fit between the sponsoring brand and the social cause. When the embedded CRM message involves high versus low brand/cause fit, consumer attitudes toward the ad and the brand are more favorable. Such positive effect of brand/cause fit, however, only emerges for consumers who are high in brand consciousness.	experiment	USA

Author/s (year)	CR domain	Dependent variables	Findings	Method	Country of research
Ramesh et al. (2019)	environmental & social	brand attitude brand image perceived quality purchase intention	CSR impacts positively purchase intention indirectly through brand image, brand attitude, and perceived quality.	online survey	India
Robinson & Wood (2018)	environmental & social	perceived product efficacy	New product trial is lower when new brands tout CSR activity than when they do not. CSR has a negative effect on new brands' perceived product performance. The negative effects for new brands can be reversed if the company explicitly signals a priority for both the product and its CSR endeavors. There is no similar negative impact of CSR on established brands.	experiment	USA
Tian et al. (2011)	environmental & social	corporate evaluation product association purchase intention	(1) Chinese consumers, who show a high level of awareness and trust of CSR, are more likely to transform a good CSR record into positive corporate evaluation, product association, and purchase intention; (2) Consumer responses to CSR vary across different product categories. Those firms selling experience products (vs search and credence products) are more likely to gain consumers' positive product associations and purchase support through CSR practices; and (3) The relationships between consumer demographics and their CSR responses are not linear, and those consumers with a middle level of age and income would respond to CSR more positively.	survey	China
van Doorn et al. (2017)	social	attitude toward the company customer retention (loyalty)	Perceived CSR can compensate for the absence of a strong brand or smaller advertising budgets, but not for lack of innovativeness. Companies that simultaneously do good and innovate are rewarded with more positive customer attitudes and higher levels of customer retention.	survey	The Netherlands

In light of the above, our study seeks to investigate whether and how do brands benefit from their CR engagement. Specifically, we propose that the extent to which CR enhances brand perception may differ depending on (a) varying combinations of brands' characteristics and (b) varying CR activities.

In the following, we focus on two fictitious brands with varying levels of performance and relationship orientation (i.e., a high performing & low relational brand, and a low performing & high relational brand) engaging in two CR domains (i.e., environmental and social). We present the preliminary results of our study concentrating on the clothing and footwear industry. The fashion industry is amongst the industries which generate most significant negative impacts (Belz & Peattie 2012), however, it is less addressed in consumer research compared with other industries, such as the food industry (Bangsa & Schlegelmilch 2020). Both environmental and social impacts are of importance in this industry (e.g., environmental pollution & working conditions). In 2019, the Global Fashion Agenda – a forum for industry collaboration on fashion sustainability – concludes in its 'Pulse of the Fashion' report that the fashion industry is unable to implement sustainable solutions in a timely manner (Global Fashion Agenda, 2019). As a result, the industry will likely fail to achieve the UN SDGs[4] or meet the UN Paris Agreement on climate change[5] (Global Fashion Agenda, 2019).

Study Results

One-hundred and sixty-eight Austrian consumers (61.9% female, 46.4% of respondents' aged between 18–25) participated in a between-subjects online study during April 2019. All participants were based in Austria and were either of Austrian origin or have been living in Austria for more than six years. At the beginning of the survey respondents were informed that the study focuses on a sportswear brand and its engagement in various activities; they were assured that the survey is completely anonymous and that there are no right or wrong answers. Participants were randomly assigned to either a *high performing & low relational* brand or a *low performing & high relational* brand condition and completed a self-administered questionnaire. Participants first read general information about the fictitious L&P sports brand after which we manipulated the brand's performance and relationship-building activities. Next, the respondents were exposed to two additional scenarios: (a) the brand's engagement in environmental issues and (b) the brand's engagement in social issues.

We used analysis of variance with multiple pairwise comparisons on the mean ratings of brand performance and relationship orientation across the two brand conditions to check the effectiveness of the brand characteristic's manipulation. Results showed that in each scenario the brand scored significantly higher on its intended characteristic. Therefore, our manipulation was successful (see Figures 5.1 and 5.2).

Our results show that both environmental and social CR activities significantly increase brand attitudes toward the two fictitious brands in our study. Furthermore, in *Scenario 1* (*high performing & low relational brand*), after introducing environmental CR engagement, the perceived performance and relational orientation of the brand also increased significantly. Similarly, the introduction of social CR engagement significantly increased the brand's relational orientation perceptions, however, it failed to increase the brand's performance perceptions significantly compared with the baseline (i.e., no CR) scenario (Figure 5.1). In *Scenario 2* (*low performing & high relational brand*), the introduction of both environmental and social

CR engagements resulted in a significant increase in the brand's perceived performance and relational orientation perceptions (Figure 5.2).

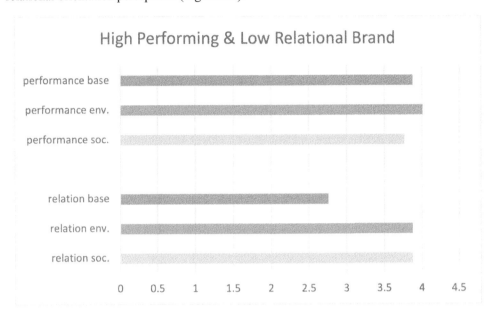

Figure 5.1   *Mean scores (Scenario 1)*

Note: Brand characteristics were measured on a 5-point Likert scale.

Further inspection of the pairwise comparisons revealed some additional interesting results. In *Scenario 1*, the introduction of social CR engagement led to balancing the perceptions of the brand's perceived performance and relational orientation, that is, social CR engagement resulted in perceptions of comparable brand performance and relational orientation, while these two brand perceptions maintained the higher performance and lower relational orientation status in the environmental CR treatment. In *Scenario 2*, although both environmental and social CR lead to a significant increase in perceptions of the brand's relational orientation, engagement in social CR resulted in a higher increase in the brand's relational orientation perceptions compared with engagement in environmental CR. The opposite holds for brand performance perceptions, where engagement in environmental CR resulted in a higher increase in performance perceptions compared with engagement in social CR. Interestingly, in *Scenario 2*, the nature of the brand perceptions (i.e., higher relational orientation compared with performance perceptions) remained constant after the manipulation of both environmental and social CR.

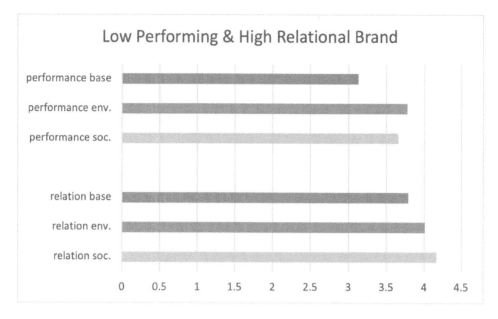

Figure 5.2   Mean scores (Scenario 2)

Note: Brand characteristics were measured on a 5-point Likert scale.

FUTURE OUTLOOK ON THE INTERSECTION OF CONSUMER AND CORPORATE RESPONSIBILITY RESEARCH

Previous studies investigating the impact of CR on brands have focused either on CR domains separately (e.g., Baskentli et al., 2019) or one brand characteristic at a time (e.g. van Doorn et al., 2017), neglecting their potential interplay. The findings on brand characteristics by van Doorn et al. (2017), for example, show that already well-performing brands have little room for improvement in terms of CR engagement and that weaker brands can most benefit from CR engagement. In our study, we point to the importance of incorporating a more fine-grained view of the relationship between the CR domains and brand characteristics. Our preliminary results indicate that one size does not fit all and that different brands (even those within the same industry) benefit differently from CR activities and that this effect depends both on the brand characteristics as well as on the CR domain these brands engage in.

Overall, our findings corroborate previous studies suggesting positive consumer responses to CR (e.g., Feldman & Vasquez-Parraga, 2013; Groza et al., 2011; Nan & Heo, 2007; Ramesh et al., 2019; Tian et al., 2011). We show that CR can positively affect consumers' brand-related beliefs and attitudes by impacting perceptions of the brand's performance and relational orientation. We further point to different ways in which brands benefit from CR activities. CR has the general ability to increase the perceptions of brands' relational orientation toward its consumers, regardless of whether the brand engaging in CR is a brand that is already scoring high on relation-oriented perceptions or one that scores lower on this characteristic. However, the ability of CR activities to increase brands' performance is contingent on the combination of the brand's characteristics (i.e., high/low performing brands with low/high relational orientation).

That is, engagement in CR leads to an increase in brand performance ratings regardless of the CR domain (i.e., environmental or social) for brands seen as weaker performers. In contrast, for brands already seen as good performers, a further increase in their performance ratings is possible, but contingent on the CR domain they engage in. For high performing brands, engagement in environmental CR further increases their already high perceptions of performance levels, whereas the positive impact of engagement in social CR is limited to brands' relational orientation scores. One reason for this might be that environmental CR is generally seen as requiring skills associated with good performers such as innovativeness and smart financial investments, leading to efficiency in energy and resource use. Environmental initiatives of successful firms, usually referred to as 'eco-efficiencies' have a spillover effect not only on firms' CR performance ratings but also increase their economic performance (Favotto et al., 2016), which again is associated with skillfulness. Social CR (e.g., supporting youth in communities), in contrast, has been connected to rather intangible gains, such as corporate reputation (e.g., Szőcs et al., 2016). While previous studies found a negative effect of CR on brands' perceived product performance (e.g., Robinson & Wood, 2018), we show that such negative effect is negligible and holds only for high performer brands (that at the same time do not emphasize and build their relations with consumers) engaging in social CR.

From a strategic point of view, previous studies have downplayed the gain of high performing brands from CR engagement (e.g., Du et al., 2011; Henderson & Arora, 2010). Currently, the advice for practicing marketing managers is unidimensional (stressing either a single brand characteristic at a time or a single CR domain) and seems to follow the route of suggesting that the stronger the brand is the lower the impact of CR on consumers' brand attitude (e.g. van Doorn et al., 2017). However, our initial findings suggest that the type of "strength" a brand is perceived to hold (i.e., relational versus performance) will determine the positive effect of CR on consumers' brand evaluations. Based on our preliminary results, high performer brands can still gain from their CR activities, especially if these activities are within the environmental CR domain. For brands exceling in relational characteristics but less so in their performance, CR represents an opportunity not only to compensate for their lower performance (as suggested, for example, by van Doorn, et al., 2017), but also to further increase their relational success.

From a practical standpoint, understanding how CR choices in conjunction with brands' characteristics will be perceived by customers is important for managers' decision-making. We find that both environmental and social CR choices are helpful in enhancing brand attitude, irrespective of brands' relational and performance characteristics. Therefore, brand managers wishing to improve attitudinal consumer outcomes toward their brands can allocate scarce resources for CR in both domains. For example, the recent 'Wear the Change' campaign of the fashion brand C&A stresses not only the brand's commitment to more environment-friendly manufacturing and consumer goods but also relates to care for employees and workers in the supply chain. Consumers' awareness of such activities may boost their overall attitude toward such brands. However, marketers need to be thoughtful about the influence of CR on their brands' positioning. Consumers tend to perceive brands in specific ways, that is, according to their relational and performance aspects (Iglesias et al., 2020). In this regard, a further implication for marketing managers striving toward establishing perceptions of a 'high performing brand' among consumers (i.e., those brands that are seen capable of delivering on their promise) and wishing to further increase their brands' perceived performance, is to engage in environmental CR. In contrast, managers marketing brands successful in relational aspects (i.e., those brands that successfully connect with their customers, having a friendly nature) and wishing to further increase their brands' relational aspects, should primarily engage in social CR, while engagement in the environmental domain will bring similar pay-offs, albeit to a slightly lesser extent.

Research on the intersection of consumer and CR research is still in its early stages, offering promising avenues for a deeper understanding of how consumers respond to various CR initiatives. While it may be likely that the majority of brands will fall within the two combinations of brand characteristics applied in our study, future research should further disentangle the interplay between CR domains and brand characteristics by investigating brands high (low) on both performance and relational characteristics. In this regard, the use of existing brands with differing combinations of relational-performance characteristics could provide additional evidence on CR's influence on consumer behavior. Moreover, adding behavioral outcome variables such as purchase intentions, willingness to pay, or actual purchase behavior in order to explain the spillover effect from brands' characteristics to behavioral consumer responses could shed more light on the two CR domains' strategic effectiveness. Given the current unprecedented circumstances for business and the global economy amid the COVID-19 pandemic, exploring this situation's effects on consumers' changing perceptions of CR is not only desirable but also necessary. Last, but not least, more research is needed on the 'dark side' of CR, namely, corporate irresponsibility, especially in the context of brands' performance and relational aspects. It is so far unclear whether the interplay between CR domains and brand characteristics would also hold in the context of irresponsible business practices and whether the expected negative effects of corporate irresponsibility would be symmetric to those of CR.

NOTES

1. https://www.unglobalcompact.org/what-is-gc/mission
2. The business case for CR is concerned with the primary questions of *What do the business community and organizations get out of CR? How do they benefit tangibly from engaging in CR policies, activities, and practices?* (Carroll & Shabana, 2010).
3. https://www.nestle.com/csv
4. https://www.un.org/sustainabledevelopment/sustainable-development-goals/
5. https://treaties.un.org/pages/ViewDetails.aspx?src=TREATY&mtdsg_no=XXVII-7-d&chapter=27&clang=_en

REFERENCES

Aaker, J. L. (1997). Dimensions of brand personality. *Journal of Marketing Research, 34*(3), 347–356.
Aguinis, H., & Glavas, A. (2012). What we know and don't know about corporate social responsibility: A review and research agenda. *Journal of Management, 38*(4), 932–968.
Ailawadi, K. L., Neslin, S. A., Luan, Y. J., & Taylor, G. A. (2014). Does retailer CSR enhance behavioral loyalty? A case for benefit segmentation. *International Journal of Research in Marketing, 31*(2), 156–167.
Andrews, M., Luo, X., Fang, Z., & Aspara, J. (2014). Cause marketing effectiveness and the moderating role of price discounts. *Journal of Marketing, 78*(6), 120–142.
Balmer, J. M., Fukukawa, K., & Gray, E. R. (2007). The nature and management of ethical corporate identity: A commentary on corporate identity, corporate social responsibility and ethics. *Journal of Business Ethics, 76*(1), 7–15.
Bangsa, A. B., & Schlegelmilch, B. B. (2020). Linking sustainable product attributes and consumer decision-making: Insights from a systematic review. *Journal of Cleaner Production, 245*, 118902.

Baskentli, S., Sen, S., Du, S., & Bhattacharya, C. B. (2019). Consumer reactions to corporate social responsibility: The role of CSR domains. *Journal of Business Research, 95*, 502–513.

Becker-Olsen, K. L., Cudmore, B. A., & Hill, R. P. (2006). The impact of perceived corporate social responsibility on consumer behavior. *Journal of Business Research, 59*(1), 46–53.

Belz, F. & Peattie, K. (2012). *Sustainability Marketing: A Global Perspective* (2nd ed). Chichester, UK: John Wiley & Sons, Ltd.

Berens, G., Van Riel, C. B., & Van Bruggen, G. H. (2005). Corporate associations and consumer product responses: The moderating role of corporate brand dominance. *Journal of Marketing, 69*(3), 35–48.

Bhattacharya, C. B., & Sen, S. (2004). Doing better at doing good: When, why, and how consumers respond to corporate social initiatives. *California Management Review, 47*(1), 9–24.

Bolton, L. E., & Mattila, A. S. (2015). How does corporate social responsibility affect consumer response to service failure in buyer–seller relationships? *Journal of Retailing, 91*(1), 140–153.

Brown, T. J., & Dacin, P. A. (1997). The company and the product: Corporate associations and consumer product responses. *Journal of Marketing, 61*(1), 68–84.

Carroll, A. B., & Shabana, K. M. (2010). The business case for corporate social responsibility: A review of concepts, research and practice. *International journal of management reviews, 12*(1), 85–105.

Chernev, A., & Blair, S. (2015). Doing well by doing good: The benevolent halo of corporate social responsibility. *Journal of Consumer Research, 41*(6), 1412–1425.

Crespo, C. F., & Inacio, N. (2019). The influence of corporate social responsibility associations on consumers' perceptions towards global brands. *Journal of Strategic Marketing, 27*(8), 679–695.

Du, S., Bhattacharya, C. B., & Sen, S. (2007). Reaping relational rewards from corporate social responsibility: The role of competitive positioning. *International Journal of Research in Marketing, 24*(3), 224–241.

Du, S., Bhattacharya, C. B., & Sen, S. (2011). Corporate social responsibility and competitive advantage: Overcoming the trust barrier. *Management Science, 57*(9), 1528–1545.

Elkington, J. (1994). Towards the sustainable corporation: Win-win-win business strategies for sustainable development. *California Management Review, 36*(2), 90–100.

Elkington, J. (1998). Partnerships from cannibals with forks: The triple bottom line of 21st-century business. *Environmental Quality Management, 8*(1), 37–51.

Elkington, J. (2018). 25 years ago I coined the phrase "triple bottom line." Here's why it's time to rethink it. *Harvard Business Review, 25*, 2–5.

Ellen, P. S., Webb, D. J., & Mohr, L. A. (2006). Building corporate associations: Consumer attributions for corporate socially responsible programs. *Journal of the Academy of Marketing Science, 34*(2), 147–157.

Favotto, A., Kollman, K., & Bernhagen, P. (2016). Engaging firms: The global organisational field for corporate social responsibility and national varieties of capitalism. *Policy and Society, 35*(1), 13–27

Feldman, P. M., & Vasquez-Parraga, A. Z. (2013). Consumer social responses to CSR initiatives versus corporate abilities. *Journal of Consumer Marketing, 30*(2), 100–111.

Ferreira, A. I., & Ribeiro, I. (2017). Are you willing to pay the price? The impact of corporate social (ir)responsibility on consumer behavior towards national and foreign brands. *Journal of Consumer Behaviour, 16*(1), 63–71.

Fournier S. (1998). Consumers and their brands: Developing relationship theory in consumer research. *Journal of Consumer Research, 24*, 343–373.

Fournier, S. (2009). Lessons learned about consumers' relationships with their brands. In: Priester, J., MacInnis, D., Park, C.W. (eds.), *Handbook of Brand Relationships* (pp. 5–23). New York: Society for Consumer Psychology and M. E. Sharp.

Garretson Folse, J. A., Niedrich, R. W., & Grau, S. L. (2010). Cause-relating marketing: The effects of purchase quantity and firm donation amount on consumer inferences and participation intentions. *Journal of Retailing, 86*(4), 295–309.

Groza, M. D., Pronschinske, M. R., & Walker, M. (2011). Perceived organizational motives and consumer responses to proactive and reactive CSR. *Journal of Business Ethics, 102*(4), 639–652.

Henderson, T., & Arora, N. (2010). Promoting brands across categories with a social cause: Implementing effective embedded premium programs. *Journal of Marketing, 74*(6), 41–60.

Hildebrand, D., Sen, S., & Bhattacharya, C. B. (2011). Corporate social responsibility: A corporate marketing perspective. *European Journal of Marketing, 45*(9/10) 1353–1364.

Holden, E., Linnerud, K., & Banister, D. (2014). Sustainable development: Our common future revisited. *Global Environmental Change, 26,* 130–139.

Homburg, C., Stierl, M., & Bornemann, T. (2013). Corporate social responsibility in business-to-business markets: How organizational customers account for supplier corporate social responsibility engagement. *Journal of Marketing, 77*(6), 54–72.

Global Fashion Agenda (2019). Pulse of the fashion industry 2019 update. Available online from: https://globalfashionagenda.com/pulse-2019-update/

Iglesias, O., Markovic, S., Bagherzadeh, M., & Singh, J. J. (2020). Co-creation: A key link between corporate social responsibility, customer trust, and customer loyalty. *Journal of Business Ethics, 163*(1), 151–166.

ILO (2020). Business and COVID-19. International Labour Organization. Available online from: https://www.ilo.org/empent/areas/business-helpdesk/WCMS_741005/lang--en/index.htm

Ind, N., Iglesias, O., & Markovic, S. (2017). The co-creation continuum: From tactical market research tool to strategic collaborative innovation method. *Journal of Brand Management, 24*(4), 310–321.

Joireman, J., Smith, D., Liu, R. L., & Arthurs, J. (2015). It's all good: Corporate social responsibility reduces negative and promotes positive responses to service failures among value-aligned customers. *Journal of Public Policy & Marketing, 34*(1), 32–49.

Kaptein, M., & Wempe, J. F. D. B. (2002). *The Balanced Company: A Theory of Corporate Integrity.* New York, USA: Oxford University Press.

Koschate-Fischer, N., Stefan, I. V., & Hoyer, W. D. (2012). Willingness to pay for cause-related marketing: The impact of donation amount and moderating effects. *Journal of Marketing Research, 49*(6), 910–927.

Krishna, A., & Rajan, U. (2009). Cause marketing: Spillover effects of cause-related products in a product portfolio. *Management Science, 55*(9), 1469–1485.

Lichtenstein, D. R., Drumwright, M. E., & Braig, B. M. (2004). The effect of corporate social responsibility on customer donations to corporate supported nonprofits. *Journal of Marketing, 68,* 16–32.

Liu, M. T., Wong, I. A., Shi, G., Chu, R., & Brock, J. L. (2014). The impact of corporate social responsibility (CSR) performance and perceived brand quality on customer-based brand preference. *Journal of Services Marketing, 28*(3), 181–194.

Luchs, M. G., Naylor, R. W., Irwin, J. R., & Raghunathan, R. (2010). The sustainability liability: Potential negative effects of ethicality on product preference. *Journal of Marketing, 74*(5), 18–31.

Lunde, M. B. (2018). Sustainability in marketing: A systematic review unifying 20 years of theoretical and substantive contributions (1997–2016). *AMS Review, 8*(3–4), 85–110.

Madden, T. J., Roth, M. S., & Dillon, W. R. (2012). Global product quality and corporate social responsibility perceptions: A cross-national study of halo effects. *Journal of International Marketing, 20*(1), 42–57.

Markovic, S., Iglesias, O., Singh, J. J., & Sierra, V. (2018). How does the perceived ethicality of corporate services brands influence loyalty and positive word-of-mouth? Analyzing the roles of empathy, affective commitment, and perceived quality. *Journal of Business Ethics, 148*(4), 721–740.

Montillaud-Joyel, S., & Otto, M. (2004). *Why Should Companies Care about Environment and Social Responsibility? The Answer Is Simple: More and More Consumers Are Asking for It.* London: Mori.

Nan, X., & Heo, K. (2007). Consumer responses to corporate social responsibility (CSR) initiatives: Examining the role of brand-cause fit in cause-related marketing. *Journal of Advertising, 36*(2), 63–74.

Öberseder, M., Schlegelmilch, B. B., & Murphy, P. E. (2013). CSR practices and consumer perceptions. *Journal of Business Research, 66*(10), 1839–1851.

Porter, M. E. & Kramer, M. R. (2002). The competitive advantage of corporate philanthropy. *Harvard Business Review, 80,*12, 56–68,

Porter, M. E., & Kramer, M. R. (2011). The big idea: Creating shared value. How to reinvent capitalism—and unleash a wave of innovation and growth. *Harvard Business Review, 89*(12), 56–69.

Ramesh, K., Saha, R., Goswami, S., & Dahiya, R. (2019). Consumer's response to CSR activities: Mediating role of brand image and brand attitude. *Corporate Social Responsibility and Environmental Management, 26*(2), 377–387.

Reputation Institute (2020). Global RepTrak – 2020's Most Reputable Companies Worldwide. Available online from: https://www.reptrak.com/global-reptrak-100/

Robinson, S., & Wood, S. (2018). A "good" new brand—What happens when new brands try to stand out through corporate social responsibility. *Journal of Business Research, 92*, 231–241.

Schwartz, M. S. (2011). *Corporate Social Responsibility: An Ethical Approach*. Toronto, Ontario: Broadview Press.

Sen, S., & Bhattacharya, C. B. (2001). Does doing good always lead to doing better? Consumer reactions to corporate social responsibility. *Journal of Marketing Research, 38*(2), 225–243.

Sen, S., Bhattacharya, C. B., & Korschun, D. (2006). The role of corporate social responsibility in strengthening multiple stakeholder relationships: A field experiment. *Journal of the Academy of Marketing Science, 34*(2), 158–166.

Sen, S., Du, S., & Bhattacharya, C. B. (2016). Corporate social responsibility: A consumer psychology perspective. *Current Opinion in Psychology, 10*, 70–75.

Shea, C. T., & Hawn, O. V. (2019). Microfoundations of corporate social responsibility and irresponsibility. *Academy of Management Journal, 62*(5), 1609–1642.

Sustainable Brand Index (2020). Available online from: https://www.sb-index.com/rankings

Szőcs, I., & Schlegelmilch, B. B. (2020). Embedding CSR in Corporate Strategies. In *Rethinking Business Responsibility in a Global Context* (pp. 45–60). Cham: Springer.

Szőcs, I., Schlegelmilch, B. B., Rusch, T., & Shamma, H. M. (2016). Linking cause assessment, corporate philanthropy, and corporate reputation. *Journal of the Academy of Marketing Science, 44*(3), 376–396.

Tian, Z., Wang, R., & Yang, W. (2011). Consumer responses to corporate social responsibility (CSR) in China. *Journal of Business Ethics, 101*(2), 197–212.

Torelli, C. J., Monga, A. B., & Kaikati, A. M. (2012). Doing poorly by doing good: Corporate social responsibility and brand concepts. *Journal of Consumer Research, 38*(5), 948–963.

Torres, A., Bijmolt, T. H. A., Tribo, J. A., & Verhoef, P. (2012). Generating global brand equity through corporate social responsibility to key stakeholders. *International Journal of Research in Marketing, 29*, 13–24.

Trudel, R., & Cotte, J. (2009). Does it pay to be good? *MIT Sloan Management Review, 50*(2), 61.

van Doorn, J., Onrust, M., Verhoef, P. C., & Bügel, M. S. (2017). The impact of corporate social responsibility on customer attitudes and retention—the moderating role of brand success indicators. *Marketing Letters, 28*(4), 607–619.

van Marrewijk, M. (2003). Concepts and definitions of CSR and corporate sustainability: Between agency and communion. *Journal of Business Ethics, 44*(2-3), 95–105.

Vlachos, P. A., Tsamakos, A., Vrechopoulos, A. P., & Avramidis, P. K. (2009). Corporate social responsibility: Attributions, loyalty, and the mediating role of trust. *Journal of the Academy of Marketing Science, 37*(2), 170–180.

WCED (1987). Report of the World Commission on Environment and Development: Our Common Future. United Nations. Available online from: https://sustainabledevelopment.un.org/content/documents/5987our-common-future.pdf

6. Promises, promises: how to showcase the authenticity of sustainability claims through digitalization

Nicholas Ind and Oriol Iglesias

It is impossible to imagine any kind of moral life without obligations, and impossible to imagine obligations without types of promises. We are always up against them. Before we ever reflect on what a promise is, we have made them and are expected to make more of them…Promises are with us like gravity. Man is a promising animal.

William Kerrigan, *Shakespeare's Promises* (1999, 7)

Organizations make promises – about their brands, about service quality and about sustainability. They promise to make our lives and those of others better, more enjoyable and exciting. Google's search engine promises us speed and efficiency, Gucci promises us desirability and status, Tesla promises us performance without guilt and Patagonia promises to help tackle the environmental crisis. However, the idea of a promise is fraught with problems when it comes to the relationship between an organization and its stakeholders. As Anker et al. (2012, 268) note, 'a promise is a relational action entailing the communication of intentions to bring about a future state of affairs beneficial to the one to whom the promise is made.' The 'relational action' illustrates the co-created nature of a promise, because while an organization can make a promise it is only realized through the actions of the recipient. This is where value is created (Grönroos and Voima, 2013). In other words, while Gucci can offer us desirability and status, that promise is only virtual, until we purchase something and wear it and receive the plaudits (or not) of others.

When organizations make promises about sustainability, there is an even greater degree of complexity. They know that sustainability is important – indeed in a study of some 60,000 respondents carried out by MIT Sloan Management Review/BCG between 2009 and 2017, it was found that 90% of global organizations consider it so (Kiron et al., 2017). Working in a sustainable way has become an expectation of stakeholders, such as, consumers, employees and investors who are pushing organizations to think and behave sustainably (Ioannou and Serafeim, 2010; Malik, 2015; Markovic et al., 2018), reduce their impacts (Vitell, 2015) and contribute to society and the environment in positive ways (Carrigan and Attalla, 2001; Walsh and Beatty, 2007). Organizations also see business and investment opportunities connected to sustainability, including reducing risks and increasing customer trust, customer loyalty and customer positive word-of-mouth recommendation (Chomvilailuk and Butcher, 2014; Kang and Hustvedt, 2014; Markovic et al., 2018).

Yet there are hurdles to making and delivering sustainability promises. First, organizations rarely deliver sustainability on their own – they are part of supply chains, involved in networks of value creation with customers and reliant on employees. For example, take sportswear brand, adidas. It has more than 50,000 employees, 1100 independent factories in its network, is a partner in the Better Cotton Initiative and Fair Labor Association and has millions of customers (Ind, 2016). Adidas can make a promise about sustainability (and it has a powerful influential role in encouraging its stakeholders to align with it), but it faces the problem of how to realize the promise. Influence is not control, and even with emerging digital technologies that can monitor performance, it is difficult to be always certain that standards and recommended best practice are adhered to by employees, partners, suppliers and customers. Customers in particular, represent a challenge, for while they demand sustainability, they are also often slow to adapt their behaviour. This is an issue that adidas has had to confront in that it can improve its production processes, such as DryDye (which uses no water) and use of materials (such as recycled fishing nets in its Parley range) but it struggles to change the way customers use, wash and dispose of products, which in terms of greenhouse gas emissions is where the biggest impacts are.

Second, even when brands can influence their different stakeholders and align them with their sustainability strategy, there can be technological constraints that do not allow them to entirely fulfil the brands' aspirations and demands. Take for example Danone, one of the leaders in the fast-moving consumer goods industry and a brand that is championing a transformation of the entire industry to become more sustainable. Even though Danone would like to have fully sustainable packaging for its products, it cannot deliver this until the packaging industry has developed the technology to make this happen. To overcome this challenge, Danone is working closely together with its packaging providers to innovate new methods of product delivery. This joint effort should help Danone to meet its objective to make every piece of packaging reusable, recyclable or compostable by 2025. Fulfilling sustainability promises, requires the development of new capabilities, which also demands collaboration and co-creation between the brand and its stakeholders.

Third, while organizations understand the importance of sustainability, its potential to influence stakeholders, and the need to co-create new technologies and capabilities, it often remains tangential and not embedded in the core of operations (Iglesias and Ind, 2016). Bhattacharya and Polman (2017) note that integrating sustainability requires more than initiatives – rather it needs to become the focus of the operation itself. While sustainability initiatives in themselves are not necessarily negative, a 'tremendous gap remains between corporate commitment and action' (Kiron et al., 2017). This leads to organizations adopting sustainability at the margins but making claims for its centrality. Not surprisingly, customers don't always greet such sustainability promises enthusiastically, which has encouraged a growing scepticism among customers and greater sensitivity to greenwashing, due to the clear gap between what organizations say and do (Nyilasy et al. 2014).The practice of sustainability can be seen as insincere and manipulative (Maxfield, 2008; Pope and Wæraas, 2016, Lim 2016); a reputation-cleaning mechanism that is an inauthentic reaction to external pressures (Marquis et al. 2016). One illustration of this has been the much parodied, Chevron's 'We Agree' campaign. For example, one of Chevron's advertisements states, 'It's time oil companies get behind the development of renewable energy. We agree.' However, as Pickl observes, Chevron remains an oil and gas business, whose main contribution to renewables has been the establishment of a $100 million Future Energy Fund (to give this context, Chevron's 2018 revenue was $158.9 billion). He notes, 'In general, Chevron's overall engagement with renewable energy is rather low, and no target, vision, or roadmap for renewable energy has been communicated' (Pickl 2019, 4).

Fourth, consumers and other stakeholders find it difficult to 'identify more or less virtuous firms' (Vogel, 2007, 60). The concept of a promise focuses on 'communication of intentions' about a future state. This is fairly clear if referring to what a bottle of Coca-Cola will deliver or the experience of staying at the Ritz-Carlton, but much less so when referring to a sustainability promise to reduce environmental impacts or to commit to recycling. For example, a company can make a commitment to only use renewable and recyclable materials in its products by 2040. This commitment is designed to convince internal and external stakeholders of a future state and connects the organization that makes the promise and its recipients. Such a promise is an act that should lead to action, but these long-term and general promises can be described as 'fuzzy' in that there is a greater degree of indeterminateness in the condition suggested (Anker et al., 2012). As consumers and citizens, we do not know quite what to expect and whether a promise is an attempt to hide inconvenient truths (Jones et al., 2008) or an authentic commitment? Consumers try to deconstruct these fuzzy promises, but the lack of simple, universal and objective standards means that they find it hard to separate those claims that are genuine from those that are questionable. The environmental and social labels attached to products (such as Fair Trade, Marine Stewardship Council and the Forest Stewardship Council) are an attempt to solve this problem (Manget et al., 2009). However, their extraordinary proliferation has made it extremely difficult for consumers to differentiate one from the other and to understand which ones are reliable (Grunert et al., 2014). In essence, consumers simply do not know how to interpret the often-complex messages they receive, and which ones to trust (Chen and Chang, 2013).

WORDS, WORDS, WORDS:[1] AUTHENTIC PROMISES

When an organization makes a promise, its authenticity is weighed up by the recipients. Here, authenticity suggests both a truth to self and a wider reference to the world beyond it. In this way, authenticity relies not only on consistency and continuity with the truth of purpose and values (Schallehn et al., 2014), but also with a valid and ethical engagement with others (Taylor, 1991). In the context of brands, Morhart et al. (2015, 202) argue that brand authenticity 'emerges to the extent to which consumers perceive a brand to be faithful and true towards itself and its consumers, and to support consumers being true to themselves.' The implication here is that a promise is authentic, when there is a clear link between the market and non-market strategy (which recognizes the broader involvement of businesses in social and political issues) (Baron, 2001; Lawton et al., 2014), and strategy and actions (Guzmán and Becker-Olsen, 2010; Morhart et al., 2015).

From an ethical perspective, Singer (2011) argues that individuals give greater moral approval to acts which demonstrate a concern for the welfare of others or a conscious desire to do what is perceived as right, than to acts rooted in self-interest. However, authenticity does not automatically connote a distinction between self-interest and the welfare of others. Banet-Weiser (2012) suggests this is not a binary argument, but rather that self-interest and social value coexist in a culture dominated by brands. Consumers buy brands both because they are desirable and because they make sustainability claims. This is to recognize one of the key roles of brands is to help people construct their identities through consumption (Holt, 2004): 'There are no distinct boundaries or divisions between the authentic and the commercial, affect and the market' (Banet-Weiser, 2012, 131). When consumers purchase soap from cosmetics company, Lush, they both buy into the market strategy of the brand as well as its non-market commitments in terms of ethical buying, vegetarian ingredients, fighting animal testing and its stance on modern slavery. That a company, such as Lush, has shown ethical and responsible commitments consistently (Du et al.,2007) and that those commitments fit with the organization's purpose, leads to differentiated perceptions of authenticity (Spiggle et al., 2012; Napoli et al., 2014; Lawton et al., 2014).

Lush, like sports brand, Patagonia and sustainable fashion pioneers, Ecoalf and Stella McCartney, typifies the sort of organizations that have built, since their inception, their value propositions around sustainability. Pirsch et al. (2007) argue that this type of approach is institutional, in that it is comprehensive and touches all aspects of the organization. Institutionalizing sustainability is important, because it enables a promise made to be kept. This orientation helps to overcome scepticism and to build connectivity with customers. However, Vogel (2007) has suggested that these types of organizations (he also references Ben & Jerry's) are typically niche and appeal primarily to those consumers and employees whose values align with those of the organizations. However, the last decade has also seen the emergence of larger organizations (such as Unilever, Danone, H&M and adidas) that are trying to integrate sustainability into their actions. While, these organizations face larger trade-offs and challenges, and inevitably are inconsistent – H&M, for example, has been both applauded for its commitments and criticized for its recent policy of burning excess stock – there is a growing appreciation that these more mainstream brands can also make authentic sustainability promises.

The contrast to the authentic are those organizations that adopt environmental and social causes and re-package them, without appreciating the context or demonstrating commitment – what Holt (2004) refers to as literacy (a nuanced understanding of social codes and idioms) and fidelity (a willingness to stand up for one's beliefs). Such organizations showcase a cause, but then fail to take a real stance, because the involvement is skin-deep or worse, disingenuous. For example, some CEOs of global companies publicly committed to support the Paris Agreement on climate change and signed an open letter to the *Wall Street Journal* while they simultaneously supported a lobbying group pushing the Trump administration to withdraw from it. This shows 'how some firms take symbolic action that sounds good in an annual report or in the newspaper while hiding the fact that they are blocking substantive progress on the political front' (Lyon et al., 2018, 10).

A DIFFERENT MODEL

Overall, even if a brand strongly and authentically commits to investing in sustainability, it is extremely difficult for consumers to form an accurate perception of each company, to demarcate one category of companies from the other, and to appreciate the true authenticity of sustainability promises. In turn, this makes it extremely difficult for companies to get an appropriate return on their investments in sustainability in terms of the development of stronger brand–customer relationships. In line with the above discussion, this is because of two key issues: (1) the coexistence of different levels of commitment to sustainability, from the superficial to the strategic; (2) the challenge of reliable standards and the proliferation of labels and certifications (see Figure 6.1).

To ensure that corporate commitment to sustainability translates into positive consumer perceptions, and delivers positive brand–consumer relationship outcomes, we propose a managerial model (see Figure 6.2), enabled by digitalization, which is based on: (1) establishing independent verification processes; (2) using blockchain and other systems to reinforce trust in the verification process; and (3) creating and communicating stories that can be supported by the verification process. This three-phase process requires organizations to use digital technologies as a way to enhance their existing assets and create new value by re-thinking their value propositions and operations (Ross, 2017). Digitalization thus goes beyond simply changing existing processes into digital versions. Rather it seeks to transmute how organizations deliver value and to ensure that the promises brands make are authentic and can be supported by the actions of all those networked partners and individuals that participate in the delivery of a seamless brand experience (Parviainen et al., 2017). As Ramaswamy notes in describing digitalized experience ecosystems, 'Every enterprise is now faced with the challenge of learning how to create valuable impacts of experienced outcomes through smarter, connected offerings and the networked interactions of individuals' (Ramaswamy, 2020, 6).

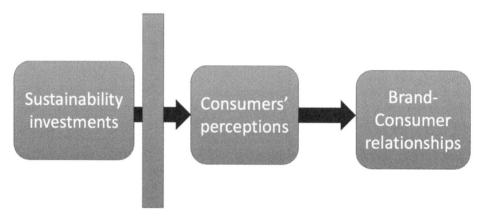

THE BARRIER TO THE SUSTAINABILITY INVESTMENTS-PERCEPTIONS LINK
1) Variable degrees of commitment towards sustainability
2) Lack of simple, universal and objective sustainability measures/standards – commutation problem

Figure 6.1   *The sustainability chain of effects*

INDEPENDENT VERIFICATION

How can an organization and its consumers be sure of the 'truth' of its sustainability strategy? In many industries, supply chains are long and complex (for example, 13 steps are typical in the food industry) and they rely both on contractual agreements and trust. The philosopher, David Hume, illustrated the importance of the latter with specific reference to farmers:

> Your corn is ripe today; mine will be so tomorrow. 'Tis profitable for us both that I shou'd labour with you today, and that you shou'd aid me tomorrow. I have no kindness for you, and know that you have as little for me. I will not, therefore, take any pains on your account; and should I labour with you on my account, I know I shou'd be disappointed, and that I shou'd in vain depend upon your gratitude. Here then I leave you to labour alone: You treat me in the same manner. The seasons change; and both of us lose our harvests for want of mutual confidence and security. (Hume, 1969, 573)

The problem that Hume refers to is a want of trust. However, if instead of a want of trust the farmers operate in an environment where there is a social convention of promising, then they should each be willing to help the other in expectation of continued reciprocal behaviour. It is the building of this social capital that enables cooperation within a supply chain. Social capital can be defined as

> the existence of a certain set of informal values or norms shared among members of a group that permits cooperation among them...The norms that produce social capital, by contrast, must substantively include virtues like truth-telling, the meeting of obligations, and reciprocity. (Fukuyama, 2000, 98–99)

With reference to the Italian coffee brand, Illy, Longoni and Luzzini (2016) show how the company used social capital as a governance method to reconstruct its green coffee supply in Brazil that led to the enhancement of two inter-twined concepts: quality and sustainability. The way Illy has realized this is by working together with farmers to build values and norms to develop an integrated supply chain. Illy does not shift responsibility to the coffee growers, but rather has built a set of trusting relationships that enable promises to be realized. This is not to ignore the importance of verification, but Hume would argue that a relationship must be first rooted in practice. An absence of trust and a pure reliance on contracts increases transaction costs, while 'trust acts like a lubricant that makes any group or organization run more efficiently' (Fukuyama, 2000, 98). Illy's processes reflect this orientation, in that the first phase was about engendering social capital, while the second concerned the external and independent verification of sustainable practice by verification company, DNV GL.

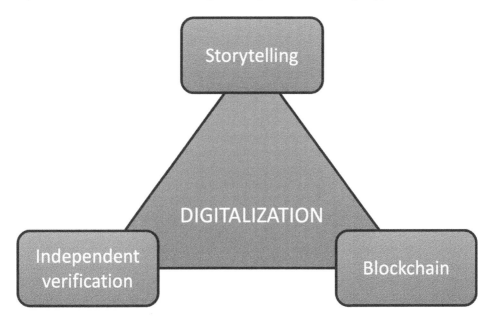

Figure 6.2   The three digital enablers of sustainability

The verification included identifying the elements and areas that needed development and then implementing systems to ensure that these were addressed. The certification, known as the Responsible Supply Chain Process (RSCP), created 'a system where individuals are treated with equity, dignity and respect; the environment is preserved and restored; and suppliers are compliant with rules and awarded for the quality and sustainability of their business' (Longoni and Luzzini, 2016, 97).

Illy illustrates two necessary components in the making of promises. First, it shows the importance of ensuring organizations and people within a network of relationships trust each other (Morgan and Hunt, 1994). This doesn't simply happen – but rather requires such mechanisms as the establishment of protocols, the sharing of best practice, building communities, developing training programmes and providing awards and recognition. Second, to affirm production processes, determine the accuracy and reliability of data and verify that claims are consistent with actions, promises require external validation. There is a temptation for organizations to be expedient or to practise corporate irresponsibility when it comes to difficult decisions in production processes or supply chains (Vogel 2019). However, these temptations can be ameliorated by the objectivity of outsiders. Verification requires neutrality. This is also a dynamic process in that it is one thing to verify at a point in time, but standards have to be maintained over time as processes and the environment changes. Verification requires the continuous use of digital technologies, such as blockchain and beacons to ensure standards continue to be met, to predict system risks and to generate knowledge that can be translated into actions.

BLOCKCHAIN AND MONITORING

When a brand makes a promise, it needs to be confident in the substance of its claims. When the process is simple, such as a farmers' market brand, where the person sitting on a market stall is also the person that made the product, it is easy to verify, but for a larger brand with many different partners, where there is distance between supply chain members and consumers, there needs to be constant monitoring. The digitalization of supply chains and manufacturing processes affords the opportunity for brand owners to accurately track and monitor all the phases from raw material production through to purchase and consumption. Transparency reduces risk and builds confidence, while enabling consumers to make informed choices. In a study of 1643 food and beverage industry professionals, 44% said their companies were using sensors and beacons, 15% blockchain and 10% smart tags. Within three years food professionals expect these to grow to 57%, 40% and 36% respectively. Notably industry leaders in food safety, see greater potential in the exploration of digital opportunities than others in their industry (DNV GL/GDFI 2019).

The value of blockchain is that it provides continuous verification through a distributed yet accurate and time-stamped record that is independent. This offers two specific benefits. First, it means one can have confidence in the stages along the blockchain. Second, because it is a single, but distributed ledger that contains all relevant information, it delivers consistency and reduces transaction costs (Werbach, 2018). From a sustainability perspective, it means that the social and environmental impacts in a process such as energy use, water consumption and labour conditions can be monitored and then optimized at each stage (FAO, 2019). It also pinpoints where failures occur. In the context of food safety this is especially significant, given that each year, the Food and Agriculture Organization of the United Nations (FAO) estimates 420,000 people die and 600 million become ill from contaminated food.

Blockchain is not a panacea. Werbach notes, 'proponents of blockchain technology describe it as a democratizing escape from the failings of territorial legal systems. Critics see it as a clever trick to avoid legal accountability' (Werbach, 2018, 489). However, there are areas where it is particularly relevant, such as those where there is the need to integrate diverse data sources and to track flows, such as in insurance, supply chains and capital markets. Here distributed ledgers can 'tackle pain points including inefficiency, process opacity, and fraud' (Higginson et al., 2019).

As an illustration of the application of blockchain, software solutions company SAP has been working with San Diego-based seafood producer, Bumble Bee Foods. Bumble Bee is a long-established business, which has a specific mission based around ocean stewardship, sustainable fishing and support for fishermen. Given this focus, Bumble Bee needs to be confident in its processes, so it is using SAP's blockchain system to trace fish from the moment they are caught through to sale. As everything in the process is date stamped and those involved from fisherman to distributor to retailer can be identified, the whole process is transparent and tamper proof. The robustness of the system lies in that each person in the chain can only input on the phase they are responsible for and they cannot alter any other information. This track and trace method culminates at the point of sale, where each individual product has a blockchain derived QR (quick response) code that can be scanned. For example, the code can tell the consumer the time and place the fish was caught, the type of fish and the sustainability of the species (i.e. whether it is being over-fished, or not), the fishing method and the process of capture, where and how the fish was processed and where it was canned. This is not simply a record of fact, but also an opportunity to provide context through video and narratives about people and processes, that aligns with Bumble Bee's ocean stewardship principles and enables consumers to personalize their experiences based on their interests and concerns.

STORYTELLING

QR codes are not a new technology. It was pioneered in the Japanese automotive industry in the mid-1990s to track parts and vehicles. Its value as a storytelling mechanism is that it has the potential to open up a lot of information while using a limited degree of space. You can now find it used on the fresh crab at the Danish restaurant, Noma, as well as on the Italian wine that accompanies a meal. This has clear value in enabling consumers to understand the social and environmental impacts of their behaviour. This is important, because as White et al. (2019) note, communications needs to overcome the lack of consumer knowledge and to persuade consumers to engage in eco-friendly actions regarding desired (and undesired) behaviours. This is why Bumble Bee's approach, which not only provides information, but also illustrates the issues and consequences, is so valuable. Citing meta-analytic reviews, White et al. further note that providing consumers with information 'has a significant albeit modest influence on pro-environmental actions' (White et al., 2019, 30).

More than just the provision of information though, organizations need to engage their stakeholders, so that the data derived from verification is translated through stories into meaningful content that generates engagement and relates to people's desire to express their identities. Stories then are not simply functional but emotional instruments that create meaning and stimulate ideas by adhering to Aristotle's three modes of persuasion: logos (rational argument), pathos (emotional connection) and ethos (moral authority) (Ind and Iglesias, 2016). How then to tell a story effectively? Organizations need to move beyond communication into transformation. Communication is transient in that it informs through words and images, which are easily forgotten (Gagliardi, 2006), whereas transformation has a cultural impact that goes beyond the immediate and becomes embedded over time, changing the way people think and behave: 'Communication needs only interest and curiosity. Proper transmission necessitates transformation if not conversion' (Debray 2000, 6). Sustainability stories need to find an approach that causes a taken-for-granted perception of a situation to move and to then build a new perception that impacts thought and action. Two elements are essential in this transformative process: authenticity and tangibility.

As we have seen, authenticity implies consistency over time and across different media, while tangibility is concerned with the ability to bring the message to life. As an illustration of this, the Dutch chocolate brand, Tony's Chocolonely, incorporates its central message into the product itself (Figure 6.3). Tony's Chocolonely didn't set out to be a brand – it was simply a protest by Dutch journalists about the use of slaves in cocoa farming in West Africa. They first built the narrative around the issue, through a TV programme produced by one the journalists, Maurice Dekkers, called *Keuringsdienst van Waarde* (Food Unwrapped) and then by one of the journalists handing himself into the police for eating a product that he knew was produced by slaves. When the case went to court, he was acquitted, but it made the issue national news.

Figure 6.3   *Outside and inside wrapper of Tony's Chocolonely bar*

In 2005, the journalists decided to challenge chocolate companies directly, by making their own brand of chocolate, called Tony's Chocolonely. They funded the production of 5000 slave-free chocolate bars and sold them through two shops and online. On the morning of the launch one of the shops in Amsterdam Central Station opened to a queue at 6.30. By 7.00, its stock of 1500 bars had sold out. In the first day, the entire production was sold, and they had orders for another 6000 bars. What were people buying into? The story that Tony's Chocolonely had been telling via the media and also the wrapper, which featured a graphic device about slave-free chocolate and the story of how cocoa was produced by slaves. In 2012 they also introduced the unequally divided chocolate bar, which featured the shapes of the cocoa producing countries of West Africa (Figure 6.4). Consumers complained about this (and still do), because the unequal shapes meant the bar could not easily be shared equally: 'This is exactly what Tony's is after – to make consumers rethink the unequal distribution in the chocolate supply chain. The chocolate bar itself has become the platform for storytelling' (Horlings, 2016). Angela Ursem, Movement Maker at Tony's Chocolonely, says about the product,

> We sold over 40 million pieces last year, and that means that there are potentially 40 million people that get in touch with our mission. So, it's a super important communication piece. And of course, this is also really where the whole Tony story started and it's also not that we created a chocolate bar, and then we created the story. No, the story was first, about the mission, that we want to eradicate child labour and modern slavery from the cocoa supply chain, and then we decided to make a chocolate bar. So, it's first the story, then the bar, and then the branding.[2]

Figure 6.4   The unequal bar

It could be argued that Tony's Chocolonely is another example of a niche brand, but as of 2019, it is the largest chocolate brand in the Netherlands. Interestingly, it has never used paid media to achieve this position. Rather it uses the product to draw people into engaging with the company's mission and then encourages its serious friends (people who are active supporters of the mission on slave-free chocolate) to co-create the story and extend it among their own personal networks. This building of social capital – similar to the process at Illy – also involves building relationships with cocoa farmers and bringing 5000 people involved in the supply chain each year to Amsterdam to exchange ideas and best practice. Tony's Chocolonely's underlying philosophy here is complete transparency, so that everyone in the chain, and indeed competitors, can see what the process of working to produce slave-free chocolate involves. To facilitate this the company has created an open supply chain called Tonysopenchain.com. Arjen Klinkenberg, Brand Guru at Tony's Chocolonely, says,

> We always say we are not a chocolate company that makes impact, but we are an impact company that makes chocolate. We believe in direct relationships, we don't use traditional paid media because we have this direct relationship with the cocoa farmers that we do business with, and we want to have this direct relationship with our chocolate fans and our retailers and our suppliers and everyone that we work with.

Chocolonely is not perfect. There have been instances of failures in the supply chain, but the company is confident enough to admit when things go wrong. It tries to ensure the substance of its promise through its support for building social capital and by the sort of monitoring and verification systems mentioned earlier in this chapter, such as a bean tracker that enables the company to track beans from the farmer to the finished product and the independent verification of its sustainability performance based on 13 key performance indicators by PwC, which is then published in the company's annual *Fair* report.

CONCLUSION

The inter-connectedness of the three elements of verification, blockchain and monitoring and storytelling enables organizations to make sustainability promises with confidence, while empowering consumers to make good (or at least, less harmful) sustainability choices. This process recognizes that the meaning of a sustainability promise is co-created as an organization and consumers come together. The argument here though is that the commitment to sustainability has to be authentic. This is often natural for organizations, such as Patagonia, Lush and Ecoalf, where the ideals of founders have fostered a strong set of beliefs from the beginning. In the case of larger organizations such as Unilever and Danone, there has also been a purposeful engagement from leaders to make the transition to integrated sustainability. This highlights the key role that top leaders can play in integrating sustainability promises into the core of the corporate identity, business strategy and operations, while reinforcing the need to foster new leadership styles that are more responsible, empathetic and participative. While some leaders and organizations are still sceptical as to the benefits of such a commitment, it has been shown that high sustainability businesses outperform low sustainability ones, especially in consumer brands and in sectors where companies compete on the basis of brands and human capital (Eccles et al., 2014).

The value of digitalization here, is that it can impact on the process, organization, business domain and societal level to improve efficiency, cut costs and transform relationships (Parviainen et al., 2017). Also, the confidence that comes with good digital verification and monitoring processes is important in three further respects. First, it encourages organizations to be transparent and willing to admit their imperfections. Companies, such as Ecoalf and Tony's Chocolonely, not only talk about their successes, but also the challenges of attaining their sustainability goals and the dilemmas they confront. This willingness to admit failings helps to create a trusting, dialogic relationship. Second, it enables organizations to let go of their brands and let consumers be active participants in co-creating sustainability strategies, telling stories and sharing experiences. This opening up of the organization and the ability to harness the power of a network, helps to create credibility and overcome the problem that consumers have in distinguishing a real sustainability commitment from the superficial. Third, while promises are only words, they also imply action. A promise is meaningless if the promise does not signify change and the will to realize it. When an organization is confident, it can motivate its internal and external stakeholders to participate in actions to deliver on a promise.

NOTES

1. *Hamlet.* Hamlet to Polonius, Act II, Scene II
2. Interviews with Angela Ursem and Arjen Klinkenberg were conducted in Amsterdam on 23 January 2020

REFERENCES

Anker, T. B., Kappel, K., Eadie, D., & Sandøe, P. (2012). Fuzzy promises: Explicative definitions of brand promise delivery. *Marketing Theory*, *12*(3), 267–287.

Banet-Weiser, S. (2012). *AuthenticTM: The Politics of Ambivalence in a Brand Culture* (Vol. 30). NYU Press.

Baron, D. P. (2001). Private politics, corporate social responsibility, and integrated strategy. *Journal of Economics & Management Strategy*, *10*(1), 7–45.

Bhattacharya, C. B., & Polman, P. (2017). Sustainability lessons from the front lines. *MIT Sloan Management Review*, *58*(2), 71–78.

Carrigan, M., & Attalla, A. (2001). The myth of the ethical consumer–do ethics matter in purchase behaviour? *Journal of Consumer Marketing*, *18*(7), 560–577

Chen, Y. S., & Chang, C. H. (2013). Greenwash and green trust: The mediation effects of green consumer confusion and green perceived risk. *Journal of Business Ethics*, *114*(3), 489–500.

Chomvilailuk, R., & Butcher, K. (2014). Effects of quality and corporate social responsibility on loyalty. *The Service Industries Journal*, *34*(11), 938–954.

Debray, R. (2000) *Transmitting Culture*. (Transmettre, 1997, Editions Odile Jacob). Trans. E. Rauth. Columbia University Press.

Du, S., Bhattacharya, C.B. & Sen, S., (2007). Reaping relational rewards from corporate social responsibility: The role of competitive positioning. *International Journal of Research in Marketing*, *24*(3), 224–241.

DNV GL/GFSI (2019). Food Safety: What's next to assure its future. Viewpoint Report. https://www.dnvgl.com/assurance/viewpoint/viewpoint-surveys/food-safety-whats-next-to-assure-its-future.html

Eccles, R. G., Ioannou, I., & Serafeim, G. (2014). The impact of corporate sustainability on organizational processes and performance. *Management Science*, *60*(11), 2835–2857.

FAO (2019). *The Future of Food Safety*. http://www.fao.org/3/CA3247EN/ca3247en.pdf

Fukuyama, F. (2000). Social Capital in Culture matters. How Values Shape Human *Progress*. Ed. L. E. Harrison and S. P. Huntington. Basic Books. 98–111.

Gagliardi, P. (2006). Exploring the aesthetic side of organizational life. In S. Clegg, C. Hardy, T. Lawrence, & W. Nord (eds.), *The Sage Handbook of Organization Studies*. Sage, pp. 701–724.

Grönroos, C., & Voima, P. (2013). Critical service logic: Making sense of value creation and co-creation. *Journal of the Academy of Marketing Science*, *41*(2), 133–150.

Grunert, K. G., Hieke, S., & Wills, J. (2014). Sustainability labels on food products: Consumer motivation, understanding and use. *Food Policy*, *44*, 177–189.

Guzmán, F. and Becker-Olsen, K. L. (2010). Strategic corporate social responsibility: A brand-building tool. In C. Louche, S. O. Idowu. and W. L. Filho (eds.), *Innovative Corporate Social Responsibility: From Risk Management to Value Creation*. Greenleaf Publishing, pp. 196–219.

Higginson, M., Nadeau, M-C., & Rajgopal, K. (2019). Blockchain's Occam problem. *McKinsey*, January 2019. https://www.mckinsey.com/industries/financial-services/our-insights/blockchains -occam-problem

Holt, D. B. (2004). *How Brands Become Icons: The Principles of Cultural Branding*. Harvard Business Press.

Horlings S. (2016). Crazy about chocolate, serious about people. In N. Ind and S. Horlings (eds.), *Brands with a Conscience: How to Build a Successful and Responsible Brand*. Kogan Page, pp. 85–101.

Hume, D. (1969). *A Treatise of Human Nature*. Originally published 1739/1740. Penguin.

Iglesias, O., & Ind, N. (2016) How to be a brand with a conscience. In N. Ind and S. Horlings (eds.), *Brands with a Conscience: How to Build a Successful and Responsible Brand*. Kogan Page, pp. 203–211

Ind, N. (2016). Influence at Adidas. In N. Ind and S. Horlings (eds.), *Brands with a Conscience: How to Build a Successful and Responsible Brand*. Kogan Page, pp. 45–49.

Ind, N., & Iglesias, O. (2016). *Brand Desire: How to Create Consumer Involvement and Inspiration*. Bloomsbury Publishing.

Ioannou, I., & Serafeim, G. (2010).The impact of corporate social responsibility on investment recommendations. *Academy of Management Proceedings, 2010* (1), 1–6).

Jones, P., Clarke-Hill, C., Comfort, D., & Hillier, D. (2008). Marketing and sustainability. *Marketing Intelligence & Planning, 26*(2), 123–130

Kang, J., & Hustvedt, G. (2014). Building trust between consumers and corporations: The role of consumer perceptions of transparency and social responsibility. *Journal of Business Ethics, 125*(2), 253–265.

Kerrigan W. (1999). *Shakespeare's Promises*. The Johns Hopkins University Press.

Kiron, D., Unruh, G., Reeves, M., Kruschwitz, N., Rubel, H., & ZumFelde, A. M. (2017). Corporate sustainability at a crossroads. *MIT Sloan Management Review, 58*(4). https://sloanreview.mit.edu/ projects/corporate-sustainability-at-a-crossroads/

Lawton, T. C., Doh, J. P., & Rajwani, T. (2014). *Aligning for Advantage: Competitive Strategies for the Political and Social Arenas*. Oxford University Press.

Lim, W. M. (2016). A blueprint for sustainability marketing: Defining its conceptual boundaries for progress. *Marketing Theory, 16*(2), 232–249.

Longoni, A., & Luzzini, D. (2016). Building social capital into the disrupted green coffee supply chain: Illy's journey to quality and sustainability. *Organizing Supply Chain Processes for Sustainable Innovation in the Agri-Food Industry, 5*, 83–108.

Lyon, T. P., Delmas, M. A., Maxwell, J. W., Bansal, P., Chiroleu-Assouline, M., Crifo, P., ... & Toffel, M. (2018). CSR needs CPR: Corporate sustainability and politics. *California Management Review, 60*(4), 5–24.

Malik, M. (2015). Value-enhancing capabilities of CSR: A brief review of contemporary literature. *Journal of Business Ethics, 127*, 419–438.

Manget, J., Roche, C., & Münnich, F. (2009). Capturing the green advantage. *MIT Sloan Management Review, 25*. https://sloanreview.mit.edu/projects/capturing-the-green-advantage/

Markovic, S., Iglesias, O., Singh, J. J., & Sierra, V. (2018). How does the perceived ethicality of corporate services brands influence loyalty and positive word-of-mouth? Analyzing the roles of empathy, affective commitment, and perceived quality. *Journal of Business Ethics, 148*(4), 721–740.

Marquis, C., Toffel, M. W., & Zhou, Y. (2016). Scrutiny, norms, and selective disclosure: A global study of greenwashing. *Organization Science, 27*(2), 483–504.

Maxfield, S. (2008). Reconciling corporate citizenship and competitive strategy: Insights from economic theory. *Journal of Business Ethics, 80*(2), 367–377.

Morgan, R. M., & Hunt, S. D. (1994). The commitment-trust theory of relationship marketing. *Journal of Marketing, 58*(3), 20–38.

Morhart, F., Malär, L., Guèvremont, A., Girardin, F., & Grohmann, B. (2015). Brand authenticity: An integrative framework and measurement scale. *Journal of Consumer Psychology, 25*(2), 200–218.

Napoli, J., Dickinson, S. J., Beverland, M. B., & Farrelly, F. (2014). Measuring consumer-based brand authenticity. *Journal of Business Research, 67*(6), 1090–1098.

Nyilasy, G., Gangadharbatla, H., & Paladino, A. (2014). Perceived greenwashing: The interactive effects of green advertising and corporate environmental performance on consumer reactions. *Journal of Business Ethics*, *125*(4), 693–707.

Parviainen, P., Tihinen, M., Kääriäinen, J., & Teppola, S. (2017). Tackling the digitalization challenge: How to benefit from digitalization in practice. *International Journal of Information Systems and Project Management*, *5*(1), 63–77.

Pickl, M. J. (2019). The renewable energy strategies of oil majors–From oil to energy? *Energy Strategy Reviews*, *26*(100370).

Pirsch, J., Gupta, S., & Grau, S. L. (2007). A framework for understanding corporate social responsibility programs as a continuum: An exploratory study. *Journal of Business Ethics*, *70*(2), 125–140.

Pope, S., & Wæraas, A. (2016). CSR-washing is rare: A conceptual framework, literature review, and critique. *Journal of Business Ethics*, *137*(1), 173–193.

Ramaswamy, V. (2020). Leading the experience ecosystem revolution: Innovating offerings as interactive platforms. *Strategy & Leadership*, *48*(3), 3–9

Ross, J. (2017). Don't confuse digital with digitization. *MIT Sloan Management Review*. https://sloanreview.mit.edu/article/dont-confuse-digital-with-digitization/

Schallehn, M., Burmann, C. and Riley, N. (2014). Brand authenticity: Model development and empirical testing. *Journal of Product & Brand Management*, *23*(3), 192–199.

Singer, P. (2011). *The Expanding Circle: Ethics, Evolution, and Moral Progress*. Princeton University Press.

Spiggle, S., Nguyen, H. T., & Caravella, M. (2012). More than fit: Brand extension authenticity. *Journal of Marketing Research*, *49*(6), 967–983.

Taylor, C. (1991). *The Ethics of Authenticity*. Harvard University Press.

Vitell, S. J. (2015). A case for consumer social responsibility (CnSR): Including a selected review of consumer ethics/social responsibility research. *Journal of Business Ethics*, *130*(4), 767–774.

Vogel, D. (2007). *The Market for Virtue: The Potential and Limits of Corporate Social Responsibility*. Brookings Institution Press.

Vogel, D. (2019). The false dawn of corporate social responsibility. *California Management Review*. 9 October 2019. https://cmr.berkeley.edu/2019/10/the-false-dawn-of-corporate-social-responsibility/

Walsh, G., & Beatty, S. E. (2007). Customer-based corporate reputation of a service firm: Scale development and validation. *Journal of the Academy of Marketing Science*, *35*(1), 127–143.

Werbach, K., (2018). Trust, but verify: Why the blockchain needs the law. *Berkeley Technology. Law Journal*, *33*, 487–550.

White, K., Habib, R., & Hardisty, D. J. (2019). How to SHIFT consumer behaviors to be more sustainable: A literature review and guiding framework. *Journal of Marketing*, *83*(3), 22–49.

7. Interactive network branding: towards a sustainability-driven strategy of small and medium-sized enterprises

Nikolina Koporcic and Jan-Åke Törnroos

INTRODUCTION

Sustainability has become a core theme in business management, while global issues and a call for sustainability thinking loom larger than ever, and with environmental degradation and climate change developing at an accelerating pace. This global surge is in line with Chabowski's et al. (2011, p. 55) argument: "More than ever, companies not only focus on obtaining economic benefits, but they also seek to deliver environmental and social benefits." This goes along with Triple Bottom Line (TBL) theory (Elkington, 1997, 2013), which represents insights into firms' actions and corporate thinking, while focusing on people, planet, and profit, in relation to sustainability. A successful example of this is The LEGO Group, being a part of the World Wildlife Fund's Climate Savers program, which is: "a program meant to aid businesses in becoming leaders of the low-carbon economy, inspiring companies to change how they think about climate solutions and develop businesses models that promote sustainability" (World Wildlife Fund blog). The Danish LEGO company has created relationships with non-governmental organizations (NGOs), suppliers, customers, consumers, universities, and third parties, with the goal to achieve 100% renewable energy capacity in its business operations, by aiming to use only sustainable materials in production processes by the year 2030.

However, although the TBL theory has introduced the practice of managing the social, economic, and environmental benefits of firms in parallel, it has not considered the challenges and potential opportunities of SMEs (small and medium-sized enterprises), related explicitly to sustainability issues. Instead, TBL researchers have mostly focused on large and multinational corporations (MNCs), taking SMEs into account often only as part of a larger business network of MNCs (for rare exceptions see, for example, Depken & Zeman, 2018; Perrini, 2006). In the current situation, companies are being perceived, as well as ranked, based on their overall corporate reputation, including their social and environmental performances. Besides being motivated by social cohesion, economic prosperity, and environmental preservation, companies have a moral obligation towards their employees, as well as customers (Perrini, 2006). This extends a company-centric approach of the marketing discipline towards one that includes business partners but also other social entities in complying with global issues concerning sustainable management (Ryan et al., 2012; Lindgreen et al., 2012). These calls of sustainability have to deal, at least, with the following key needs and demands:

- A need for a long-term perspective on managing, marketing, and developing a sustainable corporate reputation. This is due to the fact that sustainable strategies need time and long-term investments, but if it is executed in the right manner, these investments can offer new business opportunities and long-term business relationships (see, for example, Lindgreen et al., 2012).

- A need for an extended institutional perspective of marketing and branding that goes beyond the firm to include networking with its close business partners (both suppliers and customers) as well as NGOs and other societal entities (Ryan et al., 2012).
- The need to develop environmentally sound technologies and business practices, which would replace currently polluting and/or unjust business, which allows accessing resources of business counterparts that provide help and/or address similar issues and policies (Fisk, 1998).
- The need to include unpriced natural resources and the economic effects of externalities due to environmental degradation into corporate strategies (van Dam & Apeldoorn, 1996).

However, these central managerial strategic considerations are currently created and successfully executed mostly by large multinational and global corporations, such as, for example, Microsoft Corporation, Accenture plc, Owens Corning, Intel Corp., and Hasbro, Inc., who won the top five places in the Corporate Responsibility Magazine (*CR Magazine*) in its 19th annual 100 Best Corporate Citizens list. These companies are financially strong and have existed on the market for a long period of time. In comparison with MNCs, SMEs are less recognized for their sustainability-related endeavors. This reflects not only their struggle to attract funding for sustainability-driven strategies but also their long-term market survival.

Sustainability issues and strategies are also a central agenda for SMEs that employ most of the workforce across the globe and engage in production and distribution activities. They face similar issues as large firms, but with less financial, technological, and managerial power. As SMEs are numerous and have an influence across all national markets, they are also in a position to make a positive difference by improving social cohesion, economic prosperity, and environmental preservation on the market. Moreover, SMEs often act as important suppliers for larger firms. This brings additional importance for SMEs to implement sustainability as a part of successful business strategies in order to be a more attractive business partner. Furthermore, as larger firms have strategies developed for their sustainability policies, they also consider this issue to be important concerning their smaller supply firms. Thus, SMEs who already have their sustainable practices developed are more likely to be perceived as responsible and desirable partners.

Besides struggling to get a spotlight in the business world, SMEs have been undergoing less academic research in the area of sustainability, marketing, and branding, which also reflects on an existing lack of business strategies developed for this specific – but highly heterogeneous – group of companies. Shields and Shelleman (2019, p. 60) note this explicitly:

> The changing business environment and a growing perceived mandate to address sustainability intersects with the reality of resource constraints that is a feature of SMEs, highlighting the need for an organized approach to begin development of a sustainability strategy that is readily accessible to even very small businesses.

Considering the above-mentioned issues, we pose the following research question: how can SMEs create successful sustainability-driven strategies that will help them build a strong corporate reputation and position in their business markets and among stakeholders? In order to provide some relevant perspectives and implications on these issues, we introduce Interactive Network Branding (INB) as a sustainability-driven strategy that SMEs can use to prosper and survive in their business markets and achieve the desired network position. The position of an SME is evaluated by its business peers and other stakeholders in society by how it complies with its brand as a corporate reputation. INB rests on two theoretical constituents. The first is the interaction and network perspective of industrial markets (Anderson et al., 1994; Håkansson & Snehota, 1995; Möller & Halinen, 1999). The second conceptual angle is the stakeholder-oriented perspective on branding (Biraghi & Gambetti, 2015; Cornelissen et al., 2012; Koporcic & Halinen, 2018; Melewar et al., 2012). In doing this, we aim, at least partially, to close the existing gap between MNC and SME research concerning sustainability in relation to corporate branding strategy. We argue, by taking this approach, that academic research should pay more attention to developing up-to-date sustainability-driven strategies, oriented towards SMEs, as the future of sustainability lies in the hands of SMEs and their key representatives. The branding issue is important for SMEs, as having a strong reputation based on TBL issues is a strategic capability that will reflect a strong competitive advantage. This perspective is to be used based on sustainability issues and corporate acts in order to avoid greenwashing and false interpretations of companies.

This chapter is organized as follows. First, we present SMEs acting in business-to-business (B2B) markets and their specific characteristics concerning sustainability. Thereafter, we introduce the concept of INB, with its main theoretical underpinnings and its relevance for the sustainability and branding of SMEs. Next, we present INB as a sustainability-driven strategy for SMEs, by proposing and introducing its three key pillars more closely. Finally, we present the theoretical propositions and managerial implications of this conceptual-based chapter.

SMALL AND MEDIUM-SIZED ENTERPRISES IN BUSINESS-TO-BUSINESS MARKETS

As we initially noted, SMEs often have limited possibilities to invest in diversified global markets or spread their costs of service and product development (Moore & Manring, 2009). Moreover, 80% of all enterprises acting in global markets are considered to be SMEs. SMEs also occupy at least 85% of the US market; 99% of the EU market; and over 99% of the market in the UK (Moore & Manring, 2009; Koporcic, 2020). As such, SMEs are, in numbers, dominating almost all types of markets across developed as well as developing countries (Shields & Shelleman, 2019; Imram et al., 2019). Despite this fact, these companies are still facing challenges related to their branding (Koporcic, 2017) and marketing endeavors (LaPlaca, 2013; Koporcic, 2020), including sustainability.

Sustainability issues are especially relevant for SMEs in B2B markets, due to their connections and close relationships to other business actors both in upstream supply as well as in downstream markets (Ryan et al., 2012). In addition, as argued by Rudawska (2019, p. 877):

> purchasing power of business stakeholders (customers, partners in the value chain) is much higher in placing pressures on B2B organizations to be both environmentally and socially focussed. Sustainability is becoming a key determiner of the initiating the cooperation in this sector.

However, when companies collaborate closely, certain challenges related to sustainability may also come to the fore. We focus here on examining sustainability issues from a B2B SME perspective and in conjunction with the TBL theory (Elkington, 1997). As Elkington (2013, p. 26) argues: "In the simplest terms, the TBL agenda focuses corporations not just on the economic value that they add, but also on the environmental and social value that they add – or destroy." As such, the TBL became a guiding line for measuring sustainable organizational performance (Hubbard, 2009).

In this chapter, we first argue that sustainability strategies need to include those actors that are closely connected with a focal SME (i.e., main buyers, key suppliers, service providers, and investors) but also other potential stakeholders, including non-governmental actors (NGOs) and regional and governmental bodies. Second, sustainability strategies of SMEs should concern a wide array of issues, focusing specifically on the TBL theory, i.e., the alignment of environment, social, and economic components of corporate activity. These should all be jointly taken into account, as a part of the strategic endeavors of SMEs. This is in line with Moore & Manring (2009, p. 277) who argue: "A broad, multidimensional, multi-stakeholder perspective that is formed based on emerging ideas and trends should be the basis of a systematic approach towards an intentional, proactive situational analysis."

This holistic perspective is especially concerned about *managing relations* between actors both outside and inside the SME in order to achieve targets for a sustainable strategy and its dissemination to the above-mentioned key actor groups and society at large (Törnroos, 1998). Thus, we chose to use the network approach, as a leading perspective of B2B marketing, rather than a system-based viewpoint to B2B markets (Möller & Halinen, 2018). Compared with the system-based viewpoint, the network perspective has a focus on interactive business relationships between companies that are embedded in sets of connected relationships (Cook & Emerson, 1978). These connected actor firms share resources and enact their business in a semi-autonomous manner through relational exchanges and activities. These interactive business processes between connected firms can be treated as relational investments and adaptive capabilities of the actors as their resources are interdependently related to each other (Brennan & Turnbull, 1999; Hallén et al., 1991). We contend that the network approach offers a relevant viewpoint for building a sustainable network-based strategy for the SME firm (see also Ryan et al., 2012).

A sustainability-based strategy of the SME needs to be grounded on real-world, trustworthy, and actual corporate activities that deal with sustainability issues. In this sense, the corporate brand, as reflecting the firm's reputation, emerges and changes constantly as a result of ongoing business interactions between the SME and its business partners and other stakeholders. This perspective, denoted as INB (Koporcic, 2017, 2020; Koporcic & Halinen, 2018; Koporcic & Törnroos, 2019a, 2019b), thus offers a waypoint to address the role of sustainability and corporate branding from a business network perspective. In this sense, the INB approach demonstrates how well business counterparts deal with sustainability in their businesses. In forefronting this issue further, the core constituents of the INB concept are presented next, as a potential novel perspective on networking, branding, and sustainability issues of SME firms.

INTERACTIVE NETWORK BRANDING

As a relatively novel concept, INB is built up through a combination of the business network and branding literature (see Koporcic, 2017, 2020; Koporcic & Halinen, 2018; Koporcic & Törnroos, 2019a, 2019b). The INB process is complex, non-linear, and unfolding over time, precisely because of the social representatives. The "Network" denotes a B2B context of connected business actors in which INB comes to being. The "Branding" denotes the activities of SMEs, in which corporate identities and reputation are mutually influenced and created for each embedded firm. Furthermore, an INB process is "purposefully planned but, also, organically created and implemented through individuals who act on behalf of their companies" (Koporcic, 2020, p. 1181). This especially concerns SME firms, whose interpersonal and inter-organizational interactions are ultimately responsible for the co-creation of corporate identities and the reputation of all companies involved (see Figure 7.1). It is important to note that corporate *identity* is perceived as an internal INB dimension, as it is primarily built inside each firm and, secondly, influenced externally (see more details in Koporcic & Törnroos, 2019a, 2019b). Identity is often a reflection of the SME founder's personal identity and values (Iglesias et al., 2020), which is integrated into the organization as a corporate identity. Furthermore, corporate reputation is to be perceived as an external INB dimension, as it is primarily built and perceived outside of a focal firm, but also influenced internally, through the firm's actions and its strategic processes (Koporcic & Törnroos, 2019a, 2019b). That leaves us with the core of the INB concept (see Figure 7.1), representing an "in-between" space, where the internal firm's identity and the externally held reputation overlap and influence each other in a joint manner (Koporcic & Törnroos 2019a, 2019b). This "in-between" space presents the place where interaction between firms' representatives occurs. In other words, this is a place where interpersonal interactions mutually influence corporate identities and reputations of all firms involved (see Figure 7.1).

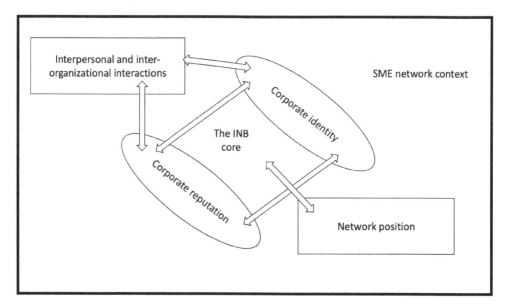

Source: Modified from Koporcic (2020).

Figure 7.1   *The Interactive Network Branding process*

Ultimately, as Koporcic and Törnroos (2019b, p. 69) argue: "INB refers to business interactions between SMEs that develop their corporate brands, while firms are acting in their roles and aiming toward the creation of desired network positions." By creating a strong identity and reputation, being in tune with the strategic intent of the firm when acting in B2B markets, companies can attract new business partners and access broader goodwill, which will further help them to achieve or maintain the desired network positions. In this manner, branding activities (i.e., identity and reputation creation) are often a result of face-to-face interactions and recommendations from current business partners (see Koporcic, 2020). As such, these branding activities overlap with networking, suggesting that: "the INB process is complex, non-linear and unfolding over time, precisely because of the social nature and dynamics of interpersonal interactions" (Koporcic, 2020, p. 1186). However, while conducting INB, SMEs need to be careful with whom they interact and with whom they are creating business relationships, as these issues will be crucial in allowing or restricting sustainability-related practices of interacting and connected firms.

INTERACTIVE NETWORK BRANDING AS A SUSTAINABILITY-DRIVEN STRATEGY OF SMES

Sustainable development is quite broadly defined as "meeting the needs of the present without compromising the ability of future generations to meet their own needs" (Brundtland, 1987, p. 43). However, as Spence et al. (2008, p. 51) argue: "Because of the broad scope of the term, most studies concentrate on one specific path [of sustainability] instead of being holistic." Thus, in order to provide a more holistic view on how SMEs can create successful sustainability-driven strategies that enable them to build their reputation and position as a sustainable company on the market, we discuss further the concept of INB as a potential waypoint for a sustainable strategy of SMEs.

The role of sustainability is concerned with, but not limited to, the role of suppliers and how they behave and manage TBL issues on their part, as this directly has a bearing on the buying firm and their potential to address sustainability-related goals that affect their corporate brands. SME firms are especially vulnerable in this regard, as they have limited resources and personnel to maintain existing and developing relations with business partners. The network approach plays an important role here as it considers both suppliers and buyer relationships to be of importance (Håkansson & Snehota 1995; Halinen & Törnroos 1998). These specific tenets of the network approach are also relevant concerning the sustainability of the SME in regards to utilizing joint and interdependent resources. In this way, TBL issues can be handled successfully for those parties that are involved in a reciprocal and interdependent manner (Håkansson & Snehota, 1995; Ryan et al., 2012). This seems quite straightforward and doable in theory, but oftentimes not in the practical management of SMEs. This also goes along with the argument presented by Spence et al. (2008, p. 55): "Although the advantages of SD [sustainable development] are put forward in the literature, in practice, SMEs face difficulties in implementing these activities."

By examining INB from a sustainability and strategic perspective, we propose next a holistic SME approach on sustainability-related issues. We start by arguing that in SME branding strategy, three intertwined levels of analysis, or approaches, play a notable role. From this perspective, INB reflects the actions and interactions of individuals (personal level), organizations (i.e., firm level), and between firms (inter-organizational level). As Oliver (1997, p. 698) argues: "At the individual level, the institutional context includes decision-makers' norms and values, at the firm level, organizational culture and politics, and at the interfirm level, public and regulatory pressures and industry-wide norms."

Moreover, this interactive multi-level process reflects – at a certain point in time – how well SMEs play a role as proactive sustainability-based actors of the network, instead of being simply passive agents (Spence et al., 2008). This will furthermore reflect on the specific reputation the firm possesses in the mindsets of its business partners and other stakeholders surrounding the SME.

Moreover, INB is especially relevant for SMEs and start-ups that have limited human, financial, and resource capabilities. In this sense, the CEOs and managers of SMEs, together with other firm representatives, are becoming leading figures for a successful sustainability-driven strategy. These representatives are responsible for developing new opportunities, for being proactive and innovative risk-takers, thus following the path of an entrepreneurial orientation, which is proposed to be an important factor for the success of an SME (Miller & Friesen, 1982; Spence et al., 2008). These individuals are acting on behalf of their firms, while following organizational rules and communicating the firm's culture and identity. Moreover, INB includes the joint efforts of business marketing, supply network management, as well as human resource departments (or alternatively, of individuals who have these responsibilities in the SME) in the deployment of a sustainability-driven approach, since these issues will reflect, either positively or negatively, on their sustainability strategies. Finally, SMEs need to keep in mind that finding suitable partners who care about the same sustainability-driven issues is their priority, as this inter-organizational aspect will influence the rest. SME firms can also learn best practices from other business actors that have already implemented successful sustainable strategies.

In order for an SME to accomplish a trustworthy sustainability strategy, we propose three main pillars that firms should take into account when planning their INB processes in this regard. This proposed theoretical model of INB (see Figure 7.2) presents the basic deployment of a sustainability-driven strategy for SMEs.

These three pillars, presented in Figure 7.2, relate to the sustainability strategies of SMEs by integrating the TBL-framework as a central component into the SME strategy process. First, as we have proposed, the sustainability-driven strategy is closely related to the *business network* of actors that the SME is dealing with (suppliers, financial bodies, customers, firms, as well as NGOs, and other potential stakeholders). This is the extended and connected environment of actors where the inter-organizational activities of INB occur. The second, *sustainability* pillar, denotes the key sustainability components that the organization is pursuing (thus denoting the organizational level of INB analysis), which is dealing with how firms can understand, develop, and manage their environmental footprints, keep their loyal employees, and sustain economic viability over the long term. However, networking is a central trait in the effectuation perspective concerning SME strategy (Sarasvathy, 2001). Thus, we suggest that SMEs need to identify key strategic partners for their TBL: business partners and shareholders for economic related issues, different entities and NGOs for the environmental aspect, and employees for the socially related issues (see Dontenwill 2005, Spence et al. 2008). The third pillar is concerned with how sustainability issues are disseminated to the key business actors and other interest groups through *branding* processes. This is central as we study the sustainability that takes place in B2B markets where branding is co-created through networking, i.e., through the business interactions of SME managers (Koporcic & Törnroos, 2019a, 2019b). This INB pillar represents the central level of INB analysis.

Figure 7.2   Three pillars of Interactive Network Branding as a sustainability-driven strategy of small and medium-sized enterprises

As a result of interactions between individuals, the corporate identities and reputations of all the involved actors are co-created and related to each other. Identity is reflected through the SME founder's personal identity, which is integrated into the organization as a corporate identity. As such, the corporate reputation that exists in the individual mindsets of external partners (representing their organizations) will affect the views of their counterparts regarding how they deal with sustainable management. By taking this approach, corporate brands are the result of interactions both within the firm (corporate identity) as well as externally (corporate reputation). The external audience is also extended towards NGOs, state and inter-governmental organizations, and other potential institutional entities that guide legislation and codes of conduct concerning sustainability issues.

It has been recognized that "demonstrating responsible corporate behaviors constitutes a potential source of benefits for the firm, because it can generate positive attitudes toward the firm and its products, which lead to competitive advantages and valuable organizational capabilities in the long run" (Lindgreen et al., 2012, p. 967). This denotes, as we have already proposed, a new, more long-term strategy and sustained development of corporations that seek a more balanced turnover and lesser risks in order to deal with sustainable management and societal demands for the future. The authors further follow a similar line of reasoning by declaring that strategic sustainable management "…is mainly a function of relationships and therefore of the brand, because brands build on dialogue with stakeholders and provide a powerful lens for comprehending organizations" (Lindgreen et al., 2012, p. 968, see also Balmer & Gray, 2003; Ryan et al., 2012). We thus propose that INB, as a sustainability-driven strategy, is dealing with the following central issues from an SME standpoint (see also Figure 7.2):

- It aims to foster currently active business relationships and develop those potential relationships that add sustainability value to current business networking activities. The goal of this is to strengthen and alleviate the corporate strategy of the SME in the future. As

Spence et al. (2008, p. 59) note: "it has been demonstrated that networks are a source of unique competencies for SMEs when implementing SD [sustainability development] strategies." This can happen proactively through the interdependencies that need to be developed to attain sustainable goals. This mutual dependence can deal, for example, with a large buyer company sharing knowledge with its smaller supply firms about how to comply with sustainable management. SMEs can also be innovative by showing how to deal with sustainability when developing their business with other firms. When sustainability issues become more of normality in business, the networking activities between firms can serve as a vital source for these sustainable interdependencies to develop. As sustainability issues are present across the supply networks of embedded companies, their activities and strategies should be in compliance with sustainability goals, for achieving mutually beneficial outcomes.

- To internally manage the firm and its personnel, it is important to implement a viable and sustainable marketing and management program, which will reflect on the firm's corporate identity. This sustainable program should be implemented carefully in the SME as a key to sustainable development and strategic change.
- The image and reputation that is held in the mindsets of external actors and entities outside the firm should be in tune with the internal associations held within the firm and its strategic vision. This should be addressed, furthermore, in business activities with upstream as well as downstream business actors and other entities (NGOs and other societal institutions).

From this viewpoint, INB offers both a strategic and sustainable perspective by denoting mutual and interdependent value mechanisms in dealing with its three sustainability pillars, while bringing an extended network-actor viewpoint to the fore. Corporate branding, thus, cannot dismiss sustainability claims and perspectives for business firms, including SMEs. The position of an SME is evaluated by its business peers and other entities in society by how they comply with their brand as a corporate reputation.

Challenges for SMEs in this setting relate, primarily, to their weak power relationships with large corporations when they act as suppliers for them (Ryan et al., 2012). In this sense, large firms can exert their power and negatively influence SME firms and their reputation concerning sustainability, especially in cases where MNCs are dismissing environmental and other sustainability issues. However, as we have pointed out, the urge for sustainability that is put upon MNCs, can also reflect positively on SMEs, offering the potential for developing their strategies (Lindgreen et al., 2012) and reputation as well (Koporcic & Törnroos, 2019a, 2019b). Other issues of many SMEs relate to their information voids, resource-scarcity, and inadequate technological innovation, lack of environmental expertise and sustainability-driven strategy, and their strategic marketing and corporate branding issues, which can all cause specific challenges in adopting sustainability-driven SME strategies. However, as Spence et al. (2008, p. 59) highlight:

> Solutions to these challenges can, however, be found or developed by owners/managers who are willing to engage in SD [sustainable development]. Their motivations would be stronger than the perceived barriers that limited resources or a hostile environment may present.

In order to present some of the potential solutions, next we turn to managerial implications.

MANAGERIAL IMPLICATIONS

In this chapter, we have examined INB from a sustainability perspective, in order to present a more holistic SME approach to sustainability-related issues. INB is especially relevant for SMEs and start-ups that have limited human, financial, and resource capabilities. In this sense, the CEOs and founders of SMEs are becoming leading figures for a successful sustainability-driven strategy. We suggest that managers need to take into account sustainability through INB activities and interactions with partners and other stakeholders. If successful, a SME will create a strong reputation as a sustainable company, in its embedded business network, which will furthermore reflect a foundation for the development of the corporate identity. This will also offer a base towards influencing the *mutually developed sustainability* issues. Moreover, if INB is managed accordingly, SMEs will become more attractive for investors who seek sustainable firms for their portfolios (e.g., the large Norwegian oil fund has this perspective as its cornerstone). Finally, INB also provides a platform for considering the TBL issues in its activities and prospects for the future.

However, an important question arises from this discussion. To what extent are SME owners or managers capable of implementing sustainability-driven strategies, owing to limited resources and other challenges that they are facing in their everyday business operations? In order to answer this question, we provide a list of suggestions and potential solutions for SMEs based on INB, TBL, and effectuation principles:

- SME representatives should establish a set of achievable sustainability goals, paying particular attention to their available resources (personal, organizational, as well as inter-firm tangible and intangible resources).
- Development of sustainable business relationships, by maintaining and enhancing existing ones and developing new ones that will contribute to the sustainability-driven goals of an SME.
- Learn from your own mistakes, but also from the mistakes of other businesses, as sustainability-related issues can quickly destroy the reputation of an SME and sometimes even its business partners.
- SMEs should aim towards developing a strong sustainability-driven strategy, as that will influence the brand of the SME, by receiving acknowledgement from its business partners and the extended group of stakeholders.

Next, we present the theoretical implications of this chapter, as well as some suggestions for future research avenues.

THEORETICAL IMPLICATIONS AND FUTURE RESEARCH SUGGESTIONS

This chapter has focused on examining sustainability, branding, and strategic marketing issues from a B2B SME perspective. Thus, theoretical implications lie in the first attempt to link INB (Koporcic, 2017, 2020; Koporcic & Halinen, 2018; Koporcic & Törnroos, 2019a, 2019b) with corporate sustainability literature in general (Chabowski et al., 2011; Lindgreen et al., 2012; Ryan et al., 2012), and with an SME context in particular (Imram et al., 2019; More & Manring, 2009; Shields & Shelleman, 2019; Spence et al., 2008). This proposal is relevant as the scope of sustainable management and marketing issues extends the contact landscape for the numerous SME companies, as they need to comply with these issues even stronger than before. Companies, including SMEs, are monitored even more carefully than previously, by external audiences, such as environmental groups, other NGOs, as well as governmental organizations, customers, and even consumers, which can all be in a position to either give or take away the legitimacy of a firm. In this chapter, we have proposed a way of managing the sustainability of SMEs by creating a strong interlinked business network with key actors and by developing a trustful and strong reputation as a viable company in sustainable terms.

These ideas offer, at this point, theoretical perspectives to explore in the future. The first issue we are proposing to be further developed deals with INB and deeper conceptualization of its three pillars, interconnected with three levels of analysis (i.e., personal, organizational, and inter-firm level). This can be used as a relevant tool in forming a base for further conceptual work in developing a sustainable marketing strategy in conjunction with branding.

Besides this, we acknowledge the process of institutionalization and how institutional actors play their role in SME branding in particular, thus offering a relevant issue for further research. How institutional theory and networking (Brito, 2001; Deligonul et al., 2013) can be aligned and used for developing a strong position of a firm, from an environmental and sustainable angle, offers an intriguing topic for further research, from both theoretical and empirical perspectives.

Another issue for further inquiry deals with international and global recognition of SME firms after they have developed a strong foothold as a sustainable firm in their home and/or nearby markets. Topics to explore can deal with how a sustainable and extended network in the home market can be developed and successfully implemented in other markets, and how international brand recognition can be attained and developed in this way.

REFERENCES

Anderson, J. C., Håkansson, H., & Johanson, J. (1994). Dyadic business relationships within a business network context. *Journal of Marketing, 58*, 1–15.

Balmer, J., & Gray, E. (2003). Corporate brands: What are they? What of them? *European Journal of Marketing, 37*(7-8), 972–997.

Biraghi, S., & Gambetti, R. C. (2015). Corporate branding: Where are we? A systematic communication-based inquiry. *Journal of Marketing Communications, 21*(4), 260–283.

Brennan, R., & Turnbull, P. W. (1999). Adaptive behavior in buyer-seller relationships. *Industrial Marketing Management, 28*(5), 481–495.

Brito, C. M. (2001). Towards an institutional theory of the dynamics of industrial networks. *Journal of Business & Industrial Marketing, 16*(3), 150–166.

Brundtland, G. H. (1987). *Our Common Future*. Oxford: Oxford University Press.

Chabowski, B. R., Mean, J. A., & Gonzalez-Padron, T. L. (2011). The structure of sustainability research in marketing, 1958–2008: A basis for future research opportunities. *Journal of the Academy of Marketing Science, 39*(1), 55–70.

Cook, K., & Emerson, R. (1978). Power, equity and commitment in exchange networks. *American Sociological Review, 43*, 712–739.

Cornelissen, J. P., Christensen, L. T., & Kinuthia, K. (2012). Corporate brands and identity: Developing stronger theory and the call for shifting debate. *European Journal of Marketing, 46*(7/8), 1093–1102.

Deligonul, S., Elg, U., Cavusgil, E., & Ghauri, P.N. (2013). Developing strategic supplier networks: An institutional perspective. *Journal of Business Research, 66*(4), 506–515.

Depken, D., & Zeman, C. (2018). Small business challenges and the triple bottom line, TBL: Needs assessment in a Midwest State, USA. *Technological Forecasting and Social Change, 135*, 44–50.

Dontenwill, E. (2005). Comment la théorie des parties prenantes permet-elle d'opérationnaliser le concept de développement durable pour les entreprises? *La revue des sciences de gestion*, January–April, *40*(211–12), 85–97.

Elkington, J. (1997). *Cannibals with Forks: The Triple Bottom Line of 21st Century Business*. Oxford, UK: John Wiley Press.

Elkington, J. (2013). Enter the triple bottom line. In A. Henriques and J. Richardson (eds.) *The Triple Bottom Line* (pp. 23–38). London, UK: Routledge.

Fisk, G. (1998). Green marketing: Multiplier for appropriate technology transfer? *Journal of Marketing Management*, *14*(1), 657–677.

Halinen, A., & Törnroos, J.-Å. (1998). The role of embeddedness in the evolution of business networks. *Scandinavian Journal of Management*, *14*(3), 187–205.

Hallén, L., Johanson, J., & Seyed-Mohamed, N. (1991). Interfirm adaptation in business relationships. *Journal of Marketing*, *55*(2), 29–37.

Håkansson, H., & Snehota I. (1995). *Developing Relationships in Business Networks*. London: Routledge & Co.

Hubbard, G. (2009). Measuring organizational performance: Beyond the triple bottom line. *Business Strategy and the Environment*, *18*(3), 177–191.

Iglesias, O., Landgraf, P., Ind, N., Markovic, S., & Koporcic, N. (2020). Corporate brand identity co-creation in business-to-business contexts. *Industrial Marketing Management*, *85*, 32–43.

Imram, M., Salisu, I., Danial, H., Aslam, H. D., Iqbal, J., & Hameed, I. (2019). Resource and information access for SME sustainability in the era of IR 4.0: The mediating and moderating roles of innovation capability and management commitment. *Processes*, *7*(211), 2–25.

Koporcic, N. (2017). *Developing Interactive Network Branding in business markets: Case studies of SMEs from developed and emerging business markets*. Åbo Akademi Dissertation, Turku, Finland.

Koporcic, N. (2020). Interactive Network Branding: Demonstrating the importance of firm representatives for small and medium-sized enterprises in emerging markets. *Journal of Business & Industrial Marketing*, *35*(7), 1179–1189.

Koporcic, N., & Halinen, A. (2018). Interactive Network Branding: Creating corporate identity and reputation through interpersonal interaction. *IMP Journal*, *12*(2), 392–408.

Koporcic, N., & Törnroos, J.-Å. (2019a). Conceptualizing Interactive Network Branding in business markets: Developing roles and positions of firms in business networks. *Journal of Business & Industrial Marketing*, *34*(8), 1681–1691.

Koporcic, N., & Törnroos, J.-Å. (2019b). *Understanding Interactive Network Branding in SME firms*. Bingley, UK: Emerald Publishing.

LaPlaca, P. J. (2013). Research priorities for B2B marketing researchers. *Revista Española de Investigacion de Marketing Esic*, *17*(2), 135–150.

Lindgreen, A., Uy, X., Maon, F., & Wilcock, J. (2012). Corporate social responsibility brand leadership: A multiple case study. *European Journal of Marketing*, *46*(7/8), 965–993.

Melewar, T. C., Gotsi, M., & Andriopoulos, C. (2012). Shaping the research agenda for corporate branding: Avenues for future research. *European Journal of Marketing*, *46*(5), 600–608.

Miller, D., & Friesen, P. H. (1982). Innovation in conservative and entrepreneurial firms: Two models of strategic momentum. *Strategic Management Journal*, *3*(1), 1–25.

Moore, S. B., & Manring, S. L. (2009). Strategy development in small and medium sized enterprises for sustainability and increased value creation. *Journal of Cleaner Production*, *17*(2), 276–282.

Möller, K. E., & Halinen, A. (1999). Business relationships and networks: Managerial challenges for a network era. *Industrial Marketing Management*, *28*, 413–427.

Möller, K. E., & Halinen, A. (2018). IMP thinking and IMM: Co-creating value for business marketing. *Industrial Marketing Management*, *69*, 18–31.

Oliver, C. (1997). Sustainable competitive advantage: Combining institutional and resource-based views. *Strategic Management Journal*, *18*(9), 697–713.

Perrini, F. (2006). SMEs and CSR theory: Evidence and implications from an Italian perspective. *Journal of Business Ethics*, *67*(3), 305–316.

Rudawska, E. (2019). Sustainable marketing strategy in food and drink industry: A comparative analysis of B2B and B2C SMEs operating in Europe. *Journal of Business & Industrial Marketing*, *34*(4), 875–890.

Ryan, A., Mitchell, I. K., & Daskou, S. (2012). An interaction and networks approach to developing a sustainable organization. *Journal of Organizational Change Management, 25*(4), 578–594.

Sarasvathy, S. D. (2001). Causation and effectuation: Toward a theoretical shift from economic inevitability to entrepreneurial contingency. *Academy of Management Review, 26*(2), 243–263.

Shields, J., & Shelleman, J. M. (2019). Integrating sustainability to SME strategy. *Journal of Small Business Strategy, 25*(2), 59–75.

Spence, M., Gherib, J., & Biwolé, V. O. (2008). A framework of SME's strategic involvement in sustainable development. In R. Wustenhagen, S. Sharma, M. Starik and R. Wuebker (eds.), *Sustainable Innovation and Entrepreneurship*. Boston: Edward Elgar, 49–70.

Törnroos, J.-Å. (1998). The environmental challenge of international industrial marketing – Problems and prospects with an example from paper industry. In H. Tikkanen (ed.), *Marketing and International Business*. Publications of the Turku School of Economics and Business Administration Series A-2: 1998, pp. 287–318.

Van Dam, Y., & Apeldoorn, A. C. (1996). Sustainable marketing. *Journal of Macromarketing, 16*, 45–56.

World Wildlife Fund blog. "Climate Savers Q&A: LEGO Group Shares Their Commitments." https://www.worldwildlife.org/blogs/sustainability-works/posts/climate-savers-q-a-lego-group-shares-their-commitments (Accessed 31 March 2020).

8. How does brand-cause fit influence the success of CrM campaigns?

Inês Padilha Campelos, Susana Costa e Silva and Joana César Machado

INTRODUCTION

In recent years, consumers have become increasingly interested in corporate issues that may affect them and society in general (Devinney, 2009; Margolis & Walsh, 2003), and they are pressuring brands to embrace genuinely sustainable social practices (Iglesias et al., 2018). Furthermore, the increasing use of social media has contributed to the development of a more transparent environment, and made consumers more aware of the effects of companies' marketing activities on the environment or on society as a whole (Markovic et al., 2018). Research suggests that consumers value companies' social development initiatives because they believe that every company action and every purchase they make has implications for the wider society (Mohr et al., 2001), and they try to reward or punish brands based on their perceptions of how environmentally and socially responsible they are (Fereira & Ribeiro, 2017; Gupta, 2015; Lerro et al., 2018). Since consumers are more aware of companies' behaviours and place an increasing value on social sustainability (Choi et al., 2016), it is advisable for companies to communicate clearly their efforts to be more socially responsible. One such way is through a cause-related marketing (CrM) strategy. CrM involves the funding of charities that support health, environmental protection or other relevant causes linked to sustainability, by donating part of the business profit (Grolleau et al., 2016). Hence, when consumers purchase a "cause-related" product, they trigger a donation by the company to an environmental or socio-economic cause (Grolleau et al., 2016). This allows consumers to feel better about their purchase decisions and about themselves (Laroche, 2017). According to the Cone Communications CSR Study (Komornicki & Komornicki, 2017), when choosing between two brands of equal quality and price, 88% of consumers are likely to switch to a cause-related brand.

CrM involves a collaborative relationship or alliance between the corporate (or product) brand and the cause supported. When two brands are presented jointly, or in the context of one another, it is likely to elicit evaluations of both brands (Broniarczyk & Alba, 1994). If the consistency between the images of the two partners in the alliance is weak, consumers might question why the brand and the cause are associated, and this can trigger undesirable judgements (Simonin & Ruth, 1998). When a company is searching for a cause to support, fit between the corporate (or product) brand and the cause is crucial, as it might influence consumers' evaluation of the CrM campaign and their intention to purchase the cause-related product (Zasuwa, 2017). Despite the relevance of brand-cause fit in the evaluation of CrM campaigns, there is a paucity of studies assessing the influence of brand-cause fit on consumer responses to CrM (Kim et al., 2015). In this study, we intend to contribute to the fulfilment of this research gap, by analysing how brand-cause fit affects the evaluation of CrM campaigns, and thus, their success. According to the findings of Zeynali and Golkar (2013), which support Varadarajan & Menon's (1988) premise that a key feature of CrM is that the firm's contribution is linked to consumers' engagement in revenue-producing transactions with the firm, and Barone et al. (2007), who suggest that consumer-cause involvement moderates consumer affinity towards a specific cause and, thus, influences his/her willingness to engage in cause-supporting activities, it is also relevant to analyse how consumer-cause involvement and corporate brand image affect the relationship between brand-cause fit and consumers' purchase intention in a CrM campaign.

In order to accomplish these goals, a qualitative study will be developed using a case study strategy with a sample of CrM campaigns that fulfil the following criteria: the campaigns should have been conducted in Portugal in the last ten years; brand-cause fit should range between a low and high level; and the campaigns should have been supported by a well-known brand. Based on these criteria, we have selected a Portuguese multinational, SONAE, and studied in detail multiple CrM campaigns conducted by this company through different brands belonging to its portfolio – namely, Worten, Zippy and Continente.

Data were collected through semi-structured in-depth interviews with the brand managers responsible for the CrM campaigns chosen. The interviews will allow researchers to identify the campaigns' objectives and the motives behind the selection of the causes supported, but also to ascertain all the relevant distinctive characteristics of the five campaigns studied, and to obtain essential data regarding the outcomes in terms of social sustainability of the different campaigns.

LITERATURE REVIEW AND RESEARCH MODEL

CrM Success and Effectiveness

CrM involves the business's commitment towards a cause, as well as the cause's commitment towards the business (Kotler & Lee, 2005). This mutual commitment is expected to generate bilateral benefits for the parties involved (Adkins, 2003) and can result in consumer engagement with the brand and the product traded (Silva & Martins, 2017). This research focuses on CrM initiatives with transactional characteristics, meaning that the company's donations to a social cause are contingent upon consumers' participation in the campaign. This approach supports Varadarajan & Menon's (1988) CrM definition and highlights that a distinctive feature of CrM is the involvement of the consumer through revenue-producing transactions and donations to the cause. Within the scope of transactional CrM, different types of campaigns can be implemented, namely: purchase-triggering donations, where the company commits to donating a portion of the profits resulting from the sale of a product or service by donating a specified amount for each product sold; buy-one-give-one, where the company matches consumers' contributions to a specific cause for each unit sold, and checkout charity, in which the company encourages consumers to make a donation at the moment of payment (Kotler and Lee, 2005; Stole, 2006; Kinard & Pardo, 2017).

The success of a CrM campaign may depend on consumers' perceptions of fit between the corporate (or product) brand and the cause supported, as brand-cause can impact consumers' evaluation of the CrM campaign and their intention to purchase the cause-related product (Gupta & Pirsch, 2006; Zasuwa, 2017). Fit can be defined as the global and abstract evaluation that consumers make regarding the connections between both brands' images (Kim and John, 2008); it may be based on the sharing of relevant associations, or on the "complementarities between the brand-unique associations that consumers have with both brands" (Bouten et al., 2011, p. 457). Brand-cause fit "refers to the extent to which the alliance between the company and the cause is logical and makes sense'' (Hassan & Abouaish, 2018, p. 245) or "the overall perceived relatedness of the brand and the cause with multiple cognitive bases" (Nan & Heo, 2007, p. 65). According to Trimble & Holmes (2013), a high brand-cause fit is present when a close relationship between the company and the cause is established.

Some studies suggest that companies should strive to support causes that reflect a high degree of brand-cause fit (Pracejus & Olsen, 2004; Zasuwa, 2017). However, other studies indicate that companies can embrace causes that have a lesser degree of brand-cause fit (Barone et al., 2007). Lafferty (2007), for example, found that consumers' evaluation of brand-cause fit does not always influence their intention to purchase the product promoted, highlighting that consumers' relationship with the cause might affect their willingness to contribute to the CrM campaign more than their evaluations of fit. In the same way, Nan and Heo (2007) added that brand-cause fit does not significantly influence the effectiveness of CrM messages, since campaigns involving cause-supporting initiatives generate more positive responses towards the company than campaigns that do not support causes, and this positive effect is not contingent on brand-cause evaluations. On the other hand, Pracejus and Olsen (2004) found that brand-cause fit favourably influences consumer response CrM campaigns, and, in particular, significantly improves consumer purchase intention. Lans et al. (2014) also found that a high brand-cause fit enhances the consumer's attitude towards the company or the brand and positively affects the image of the company. These different perspectives regarding the relevance of brand-cause fit to CrM campaigns suggest that there is a lack of consensus among researchers, with respect to the impact of brand-cause fit on consumer responses to CrM.

Studies suggest that a higher level of consumer-cause involvement can lead to more positive consumer responses to CrM initiatives. Indeed, consumer-cause involvement might affect the relationship between brand-cause fit and consumers' purchase intention in a CrM campaign (Barone et al., 2007; Zeynali & Golkar, 2013; Bui, 2017). The concept of consumer-cause involvement was introduced by Grau and Folse (2007) and is defined as "the degree to which consumers find the cause to be personally relevant to them" (p. 20). Previous research suggests that the likelihood of consumers purchasing a brand that supports causes that have a direct influence on their community is higher than the likelihood of them purchasing a brand that supports causes that do not directly affect their community (Zeynali & Golkar, 2013; Bui, 2017).

As CrM is a marketing tool, CrM success and effectiveness should be judged according to the degree of achievement of the marketing objectives of the campaign (Christofi et al., 2015). Varadarajan and Menon (1998) suggested that companies should use three different types of metrics to evaluate CrM success, namely: financial measures, consumer measures and image measures. Financial measures include sales volume, market share, purchase quantity and frequency and average purchase size; consumer measures encompass brand switching, brand loyalty and repeat purchase; and image measures, such as corporate image, brand image and media coverage. Moreover, Silva and Martins (2017) stated that "CrM does not suffer from the problem normally associated with other corporate social marketing campaigns in which the impact on sales is difficult to measure" (p. 480); the financial impact is easier to measure, since in transactional CrM campaigns, the consumer is required to purchase a specific product which is associated with the campaigns.

Research Model and Research Questions

The main objective of this research is to evaluate how brand-cause fit influences the success of a CrM campaign. Moreover, we aim to understand how consumer-cause involvement and corporate brand image affect the relationship between brand-cause fit and consumers' purchase intention in a CrM campaign, and, consequently, CrM success. In order to evaluate the success of a CrM campaign, we need to confirm whether the company was able to achieve the objectives defined for the campaign (Christofi et al., 2015).

Considering the findings of prior studies, the level of fit between the corporate (or product) brand and the supported cause should favourably influence consumers' willingness to participate in the CrM campaigns. Indeed, authors such as Gwinner and Bennett (2008), Alav and Zeynali (2013) and Pracejus and Olsen (2004) concluded that a high brand-cause fit will generate more favourable attitudes towards the campaign and the brand that conducts the campaign, and this should also increase the success of the CrM campaign. However, as previously explained, there is a lack of consensus in the literature regarding the impact of brand-cause fit on CrM's success. Therefore, we formulate the following research question:

Q1: Will brand-cause fit have a positive impact on the success of a CrM campaign?

Regarding the evaluation of the success of CrM initiatives, organisations tend to follow different criteria (Varadarajan & Menon, 1988). When conducting an analysis of how successful a CrM campaign has been, we should consider which initial objectives were set by the company when it decided to engage in the campaign. Silva and Martins (2017) note that, in transactional CrM campaigns, the financial impacts are easier to measure, since the consumer is required to purchase a specific product which is associated with the campaign. In the scope of our research, purchase intention is understood as consumers' intention to choose and purchase a product associated with a specific CrM campaign (Bui, 2017). In this study, we consider that a positive purchase intention is an appropriate measure of the success of CrM campaigns. Moreover, as previously highlighted, consumers' intention to purchase the cause-related product might be positively affected by their brand-cause fit perceptions (Zasuwa, 2017). Hence, we formulate the following research questions:

Q2: Will brand-cause fit have a positive effect on consumers' intention to purchase the product associated with the CrM campaign?
Q3: Will purchase intention have a positive effect on the success of the CrM campaign?

Zasuwa (2017) suggested that corporate/brand image and reputation are strong moderators of the influence of a consumer's evaluation of brand-cause fit on their purchase intention of the product associated with the CrM campaign. The author found that a negative corporate image weakens the positive effect of brand-cause on consumer purchase intention. Furthermore, Barone et al. (2007) concluded that consumer-cause involvement – which is defined as a consumer's affinity with a specific cause – acts as a moderator in the relationship between brand-cause fit and consumer response to CrM initiatives. Therefore, taking into consideration the findings of prior studies, we assume that a positive evaluation of the corporate brand and a strong consumer-cause involvement will favourably affect the relationship between brand-cause fit and consumers' purchase intention during the CrM campaign. Indeed, a favourable corporate brand image should reduce consumer scepticism, leading to more confidence in the company and in the campaign. Moreover, when consumers find the cause to have personal relevance, their likelihood of purchasing a brand that supports that cause will tend to be higher (Zeynali & Golkar, 2013; Bui, 2017). Ultimately, a favourable corporate brand image and strong consumer-cause involvement should also positively affect the campaign's success, since consumers' willingness to engage in commercial trades in the form of CrM campaigns will be higher. Thus, we will try to answer the following research question:

Q4: Will corporate image and consumer-cause involvement moderate the influence of brand-cause fit on consumers' purchase intention of the product associated with the CrM campaign?

This research will be guided by the research model presented in Figure 8.1.

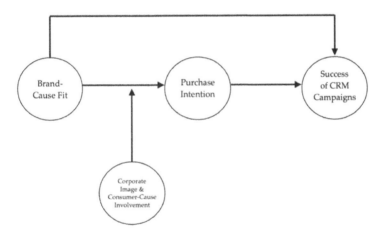

Figure 8.1   Research model and research questions

The research model assumes that, even though brand-cause fit plays an important role in the success of CrM campaigns, the influence of brand-cause fit is moderated by corporate/brand image and consumer-cause involvement. Thus, these moderating factors will be studied to understand how they affect the influence of consumer evaluations of brand-cause fit. Indeed, prior studies underline that these variables should be also considered when analysing the impact of brand-cause fit on consumers' purchase intention and on their response to CrM campaigns (Guerreiro, et al., 2015; Steffen & Günther, 2013; Melero & Montaner, 2016).

RESEARCH DESIGN

In order to investigate the research problem, we have chosen a descriptive and qualitative study, based on a case study methodology – specifically, a multiple case study design. By following a multiple case study design, we will be able to replicate findings across cases. We will focus on a reduced number of CrM campaigns and try to establish comparisons between the cases studied, identifying the similarities and differences between them. The case study will allow us to draw conclusions about CrM campaigns that have actually been implemented.

To conduct our analysis, we gathered information using different data collection procedures, including semi-structured in-depth interviews with brand managers involved in the CrM campaigns studied, and the analysis of documents relating to these campaigns. The interviews consisted of three groups of questions, containing both closed and open questions.

In the first section, respondents were asked to describe the campaign and identify the main criteria used to select the social cause supported. These questions should allow us to: understand the motivations behind the choice of cause; identify the main objectives of the CrM campaign; characterise the campaign's target consumers; identify the alignment between the cause and the consumer and the cause and the brand; identify the duration of the campaign and characterise the type of donation made. The second group of questions relate mainly to the marketing mix of the campaign. This group of questions will allow us to identify similarities and differences between the CrM campaigns studied, and to analyse the relevance of these structural elements in the success of the CrM campaigns. The third group of questions is focused mainly on the campaign's performance. The answers to this section provide managers' opinions regarding the campaigns' outcomes in terms of the impact of the campaign on consumers' purchase intention, on brand image and brand market share.

As secondary data, we used the different communication instruments used to support the CrM campaigns and the company financial reports. These financial reports were developed by the company during the time frame in which the CrM campaigns were implemented. The secondary data provided us with both quantitative and qualitative data, allowing a deeper knowledge of the impact that the CrM campaigns had on the company's performance. They are essential to support managers' answers regarding the success of the campaigns studied.

In our case study, the sample analysis will consist of a range of five CrM campaigns that fulfil the following criteria: the campaigns have been conducted in Portugal in the last ten years, they involve a brand-cause fit that ranges between a low and high brand-cause fit, they have relevant social sustainability impacts and have been supported by a well-known organisation. We have chosen campaigns that were conducted in Portugal, since our objective is to generate inferences concerning the Portuguese market, allowing marketers to better understand Portuguese consumers' motivations to engage in CrM campaigns and to adapt their CrM strategies accordingly.

In this case study we have chosen to analyse CrM campaigns developed by brands belonging to SONAE. SONAE is a multinational corporation that manages a wide portfolio of companies in retail, financial services, technology, shopping centres and telecommunications (including the retail brands Continente, Zippy, Wells, Mo, Note and Worten), operating in 90 countries. It was founded in 1959 to operate in the wood agglomerate sector. The group is one of the 20 firms listed on the Euronext PSI-20, in Lisbon. In the first semester of 2018, the company registered profits of almost €100 million, a value that is 34.5% larger than for the first semester of 2017. At the time of our study, it was the largest employer in Portugal, with

50,000 employees. Besides its reputation as the largest employer, SONAE is also known for its presence in a wide range of sectors and for the close relationship it has tried to establish with its customers.

The choice of SONAE and its brands – Worten, Zippy and Continente – to conduct the case study was based on several factors. SONAE is a company with a strong presence in the national market and the brands chosen are easily recognised by consumers. Additionally, SONAE consistently invests in sustainability initiatives, and sustainability is strongly rooted in its way of operating in the market. Indeed, since 1995, the company has consistently engaged in numerous activities linked to sustainable development and community support. Within its CSR policy the multinational sets several scopes to be addressed in the areas of climate change, nature and biodiversity, plastics, inequalities and inclusive development and community support. As CrM is part of the CSR SONAE policy, the company has undertaken several actions through the years that support its desire to contribute to the community – not only through CrM campaigns, which are the scope of our study, but also through the sponsoring of numerous institutions and projects and volunteering actions.

The choice of the three brands – Worten, Zippy and Continente – was influenced by online information about the brands' performance that was available when this exploratory research was conducted. Moreover, these three brands were chosen because they are associated with several CrM activities in the last ten years and follow different types of CrM strategies. It is important to underline that for this study we decided to analyse only transactional CrM campaigns.

In order to conduct the interviews, we contacted the brand managers of the brands studied. Table 8.1 identifies each respondent, the department he/she belongs to and the campaigns involved.

Table 8.1   Respondents' characterisation

	Respondent's characterisation		
Name	Dra. Alexandra Balão	Dra. Regina Guerner	Dra. Andreia Sousa
Company	SONAE	SONAE	SONAE
Brand	Worten	Zippy	Continente
Department	Marketing	Marketing	Marketing
Campaign	Worten & CVP (2012)	Zippy & "Make-a-Wish" (2018)	*Missão Continente* (2018)
Identification	Worten & *Terra dos Sonhos* (2014)		
	Worten & CVP (2017)		

CASE STUDIES

We will begin our analysis by briefly describing the brands chosen, namely the core business of the brand and the target market, followed by a description of the CrM campaign that will be analysed.

Zippy

Zippy is a Portuguese brand that has been operating in the retail area since 2004. The brand has a wide range of clothing and accessories, childcare products, furniture and toys, with a focus on the children's market (babies and children). In line with SONAE's desire for expansion, the brand is present in 20 countries, and has more than 100 stores.

The campaign chosen for analysis – "Zippy and Make-a-Wish Foundation Gloves" – was developed by Zippy in association with the "Make-a-Wish" Foundation during 2018/2019. The purpose of the campaign was to support an institution whose mission it is to help children accomplish their dreams. The similarity between the mission of the cause and Zippy's mission was the main reason for the development of this campaign, which led to the sale of a pair of "solidarity" gloves. This pair of gloves accommodated two hands simultaneously, ideally an adult's and a child's hand, allowing them to "walk together, hand in hand, while protecting themselves from the cold". The selling price of the pair of gloves was €9.99, and for each pair sold the brand donated €1 to the "Make-a-Wish" cause. The campaign took place between December 2018 and February 2019, covering the entire national territory.

Worten

Worten runs a chain of retail stores in the areas of home appliances, consumer electronics and entertainment. The brand has been operating in the domestic market since 1996 and offers a wide range of products and brands. Following the group's objectives, the brand pursued an expansion strategy, setting up about 180 stores in the national market. The brand has embraced an *omnichannel* strategy. Since 2016 it has been chosen as a "Trusted Brand" ("*Marca de Confiança*") by Portuguese consumers.

Worten has consistently developed several CrM campaigns throughout the years; thus, we decided to choose three of the campaigns conducted by the brand. The first campaign chosen is a campaign named "*Dê a mão por um Portugal + Feliz*" (or "Lend a Hand for a Happier Portugal"), which was developed in the years 2012/2013 in partnership with the Portuguese Red Cross. The brand has committed itself to supporting the project "*Portugal + Feliz*" ("Happier Portugal"), a programme that has been developed since 2009 as a response to the negative social consequences of the global financial and economic crisis. This programme aimed to support poor families and help them fight poverty and social exclusion. The campaign included the sale of "Christmas Wraps" at a price of €1. For each product sold, Worten donated €0.80 to the project it was supporting. In addition to the sales of the product in Worten stores, the brand developed activities on its Facebook page and created a telephone line to support the campaign. Both initiatives aimed to collect donations to the cause. The campaign took place between 16 November 2012 and 6 January 2013, covering the entire national territory from north to south.

The second campaign by Worten was developed in partnership with the institution "*Terra dos Sonhos*" ("Land of Dreams"). The goal of this campaign was to fulfil the dreams of seriously ill children, through the "*Código DáVinte*" (or "Code Give20") project. The brand committed to donating to the institution the value raised during the campaign period, plus an additional 20% of the total amount raised. The year 2013 marked the launch of "*Código DáVinte*". In this project, the decision to contribute to the campaign was not associated with the purchase of any specific product, but rather with the "act of donation". The consumer could choose, at the time of payment, how much to donate to the supported cause, as long as it was a multiple of €0.20 (minimum donation value). The campaign took place between 15 November 2013 and 6 January 2014, covering the entire national territory.

The third and last campaign was developed by Worten in partnership with the Portuguese Red Cross in 2017, with the aim of responding to the severe consequences of the fires that caused a great deal of destruction throughout the country. The objective was to raise as much money as possible, to be distributed to families to help rebuild homes and minimise the damage resulting from the fires. Once again, this CrM campaign was associated with the "*Código DáVinte*" project. The donation format was the same as that adopted in 2014: the decision to contribute to the campaign was associated with the "act of donation", and the consumer decided how much to donate to the supported cause, as long as it was a multiple of €0.20 (minimum donation value). The campaign took place between 16 November 2017 and 6 January 2018, covering the entire national territory.

Continente

Continente is a chain of hypermarkets, which has operated in the Portuguese market since 1985, and aims to fulfil a wide range of consumer needs. The brand is considered a benchmark in terms of retail in Portugal, and in polls of Portuguese consumers it has been voted a "Trusted Brand" ("*Marca de Confiança*") 11 times. Continente's marketing strategy is marked by several social initiatives with a strong impact in terms of sustainability and innovation.

In this case study, we decided to focus on the CrM initiative, "*Missão Continente*" ("Continente Mission"). This campaign was developed in 2018 with the goal of supporting projects based around the theme of food – namely healthy food, food waste and social inclusion. The campaign consisted of the sale of "solidarity mugs" with a selling price of €3. For each product (mug) sold, *Missão Continente* committed to donating €1 to the social institutions that it was supporting.

DATA ANALYSIS

Having described the brands and the campaigns selected for this study, we will next present the analysis of the data gathered through the interviews (primary data), and of the information gathered as secondary data, which will be essential to help us answer the research questions.

In the interviews, we asked respondents whether the product being promoted was developed specifically for the campaign, or if it was already part of the brand's portfolio (see Table 8.2). Additionally, in the cases where the brand developed a specific product for the CrM campaign, we asked respondents to identify the main motives and benefits of this approach. One of the main aims of these questions was to understand whether the CrM campaigns were attached to products of a hedonic nature, as suggested in the literature (Strahilevitz & Myers, 1998; Silva & Martins, 2017).

This data allowed us to conclude that, in the case of Worten in 2012, Zippy in 2018 and *Missão Continente* in 2018, the CrM campaigns were associated with specific offerings which were deliberately developed for these initiatives. Regarding Worten's 2014 and 2017 campaigns, the brand decided not to create a product, as the "product" was represented by a "barcode". In terms of product classification, the products promoted in the three campaigns fit in the utilitarian category, as these are products related to satisfying functional needs. However, prior studies suggest that CrM campaigns tend to be more successful when the product promoted is of a hedonic nature (Strahilevitz & Myers, 1998; Silva & Martins, 2017). Since none of the campaigns analysed was attached to hedonic products, further research is required to draw conclusions regarding the effectiveness of the different type of products promoted in CrM campaigns.

In the interviews, we asked brand managers about the campaign's donation structure, as this might also affect the success of CrM (see Table 8.3). Regarding the campaigns of Worten in 2012, Zippy in 2018 and *Missão Continente* in 2018, the company donation to the cause occurred when the product associated with the campaign was purchased by the consumer. Regarding Worten's 2014 and 2017 campaigns, the donation to the cause was not contingent upon the purchasing of a product.

Table 8.2   Product promoted

	Question ID	Worten & CVP (2012)	Zippy & "Make-a-Wish" (2018)	*Missão Continente* (2018)
Product	f)	Gift Box	Pair of Gloves	Mug
Motives for developing a specific product for the campaign	e1)	"The intention was to increase customer support, by promoting a product, Gift box, allied to the holiday season, were the product tends to be useful"	"To increase the perception of the emotional attributes that the product incorporates, as well as benefit from the consumption season (Christmas) which is focused on articles with a symbolic and emotional character"	"The creation of a specific product, it's important for the product to stand out and people associate it specifically with the campaign"

Table 8.3   Donation structure

	Question ID	Worten & CVP (2012)	Worten & *"Terra dos Sonhos"* (2014)	Worten & CVP (2017)	Zippy & "Make-a-Wish" (2018)	*Missão Continente* (2018)
Type of Donation	e)	Fixed Donation	Variable Donation	Variable Donation	Fixed Donation	Fixed Donation
Donation Structure	Sec. Data	Purchase-trigger donation	Check-out charity	Check-out charity	Purchase-trigger donation	Purchase-trigger donation
Product Price	j)	€1	"Act of donation"	"Act of donation"	€9.99	€3
Amount Donated	j)	€0.80	Minimum value of the donation €0.20 or multiples of €0.20	Minimum value of the donation €0.20 or multiples of €0.20	€1	€1

Our findings demonstrate that in all the campaigns carried by Worten, Zippy and *Missão Continente*, the brands chose to embrace transactional CrM, since they engaged the consumer in the campaign through commercial trade (purchase) or donation. In our case study, we can identify two different forms of transactional CrM campaigns. First, we have the "purchase-triggered donation" (Stole, 2006), illustrated by the cases of Worten 2012, Zippy

2018 and *Missão Continente* 2018, in which the company's donation to the cause is contingent on the consumer purchasing the item promoted in the CrM campaigns. Second, we also identify cases in which a "check-out charity" approach was followed (Kinard & Pardo, 2017). There are two campaigns, Worten 2014 and Worten 2017, which represent this form of transactional CrM. In these two campaigns, the company supports consumers' donations to a social cause, by encouraging consumers to donate an amount during the payment process.

In terms of the communication strategy, since our sample is composed of brands that are part of the same company, we expected that the pattern of communication would be similar across all the campaigns. In the interviews, we asked specific questions related to the communication strategy adopted (see Table 8.4), to identify the different approaches followed and understand the influence of that communication method in the success of the CrM campaigns analysed. Regarding the communication programme, in the five campaigns analysed, there were two distinct communication moments, namely before/during the implementation of the CrM campaign, and after it.

Table 8.4   Communication strategy

	Question ID	Worten & CVP (2012)	Worten & "*Terra dos Sonhos*" (2014)	Worten & CVP (2017)	Zippy & "Make-a-Wish" (2018)	*Missão Continente* (2018)
Media Coverage	g) & h)	Television; Radio; Written press	Television; Radio	Television; Radio	Radio; Event presentation	Television; Radio
Other Coverage	g) & h)	Outdoors; Social networks; Online store; Points of sale	Outdoors; Social networks; Online store; Points of sale	Outdoors; Social networks; Online store; Points of sale	Outdoors; Social networks; Online store; Points of sale; Newsletter to consumer data base	Outdoors; Social networks; Online store; Points of sale
Communication Strategy – During the Campaign	h1)	Communication in store; Media propagation of CRM message	Communication in store; Media propagation of CRM message	Communication in store; Media propagation of CRM message	Communication in store; Media propagation of CRM message	Communication in store; Media propagation of CRM message
Communication Strategy – After the campaign	h1)	Public disclosure of campaign results	Public disclosure of campaign results (through the media partner SIC); POS and Written Press	Public disclosure of campaign results (through the media partner SIC); POS and Written Press	Public disclosure of campaign results (Zippy social network)	Public disclosure of campaign results (value raised and winning institutions)

All the campaigns had extensive media coverage before and during the campaign, mainly through television and radio. However, in some of the campaigns studied, the brands involved other media partners. This was the case for Worten's 2014 CrM campaign, as the brand partnered with several media partners (e.g., Grupo Impresa – owner of well-known magazines and newspapers, such as *Visão* and *Expresso*), and for Zippy's CrM campaign, which involved the organisation of an event for the presentation of the campaign to a selected group of media and influencers. Besides these partnerships, the brands actively promoted the campaigns through outdoor advertising', social networking services (e.g., the brands' pages on Facebook), online stores, newsletters and point-of-purchase communication. In stores, the sales staff were responsible for informing consumers by means of a short briefing of the campaign's objectives.

When the campaigns were concluded, the brands actively communicated their outcomes and the amounts raised to their target audiences, using their media partners, but also through outdoor advertising, point-of-purchase communication and press releases on the brands' websites. In this respect, we should highlight the case of Worten's 2014 and 2017 campaigns, where the brand used a live interview on a famous television show (namely, "Querida Julia") to communicate the results achieved by the campaign.

In the interviews, we also asked the brand managers details about the campaign's duration (see Table 8.5). According to the information provided, the brands followed a short-term strategy, except for Missão Continente 2018, a CrM campaign that lasted for three months (nevertheless, this can still be considered short-term). However, in the case of this campaign, the first month was used to set up an application and to conduct a poll of consumers to select the institution that should receive the funds gathered through the campaign.

Regarding the geographic area, all the campaigns analysed were carried in Continental Portugal. The causes supported can be identified as foundations or organisations which target the Portuguese population.

Table 8.5   *Campaign duration*

		Worten & CVP (2012)	Worten & "*Terra dos Sonhos*" (2014)	Worten & CVP (2017)	Zippy & "Make-a-Wish" (2018)	*Missão Continente* (2018)
	Question ID					
Time Frame	d)	16/11/2012 – 6/01/2013	15/11/2013 – 6/01/2014	16/11/2017 – 6/01/2018	5/12/2018 – 12/02/2019	11/2018 – 02/2019
Duration	d)	2 months	2 months	2 months	2 months	3 months

Considering the importance of the alignment between the brand, the cause's target market and the overall campaign in terms of cause-related bundle, in the interviews, we asked questions regarding the consistency between the brand, the brand's target market and the cause supported (see Table 8.6). Additionally, we asked the brand managers to rate the relation between the brand's target consumers and the cause on a scale of 1 to 5 (where 1 is not at all related and 5 is completely related).

The congruence between the three key elements – consumer, cause and brand – is critical, because the more connected the consumer feels to the campaign, the higher the likelihood that he/she will engage in the campaign. Thus, it is fundamental that the company identifies causes and problems that are relevant to the brand's target consumers (Grau & Folse, 2007; Guerreiro et al., 2015). Moreover, Steffen & Günther (2013) pointed out that consumers' willingness to participate in CrM campaigns increases with their proximity and involvement with the cause.

Considering the importance of the alignment between these three elements, we can conclude that, in the campaigns conducted by Worten, Zippy and *Missão Continente*, the brands chose to support social causes that were relevant to their target consumers. Worten's target market is quite wide since it encompasses all Portuguese consumers or potential purchasers of household appliances. In terms of social causes, we can distinguish three situations where Worten strove to establish a connection between the brand's target market and the issues relevant to the community. In 2012, Worten supported the Portuguese Red Cross, through a project that aimed to help families in need to fight poverty and social exclusion, during the time of a severe global crisis that had a very negative impact on the Portuguese population. The choice of this project as the target of the CrM campaign demonstrates the brand's desire to find relevant social problems in the community in which the brand operates, as well as to address problems that all consumers are aware of and actively involved with.

Table 8.6   Brand-cause-consumer alignment

	Question ID	Worten & CVP (2012)	Worten & "*Terra dos Sonhos*" (2014)	Worten & CVP (2017)	Zippy & "Make-a-Wish" (2018)	*Missão Continente* (2018)
Cause supported	a)	*Cruz Vermelha Portugal*	*Association Terra dos Sonhos*	*Cruz Vermelha Portugal*	Make-a-Wish Foundation	Undefined
Criteria to support the chosen cause in the CrM campaign	a1)	Choice of an institution that was easily recognised by the Portuguese and with evidence of ground work.	Institution suggested by the advertising agency – whose goal is the realisation of the dreams of critically ill children. The choice lies in the ability to help an association whose main mission is to materialise dreams.	Due to the severity of the events of the summer of 2017. It seemed a more natural and pressing issue to support in partnership with CVP as an intermediary.	Similarity between the cause and the target audience and the brand's mission (ZIPPY).	Trends and areas with social impact, namely the food theme in the areas of healthy eating, food waste and social inclusion.
Target of the campaign	c)	All Portuguese without exception.	All Portuguese without exception.	All Portuguese without exception.	Adults who deal with children up to 9 years old and adults without children.	All Portuguese without exception.
Brand-Cause-Consumer Alignment – level of alignment in the managers opinion	c2)	5 – Completely related	5 – Completely related	5 – Completely related	5 – Completely related	5 – Completely related

Regarding Worten's 2014 campaign, the brand chose to support "Land of Dreams", an institution that operates in Portugal and aims to accomplish the dreams of ill children. Even though the target market of the cause is confined to children with severe illness, which is not as comprehensive a target as that of the causes supported in previous years, the cause linked to this CrM campaign is still of great relevance for the general public, especially for those people whose families have faced illness. We can conclude that this cause can be considered to be less aligned with the brand's target market, but does demonstrate the brand's efforts to raise awareness of a relevant social issue. In 2017, Worten engaged again in a partnership with the Portuguese Red Cross, with the aim of raising as much funding as possible for the Portuguese population affected by the destruction that resulted from the fires that plagued Portugal in that year. The goal of this campaign was to contribute to the rebuilding of infrastructure and to minimise the serious damage resulting from the fires. Thus, the company addressed a cause that was especially relevant to Portuguese people, which demonstrates the company's desire to support issues that are pertinent to its community. Therefore, we can conclude that by choosing these causes, the brand tried to approach those segments of society which required more help, or to contribute towards improving the well-being of relevant groups in society, and embraced causes that were very relevant for most of its target consumers.

Regarding Zippy's 2018 campaign, even though the brand's end users are children, the adults are the buyers and they are part of the brand's target market – specifically, adults who deal with children up to 9 years of age. In 2018, the brand partnered with the "Make-a-Wish" Foundation, a social organisation whose mission is to make children's dreams materialise. Hence, we may conclude there is a significant consistency between the consumer, the cause and the brand. Moreover, this CrM campaign demonstrates the brand's concern to support a social cause that is relevant to its target consumers. Consequently, the brand was able to develop an appropriate cause-related bundle (Guerreiro et al., 2015).

In its 2018 campaign, *Missão Continente* chose to support a social cause themed around food – namely healthy food, food waste and social inclusion. These themes have become increasingly relevant to the community over recent years. Continente targets the whole Portuguese market of retail consumers. Since one of the brand's core businesses is the food trade, we can conclude that there is a high congruence between the topics promoted and the general message conveyed by this CrM campaign, the brand's positioning and the brand's target market. Furthermore, this CrM campaign highlighted the brand's concern with supporting relevant and up-to-date issues.

In the interviews, we questioned the brand managers about the campaign's main objectives and about its general performance in terms of financial and image measures, as these are relevant evaluation metrics of the success of a CrM campaign (see Table 8.7). The questions relating to the company's performance were divided into two sets, since our intention was to obtain quantitative and qualitative data to support the answers. Unfortunately, regarding quantitative data, no information was disclosed, and for that reason we will use the qualitative and quantitative secondary data to support our analyses.

In the context of CrM, purchase intention can be understood as the consumer's choice and intention to buy and participate in CrM campaigns (Bui, 2017), which can be influenced by a number of factors, considered as moderating factors. Regarding purchase intention, Worten's 2012 campaign objective was not to boost sales but rather to engage Portuguese consumers with the causes through altruistic behaviour, and to raise the highest possible amount for the causes. The campaigns analysed were conducted during the Christmas season, which is a season of high consumption, thus consumers' willingness to be involved in this type of initiative is also amplified. In Worten's 2012 campaign, the brand was able to collect a total of €175,000 for the cause, which indicates a high level of consumer purchase intention. In terms of the amount raised by the campaigns, we were able to compare the campaigns of Worten in 2014 and 2017 (both were part of the project *"Código DáVinte"* which was launched in 2014). Through the data gathered, we can observe an increase in the amounts collected in 2017 as compared with 2014, which can be explained by an increase in consumers' awareness of the brand's project, and also by the fact that the campaign was supported by an effective communication strategy.

In terms of consumer purchase intention of the brand's products in general, the manager of Zippy's 2018 campaign stated that during the campaign there was no significant change in the brand's sales volume. Thus, we can assume that the campaign probably did not have any relevant influence on consumers' buying intention. However, in terms of consumer engagement with the campaign, the objectives were met, since according to the secondary data collected, all items placed on sale (6000 pair of gloves) were sold.

Table 8.7   *Campaign's objectives and performance*

	Question ID	Worten & CVP (2012)	Worten & "*Terra dos Sonhos*" (2014)	Worten & CVP (2017)	Zippy & "Make-a-Wish" (2018)	*Missão Continente* (2018)
Objectives of the Campaign	b)	To support a project that had an impact on the Portuguese society at a time when Portugal faced a generalised period of crisis. Involve the Portuguese and the sales teams in a meritorious cause. Position Worten as a brand that is jointly responsible and with an active role in society.	To raise the highest possible value for the institution. Involve the Portuguese and the sales teams in a meritorious cause. The campaign allowed to position Worten on the axis of social responsibility and as a brand with an active role in society.	To raise the highest possible value for the institution. Involve the Portuguese and the sales teams in a meritorious cause. The campaign allowed to position Worten on the axis of social responsibility and as a brand with an active role in society.	Reinforce the concept of togetherness – to reinforce the sense of unity between parents and children; Encourage the client to create a positive impact on society. Celebrate the Christmas spirit.	Reinforce the retailer's position as a socially responsible brand; Enhance the relevance of eating habits and food (healthy food, food waste and social inclusion); Increase consumer awareness about these topics.
Purchase Intention – Quantitative Data	k1)	Undisclosed	Undisclosed	Undisclosed	No significant changes in the brand's sales volume.	Undisclosed
Purchase Intention – Qualitative Data	k2)	Very positive impact - the objective was not to boost sales but rather to raise the highest amount of donations for the cause.	Very positive impact. The campaign allowed to position Worten in the axis of social responsibility, in a consolidated way and with a project in its own name (*Código DáVinte*).	Very positive impact. The campaign allowed to position Worten in the axis of social responsibility, in a consolidated way and with a project in its own name (*Código DáVinte*).	Positive feedback from the store teams and in the brand's digital channels, which showed a very positive response from consumers.	Considered to be very effective.
Corporate Image – Quantitative Data	l1)	Undisclosed	Undisclosed	Undisclosed	No significant changes were identified.	Undisclosed
Corporate Image – Qualitative Data	l2)	Cemented the brand's position as a leading brand and an influencer within the Portuguese society.	Positive impact in positioning Worten as a socially responsible brand.	Positive impact in positioning Worten as a socially responsible brand.	Positive impact, allowed to materialise the concept of togetherness and establish greater emotional and affective connection between the brand and the consumer.	Put Missão Continente's project at the forefront of consumers' minds, to reinforce the image of the brand as socially responsible.

	Question ID	Worten & CVP (2012)	Worten & "*Terra dos Sonhos*" (2014)	Worten & CVP (2017)	Zippy & "Make-a-Wish" (2018)	*Missão Continente* (2018)
Market Share Implications	m)	Undisclosed	Undisclosed	Undisclosed	It is not possible to directly associate the campaign with the growth in market share, and it is not expected that this would happen in a significant way.	Undisclosed
Amounts Collected	Sec. Data	€175,000	€120,000	€150,000	€6000	€240,000

Missão Continente's 2018 campaign was able to deliver €240,000 to the winning institution; this amount reveals that there was positive engagement by consumers with this CrM initiative, since 240,000 mugs were sold across Continente stores in Portugal. Regarding the image measures, in all campaigns analysed, the managers stated that one of the campaign's objectives was to position the brands as socially responsible and sustainable brands that try to effectively help the communities in which they operate. Thus, the main goal was to create a socially responsible brand image in the minds of the target consumers. Our findings show that the campaigns enhanced the position of the different brands analysed as socially responsible brands that are actively committed to their communities. Therefore, we can conclude that the objectives defined in terms of brand image were accomplished. In the case of the campaigns carried out by Worten in 2014 and 2017, besides reinforcing the brand's positioning as a socially responsible brand, this campaign raised awareness for the project "Código DáVinte".

DISCUSSION

After presenting the data gathered in the interviews, we will now discuss the main findings of this study and analyse whether the questions identified in our framework are answered.

Considering the results of two of the brands analysed, and their campaigns, Zippy and *Missão Continente*, we can provide positive answers to three of the four questions identified in our research model. Indeed, findings indicate that: brand-cause fit has a significant impact on the campaign's success (Q1), brand-cause fit will favourably influence consumers' purchase intention (Q2) and, in turn, purchase intention will have a positive effect on the success of the campaign (Q3).

In the case of Zippy, there is a high brand-cause fit, as the brand's core business is children's clothes and the brand image is strongly related to children, as well as the target and image of the cause supported. The intention of this CrM campaign, as previously explained, was to fulfil the dreams of critically ill children. Hence, there is a strong relationship between the brand's image and the image of the cause supported. Indeed, the high brand-cause-consumer fit was a fundamental criteria for the choice of the cause, as the brand manager highlights when she says that "the similarity between the cause and the target audience and the brand's mission" was a key concern (Regina Guerner, CMO Zippy).

With respect to *Missão Continente*, the brand's campaign addressed several relevant issues relating to healthy and sustainable eating habits. Hence, we can conclude that there is a high brand-cause fit, since the brand's core business is food retail, and, therefore, the brand image shares several associations with the topics supported in this CrM campaign. This conclusion is supported by the brand manager, as she points out that the decision to choose this cause was related to the fact that it concerns "trends and areas with social impact, namely the food theme in the areas of healthy eating, food waste and social inclusion" (Andreia Sousa, CMO Continente).

However, regarding Worten's campaign, we were not able reach similar conclusions. Even though the brand's target market includes the majority of the Portuguese population and the issue addressed in the three campaigns reveals the brand's concern with supporting issues that impact the community in which it operates, we cannot conclude there is a direct congruence between the brand's core business and the cause supported. Therefore, we cannot answer positively to Q1, since, even in a low brand-cause fit situation, the CrM campaigns' objectives were successfully attained. Following the same line of thought, Q2 and Q3 cannot be answered positively either, since, despite the low fit between the brand and the cause, the CrM campaign seems to have had a positive effect on consumers' purchase intentions. The brand was able to successfully engage consumers and fulfil the campaign's objectives, as consumers actively purchased the product promoted or contributed to the cause through the "act of donation".

Regarding Q4, which aims to understand whether corporate image and consumer-cause involvement moderate the influence of brand-cause fit on consumers' purchase intention, the results obtained seem to confirm the relevance of brand image as a moderating factor in this relationship, and are thus indicative of a positive answer to this question. In the case of Worten's campaigns, findings indicate that a strong and favourable brand image can contribute to a greater willingness by consumers to engage in the CrM initiatives developed by the brand, and can moderate the impact of consumers' perception of brand-cause fit. The brand presented in all its campaigns a low brand-cause fit situation. The fact that the brand was able to address issues relevant to the community – as highlighted by the manager when he said that the motive for supporting this cause was related to "the severity of the events of the summer of 2017, which seemed a more natural and pressing issue to support in partnership with the Portuguese Red Cross as an intermediary" – helped to moderate the effect of brand-cause fit on consumers' purchase intention. Thus, consumer-cause involvement positively influenced consumers' evaluation of the campaign and increased their willingness to engage in the CrM campaign in the form of purchase intention. The increase in the amounts collected by Worten in 2014 and 2017 under the project "*Código DáVinte*", allow us to support our findings regarding Q4 with respect to the moderating impact of brand image on the relationship between brand-cause fit and consumer purchase intention. In this respect, it is important to highlight that this cause is linked to a three-year project. In the brand manager's opinion, the "*Código DáVinte*" project allowed the brand "to reinforce Worten's position as a socially responsible brand and at the same time to enhance the awareness of the *DáVinte* Code project" (Alexandra Balão, CMO, Worten). Thus, we can conclude that this project resulted in an improvement in the brand's image, increasing consumers' trust in the brand. Moreover, the communication strategy employed in this project allowed Worten to create a stronger bond with its target consumers and to strengthen its position as a sustainable brand.

We can also support our findings regarding Q4 for both the *Missão Continente* and Zippy campaigns, since the decision to create a specific product for the campaign was motivated by the goal "to help the product stand out and make people associate it specifically with the campaign" (Andreia Sousa, CMO, Continente). This strategy was aimed at increasing awareness of the campaign and positively influencing consumer purchase intention.

CONCLUSION

The main contribution of this research is linked to the study of the effects of brand-cause fit in the success of CrM campaigns, considering CrM initiatives which involve consumer participation. The impact of brand-cause fit on CrM campaigns continues to raise several discussions between academics and is a relevant research topic. Pracejus and Olsen (2004), Lans et al. (2014) and Trimble and Rifon (2006) suggested that brand-cause fit is able to generate positive consumer responses to CrM initiatives, by influencing consumer motivation to engage in cause-supporting initiatives. However, our findings highlight that this is not necessarily the case. Indeed, our findings are consistent with the conclusions of Lafferty (2007) and Nan and Heo (2007), who stated that brand-cause fit does not always determine the effectiveness of CrM. The five CrM campaigns analysed in our research were considered successful, despite the fact that some of them presented a situation of high brand-cause fit (Zippy and Continente) and others of low brand-cause fit (Worten's campaigns of 2012, 2014 and 2017).

Going deeper into the analysis of the impact of brand-cause fit, Alav and Zeynali (2013) and Lans et al. (2014) concluded that CrM campaigns benefit when there is high perceived congruence between the brand and the cause in terms of brand awareness, positive attitudes towards the brand and increased brand credibility. In turn, CrM campaigns with a low brand-cause fit can result in consumer scepticism towards both the campaign and the brand, which can lead to less positive consumer responses to CrM campaigns and raise questions about the company's motivations for carrying out the campaign (Pracejus & Olsen, 2004).

Our findings suggest that even in CrM campaigns in which there is a lower brand-cause fit, successful outcomes can be achieved. In addition, our findings highlight that even though brand-cause fit has a relevant influence on consumers' evaluation of the CrM campaign, it might not be strong enough to trigger engagement in CrM initiatives. Therefore, other factors should be considered when evaluating consumer attitudes towards CrM initiatives.

The concept of consumer-cause involvement introduced by Grau and Folse (2007) can significantly influence consumer engagement behaviour in CrM campaigns, since consumers are more willing to engage in CrM campaigns that support causes that have a relevant impact on their lives and communities. This idea is in line with the conclusions of Gupta and Pirsch (2006) and Guerreiro et al. (2015), who suggested that brands should address in their CrM campaigns issues that are relevant to the brand's target audience as well as for the community in which the brand operates. These conclusions are in line with our findings, particularly in the cases of Worten's 2012, 2014 and 2017 campaigns. Worten was able to address issues that were relevant to the community at the time, and, hence stimulate a high consumer-cause involvement, which ended up significantly influencing the success of the CrM initiatives and mitigating the negative effects of a lower brand-cause fit.

Taking into account the need to address issues that matter to the brand's target market, CrM communication strategies should reflect the brand's mission, vision and core values, and the brand's target audience. Our results suggest that in all the campaigns analysed, communication was aimed at increasing consumer trust in the CrM initiatives, since the brand developed communication activities throughout the CrM campaign and after its conclusion, seeking to clearly express the campaign outcomes. Moreover, we concluded that this strategy positively influenced consumer trust in the brands' intentions, and favourably affected the image of the brands involved. For example, the increase in the amounts collected by Worten's campaigns from 2014 to 2017 can be justified by the increase in consumer awareness about the project "*Código DáVinte*" and in consumer brand trust. Thus, we may conclude that an appropriate communication strategy is essential for the success of CrM initiatives. Indeed, this will reinforce consumer trust and positively influence their perception of the brand, which will stimulate consumer engagement in the CrM initiatives, make the campaign more successful and, consequently, increase its impact in terms of sustainability.

Considering our main research question, we were not able to find evidence that brand-cause fit contributed to the success of CRM campaigns. Our findings suggest that a positive brand evaluation encourages positive consumer feelings towards the brand. Thus, it increases consumers' ability to trust in the cause supported by the brand, which will in turn influence consumer engagement in CrM campaigns. This conclusion is also applicable when there is not a high perceived fit between the brand and the cause supported. Moreover, we find that CrM campaigns that address issues that are relevant to the brand's target consumers tend to be more successful. Therefore, we conclude that this factor could moderate the impact of consumer brand-cause fit perceptions on consumers' purchase intention. In Worten's case, there is a low brand-cause fit, however the campaign was a success and the outcome was not negatively affected by the low level of fit between the brand and the cause. This suggests that the social cause supported can have an important effect on the evaluation of the CrM campaign and influence consumer participation. Findings also suggest that brands that regularly engage in CrM initiatives, by demonstrating a long-term commitment to society, stimulate positive consumer feelings towards the brand and the campaigns supported, which induces positive purchase intention in the different CrM campaigns and, thus, influences their success.

In conclusion, how does brand-cause fit influence CrM success? The success of CrM initiatives is not always directly linked to brand-cause fit. The evaluation of a CrM campaign should be measured taking into consideration several aspects and should be analysed case by case, since several moderating variables may affect the relationship between brand-cause fit and consumer responses. A high brand-cause fit can undoubtedly leverage the chances of success, however, a low brand-cause fit can also lead to success if the relevant moderating variables are present. Hence, findings are not supportive of a strong and positive relationship between brand-cause fit and the success of CrM campaigns, as we concluded that a successful CrM campaign can be achieved with both a high or low fit and that the relationship between brand-cause fit and the success of a CrM campaign is affected by several variables. When considering the development and implementation of CrM initiatives, companies should consider the effects of brand-cause fit and choose, whenever possible, causes that reveal a high congruence both with the brand and the brand target audience. Additionally, the cause or social problem supported should address issues that matter to the target consumers, to induce a higher level of consumer-cause involvement. Thus, brands should embrace causes with a national or regional geographic scope, and which have a relevant impact in terms of sustainability (social, environmental or economic) for their target consumers. Moreover, although brands should pursue a high brand-cause fit, when they have long history of CrM initiatives, they may choose relevant causes which are not perceived as highly congruent with the brand image.

Communication plays an important role in the success of CrM campaigns, with respect to consumer awareness of the campaign objectives and outcomes. A strong and well-designed communication strategy will lead to more favourable consumer behaviour, increasing the chances of success and the benefits of CrM for the brand or the corporate image in the future. Favourable corporate and brand images have been noted as positive outcomes of CrM campaigns, as companies with track records of supporting social sustainable causes are perceived as more trustworthy, which increases consumer willingness to engage in the CrM initiatives developed by these corporate or product brands. Thus, it is important that companies consider CrM initiatives as a fundamental element of their marketing strategy and consistently communicate these initiatives, so that they can build an image of a sustainable institution, which is actively engaged with relevant social, environmental or economic issues.

Like any other academic research, this study is not without limitations. The fact that the company studied did not disclose information regarding the campaign's performance was one of the main difficulties, since the impacts the campaigns we analysed had on consumer purchase intention – and their implications in terms of image and market share – were not disclosed by the managers. Thus, our analysis relies mainly on managers' subjective opinions regarding the effectiveness of each campaign. The research is based on the analysis of the responses provided by the campaign managers and of the brands' financial reports. Thus, the findings may be biased by the subjective opinions of the brand managers. However, these findings were completed with quantitative data regarding the campaigns' outcomes. Since all the campaigns chosen for this study were developed by the same company, this may also limit the relevance of the findings. Finally, given the limited sample used in this research, and its focus on one country, the results do not allow us to draw conclusions regarding consumer response to CrM initiatives, in general. These limitations could present interesting opportunities for further quantitative research that provides a deeper understanding of the relationship between brand-cause fit and consumer purchase intention in CrM initiatives, by analysing the impact of relevant moderating variables.

REFERENCES

Adkins, S. (2003). Cause-related marketing: Who cares wins. In M. J. Baker (Ed.), *The Marketing Book*, 5th Ed. Oxford: Butterworth-Heinemann, 669–693.

Alav, S., & Zeynali, S. (2013). The impact of brand/cause fit and cause's participation on consumers' purchasing intention: A case study among customers of Iranian chain stores. *Advances in Environmental Biology*, *7*(11), 3224–3233.

Barone, M. J., Norman, A. T., & Miyazaki, A. D. (2007). Consumer response to retailer use of cause-related marketing: Is more fit better? *Journal of Retailing*, *83*(4), 437–445.

Bouten, L., Snelders, D., & Hultink, E. 2011. The impact of fit measures on the consumer evaluation of new co-branded products. *Journal of Product Innovation Management*, *28*, 455–469.

Broniarczyk, S., & Alba, J. M. (1994). The importance of the brand in the brand extension. *Journal of Marketing Research*, *31*(5), 214–228.

Bui, T. (2017). *The effect of brand-cause fit on consumers' responses to cause-related marketing: A study on young Vietnamese consumers*. Master Dissertation. Aalto University School of Business, Finland.

Choi, J., Chang, Y. K., Jessica Li, Y., & Jang, M. G. (2016). Doing good in another neighborhood: Attributions of CSR motives depend on corporate nationality and cultural orientation. *Journal of International Marketing*, *24*(4), 82–102.

Christofi, M., Leonidou, E., Vrontis, D., Kitchen, P. & Papasolomou, I. (2015). Innovation and cause-related marketing success: A conceptual framework and propositions. *Journal of Services Marketing, 29*(5), 354–366.

Devinney, T. M. (2009). Is the socially responsible corporation a myth? The good, the bad, and the ugly of corporate social responsibility. *Academy of Management Perspectives, 23*(2), 44–56.

Fereira, A. & Ribeiro, I. (2017). Are you willing to pay the price? The impact of corporate social (ir) responsibility on consumer behavior towards national and foreign brands. *Journal of Consumer Behaviour, 16*, 63–71.

Grau, S., & Folse, J. (2007). Cause-related marketing (CRM): The influence of donation proximity and message-framing cues on the less-involved consumer. *Journal of Advertising, 36*(4), 19–33.

Grolleau, G., Ibanez, L., & Lavoie, N. (2016). Cause-related marketing of products with a negative externality. *Journal of Business Research, 69*(10), 4321–4330.

Guerreiro, J., Rita, P., & Trigueiros, D. (2015). Attention, emotions and cause-related marketing effectiveness. *European Journal of Marketing, 49*(11/12), 1728–1750.

Gupta, S. (2015). To pay or not to pay a price premium for corporate social responsibility: A social dilemma and reference group theory perspective. *Academy of Marketing Studies Journal, 19*(1), 24.

Gupta, S., & Pirsch, J. (2006). The company-cause-customer fit decision in cause-related marketing. *Journal of Consumer Marketing, 23*(6), 314–326.

Gwinner, K., & Bennett, G. (2008). The impact of brand cohesiveness and sport identification on brand fit in a sponsorship context. *Journal of Sport Management, 22*(4), 410–426.

Hassan, S. O., & Abouaish, E. M. (2018). The impact of strategic vs. tactical cause-related marketing on switching intention. *International Review on Public and Nonprofit Marketing, 15*(3), 253–314.

Iglesias, O., Markovic, S., Bagherzadeh, M., & Singh, J. J. (2018). Co-creation: A key link between corporate social responsibility, customer trust, and customer loyalty. *Journal of Business Ethics, 163*(1), 1–16.

Kim, H., & John, D. R. (2008). Consumer response to brand extensions: Construal level as moderator of the importance of perceived fit. *Journal of Consumer Psychology, 20*, 1–11.

Kim, K., Cheong, Y., & Lim, J. S. (2015). Choosing the right message for the right cause in social cause advertising: Type of social cause message, perceived company–cause fit and the persuasiveness of communication. *International Journal of Advertising, 34*(3), 473–494.

Kinard, B. R., & Pardo, M. L., (2017). Cause-related marketing: The effect of checkout charity requests on consumer donation behavior. *Atlantic Marketing Journal, 6*(2), 77–91.

Komornicki, S., & Komornicki, S. (2017). *2017 Cone Communications CSR Study*. Retrieved from http://www.conecomm.com/research-blog/2017-csr-study

Kotler, P., & Lee, N. (2005). *Corporate Social Responsibility: Doing the Most Good for Your Company and Your Cause*. USA: Wiley.

Lafferty, B. A. (2007). The relevance of fit in a cause-brand alliance when consumers evaluate corporate credibility. *Journal of Business Research, 60*(5), 447–453.

Lans, R., Bergh, B., & Dieleman, E. (2014). Partner selection in brand alliances: An empirical investigation of the drivers of brand fit. *Marketing Science, 33*(4), 551–566.

Laroche, S. (2017). *Cause-related marketing in five unique cultures*. Master Dissertation. Texas Christian University, USA.

Lerro, M., Vecchio, R., Caracciolo, F., Pascucci, S., & Cembalo, L. (2018). Consumers' heterogeneous preferences for corporate social responsibility in the food industry. *Corporate Social Responsibility and Environmental Management, 25*(6), 1050–1061

Margolis, J. & Walsh, J. (2003). Misery loves companies: Rethinking social initiatives by business. *Administrative Science Quarterly, 48*(2), 268–305.

Markovic, S., Iglesias, O., Singh, J. J., & Sierra, V. (2018). How does the perceived ethicality of corporate services brands influence loyalty and positive word-of-mouth? Analyzing the roles of empathy, affective commitment, and perceived quality. *Journal of Business Ethics, 148*(4), 721–740.

Melero, I., & Montaner, T. (2016). Cause-related marketing: An experimental study about how the product type and the perceived fit may influence the consumer response. *European Journal of Management and Business Economics, 25*(3), 161–167.

Mohr, L. A., Webb, D. J., & Harris, K. E. (2001). Do consumers expect companies to be socially responsible? The impact of corporate social responsibility on buying behavior. *Journal of Consumer Affairs*, *35*(1), 45–72.

Nan, X., & Heo, K. (2007). Consumer responses to Corporate Social Responsibility (CSR) initiatives: examining the role of brand-cause fit in cause-related marketing. *Journal of Advertising*, *36*(2), 63–74.

Pracejus, J. W., & Olsen, G. D. (2004). The role of brand/cause fit in the effectiveness of cause-related marketing campaigns. *Journal of Business Research*, *57*(6), 635–640.

Silva, S. C., & Martins, C. C. (2017). The relevance of cause-related marketing to post-purchase guilt alleviation. *International Review on Public and Nonprofit Marketing*, *14*(4), 475–494.

Simonin, B. L., & Ruth, J. A. (1998). Is a company known by the company it keeps? Assessing the spillover effects of brands alliances on consumer brand attitudes. *Journal of Marketing Research*, *35*(1), 30–42.

Strahilevitz, M., & Myers, J. G. (1998). Donations to charity as purchase incentives: How well they work may depend on what you are trying to sell. *Journal of Consumer Research*, *24*(4), 434–446.

Steffen, A. & Günther, S. (2013). Success factors of cause-related marketing – What developing countries can learn from a German sweets campaign. *The MENA Journal of Business Case Studies*, *13*, 1–15.

Stole I. (2006). *Cause-Related Marketing: Why Social Change and Corporate Profits Don't Mix*. Center for Media and Democracy. Retrieved from http://www.prwatch.org/node/4965

Trimble, C., & Holmes, G. (2013). New thinking on antecedents to successful CRM campaigns: Consumer acceptance of an alliance. *Journal of Promotion Management*, *19*(3), 352–372.

Trimble, C. S., & Rifon, N. J. (2006). Consumer perceptions of compatibility in cause-related marketing messages. *International Journal of Nonprofit and Voluntary Sector Marketing*, *11*(1), 472–484.

Varadarajan, P. R., & Menon, A. (1988). Cause-related marketing: A coalignment of marketing strategy and corporate philanthropy. *Journal of Marketing*, *52*(2), 61–73.

Zasuwa, G. (2017). The role of company-cause fit and company involvement in consumer responses to CSR initiatives: A meta-analytic review. *Sustainability*, *9*(6), 1–16.

Zeynali, S., & Golkar, H. (2013). The impact of cause importance and gender on consumers' purchasing intention in cause-related marketing: A case study among customers of Iranian chain stores. *Journal of Contemporary Research in Business*, *2*(2), 299–308.

PART 3

SUSTAINABILITY-DRIVEN BUSINESS STRATEGIES IN INNOVATION AND ENTREPRENEURSHIP

9. Business model innovation for sustainability: the intersections among business models, innovation, and sustainability

Stefan Markovic and Karin Tollin

INTRODUCTION

Sustainable development is an increasingly prevalent orientation in business that presupposes an integration of decision levels and processes within firms, as well as between firms and their external stakeholders (e.g., Bansal, 2005; Breuer & Lüdeke-Freund, 2017; Engert & Baumgartner, 2016; Iglesias et al., 2020; Markovic & Bagherzadeh, 2018; Schaltegger et al., 2016). A related proposition is that the business model (BM) concept enables integration, through its emphasis on co-creation across decision levels and processes within a firm's boundaries, while also recognizing the dynamic nature of businesses and interactions with external stakeholders (Berends et al., 2016; Priem et al., 2018; Spieth et al., 2016). However, some scholars have pointed at 'white fields' in literature dealing with BM, whether in isolation or in relation to innovation and/or sustainability (Dentchev et al., 2018; Foss & Saebi, 2017; Grewatsch & Kleindienst, 2017; van Bommel, 2018).

In line with these claims, this chapter aims to uncover what is known and not known about the role of the BM concept in relation to firms' innovation and sustainability endeavors. Specifically, we intend to provide an overview of the fields of BM, business model innovation (BMI), and business model innovation for sustainability (BMIfS), and to delineate issues that require further attention. To provide such an overview, we conducted a literature review of 175 articles published during the last decade in renowned journals, such as *Academy of Management Annals*, *Journal of Business Ethics*, *Journal of Management*, *Long Range Planning*, and *Strategic Management Journal*. We searched for the articles on the Business Source Complete and Scopus databases and used a set of queries (i.e., what, why, and how) to categorize the contents of the identified articles. These queries structure the presentation of our review findings.

BUSINESS MODEL

A central thesis inherent in existing definitions of the BM concept is that firms are to be understood as systems of various elements (e.g., strategies, structures, processes) that have a basis in different domains (e.g., management, marketing, finance), which in turn consist of more or less stable configurations of activities and practices (Leischnig et al., 2017; Massa & Tucci, 2014). While prior literature offers a range of approaches to capture these myriad components, any one approach is unlikely to be sufficient to capture the meaning and usefulness of the entire BM concept. Therefore, it is important to recognize the coexistence of various approaches to and, implicitly, interpretations of the BM concept (Berends et al., 2016).

What is a BM?

According to the extensive reviews conducted by Gassmann et al. (2016) and Massa and Tucci (2014), BM approaches differ in their level of abstraction. At the highest level, BMs are cognitive structures "that organize managerial understandings about the design of activities and exchanges that reflect the critical interdependencies and value creation relations in their firms' exchange networks" (Martins et al., 2015, p. 105). Thus, with the cognitive approach, a BM represents the underlying narrative or logic of an existing or envisioned way of doing business (Laasch, 2018). At the lowest level of abstraction, with an activity school approach, a BM delineates the nature and contribution of all activities enacted by a firm and its partners. A core topic from this view is the choice of one or more unifying and connecting themes, such as lock-in, complementarities, efficiency (Zott & Amit, 2010), and value co-creation (Storbacka et al., 2012).

Zott et al. (2011) identify some emergent and promising themes based on a rigorous review of BM definitions (see Table 9.1). Saebi and Foss (2015) also provide a definition that captures the defining qualities of previously recognized suggestions (see Table 9.1). Finally, a variety of other approaches range between the cognitive and activity school approaches, including the recombination school approach (Gassmann et al., 2016). In this version, a BM entails several key components and answers the following questions: customer (who is your target customer?); value proposition (VP) (what do you offer to the customer?); value chain (how is the VP created?); and profit mechanism (how is revenue created?) (Gassmann et al., 2016, p. 20).

Why Implement a BM?

A widespread view suggests that a BM represents a bridge between spheres of important, inter-related firm dimensions (Casadesus-Masanell & Heilbron, 2015; Inigo et al., 2017; Priem et al., 2018). It aligns upstream factor markets with downstream product markets and consumers (Breuer & Lüdeke-Freund, 2017; Demil et al., 2015; Gassmann et al., 2016; Priem et al., 2018; Teece, 2010). Due to this bridging capability, the BM concept arguably provides a useful tool for integrating important strategic issues and elements, such as customer segments, capabilities, and resources (Baden-Fuller & Morgan, 2010; Chesbrough & Rosenbloom, 2002; Demil et al., 2015). According to existing frameworks, this capability comes from the centrality of one particular dimension of BM, namely, the VP. Payne et al. (2017, p. 472) provide a working definition of a VP as "a strategic tool facilitating communication of an organization's ability to share resources and offer a superior value package to targeted customers."

How to Implement a BM?

A common suggestion when dealing with the application of the BM concept is to refer to a visual framework, template, or canvas (see Breuer & Lüdeke-Freund, 2017, in Table 9.1). The number of elements and the terminology used (e.g., dimensions, building blocks, components) in different visual BM frameworks vary. A common visual framework is the BM canvas by Osterwalder and Pigneur (2010), or O&P canvas. Due to interest among scholars and consultants, the O&P canvas has often been applied as a key innovation tool. Täuscher & Abdelkafi (2017) identify more than 30 versions of the O&P canvas that differ mainly in their graphical design. Despite its popularity though, other, more complex frameworks also are available, such as the BM canvas by Breuer & Lüdeke-Freund (2017). Their canvas includes normative values as foundational premises for stakeholders' values and firm–customer touch-points. However, there remain limited empirical insights regarding the application of BM in strategy processes and their relationship to a firm's performance (e.g., Täuscher, 2018). A related issue that needs further attention pertains to the prerequisites for adopting the BM concept in strategy processes. Does a BM call for a particular structure or mode of doing strategy work, or else for a set of capabilities to pursue particular strategic initiatives?

BUSINESS MODEL INNOVATION

BMI entails a strategic process oriented toward innovating a system of associated BM components (e.g., Baldassarre et al., 2017). Specifically, BMI represents a strategic 'entity' in the minds of managers (Laasch, 2018; Martins et al., 2015; Nyström & Mustonen, 2017) or a tangible device, in the form of a graphical or linguistic representation of a configuration of activities or set of BM components (Breuer & Lüdeke-Freund, 2017; Clauss, 2017; Zott et al., 2011). However, the relationship between strategy and BMI, with regard to its nature and mutual dependencies and antecedents, has not been given sufficient attention in BMI literature (Ammar & Chereau, 2018; Cortimiglia et al., 2016; Nyström & Mustonen, 2017; Spieth et al., 2016).

What is BMI?

A common perspective is that BMI is a key issue for top managers, aimed at generating 'non-trivial' innovations. One way to determine what is 'non-trivial' is to follow typologies of innovations. For example, Foss and Saebi (2017) present a typology with two dimensions: scope and novelty. The combination of these dimensions results in four types of BMI: evolutionary, adaptive, focused, and complex (Foss & Saebi, 2017). The first two types represent changes that have a bearing on the particular firm's BM, whereas the last two represent the kind of business renewal initiatives that Hamel (1998) refers to as 'strategy innovations.' These types of BMI have potential not only to create new value for end users but also to outmaneuver competitors and bring diverse advantages to the involved stakeholders. Another way to settle what is 'non-trivial' is to turn the VP into the core subject of BMI (see Baldassarre et al., 2017, and Sorescu, 2017, in Table 9.2), such that innovations are 'non-trivial' if they have a bearing on or an association with the VP. Finally, some studies suggest moving beyond the question of what is 'non-trivial' and emphasizing the systemic nature of BMI. Following this theme, as presented by Clauss (2017), BMI implies a dedication (i.e., regular, constant, and consistent) to innovation activities (incremental or radical), across and within the components of a BM.

Why Implement BMI?

Some scholars have proposed that BMI can help ensure that a 'customer-centric' and a 'holistic view' govern innovation (see Ammar & Chereau, 2018, and Demil et al., 2015, in Table 9.2).

Table 9.1   *Queries about BM*

What is a BM?	"Notably, (1) there is widespread acknowledgement—implicit and explicit—that the business model is a new unit of analysis that is distinct from the product, firm, industry, or network; it is centered on a focal firm, but its boundaries are wider than those of the firm." (Zott et al., 2011, p. 1020)
	"In line with recent literature, we define business models as the content, structure, and governance of transactions within the company and between the company and its external partners that support the company in the creation, delivery and capture of value." (Saebi & Foss, 2015, p. 204)
	"A business model describes the design or architecture of the value creation, delivery and capture mechanisms employed. The essence of a business model is that it crystallizes customer needs and ability to pay, defines the manner by which the business enterprise responds to and delivers value to customers, entices customers to pay for value, and converts those payments to profit through the proper design and operation of the various elements of the value chain." (Teece, 2010, p. 191)
	"We argue that a BM cannot be reduced to either organizational actions or cognitive representations but should be understood as a duality. Moreover, the duality of these two dimensions makes BMs inherently dynamic and generative." (Berends et al., 2016, p. 197).
	"A business model can be viewed as a template of how a firm conducts business, how it delivers value to stakeholders (e.g., the focal firms, customers, partners, etc.), and how it links factor and product markets. The activity systems perspective addresses all these vital issues, and gives managers and academics a language and a conceptual toolbox to address them and engage in insightful dialogue and creative design." (Zott & Amit, 2010, p. 222).
Why implement a BM?	"Business models are not recipes or scientific models or scale and role models, but can play any – or all – of these different roles for different firms and for different purposes: and will often play multiple roles at the same time." (Baden-Fuller & Morgan, 2010, p. 168).
	"Every new product development effort should be coupled with the development of a business model which defines its 'go to market' and 'capturing value' strategies. Clearly technological innovation by itself does not automatically guarantee business or economic success – far from it." (Teece, 2010, p. 183)
	"…because the business model concept extends beyond firm boundaries by looking both upstream toward factor markets and downstream toward product markets and consumers, it can become an important 'bridging concept' (Floyd et al., 2011) that links resource-side and demand-side strategy research, thereby contributing to a more holistic understanding of strategy-making." (Priem et al., 2018, p. 23)
How to implement a BM?	"Deliberate business modelling and innovation requires a well-structured frame of reference, i.e. a framework, verbal definition, graphical diagram, or formalized ontology. Such framing helps to explore answers to fundamental questions as: What is our business rationale? With and for whom are we creating value? And, How can we improve our current business activities?" (Breuer & Lüdeke-Freund, 2017, p. 126)
	"Business models should be designed, developed, and realized in relationships between a business and its stakeholders. A theory-based stakeholder value creation framework therefore needs to analyze relationships as a theoretical foundation for the involvement of different stakeholders in business models. A further central element to the framework is a joint purpose behind which stakeholders engage in the business model." (Freudenrich et al., 2019, p. 6)

Other scholars suggest that BMI can encourage an evolutionary and dynamic view of firms and their BM, as well as their capability to transform markets and societies (Achtenhagen et al., 2013; Schaltegger et al., 2016; Wirtz et al., 2016). In addition, firms implement BMI in response to changes in economic, environmental, or social conditions, such as a demand from customers and other stakeholders to reduce environmental impacts and improve social welfare (Schaltegger et al., 2016). However, according to our and other reviews, limited empirical research deals with the firm-level antecedents of BMI (Bashir & Verma, 2019; Foss & Saebi, 2018). In this regard, the review by Bashir and Verma (2019) of about 200 articles shows that some antecedents 'stand out' (see Table 9.2). Yet it is still difficult to propose the nature and role of each antecedent in explaining the inclination of firms to enact BMI. For example, what is the nature and role of values or behavioral orientations in enabling and implementing BMI? Finally, although a key reason to implement a BMI might be to enhance financial performance, the association between a BMI and a firm's financial performance still lacks empirical insights, due to the manifold factors involved (Foss & Saebi, 2017).

How to Implement BMI?

A prerequisite for implementing BMI that has been in the spotlight during the past decade, concerns 'customer insight' (see Karimi & Walter, 2016, and Teece, 2018, in Table 9.2), and specifically capabilities to collaborate, detect, absorb, and infuse various types of insights into BMI processes (Da Cunha Bezerra et al., 2020; Day & Schoemaker, 2020; Teece, 2018). However, literature offering concrete empirical insights into how to implement a BMI remains scarce (Ebel et al., 2016; Geissdoerfer et al., 2018; Wirtz & Daiser, 2018). This is unexpected, considering that several linguistic and graphical representations and classifications of BM frameworks and patterns have been suggested as enabling resources that can support the implementation of BMI (Breuer & Lüdeke-Freund, 2017; Chesbrough, 2010; Gassmann et al., 2014; Remane et al., 2017). However, this may be due to the fact that there are different understandings of BMI, leading to different BMI processes (Wirtz & Daiser, 2018).

BUSINESS MODEL INNOVATION FOR SUSTAINABILITY

As Dentchev et al. (2018, p. 700) state, "the extension of the business model conceptualization to the field of sustainable business models […] remains in its early stages of development." Meuer et al. (2020, p. 321) note that, despite a high production of articles dealing with corporate sustainability (CS), "the concept of corporate sustainability remains vague." Meuer et al. (2020) detect different levels of ambition (e.g., seek, demonstrate, achieve) and integration (i.e., low, medium, high) required to implement CS. In addition, they identify differences in the scope of CS. Their analysis discloses that only five of 33 definitions of CS include all four dimensions (i.e., economic, ecological, social, and intergenerational), following the definition of sustainable development in the Brundtland doctrine (World Commission on Environmental Development [WCED], 1987). The majority of definitions (22) include social and ecological dimensions but do not provide further elaboration or specification about the meaning or contents of these dimensions (Meuer et al., 2020). The findings by Meuer et al. (2020) thus correspond, in part, with our analysis of literature dealing with BMIfS. We provide a selection of definitions in Table 9.2.

In contrast with definitions that express a narrow scope, some definitions emphasize three or all four dimensions (e.g., Bocken et al., 2014; Schneider & Clauß, 2020). We also find definitions that do not mention any dimensions but instead accentuate a broad stakeholder perspective (Breuer & Lüdeke-Freund, 2017), sometimes in conjunction with a long-term view (Geissdoerfer et al., 2018).

Table 9.2   *Queries about BMI*

What is BMI?	"Business model innovation is about creating new value propositions, and the related value delivery and value capture systems, in order to generate superior economic value (Richardson, 2008). Business model innovation refers to both the transition from one business model to another within established companies (e.g. after mergers and acquisitions), and the creation of entirely new business models in new ventures (e.g. Chesbrough, 2007; Giesen et al., 2007; Mitchell and Bruckner Coles, 2004; Osterwalder et al., 2015)." (Baldassarre et al., 2017, pp. 176–177)
	"We define a BMI as 'designed, novel, and nontrivial changes to the key elements of a firm's BM and/or the architecture linking these elements.' Ultimately, BMIs will require top-management action—hence, the requirement that BMI be designed. We impose the requirement of non-triviality to avoid including minor changes in, for example, supplier relations or product portfolio; we impose the requirement of novelty to avoid including the adoption/imitation of other incumbents' BMs." (Foss & Saebi, 2017, p. 216).
	"A business model innovation is defined as a change in the value creation, value appropriation, or value delivery function of a firm that results in a significant change to the firm's value proposition." (Sorescu, 2017, p. 692)
	"Independent of the degree of innovativeness, business model innovation requires that the three outlined dimensions are changed [value creation, value proposition, value capture]. To capture business model innovation as a construct requires to measure changes in the three primary dimensions of the business model." (Clauss, 2017, p. 387).
Why implement BMI?	"Unlike other forms of innovation, such as product or process innovation, business model innovation rarely originates in a technological breakthrough, but begins with the question of 'what customer need will the new business model address?' (Amit and Zott, 2012: 45). This customer-centric view suggests important connections with the marketing and design literatures, as well as the need to understand better the micro foundations of business model design (e.g., the cognitive processes and mechanisms that enable it)." (Demil et al., 2015, p. 5)
	"As a systemic approach to innovation, BMI builds on a holistic perspective of how business is conducted (Zott and Amit, 2010). It generally describes the way in which the firm reconfigures its business model to create and appropriate new value for stakeholders by designing and operating a modified or a new activity system and recombining its existing resources and those of its partners (Amit and Zott, 2012)." (Ammar & Chereau, 2018, p. 41).
	"The first conclusion drawn from the study highlighted that organizational culture, organizational structure, leadership and technological developments are important predictor's of BMI. The second conclusion pinpoints organizational inertia as the reason behind the failure of incumbents to innovate or modify their BM as compared to new entrants." (Bashir & Verma, 2019, p. 274).
How to implement BMI?	"After scrutinizing and comparing the BMI processes on an abstract level, we could derive seven generic BMI process phases, which should be taken into account when dealing with BMI: (1) Analysis, (2) Ideation, (3) Feasibility, (4) Prototyping, (5) Decision-making, (6) Implementation, and (7) Sustainability." (Wirtz & Daiser, 2018, p. 52)
	"It [BMI] requires entrepreneurs and managers to 1) understand the "deep truth" about the fundamental needs of customers and how competitors are or are not satisfying those needs; 2) understand all technical and organizational possibilities for improvements; 3) make many informed guesses about the future behavior of customers and competitors as well as about costs; and 4) make requisite adjustments to the existing business model only after considerable trial and error learning (Sosna et al., 2010; Teece, 2010)." (Karimi & Walter, 2016, p. 344)
	"A successful business model provides a customer solution that can support a price high enough to cover all costs and leave a satisfactory profit. In most cases, the development of such a business model starts with a deep understanding of the customer's predicament (sometimes called user needs) and from familiarity with the dozens of models that exist already. In highly competitive developed economies, it is difficult, but by no means impossible, to invent an entirely new business model." (Teece, 2018, p. 45)

Of note, we find that there is limited empirical research on the links among all four dimensions (Da Cunha Bezerra et al., 2020; Lazaretti et al., 2019; Lemus-Aguilar et al., 2019; Montiel & Delgade-Ceballos, 2014; Morioka & de Carvalho, 2016).

What is BMIfS?

Most definitions of BMIfS include BM components as overall dimensions or core activities. Moreover, they often relate to "innovations that create significant positive and/or significantly reduced negative impacts for the environment and/or society" (Bocken et al., 2014, p. 44). Some studies deal with the conceptualization and implementation of sustainable BMs (see Geissdoerfer et al., 2018, in Table 9.3). Another line of research focuses on management as a general process, firms' overall logic of doing business, or values associated with BMIfS (Breuer & Lüdeke-Freund, 2017). However, according to our review, integration of management levels is not prevalent in definitions of the concept, although it is an issue that has started to gain attention in BMIfS literature (Baumgartner, 2014; Breuer & Lüdeke-Freund, 2017; Kiesnere & Baumgartner, 2019). We also find that some literature mentions the VP concept alongside other generic BM concepts but does not make a direct association between the VP and sustainable development (Bocken et al., 2014; Breuer & Lüdeke-Freund, 2017). Following literature dealing with BM and BMI, we argue that it is important to clarify the scope of BMIfS with regard to sustainable development/UN goals (e.g., economic, ecological, social), as well as the involved components of a BM (e.g., VP, customer segments). Finally, some literature suggests that BMIfS is about securing the presence of dynamic practices and organizational capabilities (Amui et al., 2017). From the review conducted by Da Cunha Bezerra et al. (2020), it is apparent that some capabilities have been widely studied, such as those for cooperating with external stakeholders in pursuing CS or absorbing and learning from knowledge acquired about CS. However, other areas call for further research, such as capabilities to motivate engagement in CS within the firm's internal environment, capabilities related to external communications about CS issues and strategies, and capabilities to respond flexibly and adaptively to CS issues.

Why Implement BMIfS?

As Lüdeke-Freund (2020, p. 677) argues,

> sustainability innovations without aligned business models fall short of improving business case drivers and are thus not successful. If this is true, larger corporations that use their traditional business models to market sustainable products or service should not wonder if they are not successful in the market.

The BM perspective can help integrate the business case with societal and environmental values, emphasizing a change of behavior and generating strategic opportunities (e.g., new value creation) (e.g., Adams et al., 2016). A BM for sustainability represents a framework or tool that aims to support managers' efforts to describe, analyze, manage, and communicate essential issues, as well as processes associated with sustainable value creation, value delivery, and value capture (Schaltegger et al., 2016). Finally, BMIfS can lead firms to a multitude of advantages, including cost and risk reduction, enhanced sales, and a stronger reputation.

However, the impact of contextual factors and business case drivers needs to be considered, as noted by Schaltegger and Burritt (2018) (see Table 9.3).

How to Implement BMIfS?

Frameworks that can support firms and their managers in implementing BMIfS include the triple-layer BM canvas (Joyce & Paquin, 2016), the sustainable balance scorecard (Hansen & Schaltegger, 2018), and the sustainability BM patterns taxonomy (Lüdeke-Freund et al., 2018). However, insights about experiences gained by firms and managers from using such frameworks are scant. In their analysis of future research issues suggested in the ten most recent and most cited publications dealing with sustainability and innovation, Lazaretti et al. (2019) note the importance of gaining more insights into the impact of networks and partnerships and of behavioral factors (e.g., employees' and customers' awareness and motivation) on driving sustainability innovations. Moreover, a firm's entrepreneurial orientation represents an important contextual factor that affects a firm's inclination to enact BMIfS. However, only a limited number of publications within the BMIfS field have dealt with this topic (Filser et al., 2019). According to Haffar and Searcy (2019, p. 5), "there is a dearth of empirical, organizational-level research that describes how firms 'think' about sustainability, the collective logic 'they' follow when faced with (inevitable) sustainability conflicts, and, crucially, how this logic translates into problem-solving behavior to overcome these tensions."

DISCUSSION AND CONCLUSION

Regardless of the specific BM approach, prior literature emphasizes that customer centrality (i.e., deep insights into customers' values and behavior) governs BM design and development processes. Moreover, the literature considers the scope of the BM concept (e.g., holistic, integrative, dynamic) and its inherent potential to act as a pivotal lens in the strategic development processes of a firm's market offerings. In the definitions or frameworks of BMI, the core subjects include the nature of BMI (e.g., discrete, continuous), the scope of BMI (e.g., component and/or architectural innovation), and the output of BMI (e.g., 'degree of novelty' from an inside-out and/or outside-in perspective). However, we still find a lack of consensus and some ambiguity about the scope of BMI with regard to the BM components (e.g., VP, value-creating processes) and sustainability dimensions to include. Moreover, whereas there are some generic frameworks for implementing BMI, insights from firms' and managers' experience of working with these frameworks remain limited, especially in relation to sustainability. Different frameworks might have different roles in different contexts and for different categories of managers (Jarzabkowski & Kaplan, 2015). Thus, studies oriented toward identifying all these differences represent an important future research avenue.

Chesbrough (2010, p. 360) argues that frameworks or tools might be useful to understand and explicate BM, "but cannot by themselves promote experimentation and innovation." Thus, internal and external factors probably have a significant role in enabling BMI and BMIfS. Our review leads us to conclude that empirical research oriented toward detecting and assessing specific internal and external factors that drive or inhibit BMI and BMIfS is still limited. One internal factor that calls for further attention is corporate culture. In relation to this, previous research indicates that market orientation is a prerequisite of CS but not a driver of commitment to CS (Tollin & Christensen, 2019). However, the interplay of market orientation with BMI and, specifically, BMIfS, could be more researched. In addition, there is limited research on the role of a firm's entrepreneurial orientation in its inclination to pursue BMI and BMIfS.

Finally, a recurrent notion in the literature, regardless of whether it deals with BM, BMI, or BMIfS, is that the concepts concern a firm's top managers. As made evident in the extensive literature review by Helfat & Martin (2015), top managers exert pivotal impacts on a firm's inclination to initiate and implement strategic changes in BM. In addition, their literature review highlights that the contents or orientation of managers' cognitions, social and human capital have a significant role in explaining the differences between firms' inclinations to change. In our review, we find that some scholars have recently dealt with managerial and organizational capabilities in the BMI and BMIfS fields (e.g., Grewatsch & Kleindienst, 2018; Haffar & Searcy, 2019). However, due to the integrative, collaborative, and dynamic nature of business that BMIfS presumes, further research is still needed to specify the dynamic managerial capabilities required to drive BMIfS within firms (i.e., across decision levels and processes), between firms and their customers, and among firms and other external partners engaged in the co-creation of value.

Table 9.3   *Queries about BMIfS*

What is BMIfS?	"Innovations that create significant positive and/or significantly reduced negative impacts for the environment and/or society, through changes in the way the organization and its value-network create, deliver value and capture value (i.e. create economic value) or change their value propositions." (Bocken et al., 2014, p. 44)
	"Values-based business model innovation describes changes in the way an organization creates, delivers, and captures value by pursuing values of its internal and external stakeholders. Their values can impact the design of value propositions, i.e. the benefits offered to target groups, as well as further business model components and configurations." (Breuer & Lüdeke-Freund, 2017, p. 136)
	"We define sustainable business models as business models that incorporate pro-active multi-stakeholder management, the creation of monetary and non-monetary value for a broad range of stakeholders, and hold a long-term perspective. We define sustainable business model innovation as the conceptualization and implementation of sustainable business models."(Geissdoerfer et al., 2018, p. 407)
Why implement BMIfS?	"The business model perspective integrates the business case with societal and environmental considerations and locates nexuses of sustainability value. The perspective also strongly indicates that sustainability is becoming less of a technical challenge than it is one of changing behaviour. To take advantage of new opportunities, societal actors and downstream entities need to be involved and invested in defining new value creation and what is sustainably valuable (e.g. performance advantages and environmental impact reduction) (Iles and Martin 2013)." (Adams et al., 2016, p. 197)
	"A business model for sustainability helps describing, analyzing, managing and communicating (i) a company's sustainable value proposition to its customers and all other stakeholders, (ii) how it creates and delivers this value, (iii) and how it captures economic value while maintaining or regenerating natural, social and economic capital beyond its organizational boundaries." (Schaltegger et al., 2016, p. 268)
	"Business cases for sustainability are realisable but do not just happen and are the result of activities and measures chosen by company managers. Among the main reasons the potential of business cases for sustainability are not realised in practice are the novelty of the area, lack of knowledge and inadequate information and lack of management motivation and commitment (e.g. Montalvo 2008; Montalvo and Kemp 2008)." (Schaltegger & Burritt, 2018, p. 243)
How to implement BMIfS?	"Usually research on sustainability is underlined by a static view, focusing on the initial development of social and environmental practices. To shift toward a new paradigm, sustainability has to be seen as a dynamic choice inside a company, and new research has to fill this gap to understand how to maintain sustainability practices as important capabilities over time." (Amui et al., 2017, p. 311)
	"A key finding is that these proposed approaches usually address individual stages of the BMI without considering the continuous activities necessary to adapt the companies' capabilities to the dynamic changes (internally or externally) required by 'CE/sustainability thinking'. Many publications do not contextualize the BMI stage in which they are contributing to, as if they assumed that BMI was only about single stages (e.g. designing BM representations)." (Pieroni et al., 2019, p. 208)
	"Firms drawing predominantly on instrumental strategies arguably stipulate the challenges since they feel hampered by and find it difficult to make sense of SBM tensions. On the other hand, accepting the myriad of these tensions as an opportunity, and following an integrative approach by working through the tensions may be a more effective route." (van Bommel, 2018, p. 838)

REFERENCES

Achtenhagen, L., Melin, L., & Naldi, L. (2013). Dynamics of business models–strategizing, critical capabilities and activities for sustained value creation. *Long Range Planning, 46*(6), 427–442.

Adams, R., Jeanrenaud, S., Bessant, J., Denyer, D., & Overy, P. (2016). Sustainability-oriented innovation: A systematic review. *International Journal of Management Reviews, 18*(2), 180–205.

Ammar, O., & Chereau, P. (2018). Business model innovation from the strategic posture perspective: An exploration in manufacturing SMEs. *European Business Review, 30*(1), 38–65.

Amui, L. B. L., Jabbour, C. J. C., de Sousa Jabbour, A. B. L., & Kannan, D. (2017). Sustainability as a dynamic organizational capability: A systematic review and a future agenda toward a sustainable transition. *Journal of Cleaner Production, 142*, 308–322.

Baden-Fuller, C., & Morgan, M. S. (2010). Business models as models. *Long Range Planning, 43*(2–3), 156–171.

Baldassarre, B., Calabretta, G., Bocken, N. M. P., & Jaskiewicz, T. (2017). Bridging sustainable business model innovation and user-driven innovation: A process for sustainable value proposition design. *Journal of Cleaner Production, 147*, 175–186.

Bansal, P. (2005). Evolving sustainably: A longitudinal study of corporate sustainable development. *Strategic Management Journal, 26*(3), 197–218.

Bashir, M., & Verma, R. (2019). Internal factors & consequences of business model innovation *Management Decision, 57*(1), 262–290.

Baumgartner, R. J. (2014). Managing corporate sustainability and CSR: A conceptual framework combining values, strategies and instruments contributing to sustainable development. *Corporate Social Responsibility and Environmental Management, 21*(5), 258–271.

Berends H., Smits, A., Reymen, I., & Podoynitsyna, K. (2016). Learning while (re)configuring: Business model innovation processes in established firms. *Strategic Organization, 14*(3), 181–219.

Bocken, N. M., Short, S. W., Rana, P., & Evans, S. (2014). A literature and practice review to develop sustainable business model archetypes. *Journal of Cleaner Production, 65*, 42–56.

Breuer, H., & Lüdeke-Freund, F. (2017). *Values-Based Innovation Management: Innovating by What We Care About*. Macmillan International Higher Education.

Casadesus-Masanell, R., & Heilbron, J. (2015). The business model: Nature and benefits. *Advances in Strategic Management, 33*, 3–30.

Chesbrough, H. (2010). Business model innovation: Opportunities and barriers. *Long Range Planning, 43*(2–3), 354–363.

Chesbrough, H., & Rosenbloom, R. S. (2002). The role of the business model in capturing value from innovation: Evidence from Xerox Corporation's technology spin-off companies. *Industrial and Corporate Change, 11*(3), 529–555.

Clauss, T. (2017). Measuring business model innovation: Conceptualization scale development, and proof of performance. *R&D Management, 47*(3), 385–403.

Cortimiglia, M. N., Ghezzi, A., & Frank, A. G. (2016). Business model innovation and strategy making nexus: Evidence from a cross-industry mixed-methods study. *R & D Management, 46*(3), 414–432.

Da Cunha Bezerra, M. C., Gohr, C. F., & Morioka, S. N. (2020). Organizational capabilities towards corporate sustainability benefits: A systematic literature review and an integrative framework proposal. *Journal of Cleaner Production, 247*, 119–114.

Day, G. S., & Schoemaker, P. J. (2020). How vigilant companies gain an edge in turbulent times. *MIT Sloan Management Review, 61*(2), 56–64.

Demil, B., Lecocq, X., Ricart. J. E., & Zott, C. (2015). Introduction to the SEJ special issue on business models. *Strategic Entrepreneurship Journal, 9*, 1–11.

Dentchev, N., Rauter, R., Jóhannsdóttir, L., Snihur, Y., Rosano, M., Baumgartner, R., Nyberg, T., Tang, X., Hoof, B., & Jonker, J. (2018). Embracing the variety of sustainable business models: A prolific field of research and a future research agenda. *Journal of Cleaner Production, 194*, 695–703.

Ebel, P., Bretschneider, U., & Leimeister, J. M. (2016). Leveraging virtual business model innovation: A framework for designing business model development tools. *Information Systems Journal, 26*(5), 519–550.

Engert, S., & Baumgartner, R. J. (2016). Corporate sustainability strategy: Bridging the gap between formulation and implementation. *Journal of Cleaner Production, 113*, 822–834.

Filser, M., Kraus, S., Roig-Tierno, N., Kailer, N., & Fischer, U. (2019). Entrepreneurship as catalyst for sustainable development: Opening the black box. *Sustainability, 11*(16), 4503.

Foss, N. J., & Saebi, T. (2017). Fifteen years of research on business model innovation: How far have we come, and where should we go? *Journal of Management, 43*(1), 200–227.

Foss, N. J., & Saebi, T. (2018). Business models and business model innovation: Between wicked and paradigmatic problems. *Long Range Planning, 51*(1), 9–21.

Gassmann, O., Frankenberger, K., & Csik, M. (2014). *The Business Model Navigator: 55 Models that will Revolutionise your Business*. Pearson, UK.

Gassmann, O., Frankenberger, K., & Sauer, R. (2016). *Exploring the Field of Business Model Innovation: New Theoretical Perspectives*. Springer.

Geissdoerfer, M., Vladimirova, D., & Evans, S. (2018). Sustainable business model innovation: A review. *Journal of Cleaner Production, 198*, 401–416.

Grewatsch, S., & Kleindienst, I. (2017). When does it pay to be good? Moderators and mediators in the corporate sustainability–corporate financial performance relationship: A critical review. *Journal of Business Ethics, 145*(2), 383–416.

Grewatsch, S., & Kleindienst, I. (2018). How organizational cognitive frames affect organizational capabilities: The context of corporate sustainability. *Long Range Planning, 51*(4), 607–624.

Haffar, M., & Searcy, C. (2019). How organizational logics shape trade-off decision-making in sustainability. *Long Range Planning, 52*(6), 101912.

Hamel, G. (1998). Opinion: Strategy innovation and the quest for value. *Sloan Management Review, 39*(2), 7–14.

Hansen, E. G., & Schaltegger, S. (2018). Sustainability balanced scorecards and their architectures: Irrelevant or misunderstood? *Journal of Business Ethics, 150*(4), 937–952.

Helfat, C. E., & Martin, J. A. (2015). Dynamic managerial capabilities: Review and assessment of managerial impact on strategic change. *Journal of Management, 41*(5), 1281–1312.

Iglesias, O., Markovic, S., Bagherzadeh, M., & Singh, J. J. (2020). Co-creation: A key link between corporate social responsibility, customer trust, and customer loyalty. *Journal of Business Ethics, 163*(1), 151–166.

Inigo, E. A., Albareda, L., & Ritala, P. (2017). Business model innovation for sustainability: Exploring evolutionary and radical approaches through dynamic capabilities. *Industry and Innovation, 24*(5), 515–542.

Jarzabkowski, P., & Kaplan, S. (2015). Strategy tools-in-use: A framework for understanding "technologies of rationality" in practice. *Strategic Management Journal, 36*(4), 537–558.

Joyce, A., & Paquin, R. L. (2016). The triple layered business model canvas: A tool to design more sustainable business models. *Journal of Cleaner Production, 135*, 1474–1486.

Karimi, J., & Walter, Z. (2016). Corporate entrepreneurship, disruptive business model innovation adoption, and its performance: The case of the newspaper industry. *Long Range Planning, 49*, 342–360.

Kiesnere, A. L., & Baumgartner, R. J. (2019). Sustainability management in practice: Organizational change for sustainability in smaller large-sized companies in Austria. *Sustainability, 11*(3), 572.

Laasch, O. (2018). Beyond the purely commercial business model: Organizational value logics and the heterogeneity of sustainability business models. *Long Range Planning, 51*, 158–183.

Lazaretti, K., Giotto, O. T., Sehnem, S., & Bencke, F. F. (2019). Building sustainability and innovation in organizations. *Benchmarking: An International Journal*. https://doi.org/10.1108/BIJ-08-2018-0254

Leischnig, A., Ivens, B. S., & Kammerlander, N. (2017). A new conceptual lens for marketing: A configurational perspective based on the business model concept. *AMS Review, 7*(3–4), 138–153.

Lemus-Aguilar, I., Morales-Alonso, G., Ramirez-Portilla, A., & Hidalgo, A. (2019). Sustainable business models through the lens of organizational design: A systematic literature review. *Sustainability, 11*(19), 5379.

Lüdeke-Freund, F. (2020). Sustainable entrepreneurship, innovation, and business models: Integrative framework and propositions for future research. *Business Strategy and the Environment, 29*(2), 665–681.

Lüdeke-Freund, F., Carroux, S., Joyce, A., Massa, L., & Breuer, H. (2018). The sustainable business model pattern taxonomy—45 patterns to support sustainability-oriented business model innovation. *Sustainable Production and Consumption, 15*, 145–162.

Markovic, S., & Bagherzadeh, M. (2018). How does breadth of external stakeholder co-creation influence innovation performance? Analyzing the mediating roles of knowledge sharing and product innovation. *Journal of Business Research, 88*, 173–186.

Martins, L. L., Rindova, V. P., & Greenbaum, B. E. (2015). Unlocking the hidden value of concepts: A cognitive approach to business model innovation. *Strategic Entrepreneurship Journal, 9*, 99–117.

Massa, L., & Tucci, C. L. (2014). Business model innovation. In M. Dodgson, D. M. Gann, & N. Phillips (Eds.), *The Oxford Handbook of Innovation Management,* 420–441. Oxford: Oxford University Press.

Meuer, J., Koelbel, J., & Hoffmann, V. H. (2020). On the nature of corporate sustainability. *Organization & Environment, 33*(3), 319–341.

Montiel, I., & Delgado-Ceballos, J. (2014). Defining and measuring corporate sustainability: Are we there yet? *Organization & Environment, 27*(2), 113–139.

Morioka, S. N., & de Carvalho, M. M. (2016). A systematic literature review towards a conceptual framework for integrating sustainability performance into business. *Journal of Cleaner Production, 136*, 134–146.

Nyström, A-G., & Mustonen, M. (2017). The dynamic approach to business models. *AMS Review, 7*(3–4), 123–137.

Osterwalder, A., & Pigneur, Y. (2010). *Business Model Generation: A Handbook for Visionaries, Game Changers, and Challengers.* John Wiley & Sons.

Payne, A., Frow, P., & Eggert, A. (2017). The customer value proposition: Evolution, development, and application in marketing. *Journal of the Academy of Marketing Science, 45*(4), 467–489.

Pieroni, M. P., McAloone, T. C., & Pigosso, D. C. (2019). Business model innovation for circular economy and sustainability: A review of approaches. *Journal of Cleaner Production, 215*, 198–216.

Priem, R. L., Wenzel, M., & Koch, J. (2018). Demand-side strategy and business models: Putting value creation for consumers center stage. *Long Range Planning, 51*(1), 22–31.

Remane, G., Hanelt, A., Tesch, J. F., & Kolbe, L. M. (2017). The business model pattern database—a tool for systematic business model innovation. *International Journal of Innovation Management, 21*(1), 1750004.

Saebi, T., & Foss, N. J. (2015). Business models for open innovation: Matching heterogeneous open innovation strategies with business model dimensions. *European Management Journal, 33*(3), 201–213.

Schaltegger, S., & Burritt, R. (2018). Business cases and corporate engagement with sustainability: Differentiating ethical motivations. *Journal of Business Ethics, 147*, 241–259.

Schaltegger, S., Lüdeke-Freund, F., & Hansen, E. G. (2016). Business models for sustainability: A co-evolutionary analysis of sustainable entrepreneurship, innovation and transformation. *Organization & Environment, 29*(3), 264–289.

Schneider, S., & Clauß, T. (2020). Business models for sustainability: Choices and consequences. *Organization & Environment, 33*(3), 384–407.

Sorescu, A. (2017). Data driven business model innovation. *Journal of Product Innovation Management, 34*(5), 691–696.

Spieth, P., Schneckenberg, D., & Matzler, K. (2016). Exploring the linkage between business model (&) innovation and the strategy of the firm. *R&D Management, 46*(3), 403–413.

Storbacka, K., Frow, P., Nenonen, S., & Payne, A. (2012). Designing business models for value co-creation. *Review of Marketing Research, 9*, 51–78.

Täuscher, K. (2018). Using qualitative comparative analysis and system dynamics for theory-driven business model research. *Strategic Organization, 16*(4), 470–481.

Täuscher, K., & Abdelkafi, N. (2017). Visual tools for business model innovation Recommendations from a cognitive perspective. *Creativity and Innovation Management, 26*, 160–174.

Teece. D. J. (2010). Business models, business strategy and innovation. *Long Range Planning, 43*, 172–194.

Teece D. J. (2018). Business models and dynamic capabilities. *Long Range Planning, 51*(1), 40–49.

Tollin, K., & Christensen, L. B. (2019). Sustainability marketing commitment: Empirical insights about its drivers at the corporate and functional level of marketing. *Journal of Business Ethics, 156*(4), 1165–1185.

van Bommel, K. (2018). Managing tensions in sustainable business models: Exploring instrumental and integrative strategies. *Journal of Cleaner Production, 196*, 829–841.

Wirtz, B., & Daiser, P. (2018). Business model innovation processes: A systematic literature review. *Journal of Business Models*, *6*(1), 40–58.

Wirtz, B. W., Pistoia, A., Ullrich, S., & Göttel V. (2016). Business models: Origin, development and future research. *Long Range Planning*, *49*(1), 36–54.

World Commission on Environmental Development [WCED] (1987). *Our Common Future*. Oxford: Oxford University Press.

Zott, C., & Amit, R. (2010). Business model design: An activity system perspective. *Long Range Planning*, *43*(2–3), 216–226.

Zott, C., Amit, R., & Massa, L. (2011). The business model: Recent developments and future research. *Journal of Management*, *37*(4), 1019–1042.

10. Social challenges within sustainable entrepreneurial ecosystems

Roberto Hernandez-Chea, Maral Mahdad and Minh Thai

INTRODUCTION

The concept of sustainable entrepreneurial ecosystems (SEEs) relates to sets of strategic partnerships among the stakeholders who work together to address sustainability-related issues through entrepreneurship. These stakeholders can be public and private actors with heterogeneous institutional forms such as universities, SMEs, public organizations, NGOs, large companies, governments and citizens. On this basis, this setting is known for high decentralization and integrated dynamic social systems that maximize mutual dependencies and interaction (Manring, 2007). Developing SEEs has become a high priority in regional development agendas because, without having an ecosystem in place, first, entrepreneurs would face difficulties in leveraging expertise and financial supports for boosting their business ideas and, second, regions would face difficulties in boosting economic development through entrepreneurship such as job creation and tackling societal issues through resilience (Alam et al., 2019). These benefits are not limited to economic metrics and also include cultural, social and material attributes that are beneficial resources to entrepreneurs (Spigel, 2017). However, Spigel (2017) argues that solely the presence of such structures does not ensure they will function efficiently and help flourishing enterprising activities. Thus, creating a nurturing environment that facilitates sustainable entrepreneurship is easier said than done (Leyden, 2016).

One reason might be that the complexities are intertwined in ecosystem structure due to the existence of various stakeholders' interactions and their influence on the ecosystem's function. Indeed, scholars call for further research on the macro-environment (e.g. ecosystem) and stakeholder collaboration in the domain of sustainable entrepreneurship (Belz & Binder, 2017). Therefore, one might say that success in stakeholder collaboration in this context could lead to better functioning of SEEs. In order to shape a functional SEE, challenges that might arise from stakeholder collaborations should be addressed. These challenges are due to the uncertainty, lack of mutual understanding among partners, timely process, high transaction costs and power asymmetries associated with multi-stakeholder collaborations. Therefore, this chapter investigates:

1. What challenges emerge when stakeholders collaborate for developing sustainable business strategies within SEEs?
2. How do actors overcome these challenges to pursue sustainable business?

Our findings are based on empirical evidence of a multiple-case study – two SEEs in East Africa involving multi-stakeholders, e.g. business incubators, universities, research institutes and private companies. The two business incubators are at the core of both SEEs by supporting youth and women entrepreneurs with help of the other stakeholders in the ecosystems. These multi-stakeholders in the SEEs have the main purpose to implement sustainable business strategies such as to stimulate the development of sustainable value propositions, and improve well-being in poor and marginalized communities, empower youth and women through support, and transfer green technologies to reduce environmental footprint. The two cases constitute a theoretically interesting context for highlighting the impact of collaborations among multi-stakeholders toward sustainability. We use concepts from stakeholder collaboration and the literature of SEEs to enhance the theoretical understanding of social challenges among multi-stakeholders.

SUSTAINABLE ENTREPRENEURIAL ECOSYSTEMS

At its simplest, sustainable entrepreneurship promises to address fundamental societal challenges such as climate change, sustainable production practices and poverty reduction. It is defined as "the discovery, creation, and exploitation of opportunities to create future goods and services that sustain the natural and/or communal environment and provide development gain for others" (Patzelt & Shepherd, 2011, p. 632). There is a strong emphasis on sustainable entrepreneurship and associated business models on linking the environmental and social dimensions into value proposition strategies (Schaltegger & Wagner, 2011). Schaltegger & Wagner (2011) showed that it is critical for societies and stakeholders to systematically orchestrate the development of sustainable entrepreneurship. The interest is not limited to government and policy makers, but it is driven from public, private and civil society actors too (Autio et al., 2018; Simatupang et al., 2015). The United Nations flagged 'partnership for goals' calls for collaborations to increase cooperation and technological innovation among diverse stakeholders, including companies, governments, universities and research institutes to address societal challenges (UN General Assembly, 2015). Therefore, the emergence of SEEs was not an unexpected phenomenon.

The concept of a SEE is an emerging and recent concept building on the nexus of entrepreneurial ecosystems literature and sustainability research streams with the aim of fostering sustainable entrepreneurship. With increasing attention from multi-stakeholders for addressing the Sustainable Development Goals (SDGs), the emergence of SEEs represents a subset of entrepreneurial ecosystems, which is "an interconnected group of actors in a local geographic community committed to sustainable development through the support and facilitation of new sustainable ventures" (Cohen, 2006, p. 3). From this perspective, organizations establish collaborations to access complementary resources, produce innovation, and deploy sustainable business strategies to create sustainable impact.

Scholars within the SEE research stream have mainly focused on investigating the nature and function of SEEs. Few scholars have investigated the process of development of SEE and its function in supporting green innovations (e.g. Uddin et al., 2015; Simatupang et al., 2015; O'Shea et al., 2021). Particularly in understanding how SEEs function, O'Shea et al. (2021) argue that SEEs help actors leverage opportunities that emerge in three stages of co-intuiting, co-interpreting, and co-integrating. Their micro-level perspective framework reflects on how different stakeholders of an ecosystem collectively comprehend, imagine, and follow opportunities within an ecosystem. Other recent research on SEEs addresses either the role of intermediary organizations in the form of incubators and accelerators (e.g. Bank et al. 2017; Theodoraki & Messeghem, 2017) or investigates the relevance of sustainable business models (e.g. Muñoz & Cohen, 2018; Neumeyer & Santos, 2018) in fostering success of SEEs by helping sustainable startups to scale up. Furthermore, Bergmann and Utikal (2021) argue that two essential ingredients of SEEs' success are a support system and supporting actors. On this basis the emphasis on stakeholders within SEEs becomes evident in this vein of research.

Indeed, research in entrepreneurial ecosystems shows that stakeholders' awareness of sustainable entrepreneurship integrated with stakeholders' collaboration toward sustainability issues positively influence the perception of SEE (Bischoff, 2019, 2021). The important role played by stakeholders and their collaborative innovation to leverage sustainability opportunities is indeed listed among required factors for entrepreneurial ecosystems to become sustainable (DiVito & Ingen-Housz, 2021). Even though the rise of SEEs brings up opportunities for sustainable entrepreneurs and stakeholders to collaborate for success, it is easier said than done. We challenge the assumption in ecosystems literature that stakeholder collaboration is one main key ingredient toward success and instead assume that it leads to success only if the challenges to emergent stakeholder collaboration are overcome or reduced. Stakeholder collaboration literature shows that collaborative efforts are not without risks and it might indeed lead to failure. To better understand the challenges that might arise in stakeholder collaborative settings, we briefly review the research on challenges in relation to stakeholder collaborations.

CHALLENGES OF MULTI-STAKEHOLDER COLLABORATIONS

SEEs' outcome relies to a great extent on orchestrating collaborations among diverse stakeholders that aim for boosting sustainable entrepreneurship as a shared goal. This entails multiple institutional settings being put together to address complex problems and accommodating the conflicting interests often engaged (Brouwer et al, 2015; Stern et al., 2015; Brockmyer & Fox, 2015). In addition, Freeman et al. (2016) argue that knowing the magnitude of the complexities in sustainability-driven problems, and higher integration and relational engagement of stakeholders are required within institutional ecosystems. In this context a stream of literature has been developed to investigate the effectiveness of multi-stakeholder collaboration initiatives (e.g. Brouwer et al., 2015) highlighting that collaboration can be a significant challenge to carry out (Kuenkel, 2019). The uncertainty, lack of mutual understanding among partners, timely processes, high transaction costs and power asymmetries are the most common risks associated with multi-stakeholder collaborations. Therefore, many multi-stakeholder collaborations are considered as inefficient (Van Tulder & Pfisterer 2013).

Despite the many discussions around the efficiency of multi-stakeholder collaborative approaches, they increasingly become common practice in different domains of research, including the sustainability domain. Aligned with this trend, Kuenkel (2019) brings three important challenges into the nexus of sustainability research and multi-stakeholder collaborations: (1) conflicting interests of multiple actors that are required to align around an issue of common concern; (2) mutual dependency of actors engaged in collaborations, their power differences and level of trust; and (3) volatile environments and complexity of context. Similarly, Van Tulder and Keen (2018) noted that stakeholders' different objectives and strategic goals put collaborations at risk and increase the probability of failure. These challenges have been investigated further in a multi-stakeholder setting but not deeply in SEEs.

Within the SEE literature, identified challenges are mostly related to resource dependencies among stakeholders in the co-innovation phases (Bergmann & Utikal, 2021). Although previous studies highlight the importance of the social dimension – i.e. network and ties –

among stakeholders within SEEs (Theodoraki et al., 2018), it is still fragmented. Therefore, we assume the social dimension plays a significant role in the success of SEEs. In this vein, newly developed entrepreneurial ecosystems might greatly suffer from liability of newness in the relationships that are formed. This particular liability that exists among all actors within ecosystems increases the risks of ecosystem failure because actors are required to learn new activities which rely to a great extent on social relationships among actors and lack of strong ties in the ecosystem network (Stinchcombe, 1965). Beside the importance of resources and resource dependencies in SEE's success, the role of social capital as a resource is undeniable. Zane and DeCarolis (2016) argue that social capital in the form of relationships among actors is the resource that helps ecosystems overcome the risks of newness and smallness. The positive influence of these relationships depends on the trustworthiness of the social environment and the terms carried out by each partner. Therefore, SEEs rely strongly on the relationships within the social settings that help in overcoming knowledge flow barriers based on trust and social capital to create sustainable impact (Fornoni et al., 2012; Muldoon et al., 2018). However, this is easier said than done in situations where a variety of actors such as resource providers, intermediary organizations, public and private institutions, large enterprises and SMEs have to act within their particular institutional settings while collaborating with each other to address social, business and environmental concerns. Scholars claim trust is one significant solution to avoid SEE failure but, on the other hand, if it is not coordinated it may foster unproductivity in entrepreneurial ecosystems (Muldoon et al., 2018). Yet, except for distrust, our understanding of what type of social uncertainties might emerge in SEE development and function is scarce. Hence, for the purpose of this explorative chapter, we investigate the open phenomenon of social challenges that emerge among stakeholders in SEEs when implementing sustainability-driven business strategies. In particular, we focus on stakeholder behaviors in the course of collaborations and investigate barriers that emerge and coping mechanisms that stakeholders implement to pursue fruitful collaborations in order to create sustainable impact from the business perspective.

METHODS

In this chapter, we explore challenges within SEEs with associated stakeholders to pursue sustainability. In doing so, we have documented events within SEEs and stakeholders' collaborative characteristics. Understanding this complex phenomenon involved investigating logics, values, perceptions, working relations, dynamics, attitudes and environmental contexts that affected stakeholder engagement/collaboration. We used a deductive-inductive research approach (Miles & Huberman, 1994). We relied on a replication strategy by conducting a multiple-case study (Eisenhardt, 1989; Yin, 2013) consisting of two case studies – two SEEs. Two considerations guided our choice of cases. First, the type of case was theoretically sampled because it constituted a SEE that involved stakeholders from academia, the public and private sectors, and entrepreneurs. In a volatile and complex context (Kuenkel, 2019) such as East Africa, multi-stakeholders have limited experience in engaging in collaborations across sectors for sustainable impact. This provides a situation in which challenges are more pronounced and observable than in the contexts where such multi-stakeholder collaborations are more institutionalized. Second, the two case studies were purposely chosen to ensure between-case variety because comparative analysis between the cases may reveal similarities and differences and provide a deep understanding of the nature of challenges and multi-stakeholder dynamics (Ryan et al., 2002, p. 145). We used a qualitative research design due to the inherent complexity of the research questions (Miles & Huberman, 1994).

Context of the Two Sustainable Entrepreneurial Ecosystems

To maintain confidentiality of our data, the two SEEs are subsequently named SEE-ONE and SEE-TWO. The two cases had the same multi-stakeholder composition, i.e. stakeholders from academia, the public and private sectors as well as business incubators at the core of each ecosystem to support entrepreneurs. They were located in two different countries in East Africa, SEE-ONE in Uganda and SEE-TWO in Kenya, and both ecosystems were established by the same international development program. Each ecosystem, thus, consisted of a business incubator, national university, public research institute and private companies as the main stakeholders to support youth and women entrepreneurs in poor and marginalized communities. In terms of management in SEE-ONE and SEE-TWO, assigned members from stakeholder organizations were part of the boards of directors and sub-committees to provide support, specifically, green technology transfer and product development to tackle sustainability issues. SEE-ONE and SEE-TWO were established to strategically improve well-being by reducing poverty through job creation, sustainable business by mitigating climate change issues, and positive societal impact by empowering youth and women in the two East African areas. The two incubators at the core of the two SEEs received seed capital from an international development cooperation agency for four years (2012–2016) to establish operations within the ecosystems. The two SEE cases represent a relevant research context to investigate stakeholders' engagement toward the implementation of sustainability-driven business strategies. The scope of this chapter is on exploring social challenges among stakeholder collaborations in SEEs to stimulate sustainable business to mitigate climate change issues through green technology transfer and product development as well as community development to tackle sustainability issues.

Data sources

Data collection was conducted during fieldwork in April–May 2015 and February–March 2016. The first period of fieldwork was used to gain an in-depth understanding of the context, the multi-stakeholder engagement, characteristics and challenges within each SEE. During the second period of fieldwork, data collection focused on obtaining detailed information about stakeholders' logics, goals, values, behaviors, collaborations, sustainable purpose and impact. We conducted follow-up interviews with key informants to verify and confirm interpretations of data along with comparisons of information across multiple data sources for triangulation purposes (Yin, 2013). Our study is based on three data sources. First, semi-structured interviews were conducted with key informants. Semi-structured interviews offer flexibility for the emergence of new and potential concepts to dig into the analysis (Ryan et al., 2002). In total, 38 interviews were conducted with main stakeholders in both SEEs, i.e. incubators, national universities, public research institutes, private companies and youth and women entrepreneurs. We conducted individual and group (three participants) interviews, each interview lasted for approximately one hour to one and a half hours. Interviews were recorded and transcribed verbatim for further analysis. The interviews included open-ended questions such as description of each stakeholder's behavior and actions, types of challenges in the ecosystem, and types of collaborations among stakeholders, which helped to identify patterns of behaviors, challenges and collaborations.

Second, during the fieldwork, the main author of the study obtained office space in the incubators as well as visits to the different stakeholder organizations. The main author took field notes and had formal and informal interviews and discussions with members from stakeholder organizations and thus a deep immersion into the reality they experienced. Moreover, observations and events were video-recorded at each stakeholder organization, including working atmosphere, meetings and events with entrepreneurs, interactions between members, and facilities to capture challenges and inter-organizational dynamics related to sustainability-driven business strategies and implementation. Lastly, we collected archival materials such as annual reports, manuals, marketing brochures, business plans and sustainability strategy reports.

Data analysis

For our analysis, we applied a qualitative analysis (Miles & Huberman, 1994) by using concepts from stakeholder collaborations and the literature of SEEs to identify challenges within ecosystems. Yet, we were also attentive to emerging concepts from empirical data. First, we classified the multiple data sources by assigning codes with the respective information of every interviewee, place and date. We carefully compiled transcripts from our interviews, observation field notes, informal discussion notes and archival materials using QSR NVivo software. We familiarized ourselves with the data from the two case studies through reading transcripts and field notes several times. Second, we coded the data, using a coding scheme based on concepts from literature, but we also expanded the initial framework by coding new categories that emerged from the data. Third, we refined our preliminary categories through discussions among the authors resulting in revisions and adjustments of initial interpretations. We analyzed quotes, concepts and categories within and across the cases with an emphasis on avoiding individual bias. Finally, we grouped categories into themes (Miles & Huberman, 1994) and identified their relationships. We went back and forth between the literature and our empirical findings to develop and support emerging concepts and establish the relationship with the existing literature.

RESULTS

In this section, we present empirical evidence and focus on the challenges that emerged in two SEEs as a result of multi-stakeholder collaborations. The challenges occurred during two phases of sustainable enterprising functions within the SEEs: green technology transfer and sustainable product development.

Findings evidenced that SEEs composed of incubators, universities, research institutes and private companies supported sustainable businesses of youth and women entrepreneurs by providing assistance in innovation through green technologies and product development to tackle sustainability issues. Within such support given by the multi-stakeholders, the incubators, in the two SEEs, served as platforms to complement and share resources and thus collectively help develop youth and women's sustainable businesses to scale up. Each of the stakeholders provided support and resources based on their competences and capacities.

In SEE-ONE, for instance, the research institute had the role to provide green technologies, i.e. farming technologies related to plant disease-resistant varieties, which resulted in less use of pesticides and therefore better health and safety as well as efficient crop production in rural communities of Uganda. The private company in SEE-ONE was responsible for supporting commercialization of such green technologies among youth and women, and for supporting commercialization of their crop production through international networks. Meanwhile, the university had the role of supporting youth and women in product development by providing lab equipment, machinery and technical know-how for experimentation and prototyping. Among the products developed by youth and women were coffee by-products from reusing and upcycling waste, e.g. coffee liquor as well as more environmentally friendly charcoal with low-carbon emissions.

In SEE-TWO in Kenya, the roles of stakeholders for green technology transfer and product development were similar to the above-mentioned. The research institute was responsible for assisting with green technologies, i.e. animal feed formulations that offered a sustainable nutrition management and efficient production, and improved seed varieties that implicated high yields and resistance to extreme weather conditions for climate change resilience. The university in SEE-TWO had the role of supporting product development, for instance by assisting with food-processing technologies (i.e. food baking facilities and equipment for improving quality and energy consumption). The two private companies involved in SEE-TWO adopted different roles. One company engaged in supporting commercialization of improved seed varieties as well as packaging activities. The other company had the role of providing commercialization support of products developed by youth and women.

Green Technology Transfer

We identified that transfer of green technology in SEE-ONE presented some challenges that limited the research institute and the incubator from getting actively involved in their roles. Framed by the public-service interest and bureaucratic procedures, the research institute faced a conflict with the incubator – implementing a market-oriented approach – since public organizations need to provide free services to society. As mentioned by one researcher from the research institute:

> It has been a challenge to actually transitioning from the core single-mindedness as a scientist that we start coming out by providing technologies for commercialization during the incubation process… One of the big challenges is to address issues of policy with the public institute, so that we can effectively operate as business because the mindsets and bureaucratic processes in the public institutes may not favor business operation.

Besides the conflicting interests, informality was also reflected in managing technology transfer, as there was a lack of clear agreements in terms of intellectual property rights and a profit sharing scheme between the parties. This situation led to defective behavior – failure to contribute fully as stipulated – from the research institute, since the conflicting interests and the informal governance influenced its reluctance to transfer green technologies for the benefit of youth and women in rural communities. We noted that the research institute initially perceived risk about technology transfer, which constrained its engagement in its role.

In SEE-TWO, we observed that green technology transfer for improved seed varieties was simpler compared with animal feed formulation since the former technology was handled by the research institute unit that knew about the collaborative initiative with the incubator and the other stakeholders in SEE-TWO. Nonetheless, the research institute unit that handled the animal feed formulation was initially unaware about the collaborative initiative to support youth and women in SEE-TWO. This was because the research institute is a large institute composed of various units and employees. One member of the incubator management team said: "The research institute is very big, they have 17 offices that I have mentioned and not all the offices know about our collaboration, so in many of their offices I need more introduction and discussion before you get support."

Besides unawareness of support given, parties did not have an established memorandum of understanding specifying how to handle the technology transfer of animal feed formulation, how to commercialize it, and the benefits for the research institute. In this situation, the research institute unit adopted defective behavior as a defensive mechanism due to the limited capacity in understanding the collaborative initiative and support to provide as well as the informal governance in managing technology transfer agreements. The research institute perceived risk to transfer technology and had misconceptions regarding the given support.

Product Development

In SEE-ONE, the university and the incubator mainly supported product development of youth and women's sustainable business ideas. However, a structural change in the university's top management led to a change of a new authority who could decide to support youth and women to develop products. The new authority was unfamiliar with the collaborative initiative and incubation concept, which resulted in an initial unwillingness to support product development activities. Such structural change and limited capacity to understand incubation constrained the new authority in assimilating knowledge of incubation and understanding benefits, which led to adoption of ambiguous behaviors – differing in perceptions and attitudes to support – as the new authority was unclear how to engage in providing support. Consequently, the new authority misconception of the nature of incubation, led to suspension of the university's initial collaborative intent.

In SEE-TWO, one private company supported product development through commercialization of improved varieties – as raw material for production – as well as a packaging service. Despite the packaging service not being part of the original role of the private company, the private company adjusted such support to help youth and women. We observed the private company lacked capacity and resources to support. Therefore, the incubator helped with equipment for packaging in the hope of implementing the sustainable business strategy of diffusing improved varieties in poor communities to mitigate climate change issues and empower youth and women. This support for product development raised concerns among the other stakeholders, especially the incubator, regarding the type of support given by the private company and the outcomes, including the benefits of such support.

From this product development situation in SEE-TWO, we noticed that there was informality from the private company regarding performing the role that was originally established in agreements, i.e. the memorandum of understanding. Moreover, there was little understanding about the incubation concept, since the private company believed they were entitled to be beneficiaries in terms of getting support given by the incubator rather than providing support with their own resources to youth and women. A member of the university stated:

> You can find the private company is bringing business, they have started their own business using funding from the incubator [given by a donor] but nobody thinks that is wrong, other people don't

know… That is the question, they are benefiting, and they are generating revenue, using the money the incubator gave them. Are we getting anything? You see there is no, there was not agreement. For instance, we gave the private company USD 40,000.00 to start a business, after sometime they started generating revenue. Since there is not agreement between the incubator and them, we are not really entitled to whatever they are generating.

The incubator and other stakeholders within SEE-TWO adopted ambiguous behaviors regarding the role performed by the private company to do business at the expense of incubation. They perceived that the private company had misinterpreted its role in the way to support youth and women entrepreneurs in the incubation process. Regardless of it, youth and women still got benefits by obtaining access to improved varieties and the packaging service.

Managing Social Challenges to Enable the Implementation of Sustainable Business Strategies

In the previous section, having identified different challenges during green technology transfer and product development phases for sustainable business, social uncertainty emerged during such processes. Social uncertainty emerged from the combination of unfavorable contextual factors, negative perceptions and behaviors associated with stakeholders during the two phases for sustainable enterprising in the two SEEs. This led to ambiguities in stakeholders' actions, which threatened the collaborative initiatives. Table 10.1 describes the components involved during the emergence process of social uncertainty.

Table 10.1   The emergence of social uncertainty threatening green technology transfer and product development for sustainable business

Phases of sustainable enterprising	Social uncertainty		
	Contextual factors	Perceptions	Behaviors
Green technology	Conflicting interests, informal governance	Risk and misconception	Defective behaviors
	Limited capacity, informal governance		
Product development	Structural change, limited capacity	Misconception	Ambiguous behaviors
	Limited capacity, informal governance	Misinterpretation	

We now turn to the question of when and how such a social uncertainty can be managed constructively. In the process of social uncertainty emergence, we observed that some actions were taken to minimize social uncertainty among stakeholders and facilitate the transformation of defective and ambiguous behaviors into collaborative behaviors. These actions were, first, to collectively elaborate formal agreements, for example, on technology transfer procedures, intellectual property management and profit sharing schemes. Second, to align their interests and agree on mutual benefits of collaborative initiatives. Third, to apply an adaptive management approach to allow strengthening stakeholders' participation by adapting to changes in the stakeholder organizations. Lastly, to clarify resource contributions and support each other's activities. These actions indicated that multi-stakeholders engaged in accordance with their jointly defined roles and tasks in order to enable green technology transfer and product development to tackle sustainability issues. These actions reflected joint efforts to foster the continuity of the collaborative initiatives.

Formal agreements, which imply formal governance such as contractual agreements, helped control competition and opportunism among stakeholders during technology transfer and product development. Within the two SEEs, stakeholders needed to develop formal agreements that created mutual understanding of how to manage technologies and benefits in sharing those technologies to reduce risks. To enable formal governance, stakeholders worked closely and had continuous dialogues, facilitating understanding for their contributions.

With regard to *alignment of interests*, particular stakeholders, e.g. the incubator manager and the CEO of the private company, promoted a sustainable business vision in empowering poor communities through green technologies and sustainable products, and therefore a moral obligation and a common ground to provide green technologies, facilities and equipment for product development. The incubator manager also insisted and coordinated regular meetings with stakeholders to share opinions, interests and alternative solutions to facilitate support to youth and women entrepreneurs.

An *adaptive management* approach was derived because of structural changes in stakeholder organizational structures, which led to involving the new member, i.e. from the university, in the board of directors where all stakeholders from SEE-ONE met to discuss strategic directions. Since the new board member was unfamiliar with the collaborative initiative and incubation concept, dialogues helped clarify issues as the incubator manager expressed: "We have looked at and handled issues strategically. For example, we clarified the mutual benefits with the new principal executive director [in the research partner organization] to prevent confusion and disorder."

In terms of clarifying *resource contribution and supporting each other's activities*, despite the limited understanding of certain stakeholders of their roles or how they should support youth and women entrepreneurs, they were motivated to clarify and adjust roles, agreements and benefits to enable support and achievement of the sustainable business vision associated with product development to tackle sustainability issues. This situation involved willingness to work together to clarify how to proceed with support, how to share benefits and reach agreements mainly on profit sharing.

The previous four counteractions facilitated the transformation of defective and ambiguous behaviors into collaborative behaviors through encouraging stakeholders to overcome doubts and thereby diminish social uncertainty among stakeholders. Due to the counteractions, stakeholders indicated that negative perceptions were transformed into positive perceptions that reflected: (1) mutual understanding for green technology transfer and product development; (2) common vision and goals; (3) agreement on distribution of benefits; and (4) mutual trust due to transparency about contributions. Under the influence of positive perceptions, stakeholders pursued sensible responses and joint actions that we refer to as collaborative behaviors. Through these behaviors, stakeholders clarified doubts and transformed delays into the continuity of collaborative initiatives.

Based on our findings, we identified three distinct strategies, depicted in Figure 10.1, used in the two SEEs to manage social uncertainty as the main cause of stakeholder collaboration challenges. The first strategy was *joint learning*. This strategy was used to manage conflicting interests and structural changes. To facilitate this learning, the incubators as platforms ensured regular training among multi-stakeholders on incubation concepts, formal governance mechanisms, teamwork and interactions for collaborations. Multi-stakeholders engaged in open dialogues about their interests, contributions and benefits for gaining mutual understanding and harmonizing interests, beliefs and practices. There was also a joint review of the strategy over time according to structural changes and adjustments for involving new members (e.g. adding the new authority from the university as a board member) and developing mutual understanding about terms for continued collaboration.

The second strategy was *coordination* to stimulate stakeholders' efforts to effectively manage the continuity of collaborations and diminish social uncertainty. Stakeholders relied on two coordination mechanisms. First, they implemented a formal governance structure, especially in relation to policies and procedures, for intellectual property and profit sharing between stakeholders. Formal agreements also enhanced mutual understanding about support given, roles and contributions. Second, stakeholders agreed to establish the incubator as the central platform for coordination of collaborations.

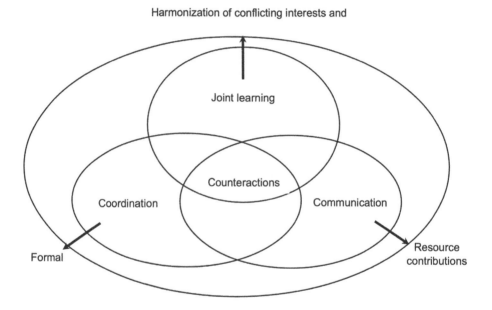

Figure 10.1   Strategies to manage social uncertainties in SEE

The third strategy was to ensure *communication* as a means of developing cohesiveness and reciprocity among stakeholders within the SEEs and to manage clarifications of resource contributions and support. To enhance the communication, all multi-stakeholders had members in both boards of directors and sub-committees. The frequent board and sub-committee meetings marked the difference to move forward and created mutual understanding among stakeholders, and actively ensured their engagement in open dialogues to perform their roles. Moreover, dialogues motivated stakeholders to participate and obtain a sense of ownership, and enhance their commitment to support youth and women in poor communities.

Overlaps between the circles in Figure 10.1 indicated the complementarity between the three different strategies. For example, communication can often help to achieve better coordination and joint learning and vice versa, and this helps in managing social uncertainty.

Mechanisms that contribute to establishing overlaps between communication, coordination and joint learning strategies were (1) collective involvement in constructive dialogues to facilitate understanding of each other's role and contribution; and (2) openness to discussion of and learning about stakeholders' intentions and behaviors.

DISCUSSION

The findings suggest different contextual factors influence perceptions and result in different types of behaviors, e.g. defective and ambiguous. We call this process the emergence of social uncertainty, which has been emphasized in previous studies that investigated social challenges in collaborations (e.g. Dirks, 2019; Ishiguro & Okamoto, 2013; Messick et al., 1988). Social uncertainty has been previously described as the situation where actors have incomplete information about the behaviors of others (Dirks, 2019). Our analysis provides a better understanding of social uncertainty from the process-based perspective.

Our analysis indicates that defective behaviors hinder green technology transfer. The conflicting interests among stakeholders were manifested through identity-related actions. Stakeholders perform identity-related actions by emphasizing their own organizational standards and routines as the best approach for collaborations and outcomes of collaborations. Meanwhile, when stakeholders were unsure about collaborations, they were passively participating in providing support, resulting in limited provision of technologies. Based on the analysis, stakeholders with green technologies employed both identity-related and passive actions for controlling contributions, reflecting defensive mechanisms, which is in line with previous studies (Brouwer et al., 2015; Stern et al., 2015) that suggest that institutional settings often accommodate conflicting interests that can result in particular actions.

Our analysis also identified ambiguous behaviors that hinder sustainable product development. Stakeholders adopted a behavior of suspending actions by suspending the collaboration until further clarification of outcomes and benefits, e.g. supporting youth and women. Second, adjusting role actions occur when taking advantage of opportunities from collaborations. Therefore, stakeholders become uncertain about the consequences of collaborations that can be considered inefficient (Van Tulder & Pfisterer 2013). We suggest that before a collaboration is considered inefficient, there is ambiguity among stakeholders within SEEs in terms of collaboration outcomes and benefits, e.g. beneficiaries, and such an ambiguity can be reduced prior to becoming a collaboration failure.

Finally, our analysis offers four types of counteractions that can be utilized by stakeholders to deal with defective and ambiguous behaviors to continue collaborating for green technology transfer and product development. First, stakeholders collectively negotiate and elaborate formal agreements to manage intellectual property and profit sharing issues. Second, stakeholders align their interests and agree on mutual benefits. Third, stakeholders apply an adaptive management approach to allow strengthening participation of the stakeholders by adapting to changes in stakeholder organizations. Lastly, stakeholders clarify resources contributions and support to each other's activities. These behaviors indicated that stakeholders engaged in accordance with tasks to support the development of entrepreneur sustainable businesses with green technologies and sustainable products.

Social uncertainty can lead to inefficient collaborations within SEEs (Dirks, 2019; Van Tulder & Pfisterer, 2013). Therefore, it is critical to manage contextual factors, negative perceptions and behaviors. Contextual factors may start inducing the emergent process of social uncertainty. For instance, even though public organizations e.g. research institutes are encouraged to do the common good, sometimes their interests are embedded in complex systems that limit fully engagement and support of sustainable business strategies within SEEs. This can limit addressing the SDGs; for example, partnerships for the goals, which calls for creative ways of taking actions to secure public engagement in collaborations with multi-stakeholders, especially with private companies with a market-oriented approach.

CONCLUSION

In this chapter, we address stakeholder collaboration challenges within SEEs in two phases of sustainable enterprising, i.e. green technology transfer and product development, to tackle sustainability issues. We found social uncertainty as the main cause of stakeholder collaboration challenges in SEEs. The emergence of social uncertainty involves contextual factors, negative perceptions and defective and ambiguous behaviors that threaten the continuity of collaborative initiatives. Findings also suggest that multi-stakeholders within SEEs can employ counteractions related to joint learning, coordination and communication strategies to manage social uncertainty, overcome challenges and pursue sustainable businesses.

This chapter has contributions to theory and practice. We contribute to theory by linking the literature of SEEs and stakeholder collaboration from the social dimension perspective, which has been overlooked (Theodoraki et al., 2018). We conceptualize the phenomenon of social uncertainty as a process associated with different contextual factors, perceptions and behaviors and their consequences that may damage stakeholder collaborations within SEEs. The conceptualization moves beyond the traditional focus on theorizing social uncertainty as a source of uncertainty related to lack of knowledge on the sustainable impact (Morone & Govoni, 2020). We extend such a conceptualization by explaining its emergence process with antecedents, i.e. contextual factors and negative perceptions, and consequences that result in defective and ambiguous behaviors. This process draws special attention to the micro level of the social dimension, i.e. network and ties within SEEs (Theodoraki et al., 2018).

Our study contributes to practice by identifying contextual factors that can lead to defective and ambiguous behaviors and therefore damage stakeholder collaborations. Practitioners can focus on the uncovered strategies discussed in this chapter to manage social uncertainty. Such strategies involve counteractions that are critical to change perceptions and behaviors and thereby foster the continuity of green technology transfer and sustainable product development within SEEs.

Our study has some limitations that can be addressed in future research. First, the scope of our study was limited to sustainable business and green co-innovation in terms of green technology transfer and sustainable product development. Further, we covered two years of data collection for two SEEs. Since stakeholder collaboration and SEEs are dynamic by nature, future research can conduct longer longitudinal data collection with more SEEs and different types of collaborations. Second, we identified contextual factors related to social uncertainty in the East African context, which represents a volatile and complex environment (Kuenkel, 2019). However, future research can replicate our study in other contexts to compare if contextual factors vary according to where SEEs are located, for instance, some areas with more sustainable policies and regulations, more institutionalized settings, and/or more stakeholders embedded in SEEs. Lastly, our study is based on empirical evidence of two SEEs in East Africa, which is difficult for generalization; therefore, future quantitative studies can consider large samples and investigate the degree of significance of proposed concepts discussed in this study.

REFERENCES

Alam, J., Ibn-Boamah, M., & Johnson, K. (2019). Exploring the entrepreneurial ecosystem: Some local Canadian perspectives. *Strategic Change, 28*(4), 249–254.

Autio, E., Nambisan, S., Thomas, L. D., & Wright, M. (2018). Digital affordances, spatial affordances, and the genesis of entrepreneurial ecosystems. *Strategic Entrepreneurship Journal, 12*(1), 72–95.

Bank, N., Fichter, K., & Klofsten, M. (2017). Sustainability-profiled incubators and securing the inflow of tenants–The case of Green Garage Berlin. *Journal of Cleaner Production, 157,* 76–83.

Belz, F. M., & Binder, J. K. (2017). Sustainable entrepreneurship: A convergent process model. *Business Strategy and the Environment, 26*(1), 1–17.

Bergmann, T., & Utikal, H. (2021). How to support start-ups in developing a sustainable business model: The case of a European social impact accelerator. *Sustainability, 13*(6), 3337.

Bischoff, A. K. (2019). *Stakeholder Support and Collaboration in Entrepreneurial Ecosystems: An Analysis of the Roles of Sustainability, Education and Culture.* BoD – Books on Demand.

Bischoff, K. (2021). A study on the perceived strength of sustainable entrepreneurial ecosystems on the dimensions of stakeholder theory and culture. *Small Business Economics, 56*(3), 1121–1140.

Brockmyer, B., & Fox, J. A. (2015). Assessing the evidence: The effectiveness and impact of governance-oriented multi-stakeholder initiatives. *Transparency & Accountability Initiative,* September.

Brouwer, J. H., Woodhill, A. J., Hemmati, M., Verhoosel, K. S., & van Vugt, S. M. (2015). *The MSP Guide: How to Design and Facilitate Multi-stakeholder Partnerships.* Centre for Development Innovation Wageningen UR.

Cohen, B. (2006). Sustainable valley entrepreneurial ecosystems. *Business Strategy and the Environment, 15*(1), 1–14.

Dirks, S. (2019). *On the Determinants of Risk and the Pro-social Preferences and their Role in Cooperation under Social Uncertainty.* Wageningen University, Environmental Economics and Natural Resources Group, Wageningen, the Netherlands.

DiVito, L., & Ingen-Housz, Z. (2021). From individual sustainability orientations to collective sustainability innovation and sustainable entrepreneurial ecosystems. *Small Business Economics, 56*(3), 1057–1072.

Eisenhardt, K. M. (1989). Building theories from case study research. *Academy of Management Review, 14*(4), 532–550.

Fornoni, M., Arribas, I., & Vila, J. E. (2012). An entrepreneur's social capital and performance: the role of access to information in the Argentinean case. *Journal of Organizational Change Management, 25*(5), 682–698.

Freeman, C., Wisheart, M., Hester, K., Prescott, D., & Stibbe, D. (2016). *Delivering on the Promise: In-country Multi-stakeholder Platforms to Catalyse Collaboration and Partnerships for Agenda 2030.* World Vision International and The Partnering Initiative.

Ishiguro, I., & Okamoto, Y. (2013). Two ways to overcome social uncertainty in social support networks: A test of the emancipation theory of trust by comparing kin/nonkin relationships. *Japanese Psychological Research, 55*(1), 1–11.

Kuenkel, P. (2019). Stewarding sustainability transformations in multi-stakeholder collaboration. In *Stewarding Sustainability Transformations,* Cham: Springer, pp. 141–205.

Leyden, D. P. (2016). Public-sector entrepreneurship and the creation of a sustainable innovative economy. *Small Business Economics, 46*(4), 553–564.

Manring, S. L. (2007). Creating and managing interorganizational learning networks to achieve sustainable ecosystem management. *Organization & Environment, 20*(3), 325–346.

Messick, D. M., Allison, S. T., & Samuelson, C. D. (1988). Framing and communication effects on group members' responses to environmental and social uncertainty. *Applied Behavioral Economics*, 2, 677–700.

Miles, M. B., & Huberman, A. M. (1994). *Qualitative Data Analysis: An Expanded Sourcebook.* Thousand Oaks, CA: Sage.

Morone, P., & Govoni, F. (2020). Chapter 1: Introduction: Tackling uncertainty in the biobased economy through science. In Morone, P. and Clark, J. H. (eds) *Transition Towards a Sustainable Biobased Economy*, London, UK: Royal Society of Chemistry, pp. 1–11.

Muldoon, J., Bauman, A., & Lucy, C. (2018). Entrepreneurial ecosystem: Do you trust or distrust? *Journal of Enterprising Communities: People and Places in the Global Economy*, 12(2), 158–177. https://doi.org/10.1108/JEC-07-2017-0050

Muñoz, P., & Cohen, B. (2018). Sustainable entrepreneurship research: Taking stock and looking ahead. *Business Strategy and the Environment*, 27(3), 300–322.

Neumeyer, X., & Santos, S. C. (2018). Sustainable business models, venture typologies, and entrepreneurial ecosystems: A social network perspective. *Journal of Cleaner Production*, 172, 4565–4579.

Patzelt, H., & Shepherd, D. A. (2011). Recognizing opportunities for sustainable development. *Entrepreneurship Theory and Practice*, 35(4), 631–652.

O'Shea, G., Farny, S., & Hakala, H. (2021). The buzz before business: A design science study of a sustainable entrepreneurial ecosystem. *Small Business Economics*, 56, 1097–1120. https://doi.org/10.1007/s11187-019-00256-4

Ryan, B., Scapens, R. W., & Theobald, M. (2002). *Research Method and Methodology in Finance and Accounting* (2nd ed.). Padstow: Thomson.

Simatupang, T. M., Schwab, A., & Lantu, D. (2015). Introduction: Building sustainable entrepreneurship ecosystems. *International Journal of Entrepreneurship and Small Business*, 26(4), 389–398.

Schaltegger, S., & Wagner, M. (2011). Sustainable entrepreneurship and sustainability innovation: Categories and interactions. *Business Strategy and the Environment*, 20(4), 222–237.

Spigel, B. (2017). The relational organization of entrepreneurial ecosystems. *Entrepreneurship Theory and Practice*, 41(1), 49–72

Stern, A., Kingston, D., & Ke, J. (2015). *More than the Sum of its Parts: Making Multi-stakeholder Initiatives Work.* Washington DC: Global Development Incubator (GDI).

Stinchcombe, A. L. (1965). Social structure and organizations. In J. March (Ed.), *Handbook of Organizations*. Chicago: Rand McNally, pp. 142–193.

Theodoraki, C., & Messeghem, K. (2017). Exploring the entrepreneurial ecosystem in the field of entrepreneurial support: A multi-level approach. *International Journal of Entrepreneurship and Small Business*, 31(1), 47-66.

Theodoraki, C., Messeghem, K., & Rice, M. P. (2018). A social capital approach to the development of sustainable entrepreneurial ecosystems: An explorative study. *Small Business Economics*, 51(1), 153–170.

Uddin, M., Hindu, R. C., Alsaqour, R., Shah, A., Abubakar, A., & Saba, T. (2015). Knowledge management framework using green IT to implement sustainable entrepreneur ecosystem. *Applied Mathematics & Information Sciences*, 9(5), 2703.

UN General Assembly. (2015). Resolution adopted by the General Assembly on 19 September 2016. A/RES/71/1, 3 October 2016 (The New York Declaration).

Van Tulder, R., & Keen, N. (2018). Capturing collaborative challenges: Designing complexity-sensitive theories of change for cross-sector partnerships. *Journal of Business Ethics*, 150(2), 315–332.

Van Tulder, R., & Pfisterer, S. (2014). Creating partnering space: Exploring the right fit for sustainable development partnerships. In M. M. Seitanidi & A. Crane (eds) *Social Partnerships and Responsible Business: A Research Handbook*, Hoboken: Taylor and Francis, pp. 105–125.

Yin, R.K. (2013), Validity and generalization in future case study evaluations. *Evaluation*, 19(3), 321–332.

Zane, L. J. and DeCarolis, D. M. (2016). Social networks and the acquisition of resources by technology-based new ventures. *Journal of Small Business & Entrepreneurship*, 28(3), 203–221.

11. The UN Global Compact SDG Action Manager: how benefit corporations and purpose-driven businesses are driving the change

Giorgia Nigri, Armando Agulini and Mara Del Baldo

INTRODUCTION

Contemporary social and environmental challenges have accelerated the depletion of natural resources and disrupted the balance called for by sustainability, underlining the need to strictly abide by the 2030 United Nations Agenda (Baumgartner, 2014; Kaur & Nguyen, 2018; SDG Compass, 2015). It has been made evident how many of the issues facing humankind today, such as inequality, desertification, water scarcity, and poverty, can only be resolved at a global level by promoting sustainable development (Amini & Bienstock, 2014; Bebbington & Unerman, 2018; Blewitt, 2015; Boons & Lüdeke-Freund, 2013; Rodriguez et al., 2002; Sachs, 2015) and sustainability-driven practices.

Defined as the state of society where living conditions and resources used continue to meet human needs without undermining the integrity and stability of the natural system upon which the economy and society depend (UNWCED, 1987), sustainable development poses a significant dilemma for both institutions, governments and business, which is to weigh care for the environment and social well-being against economic growth (Babiak & Trendafilova, 2011; Cintra & Carter, 2012; Lozano, 2015).

Institutional forms that reflect hybrid business purposes and governance regimes (Bruni & Zamagni, 2004; Charter et al., 2008; Schaltegger et al., 2016) have been envisioned in various configurations over the past decades (Billis, 2010; Dillard et al., 2008), such as the low-profit limited liability companies (Rawhouser et al., 2015) and the community interest companies (Castellani et al., 2016; Nigri et al., 2017), benefit corporations (Alcorn & Alcorn, 2012; Baudout et al., 2018; Munch, 2012; Murray, 2012) and social purpose companies (Levillain & Segrestin, 2014; Segrestin et al., 2016), or territorial-based companies (Del Baldo, 2012; Laloux, 2014).

Management scholars and practitioners in the field are thus forced continuously to rethink business paradigms and economic models (Bruni, 2010; Dyllick & Hockerts, 2002; Johnson, 2010; Ketola, 2008; Schaltegger et al., 2012, 2016; Zadek, 2006; Zamagni, 1995, 2007) taking into consideration sustainability issues (Bruni & Zamagni, 2004; Charter et al., 2008; Schaltegger et al., 2016). This brought new business-driven paradigms and practices – such as teal (Laloux, 2014) and flourishing (Laszlo et al., 2014) – that make use of traditional methods of business but are geared toward socially beneficial goals as well (Nicholas & Sacco, 2017; Nicholls, 2010)

The benefit corporation movement, which started in 2010 and in just nine years has grown extensively, is a perfect example of a business-driven shift in paradigm (Sabeti, 2010; Hiller,

2013; Baudout et al., 2018; Di Cesare & Ezechieli, 2017) which developed and deployed a sustainability-focused strategy (Brinkmann & Garren, 2018; Longoni et al., 2014; Nidumolu et al., 2009). Certified B Corps and benefit corporations offer a legal framework, a certification platform, and rating standards (Brinkmann & Garren, 2018; Nigri & Del Baldo, 2018). The Benefit Act introduced by Maryland in 2010 gives companies that want to incorporate as benefit corporations the legal protection to pursue a public benefit while expanding the obligations of boards, requiring them to consider environmental and social factors as well as the financial interests of shareholders (Camm, 2012; Nigri, 2018). B Lab,[1] a private standard-setting and certifying non-profit organization based in the US (Alcorn & Alcorn, 2012) developed a robust, transparent, and effective protocol to measure impacts on workers, the community, the environment, governance, and the overall business model of each company (Castellani et al., 2016; Di Cesare & Ezechieli, 2017; Nigri et al., 2017). B Lab's certification process provides a seal of fitness to B Corp standards if companies achieve a score of 80 or above – which indicates value creation on top of profits – when taking the Benefit Impact Assessment (BIA) (Bell & Morse, 2018; Nicholas & Sacco, 2017).

In view of the increasing sophistication of sustainability-business-driven strategies, the aim of this chapter would be to shed light on the new SDG (Sustainable Development Goals) Action Manager adopted by the United Nations Global Compact (UNGC) and pinpoint how the integration with the BIA can drive the shift in paradigm.

To follow this path, we decided to structure the article as follows. First, we briefly analyze the sustainability literature as treated in the impact assessment field (Dumay et al., 2016; Nigri & Michelini, 2019) to develop a theoretical framework useful for classifying the different approaches to sustainability-driven practices. Second, we present the benefit impact indicator and SDG Action Manager to analyze the correlation between the overall strategy and the level of deployment of sustainability-driven activities. Finally, we introduce some practical implications for management and our conclusions.

We believe our contribution to the literature to be twofold. On the one hand, we explain a new indicator able to extend the effectiveness of practices in line with SDGs and benchmark against other company results. On the other hand, we contribute to the impact assessment debate by analyzing the two indicators in comparison, introducing a specific lens through which sustainability practices can be viewed.

LITERATURE REVIEW

Reporting SDGs

Sustainability emphasizes the need to balance economic goals, environmental impact, and social development (Schlange, 2009), and translates to the corporate context through the triple bottom line (TBL) framework (Brown et al., 2008; Garcia et al., 2016; Hussain et al., 2018; Miller et al., 2007; Savitz & Weber, 2014; Vanclay, 2004).

Many models (Christensen et al., 2013; Morioka & Carvalho, 2016a, 2016b; Nigri et al., 2016) are available in the literature that propose effective implementation of sustainability-driven activities (Fletcher, 2012; Leal Filho et al., 2015; Leal Filho et al., 2018), but, given that most stakeholders are external to the company, they cannot directly observe sustainable activities and actions even though these are gaining strategic managerial importance. This results in information asymmetry between managers and stakeholders, and sustainable reporting (SR) is the most appropriate tool for reducing it (Thijssens et al., 2016; von Schwedler, 2016). SR reporting is thus proliferating, both regarding the number of companies engaging in this activity, and the comprehensiveness of the data included in the reports (Deegan & Rankin, 1996; Gray et al., 1995; Kolk, 2003; KPMG, 2011), turning the TBL into a more operational approach, with the creation of standards, codes, and metrics (Garcia et al., 2016) which brought the introduction of new impact assessments (Nigri & Michelini, 2019). Environmental and social indicators were added, since, focusing only on economic impacts, left a tightly defined data set, frequently presenting a rather narrow picture of the results of intervention (Kusek & Rist, 2004).

Managing, measuring, and reporting the three elements of an organization's economic impacts together with social and environmental factors gained prominence during the late 1990s and early 2000s starting from John Elkington's (1997) book *Cannibals with Forks: The Triple Bottom Line of 21st Century Business*, which is accredited with starting new non-financial reporting frameworks from a social and environmental perspective (Dumay et al., 2016) aimed at completing traditional financial reporting (ASVIS, 2018; Gray et al., 2014; Gray, 2006).

Several authors have proposed frameworks for sustainable management with a focus on collaborative management tools for the implementation, monitoring, and continuous improvement of the SDGs (Deloitte, 2015). Since the publication of the 2030 Agenda (UN, 2015), numerous contributions have nurtured the international debate on SDGs and the SDG reporting, coming not only from the academic world but also from accounting and professional practice (Acca, 2017). Among the relevant international documents (such as guidelines and research reports), one can mention the *SDG Compass. The Guide for Business Action on the SDGs*;[2] and the *CEO Guide to Sustainable Development Goals* (WBCSD, 2016), which propose examples of business solutions aimed to implement sustainable development objectives. Other relevant sources include the document released by Adams (2017a), *The Sustainable Development Goals, Integrated Thinking and the Integrated Report* that illustrates how SDG-related targets can be reconciled with value creation through integrated thinking (Dumay et al., 2016); and the report *Walking the Talk*, published by Oxfam (Oxfam, 2018), an NGO operating on a global scale, that analyzes the content of SDG-based information in the financial statements of large companies. The latter pointed out the lack of a coherent approach in prioritizing SDGs; low impact of SDGs in sustainability strategies and plans, reduced linkage between human rights policies and risks and SDGs, and finally, fragmented and often inconsistent budget reporting on SDGs. With specific regard to the Italian context, the ASVIS Report (ASVIS, 2018), provides a detailed review of the results achieved by Italy in terms of SDGs according to a territorial-based approach (Lozano, 2015; Del Baldo & Demartini, 2012) and a scoring system which records the results in achieving the 17 goals.

The role and potential of SDGs in guiding governments, businesses, and civil society toward shared and sustainable development has been widely recognized in governance and accounting studies (Hajer et al., 2015). In this context, a number of contributions, since the Brundtland Report, have fed into the scientific debate on sustainable development (Lozano, 2015) and sustainability, emphasizing the role of companies in the advancement of the Sustainable Development Agenda 2030. When the pursuit of SDGs is integrated into business strategies, it facilitates innovative solutions to address global challenges and innovate the business model (Boons & Lüdeke-Freund, 2013), supports the implementation at the political and managerial level (Bebbington et al., 2017; Bebbington & Unerman, 2018), and raises awareness among practitioners and regulators. Regarding the latter, two main lines of research have emerged, a brief summary of which is provided below.

The first body of studies focused on contingent factors that influence the implementation of sustainable development objectives (Lozano, 2015; GRI, 2018) and SDG reporting (Hák et al., 2016) investigating exogenous and endogenous variables, i.e. external and internal (organizational) contingent factors that hinder or facilitate the decision of organizations to pursue and report on sustainability objectives (Hahn & Kühnen, 2013; Liu & Anbumozhi, 2009). On the one hand, country-level institutional factors include economic and finance; sustainability; education and labor; politics and law; society and culture; technology and innovation. On the other hand, the promotion of social and environmental responsibility in companies is driven by professionals, managers, entrepreneurs, as well as public officials and governing bodies whose decisions affect SDGs by identifying sustainable-driven strategies and management models (with specific regard to corporate vision, strategic approach, planning, accountability, and risk management); carrying out internal operating processes (in the broad spectrum of activities relating to operational management, accounting, disclosure, and the adoption of information tools); and reporting (with a view to implementing a coherent system of sustainability disclosure and processes of asseveration and control). Within this research stream the importance of sustainability reporting in promoting the advancement of SDGs has been addressed by several authors (GRI, 2018; Lozano, 2015; Siebenhüner & Arnold, 2007), who pointed out both its relevance as a driver for the implementation of sustainability-oriented investments and strategies (Adams, 2017b), and the contribution of SDGs to the advancement of sustainability reporting (Bebbington et al., 2017), disclosure, and dissemination of an action-oriented disclosure framework (Annan-Diab & Molinari, 2017; Garcia-Torres et al., 2017; Schaltegger et al., 2017).

Among the factors affecting TBL disclosure (Rosati & Faria, 2019), we find the socio-cultural system (it is more widespread in countries with a lower level of power distance); the education/training and labor system (companies releasing SDGs reporting belong to countries marked by high investments in tertiary education and academic knowledge); the level of individualism and short-term orientation (Vachon, 2010; Slawinski & Bansal, 2015; Slawinski et al., 2017); the policy-makers' orientation to social responsibility; and the level of vulnerability to climate change that nurtured a greater political and social pressure on companies (Horn & Grugel, 2018). Addressing the attention to internal factors, key features are represented by the company's structural and organizational characteristics (company size, endowment of resources, level of skills and intangibles, level of commitment and sustainability performance, presence of external assurance), and individual motivations. The correlation among the aforementioned factors has been proved through empirical analyses (Rosati & Faria, 2019): TBL and SDG reporting is more diffused among large companies that possess a high level of intangibility; submit their report to external assurance; experience a greater commitment to sustainability; are characterized by governance with significant shares of female councilors and a younger board (more prone to assume as "core" environmental and social aspects).

The second body of studies developed a thematic analysis on SDGs and investigated the connectivity among specific goals, fueling a debate on the need to achieve the integration between the different objectives (Hajer et al., 2015; Horn & Grugel, 2018; Le Blanc, 2015; Salvia et al., 2019; Storey et al., 2017) as we will see below.

Measuring SDGs

SDG-related research in business and management has begun to raise attention and grow, guiding organizational policy and action (Annan-Diab & Molinari, 2017; Schaltegger et al., 2017; Storey et al., 2017). Each goal incorporates social and environmental dimensions on top of economic ones (Balog et al., 2014; Griggs et al., 2014, p. 49; Storey et al., 2017) and has become integrated into a governmental, corporate, and civil society vision for shared and lasting prosperity (Hajer et al., 2015, p. 1657; Le Blanc, 2015). Among the 1000 respondents to the Accenture (2017) survey, 89 percent indicated that commitment to sustainability had a direct impact on their business and 70 percent regarded the goals as a robust framing within which to act toward sustainable development.

Moreover, the sustainable development agenda calls for a global partnership at all levels and between all countries and stakeholders who are called to work together to achieve the stated goals and targets, thus also mobilizing the academic and professional communities. The current concepts of sustainable development are increasingly more valuable than they were two decades ago, overcoming strictly environmental, economic, and social development concerns and impacting people's very survival (Gupta & Vegelin, 2016; Gusmão Caiado et al., 2018). Accordingly, operational solutions are needed to monitor, measure, and evaluate the implementation of SDGs and overall sustainability because such assessment is being increasingly recognized as essential for the tracking of SDGs and is required for the UN member states.

According to Sachs (2012), the path to sustainable development should follow a bottom-up approach and should be grounded on networks involving multiple actors capable of operationalizing solutions and develop concrete projects for the SDGs achievement (Gusmão Caiado et al., 2018, p. 1279). Education to sustainable development emphasizes the integration of key-matters through teaching and participative methods in order to empower young generations to adopt measures for sustainable development and allow the sharing of knowledge through interdisciplinary multi-stakeholder approaches.

While the goals provide an indication of the aspects that are considered critical, they do not illuminate how indicator sets can be used to steer and coordinate actions and outcomes (Selomane et al., 2015), nor the underlying drivers of the impacts that the SDGs seek to address (Griggs et al., 2014). There are goals within the SDGs that are pivotal to social and environmental outcomes (Balog et al., 2014; Fearon et al., 2010; Storey et al., 2017). Thus, to develop new SDG-related drivers requires moving from organization-centric responsibility, performance, and accountability, to novel types of performance indicators (Agostino & Sidorova, 2017; Bellucci & Manetti, 2017; Nigri & Del Baldo, 2018). Social and environmental sustainability accounting needs to develop and adopt new conceptual frames and indicators (Unerman & Chapman, 2014) as the challenges that gave rise to the SDGs as well as the integrated nature of the goals require re-examining the conceptual basis of sustainability from a responsibility and accountability perspective.

PwC has developed tools in this area – such as their SDG Selector and SDG Navigator (Wilson, 2017) as 71 percent of the business respondents to their survey indicated that they were actively planning how to engage and assess their impact on the SDGs (PwC, 2015). Many sustainability frameworks have also been developed at the national level, such as the SDG Index (Schmidt-Traub et al., 2017), by different organizations, such as the United Nations (United Nations, 2015), OECD (2017), RobecoSam (RobecoSam, 2018), to better manage a country's sustainability (Muff et al., 2017) and show the increasing importance of the issues and challenges addressed. Likewise, many scholars and academics have created (Leal Filho et al., 2015) frameworks of indicators to monitor progress, inform policy and ensure accountability by all stakeholders. A global indicator framework was adopted by the General Assembly in 2017 and two reports were published highlighting both gains and challenges of the full realization of the 2030 Agenda principles (United Nations, 2016). The approach used to monitor the goals and their achievements has also been published in other reports, related to countries' performances (OECD, 2017; Sachs, 2012; World Bank, 2017).

We do not go into further depth in thematic analysis on SDGs, or analyze all previous tools, since it does not constitute the core of our contribution in this paper. Step-by-by step tools, such as the SDG Compass, are relevant to all types of companies and are available online. However, we want to shed light on the most updated tool, the SDG Action Manager, which was launched on 29 January 2020 as a joint effort between B Lab and the UNGC. This new online impact-management assessment, as we will discuss below, draws from the BIA and incorporates the Ten Principles of the UNGC, providing businesses with a tool to manage and directly improve their sustainability performance, and therefore, contribute to the growth of the enterprise at several levels (Global Compact, 2020).

METHODOLOGY

A literature review was performed to frame the theoretical background on impact assessment (Nigri & Michelini, 2019) and SDG-related indicators. We defined the specific aims of the research and focused on scholarly journals as these can be considered validated knowledge and are likely to have the highest impact in the field, followed by books and e-books (Nigri & Michelini, 2019). The analysis was developed following Webster and Watson (2002). The key data sources were extracted from scientific databases,[3] using the following keywords: impact assessment, social impact assessment, benefit impact assessment, sustainable development goals indicator, SDGs, to be found in both 'title' and 'abstract'.

All articles were analyzed using content analysis (Hsieh & Shannon, 2005; Mayring, 2004; Mazzoleni, 2015) analyzing the abstract and comparing it with similar reviews (Coviello & Jones, 2004; Keupp & Gassmann, 2009). A comparison was also made with previous research (Nigri, 2018; Nigri et al., 2016, 2017, 2020; Nigri & Del Baldo, 2018). Finally, coding (Pisoni et al., 2018) was used to link the literature analysis results to the newly presented documents by B Lab and the Global Compact.[4]

These two indicators were chosen as they are complementary and have proved to be very effective (Nigri & Del Baldo, 2018). From its start in 2010, the B Corp movement counts over 3300 certified B Corps in 70 countries from 150 different sectors and over 120,000 companies have applied to take the BIA.[5]

Through commitment to the ten UNGC Principles, the private sector can reduce its negative impacts and generate positive results in social, environmental, and governance terms. According to its members, the Global Compact has helped to increase sustainability in the company by 80 percent, increase sustainability reporting by 66 percent, promote the implementation of sustainability policies and practices (68 percent), and shape a new corporate vision (48 percent) (Global Compact, 2020).

Thus, in our perspective, a combination of these two indicators is worth the analysis, as we will see below.

THE BENEFIT IMPACT ASSESSMENT AND THE SDG ACTION MANAGER

Overview

In order to translate sustainability-driven actions effectively to business, two significant assessments have been recently developed: the B Lab BIA, in 2007 (with the last version launched in 2019)[6] and the newly released SDG Action Manager in 2020.

The BIA was introduced by B Lab and evaluates a benefit corporation's impact on workers, community, environment, customers, and governance (Nigri et al., 2016). The BIA helps to identify those companies – certified B Corps – that produce an overall measured benefit for the company and the environment, as well as a profit for shareholders.

The B Lab interactive platform allows B Corps to quickly receive information on the areas of improvement of the company. Every company that intends to be certified must complete a questionnaire and obtain at least 80 points, on a scale from 0 to 200. After this self-assessment step, the company can ask B Lab to validate their score, which requires analysis and verification on behalf of B Lab analysts of all the practices and results achieved by the company. After this screening, which lasts about six weeks, the company can become a certified B Corp and add the B Corp certification to its products and website (Di Cesare & Ezechieli, 2017; Nigri et al., 2016). Results can also be used to prepare the annual Benefit Report, which benefit corporations are required (Nigri, 2018) to publish (except in Delaware) to describe the benefits produced.[7]

The SDG Action Manager was developed by B Lab and the UNGC, along with the work and feedback of a range of expert stakeholders in their field and content advisors that include institutions – such as the Global Reporting Initiative (GRI), the Impact Management Program, the World Benchmarking Alliance, the Danish Institute for Human Rights, and the United Nations Development Programme (UNDP) – and academia – such as the University of Colorado, the Universitè de Geneve, and the Leeds School of Business. The tool brings together B Lab's B Impact Assessment, the SDGs and the Ten Principles of the UNGC, to enable businesses to assess where they stand and to take action on the SDGs.[8]

The SDG Action Manager, like the BIA, begins with a self-assessment. First, there are a series of SDG-related questions that cover all 17 SDGs, constructed on the Ten Principles of the UNGC and the World Benchmarking Alliance Seven transformations. Each company has a recommended set provided based on industry, sector, and size.[9] The self-assessment determines the starting point and opens up a specific set on the assessment platform that matches the company's needs and starts from the SDGs the company wants and needs to focus most upon. By answering the questions and going through the various steps a company is able to get a snapshot of how their operations, supply chain, and business model can create positive impacts. At the same time it helps to identify risk areas for each SDG. The assessment has a compartmentalized module approach. First, a manager can access the specific module and add team members and then navigate into each question. Because some questions are harder to answer and require more detail, documentation may be required in support (as for the

BIA, only that in this case, the request is not prompted by B Lab).[10] Once the questions are completed, the company can view the comprehensive assessment baseline score as it stands today and elaborate an SDG Performance report. The report assesses the business model, how it contributes and what operations support impact. Like the GRI, it has a strong materiality approach (UNGC Academy, 2020).

In detail, The SDG Action Manager allows one to:

- identify which SDGs are most compatible with the company profile and strategically plan to obtain results in that direction;
- get a clear vision of how operations, the supply chain, and the business model generate a positive impact and identify the risk areas for each SDG;
- set goals and monitor performance through the control panel;
- strengthen internal collaboration by inviting colleagues to subscribe to the Action Manager SDG platform for contributions of experts and test real-time progress and performance;
- prompt continuous leaning through high-impact implementable actions based on key questions, industry benchmarks, and improvement guidelines (Global Compact, 2020).

The action manager allows one to add, during the procedure, potential unmet goals and to visualize progress on the SDG Action Manager dashboard, thus eliciting a continuous and fertile learning process. It also allows one to access extra relevant resources from the UN database and improvement guides such as the UNGC smart resource library.[11] The online manager helps to determine high-impact action based on actionable assessment questions, which can also be compared with other companies taking the same assessment as a benchmarking function (UNGC Academy, 2020). This is where companies can view their performance compared with all the companies that have also completed the questionnaires.

Finally, companies taking the B Lab BIA can integrate the SDG Action Manager, i.e. B Corp data is automatically used for the SDG Action Manager and vice versa, as the platforms are connected.

Advantages and Disadvantages

The advantages of the partnership between the B Lab-led assessment and the SDG Action Manager include, on the one hand, the B Impact Assessment & B Analytics technical approach, B Lab's high experience and competence in measuring sustainability, and their specific expertise on small and medium sized businesses (SMEs). On the other hand, the Global Compact global extension, content expertise, UN databases, libraries, and initiatives together with the SDG drive as part of the mission, pinpoint the overall competence of the Global Compact.

For the first time, a single, free and accessible to all, international reference tool is available, which helps companies identify the most relevant SDGs for their business and identify the actions to be implemented to contribute to their achievement as each question measures materiality and opportunity, and the final score gives an overarching result.

Some of the limitations that have already emerged even though the assessment has just been launched include, first, that it is an internal tool. The SDG Action Manager serves to evaluate and assess company performance against SDGs, analyzes what to adopt to improve results, and pinpoints what practices may be inhibiting solutions.

It is a continuous improvement tool though and not a reporting or certification tool. In fact, today, it does not substitute for the Communication on Progress (COP) of Global Compact companies needed to maintain membership reviewing content and it is only complementary to ESG reporting.

The action manager is a compartmentalized in-depth assessment while the BIA gives a better overall outlook. Although both indicators are not intended as a reporting tool, companies that deem it useful can use it to set up their sustainability reporting even though both assessments lack an effective reporting structure. The strong drive towards a materiality approach and the GRI as an SDG Action Manager partner aim toward better reporting in the future.

DISCUSSION AND CONCLUSION

The release of the SDGs coincides with a new questioning by business of its approach to issues of environmental sustainability and development impact (Adams, 2017b; United Nations, 1992). In the most recent iteration of the global sustainable development agenda, the United Nations' 2030 Agenda has rapidly gained traction and salience among a broad range of actors, starting from the member states who unanimously endorsed them, to public policy bodies, NGOs, public and private sector organizations – including many businesses and professional institutions (Bebbington & Unerman, 2018) – and the academic world (Annan-Diab & Molinari, 2017; Schaltegger et al., 2017; Storey et al., 2017). There seems to be a strong commitment to the planet and more importantly to ensure long-term sustainable growth by experts in corporate sustainability, civil society, UN, and academia as without longlasting sustainable business, companies will fail to achieve the SDGs by 2030 and bring a shift in paradigm.

The SDGs, and their sub-targets, represent the best long-term strategic market outlook even though some companies will entail increased risks because of regulations or varied consumer behavior; others will drive added costs; some will experience market growth. In general, many companies are still struggling to define the next steps to align their strategies with the SDGs and to manage and measure their impacts. Both the BIA and the SDG Action Manger are business-driven sustainability indicators inspired on the one hand by the Certified B Corp community and on the other hand by participating companies of the UNGC.[12]

Although, to date, both assessments have some limitations, especially in reporting that is still "missing" and requires additional efforts to improve its diffusion among/within organizations (GBS, 2019), succeeding with this strategy will bring to a much stronger inclusion of sustainability perspectives in business strategy development and execution as the SDG agenda increasingly drives business, sustainability, and policy interests closer together.

According to our analysis, the partnership between the BIA and the SDG Action Manager can be considered as a tangible application of the theoretical principles of a sustainability approach that drives toward positive deviance (Laszlo, 2019). Ultimately, this theoretical chapter may advance the existing literature in a sustainability context as it enhances from a managerial perspective all three dimensions of sustainability – social, environmental, and economic. Benefit corporations are for-profit companies that provide an additional benefit for society, both social and environmental and Global Compact companies abide to the ten Global Compact principles that do the same.

Through the BIA, companies have a way to measure their overall impact and know how to intervene to generate a benefit for the community they live in and society as a whole. The SDG allows, in the same way, one to measure against effective SDG implementation and strategically plan to improve sustainable practices while avoiding sustainability inhibitors. Both these tools help to measure and implement sustainability in an organization, thus contributing to an effective operationalization, and also to benchmark results with other companies finding a joint strategy toward sustainability.

We, therefore, believe that there is a need among accounting academics and institutions (Bebbington et al., 2017; Bebbington & Unerman, 2018) to raise awareness toward the measurement of company business models and SDG-related practices, and call for an increase in their involvement to help in the initiation, scoping, and development of high-quality research projects in the area. In this regard it should be argued that the field research approach (based on the direct involvement of companies, professionals, and scholars), and the usefulness of analyzing business cases aimed at investigating both methods and subject matter of business reporting on TBL and SDGs (Bebbington and Unerman, 2018), which has been particularly felt in the areas of accounting and accountability (Godemann, Bebbington, et al., 2014; Godemann, Haertle, et al., 2014), should be further improved, confirming its usefulness to actively "mould" the reality and face the relative challenges.

ACKNOWLEDGEMENT

All authors have contributed equally.

NOTES

1. B Lab was founded in Pennsylvania in 2006. It develops standards around responsible business conduct and provides the B Corp certification. For additional information see the B Lab website, www.bcorporation.net
2. https://sdgcompass.org/
3. Scopus, JSTOR, Science Direct, Emerald, and G-Scholar.
4. Official presentations, webinars and their website.
5. https://bcorporation.eu/about-b-lab
6. https://bcorporation.net/news/v6-b-impact-assessment-coming-january-2019
7. https://bcorporation.net/certification
8. https://bcorporation.net/welcome-sdg-action-manager
9. https://www.unglobalcompact.org/take-action/sdg-action-manager
10. https://sdghub.com/project/sdg-action-manager-tool/
11. https://www.unglobalcompact.org/library
12. Gruppo Hera, Chiesi Farmaceutic, Nativa, Singularity contributed to develop the indicator.

REFERENCES

Acca. (2017). *The Sustainable Development Goals: Redefining Context, Risk and Opportunity*. https://www.accaglobal.com/content/dam/ACCA_Global/professional-insights/The-sustainable -development-goals/pi-sdgs-accountancy-profession.pdf

Accenture (2017). Compliance: Dare to be different. 2017 compliance to risk study. Accenture consulting. https://www.accenture.com/us-en/insights/financial-services/compliance-risk-study-2017 -financial-services

Adams, C. A. (2017a). *The Sustainable Development Goals, Integrated Thinking and the Integrated Report*. https://pdfs.semanticscholar.org/3d66/cfded85ad8281dcad2ec35a4d1332bfc7f36.pdf?_ga=2 .48529381.2133768210.1585398516-1449654141.1570697049

Adams, C. A. (2017b). *The Sustainable Development Goals, integrated thinking and the integrated report*. https://integratedreporting.org/wp-content/uploads/2017/09/SDGs-and-the-integrated-report_full17.pdf

Agostino, D., & Sidorova, Y. (2017). How social media reshapes action on distant customers: Some empirical evidence. *Accounting, Auditing & Accountability Journal, 30*(4), 777–794. https://doi.org/10.1108/AAAJ-07-2015-2136

Alcorn, S., & Alcorn, M. (2012). Benefit corporations: A new formula for social change. *Associations Now*. https://www.asaecenter.org/Resources/ANowDetail.cfm?ItemNumber=179687

Amini, M., & Bienstock, C. C. (2014). Corporate sustainability: An integrative definition and framework to evaluate corporate practice and guide academic research. *Journal of Cleaner Production, 76*, 12–19. https://doi.org/10.1016/j.jclepro.2014.02.016

Annan-Diab, F., & Molinari, C. (2017). Interdisciplinarity: Practical approach to advancing education for sustainability and for the Sustainable Development Goals. *The International Journal of Management Education, 15*(2), 73–83. https://doi.org/10.1016/j.ijme.2017.03.006

ASVIS. (2018). *Introducing an Actionable Management Platform for Businesses to Deliver on the Sustainable Development Goals by 2030*. http://asvis.it/public/asvis/files/B_Lab_and_the_SDGs_One_Pager_2_.pdf

Babiak, K., & Trendafilova, S. (2011). CSR and environmental responsibility: Motives and pressures to adopt green management practices. *Corporate Social Responsibility and Environmental Management, 18*(1), 11–24. https://doi.org/10.1002/csr.229

Balog, A. M., Baker, L. T., & Walker, A. G. (2014). Religiosity and spirituality in entrepreneurship: A review and research agenda. *Journal of Management, Spirituality & Religion, 11*(2), 159–186. https://doi.org/10.1080/14766086.2013.836127

Baudout, K. L., Dillard, J., & Pencle, N. (2018). *The Emergence of Benefit Corporations: A Cautionary Tale of Responsible Business Conduct and the Common Good* [Conference]. 41th Annual Congress of EEA, European Accounting Association, Milan, Bocconi University.

Baumgartner, R. J. (2014). Managing corporate sustainability and CSR: A conceptual framework combining values, strategies and instruments contributing to sustainable development: Managing corporate sustainability and CSR. *Corporate Social Responsibility and Environmental Management, 21*(5), 258–271. https://doi.org/10.1002/csr.1336

Bebbington, J., Russell, S., & Thomson, I. (2017). Accounting and sustainable development: Reflections and propositions. *Critical Perspectives on Accounting, 48*, 21–34. https://doi.org/10.1016/j.cpa.2017.06.002

Bebbington, J., & Unerman, J. (2018). Achieving the United Nations Sustainable Development Goals: An enabling role for accounting research. *Accounting, Auditing & Accountability Journal, 31*(1), 2–24. https://doi.org/10.1108/AAAJ-05-2017-2929

Bell, S., & Morse, S. (2018). *Routledge Handbook of Sustainability Indicators*. Routledge.

Bellucci, M., & Manetti, G. (2017). Facebook as a tool for supporting dialogic accounting? Evidence from large philanthropic foundations in the United States. *Accounting, Auditing & Accountability Journal, 30*(4), 874–905. https://doi.org/10.1108/AAAJ-07-2015-2122

Billis, D. (A c. Di). (2010). *Hybrid Organizations and the Third Sector: Challenges for Practice, Theory and Policy*. Palgrave Macmillan.

Blewitt, J. (2015). *Understanding Sustainable Development* (Second edition). Routledge.

Boons, F., & Lüdeke-Freund, F. (2013). Business models for sustainable innovation: State-of-the-art and steps towards a research agenda. *Journal of Cleaner Production, 45*, 9–19. https://doi.org/10.1016/j.jclepro.2012.07.007

Brinkmann, R., & Garren, S. J. (2018). *The Palgrave Handbook of Sustainability: Case Studies and Practical Solutions*. Springer.

Brown, D., Dillard, J., & Marshall, R. S. (2008). Triple bottom line: A business metaphor for a social construct. In *Understanding the Social Dimension of Sustainability*. [Working Paper]. http://archives.pdx.edu/ds/psu/18442

Bruni, L. (2010). *L'impresa civile: Una via italiana all'economia di mercato*. books.google.com. https://books.google.it/books?hl=it&lr=&id=u3KVCwAAQBAJ&oi=fnd&pg=PT4&dq=Economia+civile.+Efficienza,+equit%C3%A0,+felicit%C3%A0+pubblica+L+Bruni,+S+Zamagni&ots=KDVmG6mirM&sig=OG5Nr_1iKf7jwsjxTi8tnk3PQEw#v=onepage&q=Economia%20civile.

%20Efficienza%2C%20equit%C3%A0%2C%20felicit%C3%A0%20pubblica%20L%20Bruni%2C %20S%20Zamagni&f=false

Bruni, L., & Zamagni, S. (2004). *Economia civile*. Il Mulino.

Camm, E. (2012). *Benefit Enforcement Proceedings for the Benefit Corporation – What are they and how will they work?* Apex Law Group. http://apexlg.com/benefit-enforcement-proceedings-for-the -benefit-corporation-what-are-they-and-how-will-they-work/

Castellani, G., De Rossi, D., & Rampa, A. (2016). *Le Società Benefit: La nuova prospettiva di una Corporate Social Responsability con commitment*. Fondazione Nazionale dei Commercialisti. http:// www.fondazionenazionalecommercialisti.it/node/1006

Charter, M., Gray, C., Clark, T., & Woolman, T. (2008). Review: The role of business in realising sustainable consumption and production. In A. Tukker, M. Charter, C. Vezzoli, E. Stø, & M. M. Andersen (Eds.), *Perspectives on Radical Changes to Sustainable Consumption and Production*. London, UK: Routledge, pp.46–69.

Christensen, L. T., Morsing, M., & Thyssen, O. (2013). CSR as aspirational talk. *Organization, 20*(3), 372–393. https://doi.org/10.1177/1350508413478310

Cintra, Y., & Carter, D. (2012). Internalising sustainability: Reflections on management control in Brazil. *International Journal of Strategic Management, 12*(2), 108–125.

Coviello, N. E., & Jones, M. V. (2004). Methodological issues in international entrepreneurship research. *Journal of Business Venturing, 19*(4), 485–508. https://doi.org/10.1016/j.jbusvent.2003.06.001

Deegan, C., & Rankin, M. (1996). Do Australian companies report environmental news objectively?: An analysis of environmental disclosures by firms prosecuted successfully by the Environmental Protection Authority. *Accounting, Auditing & Accountability Journal, 9*(2), 50–67. https://doi.org/10 .1108/09513579610116358

Del Baldo, M. (2012). Corporate social responsibility and corporate governance in Italian SMEs: The experience of some "spirited businesses". *Journal of Management & Governance, 16*(1), 1–36. https://doi.org/10.1007/s10997-009-9127-4

Del Baldo, M., & Demartini, P. (2012). Bottom-up or top-down: Which is the best approach to improve CSR and sustainability in local contexts? Reflections from Italian experiences. *Journal of Modern Accounting and Auditing, V8*(3), 381–400.

Deloitte. (2015). *CSR Managers Survey 2015 in Central Europe. How CSR has Influenced Central European Societies and Economies. Lessons Learnt and Future Trend.* https://www2.deloitte.com/ru/ en/pages/risk/articles/2016/csr-managers-survey-in-central-europe-2015.html

Di Cesare, P., & Ezechieli, E. (2017). *Le Benefit Corporation e l'evoluzione del Capitalismo* (1.0) [Computer software]. Università Ca' Foscari Venezia, Italia. https://doi.org/10.14277/6969-188-1/ LCF-4-4

Dillard, J., Dujon, V., & King, M. C. (2008). *Understanding the Social Dimension of Sustainability*. books.google.com. https://books.google.it/books?hl=it&lr=&id=Ps6SAgAAQBAJ&oi=fnd&pg=PP1 &dq=jesse+dillard&ots=Kdl28Ky9nU&sig=exeEcB6z14qgCxXuFwGU2jLaSv4#v=onepage&q= jesse%20dillard&f=false

Dumay, J., Bernardi, C., Guthrie, J., & Demartini, P. (2016). Integrated reporting: A structured literature review. *Accounting Forum, 40*(3), 166–185. https://doi.org/10.1016/j.accfor.2016.06.001

Dyllick, T., & Hockerts, K. (2002). Beyond the business case for corporate sustainability. *Business Strategy and the Environment, 11*(2), 130–141. https://doi.org/10.1002/bse.323

Elkington, J. (1997) *Cannibals with Forks: The Triple Bottom Line of 21st Century Business*. Capstone.

Fearon, R. P., Bakermans-Kranenburg, M. J., van Ijzendoorn, M. H., Lapsley, A.-M., & Roisman, G. I. (2010). The significance of insecure attachment and disorganization in the development of children's externalizing behavior: A meta-analytic study. *Child Development, 81*(2), 435–456. https://doi.org/10 .1111/j.1467-8624.2009.01405.x

Fletcher, K. (2012). Durability, fashion, sustainability: The processes and practices of use. *Fashion Practice, 4*(2), 221–238. https://doi.org/10.2752/175693812X13403765252389

Garcia, S., Cintra, Y., Torres, R. de C. S. R., & Lima, F. G. (2016). Corporate sustainability management: A proposed multi-criteria model to support balanced decision-making. *Journal of Cleaner Production, 136*, 181–196. https://doi.org/10.1016/j.jclepro.2016.01.110

Garcia-Torres, S., Rey-García, M., & Albareda-Vivo, L. (2017). Effective disclosure in the fast-fashion industry: From sustainability reporting to action. *Sustainability*, *9*(12), 2256. https://doi.org/10.3390/su9122256

GBS. (2019). *The SDGs in the Reports of the Italian Companies*. Franco Angeli Milano. http://www.gruppobilanciosociale.org/wp-content/uploads/2019/11/436-99Z_Book-Manuscript-2075-1-10-20191113.pdf

Global Compact. (2020). *La valutazione delle performance di sostenibilità delle imprese: UNGC SDG Action Manager*. GCNI WEBINAR.

Godemann, J., Bebbington, J., Herzig, C., & Moon, J. (2014). Higher education and sustainable development: Exploring possibilities for organisational change. *Accounting, Auditing & Accountability Journal*, *27*(2), 218–233. https://doi.org/10.1108/AAAJ-12-2013-1553

Godemann, J., Haertle, J., Herzig, C., & Moon, J. (2014). United Nations supported principles for responsible management education: Purpose, progress and prospects. *Journal of Cleaner Production*, *62*, 16–23. https://doi.org/10.1016/j.jclepro.2013.07.033

Gray, R. (2006). Social, environmental and sustainability reporting and organisational value creation?: Whose value? Whose creation? *Accounting, Auditing & Accountability Journal*, *19*(6), 793–819. https://doi.org/10.1108/09513570610709872

Gray, R, Adams, C., & Owen, D. (2014). *Accountability, Social Responsibility and Sustainability. Accounting for Society and the Environment*. Pearson.

Gray, R, Kouhy, R., & Lavers, S. (1995). Corporate social and environmental reporting: A review of the literature and a longitudinal study of UK disclosure. *Accounting, Auditing & Accountability Journal*, *8*(2), 47–77. https://doi.org/10.1108/09513579510146996

GRI. (2018). *Global Reporting Initiative*. https://www.globalreporting.org/information/news-and-press-center/newsarchive/Pages/2018.aspx

Griggs, D., Stafford Smith, M., Rockström, J., Öhman, M. C., Gaffney, O., Glaser, G., Kanie, N., Noble, I., Steffen, W., & Shyamsundar, P. (2014). An integrated framework for sustainable development goals. *Ecology and Society*, *19*(4). https://doi.org/10.5751/ES-07082-190449

Gupta, J., & Vegelin, C. (2016). Sustainable development goals and inclusive development. *International Environmental Agreements: Politics, Law and Economics*, *16*(3), 433–448. https://doi.org/10.1007/s10784-016-9323-z

Gusmão Caiado, R. G., Leal Filho, W., Quelhas, O. L. G., Luiz de Mattos Nascimento, D., & Ávila, L. V. (2018). A literature-based review on potentials and constraints in the implementation of the sustainable development goals. *Journal of Cleaner Production*, *198*, 1276–1288. https://doi.org/10.1016/j.jclepro.2018.07.102

Hahn, R., & Kühnen, M. (2013). Determinants of sustainability reporting: A review of results, trends, theory, and opportunities in an expanding field of research. *Journal of Cleaner Production*, *59*, 5–21. https://doi.org/10.1016/j.jclepro.2013.07.005

Hajer, M., Nilsson, M., Raworth, K., Bakker, P., Berkhout, F., de Boer, Y., Rockström, J., Ludwig, K., & Kok, M. (2015). Beyond cockpit-ism: Four insights to enhance the transformative potential of the sustainable development goals. *Sustainability*, *7*(2), 1651–1660. https://doi.org/10.3390/su7021651

Hák, T., Janoušková, S., & Moldan, B. (2016). Sustainable Development Goals: A need for relevant indicators. *Ecological Indicators*, *60*, 565–573. https://doi.org/10.1016/j.ecolind.2015.08.003

Hiller, J. S. (2013). The benefit corporation and corporate social responsibility. *Journal of Business Ethics*, *118*(2), 287. https://doi.org/10.1007/s10551-012-1580-3

Horn, P., & Grugel, J. (2018). The SDGs in middle-income countries: Setting or serving domestic development agendas? Evidence from Ecuador. *World Development*, *109*, 73–84. https://doi.org/10.1016/j.worlddev.2018.04.005

Hsieh, H.-F., & Shannon, S. E. (2005). Three approaches to qualitative content analysis. *Qualitative Health Research*, *15*(9), 1277–1288. https://doi.org/10.1177/1049732305276687

Hussain, N., Rigoni, U., & Orij, R. P. (2018). Corporate governance and sustainability performance: Analysis of triple bottom line performance. *Journal of Business Ethics*, *149*(2), 411–432. https://doi.org/10.1007/s10551-016-3099-5

Johnson, M. W. (2010). *Seizing the White Space: Business Model Innovation for Growth and Renewal*. Harvard Business Press.

Kaur, M., & Nguyen, M. (2018). *Leveraging the business sector for a sustainable future* [May 2018 Report].   https://ghd.georgetown.edu/wp-content/uploads/2018/12/Business-Sector-and-the-SDGs -Final-Report.pdf

Ketola, T. (2008). A holistic corporate responsibility model: Integrating values, discourses and actions. *Journal of Business Ethics, 80*(3), 419–435. https://doi.org/10.1007/s10551-007-9428-y

Keupp, M. M., & Gassmann, O. (2009). The past and the future of international entrepreneurship: A review and suggestions for developing the field. *Journal of Management, 35*(3), 600–633. https:// doi.org/10.1177/0149206308330558

Kolk, A. (2003). Trends in sustainability reporting by the Fortune Global 250. *Business Strategy and the Environment, 12*(5), 279–291. https://doi.org/10.1002/bse.370

KPMG. (2011). *International Survey of Corporate Responsibility Reporting.* KPMG.

Kusek, J. Z., & Rist, R. C. (2004). *Ten Steps to a Results-based Monitoring and Evaluation System: A Handbook for Development Practitioners.* World Bank.

Laloux, F. (2014). *Reinventing Organizations: A Guide to Creating Organizations Inspired by the Next Stage of Human Consciousness* (First edition). Nelson Parker.

Laszlo, C. (2019). Strengthening humanistic management. *Humanistic Management Journal, 4*(1), 85–94.

Laszlo, C., Brown, J., Ehrenfeld, J., Gorham, M., Barros-Pose, I., Robson, L., Saillant, R., Sherman, D., & Werder, P. (2014). *Flourishing Enterprise: The New Spirit of Business.* Stanford Business Books, an imprint of Stanford University Press.

Le Blanc, D. (2015). Towards integration at last? The sustainable development goals as a network of targets. *Sustainable Development, 23*(3), 176–187. https://doi.org/10.1002/sd.1582

Leal Filho, W., Manolas, E., & Pace, P. (2015). The future we want: Key issues on sustainable development in higher education after Rio and the UN decade of education for sustainable development. *International Journal of Sustainability in Higher Education, 16*(1), 112–129.

Leal Filho, W., Brandli, L. L., Becker, D., Skanavis, C., Kounani, A., Sardi, C., Papaioannidou, D., Paço, A., Azeiteiro, U., de Sousa, L. O., Raath, S., Pretorius, R. W., Shiel, C., Vargas, V., Trencher, G., & Marans, R. W. (2018). Sustainable development policies as indicators and pre-conditions for sustainability efforts at universities: Fact or fiction? *International Journal of Sustainability in Higher Education, 19*(1), 85–113. https://doi.org/10.1108/IJSHE-01-2017-0002

Levillain, K., & Segrestin, B. (2014). *The Blind Spot of Corporate Social Responsibility: Changing the Legal Framework of the Firm.* EURAM, Jun 2014, Valence, Spain. hal-00969099

Liu, X., & Anbumozhi, V. (2009). Determinant factors of corporate environmental information disclosure: An empirical study of Chinese listed companies. *Journal of Cleaner Production, 17*(6), 593–600. https://doi.org/10.1016/j.jclepro.2008.10.001

Longoni, A., Golini, R., & Cagliano, R. (2014). The role of New Forms of Work Organization in developing sustainability strategies in operations. *International Journal of Production Economics, 147*, 147–160. https://doi.org/10.1016/j.ijpe.2013.09.009

Lozano, R. (2015). A holistic perspective on corporate sustainability drivers. *Corporate Social Responsibility and Environmental Management, 22*(1), 32–44. https://doi.org/10.1002/csr.1325

Mayring, P. (2004). Qualitative content analysis. In *A Companion to Qualitative Research* (Vol. 1, pp. 159–176). Sage Publications.

Mazzoleni, G. (A c. Di). (2015). *The International Encyclopedia of Political Communication* (First edition). Wiley. https://doi.org/10.1002/9781118541555

Miller, E., Buys, L., & Summerville, J. (2007). Quantifying the social dimension of triple bottom line: Development of a framework and indicators to assess the social impact of organisations. *International Journal of Business Governance and Ethics, 3*(3), 223. https://doi.org/10.1504/IJBGE.2007.014314

Morioka, S. N., & Carvalho, M. M. (2016a). A systematic literature review towards a conceptual framework for integrating sustainability performance into business. *Journal of Cleaner Production, 136*, 134–146. https://doi.org/10.1016/j.jclepro.2016.01.104

Morioka, S. N., & Carvalho, M. M. (2016b). Measuring sustainability in practice: Exploring the inclusion of sustainability into corporate performance systems in Brazilian case studies. *Journal of Cleaner Production, 136*, 123–133. https://doi.org/10.1016/j.jclepro.2016.01.103

Muff, K., Kapalka, A., & Dyllick, T. (2017). The gap frame—Translating the SDGs into relevant national grand challenges for strategic business opportunities. *The International Journal of Management Education, 15*(2), 363–383. https://doi.org/10.1016/j.ijme.2017.03.004

Munch, S. (2012). Improving the benefit corporation: How traditional governance mechanisms can enhance the innovative new business forms. *Northwestern Journal of Law & Society, 7*(1), 170–195.

Murray, J. (2012). Choose your own master: Social enterprise, certifications and benefit corporation statutes. *American University Business Law Review, 2*(1), 1–54.

Nicholas, A. J., & Sacco, S. (2017). *People, Planet, Profit: Benefit and B Certified Corporations— Comprehension and Outlook of Business Students* [Articles & Papers Faculty and Staff]. Salve Regina University. https://digitalcommons.salve.edu/cgi/viewcontent.cgi?article=1069&context=fac_staff _pub

Nicholls, A. (2010). The legitimacy of social entrepreneurship: Reflexive isomorphism in a pre-paradigmatic field. *Entrepreneurship Theory and Practice, 34*(4), 611–633. https://doi.org/10 .1111/j.1540-6520.2010.00397.x

Nidumolu, R., Prahalad, C. K., & Rangaswami, M. R. (2009). *Why Sustainability Is Now the Key Driver of Innovation.* https://hbr.org/2009/09/why-sustainability-is-now-the-key-driver-of-innovation

Nigri, G. (2018). Benefit Corporations and B Corps. In *Scholarly Community Encyclopedia.* Sustainability, MDPI. https://encyclopedia.pub/item/revision/c8f242184dfc97c8c19c4cb162cfa16e

Nigri, G., & Del Baldo, M. (2018). Sustainability reporting and performance measurement systems: How do small- and medium-sized benefit corporations manage integration? *Sustainability, 10*(12), 4499. https://doi.org/10.3390/su10124499

Nigri, G., Del Baldo, M., & Agulini, A. (2020). Integrated sustainable performance management systems: A case study on Italian benefit corporations. *Corporate Ownership and Control, 17*(2), 65–76. https://doi.org/10.22495/cocv17i2art6

Nigri, G., & Michelini, L. (2019). A systematic literature review on social impact assessment: Outlining main dimensions and future research lines. In R. Schmidpeter, N. Capaldi, S. O. Idowu, & A. Stürenberg Herrera (A c. Di), *International Dimensions of Sustainable Management* (pp. 53–67). Springer International Publishing. https://doi.org/10.1007/978-3-030-04819-8_4

Nigri, G., Michelini, L., & Grieco, C. (2017). Social impact and online communication in B-Corps. *Global Journal of Business Research, 11*(3), 87–104.

Nigri, G., Michelini, L., Grieco, C., & Iasevoli, G. (2016). B Corps and their social impact communication strategy: Does the talk match the walk? *SIM Conference 2016.* XIII Convegno Annuale della Società Italiana Marketing, Università di Cassino.

OECD. (2017). *Going for Growth.* http://www.oecd.org/economy/growth/going-for-growth-2017/

Oxfam. (2018). *Walking the Talk.* https://oxfamilibrary.openrepository.com/bitstream/handle/10546/ 620550/dp-walking-the-talk-business-sdgs-240918-en.pdf

Pisoni, A., Michelini, L., & Martignoni, G. (2018). Frugal approach to innovation: State of the art and future perspectives. *Journal of Cleaner Production, 171,* 107–126. https://doi.org/10.1016/j.jclepro .2017.09.248

PwC. (2015). *Making it Your Business: Engaging with the Sustainable Development Goals.* PwC London.

Rawhouser, H., Cummings, M., & Crane, A. (2015). Benefit corporation legislation and the emergence of a social hybrid category. *California Management Review, 57*(3), 13–35. https://doi.org/10.1525/ cmr.2015.57.3.13

RobecoSam. (2018). *Measuring Intangibles.* https://www.robecosam.com/media/b/3/7/b37010e6273b 82fb33528754e55051b1_measuring-intangibles-csa-methodology_tcm1012-15720.pdf

Rodriguez, M. A., Ricart, J. E., & Sanchez, P. (2002). Sustainable development and the sustainability of competitive advantage: A dynamic and sustainable view of the firm. *Creativity and Innovation Management, 11*(3), 135–146. https://doi.org/10.1111/1467-8691.00246

Rosati, F., & Faria, L. G. D. (2019). Addressing the SDGs in sustainability reports: The relationship with institutional factors. *Journal of Cleaner Production, 215,* 1312–1326. https://doi.org/10.1016/j.jclepro .2018.12.107

Sabeti, H. (2011). The for-benefit enterprise. *Harvard Business Review, 89*(11), 98–104.

Sachs, J. (2012). From Millennium Development Goals to Sustainable Development Goals. *The Lancet, 379*(9832), 2206–2211. https://doi.org/10.1016/S0140-6736(12)60685-0

Sachs, J. (2015). *The Age of Sustainable Development*. Columbia University Press.

Salvia, A. L., Leal Filho, W., Brandli, L. L., & Griebeler, J. S. (2019). Assessing research trends related to Sustainable Development Goals: Local and global issues. *Journal of Cleaner Production, 208*, 841–849. https://doi.org/10.1016/j.jclepro.2018.09.242

Savitz, A. W., & Weber, K. (2014). *The Triple Bottom Line: How Today's Best-run Companies are Achieving Economic, Social, and Environmental Success – And How You Can Too* (Revised and updated). Jossey-Bass, a Wiley brand.

Schaltegger, S., Etxeberria, I. Á., & Ortas, E. (2017). Innovating corporate accounting and reporting for sustainability – attributes and challenges: Innovating accounting and reporting for sustainability. *Sustainable Development, 25*(2), 113–122. https://doi.org/10.1002/sd.1666

Schaltegger, S., Hansen, E. G., & Lüdeke-Freund, F. (2016). Business models for sustainability: Origins, present research, and future avenues. *Organization & Environment, 29*(1), 3–10. https://doi.org/10.1177/1086026615599806

Schaltegger, S., Lüdeke-Freund, F., & Hansen, E. G. (2012). Business cases for sustainability: The role of business model innovation for corporate sustainability. *International Journal of Innovation and Sustainable Development, 6*(2), 95–119.

Schlange, L. E. (2009). Stakeholder identification in sustainability entrepreneurship: The role of managerial and organisational cognition. *Greener Management International, 55*, 13–32.

Schmidt-Traub, G., Kroll, C., Teksoz, K., Durand-Delacre, D., & Sachs, J. D. (2017). National baselines for the Sustainable Development Goals assessed in the SDG Index and Dashboards. *Nature Geoscience, 10*(8), 547–555. https://doi.org/10.1038/ngeo2985

SDG Compass. (2015). *SDG Compass. The Guide for Business Action on the SDGs*. http://sdgcompass.org/wp-content/uploads/2015/12/019104_SDG_Compass_Guide_2015.pdf

Segrestin, B., Levillain, K., & Hatchuel, A. (2016). Purpose-driven corporations: How corporate law reorders the field of corporate governance. *EURAM 2016*, Jun 2016, Paris, France. hal-01323118

Selomane, O., Reyers, B., Biggs, R., Tallis, H., & Polasky, S. (2015). Towards integrated social–ecological sustainability indicators: Exploring the contribution and gaps in existing global data. *Ecological Economics, 118*, 140–146. https://doi.org/10.1016/j.ecolecon.2015.07.024

Siebenhüner, B., & Arnold, M. (2007). Organizational learning to manage sustainable development. *Business Strategy and the Environment, 16*(5), 339–353. https://doi.org/10.1002/bse.579

Slawinski, N., & Bansal, P. (2015). Short on time: Intertemporal tensions in business sustainability. *Organization Science, 26*(2), 531–549. https://doi.org/10.1287/orsc.2014.0960

Slawinski, N., Pinkse, J., Busch, T., & Banerjee, S. B. (2017). The role of short-termism and uncertainty avoidance in organizational inaction on climate change: A multi-level framework. *Business & Society, 56*(2), 253–282. https://doi.org/10.1177/0007650315576136

Storey, M., Killian, S., & O'Regan, P. (2017). Responsible management education: Mapping the field in the context of the SDGs. *The International Journal of Management Education, 15*(2), 93–103. https://doi.org/10.1016/j.ijme.2017.02.009

Thijssens, T., Bollen, L., & Hassink, H. (2016). Managing sustainability reporting: Many ways to publish exemplary reports. *Journal of Cleaner Production, 136*, 86–101. https://doi.org/10.1016/j.jclepro.2016.01.098

UN. (2015). *United Nations Sustainable Development Summit 2015*. https://sustainabledevelopment.un.org/post2015/summit

Unerman, J., & Chapman, C. (2014). Academic contributions to enhancing accounting for sustainable development. *Accounting, Organizations and Society, 39*(6), 385–394. https://doi.org/10.1016/j.aos.2014.07.003

UNGC Academy. (2020). *Managing Corporate Sustainability Performance through the SDG Action Manager*.

United Nations. (1992). *Rio Declaration of the United Nations on Environment and Development*. http://www.unesco.org/education/pdf/RIO_E.PDF

United Nations. (2015). *Transforming Our World: The 2030 Agenda for Sustainable Development*. United Nations, New York. https://sustainabledevelopment. un.org/content/documents/21252030%20Agenda%20for%20Sustainable%20Development%20 web.pdf

United Nations. (2016). *The Sustainable Development Goals Report*. United Nations, New York.

UNWCED. (1987). *Our Common Future (The Brundtland Report)*. Oxford University Press. http://www
.un-documents.net/our-common-future.pdf

Vachon, S. (2010). International operations and sustainable development: Should national culture
matter? *Sustainable Development*, *18*(6), 350–361. https://doi.org/10.1002/sd.398

Vanclay, F. (2004). The triple bottom line and impact assessment: How do TBL, EIA, SIA, SEA and
EMS relate to each other? *Journal of Environmental Assessment Policy and Management*, *6*(3),
265–288. https://doi.org/10.1142/S1464333204001729

von Schwedler, M. (2016). Accounting and sustainable development: An exploration. *Social and
Environmental Accountability Journal*, *36*(2), 165–165. https://doi.org/10.1080/0969160X.2016
.1197623

WBCSD. (2016). *Communicating on the Sustainable Development Goals*. https://www.wbcsd.org/
Programs/Redefining-Value/External-Disclosure/Reporting-matters/Resources/Reporting-matters
-2016

Webster, J., & Watson, R. (2002). Analyzing the past to prepare for the future: Writing a literature
review. *MIS Quarterly*, *26*. https://doi.org/10.2307/4132319

Wilson, P. (2017). Goal setters. *Economia*, *57*, 40–44.

World Bank. (2017). *World Bank Annual Report*. http://documents.worldbank.org/curated/en/
143021506909711004/World-Bank-Annual-Report-2017

Zadek, S. (2006). Responsible competitiveness: Reshaping global markets through responsible business
practices. *Corporate Governance: The International Journal of Business in Society*, *6*(4), 334–348.
https://doi.org/10.1108/14720700610689469

Zamagni, S. (1995). *The Economics of Altruism*. E. Elgar.

Zamagni, S. (2007). *L'economia del bene comune*. Citta` Nuova.

PART 4

SUSTAINABILITY-DRIVEN BUSINESS STRATEGIES IN OPERATIONS AND INFORMATION SYSTEMS

12. SMEs, environmental sustainability and waste management: a comparative empirical study of Spain and Chile

Francisco Villegas Pinuer, Joan Llonch Andreu and Pilar López Belbeze

INTRODUCTION

Human society and the planet are currently facing major challenges regarding the environment. With climate change and resource scarcity as core sustainability issues, the world today requires a global commitment to overcome the difficulties it is facing. To this end, the United Nations (UN) has developed 17 Sustainable Development Goals (SDGs) for the UN2030 agenda, with member states expected to cooperate to balance economic growth, social equality and environmental protection (United Nations, 2015). In a practical sense, sustainability is the basis for building a society that balances economic, social and environmental aims and that pursues ethical business practices, sustainable employment and value for company stakeholders (Székely & Knirsch, 2005). Finding the way to achieve sustainable growth and development has become a priority for most world societies.

In regard to the environmental agenda and their own environmental sustainability (ES), companies have an enormous responsibility to bear as they must become capable of balancing economic and financial objectives with the proper use of resources (including avoidance of overexploitation), while ensuring their continuity in time. In analysing the private sector, researchers have tended to focus on large companies due to the sheer volume of their operations. Examples in the literature cover ES practices and applications (Hörisch et al., 2015; Ndubisi & Nygaard, 2018), management (Arnold, 2017; De Oliveira et al., 2016), corporate social responsibility (Helfaya & Moussa, 2017; Quarshie et al., 2016), sustainability investments (De Mendonca & Zhou, 2019) and environmental incentives and policies (Dahlmann et al., 2017).

The role played by small and medium enterprises (SMEs) in generating socioeconomic growth and employment (Acs et al., 2012) tends to be overlooked by researchers, but may, in fact, be more crucial to accomplishing ES than previously thought. In the European Union (EU), for instance, SMEs represent 99.8% of companies, 61.4% of total employment and 54.5% of gross domestic product (GDP) (European Commission, 2019). SMEs also have an environmental impact, as they account for approximately 60–70% of environmental pollution (Aragón-Correa et al., 2008) and have a particular impact on waste management in cities (Sáez-Martínez et al., 2016). These impacts tend to be underestimated, due to the relatively smaller size of SMEs and under-measurement of their management and production indicators (Szilagyi & Mocan, 2018).

As for ES in SMEs, the existing academic literature is scarce and overly general (lack of depth). Nonetheless, researchers are developing an interest in studying the application of ES principles and practices in SMEs to help them integrate critical environmental issues with their organizational and market objectives. However, such a strategy, which profoundly affects SME development and management, requires in-depth analyses due to the focalized nature of its implementation (Johnson & Schaltegger, 2016). Bakos et al. (2020), for instance, emphasize the imperative need to better understand the reality of SMEs in terms of characteristics such as size, sector and stance on environmental issues.

Our comparative study focuses on SMEs in Spain – 99.83% of companies and 71.9% of total employment (Ministerio de Industria – Comercio y Turismo, 2019) and in Chile – 97% of companies and 70% of total employment (Ministerio de Economia – Fomento y Turismo, 2019). In particular, we examine two main regions within these countries: Catalonia and Santiago. Catalonia is the second most populated region of Spain (7,488,717 inhabitants), contributing 19.1% of the country's GDP (Instituto Nacional de Estadística de España, 2019). In retrospect, Santiago is the second most populated region of Chile (7,915,199 inhabitants) (Instituto Nacional de Estadísticas de Chile, 2019) accounting for almost half (43.6%) of Chilean GDP (Banco Central de Chile, 2018). Note, while in the case of Latin America SMEs account for similar levels of shares in companies (99.5%) and employment (61%) as in the EU (Comisión Económica para América Latina y el Caribe, 2018), GDP input tends to be much lower; 25% in Latin America (Comisión Económica para América Latina y el Caribe, 2018) compared with 54.5% in the EU (European Commission, 2019).

Spain's environmental approach has been heavily governed by the EU environmental framework for the last 20 years, through directives related to waste hierarchy, separate waste collection, expanded producer responsibility (EPR), and more (European Commission, 2008). In contrast, Chile's regulations have been developed under its own impetus, as Latin America does not have a common environmental and waste framework. Hence, Chile's initiatives are more recent than those of the EU, e.g., specific law governing EPR dates from 2016 (Ministerio del Medio Ambiente, 2016), and the ban on plastic bags was recently implemented in 2018 (Ministerio del Medio Ambiente, 2018).

The research described in this chapter, which focuses on issues such as environmental regulations, waste management and raw materials, among others, analyses ES in SMEs through the circular economy (CE) in supply chains, considering production inputs and resources as well as waste generation (Geissdoerfer et al., 2017), bearing in mind that the method of how companies operationally manage their supply chain is highly relevant to the environment. Thus, we consider the characteristics, motivators and inhibitors that affect ES practices in the supply chain (Reyes-Rodríguez et al. 2016), as well as how the economic and legal context for SMEs affects management decisions and business practices (Zamfir et al., 2017).

The research was based on in-depth interviews with Spanish and Chilean SME managers and decision-makers, who provided insights regarding ES in their businesses, including perspectives on resource efficiency factors, limitations, economic/societal barriers and obstacles, waste regulations and personal and corporate motivations in relation to environmental issues. Such experiences provide insights that enrich applications in the real world, and they also help visualize practical similarities and differences between sectors or regions. Specifically, we further explored the subject through open questions with interviewees such as:

1. What is the impact of environmental regulations on SMEs?
2. How do city or regional waste management systems impact ES for SMEs?
3. What is the situation regarding raw materials and their waste management in SMEs?

4. How do the above-mentioned factors affect ES in the CE supply chains for SMEs?

Freedom to answer such questions allowed the study to obtain valuable insights in the topic of ES and CE in SMEs. This chapter is organized as follows: the next section provides the theoretical background on ES, the CE and waste management, the links between them, and their applications. The third section describes the research methodology, the sample, and data collection and analysis. The fourth section reports the results. The fifth section discusses findings in relation to their implications for SME management and policy-maker decisions. The final section highlights the limitations of the research.

THEORETICAL BACKGROUND

The theoretical aspects are addressed in this section, while Figure 12.1 depicts an analytical framework of conceptual lines.

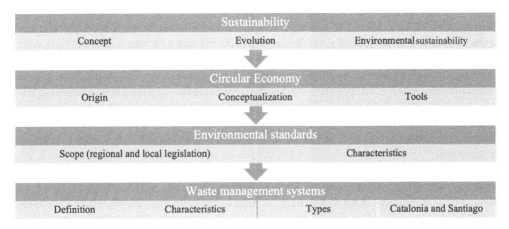

Figure 12.1   The analytical framework for ES in the SME supply chain

The Evolution of Sustainability and its Relationship with the Environment

The manner in which companies develop their operational supply management activities affects the sustainability of the planet in the broadest sense. Productive system decisions are therefore becoming an increasingly relevant topic, with ecological perspectives becoming increasingly important not only in society, but also in business (Dyllick & Hockerts, 2002). One of the earliest definitions of sustainability was provided by the Brundtland Commission in 1987, which established a framework for its scope: "development that meets the needs of the present without compromising the ability of future generations to meet their own needs" (World Commission on Environment and Development, 1987).

Naturally, the concept of sustainability and ES has changed over time, evolving into further tangible and concrete concepts in the past 30 years. What had previously been theoretical has now become a transdisciplinary concept that includes areas as diverse as business, design, mechanics and chemistry, with each discipline making its own contribution to the subject

(Sakao & Brambila-Macias, 2018). As a result of this development, some perspectives focus on the concepts of transparency, support systems and proposals and ideas that generate an ethical and civic force for contributions to society (Ciasullo and Troisi, 2013). Other researchers, such as Missimer et al. (2017), emphasize the relevance of our dependence on the ecological and social system, establishing that essential aspects must be sustained or restored to enable us to meet our present and future needs. Geissdoerfer et al. (2017) underlines the importance of achieving balanced and systemic integration of intra- and intergenerational economic, social and environmental performance, emphasizing intragenerational prosperity that simultaneously preserves the support systems needed to meet intergenerational needs. Contributing to this definition, Lozano and von Haartman (2018) refer to the holistic importance of ES drivers for companies and their importance in economic and social terms. Hence, as can be seen, the evolution and development of ES research points to its multilateralism and the boundary conditions (limits) that need to be set.

Environmental Sustainability and SMEs: Antecedents and Evidence

Bearing in mind the existence of multiple perspectives on sustainability, this chapter focuses on the environmental perspective, which involves different actors in society. For example, over the last 20 years, Goodland (1995) has argued that the development of sustainable levels of consumption and production has to take into consideration the maintenance of natural capital (human-made capital, not a substitute) to emphasize the relevance of resources. Following this idea, Morelli (2013) defines ES as "meeting the resource and services needs of current and future generations without compromising the health of the ecosystems that provide them". This definition highlights the importance of ecosystem stability and the use and management of resources.

When focusing on the case of SMEs, special attention must be paid to their problems regarding survival and development in the long term (Sallem et al., 2017). These problems are due to a lack of technical skills and strategic orientation (Arasti et al., 2014), where the importance and development of resources and capabilities become very relevant when attempting to achieve ES. Some of the antecedents are stated by Darcy et al. (2014), who maintains that SMEs need to ensure that they have the right human resources and skill set in the early stages of their development to achieve stable growth. This evidence is consistent with the relevance of the firm's strategic orientation with regard to its commitment to ES (Jansson et al., 2017; Reyes-Rodríguez et al., 2016). The importance of SMEs is that the implementation of sustainability agendas in different areas can allow the achievement of long-term competitive advantages and, hence, generate more probabilities for survival while stabilizing the market through ecological issues (Jansson et al., 2017).

Worryingly, and despite evidence that suggests a positive relationship, the popular view is that ES is an undesirable risk as there are other more profitable areas for SMEs to develop and exploit. In this regard, Ormazabal et al. (2018) affirm that SMEs do not think that ES could help to improve their financial results and profitability due to limited resources, short-term vision and lack of time on a daily basis. Supporting these arguments, Cantele and Zardini's (2018) research found that environmental practices did not have a significant impact on competitive advantage, as entrepreneurs felt that the market was not (and is still not) strongly committed to ES issues. Therefore, the challenge for SMEs is to incorporate and implement

ES-related practices in their businesses as these can have a positive effect on SME development, in incorporating all actors in society and thus presenting the CE as a viable option.

The Circular Economy (CE) and Environmental Sustainability (ES) in Production and Supply Systems

The CE is an expression of ES that has gained enormous traction among scholars and practitioners and – gradually – in society. A CE can be understood as an economy that is restorative and regenerative by design (Ellen MacArthur Foundation, 2013). This premise differs from a linear economy, which is based on a 'take-make-dispose' approach.

However, this concept is not a new or a novel paradigm. As far back as the 1970s, renowned Romanian economist Georgescu-Roegen, in *The Entropy Law and the Economic Process*, stated the importance of understanding how goods and services are produced; his research, undertaken 40 years ago, had already identified current problems such as environmental pollution, global warming and waste management. Georgescu-Roegen emphasized the lack of knowledge regarding the relationship between the economic and biological factors in the economy as a whole, where people's satisfaction is measured based on the production function for goods (in line with economic theory). This school of thought explains that when a society has satisfied its basic needs, it will tend to consume and produce more goods, hence generating productive overcapacity. However, even as society continues to produce, natural resources are finite and the flow of solar energy is a resource that cannot be controlled. Consequently, as Georgescu-Roegen explains, establishing the production function without considering inputs, natural resources, capital maintenance, waste and time and their relationship with capital and work assumes a very simplified reality (Georgescu-Roegen et al., 1996).

Following this idea, one of the main current conceptualizations is a regenerative system in which resource input and waste, emissions and energy leakage are minimized by slowing, closing and narrowing material and energy loops (Geissdoerfer et al., 2017). Hence, an understanding of productive processes and supply chain management within companies is fundamental to achieving a balance in the sustainable development of nations.

A clear example of the lack of balance can be identified in the EU. In 2016, an average of 12% of material resources used in the EU originated from recycled products and recovered materials. Nevertheless, as a whole, the EU has a high recycling rate of approximately 40% (Eurostat, 2019b). Given these statistics, Geissdoerfer et al. (2017) state the importance of the CE in aligning itself with the supply chain, since in this way it can contribute to sustainable development by promoting the economic, environmental and social goals of SMEs.

An in-depth examination of the CE shows that it is a concept that has evolved over time, particularly in relation to the well-known 3Rs: reduce, reuse and recycle. Reducing minimizes the input of initial energy, raw materials and waste by improving efficiency in production and consumption processes. Reusing means ensuring that products or components are not wasted and are used again for the same purpose for which they were conceived. Recycling is defined as any recovery operation by which waste materials are reprocessed into products, materials or substances, whether for the original or other purposes (King et al., 2006; Su et al., 2013). A more recent operationalization process corresponds to Potting et al (2017), who understand this last definition as a more complete representation that points to the different CE tools incorporating a less linear and more circular business perspective (see Table 12.1).

SMEs can use the CE tools to apply ES to their business via their supply chain. However, it is necessary to understand how SMEs close the loop of material flows and how waste management plays a prominent role in the implementation of the CE tools (Mura et al., 2020).

Regulatory Environmental Frameworks in Spain and Chile

The environmental situation is quite different in Spain and Chile. According to 2018 data, Spain has a domestic material consumption (DMC) of 9110 kg per capita, ranking 37th in the world, while Chile has a DMC of 40,400 kg per capita, making it the country with the largest DMC worldwide (OECD.Stat, 2020). The environmental framework determining the configuration of rules and mechanisms imposed on companies to reduce their adverse effects on the environment and society is therefore crucial. The correct establishment of standards and mechanisms plays a central role in the environmental responses of companies, especially SMEs (Lynch-Wood & Williamson, 2014). Spain is subject to the legal framework of the EU, which established the first environmental standard for all its member states in 1986. This framework established: (1) general rules to preserve, protect and improve the quality of the environment; (2) the first steps of the 'polluter pays' principle; and (3) the measurement of environmental conditions in the regions (European Commission, 1987). This general standard has been updated by a variety of treaties and agreements, including those of Maastricht, Lisbon and Helsinki (European Commission, 2017a).

Table 12.1   Circular economy tools

Purpose	Tool	Definition
Smarter product manufacture and use	Refuse	Make product redundant by abandoning its function, or by offering the same function with a radically different product
	Rethink	Make product use more intensive (e.g., by sharing the product)
	Reduce	Increase efficiency in product manufacture or use by consuming fewer natural resources and materials
Extension of product/ component lifespans	Reuse	Reuse a discarded product which is still in good condition and fulfils its original condition (e.g., by another consumer)
	Repair	Repair and maintain a defective product so it can be used with its original function
	Refurbish	Restore an old product and bring it up to date
	Remanufacture	Use parts of a discarded product in a new product with the same function
	Repurpose	Use a discarded product or its parts in a new product with a different function
Useful material application	Recycle	Process materials to obtain the same (high-grade) or lower (low-grade) quality
	Recover	Incinerate material to recover energy

Source: Authors, adapted from Kirchherr et al. (2017) and Potting et al. (2017).

In recent years, one of the EU's principal concerns has been to encourage SMEs to adopt CE principles and practices. In 2017, the CE generated approximately 3985 million jobs in the EU, corresponding to 1.69% of total employment (Eurostat, 2019a). The EU launched a CE Package in 2018 that emphasized the development of tools to support waste hierarchy objectives at all appropriate levels. It also focuses on promoting and incentivizing CE practices within SMEs (European Commission, 2018). In the same focus, the EU established a new CE Action Plan in March 2020. This ambitious plan is based on a closer relationship with customers and a sharing and collaborative economy powered by big data, blockchain and artificial intelligence. The plan will seek not only to accelerate circularity but also to dematerialize the economy and make the EU less dependent on primary materials (European Commission, 2020). Under this framework, Spain has launched a Spanish CE Strategy, with a number of objectives, including: (1) to reduce the national consumption of materials by 30% in relation to GDP (using 2010 as the reference year); (2) to reduce waste generation by 15% with respect to 2010; and (3) to improve reuse to the point where 10% of municipal waste is regenerated (Ministerio para la Transición Ecológica y el Reto Demográfico, 2020). This multidimensional strategy provides the impetus for a new production and consumption model that maintains the value of products, materials and resources for as long as possible – an issue that becomes especially important in the post-pandemic world.

Environmental legislation in South America varies from country to country and region to region, as there is no shared environmental framework. In the case of Chile, the environmental framework originated in 1994, when a general law founded and established the Ministry of the Environment, creating a general basis for environmental concerns that incorporates citizens' rights, pollution, education, information and other issues (Ministerio Secretaría General de la Presidencia, 1994). This law publicly made companies and society responsible for environmental issues for the first time ever. Following its enactment, Chile established bilateral environmental agreements with the USA, EU and Canada (2003). The current environmental framework is developed on the basis of EPR, which refers to waste management.

Waste Management Implications for Environmental Sustainability in Catalonia and Santiago

Waste management: origins and concepts

One of the outcomes of the production processes of any company is the waste generated. The concept of waste does not have a clear definition in the literature (Adipah & Kwame, 2019). The conceptual range is extensive; compare a discardable object (European Council, 1991) to substances or objects that can be disposed of and/or recovered depending on the final destination of a material (OECD, 2009). This last conceptualization suggests that the use-value of waste depends on how it is viewed by a society. In this sense, one of the main aspects of ES in a city and society is waste management (Jones & Comfort, 2018). For context, waste management covers the collection, processing, transport, recovery and disposal of waste, including the supervision of operations and after-care of disposal sites (European Council, 1991). There are a variety of ways in which a territorial unit (town, city, municipality and local authority) can take care of generated waste. The processes for collecting different materials and the range of respective treatments, from landfilling, incineration and composting to recovery, constitute a waste management system (Eriksson et al., 2002). This type of system, covering both companies and households, is typically managed by local authorities. Moreover, this system has a central issue in its development: traceability, which refers to the monitoring and control of the different stages within a waste management system (Briassoulis et al., 2014), allowing for the evaluation of the performance and effectiveness of waste management systems.

Waste management in Spain and Chile

A waste management system is an expression of the waste management legislation of a country. Legislation differs according to geographic location and this consideration is imperative to understanding the characteristics of the legislation. The characteristics of waste management systems in Catalonia and Santiago are described as follows.

Spain

In Spain, waste legislation is the extension of the EU framework enacted in 1998, subsequently updated in 2008 (European Commission, 2008). This legislation establishes concepts such as waste hierarchy, separate waste collection and EPR. A law regulating EPR was enacted in 2011 and updated in 2015, based on the principle 'the polluter pays', i.e., the law forces companies to be responsible for their waste (individually or as a group of firms), through separate, non-profit waste collection systems (Ministerio para la Transición Ecológica y el Reto emográfico, 2011). In terms of waste reduction, the European framework has developed municipal objectives, establishing strict standards and targets for urban waste as follows: 55% in 2025, 60% in 2030 and 65% in 2035 (the percentages refer to reuse and recycling of all waste). In addition, all plastic packaging must be recyclable by 2030, and certain types of waste will also begin to be collected selectively: hazardous household waste in 2022, biological waste in 2023 and textile waste in 2025 (European Environment Agency, 2017). All EU member states must comply with those goals, where Spain has established several standards relating to specific materials: hazardous substances (1988), packaging (1997), batteries (2008), electronic devices (2015) and vehicles and tyres (2017) (Ministerio de la Presidencia – Relaciones con las Cortes y Memoria Democrática, 2018).

Chile

In Chile, waste legislation is based on a law that regulates EPR (Extended Producer Responsibility). Waste legislation enacted in 2016 refers to producer responsibility for waste arising in the production process (this law is similar to the Spanish law, taking elements of their norms), and provides for the implementation of a plan to establish the separate collection of waste by integrated waste management systems. Furthermore, the law establishes priority areas and materials-to-waste collection objectives (Ministerio del Medio Ambiente, 2016). These goals were upgraded in the updated waste legislation enacted in 2019 (specific goals which are gradually increasing in scope). Priority areas were defined as follows: (1) tyres (50% collection and 25% reuse by 2021); (2) packaging (70% reuse of non-household packaging and 60% of household packaging by 2022 and by 2030, respectively). However, the aforementioned packaging goal was further updated by a ministerial council and decree-law on 7 May 2020, which targets various issues such as (1) non-household and household packaging goals to be delayed to the 9th and 12th years (respectively) following implementation; and (2) efforts to achieve the set goals would be delayed to 30 months after publication of the legislation (which would begin in 2023). This change in the date of implementation was motivated by the pandemic situation, however there is no launch date established for other materials such as lubricant oil, electronic devices and batteries, and thus these will go ahead during 2020 according to Chile's Ministry of the Environment. Another measure is a law enacted in 2018 that forbids commercial establishments from issuing plastic bags to customers (understood as bags that are made of plastic polymers and produced from oil), with a compliance deadline set for 2018 for large companies and 2020 for SMEs (Ministerio del Medio Ambiente, 2018).

It must be noted that the law regulating EPR is the first general law on waste in Chile's history, hence representing the country's environmental framework. Prior to 2016, industrial waste was subject to controls and mechanisms managed by the corresponding government bodies (e.g., ministries of mining, of agriculture, and so on). In lieu, the 20.416 Law refers to special standards for SMEs, based on 'the principle of proportionality' (Ministerio de Economia – Fomento y Turismo, 2010). This law establishes the relevance of the municipal waste management system for SME (based on Law 20.416) and household waste. Table 12.2 summarizes legislation and characteristics at the regional, country and local levels in Catalonia and Santiago.

Waste Management Characteristics and Implementation in Catalonia and Santiago

Catalonia: separated waste collection and the tax rate

Catalonia, which produced an average of 504.93 kg of waste per citizen in 2018 (Generalitat de Catalunya, 2018), has separate waste collection systems for different materials (plastic, paper, metal, organic material, glass and non-recyclable elements). Note that in 1993, Catalonia imposed a separate waste collection regulation governing all municipalities with more than 5000 inhabitants (Presidencia de la Generalitat de Cataluña, 1993). The system is financed by integrating various waste management systems, which are, in turn, managed and administered by the municipalities. The system ensures the availability of rubbish bins located at a distance of 100–150 metres from every household. When citizens buy a product (which is part of this system), they pay a 'green point' levy that is used to fund management of the waste generated by the product.

Table 12.2   Environmental regulations in force in Catalonia and Santiago

Regulations	Catalonia	Santiago
Supra-national	*EU*	*Latin America*
	Waste management legislation; goals imposed for separate collection, recycling and recycled materials in 1998 (updated in 2018). Law to regulate EPR enacted in 2011 (updated in 2015).	No common legislation. Every country establishes its own legislation and goals.
National	*Spain*	*Chile*
	Specific legislation for materials (hazardous substances (1988), packaging (1997), batteries (2008), electronic devices (2015) and vehicles and tyres (2017). This legislation was updated in 2018 by the CE Package, and in 2020 by the EU's New CE Action Plan.	No legislation for separate waste collection management in municipalities. Law regulating EPR enacted in 2016 (updated in 2019 and 2020), to be implemented gradually: tyres (2021), packaging (2023), lubricant oil and electronic devices and batteries (2020). Law prohibiting plastic bags derived from oil (enacted in 2018), implemented gradually for SMEs.
Local	*Catalonia*	*Santiago*
	Separate waste collection management from 1993 (municipalities with more than 5,000 inhabitants).	Waste collection and management is organized independently by municipalities.

Source: Authors, based on data from the European Commission (2015, 2018, 2020); Ministerio del Medio Ambiente (2016); Ministerio para la Transición Ecológica y el Reto Demográfico (2011).

Furthermore, households pay a fixed cost, which is added to their water amenities bill, regardless of that household's consumption (Área Metropolitana de Barcelona, 2009). This cost results in the existence of a two-tier payment system for the separate collection and management of waste. Moreover, Catalonia, with the implementation of new legislation, introduces a waste rate between €27–51 annually (to take effect in May 2020) to improve the waste collection and treatment. This legislation contemplates a discount for citizens who use the city's 'green points' (recycling points where waste is collected and separated for recycling), whose users will benefit from reductions of up to 14% in their waste tax. This new mechanism is seen as a first step to achieve a fair waste rate with regard to the generation of waste by households (Ajuntament de Barcelona, 2020).

In the case of companies, there are two alternatives: (1) to hire a private waste management service, which must be accredited/validated by the municipality or a local entity with authority; or (2) to pay the public price to municipalities or local entities. This second option considers the cost as based on a combination of economic activity (classification of activities), the surface area of the company, and the volume of generated waste (minimum, small, medium, large) (Ajuntament de Barcelona, 2018). In terms of cost, Catalonia spent approximately €953 million on waste management (including street cleaning) in 2018, which represents around 12.86% of its total municipal budget (Secretaría de Estado de Presupuestos y Gastos, 2018).

Santiago: non-separated waste collection system and a fixed tax rate
Santiago produced 485.72 kg of waste per inhabitant in 2017 (Ministerio del Medio Ambiente, 2019). Chile's capital does not have a uniform system of waste collection (waste is generally collected by municipal trucks and disposed of in landfill sites). A mix of private initiatives has been organized by organizations that work with local municipalities, with collection systems that, operating in parallel with the municipal collection trucks, still remain independent. Like other Latin American cities (and in the macro-sense, countries), Santiago has a large number of informal recyclers whose working conditions are far from optimal (Comisión Económica para América Latina y el Caribe, 2016). This situation is being addressed in the decree-law mentioned above, through formalization of the work of informal recyclers; a similar approach which is being taken in Colombia (Ministerio del Medio Ambiente, 2020a). In lieu, a new system called 'Recycle at home' has been launched in Chile, based on a platform that connects citizens to recyclers; thus, while the pandemic situation and quarantine is ongoing, these recyclers remove household waste directly from the source and take it for disposal (Ministerio del Medio Ambiente, 2020b). However, the plan is causing some concern due to a number of technical issues that remain unresolved, related to: (1) the amount of waste and the certificate of disposal supplied to households; (2) traceability processes to ensure that waste ends up in recycling plants; and (3) the amount of recycled raw materials that return to the market.

Households pay for waste collection in the form of a fixed municipal fee (territorial tax for property owners) that varies by municipality depending on how costs are defined (tax assessment, waste system costs), and apply exemptions to households in situations and/or conditions of poverty. In the case of companies, the payment for waste collection is included in municipal business permits, which companies need to be able to operate (Ministerio del Interior, 1996). Like Spain, Santiago also has a system of green points, managed and coordinated by private waste management companies and municipalities that is non-homogeneous. The law on EPR provides for a plan to establish separated waste collection systems, establishing an obligation (from 2023) to install infrastructure that includes one green point per 40,000 inhabitants and an additional green point for each additional 80,000 inhabitants. A process of waste collection from households will, therefore, gradually be established, beginning with 10% of households in around 2023. Santiago spends approximately €200.2 million[1] on waste management (including cleaning services), representing 7.61% of the total municipal budget (Secretaría de Estado de Presupuestos y Gastos, 2018). Figure 12.2 provides a comparative overview of expenditure per capita for the 50 municipalities in Catalonia and Santiago with the largest populations.

The collection rate for recyclable waste materials in Catalonia is 41.76% (Generalitat de Catalunya, 2018), compared with only 3% in Santiago (Ministerio del Medio Ambiente, 2019), reflecting a strongly asymmetric situation in waste management in the two regions despite similar levels of strong public investment. The Appendix summarizes the characteristics and differences of the two waste management systems.

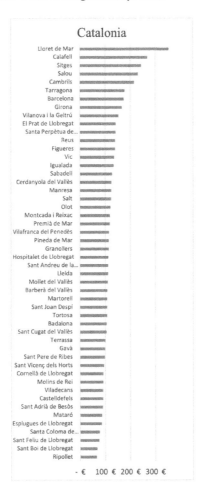

METHOD

The primary data for this research was collected from SMEs in Catalonia (Spain) and Santiago (Chile). The definition of SME in Spain and in Chile is a company with up to 250 employees and an annual income of less than €50 million (European Commission, 2017b) and up to 200 employees and an annual income of less than (approximately) €3.21 million[2] (Ministerio de Economía, 2014), respectively. The two regions are comparable in terms of their economic contribution to their respective countries. Spain has 2,829,754 SMEs (Ministerio de Industria – Comercio y Turismo, 2020), a fifth of which (22.1%; 625,465 companies) are from Catalonia (Idescat, 2018). Chile has 1,257,710, with nearly half (42.9%; 539,839) based in Santiago (SII, 2017). GDP participation of SMEs in the respective countries (as mentioned in the Introduction) is 19.1% and 43.6% for Spain and Chile, respectively.

Source: Authors, based on data from Secretaría de Estado de Presupuestos y Gastos (2018); Subsecretaría de Desarrollo Regional y Administrativo (2019).

Figure 12.2   *Per capita spending on waste management (50 most populated municipalities) in Catalonia (Spain) and Santiago (Chile)*

In terms of regulations governing SMEs, small business legislation in Spain states the following aims: (1) to promote entrepreneurship in Europe; (2) to simplify the environmental policy; (3) to promote access to finance; and (4) to enhance access to international markets (European Commission, 2011). In Chile, SMEs are governed by the 20.416 Law, which supports, among other issues, business incubation, operation and dissolution (Ministerio de Economia – Fomento y Turismo, 2010).

Fieldwork took place in Catalonia between January and April 2019, and between July and September 2019 in Santiago. To pre-select target companies, researchers used the SABI database of Spanish and Portuguese companies for Catalonia and the database of the University of Chile for Santiago. Data collection was of qualitative nature, based on 16 in-depth interviews and one group interview conducted in Catalonia, and 22 in-depth interviews and three group interviews in Santiago (the in-depth interviews were held with a single manager per company, while group interviews were held with more than one manager per company). This method has previously been used in different sustainability investigations of firms and companies (Panwar et al., 2016; Soto-Acosta et al., 2016). In-depth interviewing is highly recommended to explain complex phenomena such as sustainability (Reinecke et al., 2016), as it offers the possibility of providing insights on supply chain management from real business context (Oelze et al., 2016). This approach has also been used to study different aspects of sustainability, including product innovation (Hallstedt et al., 2013), ISO14001 certification (Granly & Welo, 2014) and the environmental engagement of SMEs (Williams & Schaefer, 2013).

The selected companies met the following criteria: (1) they belonged in productive and service sectors that allow the possibility of applying ES and CE, (2) they had an annual income of less than €50 million, and (3) they had more than five employees. Excluded were companies that generated no waste in their production processes. The sample represented different economic sectors in Catalonia (industrial 47%, commerce 29%, food services 12% and consulting services 12%) and Santiago (food services 32%, commerce 28%, consulting services 24%, industrial 12% and financial 4%). Table 12.3 summarizes basic characteristics of the interviewees (primarily male, primarily aged 45–54 years, and primarily university-educated) and companies (mainly well established and employing between 11 and 50 workers).

Table 12.3   Characteristics of the interviewees

Variables		Catalonia	Santiago
Gender	Male	61.1%	44.8%
	Female	38.9%	55.2%
Age, years	25–34	11.1%	41.4%
	35–44	22.2%	27.7%
	45–54	44.4%	10.3%
	55–64	16.7%	10.3%
	Over 65	5.6%	10.3%
Education	Secondary	0%	6.9%
	University	44.4%	79.3%
	Post–graduate	44.4%	13.8%
	Doctorate	11.2%	0%
Company workers	5–10	16.7%	62.1%
	11–50	44.4%	31%
	51–100	16.7%	6.9%
	Over 100	22.2%	0%
Company age, years	1–5	22.2%	37.9%
	6–10	0%	34.5%
	11–20	11.1%	10.3%
	Over 20	66.7%	17.3%

The interviews, conducted and recorded in the Spanish language, each lasted approximately 50–70 minutes. Interview content was previously reviewed by researchers of the Autonomous University of Barcelona and the University of Chile to validate and harmonize concepts and expressions and so enhance understanding of the questions by interviewees. The interviews were semi-structured, ensuring discussion of theoretical aspects and the capture of emerging themes and issues (Reynolds et al., 2018). They were based on two parts: general information about the company, its characteristics and the market; and ES and its application in the company. Interviews thus began with questions about the company (annual income, number of workers, years in existence, etc.) and about the interviewee themselves (position in the company, age, etc.), and continued with questions regarding ES and related matters, such as application, regulations, education, society, industry and clients.

Exploration of the content of interviews was implemented through thematic analysis and a dual coding process. The first stage was manual coding to identify different factors and elements that emerged from the interviews. The second stage, automated using NVIVO 11 software, clustered themes in nodes in order to visualize relationships and patterns in emerging concepts. Table 12.4 summarizes the coding process and resulting codes by theme in Catalonia and Santiago.

Table 12.4   NVIVO codebook of themes and subthemes for Catalonia and Santiago

Catalonia codebook			Santiago codebook		
Variables	Themes	Subthemes	Variables	Themes	Subthemes
Supply chain ES	Raw materials	Availability Management Knowledge	Supply chain ES	Raw materials	Availability Management Knowledge
	Recycled raw materials	Quality Price		Employees	
	Employees			Costs	
	Costs				
Waste management	Company waste	Process Payment rate	Waste management	Company waste	Processes Physical space
	Traceability	Waste management Final waste disposal			Municipal system Private system
				Household waste	
				Traceability	
Regulations	Characteristics		Regulations	Characteristics	
	Adoption	Certification		Adoption	Complementary systems
	Government role	Communication Subsidies Training		Government role	Communication
				Collaboration	Lack of opportunities
	Obstacles			Influence	
	Influence				

RESULTS

Regulations and their Impact on Environmental Sustainability

The regulation of environmental aspects of business is of growing importance in the current global economy.

In Catalonia, respondents point to the key role played by legal aspects through ES regulations governing companies, which are recognized by SME managers in general to be rigorous and strict. ERP legislation from 1996 – as adopted by companies – determines that waste can be handled by paying a private waste collection service or by paying a public price for the municipal separated waste collection system. However, according to the respondents, the regulations do not consider the reality faced by SMEs in their respective environments. In essence, EPR is more prohibitive than it is proactive, as it regulates and demands rather than proposes or encourages initiatives aimed at increasing the adoption of ES principles and practices. In retrospect, when regulations are more lax, companies rely on this broader framework to act without taking ES into account. With regard to ISO 9000 (quality management) and ISO 14000 (environmental management) certification, some companies only implement compliance with these standards when the market attributes them value or when the customer demands it.

The interviewees indicated that they would be willing to implement sustainable actions if they received co-financing subsidies or grants from public or government bodies. As pointed out, many large companies and corporations do receive such specific subsidies. The interviewees also emphasized the lack of regulations regarding communications, indicating that it is insufficient to sensitize companies to sustainable actions. The managers suggested that the development of a road map could set out clearer and better ES parameters for SMEs and would ensure that state institutions disseminated information on proper practices and thus aid the adoption of ES practices.

In Santiago, there was unanimous agreement of a severe lack of environmental regulations that could directly affect their operations. In essence, existing regulations only focus on the security and safety of operations and are particularly weak in terms of influencing environmental aspects. When interviewees were asked regarding the ISO 9000 and ISO 14000 standards, many did not fully understand what they meant nor did they feel any pressure (by government or society) to implement them. In Chile, SMEs are aware of the concept of EPR as a main environmental principle but also feel that inspections of 'failure to comply' (by state and/or government agents) are largely non-existent. Interestingly, Chilean managers have expressed concerns regarding the regulation of recycling and waste collection in their country.

Retrospectively, SMEs recognize that ERP and legislation (like that of limiting plastic bag use) can generate positive change in the behaviour of the population. However, their criticism is that the focus is misplaced; instead of regulating and forbidding, states should develop proper infrastructure and implement educational campaigns aimed at changing behaviour. The government has failed to develop an agenda for ES implementation in SMEs. Therefore, for change to happen, a major commitment is necessary as the impact of the deteriorating state of the environment is reflected in externalities in the economic system. Moreover, there are no incentives for SMEs to adopt ES practices, not only in financial terms (e.g., tax exemptions and rebates) but also in terms of the absence of company collaboration networks to share resources and waste. This situation would suggest that the issue is not an economic one, but one of state policy, given that the environment is not an externality but is part of the system.

The experiences of SMEs in Catalonia and Santiago in relation to environmental regulations (taking into account differences in progress and implementation) would suggest a common sensation of obstacles placed on SMEs. The lack of concrete and clear guidelines in the form of a CE road-map for SMEs and of financial subsidies and educational programmes further highlights that the regulations are limited and fail to offer specific guidance and proposals. Table 12.5 illustrates this issue with some quotes regarding regulations, standards and specific concerns.

Table 12.5   Interviewee quotes on standards and regulations

Catalonia
"I have the whole hotel with LED lights, big companies are given a prize for it, but for my volume, not me. They get a subsidy, and I don't because it cost me less money than it cost them. Small and medium-sized companies I think do many things, but we are not taken into account at all." (Monica, owner of an eco-hostel)
"I think it happens to be closer to companies. It is not only to create a standard, a law, how it can be applied, send a road map to companies, what can be done, what cannot be done. Help the company more than say, here it is." (Montserrat, marketing director of a packaging company)
Santiago
"If these types of regulations begin to come out, they are positive, but we do not prohibit everything. More than prohibitions, we generate things that favour environmental actions." (Sebastian, owner of an environmental education company)
"The ERP law is focused on big companies, but also the waste is not just from the big companies, maybe SMEs generate much more in volume. Moreover, they enact an ERP law without recycling plants." (Álvaro, manager of an environmental consultancy)

Waste Management and Supply Chain Characteristics and Limitations

A crucial issue for production processes and supply chains in SMEs is waste management. In Catalonia, local entities or municipalities regulate separated waste collection by SMEs, which can choose one of two approaches: payment of a public price, based on their business activity and volume of waste, or payment of a private waste collection service approved by the municipality or local entity. Waste collection companies, representing the SME's guarantee regarding waste management, are responsible for accounting, for recording and removing waste, and for delivering a report of waste materials collected by type and quantity.

However, a problem with private waste collection services – pointed out by interviewees in Catalonia – is the lack of guarantees that the waste will be recycled and its poor level of traceability. The concept of traceability of materials and the corresponding recycling and recovery activities is central to the CE. The interviewees confirm that managers opt to ignore what ultimately happens to the waste, given that there is no proper method to ensure that private companies are functioning as intended (or as they promised).

In Santiago, interviewees explain that municipalities do not have separated waste collection systems. Hence, SME waste typically ends up being collected by municipal trucks to be taken to landfills for final disposal. Furthermore, there is no major difference between SMEs and households in terms of waste collection and waste separation before collection; in other words, there is no distinction between business and household waste collection in the Chilean capital.

Chile, like Spain, has green points with specific containers to separate waste before collection, but, according to Chilean SME managers, they are few in number and irregularly distributed between districts. Furthermore, while people can bring their waste for separated collection, they have little real idea of what happens to the waste in terms of recycling.

Table 12.6   Interviewee quotes on waste management

Catalonia
"There are not enough recycling plants, in the case of England, for example, it is already committed to a dairy company, and all the bottles that the only the plant in England can produce are already fully committed." (Melania, acquisitions manager of a pharmaceutical company)
"Companies mix everything on the initiative of the waste manager and place no value on it. The manager signs the waste collection and everyone is happy, but what the manager has taken away, how much money has been lost, what materials may have been re-used but are lost forever, we will never know." (Monica, manager of a business fostering centre)
Santiago
"The creation of products from waste is not quantified. There is no traceability. Waste managers generate the entry document, where they say they receive so many kilos of waste, and I keep that document, that is my proof that my part of the job is done." (Pilar, manager of an environmental consulting firm)
"We pay a person to go through the waste, and we have no idea where they are taken if recycled or if separated. Because of our lack of storage, sometimes we throw things out that we could use but we have nowhere to store them." (José Luis, owner of an interior design company)

SME managers also explained that some municipalities have agreements with private companies for separated waste collection. These companies typically require inhabitants to separate out packaging types (separating cardboard and plastic from food packaging, for instance) and to deliver items (e.g., bottles) clean. The respondents point out their concerns regarding "working for a private company that takes the economic benefits of recycling", raising doubts about this kind of private waste management system and forcing many to ask why the service is not public. Here again, no distinction is drawn between waste from SMEs and households, with both expected to prepare waste for collection by private entities that benefit greatly from the omission of this service. Interviewees emphasized two especially important issues:

1. SMEs have no practical reasons (only ethical reasons) to recycle due to the failure of municipalities in their collection systems, to separate different types of waste (plastic, glass, metal, paper, organic, etc.). This means that if SMEs separate materials, the materials will still end up in a landfill (defeating the purpose of reuse and recycling). An alternative option is to use private waste collection services; however, this would affect SME finances (increased spending on waste management). Besides, the problem with traceability remains, as the law does not ensure that collectors register or record what happens with collected waste materials, and this affects trust in CE activities such as recycling, recovery and reuse. In view of this uncertainty, companies would prefer natural persons (citizens) to act as informal collectors who remove the waste to sell it on to companies. These informal collectors would obtain an economic benefit and the materials would be more likely to be reused or recycled. This type of action could mitigate the lack of transparency regarding waste collection by private entities and would help avoid landfills becoming choked with reusable and recyclable materials. Nevertheless, these actions are not enough to resolve the situation. The traceability problem affects many different aspects of the waste management system (collection, disposal, recovery, etc.).
2. Physical space is often mentioned as a major factor affecting waste management by SMEs. Companies state that most do not possess (or cannot use) space in their limited premises

for recycling purposes. Even though many SMEs would participate in recycling, their lack of space forces them to depend on the municipal system. As a consequence, options to recycle and reuse as part of the CE are sharply diminished at the local economy level. Table 12.6 shows some quotes of the interviewees about their perception of waste management. The Appendix summarizes traceability characteristics and differences in Catalonia and Santiago.

The summary of traceability characteristics, and differences in Catalonia and Santiago are presented in Table 12.7.

Table 12.7   Waste traceability in Catalonia and Santiago: characteristics and differences

Variables	Catalonia	Santiago
Household waste traceability	Separated waste goes to treatment plants or eco-parks for recycling. Non-recoverable materials go to landfills.	Non-separated waste goes to treatment plants and then to landfills. Recycling is only done by private companies according to their capacity.
Company waste traceability	Companies keep records of withdrawn waste but have no traceability information on the recycling rate from waste managers. Material that is not recycled goes to landfills.	Private companies treat the waste and sell recycled material to companies. Informal waste collectors sell materials to recycling companies or other users. No traceability.

Source: Authors.

Raw Material Management, Availability, Cost and Knowledge

Interviewee input regarding the adoption of ES practices suggests that raw materials is an especially important issue in ES as a whole.

In Catalonia, this issue is mainly voiced as follows:

1. Interviewees recognize the existence of different kinds of materials (some more sustainable than others) used in different supply chain processes in primary and secondary activities. The fact that recycled raw materials cost more than virgin raw materials hinders their adoption and frequent use. In the case of resources used mainly for primary activities, available materials are scarce and suppliers often do not have enough capacity to meet demand. SME managers are concerned that increased adoption of recycled materials may lead to scarcity as suppliers may be unable to meet demand (current production capacity may not be enough to deal with any increase in demand).

2. Interviewees are aware of the financial impact of adopting more sustainable materials, as switching to more sustainable resources implies an increased production cost. Some companies, but not all, can assume the cost differential, an issue that is strongly related to the value perceived by customers and their willingness to pay for sustainable products.

In Santiago, interviewees identify key issues regarding ES and raw materials as follows:

1. Interviewees recognize the importance of using sustainable raw materials in their production processes (more important for some industries than others). However, the main issue is the management of these resources, as companies focus on satisfying customers' needs. In many cases, this may lead to an action contrary to ES concerns/ideals, e.g., an excessive

amount of raw materials such as plastic, aluminium and expanded polystyrene used to protect the product and ensure safe and secure delivery. This situation represents another perspective that affects the CE in relation to resources.

2. Interviewees emphasize the importance of knowledge regarding the characteristics of raw materials so as to generate use that goes beyond a single-use. Another problem is that a product thrown away without an understanding of its components leads to improperly mixed waste (for instance, a box with a plastic component cannot be recycled with cardboard). When SMEs have a surplus of materials that they do not know how to dispose of properly, they need additional technology and/or technical know-how to discard of the waste properly or to enhance use of CE tools such as reuse or reduce.

3. Cost is a substantial barrier to increasing sustainable raw material use. SME managers indicate that they have to make a conscious effort to adopt ES principles in their business, especially as their business margin often does not allow them to generate the changes they aspire to.

In summary, Catalonia is one step ahead with the specific problem of availability, whereas Santiago is faced with a lack of in-depth knowledge of materials and a high-cost barrier. Table 12.8 shows quotes regarding raw material management and availability and the practical experiences of SMEs.

Table 12.8   Interviewee quotes on raw material management and availability

Catalonia
"At the moment, you cannot be biodegradable given the durability of the raw materials. The clients want a product that lasts a long time in the field so as not to have to make refills. However, the biodegradable ones that we have tried do not last at all." (Mireia, quality manager of a chemical company)
"Right now there are raw materials on the market that are recycled. Currently, the cost is very high because there is not enough infrastructure to manufacture all these raw materials. Raw materials that come from recycled sources are more expensive than newly manufactured material." (Melania, acquisitions manager of a pharmaceutical company)
Santiago
"The problem with raw materials such as plastic is that people and companies do not take enough care to give it more of a useful life. Plastic is an excellent alternative if you know how to use it." (Carolina, director of a clean products company)
"Being honest, the truth is that we have not changed suppliers because the product comes in a plastic or cardboard box. Unfortunately, today we are making provider decisions on a cost-benefit basis." (Kurt, owner of a veterinary company)

The summary of the raw material situation between Catalonia and Santiago is presented in Table 12.9.

Table 12.9   Raw materials in Catalonia and Santiago: main differences

Variables	Catalonia	Santiago
Raw material availability and cost	There are recycled materials available but their cost is very high. The stock is not enough if many companies begin to use recycled materials, so availability could be a problem.	There are recycled materials available but their cost is very high, so companies do not use them because their profitability would be greatly affected. Availability is not a concern at present
Raw material quality	The quality of recycled raw materials is poor, due to the central separate waste collection system that receives all types of waste (e.g., all type of plastics), generating raw materials with high possibilities of decrease for companies which use recycled materials.	In view of their low use, quality is not a concern at present.
Raw material knowledge	Companies are knowledgeable about the characteristics of raw materials.	Companies lack knowledge about the characteristics of raw materials. The main concern is product protection, which implies overuse of packaging.

Source: Authors.

Node Clustering: Principal Differences Between Catalonia and Santiago

To analyse the nodes resulting from the coding process in an integrated manner we used the cluster analysis function in NVIVO11 software. This tool allowed visualization of the relationships between the concepts that emerged in the interviews with the SME managers in Catalonia and Santiago, highlighting the different situations that must be addressed (see Figure 12.3).

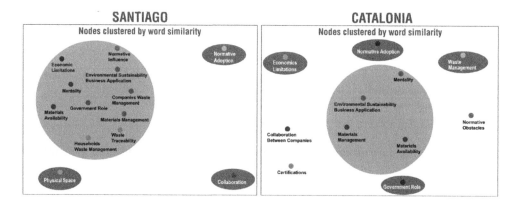

Note: The grey circles reflect more related concepts with higher Pearson correlation with ES business application. The black circles represent less closely related concepts with lower Pearson correlation with ES business application.

Figure 12.3   Word clusters for Catalonia and Santiago

In Catalonia (Figure 12.3), associations are strong between ES application to business factors (such as the mentality of the manager), material management and availability, and both regulation/standard adoption and obstacles. Although the government's role is somewhat limited (as indicated by the distance in Figure 12.3), it does help with the development of standards, where it is important for SMEs to comply with the law yet benefit from the incentives of ES. Neither economic limitations nor waste management are associated with ES business application, possibly due to the problem of final-stage waste management for SMEs. Recycling and separated waste collection do not represent an issue for SMEs.

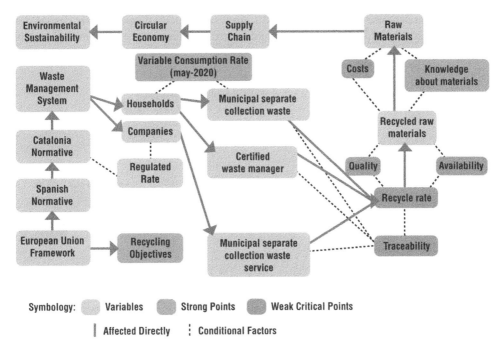

Source: Authors. The solid lines represent a direct effect of a variable and/or a sequential relationship on other variables. The broken lines represent variables that have a conditional effect, depending on their implementation or efficiency, on other variables.

Figure 12.4   Environmental sustainability in Catalonia

In Santiago (Figure 12.3: left), the adoption of standards/regulations is a very isolated concept, almost an entirely different subject in the eyes of SMEs. SMEs do not perceive the influence of standards and regulations and do not feel pressure to comply, considering the lack of inspection. Moreover, SMEs see it as difficult to adopt ES practices in their businesses. A clear example is related (as mentioned above) to the physical space available in SMEs for properly separating waste before collection. The issues of raw material management and availability are similar to those in Catalonia. However, the waste management system (companies and households without proper waste collection systems) and their traceability are especially relevant. The failures and weaknesses of this system are translated into diminished possibilities of ES-based supply chains, considering the difficulties posed by implementing CE tools such as effective recycling, recovery and reuse.

These constraints are crucial to how SME managers are able or unable to visualize ES in the business application, which can clearly be seen in the contrasting roles of governments in Santiago versus Catalonia.

Environmental Sustainability flows in Catalonia and Santiago

Based on the results obtained for the literature review, the information elaborated from government data and the analysis of the SME interview content, diagrams were designed to depict the situations in Catalonia and Santiago. Figure 12.4 shows the environmental outlook in Catalonia.

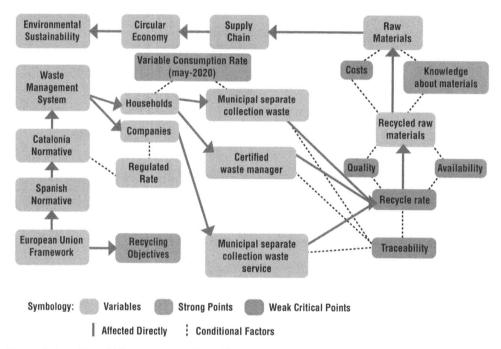

Source: Authors. The solid lines represent a direct effect of a variable and/or a sequential relationship on other variables. The broken lines represent variables that have a conditional effect, depending on their implementation or efficiency, on other variables.

Figure 12.5   *Environmental sustainability in Santiago*

The ES situation in Catalonia reveals specific problems in the final stages. In the early stages, environmental and municipal waste regulations have been established with clear conduits for the process for companies and households. The waste management system functions in the collection and separation phases. However, the waste processing stage is problematic in terms of the transformation of waste into recycled raw materials.

The traceability of waste from different waste management systems in the final stage is affected by the recycling rate of materials. The municipal service (for SMEs and households) may have to deal with the problem of the quality of collected waste, which ultimately affects the recycling rate in processing plants, whereas the private waste collection service generates a lack of certainty as to the ultimate destination of separated waste, thereby also directly affecting the recycling rate. The quality and availability of recycled raw materials after the recycling process are thus affected. Recycled materials (as previously mentioned) cost more due to their scarcity, which in turn produces a secondary effect of decreased production in companies that use recycled raw materials.

The strong points in Catalonia are as follows: (1) the recycling objectives imposed by the EU represent continuous pressures to do things right; (2) the new variable consumption rates for households contribute to diminishing waste generation; and (3) knowledge regarding materials allows SMEs to adopt the CE given appropriate incentives.

The ES situation in Santiago is somewhat different from that in Catalonia, considering the different states and applications of environmental and waste management standards and regulations. Figure 12.5 shows the environmental outlook in Santiago.

More difficulties in the different stages of waste management are evident for Santiago in comparison with Catalonia, in view of the fact that environmental and waste management regulation is relatively recent in Chile. Furthermore, Latin America has no common waste framework that might generate regional pressure regarding objectives, while, in Chile, pressures have only increased superficially and gradually (e.g., recycling objectives and their stepped aims). Municipal waste management in Chile lags behind that of the EU, as exemplified by the lack of separated waste collection from companies and households. Mainly informal or private options exist (in some cases in collaboration with municipalities), but they generate traceability issues from the outset of the process (although this may change with ERP legislation implementation in upcoming years).

Therefore, the quality and availability of recycled products is not yet an issue, given the scarce demand for such materials (and the lack of a proper waste separation system). However, if sustainable materials are adopted widely, this could become a critical problem for the supply chain of companies. The lack of recycled materials raises prices, which in lieu of the region's lack of knowledge and technical know-how regarding materials, means that adoption will be slow. This lack of an integrated structure strongly affects the recycling rate, as structural changes in the different stages are required to reduce use of new virgin materials in production processes and increase the use of recycled raw materials in the SME supply chain. At the same time, the implementation of CE tools is also affected.

DISCUSSION AND IMPLICATIONS

Discussion

This chapter discussed environmental and waste management regulations and standards, their effect on ES through CE tools in the supply chain, and key enabling and inhibiting factors affecting implementation. Theoretical contributions to the growing literature on these topics include the following.

1. The comparison of two regions (Catalonia and Santiago) at different development stages in environmental themes offers novel evidence that contributes to addressing a gap in the

literature. Thus, we are faced with the challenge of deepening knowledge regarding environmental issues which needs to be more specific (Bakos et al., 2020).

2. Insights are provided on the characteristics of waste management systems (public or private systems), rates (fixed or variable) and waste collection (separated or non-separated) and on the importance of waste management in the SME supply chain; as pointed out by Mura et al. (2020), who highlight the importance of waste management in implementing CE strategies, and Singh and Ordoñez (2016), who emphasize the importance of waste management in relation to raw materials in CE strategies.

3. The identification of barriers and challenges in the application of ES in the supply chain, related to technical knowledge, and the capacity to exploit raw materials and costs confirm Ormazabal et al's. (2018) findings regarding SMEs in Spain, which highlights the importance of such hard barriers in the application of CE strategies.

4. The analytical scheme used in this chapter provides a structured view of the complex relationships between environmental and waste management regulations and standards, and raw materials in the SME supply chain, contributing to clarifying how different aspects facilitate or hamper the CE for SMEs (Levänen et al., 2018).

Consequently, we pose the following questions: (1) Are existing regulations and standards appropriate for reducing waste and developing ES according to the current realities of Catalonia and Santiago? (2) Have environmental and waste regulations that impose obligations influenced current waste management practices, when perhaps what is needed are motivations based on incentives to reduce, reuse and recycle? (3) What are the possibilities to enhance and improve the environmental situation in Catalonia and Santiago from the perspective of SMEs?

Implications and Managerial Contributions for Catalonia

In managerial aspects, environmental regulations in Catalonia are stable and precise, but their communication and diffusion generate doubts and uncertainty for SMEs, especially in relation to waste management, e.g., when a city such as Barcelona has a separated waste collection system that generates certain problems related to traceability and the quality of recycled materials, what would happen to less developed cities? Haupt et al. (2017) describe the Swiss waste management system as closed-loop (recycled material used in the same product) and open-loop (recycled material for secondary use), while our research highlights the importance of the quality of recycled materials; a key example is that blue and colourless PET recycled materials can be used for the same product, whereas green PET is valid only for secondary use.

Catalonia's separated waste collection system directly affects the quality of recycled raw materials. The monopolistic condition of the municipal separated waste collection system negatively affects the final quality of the recycled raw materials. This situation, in turn, reduces demand for said materials, and, therefore, diminishes their use by recyclers. A concern of SMEs regarding raw materials is that recycled materials are more costly and undergo significant shrinkage, this affects their finances as well as the ES of the system. The scarcity and quality of raw materials are crucial factors in enhancing ES adoption, and the potential scarcity of raw materials implies that SMEs need to play a more proactive role in their supply chain (Kalaitzi et al., 2018). This reality contrasts enormously with the EU plan to promote recycled material use as a means to decouple the economy from natural resource use (European Commission, 2020).

The traceability of recycled waste is crucial in terms of the incorporation of recycled materials into production processes (Sandvik & Stubbs, 2019). A positive global effect may be achieved by combining waste systems with options such as deposit-refund schemes (DRS), widely adopted in countries such as Germany and Denmark. DRS combines two mechanisms: a tax on purchase of a product, and a subsidy on separated waste collection of the same product in the after-use stage (Linderhof et al., 2019). The drawback of the DRS is that the implementation cost is high and it also requires accurate analyses for effective implementation. The EU proposes harmonizing separated waste collection systems in its CE plan for 2020, so as to ensure effective combination of separated collection models (European Commission, 2020).

An in-depth analysis of system characteristics is relevant to describing the waste collection tax for companies. Current options are the payment of a private waste collection service and payment of a public price to municipalities or local authorities. The public price for SMEs is determined by their economic activity (according to a classification of activities), the surface area of their premises and the volume of waste generated. While this polynomial system generates an equal standard, it does not generate incentives to reduce waste. The relationship between the price that SMEs pay and the waste collection system has an immediate effect on the situation of SMEs. In Catalonia, the fee has this same problem of providing weak incentives and, as a consequence, there is little interest in implementing CE practices of recycling, reusing and reducing waste. Puig-Ventosa and Sastre Sanz (2017) point to the dual relevance of waste collection pricing: first, the fixed fee (which effectively penalizes responsible behaviour) versus the variable fee (taking into account waste generation and water consumption); and, second, waste management system financing, the percentage covered by fees, and its impact on the possibility of reorienting policies (e.g., the effect of charging a fee except as a social assistance mechanism for people with lower incomes).

The focus of public policies has always been on regulations and standards centred on compliance rather than on incentives or rewards (technical or economic knowledge). CE implementation could be facilitated by a system of appropriate incentives, as the transition to CE is tightly linked to a shift in the way that companies conceive, systematize and apply regulatory and institutional systems (Desing et al., 2020). The lack of incentives means that CE tools, such as recycle, reuse and reduce, are viewed more as an obligation; this reduces the possibility of companies finding real value in addressing environmental issues. In essence, companies and societies are failing to switch perceptions from resources with exploitation and economic potential to the association of resources with moral and environmental values.

Implications and Managerial Contributions for Santiago

Several aspects need to be considered in relation to ES adoption by SMEs in Santiago. The first point is environmental regulations. The 20.416 Law considers the application of the proportionality principle, important for SMEs considering their reality, but representing only an initial step. The first responsibility of SMEs is to survive, while tackling environmental issues needs belief and, in turn, knowledge, guidance and infrastructure (Kornilaki & Font, 2019).

For this reason, the regulatory approach is critical to enhancing CE tool implementation by SMEs. In Chile, this work is in a very early phase still, and is a very long way from achieving the standards of European countries. And given the lack of incentives, the small numbers of SMEs with environmental certification and the absence of inspections is a crude reality of the economy.

Another discussion point refers to the importance and impact of the waste management system on SMEs. In Santiago, the lack of collection systems based on properly separated waste (Ministerio del Medio Ambiente, 2019) has produced a chain reaction that has been detrimental to the economy. Households need to find other ways to implement CE practices in waste disposal, such as the use of green points. Moreover, requiring further analyses are the duration of the launched "Recycle at home" programme, its longer-term perspectives and the perception of a triple payment by households (waste collection fees, product levies according to EPR principles and charges for recyclers that collect waste directly from households). However, the main problem is that SMEs use the same system as households. This situation means that SMEs need to figure out their own system to separate waste while taking possibly incomplete traceability and the lack of a trustworthy register into account. Traceability is critical to waste reduction and to possibilities for material recovery and reuse (Molina-Moreno et al., 2017). The ERP legislation (updated in 2019 and 2020) tackles this aspect with the instauration of waste managers, although what remains relevant is the issue of inspections to ensure compliance with the law.

In Chile, as the rate of separated waste collection of recyclable raw materials is only 1.72% (Valenzuela-Levi, 2019), the initial situation does not represent a significant problem in terms of volumes. Nevertheless, adopting a mid-term perspective, difficulties may arise if/when the volume of recycled materials increases. The ERP legislation tackles separated waste collection, principally through an integrated waste management system of producers. Correct implementation has direct effects on the availability and quality of recycled materials. However, caution will be required with the operating conditions for ERP, including (1) the fixing of system costs and the percentage to be borne by the customer; (2) the utilities of the system and reinvestment mechanisms; and (3) adequate representation of stakeholders in decision-making processes. Most especially, transparency and honesty will be crucial for success of the system.

The above-described situation has direct repercussions for CE tool adoption by SMEs. EU evidence highlights the difficulties of using recycled raw materials in production processes due to the need for a reassessment of resources (Bassi & Dias, 2019). If the situation is difficult for countries with developed regulatory systems, it is even more critical (and difficult) for countries such as Chile.

Another issue in relation to Santiago is the payment concept for the waste collection system. SMEs indicate that they pay a specific amount for separated waste collection (in Chile, only SMEs are genuinely committed to ES to employ a waste manager). The fixed rate for SMEs is included in the payment of the municipal licence to launch and continue a commercial activity. This rate is independent of the amount of generated waste (the same method as used for households, except that exemptions are allowed on the basis of socioeconomic criteria). This situation greatly influences the possibility of reducing waste, as SMEs do not have any real financial incentive to be more sustainable, and the situation is the same for households. The waste management system therefore needs to be viewed as multi-dimensional, with municipalities in developing countries needing to consider the environmental, sociocultural, legal, institutional and economic aspects of ES (Guerrero et al., 2013).

In general terms, the issue is viewed as one of rules versus incentives, with the former not viewed as a priority by SMEs. Government legislation needs to enable not hinder (Govindan & Hasanagic, 2018) the adoption of ES principles and practices in SME supply chains and CE tools. SMEs need further input on the importance of ES practices for business performance, especially an educational programme that provides the information necessary so that managers can make appropriate changes in their businesses and take advantage of the potential benefits of ES (Redmond et al., 2008).

Policy-makers and Government Institutions

The theoretical and empirical issues reviewed in this chapter enable several guidelines to be proposed so that policy-makers and practitioners can enhance the possibilities for SMEs to achieve supply chain ES.

1. Waste management covers a variety of systems and variables, including waste managers, deposit refund schemes (DSR), municipal collection, different fee structures, among others. However, perhaps the most important issue is to understand the reality of a city or region and its SMEs. It is not recommended to simply imitate models or centralize waste management (as in Santiago and Catalonia, respectively), but to analyse and implement the best solution considering the characteristics of both the population and the companies.
2. Different variables affect ES in the supply chain, including: (a) the technical knowledge of companies, (b) economic barriers and (c) the availability and management of raw materials. To implement a waste hierarchy in the CE, SMEs need to see CE as an investment and not as a cost in their supply chain. Consumers consequently need to attach more importance to their purchase behaviour, while environmental education at different levels of society is a pending issue (Aikens et al., 2016). However, this education needs to be provided in simple terms (especially in Santiago) so as to lay a knowledge base for reinforcement of the importance of climate change and awareness of world environmental challenges.
3. Flexible regulations and standards are needed to support ES adoption in SME supply chains, as indicated by international experiences (Mura et al., 2020), as well as incentives such as (a) financing, (b) subsidies, (c) tax reductions and rebates, (d) collaboration networks for companies and government and (e) training in environmental themes (ES, CE, raw materials, etc).
4. For SMEs to adopt ES in their supply chains, clear communication with specific guidelines is needed, as lack of knowledge is a major barrier to ES adoption. Sanctions and fines (under ERP legislation) will not be effective, especially for companies that do not fear them based on their practical experience (Santiago) or that do not have sufficient incentives to adopt them (Catalonia). The approach used to encourage ES in SMEs is crucial, given their economic, social and environmental impact.

Implementing Environmental Sustainability in SMEs' Supply Chain

As seen throughout the chapter, SMEs are fundamental to achieving ES. Considering their resources, SMEs could adopt ES practices as follows.

1. By spending time on the selection of raw materials, considering aspects such as costs, environmental impact and the possibility of applying CE tools (reduce, reuse, repair, recycle, recover, etc.) from the outset of production processes. Conscious selection from the outset ensures more possibilities to adapt the supply chain to changes in environmental regulations.
2. To avoid as far as possible the use of mixed materials in production processes. The use of mixed materials greatly reduces the possibility of applying CE tools, while difficulties

in separating materials generate poorer quality and smaller quantities of recycled raw materials.

3. To monitor environmental and waste regulations on an ongoing basis. Regulatory changes can require modifications in production processes and the supply chain, so earlier detection enhances adaptation possibilities.

4. To collaborate with other SMEs in terms of exchanging knowledge in general, but especially on raw materials and ES and CE principles and practices. A lack of knowledge is a limitation, so a practical way to diminish this gap – closer to the reality of SMEs – is to share existing knowledge and learn from other SMEs' experiences.

5. To analyse the importance awarded by customers to ES principles by listening to them. While ES tends to be socially desired, SMEs, nonetheless, need to balance economic and environmental issues (optimizing the investment in resources). Information on customers gives valuable insights into the phases in which an SME can foster ES practices (design, materials, diffusion, communication, etc.) and helps visualize alternatives, e.g., incentivizing product-as-a-service or other models retaining ownership of the product.

LIMITATIONS

This study focuses on the importance of ES for different supply chain issues for SMEs in Catalonia and Santiago, considering the lack of in-depth comparative studies on the operationalization of ES (Farooq et al., 2019). Environmental aspects such as regulations and waste management differ in both areas, as Catalonia is substantially more advanced than Santiago. However, SMEs in both regions believe in the importance of ES in the supply chain while recognizing that adoption and implementation are highly challenging due to the lack of knowledge and of government support and given the existing waste management setup (especially in Chile).

The main limitation of this study is that the sample is representative only of SMEs in Catalonia and Santiago. Future research could consider other regions in those countries and in other countries to enhance comparison at the international level. Quantitative research could also complement and validate the generalizations of this study at the aggregate level and would throw light on how SMEs could incorporate functional ES principles in business development and growth. Finally, sectorial analyses could provide specific insights by industry that enrich both overall and sectoral knowledge on ES.

ACKNOWLEDGEMENTS

The first author was financially supported by the National Agency for Research and Development (ANID)/Scholarship Program/DOCTORADO BECAS CHILE/2018–72190184 doctoral grant.

NOTES

1. This amount correspond to the conversion of Chilean pesos to euros (at exchange rate of December 2018).
2. Chilean pesos converted to euros (exchange rate May 2020).

REFERENCES

Acs, Z. J., Audretsch, D. B., Braunerhjelm, P., & Carlsson, B. (2012). Growth and entrepreneurship. *Small Business Economics*, *39*(2), 289–300. https://doi.org/10.1007/s11187-010-9307-2

Adipah, S., & Kwame, N. (2019). A novel introduction of municipal solid waste management. *Journal of Environmental Science and Public Health*, *3*(2), 147–157. https://doi.org/10.26502/jesph.96120055

Aikens, K., McKenzie, M., & Vaughter, P. (2016). Environmental and sustainability education policy research: A systematic review of methodological and thematic trends. *Environmental Education Research*, *22*(3), 333–359. https://doi.org/10.1080/13504622.2015.1135418

Ajuntament de Barcelona. (2009). *Recogida de residuos comercios y grandes generadores | Ecología, Urbanismo, Infraestructuras y Movilidad*. https://ajuntament.barcelona.cat/ecologiaurbana/es/servicios/la-ciudad-funciona/mantenimiento-del-espacio-publico/gestion-de-limpieza-y-residuos/recogida-de-residuos-comercios-y-grandes-generadores

Ajuntament de Barcelona. (2018). *Explicación del precio público para la recogida de residuos | Institut Municipal d'Hisenda de Barcelona*. https://ajuntament.barcelona.cat/hisenda/es/explicación -del-precio-público-para-la-recogida-de-residuos

Ajuntament de Barcelona. (2019). *Anexo III – Precios públcos del área de ecología urbana 3.1 Precios públicos de los servicios de recogida de residuos comerciales e industriales asimilables a los municipales 2018* [Boletin Oficial de la provincia de Barcelona].

Ajuntament de Barcelona. (2020). *Tramitación de una nueva ordenanza fiscal 3.18 de tasas por el servicio de recogida de residuos municipales generados en los domicilios particulares | Transparencia*. https://ajuntament.barcelona.cat/transparencia/es/tasa-recogida-residuos-solidos-urbanos

Aragón-Correa, J. A., Hurtado-Torres, N., Sharma, S., & García-Morales, V. J. (2008). Environmental strategy and performance in small firms: A resource-based perspective. *Journal of Environmental Management*, *86*(1), 88–103. https://doi.org/10.1016/J.JENVMAN.2006.11.022

Arasti, Z., Zandi, F., & Bahmani, N. (2014). Business failure factors in Iranian SMEs: Do successful and unsuccessful entrepreneurs have different viewpoints? *Journal of Global Entrepreneurship Research*, *4*(1), 10. https://doi.org/10.1186/s40497-014-0010-7

Área Metropolitana de Barcelona. (2009). *Tasa metropolitana de tratamiento de residuos – Àrea metropolitana de Barcelona*. http://www.amb.cat/s/es/web/medi-ambient/gestio-i-organitzacio/taxa -metropolitana-de-tractament-de-residus.html

Arnold, M. (2017). Fostering sustainability by linking co-creation and relationship management concepts. *Journal of Cleaner Production*, *140*, 179–188. https://doi.org/10.1016/j.jclepro.2015.03.059

Bakos, J., Siu, M., Orengo, A., & Kasiri, N. (2020). An analysis of environmental sustainability in small & medium-sized enterprises: Patterns and trends. *Business Strategy and the Environment*, bse.2433. https://doi.org/10.1002/bse.2433

Banco Central de Chile. (2018). *PIB regional – Banco Central de Chile*. Banco Central de Chile. http:// www.bcentral.cl/pib-regional

Bassi, F., & Dias, J. G. (2019). The use of circular economy practices in SMEs across the EU. *Resources, Conservation and Recycling*, *146*, 523–533. https://doi.org/10.1016/j.resconrec.2019.03.019

Briassoulis, D., Hiskakis, M., Karasali, H., & Briassoulis, C. (2014). Design of a European agrochemical plastic packaging waste management scheme – Pilot implementation in Greece. *Resources, Conservation and Recycling*, *87*, 72–88. https://doi.org/10.1016/j.resconrec.2014.03.013

Cantele, S., & Zardini, A. (2018). Is sustainability a competitive advantage for small businesses? An empirical analysis of possible mediators in the sustainability–financial performance relationship. *Journal of Cleaner Production*, *182*, 166–176. https://doi.org/10.1016/j.jclepro.2018.02.016

Ciasullo, V. M., & Troisi, O. (2013). Sustainable value creation in SMEs: A case study. *The TQM Journal*, *25*(1), 44–61. https://doi.org/10.1108/17542731311286423

Comisión Económica para América Latina y el Caribe. (2016). *Guía general para la gestión de residuos sólidos domiciliario Publicación.* https://www.cepal.org/es/publicaciones/40407-guia-general-la-gestion-residuos-solidos-domiciliarios

Comisión Económica para América Latina y el Caribe. (2018). *Mipymes en América Latina: un frágil desempeño y nuevos desafíos para las políticas de fomento.* https://repositorio.cepal.org/bitstream/handle/11362/44148/1/S1800707_es.pdf

Dahlmann, F., Branicki, L., & Brammer, S. (2017). 'Carrots for corporate sustainability': Impacts of incentive inclusiveness and variety on environmental performance. *Business Strategy and the Environment, 26*(8), 1110–1131. https://doi.org/10.1002/bse.1971

Darcy, C., Hill, J., McCabe, T., & McGovern, P. (2014). A consideration of organisational sustainability in the SME context. *European Journal of Training and Development, 38*(5), 398–414. https://doi.org/10.1108/EJTD-10-2013-0108

De Mendonca, T., & Zhou, Y. (2019). When companies improve the sustainability of the natural environment: A study of large U.S. companies. *Business Strategy and the Environment,* bse.2398. https://doi.org/10.1002/bse.2398

De Oliveira, J. A., Oliveira, O. J., Ometto, A. R., Ferraudo, A. S., & Salgado, M. H. (2016). Environmental Management System ISO 14001 factors for promoting the adoption of cleaner production practices. *Journal of Cleaner Production, 133*, 1384–1394. https://doi.org/10.1016/j.jclepro.2016.06.013

Desing, H., Brunner, D., Takacs, F., Nahrath, S., Frankenberger, K., & Hischier, R. (2020). A circular economy within the planetary boundaries: Towards a resource-based, systemic approach. *Resources, Conservation and Recycling, 155*, 104673. https://doi.org/10.1016/j.resconrec.2019.104673

Dyllick, T., & Hockerts, K. (2002). Beyond the business case for corporate sustainability. *Business Strategy and the Environment, 11*(2), 130–141. https://doi.org/10.1002/bse.323

Ellen MacArthur Foundation. (2013). *Circular Economy Overview.* Www.Circularfoundation.Org.

Eriksson, O., Frostell, B., Björklund, A., Assefa, G., Sundqvist, J. O., Granath, J., Carlsson, M., Baky, A., & Thyselius, L. (2002). ORWARE – A simulation tool for waste management. *Resources, Conservation and Recycling, 36*(4), 287–307. https://doi.org/10.1016/S0921-3449(02)00031-9

European Commission. (1987). *Single European Act.* Official Journal of the European Communities. https://europa.eu/european-union/sites/europaeu/files/docs/body/treaties_establishing_the_european_communities_single_european_act_en.pdf

European Commission. (2008). *Directive 2008/98/EC of the European Parliament and of the Council of 19 November 2008 on Waste and Repealing Certain.* Official Journal of the European Union. http://eur-lex.europa.eu/legal-content/EN/TXT/PDF/?uri=CELEX

European Commission. (2011). *The Small Business Act for Europe | Internal Market, Industry, Entrepreneurship and SMEs.* https://ec.europa.eu/growth/smes/business-friendly-environment/small-business-act_en

European Commission. (2015). Closing the loop – An EU action plan for the circular economy. In *Com, 2*(12). https://eur-lex.europa.eu/resource.html?uri=cellar:8a8ef5e8-99a0-11e5-b3b7-01aa75ed71a1.0012.02/DOC_1&format=PDF

European Commission. (2017a). *Multilateral Agreements – Environment – European Commission.* http://ec.europa.eu/environment/international_issues/agreements_en.htm

European Commission. (2017b). *What is an SME? | Internal Market, Industry, Entrepreneurship and SMEs.* European Commission. https://ec.europa.eu/growth/smes/business-friendly-environment/sme-definition_en

European Commission. (2018). *Circular Economy Strategy – Implementation of the Circular Economy Action Plan.* https://ec.europa.eu/environment/circular-economy/

European Commission. (2019). *Annual Report on European SMEs 2018/2019.*

European Commission. (2020). *Communication COM/2020/98: A New Circular Economy Action Plan for a Cleaner and More Competitive Europe | Knowledge for Policy.* https://ec.europa.eu/knowledge4policy/publication/communication-com202098-new-circular-economy-action-plan-cleaner-more-competitive-europe_en

European Council. (1991). *European Council. Council Directive 75/442/EEC Modified by Directive 91/156/EEC on Waste, 1991.*

European Environment Agency. (2017). *Recycling of Municipal Waste, European Environment Agency.* 2017. https://www.eea.europa.eu/airs/2017/resource-efficiency-and-low-carbon-economy/recycling-of-municipal-waste

Eurostat. (2019a). *Eurostat – Tables, Graphs and Maps Interface (TGM) Table.* Eurostat. https://ec.europa.eu/eurostat/tgm/table.do;jsessionid=9NfjbF_FygohKRFGrq5-0hLvHt9D1iP-0AL8QdXMdpI

xKGX0LABW!-755574875?tab=table&plugin=1&language=en&pcode=cei_wm011%0Ahttp://epp
.eurostat.ec.europa.eu/tgm/table.do?tab=table&init=1&plugin=1&language=en&pcod

Eurostat. (2019b). *Record Recycling Rates and Use of Recycled Materials in the EU*. https://ec.europa
.eu/eurostat/documents/2995521/9629294/8-04032019-BP-EN.pdf/295c2302-4ed1-45b9-af86
-96d1bbb7acb1

Farooq, O., Farooq, M., & Reynaud, E. (2019). Does employees' participation in decision making
increase the level of corporate social and environmental sustainability? An investigation in South
Asia. *Sustainability (Switzerland)*, *11*(2), 511–523. https://doi.org/10.3390/su11020511

Geissdoerfer, M., Savaget, P., Bocken, N. M. P., & Hultink, E. J. (2017). The circular economy – A new
sustainability paradigm? *Journal of Cleaner Production*, *143*, 757–768. https://doi.org/10.1016/j
.jclepro.2016.12.048

Generalitat de Catalunya. (2018). *Estadístiques de residus municipals. Agencia de residus de catalunya*.
http://estadistiques.arc.cat/ARC/#

Georgescu-Roegen, N., Naredo, J. M., & Grinevald, J. (1996). *La ley de la entropía y el proceso económ-
ico*. Fundación Argentaria.

Goodland, R. (1995). The concept of environmental sustainability. *Annual Review of Ecology and
Systematics*, *26*, 1–24. https://doi.org/10.1146/annurev.es.26.110195.000245

Govindan, K., & Hasanagic, M. (2018). A systematic review on drivers, barriers, and practices towards
circular economy: A supply chain perspective. *International Journal of Production Research*,
56(1–2), 278–311. https://doi.org/10.1080/00207543.2017.1402141

Granly, B. M., & Welo, T. (2014). EMS and sustainability: Experiences with ISO 14001 and
Eco-Lighthouse in Norwegian metal processing SMEs. *Journal of Cleaner Production*, *64*, 194–204.
https://doi.org/10.1016/j.jclepro.2013.08.007

Guerrero, L. A., Maas, G., & Hogland, W. (2013). Solid waste management challenges for cities in
developing countries. *Waste Management*, *33*(1), 220–232. https://doi.org/10.1016/j.wasman.2012
.09.008

Hallstedt, S. I., Thompson, A. W., & Lindahl, P. (2013). Key elements for implementing a strategic sustainability perspective in the product innovation process. *Journal of Cleaner Production*, *51*, 277–288.
https://doi.org/10.1016/j.jclepro.2013.01.043

Haupt, M., Vadenbo, C., & Hellweg, S. (2017). Do we have the right performance indicators for the
circular economy? Insight into the Swiss waste management system. *Journal of Industrial Ecology*,
21(3), 615–627. https://doi.org/10.1111/jiec.12506

Helfaya, A., & Moussa, T. (2017). Do board's corporate social responsibility strategy and orientation influence environmental sustainability disclosure? UK evidence. *Business Strategy and the
Environment*, *26*(8), 1061–1077. https://doi.org/10.1002/bse.1960

Hörisch, J., Ortas, E., Schaltegger, S., & Álvarez, I. (2015). Environmental effects of sustainability
management tools: An empirical analysis of large companies. *Ecological Economics*, *120*, 241–249.
https://doi.org/10.1016/J.ECOLECON.2015.11.002

Idescat. (2018). *Idescat. Anuario estadístico de Cataluña. Empresas y establecimientos a 1 de enero.
Por sectores de actividad y número de asalariados*. https://www.idescat.cat/pub/?id=aec&n=975&
lang=es

Instituto Nacional de Estadística de España. (2019). *España en cifras 2019*. https://www.ine.es/prodyser/
espa_cifras/2019/31/

Instituto Nacional de Estadísticas de Chile. (2019). *Estimaciones y proyecciones de la población de Chile
2002-2035. Totales regionales, población urbana y rural*. www.ine.cl

Jansson, J., Nilsson, J., Modig, F., & Hed Vall, G. (2017). Commitment to sustainability in small and
medium-sized enterprises: The influence of strategic orientations and management values. *Business
Strategy and the Environment*, *26*(1), 69–83. https://doi.org/10.1002/bse.1901

Johnson, M. P., & Schaltegger, S. (2016). Two decades of sustainability management tools for SMEs:
How far have we come? *Journal of Small Business Management*, *54*(2), 481–505. https://doi.org/10
.1111/jsbm.12154

Jones, P., & Comfort, D. (2018). Sustainability and the UK waste management industry. *European
Journal of Sustainable Development Research*, *2*(1). https://doi.org/10.20897/ejosdr/79227

Kalaitzi, D., Matopoulos, A., Bourlakis, M., & Tate, W. (2018). Supply chain strategies in an era of
natural resource scarcity. *International Journal of Operations and Production Management*, *38*(3),
784–809. https://doi.org/10.1108/IJOPM-05-2017-0309

King, A. M., Burgess, S. C., Ijomah, W., & McMahon, C. A. (2006). Reducing waste: Repair, recondition, remanufacture or recycle? *Sustainable Development, 14*(4), 257–267. https://doi.org/10.1002/sd.271

Kirchherr, J., Reike, D., & Hekkert, M. (2017). Conceptualizing the circular economy: An analysis of 114 definitions. *Resources, Conservation and Recycling, 127*, 221–232. https://doi.org/10.1016/J.RESCONREC.2017.09.005

Kornilaki, M., & Font, X. (2019). Normative influences: How socio-cultural and industrial norms influence the adoption of sustainability practices. A grounded theory of Cretan, small tourism firms. *Journal of Environmental Management, 230*, 183–189. https://doi.org/10.1016/j.jenvman.2018.09.064

Levänen, J., Lyytinen, T., & Gatica, S. (2018). Modelling the interplay between institutions and circular economy business models: A case study of battery recycling in Finland and Chile. *Ecological Economics, 154*, 373–382. https://doi.org/10.1016/j.ecolecon.2018.08.018

Linderhof, V., Oosterhuis, F. H., van Beukering, P. J. H., & Bartelings, H. (2019). Effectiveness of deposit-refund systems for household waste in the Netherlands: Applying a partial equilibrium model. *Journal of Environmental Management, 232*, 842–850. https://doi.org/10.1016/j.jenvman.2018.11.102

Lozano, R., & von Haartman, R. (2018). Reinforcing the holistic perspective of sustainability: Analysis of the importance of sustainability drivers in organizations. *Corporate Social Responsibility and Environmental Management, 25*(4), 508–522. https://doi.org/10.1002/csr.1475

Lynch-Wood, G., & Williamson, D. (2014). Understanding SME responses to environmental regulation. *Journal of Environmental Planning and Management, 57*(8), 1220–1239. https://doi.org/10.1080/09640568.2013.793174

Ministerio de Economía. (2014). *Antecedentes para la revisión de los criterios de clasificación del Estatuto Pyme.*

Ministerio de Economia – Fomento y Turismo. (2010). *Ley 20.416 - Fija normales especiales para las empresas de menor tamaño.* https://www.leychile.cl/Navegar?idNorma=1010668

Ministerio de Economia – Fomento y Turismo. (2019). *Quinta Encuesta Longitudinal de Empresas (ELE5) – Ministerio de Economía, Fomento y Turismo.* https://www.economia.gob.cl/2019/03/12/quinta-encuesta-longitudinal-de-empresas-ele5.htm

Ministerio de Industria – Comercio y Turismo. (2019). *Cifras PYME.* Portal PYME. http://www.ipyme.org/es-ES/publicaciones/Paginas/estadisticaspyme.aspx

Ministerio de Industria – Comercio y Turismo. (2020). *Cifras PYME. Datos abril 2020.*

Ministerio de la Presidencia – Relaciones con las Cortes y Memoria Democrática. (2018). *Código de residuos y sustancias peligrosas.* https://www.boe.es/biblioteca_juridica/codigos/codigo.php?id=156&modo=2&nota=0&tab=2

Ministerio del Interior. (1996). *Decreto ley No 3.063. Fija texto refundido y sistematizado de 1979, sobre rentas municipales.* https://www.leychile.cl/Navegar?idNorma=18967

Ministerio del Medio Ambiente. (2016). *Ley 20.920 Gestión de residuos, la responsabilidad extendida del productor y fomento al reciclaje* (1–16). Ministry of Environment. https://www.leychile.cl/N?i=1090894&f=2016-06-01&p=

Ministerio del Medio Ambiente. (2018). *Ley 21.100 Prohibe la entrega de boldas plásticas de comercio en todo el territorio nacional.* 1–3. https://www.leychile.cl/N?i=1121380&f=2019-02-03&p=

Ministerio del Medio Ambiente. (2019). *Sistema Integrador de Información Ambiental.* http://sistemaintegrador.mma.gob.cl/mma-centralizador-publico/indicador/vistaIndicador.jsf?id=58AA51D2-E6A5-2CBC-84F9-7ADF41082274&subtema=6

Ministerio del Medio Ambiente. (2020a). *Decreto supremo que establece metas de recolección y valorización y otras obligaiones asociadas de envases y embalajes.*

Ministerio del Medio Ambiente. (2020b). *Ministerio del Medio Ambiente lanza plataforma para reciclar sin salir de la casa.* https://mma.gob.cl/ministerio-del-medio-ambiente-lanza-plataforma-para-reciclar-sin-salir-de-la-casa/

Ministerio para la Transición Ecológica y el Reto Demográfico. (2011). Ley 22/2011, del 28 de julio, de residuos y suelos contaminados. Responsabilidad ampliada del productor. *Boletín Oificial Del Estado, 181, 28 de julio*, 85650. https://www.boe.es/boe/dias/2011/07/29/pdfs/BOE-A-2011-13046.pdf

Ministerio para la Transición Ecológica y el Reto Demográfico. (2020). *Estrategia Española de Economía Circular. España Circular 2030.*

Ministerio Secretaría General de la Presidencia. (1994). *Ley 19.300 Bases generales del medio ambiente.* https://www.leychile.cl/Navegar?idNorma=30667

Missimer, M., Robèrt, K. H., & Broman, G. (2017). A strategic approach to social sustainability - Part 2: A principle-based definition. *Journal of Cleaner Production, 140*, 42–52. https://doi.org/10.1016/j.jclepro.2016.04.059

Molina-Moreno, V., Leyva-Díaz, J., Sánchez-Molina, J., & Peña-García, A. (2017). Proposal to foster sustainability through circular economy-based engineering: A profitable chain from waste management to tunnel lighting. *Sustainability, 9*(12), 2229. https://doi.org/10.3390/su9122229

Morelli, J. (2013). Environmental sustainability: A definition for environmental professionals. *Journal of Environmental Sustainability, 1*(1), 1–10. https://doi.org/10.14448/jes.01.0002

Mura, M., Longo, M., & Zanni, S. (2020). Circular economy in Italian SMEs: A multi-method study. *Journal of Cleaner Production, 245*, 118821. https://doi.org/10.1016/j.jclepro.2019.118821

Ndubisi, N. O., & Nygaard, A. (2018). The ethics of outsourcing: When companies fail at responsibility. *Journal of Business Strategy, 39*(5), 7–13. https://doi.org/10.1108/JBS-03-2018-0037

OECD. (2009). Guidance manual for the control of transboundary movements of recoverable wastes. In *Guidance Manual for the Control of Transboundary Movements of Recoverable Wastes*. https://doi.org/10.1787/9789264060753-en

OECD.Stat. (2020). *Material resources: Domestic Material Consumption per Capita*. https://doi.org/10.1007/978-1-349-11075-9_26

Oelze, N., Hoejmose, S. U., Habisch, A., & Millington, A. (2016). Sustainable development in supply chain management: The role of organizational learning for policy implementation. *Business Strategy and the Environment, 25*(4), 241–260. https://doi.org/10.1002/bse.1869

Ormazabal, M., Prieto-Sandoval, V., Puga-Leal, R., & Jaca, C. (2018). Circular economy in Spanish SMEs: Challenges and opportunities. *Journal of Cleaner Production, 185*, 157–167. https://doi.org/10.1016/j.jclepro.2018.03.031

Panwar, R., Nybakk, E., Hansen, E., & Pinkse, J. (2016). The effect of small firms' competitive strategies on their community and environmental engagement. *Journal of Cleaner Production, 129*, 578–585. https://doi.org/10.1016/j.jclepro.2016.03.141

Potting, J., Hekkert, M., Worrell, E., & Hanemaaijer, A. (2017). *Circular Economy: Measuring Innovation in the Product Chain. Policy Report.* http://www.pbl.nl/sites/default/files/cms/publicaties/pbl-2016-circular-economy-measuring-innovation-in-product-chains-2544.pdf

Presidencia de la Generalitat de Cataluña. (1993). *Ley 6/1993, 15 de Julio, Reguladora de los residuos.*

Puig-Ventosa, I., & Sastre Sanz, S. (2017). An exploration into municipal waste charges for environmental management at local level: The case of Spain. *Waste Management & Research : The Journal of the International Solid Wastes and Public Cleansing Association, ISWA, 35*(11), 1159–1167. https://doi.org/10.1177/0734242X17727067

Quarshie, A. M., Salmi, A., & Leuschner, R. (2016). Sustainability and corporate social responsibility in supply chains: The state of research in supply chain management and business ethics journals. *Journal of Purchasing and Supply Management, 22*(2), 82–97. https://doi.org/10.1016/J.PURSUP.2015.11.001

Redmond, J., Walker, E., & Wang, C. (2008). Issues for small businesses with waste management. *Journal of Environmental Management, 88*(2), 275–285. https://doi.org/10.1016/j.jenvman.2007.02.006

Reinecke, J., Arnold, D. G., & Palazzo, G. (2016). Qualitative methods in business ethics, corporate responsibility, and sustainability research. *Business Ethics Quarterly, 26*(4), xiii–xxii. https://doi.org/10.1017/beq.2016.67

Reyes-Rodríguez, J. F., Ulhøi, J. P., & Madsen, H. (2016). Corporate environmental sustainability in Danish SMEs: A longitudinal study of motivators, initiatives, and strategic effects. *Corporate Social Responsibility and Environmental Management, 23*(4), 193–212. https://doi.org/10.1002/csr.1359

Reynolds, O., Sheehan, M., & Hilliard, R. (2018). Exploring strategic agency in sustainability-oriented entrepreneur legitimation. *International Journal of Entrepreneurial Behaviour and Research, 24*(2), 429–450. https://doi.org/10.1108/IJEBR-03-2016-0100

Sáez-Martínez, F. J., Díaz-García, C., & González-Moreno, Á. (2016). Factors promoting environmental responsibility in European SMEs: The effect on performance. *Sustainability (Switzerland), 8*(9). https://doi.org/10.3390/su8090898

Sakao, T., & Brambila-Macias, S. A. (2018). Do we share an understanding of transdisciplinarity in environmental sustainability research? *Journal of Cleaner Production, 170*, 1399–1403. https://doi.org/10.1016/j.jclepro.2017.09.226

Sallem, N. R. M., Nasir, N. E. M., Nori, W. M. N. W., & Che Ku Kassim. (2017). Small and medium enterprises: Critical problems and possible solutions. *International Business Management, 11*(1), 47–52. https://doi.org/10.3923/ibm.2017.47.52

Sandvik, I. M., & Stubbs, W. (2019). Circular fashion supply chain through textile-to-textile recycling. *Journal of Fashion Marketing and Management, 23*(3), 366–381. https://doi.org/10.1108/JFMM-04 -2018-0058

Secretaría de Estado de Presupuestos y Gastos. (2018). *Presupuestos Comunidades Autónomas.* https://www.sepg.pap.hacienda.gob.es/sitios/sepg/es-ES/Presupuestos/OtrosPresupuestos/ PresupuestosCCAA/Paginas/PresupuestosCCAA.aspx

SII. (2017). *SII | Servicio de Impuestos Internos.* Estadisticas de Empres Servicio de Impuestos Internos. http://www.sii.cl/sobre_el_sii/estadisticas_de_empresas.html%0Ahttp://www.sii.cl/valores _y_fechas/dolar/dolar2019.htm%0Ahttp://www.sii.cl/sobre_el_sii/estadisticas_de_empresas.html %0Ahttp://www.sii.cl/valores_y_fechas/dolar/dolar2018.htm%0Ahttp://www.sii.

Singh, J., & Ordoñez, I. (2016). Resource recovery from post-consumer waste: Important lessons for the upcoming circular economy. *Journal of Cleaner Production, 134*, 342–353. https://doi.org/10.1016/j .jclepro.2015.12.020

Soto-Acosta, P., Cismaru, D.-M., Vătămănescu, E.-M., & Ciochină, R. (2016). Sustainable entrepreneurship in SMEs: A business performance perspective. *Sustainability, 8*(4), 342–353. https://doi.org/10 .3390/SU8040342

Su, B., Heshmati, A., Geng, Y., & Yu, X. (2013). A review of the circular economy in China: Moving from rhetoric to implementation. *Journal of Cleaner Production, 42*, 215–227. https://doi.org/10 .1016/J.JCLEPRO.2012.11.020

Subsecretaría de Desarrollo Regional y Administrativo. (2019). *Sistema Nacional de Información Municipal.* http://datos.sinim.gov.cl/datos_municipales.php

Székely, F., & Knirsch, M. (2005). Responsible leadership and corporate social responsibility: Metrics for sustainable performance. *European Management Journal, 23*(6), 628–647. https://doi.org/10 .1016/j.emj.2005.10.009

Szilagyi, A., & Mocan, M. (2018). Scaling up resource efficiency and cleaner production for an sustainable industrial development. *Procedia – Social and Behavioral Sciences, 238*, 466–474. https://doi.org/ 10.1016/j.sbspro.2018.04.025

United Nations. (2015). Transforming Our World, the 2030 Agenda for Sustainable Development. In *General Assembly Resolution A/RES/70/1.* https://www.un.org/ga/search/view_doc.asp?symbol=A/ RES/70/1&Lang=E

Valenzuela-Levi, N. (2019). Factors influencing municipal recycling in the Global South: The case of Chile. *Resources, Conservation and Recycling, 150*, 104441. https://doi.org/10.1016/j.resconrec.2019 .104441

Williams, S., & Schaefer, A. (2013). Small and medium-sized enterprises and sustainability: Managers' values and engagement with environmental and climate change issues. *Business Strategy and the Environment, 22*(3), 173–186. https://doi.org/10.1002/bse.1740

World Commission on Environment and Development. (1987). *Brundtland Report: Our Common Future. United Nations.* https://doi.org/10.1016/0022-2364(91)90424-R

Zamfir, A.-M., Mocanu, C., Grigorescu, A., Zamfir, A.-M., Mocanu, C., & Grigorescu, A. (2017). Circular economy and decision models among European SMEs. *Sustainability, 9*(9), 1507. https://doi .org/10.3390/su9091507

APPENDIX 12.1   WASTE MANAGEMENT SYSTEMS IN CATALONIA AND SANTIAGO: CHARACTERISTICS AND DIFFERENCES

Table 12.1A   *Waste management systems in Catalonia and Santiago: characteristics and differences*

Variables	Catalonia	Santiago
Waste management system households	Separated waste collection system operated by municipalities and funded integrated management waste systems for different materials.	Non-separated waste collection system operated independently by each municipality, terminating in landfill. Small number of green points and private systems that accept waste (clean, unlabelled, and unpackaged). Independent waste withdrawal for recycling or reuse.
Waste management rate households	Households pay a rate according to their water consumption (new system from May 2020).	Households pay a fixed rate, which varies by municipality.
Waste management system companies	Certified waste managers. Municipal system for separated waste collection.	Non-certified waste managers. Informal collectors. Municipal systems for non-separated waste collection (same system as households).
Waste management rate companies	Regulated payment to certified waste managers. Public price to the municipal system according to type of waste, commercial sector, volume, size (sq m).	Non-regulated payment to non-certified waste managers. Non-regulated payment to informal waste collectors.

Source: Authors, based on Ajuntament de Barcelona (2009, 2018, 2019, 2020); Ministerio del Interior (1996); Ministerio del Medio Ambiente (2020a).

13. Adoption of environmental management systems: perspectives from UK, Finland and Thailand

David B. Grant, Sarah Shaw, Siriwan Chaisurayakarn and Alex Nikolai Shenin

INTRODUCTION

Environmental performance measurement and management within supply chains has increased during this century due to climate change, diminishing raw materials, excess waste production and increasing levels of pollution, and has garnered some attention in the academic literature (Sarkis et al., 2011). Consideration of the natural environment has also been promoted as a good source of competitive advantage (Lee et al., 2012). This has led to research into environmental supply chain performance measurement (ESCPM), which is positioned within the broader domain of sustainability (Carter and Rogers, 2008; Carter and Easton, 2011).

ESCPM enables organizations to measure how well they are mitigating their impact on the natural environment and to report their environmental performance externally, for example through public disclosure programmes or for benchmarking. It also helps organizations to internally control and assess their environmental performance so they can understand their business better and continually improve (Holt and Ghobadian, 2009). Finally, the International Organization for Standardization (ISO) notes in its social responsibility standard that organizations no longer operate in a vacuum and their relationship to society and the environment they operate within is a critical factor for them to do so effectively (ISO 26000, 2020). As a result, environmental management systems (EMS) have emerged as a method to measure and report sustainable performance as part of an organization's certifications or accreditations, allowing them to demonstrate their supply chains operate sustainability, responsibly and ethically.

Research has considered developing and incorporating wider sustainability measures into the existing bank of supply chain performance measures, however this work has been limited in scope and amount (Beske-Janssen et al., 2015). Further, academics and organizations may be confused by a plethora of measures and related 'certifications and accreditations' and how they might underlie an effective EMS. Finally, there has also been a substantial gap regarding the use of reporting tools and the adoption of EMS or standards such as ISO 14001 (2020) or the European Union's Eco-Management and Audit Scheme (EMAS, 2020) in which to position and report measures (Iraldo et al., 2009). As a result, little work has been done to assess the use or adoption of appropriate environmental reporting tools and EMS (Shaw et al., 2010).

This chapter investigates organizational adoption of an EMS as well as related and appropriate ESCPM measures for reporting by synthesizing and analysing findings from three independent empirical studies on supply chain sustainability in the UK, Finland and Thailand. The chapter's objective is to determine the important EMS adopted in each of the three countries and shortcomings related to less popular EMS techniques. Finally, the chapter identifies important ESCPM used by developing a consensus on what is currently used in practice and why. The next section provides a background to these issues as well as a discussion of the theoretical lens use to view it.

LITERATURE REVIEW

Performance measures are essential for organizations to manage operations and navigate through turbulent and competitive global markets. They allow organizations to track progress against strategy, identify areas of improvement and act as a good benchmark against industry leaders (Lee et al., 2012). Much has been published on performance measurement; Taticchi et al. (2010) analysed the ISI Web of Knowledge database using the key word 'performance measurement' in the title or abstract and found over 6600 papers published in almost 550 journals between 1970 and 2008.

A general issue with supply chain performance measures is an abundance of too many measures. Some organizations are using hundreds, which are often not aligned to the organization's strategy (Gunasekaran and Kobu, 2007). This can lead to confusion and presents difficulties in conducting benchmarking exercises, and thus organizations are faced with a challenge of what measures to select, use and report. They can, however, obtain quality certifications or accreditations such as ISO 9000 (2020) to assist with that process.

Traditionally, supply chain performance measures have been retrospective, quantitative and orientated around measuring cost, time and accuracy (Gunasekaran et al., 2004). ESCPM has become important over the last decade as it enables organizations to internally set, control and analyse their performance as regards the natural environment and understand their business better by improving and externally reporting their environmental performance to various stakeholders (Çankaya and Sezen, 2019). This allows firms to broaden their performance measurement focus to include ESCPM where the need to integrate and share data from multiple firms, i.e. beyond the dyad, is critical (Maestrini et al., 2017).

ESCPM has focused on greenhouse gas (GHG) emissions, particularly carbon dioxide or CO_2, due to their importance in the fight against climate change (Shaw et al., 2010) but organizations are starting to consider broader sustainable management issues not only from a mitigation and legislative perspective, but also from an adaptation perspective (Grant et al., 2017).

Further, a significant number of environmental and sustainability schemes have been created and developed to assist organizations in managing their environmental and sustainable performance (Grant and Shaw, 2019). For example, ISO 14031:2013 is part of the ISO 14000 (2020) series on environmental management and provides organizations with specific guidance on the design and use of environmental performance evaluation and the identification and selection of indicators or measures. The standard divides these indicators into three classifications: management performance (e.g. environmental costs or budget in dollars per year or the percentage of environmental targets achieved); operational performance (e.g. kilogrammes of raw materials used per unit of product or average fuel consumption of vehicle fleet in litres per 100 kilometres); and the external environment condition (e.g. frequency of photochemical smog events or contaminant concentration in ground or surface water in milligrams per litre).

However, a shortcoming with many supply chain schemes is that they fail to acknowledge the impact of supply chains on the natural environment, which is a critical component for measuring supply chain sustainability (Carter and Rogers, 2008, Shaw et al., 2010, Carter and Easton, 2011). Further, it is unclear from the literature what supply chain performance measurement tools organizations are currently using.

EMS and related certification or accreditation schemes range in scope from generic business certifications such as ISO 14000 (2020), ISO 26000 (2020) and EMAS (2020), through to more industry-specific certifications such as BREEAM (2019), which measures sustainability in the UK building and construction sector. Other environmental reporting tools include the expansion of the balanced scorecard to integrate environmental performance measures (Hervani et al., 2005; Grant and Shaw, 2019). Further, a 'green' Supply Chain Operations Reference (SCOR) or GreenSCOR model was developed to enable organizations to incorporate environmental management within supply chain management and track environmental impacts simultaneously (Metta, 2011), while the life cycle analysis tool assesses the environmental impacts of a product from cradle to grave (Hagelaar and van der Vorst, 2001). Finally, the Global Reporting Initiative (GRI) developed in the late 1990s encourages the disclosure of sustainability performance data by organizations. GRI provides an alternative perspective on how organizations can measure and report on their environmental performance, designed as an external sustainable reporting tool to aid external benchmarking, and, although it provides a useful guide of what ESCPMs to measure, there is no indication of how these are applied in an end-to-end supply chain (Grant and Shaw, 2019).

The diversity of available certifications is another challenge for organizations when selecting the most appropriate certification or accreditation; for example, one report identified 15 sustainability certifications for the mining sector (Mori Jr. et al., 2015). Another challenge is the differing scope and level each certification follows such as country, industrial sector, type of organization, type of supply chain and/or global presence (Khan, 2008).

Björklund et al. (2012) argue ISO 14001 and EMAS are the two most-common EMS in use. For reference, there are currently about 320,000 ISO 14000 certifications around the globe, including 17,824 in the UK, 1466 in Finland and 3025 in Thailand (ISO 14000, 2020). On a per capita basis there are about 275 certifications per million of population in the UK and Finland and about 45 in Thailand. The annual increase in ISO 14001 adoption from 2014 to 2015 was 8% across the globe, but that rate was inconsistent across many regions, for example, Africa grew by 19%, East Asia and the Pacific by 14%, North America by 6%, and Europe by 1%.

Total EMAS organizational certifications were about 3652 in April 2020 and included about 12,515 sites (EMAS, 2020). Germany leads the number of organization registrations with 1134, followed by Italy with 991 and Spain with 809. The next highest number of organizations registrations is Austria with 264. The leading industrial and service sectors by Nomenclature des Activités Économiques dans la Communauté Européenne or NACE code (NACE, 2020) for certification did not include any logistics or supply chain activities contained in NACE codes 49–52. NACE code 49, Specialized construction activities, leads the sectors with about 1300 organizations, followed by code 20 Manufacture of food products with a little over 600 and code 84 Public administration with a little under 600.

From a theoretical perspective, larger firms 'financially back' the implementation of environmental and sustainability certifications as they have 'in house' resources and capabilities to do so. In contrast, small and medium-sized firms (SMEs) often struggle and see little benefit in doing so (Hillary, 2004; Rațiu and Mortan, 2014). This behaviour can be explained by the Natural Resource Based View theory or NRBV (Hart, 1995, Hart and Dowell, 2011).

NRBV emerged from the resource-based view of the firm developed by Penrose (1959), who defined a firm as a collection of resources where growth is limited by its resource endowment. Barney (1991) enhanced this view contribution of the value, rareness, imperfect imitability and substitutability characteristics of a resource. However, Barney focused on exogenous factors, i.e. outside the firm, whereas Penrose focused on endogenous factors, i.e. within the firm, which are more relevant to discussions of ESCPM (Kor and Mahoney, 2004). As the nature and range of these resources vary from firm to firm, so do the respective resource constraints. Penrose and Barney both suggest that a firm's resources and its capability to convert these resources to provide sustainable competitive advantage are the key to superior performance.

In general, resources are referred to as physical, financial, individual and organizational capital for a firm and are necessary inputs for producing the final product or service and form the basis for a firm's profitability. They may be considered both tangible assets such as plants and equipment and intangible assets such as brand names and technological know-how. Resources can also be traded, but few resources are productive by themselves. They only 'add value' when they are converted into a final product or service.

Hart (1995) proposed NRBV to determine strategic directions for organizations seeking sustainability as a competitive advantage. NRBV incorporates resources in the natural environment in a three-part framework of pollution prevention, product stewardship and sustainable development. Such resources must also possess certain properties: they must be valuable and non-substitutable, tacit or inferred, socially complex, or rare (Hart, 1995). Markley and Davis (2007) argued that NRBV emphasizes the importance of stakeholder value on sustainable competitive advantage and their research looked specifically at correlations between organizational stakeholders of customers, employees and general society, and the relationships these have with financial outcomes. According to NRBV concepts, organizations employing a stronger focus on creating sustainable supply chains that emphasize lower negative interactions with society and the environment, in addition to employing higher codes of ethics, should have stronger ratings on scales of sustainability measures, customer and employee satisfaction, corporate social responsibility (CSR) and profitability measures.

Hart and Dowell (2011) revisited the NRBV and further delineated sustainable development into two major themes: clean technology and base of the pyramid (BoP). Clean technology deals with the way that firms build new competencies and position themselves for competitive advantage as their industries evolve. Reduced material and energy consumption occur through the pursuit of clean technologies that provide for human needs without straining the planet's resources. This includes cleaner production through reduced resource and toxic resource use, better packaging, and dealing with end-of-life products and materials (Grant et al., 2017).

Further, BoP has evolved due to increased attention to the role of firms in alleviating poverty for the poorest of the world's citizens. This is much more of a CSR concept but there are supply chain implications as well (Gold et al., 2013). However, in the main, NRBV provides a useful lens to evaluate EMS adoption, as it suggests organizations should utilize their resources appropriately to address potential issues occurring in the natural environment as a result of their activities.

However, there is a risk that organizations may simply adopt such techniques for marketing purposes, referred to as 'green washing', without providing any real substance behind their efforts, misleading customers and other stakeholders, and showing little regard for the natural environment (Saha and Darnton, 2005; Delmas and Burbano, 2011; Lyon and Maxwell, 2011). This behaviour represents an ethical and reputational risk for firms besides any commercial and/or punitive risk but is a challenge to mitigate in contexts of limited and uncertain regulation and hence voluntary schemes may be open to such activities. Delmas and Burbano (2011) suggest that, besides facilitating and improving knowledge about 'green washing', increasing transparency of environmental performance by policy-makers and firms and effectively aligning intrafirm structures, process and incentives by firms, i.e. in concert with views of Penrose, will address these risks.

There is also a difference in EMS or certification uptake between public and private organizations, with public organizations, such as local authorities and healthcare, being placed under greater pressure from government bodies to demonstrate their sustainable credentials (Walker et al., 2008). Finally, not implementing EMS may be an inhibitor for developing nations trading with developed nations within globalized production and supply chain business environments (Prajogo et al., 2012; To & Tang, 2014).

Despite the importance of this topic, very little empirical work has been completed to date on EMS and ESCPM reporting. Although multiple reporting tools are discussed in the literature, there has been no assessment of which tools are currently adopted and appropriate to position and report ESCPMs (Hervani et al., 2005, Shaw et al., 2010, Beske-Janssen et al., 2015).

Wong et al. (2015) conducted a literature review and revealed that literature on green or environmental supply chains is diverse, lacks a holistic understanding on how different functions, supply chain partners and stakeholders may integrate environmental management efforts in supply chains by identifying the relevant stakeholders and key resources to be orchestrated. They identified four important practices to do so: internal, supplier, customer and community stakeholder integration.

Wong et al. (2020) extended this work by establishing a model differentiating how small and large firms use integrated EMS to enhance practices. Their study revealed two distinct resource allocation patterns: large firms use resource-demanding practices while small firms use resource-light practices to improve environmental and cost-reduction performance, supporting Penrose (1959) and Barney (1991).

Johnstone (2020) explored the relationship between implementation of an EMS and environmental performance from a management accounting and control perspective and found environmental performance is a multidimensional construct and that there are limitations in trying to capture it solely as an output at the intraorganizational level through quantitative items from accounting statements. Mohd-Jamal et al. (2019) also found a dichotomy between knowledge integration of supply chain management and management accounting practices. Hence, there is need not only for interdisciplinary integration within firms but also research across academic domains.

Some work has discussed key enablers and inhibitors for environmental supply chain practices and adoption or use of an EMS (Walker et al. 2008; Diabat and Govindan, 2011; Heras-Saizarbitoria et al., 2011; Shaw et al., 2021). Key enablers for an organization, both internal and external, range from improving environmental performance and waste reduction through to enhancing the corporate image (Holt and Ghobadian, 2009; Psomas et al., 2011; Prajogo et al., 2012).

In contrast, key inhibitors for EMS implementation relate to firm size, with smaller organizations seeing little or no benefit of implementing EMS. For example, Rațiu and Mortan (2014) identified both internal and external inhibitors in SMEs, such as a lack of recognition and positive rewards by public institutions, lack of customer interest and awareness, unclear benefits or insufficient enablers for EMS adoption, and difficulty in involving and motivating employees.

Psomas et al. (2011) also found the most significant inhibitors to EMS implementation were divided into two groups, ISO 14001 requirements of periodic audits, knowledge and experience in environmental management issues and required resources, and determining the key issues of environmental performance such as determining objectives and measurable aims, identifying environmental issues and determining employees' tasks and responsibilities. Thus, organizational demographics, such as country, industry sector and company size potentially influence EMS adoption, and while some larger organizations may experience significant benefits to EMS implementation, this is not necessarily true for SMEs (Wiengarten et al., 2013).

However, some firms may not adopt EMS or even remove themselves from formal schemes. Mosgaard and Kristensen (2020) investigated why Danish companies chose to discontinue their ISO 14001 certification and found two primary reasons: some decertified for another system but continued their environmental practice, while some decertified for cost-benefit reasons and instead focused on production and resource efficiency.

In summary, the need for, adoption of and current use of ESM for ESCPM is fraught with difficulty because of the multiple tiers and dimensions that exist in a supply chain. Overcoming inhibitors to successful ESCPM implementation and management is not trivial and requires significant resources, capabilities and coordination among different supply chain actors. Managing environmental performance also requires unique interdisciplinary resources and capabilities in the form of intrafirm finance, people, systems and processes, which may be readily available in larger firms but not necessarily SMEs (Nawrocka et al., 2009).

The genesis for the study in this chapter was a conference where the authors met and discovered they were independently researching foregoing issues about ESM and ESCPM adoption, reporting and measuring. The authors chose to collectively evaluate these three studies, across three different contexts, to look for similarities and differences to further inform the ESM/ESCPM debate. The next section discusses the methodology and methods used to evaluate these empirical studies.

METHODOLOGY AND METHODS

The evaluation was not a meta-analysis, which is a statistical technique for estimating means and variances of underlying population effects from a collection of empirical studies ostensibly addressing the same research question (Field and Gillett, 2010). This is due to the different research foci and methods used in each study. Rather, this approach was an analytical autoethnography.

Ethnography is a wellknown and rigorous approach qualitatively analysing institutional contexts and is well suited to providing researchers with rich insights into human, social and organizational aspects in such contexts (Harvey and Myers, 1995). Autoethnography is an autobiographical form of ethnography where the ethnographer meets three criteria: a full member in the research group or setting, visible as such a member in published texts, and committed to developing theoretical understandings of broader social phenomena (Anderson, 2006). This approach was considered suitable, rigorous and relevant for the exploratory nature of this study.

A textual content analysis (Krippendorf, 2004, Bowen, 2009) of the three studies, in conjunction with ESCPM and EMS literature discussed in the preceding section, was conducted by the authors to provide a comparison and contrast among the ESCPM reporting tools used and EMS adopted.

The three studies, conducted in the UK, Finland and Thailand, adopted a range of inductive and deductive tools, i.e. a mixed methods approach to explore and answer their respective research questions. A commonality across all three studies was the focus on the transport and third-party logistics service provider (LSP) market in the different country contexts. It is worth noting that a significant amount of CO_2 emissions are generated annually, due to multi-modal transport activities globally, and transport and LSP activities have come to the fore for governments because of their negative impact on climate change. Thus, there is a huge amount of pressure on organizations to find alternative fuels and transportation modes and to begin scrutinizing their ESCPM to help determine their level of impact on the environment in order that they develop more environmentally friendly supply chain practices (Ghadge et al., 2020).

Again, while this chapter's synthesis and analysis do not represent a true meta-analysis, the approach used nevertheless provides important and distinguishable findings and themes that should inform academics and practitioners interested in these issues to carry out future research. The methods used in each of the three studies are described below.

United Kingdom

The UK study (Shaw et al., 2021) employed a three-phase, mixed method approach. The first phase was inductive and involved conducting focus groups with leading logistics/supply chain managers and directors to generate a list of reporting tools and EMS practices. The second phase was deductive and involved testing these tools and EMS practices and their adoption in a survey of 388 members of the Chartered Institute of Logistics & Transport (UK). Finally, the third phase was again inductive and consisted of conducting a focus group with a different group of logistics/supply chain managers and directors to verify the overall research findings.

Finland

The Finnish empirical study (Shenin and Grant, 2015) was exploratory to determine which EMS or environmental reporting tools Finnish LSPs are using, the motivation to do so, the benefits or enablers and inhibitors for adopting and implementing an EMS, and what should be done in Finland in order to increase adoption of EMS. Semi-structured interviews were conducted across nine organizations that represented a wide range of size and core supply chain activities, comprising three micro, two small, three medium and one large, state-owned organizations.

Thailand

The Thai empirical study (Chaisurayakarn et al., 2016) also employed a three-phase process, like the UK study, and investigated how a Thai LSP's overall performance is dependent upon logistics service quality and 'green' or environmental service quality. Eight different company interviews were conducted in the first phase to determine all issues of interest, a survey of 429 companies (231 LSP customers and 198 LSPs) in the second phase tested these issues, and 15 company and other organization interviews in the third phase validated the first two phases.

Two studies, Shaw et al. (2021) and Chaisurayakarn et al. (2016), had wider-ranging objectives beyond environmental reporting tools and EMS and thus the analysis only pertains the relevant portions of the three studies to address the objectives set out in the Introduction.

The qualitative data in all three studies (semi-structured interviews and focus groups) were audio recorded, fully transcribed and coded into themes (Miles and Huberman, 1994). Further, the quantitative data from the UK and Thai surveys were analysed using descriptive and multi-variate analysis to identify underlying constructs and variables. The authors then met multiple times, to review each study systematically, to compare and contrast the key variables and trends (such as EMS systems adopted, enablers, benefits and inhibitors), from both the qualitative and quantitative aspects of their studies, relating specifically to the adoption of EMS.

FINDINGS

United Kingdom

In total, nine ESPCM reporting tools/EMS shown in Table 13.1 were identified and validated by practitioners across all three phases of the research – these nine did not include EMAS, which is not a surprise given a lack of EMAS certifications noted in the literature review. One question posed to focus group participants was whether their organization uses an EMS such as ISO 14001 or EMAS. Many were not aware of what EMS their organizations adopted; responses included "Probably do, but not aware", "Yes we do, but not sure, possible Carbon Trust" and "Ditto, we have a green centre initiative, so I am sure we do". These responses demonstrate a disconnect between supply chain management and environmental management practices in organizations, which requires further exploration and thus has implications on future ESCPM/EMS research and practice.

Table 13.1   *UK ESCPM reporting tool/MS use in order and appropriateness score*
            (1=very inappropriate, 5=very appropriate)

ESCPM reporting tool/EMS	1	2	3	4	5	Average score
Own company reporting	1	4	51	130	52	3.96
ISO 14001	5	11	94	95	33	3.59
Balanced Scorecard (BSC)	7	15	96	101	19	3.46
Carbon Reduction Commitment (CRC)	7	13	117	77	24	3.41
Supply Chain Operations Reference (SCOR)	10	19	130	68	11	3.21
Six Sigma	12	26	126	57	17	3.17
Global Reporting Initiative (GRI)	11	19	143	52	13	3.16
SAP Reporting	16	24	137	49	12	3.07
Defra Reporting	17	22	145	50	4	3.01

An interesting theme emerging from the set of focus groups is that ESCPM reporting is driven by large customers; comments included "This requirement goes into all of our tenders and contracts, if they do not have it they/we do not get it" and "This whole green agenda is going to be driven by what the retailers want. They want to preserve their USP for their own customers and push more onto suppliers". Thus, customers appear to be dictating which ESCPM measures suppliers use and are driving the ESCPM measurement and reporting agenda.

A consensus from survey respondents was that ESCPM could integrate into their existing supply chain performance frameworks, and practitioners saw some benefit in doing so. However, little evidence existed that this was taking place and it is suggested that environmental management is increasingly viewed as separate from, and managed outside of, normal business strategy.

A key finding was that the most significant reporting tool used by organizations is their own in-house company reporting (72% of survey respondents), followed closely by ISO 14001 and the balanced scorecard. There was also a difference regarding organization size. For example, one large, UK-based multinational organization commented they used their own "global metric system, so every operation in [their] supply chain will have the same things to report on and the same explicit definitions of how to collect the data and what to feed into the system". In contrast, SMEs seemed less certain about what measurement reporting tools they used, with many unclear on what they measure and report, e.g. "I do not think we do a lot of direct monitoring at the moment".

This suggests that organization size has an impact on the capability or need to report ESCPM as larger organizations have greater resources to invest in reporting than SMEs, supporting some findings in the literature (e.g. Psomas et al., 2011; Raţiu and Mortan, 2014; Wong et al., 2020). Over 68% of survey respondents answered 'agree' or 'strongly agree' to the question as to whether ESCPM can be incorporated into existing supply chain reporting tools, and over 65% answered likewise that there is a benefit to doing so.

Survey respondents also identified the appropriateness of the nine reporting tools for ESCPM integration as shown in Table 13.1. The most significant difference categories using a Pearson Chi-square test were found for 'own company reporting' across 'very appropriate' and 'appropriate', suggesting most respondents consider their own company reports are the most appropriate tools to integrate ESCPM, i.e. supporting notions found by Mosgaard and Kristensen (2020). There was also a significant difference for the category 'appropriate' for both ISO 14001 and balanced scorecard reporting, also indicating their importance.

Finally, many of the reporting tools discussed in the background literature such as SCOR/GreenSCOR or GRI are not extensively used in the UK. Thus, it appears that 'no one size fits all' in terms of ESCPM reporting, with many organizations developing 'own company designed' reporting tools, which also presents challenges for external ESCPM benchmarking and the future of ESCPM reporting and EMS, particularly for frameworks such as GRI which rely on standardized results.

Finland

A profile of the nine interviewed firms is presented in Table 13.2. Four organizations use ISO 14001, one uses its own annual environmental reports, one will adopt "something in the near future", while three do not use any EMS at all. There was no discussion of EMAS, which again is not a surprise given the lack of certifications. All organizations were able to identify general motivations, benefits and/or inhibitors to adopt EMS. Organizations A, B and C, which did not adopt any form of EMS, were weak on identifying potential benefits to their organization if they did so.

Table 13.2   Profile of Finnish interviewee organizations

Organization	Turnover (€)	Employees	Core activity	Size	EMS used
A	1M	6	Road transports	Micro	None
B	1–2M	5–9	Road transports	Micro	None
C	1.1M	20–49	Courier and road transports	Small	None
D	3.3M	10–19	Full Service LSP	Small	ISO14001
E	26M	417	Moving and logistics services	Medium	In near future
F	44.4M	146	Forwarding and LSP	Medium	ISO14001
G	18.3M	10–19	Taxi and road transports	Small	ISO14001
H	1437,8M	10 000	Railroad and LSP	Large state-owned	ISO14001
I	20M	150	Refrigerated road transports	Medium	Annual environmental reports

Organization A identified general benefits such as standardized working routines, standardized reporting and clear guidelines for different practical tasks such as managing warehouses, waste and chemicals while the interviewee from organization B stated that "some customers in our case would probably value this [EMS] but they should also advertise it further that's how they transport their products" and thought EMS could help the organization by reducing costs due to fuel efficiencies. Organizations A and B also raised non-existent motives or enablers such as tax benefits and other state-incentives. The interviewee from organization I did not identify any possible direct benefits but the organization is already working according to strict environmental practices and has a quality management system and its own environmental reporting system.

The ISO 14001 certified organizations and organization E provided examples of direct benefits, including better overall routines, less customer reclamations and cost-savings due to increased cost-efficiency and waste handling. Four organizations indicated that EMS has or will provide greater transparency of different operations both internally among the staff and externally among customers and partners, while three recognized a marketing value for EMS where the ISO14001 certificate has been used to draw customer attention that enhances firm image, which in turn increases customer acceptance and provides organizations with a competitive edge. Another aspect that emerged from several firms is that they have been able to better track and measure their environmental performance, e.g. organization F said that "the audit [ISO14001 certification] pushed us to realize the true potential of EMS and that green performance measuring and measurement of other activities is, in fact, possible" .

All perceived and actual benefits and enablers of EMS discussed by the Finnish organizations support the literature (e.g. Walker et al. 2008, Diabat and Govindan, 2011, Heras-Saizarbitoria et al., 2011). Additionally, the ISO14001 certified organizations were able to link having environmental practices to a competitive advantage over competitors in efficiency, brand image and customer satisfaction. This also supports the NRBV (Hart, 1995, Hart and Dowell, 2011).

All interviewees identified inhibitors for EMS adoption but organizations C, G, H and I reported that inhibitors were not substantial. Organizations A and B reported that the inhibitors were too large for them to adopt EMS, supporting issues found by Psomas et al. (2011) and Rațiu and Mortan (2014) much like the UK findings, while organizations D, E and F reported there were some inhibitors but that they were able to overcome them.

Some organizations failed to recognize the value added an EMS brings; all mentioned additional costs and extra workload that would apply as adopting an EMS would require additional staff, which the organizations could not afford. Additionally, a lack of incentives from the state are considered an inhibitor. Organization I, who has an EMS modus operandi but is not certified, stated that the only inhibitors stopping them from acquiring an ISO14001 certificate in addition to ISO9001 is the fact that customers do not demand it.

All organizations without EMS expressed two unanimous motivations for adopting an EMS, which were value recognition from customers and any kind of legislative or tax-incentives from the state. Interestingly, firm H, which is a large state-owned firm, noted that "a new state-incentive for large companies (not for SMEs) lets them by-pass an annual energy-review of the company if they are ISO14001-certified". This might be an indication that legislative and institutional forces are not promoting the issues surrounding EMS well enough, since all but one of the non-users of EMS in this study indicated a lack of overall knowledge in EMS.

Thailand

Table 13.3 summarizes comments from the qualitative interviews conducted in Thailand before and after the second phase survey from both customer (C) and LSP (L) perspectives regarding adopting EMS. ISO 14001 adoption was evident and growing as a lack of ISO 14001 certification is seen as a key inhibitor to trading with organizations in the developed west. Thai organizations wanting to work with western customers are cognizant of the need to enhance their sustainability credentials, supporting Psomas et al. (2011) and Rațiu and Mortan (2014). The adoption of EMAS never surfaced in any of the research phases, but if Thai organizations are concerned about doing business in Europe, they should be aware of its basic parameters.

Of interest was a focus on working conditions and staff health and safety, which Grant et al. (2017) addresses as the social or people issue in the classical triple-bottom line for sustainability of social (people), environment (planet) and economic (profit). This suggests that sustainability or environmental issues may be considered at lower levels in developing countries than in developed countries, and that ESCPM and EMS adoption might be based on the supply chain and economics maturity of a country.

The 13 ESCPM variables used in the Thai survey related to reporting tools and EMS and were combined in a construct entitled 'Green Safety, Regulations and Collaboration' (GSRC) shown in Table 13.4. In examining each variable in that construct, four main sub-constructs emerge including: organizational collaboration; sustainability; green regulation and standardization; and vehicle technology and logistics design.

Table 13.3   Thailand interviewees' comments about EMS

Organization: C=Customer L=LSP	Interviewee comments
C-11	At the first time implementing a kind of environmental system, no firm wants to do this, but they get pressure from customers to do it to get a new customer and secure an existing customer. After that, some firms just do it when they have to, but some firms learn from this implementation that a process system in their companies seems systematic and also have no trouble with society. This also helps to screen any person that wants to join a company because (s)he will have to follow many regulations to deserve the certificates. People who join a company should have attitudes of a similar direction as the company. Eventually, the level of service will be increased automatically.
L-11	In my opinion, ISO is one of the trade barriers. It is unnecessary for you to have a kind of certificate, and this certificate isn't relative to service quality. For example, our company don't have the EMS/ISO 140001, but we have our own regulations and standards that our customers accept as the same as ISO 14001. It depends on the standard of the service quality that your company has. If your company's management isn't systematic, this kind of certificate may help you to set up a standard of processes and increase the quality of service.
L-12	It can relate to the quality of service about 30–40% of the time as some customers don't require this kind of certificate as one of the service requirements. Some new customers say it is preferable if the LSP has a certificate. In this case, we can tell customers that we haven't had this kind of certificate, but we have a standard of service which seems to cover most of your requirements. He thinks that EMS will help a firm in their process improvement in terms of service quality. If a firm can achieve this kind of certificate, the firm has a standard of service. Therefore, it can relate to the quality of service indirectly. It also helps companies for their internal development.
C-12	It isn't necessary that an LSP has a kind of environmental certificate to provide a good quality of service. It depends on what its customers require and whether the LSP can do it or not. EMS and other certificates absolutely help a LSP to set up a standard for its processes. Though our company has launched ISO 14001, we haven't pushed our suppliers like the LPSs to have this certificate too.
L-13	It is quite important to the service quality to set up a standard and also expand into the new market with concerns about green issues. If you have this kind of certificate, customers will have confidence that you will get all as promised about green issues.
L-14	It is beneficial to business, but it is unnecessary to have this kind of certificate. Some customers may require this certificate, but some don't. It is up to the customer's requirements. EMS may be like a guideline to take a greener approach in business but in the business competition in Thailand, cost is the first priority that customers will consider. EMS may be relative to the service quality but not much, especially in high value or health products.
C-13	It is relative to the service quality as a set of standards of process. Some companies require the EMS as a condition. It appears that EMS can help LSP to serve with a better quality of service.
C-14	It is relative to service quality but not much. This kind of certificate can set up a standard of processes and this will help the quality of service indirectly. It also guarantees that the LSP will deliver all the services as promised by the certificate. Though some LSPs may have their own way to undertake the green approach, I think an LSP which has a certificate/ EMS will have more chance to approach the market.

Table 13.4   Thailand ESCPM variables for EMS and their importance

	Variable name	Mean rank
1	Environmental regulations	1
2	Accident rate reduction	4
3	Operational efficiency	6
4	LSP stakeholders' green awareness	8
5	CO_2 emissions by vehicle technology	9
6	Staff fully trained on environment and safety	10
7	Environmental collaboration enhancement	11
8	Environmental targets achievement	12
9	CO_2 emission by behavioural aspects	13
10	Environmental aspects changes	14
11	Distribution network improvement	17
12	CO_2 emission from awareness of LSP stakeholders	19
13	Knowledge sharing on environmental	21

Regulatory pressures can play a major role in operational processes as they oblige companies to adopt sustainable supply chain practices. According to Björklund et al. (2012), one of the most commonly applied environmental demands in Sweden is the ISO 14001 certificate. This also holds in Thailand where EMS are implemented in some Thai companies to help manage the four categories (emission to air; emission to land; emission to water; and resources used) including ISO 14031 with green regulation and standardization leading directly to improved LSP service quality.

A cross-country comparison of all three studies has revealed a significant lack of implementation of EMAS in the UK, Finland and Thailand, with the UK and Finland showing single-figure adoptions in the bottom decile of European Union countries, which is interesting given its origin and development within Europe. The EMS of choice is ISO 14001 governed by the ISO, which was developed in 1947, with a global reach. Perhaps this is because many large organizations have already established ISO standards (i.e. ISO 9001) and it has consequentially been easier to adopt ISO 14001 certification as part of this or at least as a first step. In addition, EMAS was developed more latterly in 1993, so perhaps is a less well established 'stand-alone' system for adoption. Nonetheless, the reasons for this require further investigation. Finally, the Thailand study also revealed the key driver for adopting of ISO 14001 in Thailand is to enable trading with the western developed economies, thus reinforcing ISO 14001's global adoption and popularity.

CONCLUSION

The findings from the analysis meet the objective set out at the beginning of this chapter, and the synthesis of the three studies found that the most commonly adopted EMS is ISO 14001 in the ISO 14000 series. This may appear intuitive and trite but suggests that this well-recognized scheme is understood by firms as one that is truly extensive and global in perspective. Whither other schemes then?

Key enablers and benefits for reporting tool adoption were financially linked to customer requirements, reducing waste and operating more efficiently. Key inhibitors to effective implementation included a lack of standard ESCPM reporting and measurement tools and government direction, and the complexity of the supply chain.

The findings also provide several deeper insights and suggest several implications for ESCPM use and EMS adoption. First, size and motivation continue to be issues regarding adoption. SMEs do little reporting at all, and while larger organizations internally report ESCPM, they may not do so externally unless required by government or legislation. This supports the literature that reporting and benchmarking of ESCPM and EMS adoption are still very much in their infancy, but also because many organizations do not feel under any pressure to report and are also struggling with the initial concept of "what to measure" and "how to measure it".

However, while ISO 14001 alongside own company reporting continues to be the most widely used in practice and thus the most favourable and relevant EMS for ESCPM integration, it has been inconsistently adopted across the three contexts. For example, many UK logistics practitioners have developed their 'own company designed' reporting tools. Further, supply chain practitioners in all countries indicated a lack of understanding of EMS with small firms demonstrating no reporting at all. We conclude that industry is leading rather than following academia on ESCPM and reporting, i.e. there is a clear divergence between normative theory and practice. This presents challenges for standardization and benchmarking across different companies and industrial sectors.

This lack of understanding and knowledge about environmental management practices amongst the supply chain community, i.e. participants were unclear about what EMS their organization adopted in some of the studies, suggests that practitioners require information and education in this area, if they are to successfully assist their organization in reducing its environmental impact. This demonstrates a disconnect between supply chain management and environmental management practices in organizations, which requires further exploration and has implications on the future of ESCPM and EMS research and practice.

The lack of take-up of EMAS in UK and Finland is also interesting as their single-figure adoptions are in the bottom decile of European Union countries. Is EMAS redundant to ISO or has the promotion of it been lacking? Also, how do countries outside the European Union, especially those doing business in Europe, such as Thailand, engage with EMAS? These are issues for further research about EMS generally and EMAS particularly.

Second, the issue of cost and resources for adoption emerged in both the literature and the analysis findings, especially micro firms struggling with few staff and limited resources, and thus the NRBV theory is very applicable for investigating the ESPCM and EMS domains. Further research should make use of NRBV to investigate firm motivations and behaviour toward EMS and ESCPM adoption and use, particularly as they impact on firm performance. In addition, the capabilities and resources that firms need to implement such systems may be evident in larger but not necessarily smaller firms.

Regarding these issues emerging from the analysis, it is proposed that institutions providing EMS certifications, i.e. ISO, devise simplified versions of their EMS standard certificates that smaller firms would have an easier time adopting and complying with, e.g. 'ISO 14001-Lite' or equivalent. In addition, the findings indicate that government benefits such as tax-breaks would probably have some effect on EMS adoption for Finnish LSPs, but this is not something that organizations can affect themselves, i.e. it is an externality. It is likely such benefits would also apply in the UK and Thailand.

The business of LSPs is an interlaced network of customers and contractors where price and cost-efficiency are paramount and where there may be too little room for EMS to play a significant role, even if it provides a competitive advantage. Thus, it may not be the natural environment that dictates the terms for doing business or, as organization F in Finland said: "money comes first, the environment just benefits from cost-efficient decisions". Therefore, EMS may simply be a tool for implementing environmental considerations better into the equation of cost-efficient businesses. Again, further research should more deeply investigate motivations and behaviour of organizations regarding EMS adoption.

A clear enabler or motivation for some organizations is customers demanding EMS certification from their contracting LSPs to provide an edge in competitive-bidding scenarios. However, this would require a unanimous mindset in terms of EMS being a competitive advantage in the highly cost-competitive industry of logistics.

Lastly, as practice appears to be leading rather than following academia on supply chain performance reporting, particularly in a Thai context where, despite small numbers, organizations consider having ISO 14001 as a necessary pre-requisite to doing business with the west. This presents challenges for standardizing and benchmarking ESCPM reporting, i.e. selection of an appropriate EMS, across different countries, companies and industrial sectors, and may suggest there is a supply chain and economic maturity factor at play here, i.e. Thailand or other developing nations versus the west regarding issues of importance. Many interviewees noted they prefer legislation to level the playing field to prevent a competitive disadvantage occurring.

As with all studies there are several limitations and therefore productive avenues for future research. First, this study used an autoethnographic approach and textual content analysis of extant literature and three exploratory empirical studies, which were somewhat disparate. Thus, the findings cannot be generalized to other contexts but nevertheless were conducted in a rigorous manner and provide a good direction of travel. Second, the empirical studies analysed focused predominately on the transport and LSP sector. Thus, there is a need to conduct similar studies in other supply chain activities and sectors with other organizations to see if there are any other significant differences. Finally, the analysis focused on aspects of the natural environment, which was inherent in the three empirical studies, and thus there is an opportunity to extend the scope to look at broader issues of sustainable supply chain performance measurement reporting, including economic (profit) and social (people) aspects, to complete a triple-bottom line approach.

REFERENCES

Anderson, L. (2006). Analytic autoethnography. Journal of Contemporary Ethnography, 35(4), 373–395. https://doi.org/10.1177/0891241605280449

Barney, J. (1991). Firm resources and sustained competitive advantage. *Journal of Management, 17*(1), 99–120. https://doi.org/10.1177/014920639101700108

Beske-Janssen, P., Johnson, M. P. & Schaltegger, S. (2015). 20 years of performance measurement in sustainable supply chain management – what has been achieved? *Supply Chain Management: An International Journal, 20*(6), 664–680. http://dx.doi.org/10.1108/SCM-06-2015-0216

Björklund, M., Martinsen, U. & Abrahamsson, M. (2012). Performance measurements in the greening of supply chains. *Supply Chain Management: An International Journal, 17*(1), 29–39.

Bowen, G. A. (2009). Document analysis as a qualitative research method. *Qualitative Research Journal, 9*(2), 27–40. https://www.researchgate.net/profile/Glenn_Bowen/publication/240807798

_Document_Analysis_as_a_Qualitative_Research_Method/links/59d807d0a6fdcc2aad065377/Document-Analysis-as-a-Qualitative-Research-Method.pdf

BREEAM. (2019). *BREEAM.* Retrieved 3 December 2019 from http://www.breeam.com

Çankaya, S. Y. & Sezen, B. (2019). Effects of green supply chain management practices on sustainability performance. *Journal of Manufacturing Technology Management, 30*(1), 98–121. https://doi.org/10.1108/JMTM-03-2018-0099

Carter, C. R. & Rogers, D. S. (2008). A framework of sustainable supply chain management. *International Journal of Physical Distribution & Logistics Management, 38*(5), 360–387. http://dx.doi.org/10.1108/09600030810882816

Carter, C. R. & Easton, P. L. (2011). Sustainable supply chain management: evolution and future directions. *International Journal of Physical Distribution & Logistics Management, 41*(1), 46–62. http://dx.doi.org/10.1108/09600031111101420

Chaisurayakarn, S., Grant, D. B. & Talas, R. (2016). The effect of green logistics service quality on Thai logistics service provider performance. *Proceedings of the 21st Annual Logistics Research Network (LRN) Conference*, September, University of Hull, Hull, UK.

Delmas, M. A. & Burbano, V. A. (2011). The drivers of greenwashing. *California Management Review, 54*(1), 64–87. https://doi.org/10.1525/cmr.2011.54.1.64

Diabat, A. & Govindan, K. (2011). An analysis of the enablers affecting the implementation of green supply chain management. *Resources, Conservations and Recycling, 55*(6), 659–667. http://dx.doi.org/10.1016/j.resconrec.2010.12.002

EMAS. (2020). *European Commission Eco-Management and Audit Scheme.* Retrieved 10 July 2020 from http://ec.europa.eu/environment/emas/index_en.htm

Field, A. P. & Gillett, R. (2010). How to do a meta-analysis. *British Journal of Mathematical and Statistical Psychology, 63*, 665–694. https://doi.org/10.1348/000711010X502733

Ghadge, A., Wurtmann, H. & Seuring, S. (2020). Managing climate change risks in global supply chains: a review and research agenda. *International Journal of Production Research, 58*(1), 44–64. https://doi.org/10.1080/00207543.2019.1629670

Gold, S., Hahn, R. & Seuring, S. (2013). Sustainable supply chain management in 'Base of the Pyramid' food projects – a path to triple bottom line approaches for multinationals? *International Business Review, 22*(5), 784–799. https://doi.org/10.1016/j.ibusrev.2012.12.006

Grant, D. B. & Shaw, S. (2019). Environmental or sustainable supply chain performance measurement standards and certifications. In J. Sarkis (Ed.), *Handbook on the Sustainable Supply Chain.* (pp 357–376). Cheltenham,

UK and Northampton, MA: Edward Elgar.

Grant, D. B., Trautrims, A. & Wong, C. Y. (2017). *Sustainable Logistics and Supply Chain Management* (2nd ed.). London: Kogan Page.

Gunasekaran, A. & Kobu, B. (2007). Performance measures and metrics in logistics and supply chain management: a review of recent literature (1995-2004) for research and applications. *International Journal of Production Research, 45*(12), 2819–2840. http://dx.doi.org/10.1080/00207540600806513

Gunasekaran, A., Patel, C. & McGaughey, R. F. (2004). Framework for supply chain performance measurement. *International Journal of Production Economics, 87*, 333–347. http://dx.doi.org/10.1016/j.ijpe.2003.08.003

Hagelaar, G. J. L. F. & Van der Vorst, J. G. A. J. (2001). Environmental supply chain management, using life cycle assessment to structure supply chains. *The International Food and Agribusiness Management Review, 4*(4), 399–412. http://dx.doi.org/10.1016/S1096-7508(02)00068-X

Hart, S. L. (1995). A natural resource based view of the firm. *Academy of Management Review, 20*(4), 986–1014. http://dx.doi.org/10.5465/AMR.1995.9512280033

Hart, S. L. & Dowell, G. (2011). A natural resource based view of a firm: fifteen years after. *Journal of Management, 37*(5), 1464–1479. https://dx.doi.org/10.1177/0149206310390219

Harvey, L. J. & Myers, M. D. (1995). Scholarship and practice: the contribution of ethnographic research methods to bridging the gap. Information Technology & People, 8(3), 13–27. https://doi.org/10.1108/09593849510098244

Heras-Saizarbitoria, I., Landín, G. A. & Molina-Azorín, J. F. 2011. Do enablers matter for the benefits of ISO 14001? *International Journal of Operations & Production Management, 31*(2), 192–216. http://dx.doi.org/10.1108/01443571111104764

Hervani, A. A., Helms, M. M. & Sarkis, J. (2005). Performance measurement for green supply chain management. *Benchmarking: An International Journal, 12*(4), 330–353. http://dx.doi.org/10.1108/14635770510609015

Hillary, R. (2004). Environmental management systems and the smaller enterprise. *Journal of Cleaner Production, 12*, 561–569. http://dx.doi.org/10.1016/j.jclepro.2003.08.006

Holt, D. & Ghobadian, A. (2009). An empirical study of green supply chain management practices amongst UK manufacturers. *Journal of Manufacturing Technology Management, 20*(7), 933–956. http://dx.doi.org/10.1108/17410380910984212

Iraldo, F., Testa, F. & Frey, M. (2009). Is an environmental management system able to influence environmental and competitive performance? The case of the eco-management and audit scheme (EMAS) in the European Union. *Journal of Cleaner Production, 17*, 1444–1452. http://dx.doi.org/10.1016/j.jclepro.2009.05.013

ISO 9000. (2020). *International Organization for Standardization (ISO) 9000 – Quality Management.* Retrieved 10 July 2020 from http://www.iso.org/iso/home/standards/management-standards/iso_9000.htm

ISO 14000. (2020). *International Organization for Standardization (ISO) 14000 – Environmental Management.* Retrieved 10 July 2020 from http://www.iso.org/iso/iso14000

ISO 26000. (2020). *International Organization for Standardization (ISO) 26000 – Social Responsibility.* Retrieved 10 July 2020 from http://www.iso.org/iso/home/standards/iso26000.htm

Johnstone, L. (2020). The construction of environmental performance in ISO 14001-certified SMEs. *Journal of Cleaner Production, 263*. https://doi.org/10.1016/j.jclepro.2020.121559

Khan, Z. (2008). Cleaner production: an economical option for ISO certification in developing countries. *Journal of Cleaner Production, 16*, 22–27. http://dx.doi.org/10.1016/j.jclepro.2006.06.007.

Kor, Y. Y. & Mahoney, J. T. (2004). Edith Penrose's (1959) contributions to the resource-based view of strategic management. *Journal of Management Studies, 41*, 183–191. https://doi.org/10.1111/j.1467-6486.2004.00427.x

Krippendorf, K. (2004). *Content Analysis: An Introduction to Its Methodology* (2nd ed.). Thousand Oaks, CA: Sage Publications.

Lee, S. M., Kim, S. T. & Choi, D. (2012). Green supply chain management and organizational performance. *Industrial Management & Data Systems, 112*(8), 1148–1180. http://dx.doi.org/10.1108/02635571211264609

Lyon, T. P., & Maxwell, J. W. (2011). Greenwash: corporate environmental disclosure under threat of audit. *Journal of Economics & Management Strategy, 20*(1), 3–41. http://dx.doi.org/10.1111/j.1530-9134.2010.00282.x

Markley, M. J. & Davis, L. (2007). Exploring future competitive advantage through sustainable supply chains. *International Journal of Physical Distribution & Logistics Management, 37*(9), 763–774.

Maestrini, V., Luzzini, D., Maccarone, P. & Caniato, F. (2017). Supply chain performance measurement systems: a systematic review and research agenda. *International Journal of Production Economics, 183*, 299–315, https://doi.org/10.1108/09600030710840859

Metta, H. (2011). A Multi-Stage Decision Support Model for Coordinated Sustainable Product and Supply Chain Design. *University of Kentucky Doctoral Dissertations 137*. Retrieved 3 December 2019 from https://uknowledge.uky.edu/gradschool_diss/137

Miles, M. B. and Huberman, A. M. (1994). *Qualitative Data Analysis* (2nd ed.). London: Sage Publications.

Mohd-Jamal, N., Tayles, M. & Grant, D. B. (2019). Investigating the relationship between supply chain management and management accounting practices. Journal of Supply Chain Management: Research & Practice, 13(2), 1–22. https://jscm.au.edu/index.php/jscm/article/view/173

Mori Jr., R., Franks, D. M. & Ali S. H. (2015). *Designing Sustainability Certification for Impact: Analysis of the Design Characteristics of 15 Sustainability Standards in the Mining Industry.* Centre for Social Responsibility in Mining, University of Queensland, Brisbane, Australia.

Mosgaard, M. A., & Kristensen, H. S. (2020). Companies that discontinue their ISO14001 certification – Reasons, consequences and impact on practice. *Journal of Cleaner Production, 260*. https://doi.org/10.1016/j.jclepro.2020.121052

NACE. (2020). *NACE Rev. 2: Statistical Classification of Economic Activities in the European Community*. Retrieved 10 July 2020 from http://ec.europa.eu/eurostat/documents/3859598/5902521/KS-RA-07-015-EN.PDF

Nawrocka, D., Brorson, T. & Lindhqvist, T. (2009). ISO 14001 in environmental supply chain practices. *Journal of Cleaner* Production, 17, 1435–1443. https://doi.org/10.1016/j.jclepro.2009.05.004

Penrose, E. (1959). *The Theory of the Growth of the Firm*. Oxford, UK: Oxford University Press.

Prajogo, D., Tang, A. K. Y. & Lai, K-H. (2012). Do firms get what they want from ISO 14001 adoption? An Australian perspective. *Journal of Cleaner Production, 33*, 117–126. http://dx.doi.org/10.1016/j.jclepro.2012.04.019

Psomas, E. L., Fotopoulos, C. V. & Kafetzopoulos, D. P. (2011). Motives, difficulties and benefits in implementing the ISO 14001 environmental management system. *Management of Environmental Quality: An International Journal, 22*(4), 502–521. http://dx.doi.org/10.1108/14777831111136090

Rațiu, P. & Mortan, M. (2014). EMAS Implementation in SMES: driving forces and barriers. *Managerial Challenges of the Contemporary Society Proceedings, 7*(2), 73–79, Babeș-Bolyai University, Cluj-Napoca, Romania.

Saha, M. & Darnton, G. (2005). Green companies or green con-panies: are companies really green, or are they pretending to be? *Business and Society Review, 110*(2), 117–157. http://dx.doi.org/10.1111/j.0045-3609.2005.00007.x

Sarkis, J., Zhu, Q. & Lai, K-H. (2011). An organizational theoretic review of green supply chain management literature. *International Journal of Production Economics, 130*, 1–15. http://dx.doi.org10.1016/j.ijpe.2010.11.010

Shaw, S., Grant, D. B. & Mangan, J. (2010). Developing environmental supply chain performance measures. *Benchmarking: An International Journal, 17*(3), 320–339. http://dx.doi.org/10.1108/14635771011049326

Shaw, S., Grant, D. B. & Mangan, J. (2021). A supply chain practice-based view of enablers, inhibitors and benefits for environmental supply chain performance measurement. *Production Planning & Control, 32*(5), 382–396.

Shenin, N. & Grant, D. B. (2015). Investigating the adoption of environmental management systems in the Finnish logistics sector. *Proceedings of the 20th Annual Logistics Research Network (LRN) Conference*, September, University of Derby, Derby, UK.

Taticchi, P., Tonelli, F. & Cagnazzo, L. (2010). Performance measurement and management: A literature review and a research agenda. *Measuring Business Excellence, 14*(1), 4–18. http://dx.doi.org/10.1108/13683041011027418

To, W. M. & Tang, M. N. F. (2014). The adoption of ISO 14001 environmental management systems in Macao SAR, China: trend, motivations, and perceived benefits. *Management of Environmental Quality: An International Journal, 25*(2), 244–256. http://dx.doi.org/10.1108/MEQ-01-2013-0002

Walker, H., Di Sisto, L. & McBain, D. (2008). Drivers and inhibitors to environmental supply chain management practices: lessons from the public and private sectors. *Journal of Purchasing & Supply Management, 14*(1), 69–85. http://dx.doi.org/10.1016/j.pursup.2008.01.007

Wiengarten, F., Pagell, M. & Fynes, B. (2013). ISO 14000 certification and investments in environmental supply chain management practices: identifying differences in motivation and adoption levels between Western European and North American companies. *Journal of Cleaner Production, 56*, 18–28. http://dx.doi.org/10.1016/j.jclepro.2012.01.021

Wong, C. Y., Wong, C. W. & Boon-itt, S. (2015). Integrating environmental management into supply chains: a systematic literature review and theoretical framework. *International Journal of Physical Distribution & Logistics Management, 45* (1/2), 43–68. https://doi.org/10.1108/IJPDLM-05-2013-0110

Wong, C. W. Y., Wong, C. Y. & Boon-itt, S. (2020). Environmental management systems, practices and outcomes: differences in resource allocation between small and large firms. *International Journal of Production Economics, 228*. https://doi.org/10.1016/j.ijpe.2020.107734

14. The role of purchasing in the diffusion of sustainability in supply networks

Thomas E. Johnsen, Federico Caniato and Toloue Miandar

BACKGROUND

Sustainable supply chain management (SCM) has received increasing attention in recent years (Miemczyk et al., 2012; Seuring and Müller, 2008; Carter and Rogers, 2008). There are plenty of well-publicized accounts of social sustainability problems; consider the infamous collapsing Rana Plaza factory in Bangladesh, killing over 1100 workers, or the BP oil spill in the Mexican gulf in 2010. Despite the increasing attention, these reports do not go away. For example, a UK Channel 4 investigation in March 2020 documented child labour in the coffee supply chain in Guatemala, potentially damaging the brands of Starbucks and Nespresso at the centre of this report. The persistence of these problems suggests that they are all but simple to tackle.

One key challenge is that sustainability problems often occur in sub-tier supplier operations (Villena and Gioia, 2020). Few companies have visibility of what goes on in their extended supply networks and addressing these issues requires implementing sustainability across, or *diffusing* sustainability into, a company's extended supply network (Meqdadi et al., 2017; Moretto et al., 2018). Companies apply different strategies to diffuse sustainability into supply networks. Supplier monitoring, such as supplier auditing, and supplier mentoring, such as supplier training programmes, are popular but are insufficient on their own to ensure a sustainable supply network (Meqdadi et al., 2020). Therefore, there is a need to apply a wider range of strategies (Akhavan and Beckmann, 2017). In this chapter, our first aim is to explore different strategies and practices for the diffusion of sustainability along the supply chain.

Our second aim is to explore which organizational function should take the lead in diffusing sustainability to suppliers. What is the role of purchasing (or 'procurement') in this process? Considering which organizational functions influence the implementation of sustainable supply chains, Purchasing & Supply Management (PSM) stands out because of its critical role in managing the external supply base of the firm (Schultze et al., 2019).

These are the questions we seek to answer in this chapter. Specifically, this chapter seeks to:

- Identify and classify the range of strategies and practices for the diffusion of sustainability in supply networks and to explore the role of purchasing in this process (based on a literature review).
- Report on a small set of pilot interviews conducted within the Italian fashion and food industries, to understand if and how such strategies are adopted, and the role performed by the purchasing function.

Building on existing literature, we begin this chapter by giving a brief overview of the strategies that companies typically apply to diffuse sustainability into supply networks and the role of PSM in this process. In terms of the scope of practices we take both internal and external practices into consideration, provided that they focus on the diffusion of sustainability throughout supply networks. We then report on a set of pilot cases that we have carried out in the Italian fashion and food industries before drawing conclusions on what this means for the role of PSM in diffusing sustainability into supply networks.

WHICH STRATEGIES DO COMPANIES DEPLOY TO DIFFUSE SUSTAINABILITY TO SUPPLY NETWORKS?

Inspired by Akhavan and Beckmann's (2017) study, we have divided the strategies for the diffusion of sustainability in supply networks into six categories: internal integration, supplier selection, supplier monitoring, supplier development, joint development projects and stakeholder management. We apply this classification throughout the chapter.

Considering external strategies, we include supplier selection, supplier monitoring, supplier development, joint development projects and stakeholder management. The PSM literature has traditionally included research on sourcing processes, including supplier selection (Backstrand et al., 2019). In addition, there is a large body of research on supplier selection from a sustainability perspective, typically under the label 'green supplier selection' (Govindan and Sivakumar, 2016). Clearly, sourcing from sustainable suppliers is a critical first step in ensuring a sustainable supply chain and there are various ways in which companies can achieve this. Important practices include developing clear guidelines and codes of conduct that suppliers must comply with as well as certifications (Wilhelm et al., 2016). Other common practices include the use of sustainability-related key performance indicators (KPIs) in the selection process and sustainability risk assessment in order for suppliers to become approved (Foerstl et al., 2010).

Various supplier monitoring practices are designed to assess or evaluate the sustainability performance of suppliers. Supplier audits are often considered the first port of call, but other practices can be used to monitor supplier sustainability compliance such as self-assessment questionnaires and supplier self-reporting (Meqdadi et al., 2020). These practices can be applied to prove due diligence but often supplier monitoring practices are limited in that it can be very difficult to get a reliable and accurate picture of supplier compliance purely through these methods (Gualandris et al., 2015). It is also difficult to reach beyond first-tier suppliers with these practices.

Companies with well-established sustainable PSM practices often follow up supplier monitoring with supplier development, i.e. corrective actions plans. These comprise activities to help the supplier to rectify the problems that have been identified. Where traditional supplier development programmes focus on helping suppliers to make operational improvements, such as quality improvements or the implementation of lean production practices, supplier development can now also be focused on sustainability. The main purpose is to work together with suppliers to develop their capabilities through developmental programmes. This strategy is sometimes described as supplier mentoring (Gimenez and Tachizawa, 2012; Meqdadi et al., 2020), as it involves helping suppliers to really appreciate the relevance and need for sustainability implementation, i.e. to create a change of mindset.

Joint development with suppliers to co-develop, for example, new green (or 'eco') product designs or packaging (Pullman and Wikoff, 2017) is another way to diffuse sustainability.

Such projects typically aim to increase the use of renewables, avoid the use of toxic and hazardous materials (Li et al., 2016), and increase the use of recycled material (Tate et al., 2012).

This is linked to another strategy focused on external partnering: stakeholder engagement with, for example, NGOs (Gualandris et al., 2015), industrial associations (Kourula and Delalieux, 2016) and providers of platforms, such as Sedex or Ecovadis, that provide sustainability assessment and development services to companies across industries. Engaging with stakeholders is important especially as stakeholder standards are more likely to penetrate into supply networks than any single company's requirements (Villena, 2019).

In addition to externally focused strategies, it is important to consider the need for internal integration to ensure that these are supported by standards, policies and capabilities within the company. Internal integration includes, for example, internal training, top management commitment and inter-departmental collaboration. There is a need to share and communicate sustainability across different functional areas and organizational levels. In practice, this involves establishing functions and activities at corporate level and a structured and consistent set of processes, policies, communication and training activities that span the entire organization. This question is particularly relevant in this chapter because it is about which organizational function takes the lead in which practices, that is, what is the role of PSM?

THE ROLE OF PSM IN DIFFUSING SUSTAINABILITY

There has been a strong growth in research on sustainable SCM. However, there is a real lack of research on the role of PSM in developing sustainable supply networks. Scattered research has examined, for example, how the PSM function can take the lead to ensure that suppliers comply with corporate codes of conduct and do not act against environmental and social requests (Reuter et al., 2010). Other research has investigated the involvement of PSM in joint projects with suppliers for the development of new greener product designs (Yen and Yen, 2012). A few research projects have explored cross-functional collaboration between PSM and the sustainability department or R&D (Testa et al., 2016). Walker and Jones (2012) focused on the role of PSM in supporting and training key suppliers and to build strong relationships with these; this requires sufficient resources to be allocated. Likewise, the PSM function can foster sustainability development by encouraging first-tier suppliers to work with small local businesses, contracting with voluntary organizations or replacing hazardous materials in product design (Preuss, 2009).

A recent major study by Villena (2019) finds that PSM is 'the missing link' in diffusing sustainability in supply networks. She focused on how companies rely on first-tier suppliers to cascade requirements to their own suppliers but finds that this often fails as these have limited resources and do not prioritize sustainability. Her study suggests that for cascading to succeed the buyer's PSM unit needs to directly engage the supplier's PSM unit as otherwise the supplier's PSM personnel are not informed of the requirements from the buying company and cannot transmit these to their suppliers. Often, a lack of collaboration between PSM and other internal functions, i.e. sustainability and R&D, as well as external stakeholders, limits the promotion of sustainability throughout the supply network.

One challenge is that PSM is traditionally not well equipped to take a leading role in sustainability implementation so at least requires training in order to increase awareness about environmental, social and ethical issues (Koplin et al., 2007). In addition, PSM is foremost measured by its ability to save costs whilst ensuring quality and delivery performance and may therefore downplay sustainability as an important KPI. In most organizations cost is the number one KPI for PSM, so purchasing and supply managers have little incentive to focus on sustainability. To summarize, there is therefore scope for PSM to assume a key role in diffusing sustainability but also many obstacles. We set out to investigate these issues in our study of the food and fashion industries.

Table 14.1   Overview of the companies

	Industry	Description	Turnover
FashionHouse	Fashion	Large European company in upper premium segment of global apparel. Four production sites in Europe.	Circa €3 bill. (2017) + 10,000 employees
SustainFashion	Fashion	Italian clothing SME, part of larger group. Markets 100% animal free clothing. Offices in Italy and China.	Circa €30 mill. (2017) Under 50 employees
HauteCouture-House	Fashion	Independent British global haute couture house. Headquarters in London and Italy.	Circa €50 mill. (2017) + 250 employees
ItalCoffee	Food	Italian coffee roaster with six production plants in Europe and hubs in Brazil and India.	Circa €2 bill. (2017) +1000 employees
ItalMeat	Food	Part of a larger group with strong position in Italy and a major European player in the food sector. Product lines in burgers, canned meat and steaks. 20 production plants (mainly in Italy but also abroad), four farms and a large number of distribution platforms.	Circa €2 bill. (2017) +5000 employees

METHODOLOGY

We report on five pilot cases focusing on the Italian luxury fashion and food industries. We chose these industries as they have both experienced a range of sustainability challenges, including social sustainability problems, such as child labour, and environmental sustainability issues such as the use of hazardous chemicals and waste. Within these two industries we specifically looked for companies with multiple tiers of suppliers and with evidence of supply network sustainability initiatives. We also deliberately searched for companies with different levels of sustainability maturity and different sizes to better understand how this would impact the strategies and practices adopted by the companies.

In order to cover all questions related to supply chain organization, sustainability strategy and purchasing involvement we aimed to interview managers from purchasing and sustainability departments. We contacted 20 companies and from this ended up with five companies that fitted our criteria and were willing to participate in our study (see Table 14.1). In addition to the interviews, we collected various documentary data through the company websites and their sustainability reports; some of the companies had very detailed annual sustainability reports which we were able to use to triangulate the data from the interviews. We also had the chance to interact with the companies at various events.

FINDINGS

We begin this section by briefly describing the backgrounds of the five companies to give an idea of the context of each case. We focus on the specific sustainability risks faced by the companies and explain how they apply different strategies for diffusing sustainability within their supply networks and the role of the PSM function. Having introduced each of the cases, we then compare these to see the patterns of sustainability activities across the cases.

FashionHouse

"FashionHouse" is a large European fashion house focused on the high end of the market and with a global footprint. With traditional product lines of clothing and accessories targeting men, women and children, the company has become increasingly focused on sustainability; they publicly state: "We act responsibly".

FashionHouse was incorporated into the Dow Jones Sustainability Index (DJSI) in 2017 and has implemented a sustainability management function to ensure that all actions are consistently implemented. A sustainability committee controls the sustainability strategy, chaired by the Chief Executive Officer (CEO) and including 15 managers from relevant central functions, e.g. Brand and Creative Management, Business Solutions, Central Services, Communications, Finance, Human Resources, Investor Relations, Legal Affairs, Logistics, Operations, Retail and Sustainability.

The sustainability department oversees the organizing of official training programmes and the writing of sustainability reports. The company has developed standards and policies that are used internally and shared externally with various stakeholders; this includes codes of conduct, social standards, statement on the UK modern slavery act, environmental commitment, health and safety commitment, stakeholder engagement commitment and cotton commitment.

FashionHouse's supply network is composed of first-tier suppliers that provide finished goods (in addition to those produced internally), second-tier suppliers that deliver raw materials such as fabric (cotton, silk, wool, synthetic), tanned leather and various other parts including zippers, soles, buttons, etc. These suppliers are managed directly by the focal company in the case of contract manufacturing, even if they deliver through first-tier supplies. In the case of merchandise, suppliers are managed autonomously by first-tier suppliers. Third-tier suppliers deliver, for example, yarn, untanned leather, or provide washing or dyeing services. The company deals with different sizes of suppliers and has created stable and strong relationships with the most strategic suppliers.

All FashionHouse suppliers must go through three steps to become approved:

1. *Complete questionnaires*: general company information, information about social and environmental aspects, compliance and customs;
2. *Sign a contract*: defining the general purchase terms and conditions, agree on FashionHouse social standards, Restricted Substance List (RSL) and other important codes;
3. *Allow verifications on site*: social compliance audit for first-tier suppliers, social compliance self-assessment requested at second-tier and for both custom audit, financial checks and evaluation of country risk.

FashionHouse monitors suppliers on an ongoing basis. The company performs traditional vendor rating twice a year, for both first-tier and second-tier suppliers, including a section based on sustainability and social compliance. A third party verifies the results of the questionnaires; in case of non-compliance, a corrective action plan will be set in motion. Moreover, audits are carried out to investigate social and environmental compliance issues. Audit results lead to risk classification of suppliers and future audits to follow up on suppliers 'at risk'. Second-tier suppliers likewise must fill in a self-assessment questionnaire, checked by a third party every 12 to 18 months. Ultimately, production from non-complying suppliers can be blocked and suppliers banned. Supplier monitoring can be followed up by on-site training for suppliers that were issued with a corrective action plan. In the case of strategic suppliers, FashionHouse organizes supplier days, with the aim of informing its partners about future developments.

FashionHouse collaborates with key suppliers in the co-development of new sustainability projects, for example, new 'vegan shoes'. Moreover, the company participates in the Better Cotton Initiative (BCI) to define an action plan for cotton commitment and a sourcing strategy in collaboration with suppliers. FashionHouse is also a member of other associations and initiatives including: the Leather Working Group (LWG), Apparel and Footwear International RSL Management (AFIRM), the Zero Discharge of Hazardous Chemicals (ZDHC) and the FLA (Fair Labour Associations). For example, as part of its work with the LWG, the company is developing a protocol to assess the environmental performance of leather manufacturers and to promote sustainable business practices; 55% of the leather used in its products is procured from LWG-certified tanners (2018).

FashionHouse does not have a centralized purchasing department as each product group has its own team in charge of product development, planning, sourcing and production. The purchasing managers of each product group are deeply involved in sustainability initiatives and are responsible for selecting and monitoring suppliers, including first-tier and second-tier suppliers, applying sustainability criteria and the various tools, e.g. a Vendor Rating and Sustainability Scorecard. Moreover, the PSM function is involved in training suppliers and joint projects with suppliers. According to the latest sustainability report, 86% of all active finished goods suppliers have undergone face-to-face sustainability training sessions (accounting for 95% of the purchasing volume). There are regular training sessions concerning the topic of circularity, recycling and the use of sustainable materials for all employees in the design, production and procurement departments. The function works in close collaboration with the sustainability department in order to achieve the sustainability goals. In sum, the PSM function of FashionHouse has a central role in diffusing sustainability in its supply networks.

SustainFashion

This company is strongly positioned in terms of sustainability issues, with a focus on protecting animal rights. Sustainability is at the heart of the company's business model. The company has won several sustainability awards in the past years such as 'animal free fashion' certification.

As a smaller operation, SustainFashion does not have a sustainability department, but one person inside the company oversees sustainability projects coordinating between departments. As sustainability is embedded in the company all departments are deeply involved in these subjects. The company did not publish a sustainability report or structured methodology to measure sustainability until 2019. As the company grows, it is planning to build a more structured method. The company did not want to fully disclose its sustainability plans until they felt confident about exposing themselves to public opinion.

SustainFashion's supply chain is composed of two tiers: first-tier suppliers are finished goods manufacturers and the second-tier are raw materials suppliers, mainly from China. There are few manufacturers, but these manufacturers produce around 600,000 pieces per year so are high volume.

Supplier selection is a team process that involves the designer, the product manager and the merchandiser in Italy and China. Selecting purely sustainable suppliers, the company requires

- *Certifications*: suppliers are required to have certifications and standards, e.g. Bluesign.
- *RSL*: suppliers (first and second tier) must countersign the RSL to ensure that they know about chemicals requirements.
- *On-site control*: all suppliers are visited to check their compliance with social and environmental standards.

SustainFashion uses the RSL testing programme for chemical and physical monitoring of finished garments both for first-tier and second-tier suppliers. The company audits suppliers with two foci. For chemicals auditing, the company relies on UL (Underwriters Laboratories), whereas social audits are done through the BSCI (Business Social Compliance Initiative). To monitor second-tier suppliers, only the RSL is used for chemicals, but no social audits are conducted due to the difficult market situation in China.

Problems emerging from supplier monitoring are jointly discussed with suppliers and lead to BSCI recovery plans for rectification. Monitoring is performed continuously until a resolution has been found and the company emphasizes the importance of maintaining a continuous open discussion with suppliers and developing long-term relationships with suppliers based on trust: "human relationships are fundamental for us and this goes beyond a rating achieved in an audit".

Joint projects with suppliers include a new 'Ocean is my Home' collection and a 'Recycled Collection'. The basic principle in both collections is that only recycled materials are used. SustainFashion also collaborates with external stakeholders, such as third-party associations (UL and BSCI) for the monitoring and development of suppliers. There are also collaborations with several NGOs, e.g. WWF and Oxfam, and SustainFashion channels a percentage of its income to these NGOs.

SustainFashion does not have a structured purchasing function so the production and the merchandizing departments are involved in the purchasing process. These two functions also manage joint projects with suppliers and work closely together with the sustainability manager. SustainFashion's sustainability report emphasizes its strong commitment to animal welfare and cruelty free procurement. Along the supply chain the company has structured its business by allocating the production of garments to external suppliers (Tier 1), which in turn independently procure components, semi-finished goods and materials from around 20 second-tier suppliers, the majority of whom are appointed by the focal company. Over time, in order to increase control over first-tier suppliers, the company has concentrated spend on a restricted group of suppliers located in China.

HauteCouture-House

"HauteCouture-House" is a well-known luxury fashion company renowned for its stylish fashion range. The founder of the company is personally committed to sustainability and decided to position and market the company through its commitments to campaigns that include the 'Climate Revolution' and 'Save the Arctic'. As a typical haute couture company, the traditional focus is more on creativity than defined rules, regulations or policies. As an illustration of the company culture, the founder of the company recently chose to participate in a demonstration instead of the annual general meeting at which new strategies were to be discussed. A code of ethics and a supplier code of conduct was introduced in 2017–2018.

There is a strong focus on animal welfare, and animal sourcing principles have been developed. These principles are put in place to uphold the highest animal welfare standards internally as well as in the supply chain. These principles apply to the capture, maintenance, breeding, raising, transportation, handling and slaughter of animals and are mandatory for all suppliers to ensure that they do not use any material in the products that may harm animal welfare or have a negative impact on biodiversity. It is the suppliers' responsibility to ensure that all animal-derived materials are sourced, processed and manufactured in accordance with these principles, and suppliers should be able to provide evidence demonstrating their compliance when required. The company provides support to help suppliers understand and implement these principles.

The UK company oversees design and marketing activities, with production and operations departments in Italy. For the business lines that are managed in Italy, 90% is sourced locally in Italy. In comparison, for the UK, business lines sourcing is mainly from Asia. The company has limited supply network visibility, but in the last ten years the company moved from a licensing model to bring more activities in-house. Interviewees stated that the company can check up to 90% of first-tier suppliers but is aware that its recent commitment to the Modern Slavery Act obliges the company to start mapping its entire supply chain.

The production department in Italy is responsible for the procurement process for each business line. There is currently a CSR expert based in the UK but to date no sustainability department has been established. In Italy, the production department is responsible for sustainability issues and has launched internal training programmes. HauteCouture-House's Italian subsidiary has begun to participate in roundtables organized by various institutions and universities and is now benchmarking against other brands to better understand their level of commitment concerning sustainability.

Supplier relationships are generally long-term and based on trust. The recently developed supplier code of conduct emphasizes sustainability requirements. When new suppliers are introduced, certifications are required and there is a general desire to select sustainable suppliers. The company relies on its first-tier suppliers to select and manage their own sub-tier suppliers but without formal requirements for first-tier suppliers to do so.

HauteCouture-House does not perform audits but has started to informally control some Asian suppliers in order to solve 'grey market' problems, and the company believes that this may help them to control sustainability. In response to customer pressure, the company has launched sustainability questionnaires for suppliers; for the time being, these are not aligned with any standard, but the plan is to base these on the company's ethical code. No monitoring activities for sub-tier suppliers are in place and there are no supplier development or training activities in place.

HauteCouture-House is engaged in a range of initiatives with external stakeholders. The company's ethical fashion Africa collection, in collaboration with the UN's International Trade Centre and Ethical Fashioning Initiative (EFI), helps to dignify long-term employment for some of the world's most marginalized people while protecting the environment. This programme supports over 7000 women who have a strong desire to improve their lives. The programme was initiated by the founder ten years ago in Kenya and another one in Nepal with the same aim has just been launched. Last year, the Italian branch collaborated with a partner company to contrast the use of plastic bottles and a part of the profit was donated to an NGO. The company also supports environmental and ethical causes and charities, including the United Nations Environment Programme (UNEP) and Amnesty International. Furthermore, through a climate campaign launched in January 2013, the founder continues to ask the public to petition, act and protest for a more sustainable future.

In sum, HauteCouture-House has an immature purchasing function. Since the company does not produce anything internally, the production department is de facto responsible for purchasing. Moreover, despite the founder's commitment, the company has a low level of sustainability diffusion in the supply network, working predominantly with first-tier suppliers, although some initiatives are beginning to address sub-tier supplier compliance issues.

ItalCoffee

ItalCoffee is a historical Italian coffee roaster, still owned by the founding family, which has become a global player through the acquisitions of international brands. The company's culture is based on sustainability principles: the company maps its supply chain with a focus on sustainability, issues annual sustainability reports, uses global reporting initiative (GRI) standards and sets its goals based on the SDGs (sustainable development goals). The company wants to further emphasize its commitment to sustainability by "going from sustainability as a task to sustainability as a strategy".

A few years ago, a CSR department was introduced to align customers and suppliers with the company's strategies, reporting directly to the CEO. There is cross-department collaboration, notably between purchasing and CSR, for example, on supplier development. As part of this, our interviewees also highlighted collaboration with the NGO Save the Children. Another cross-departmental collaboration sees the CSR, quality and R&D departments working together on new sustainable packaging designs.

ItalCoffee distinguishes between two fundamentally different purchases in the supply chain: green coffee beans and other items. For coffee beans, the coffee buying department typically deals with 50–60 suppliers who are international traders and who source coffee mostly from farmers located in Central and South America, South-East Asia and Africa. The purchasing department, which procures everything but coffee, manages approximately 2000 suppliers, including both multinational companies and SMEs that span European and Asian suppliers; the company buys coffee machines or components for coffee machines exclusively from Asia. In comparison, packaging is procured mainly from European suppliers located predominantly in Italy and central Europe.

For supplier selection and ongoing monitoring for non-coffee items, the company relies on questionnaires and audits for the qualification and validation phase. Questionnaires are generic but include specific questions related to sustainability. As part of supplier audits the company has introduced a section related to CSR requirements and suppliers are required to sign the

Code of Ethics and the Supplier Code of Conduct. These procedures are used to monitor first-tier suppliers; the company relies on first-tier suppliers to select second-tier suppliers, specifying that these must comply with ItalCoffee's sustainability principles. Additional audits and verifications are carried out for Asian suppliers either by ItalCoffee or third parties; these go deeper into how suppliers manage CSR, such as issues concerning salaries, living conditions and workers management. The company will occasionally send self-assessment questionnaires to suppliers when requested for a specific project; currently only first-tier suppliers are monitored with second-tier suppliers checked only where problems have been reported.

An event to foster supplier development was launched a few years ago with the aim of pushing suppliers to propose new less-costly but sustainable solutions. A project was created to share best practices with suppliers, depending on their country of origin: for Asian suppliers, the company collaborates with Save the Children to address working conditions, safety, employee management and to develop the social community; for European suppliers, improvement plans typically focus on joint new product development projects, e.g. with packaging suppliers to develop more sustainable packaging materials and processes to reduce waste and resource consumption. From the coffee side, sustainability projects with farmers are managed by the company's own foundation, but there is not necessarily a direct link between the farmers benefiting from these initiatives and the coffee sourced by the company. As ItalCoffee has no direct relationships with growers but source through international traders, they leave it to the latter to develop sustainability initiatives with growers.

ItalCoffee's purchasing department has a leading role in diffusing sustainability. It is involved in the strategic decision-making related to sustainability, and works directly with the CSR department in order to develop more extensive sustainable sourcing and monitoring guidelines. The collaborations with Save the Children and Oxfam also entail training and developing foreign suppliers. In 2018, the CSR department began to collaborate with Save the Children to carry out specific projects in support of Children's Rights and Business Principles (CRBP), with a focus on the supply chain. Two projects were launched in collaboration with suppliers: one in China, with a focus on coffee machine suppliers, and another in Vietnam, devoted to the local communities where the company procures green coffee.

In traditional green coffee trading practices, coffee is purchased following common international standards. Beyond that the company has defined its own purchasing standards. ItalCoffee won an Italian procurement award in the category of Ethical and Sustainable Procurement for its work in 2018 by its purchasing department with the aim of ensuring that social and environmental issues be recognized and respected by the entire community of suppliers.

ItalMeat

ItalMeat is one of the largest European actors in the beef meat industry, with an integrated supply chain that includes farms, slaughterhouses, processing plants and distribution centres, and a clear commitment to sustainability. ItalMeat follows GRI's G4 standard, issues sustainability reports, aligns its objectives with the UN Agenda 2030 and sets sustainability KPIs to internally monitor the performance related to the three pillars of the triple bottom line.

Until recently, sustainability was not integrated in the company goals: there were a set of actions, such as the reduction of CO_2 and water usage, but these objectives were not integrated in the strategy plan of the company. The company decided to define a sustainability plan in order to protect itself from external criticisms and to protect the beef sector reputation after the BSE scandal (the so-called 'mad cow' disease). As a result, the beef sector created international and local associations in order to promote sustainability across the industry and set regulations, for instance partnering in the Global Roundtable for Sustainability Beef (GRSB).

ItalMeat's first-tier suppliers are farmers: 20,000 farms of varying sizes. The company's three purchasing departments act independently for the purchasing of animals, purchasing of meat and subsidiary products (e.g. packaging or flavouring), and various services. Together with the compliance department, the sustainability department decides the rules that the purchasing department must follow and the code of ethics.

The company has two different approaches for supplier selection, depending on the type of suppliers: breeders or subsidiary product suppliers. There is a standard process for supplier assessment and a dedicated portal on the company website, but the sustainability criteria are asked only of subsidiary product suppliers. Before starting a new contract, suppliers are required to fill in a questionnaire and attach the requested certification such as IFS (International Food Standards), ISO9000, ISO14000 and OCSE. There are also on-site visits during the selection phase and breeders are asked to provide certifications for food and animal safety, but currently there is no standard supplier assessment process. Supplier monitoring is mainly focused on meat quality inspections by the quality department and there is no systematic ongoing supplier monitoring although the sustainability department will occasionally check suppliers regarding labour rights through third-party auditors.

ItalMeat has a standardized approach for supplier development, depending on the type of problem emerging from the supplier monitoring process. For low compliance, suppliers receive a notice requesting the correction of the problem. For more serious issues, in addition to the notice, the company inspects if the problem has been solved and, if needed, supports the suppliers in adopting new solutions. If the problem is critical, the company stops the supply until the problem is solved. Ultimately, relationships with suppliers can be terminated. The company collaborates with a range of stakeholders including customers, NGOs, farmer associations and scientific bodies.

ItalMeat is a large multinational with a structured purchasing department, but also a structured sustainability department and compliance office. The purchasing function does not have a leading role in sustainability diffusion but follows the sourcing guidelines and standards imposed by the sustainability department.

CASE COMPARISON AND OBSERVATIONS

Table 14.2 gives an overview of the strategies, and the specific practices within these, that the five companies have in place to diffuse sustainability in their supply networks.

Overall, FashionHouse, ItalCoffee and ItalMeat are the companies with the most extensive development of internal organizational policies and implementation of standards (e.g. ISO standards, labour standards, health and safety and Modern Slavery Act). These companies all have standardized processes of reporting of sustainability practices: they all publish a sustainability report, developed through GRI G4 standards, they are in line with the Agenda 2030 and SDGs, and have developed a programme outlining their sustainability targets. All these companies have activities related to internal training of employees, focusing on training of the sustainability department.

Table 14.2   Strategies and practices for diffusion of sustainability in supply networks

	Fashion	Sustain	Haute	Coffee	Meat
Internal integration					
Organizational policies/regulations/certifications/guidelines/ sustainability report/life-cycle analysis	X	X	X	X	X
Awards	X	X	–	X	X
Internal training/increasing awareness	X	X	X	X	X
Top management commitment/CEO commitment	X	X	X	X	X
Reward and incentive for employees	X	–	–	X	–
Sustainable KPIs/target setting/internal monitoring	X	–	–	X	–
Cross-functional collaboration between departments	X	X	–	X	X
Centralized sustainable department/function	X	–	–	X	X
Supplier selection					
Guidelines/certifications/standards/code of conduct/ethical sourcing code/ sustainability report/supplier policies/legal requirements – (1st tier)	X	X	X	X	X
Guidelines/certifications/standards/code of conduct/ethical sourcing code/ sustainability report/supplier policies/legal requirements – (2nd tier)	X	X	–	–	–
Questionnaires for the qualification phase – (1st tier)	X	–	–	X	X
Questionnaires for the qualification phase – (2nd tier)	X	–	–	–	–
Audits for the qualification phase – (1st tier)	X	X	–	X	X
Supplier monitoring					
Audits – (1st tier)	X	X	–	X	X
Audits – (2nd tier)	–	X	–	–	–
Managing compliance/standardized process for supplier compliance and non-compliance	X	X	–	–	X
Supplier questionnaire	X	–	X	X	–
Vendor rating – (1st tier)	X	–	–	X	–
Supplier development					
Collaboration/cooperation/partnership/coordination with suppliers/sharing best practices	X	X	–	X	X
Training suppliers	X	–	–	X	X
Reward and incentive system for suppliers/supplier engagement	X	–	–	X	X
Communication of monitored results	X	X	–	–	X
Joint development projects					
Green design/eco-design/green product/green packaging	X	X	–	X	X
Green manufacturing	X	–	–	–	X
Stakeholder management					
Collaboration/cooperation/partnership with stakeholders	X	X	X	X	X
Philanthropic practices	X	X	X	X	X
Stakeholders engagement/structured tools to manage stakeholders	X	–	–	X	X

Supplier selection is performed in all cases according to criteria and guidelines that include sustainability, suppliers are requested to adhere to the customer's code of conduct and sustainability-related certifications are required. This applies in all cases to first-tier suppliers, but FashionHouse and SustainFashion both extend their criteria to second-tier suppliers. The larger firms, i.e. FashionHouse, ItalCoffee and ItalMeat, also issue questionnaires to, and audit, first-tier suppliers, but only FashionHouse extends these practices to the second-tier. A similar picture emerges from supplier monitoring: all the companies carry out some monitoring, typically audits and questionnaires, but only FashionHouse and SustainFashion extend these practices to their second-tier suppliers.

Supplier development is important for all the companies, except HauteCouture-House which is less advanced in this respect. Our three largest companies all engage in training their suppliers, as follow-up action to non-compliance problems that have been detected during supplier monitoring, with different degrees of commitment depending on each company's maturity level. We also observe joint development projects with suppliers across all the companies, with the main projects related to green product design (FashionHouse and SustainFashion), and green packaging (ItalCoffee).

External stakeholder management is the strategy where companies have the most information available to the public, which is probably due to the need to increase reputation with consumers, investors and public opinion in general. This is true also for the companies with a lower level of maturity concerning sustainability. All five companies have collaboration or partnerships with stakeholders, such as NGOs, third-party auditors or industry associations. Such stakeholders provide specialized competences as well as legitimacy, as they are independent trusted parties with strong sustainability knowledge. Also, the largest companies in our sample explained the need to act together with industry associations to establish standards and reach a critical mass to drive the industry and the supply chain. The management of relationships with external stakeholders, however, is often the responsibility of the CSR function, rather than PSM, which is involved only when such stakeholders perform activities such as supplier auditing or development.

The PSM function of FashionHouse has an active role in diffusing sustainability in its supply networks. Although the company does not have a centralized purchasing department, the purchasing managers of each product group are deeply involved in sustainability initiatives. SustainFashion does not have a structured purchasing function and it is the production and the merchandizing departments that are involved in the purchasing process. The company has limited procurement from a restricted group of suppliers, mainly located in China. HauteCouture-House has an immature purchasing function. Moreover, the company has a low level of sustainability diffusion. On the other hand, ItalCoffee has a mature purchasing function and has defined its own purchasing standards. The company is an award winner in the category of Ethical and Sustainable Procurement for the work done in 2018 by its purchasing department. ItalMeat has both PSM and departments that are structured and mature. Its sustainability department has the leading role in the diffusion of sustainability and the PSM function follows the sustainability guidelines in the diffusion of sustainability in the supply networks.

In summary, we observe that when a structured and mature purchasing function is in place, it is also responsible for the diffusion of sustainability in the supply network, in collaboration with the sustainability department (where it exists); when purchasing does not have its own department, but is performed inside other departments such as production and planning, it is also less involved and effective in diffusing sustainability.

CONCLUSION

Our pilot cases show marked differences in terms of sustainability maturity levels: intentions may be in place but not necessarily followed by adequate actions. The strategies of internal integration, supplier selection, supplier monitoring, supplier development, joint development projects and stakeholder management are observed across all cases but with significant variation. We also find that PSM has an active role in the sustainability diffusion in collaboration with corporate CSR/sustainability and R&D (especially for environmental projects).

The first aim of this chapter was to identify and classify strategies and practices for sustainability diffusion in the supply network. We have done so by proposing a framework that includes not only all the processes of managing suppliers during the relationship with the focal firm, but also the integration of sustainability inside and outside the company. The differences observed in the sample in terms of breadth and depth of adoption of these strategies and practices can be explained according to several drivers: first, company size of course plays a role, since larger and more structured companies are better organized and equipped to adopt systematic processes, tools and methods, and this is clear from our results. Smaller firms, however, may compensate their structural limitations through a clear commitment to sustainability that is rooted in the company's identity and business model, as in the case of SustainFashion, which is a typical case of a 'born sustainable' firm. Second, implementing strategies and practices beyond the first tier, in order to diffuse sustainability in the entire supply network, is still limited to the most mature companies, and even in these cases there is still a long way to go. There are several major challenges, including the complexity, fragmentation and global spread of supply networks, the lack of maturity and resources, and a tendency to 'leave it' to first-tier suppliers. As Villena (2019) suggests, the first step would be to involve first-tier suppliers' PSM personnel in audits and training. Third, all firms collaborate with external stakeholders, of various types, for various reasons. For sure, legitimacy and reputation play a role for all companies, but less mature ones also need expertise and knowledge to help them develop sustainability competences, but also more mature companies need the help of industry associations or large NGOs to reach a critical mass to influence the supply network, which is also in line with Villena (2019).

The second aim of this chapter was to investigate the role of the PSM function in the diffusion of sustainability in the supply network. In most of the companies we analysed, the PSM functions are very actively involved in cross-functional collaboration between different departments (e.g. sustainability department, R&D) and PSM performs a critical role in dealing with suppliers in sourcing, monitoring, development and joint projects. Less relevant is the involvement of the PSM function in projects (e.g. charity) with external stakeholders, unless these are directly involved in activities such as supplier auditing or development. An exception was observed in ItalMeat: even if the PSM function of this company is well structured, it has a passive role because there is a highly organized sustainability department; as there is limited collaboration between the two departments, PSM follows the guidelines dictated by sustainability.

Our study illustrates the critical role performed by an active PSM function in diffusing sustainability into supply networks, because buyers act as intermediaries between the company and suppliers. A proactive PSM function can play a key role in management of sustainability in supplier selection, monitoring and development and a higher visibility of the supply network actions. Moreover, our findings emphasize the importance of developing collaboration between departments, especially between the PSM function and the sustainability department.

The managerial implications that can be underlined are: first, the list of strategies and practices can be a useful tool for companies as a starting point to set up their specific strategies and practices in sustainability diffusion. The second managerial implication relates to the role of the PSM function and the importance of having an active function: as PSM is the interface between the company and its suppliers, a proactive role could result in more control of sub-tier suppliers, and thereby diffusion of sustainability in the network. Finally, PSM can play a proactive role in managing the relationship with external stakeholders, when these are involved in supplier-related activities for sustainability purposes, with the goal of coordinating the process of sustainability diffusion.

REFERENCES

Akhavan, R. M., & Beckmann, M. (2017). A configuration of sustainable sourcing and supply management strategies. *Journal of Purchasing and Supply Management*, 23(2), 137–151.

Backstrand, J., Suurmond, R, van Raiij, E.M., & Chen, C. (2019). Purchasing process models: Inspiration for teaching purchasing and supply management. *Journal of Purchasing and Supply Management*, 25(5), Article 100577.

Carter, C.R., &, Rogers, D.S. (2008). A framework of sustainable supply chain management: Moving toward new theory. *International Journal of Physical Distribution & Logistics Management*, 38(5), 360–387.

Foerstl, K., Reuter, C., Hartmann, E., & Blome, C. (2010). Managing supplier sustainability risks in a dynamically changing environment—Sustainable supplier management in the chemical industry. *Journal of Purchasing and Supply Management*, 16(2), 118–130.

Gimenez, C., & Tachizawa, E. M. (2012). Extending sustainability to suppliers: A systematic literature review. *Supply Chain Management: An International Journal*, 17(5), 531–543.

Govindan, K., & Sivakumar, R. (2016). Green supplier selection and order allocation in a low-carbon paper industry: Integrated multi-criteria heterogeneous decision-making and multi-objective linear programming approaches. *Annals of Operations Research*, 238(1–2), 243–276.

Gualandris, J., Klassen, R.D., Vachon, S., & Kalchschmidt (2015). Sustainable evaluation and verification in supply chains: Aligning and leveraging accountability to stakeholders. *Journal of Operations Management*, 38, 1–13.

Koplin, J., Seuring, S., & Mesterharm, M. (2007). Incorporating sustainability into supply management in the automotive industry – the case of the Volkswagen AG. *Journal of Cleaner Production*, 15(11-12), 1053–1062.

Kourula, A., & Delalieux, G. (2016). The micro-level foundations and dynamics of political corporate social responsibility: Hegemony and passive revolution through civil society. *Journal of Business Ethics*, 135(4), 769–785.

Li, S., Jayaraman, V., Paulraj, A., & Shang, K. C. (2016). Proactive environmental strategies and performance: Role of green supply chain processes and green product design in the Chinese high-tech industry. *International Journal of Production Research*, 54(7), 2136–2151.

Meqdadi, O., Johnsen, T. E., & Johnsen, R. E. (2017). The role of power and trust in spreading sustainability initiatives across supply networks: A case study in the bio-chemical industry. *Industrial Marketing Management*, 62, 61–76.

Meqdadi, O., Johnsen, T.E., Johnsen, R.E., & Salmi, A. (2020). Strategies for diffusing sustainability in supply networks: Case study findings. *Supply Chain Management: An International Journal*, 25(6), 729–746.

Miemczyk, J. Johnsen T., & Macquet, M. (2012) Sustainable purchasing and supply management: A structured literature review of definitions and measures at dyad, chain and network levels. *Supply Chain Management: An International Journal*, 17(5), 478–496.

Moretto, A., Macchion, L., Lion, A., Caniato, F., Danese, P., & Vinelli, A. (2018). Designing a roadmap towards a sustainable supply chain: A focus on the fashion industry. *Journal of Cleaner Production*, 193, 169–184.

Preuss, L. (2009). Ethical sourcing codes of large UK-based corporations: Prevalence, content, limitations. *Journal of Business Ethics*, 88(4), 735–747.

Pullman, M., & Wikoff, R. (2017). Institutional sustainable purchasing priorities: Stakeholder perceptions vs environmental reality. *International Journal of Operations & Production Management*, 37(2), 162–181.

Reuter, C., Foerstl, K. A. I., Hartmann, E. V. I., & Blome, C. (2010). Sustainable global supplier management: The role of dynamic capabilities in achieving competitive advantage. *Journal of Supply Chain Management*, 46(2), 45–63.

Schultze, H., Bals, L., & Johnsen, T.E. (2019). Individual competences for sustainable purchasing and supply management (SPSM): A literature and practice perspective. *International Journal of Physical Distribution & Logistics Management*, 49(3), 287–304.

Seuring, S., & Müller, M. (2008). From a literature review to a conceptual framework for sustainable supply chain management. *Journal of Cleaner Production*, 16, 1699–1710.

Tate, W. L., Ellram, L. M., & Dooley, K. J. (2012). Environmental purchasing and supplier management (EPSM): Theory and practice. *Journal of Purchasing and Supply Management*, 18(3), 173–188.

Testa, F., Annunziata, E., Iraldo, F., & Frey, M. (2016). Drawbacks and opportunities of green public procurement: An effective tool for sustainable production. *Journal of Cleaner Production*, 112, 1893–1900.

Villena V. H., & Gioia D. (2018). On the riskiness of lower-tier suppliers: Managing sustainability in supply networks. *Journal of Operations Management*, 64, 65–87.

Villena V. H. (2019). The missing link? The strategic role of procurement in building sustainable supply networks. *Production and Operations Management*, 28 (5), 1149–1172.

Walker, H., & Jones, N. (2012). Sustainable supply chain management across the UK private sector. *Supply Chain Management: An International Journal*, 17 (1), 15–28.

Wilhelm, M.M., Blome, C., Bhakoo, V., & Paulraj, A. (2016). Sustainability in multi-tier supply chains: Understanding the double agency role of the first-tier supplier. *Journal of Operations Management*, 41, 42–60.

Yen, Y. X., & Yen, S. Y. (2012). Top-management's role in adopting green purchasing standards in high-tech industrial firms. *Journal of Business Research*, 65(7), 951–959.

15. Sustainability assessment in the food supply chain

Verónica León-Bravo and Federico Caniato

INTRODUCTION

Sustainable supply chain management responds to increasing pressures from stakeholders, policymakers and consumers for companies to devote efforts to environmental and social sustainability (Gualandris et al., 2015; FAO, 2014; European Commission, 2014). Accordingly, the literature has grown with studies on sustainable practices, drivers and performance indicators in different industries and with different supply chain scopes.

This chapter focuses on the measurement of sustainability performance in the supply chain, with reference to the application of groups of measures for different stages of the chain (Beamon, 1999), and particularly the sustainability assessment that involves the application of different measures in the environmental, social and economic areas. Furthermore, the chapter considers arguments presented in the literature in which authors claim that the use of indicators and/or measures for assessing sustainability in different stages of the chain increases the complexity of developing an effective assessment system (Gualandris et al., 2015; Trienekens et al., 2012; León-Bravo et al., 2019). Furthermore, given the diversity of sustainability indicators in the literature, risk assessments are ineffective when companies do not know how practices should be evaluated and for what reasons (Bourne et al., 2002). Therefore, the need to understand how companies in the supply chain assess sustainability arises together with that of identifying the company features that influence sustainability assessment.

However, measuring sustainability is highly complex given that it involves social and environmental issues that cannot easily be translated into economic indicators. Some authors have proposed frameworks for dealing with the measurement of sustainability in the supply chain for different industries. They have mostly concentrated on determining the areas to be evaluated and defining the measures or indicators, e.g., Aramyan et al. (2007); Fritz and Matopoulos (2008); Varsei et al. (2014); Yakovleva (2007); Bloemhof et al. (2015); Ilbery and Maye (2005), Arena and Azzone (2012). Moreover, growing attention to the adoption of sustainability measures for different practices in more than two stages of the supply chain is shown as companies might respond to different motivations or strategies determined by specific characteristics.

The sustainability challenges in the food industry include the scarcity of natural resources, climate change, consumer health and safety, and the economic development of communities (Pullman et al., 2009; Maloni & Brown, 2006; Beske et al., 2014). Unsurprisingly, this industry deals with increasing stakeholder demands for better sustainability performance in the triple bottom line (environmental, social and economic) and the industry is widely implementing and assessing sustainability practices, as well as establishing standards and reporting mechanisms (Bloemhof et al., 2015; Trienekens et al., 2012; Bourlakis et al., 2014).

The aims of this study are twofold. First, to understand how different stages in the food supply chain address sustainability assessment. Second, to identify the elements that motivate sustainability assessment in the food supply chain. With these objectives in mind, this study analyses the fresh fruit and vegetables (FF&V) sector given the relevance for Italy's economy: Italy is the second main fruit and third vegetables producer; the third main exporter; and, the first processor in Europe (Eurostat, 2019). We study 12 companies of different sizes and with different locations in the country with operations in one or more supply chain stages.

Companies implement sustainability to gain competitive advantage and to respond to stakeholder pressures, thus, this study applies the stakeholder theory and resource-based view (RBV) theory (Sarkis et al., 2011; Barney, 1991). Given that the pressures exerted by stakeholders are important for companies, it becomes crucial to measure the company's ability to respond effectively (Freeman et al., 2010) while generating or keeping their competitive advantage by creating value that is appreciated in the market.

This chapter presents a comprehensive literature review of the sustainability and assessment of the food supply chain. Each aspect of the study is then described: research questions, methodology, findings and discussion.

CONCEPTUAL BACKGROUND

Sustainability of the Food Supply Chain

The food industry deals with increasingly demanding expectations of product quality and availability for the growing population, as well as accelerating environmental and social impact assessment policies and standards to respect (Bloemhof et al., 2015; Fritz & Matopoulos, 2008; Banterle et al., 2013). Consumers are becoming more concerned with the products they consume, including their origin, the inputs used during production, the labour standards implemented and the environmental impact of production (Trienekens et al., 2012; Maloni & Brown, 2006; Pullman et al., 2009). Hence, as Schmitt et al. (2017) mentioned, the sustainability of food production is implicitly multidimensional, involving environmental care, social wellbeing and economic performance.

Accordingly, the significance of sustainability in the food industry is revealed by the vast number of practices, projects and/or initiatives deployed, and the increasing contributions in literature regarding the study of environmental and social sustainability practices. Maloni and Brown (2006), Banterle et al. (2013), Beske et al. (2014), Pullman et al. (2009), Trienekens et al. (2012) have identified different sets of sustainability practices to be applied in the food supply chain, which, together with guidelines provided by international organizations (UN Global Compact, 2012; FAO, 2014; European Commission, 2014; IFOAM, 2005; ISEAL, 2014), can be summarized in the following seven categories:

- *Emissions reduction and resource preservation*: this category refers to all the practices involving actions and techniques in food production, processing, packaging and transportation that aim to reduce emissions and the use of pollutant chemical substances, e.g., responsible farming methods (reducing fertilizer and pesticides), eliminating contaminant and pollutant agents, reducing CO_2 emissions and GHGs, all reduce pollution.

- *Resource efficiency*: this category includes the practices that improve sustainability by increasing resources and process efficiency, for instance reducing water consumption, efficient water use, wastewater reuse and recovery. Other practices include reducing energy use, energy conservation, reducing the use of other input materials, reducing fuel consumption and optimization of transportation and logistics.
- *Waste reduction and packaging*: this category includes the practices and initiatives to reduce waste, which could be food or packaging material, for example reducing waste throughout the production, packing, transportation and storing processes; decreasing and/ or eliminating hazardous materials; composting organic waste; producing renewable energy or animal feed with food waste; food and material recycling; and, particularly regarding packaging: reuse and recycling, reducing packaging, using reusable/recyclable packaging, sustainable packaging design (e.g., appropriate packaging can allow longer food preservation and reducing food waste).
- *Health and safety*: refers to the practices that help to ensure and increase consumer health and safety, i.e., product quality and control, reducing contamination risk (food safety and security), traceability, promotion of healthier products and diets, communication and education to consumers.
- *Labour and human rights*: all the practices to improve the working conditions and enhance workers' wellbeing, for example regular employment, training, education, respect of worker rights, safe working environment, fair compensation. These practices can be either regulated or voluntarily applied by the companies in the supply chain.
- *Community*: this category refers to the practices aimed at supporting local communities, philanthropic initiatives, contributions to improve quality of life in the community, educational projects, health campaigns, gender equality and diversity, and local biodiversity.
- *Ethical trade:* This category refers to several certification schemes that promote ethical practices and transparency between buyers and suppliers to improve the quality of life thanks to a premium price for sustainable-grown products, respect and fairness.

The identification of practices implemented in different supply chain stages along with their relationships with performance has recently been studied (León-Bravo et al., 2019) but the actual assessment of sustainability per stage is still to be understood and analysed. As Gualandris et al. (2015) mentioned, the range of issues or dimensions that a company considers in its sustainability efforts will determine the scope of the sustainability evaluation. Hence, it is important to identify the sustainability practices implemented per supply chain stage prior to determining an assessment system.

Sustainability Assessment in the Supply Chain

Increasing strict regulations and public awareness are among the main motivations not only for implementing sustainability but for assessing its performance, communicating it and for reducing risks (Schöggl et al., 2016; Fritz et al., 2017). Hence, sustainability performance is key for evaluating whether sustainability goals are achieved and stakeholder requirements met (Grosvold et al., 2014; Schaltegger & Burritt, 2014; Fritz et al., 2017).

Some authors have proposed frameworks to deal with sustainability measurement in the supply chain for different industries and for food in particular. They have mostly concentrated on determining the areas to be evaluated and defining the measures or indicators, e.g.,

Aramyan et al. (2007), Fritz and Matopoulos (2008), Varsei et al., (2014), Yakovleva (2007), Bloemhof et al. (2015), Ilbery and Maye (2005), Arena and Azzone (2012). However, the vast number of indicators in the literature risks making the assessment ineffective, especially when companies do not know how and why practices should be evaluated (Bourne et al., 2002). Along this line, Genovese et al. (2017) pointed out that the main challenge for companies is to identify which indicators to apply without overloading users with too many measures and avoiding information redundancies, thus evidencing the need for simpler assessment with core indicators.

In addition, regarding sustainability assessment in the supply chain, Gualandris et al. (2015) define sustainable evaluation and verification in the extended supply chain as all the activities related to the identification of measures, data collection and processing, data verification and disclosure. The authors discuss how key companies in a supply chain could deploy a sustainability evaluation strategy, considering different stakeholder requirements, company capabilities and the degree of supply chain integration. Consequently, the sustainability assessment system (methods/techniques applied for measuring, monitoring and controlling sustainability) will vary between companies in the supply chain according to the scope or range of issues to be measured and how are they measured, if they are.

In order to better understand how companies in the supply chain are assessing their sustainability efforts, we identified the main sustainability assessment methods mentioned in literature and summarized them in the following groups:

- *Absent*: when there is no sustainability assessment even if one or more sustainability practices are implemented.
- *Non-structured*: refers to the cases when sustainability practices are assessed in some way, but the assessment is limited to another perspective rather that sustainability. For example, the dimensions proposed by Aramyan et al. (2007): efficiency, flexibility, responsiveness; or as Varsei et al. (2014) proposed, cost and service level performances; or measuring productivity as proposed by Fritz & Matopoulos (2008). In these cases, data is not used to assess sustainability per se.
- *Structured*: the case when there is an established and structured performance measurement system that is integrated with other systems in the company; for instance, measurement systems that are integrated with the accounting, planning and/or manufacturing areas and are used for the control, evaluation, coordination and benchmarking of activities (De Toni & Tonchia, 2001). Particularly for sustainability purposes, some measurement and reporting schemes proposed in the literature and industry, such as the GRI (Global Reporting Initiative) and LCA (lifecycle assessment), are increasingly being used. The former, provides a set of indicators for the sustainability triple bottom line, along with guidelines for different industries and processes. The latter provides a method to determine the environmental impact of a product along the lifecycle processes. Moreover, the industry has developed other in-house reporting systems, codes of conduct and own sustainability reports.
- *Certification*: the most formal performance measurement system. Certifications are structured, provide standardized guidelines that are shared with all the actors adopting them, and are assessed by specialized third parties (i.e., certification bodies). Sustainability certification schemes are usually complex and demanding in terms of time and resource investment requirements because they imply interactions with external actors or organiza-

tions (Gualandris et al., 2015), but they are internationally recognized and help companies to ensure compliance, to gain competitive advantage, to optimize processes and reduce risks (Trienekens et al., 2012; Gualandris et al., 2015). Specifically, for the food supply chain, some of the most renowned sustainability certifications are the BRC (British Retail Consortium), IFS Food (International Featured Standards), FTI (Fair Trade international), RFA (Rain Forest Alliance), IFOAM (organic food consortium) and UTZ Certified (member of the RFA) (Trienekens et al., 2012; Gualandris et al., 2015).

The four abovementioned groups refer to the different levels of assessment that a company can apply for one or more of the sustainability practices implemented. All of them, however, focus mainly on single companies, sometimes including the relationships with supply chain partners, but, to our knowledge, none of these frameworks explains the way different supply chain stages assess different sustainability practices. Authors underline that sustainability performance assessment studies considering multiple tiers in the supply chain have mostly remained conceptual and firm-centred (Tachizawa & Wong, 2014). This issue becomes relevant as it is necessary to consider that each stage has its own objectives, capabilities and strategies, and may face different pressures or challenges for performance measurement (Genovese et al., 2017). Furthermore, as Gualandris et al. (2015) and Trienekens et al. (2012) posit, sustainability assessment and transparency vary among companies and among supply chains according to intrinsic and extrinsic food product attributes, company capabilities, stakeholder's importance, and supply chain integration. Hence, in this study we address the need to identify how sustainability practices are assessed in different supply chain stages and the company features that foster the evaluation of sustainability.

CONTEXT OF THE STUDY

The food industry is characterized by unique sustainability challenges. Scarce natural resources that need to be preserved, attention to consumer health and safety, community economic development around the world are only some of them (Pullman et al., 2009; Maloni & Brown, 2006; Beske et al., 2014). Furthermore, consumers are becoming more concerned with the products they consume, including their origin, the inputs used during production, labour standards and the environmental impact of production (Trienekens et al., 2012; Maloni & Brown, 2006; Pullman et al., 2009). Hence, as Schmitt et al. (2017) mentioned, the sustainability of food production is implicitly multidimensional, involving environmental care, social wellbeing and economic performance. Unsurprisingly, this industry, which deals with increasing stakeholder demands for better sustainability performance in the triple bottom line (environmental, social and economic), has started developing assessment policies, standards and reporting (Bloemhof et. al., 2015; Trienekens et al., 2012; Bourlakis et al., 2014) in the attempt to fulfil such expectations.

In Italy, the food industry is the second most important economic sector in terms of production volumes, import and export, representing a turnover of €140 billion in 2018,[1] 56,500 companies, and employs more than 380,000 people (FoodDrink Europe, 2018), and is thus one of the main income sources for the country. In the EU, Italy is the second main fruit and third vegetables producer thanks to the various microclimates that characterize the food variety in the country. Furthermore, Italy is the third main exporter and the first processor (Eurostat,

2019). Hence, this study concentrates on the FF&V supply chain, analysing four stages: growers, processors, wholesalers and retailers. The characteristics of this supply chain provide an interesting scenario in which the complexity of the implementation and assessment of sustainability exists: high perishability, high product variety and packaging sizes, long production times, long set-up times and high set-up costs (Kaipia et al., 2013).

Growers cultivate and harvest the fruit and/or vegetables. Usually, they clean and sell the product in bulk without particular packaging. *Processors* are the companies in charge of some kind of product processing or transformation, e.g., portioning, boiling, grinding, squeezing. They also classify, weigh and pack the product before selling. *Wholesalers* are in charge of collecting and warehousing the fruit and/or vegetables prior to distributing them to retail. Quality control and reconditioning are some additional activities that these companies may perform. Lastly, *Retailers* are the companies that sell the products directly to consumers. Before displaying the product on the shelves, one or more points of quality control may be performed, as well as reconditioning the product in different packaging presentations (e.g., carton boxes, plastic or Styrofoam trays, plastic or paper bags). In addition, these companies commonly handle product waste recovery that can be destined to processing, re-processing, re-selling or donation.

In a first screening, we selected companies in the FF&V food industry registered in a national database, associations and cooperatives databases. Subsequently, companies were selected because they have set up a sustainability strategy in their operations within different axes of action: specific sustainability strategy, development of organic product lines, higher attention to product quality and traceability, sustainability reporting, etc. Lastly, cases were selected according to their availability and willingness to participate in the research. Thus, the companies selected provide a pertinent scenario to study the diverse implementation and assessment of sustainability practices across the FF&V supply chain, that is in multiple stages and with companies of various characteristics (see Table 15.1).

RESEARCH QUESTIONS AND METHODOLOGY

This study focuses on the sustainability assessment that companies apply in different stages of the FF&V supply chain and if there are specific elements that motivate such assessment. The theoretical lenses applied in this study are the stakeholder theory and the RBV theory, as the implementation of sustainability in the food supply chain suggests the expectation of gaining competitive advantage and because such implementation is considered essential due to various stakeholder pressures (Sarkis et al., 2011; Barney, 1991). First, according to the stakeholder theory, companies should consider how well a specific practice helps them to achieve their objectives and to deal with stakeholder influences (Freeman et al., 2010). Therefore, the sustainability assessment is necessary to understand if the company is attaining its performance objectives and improving relationships with stakeholders as well (Freeman et al., 2010; Clarkson, 1995). Second, as Sarkis et al. (2011) exemplified with the RBV theory application in green [sustainability] studies, companies can generate competitive advantages by developing capabilities when implementing sustainability.

Table 15.1   Cases under study

Case	Product	Sales [mln €/year]	Interviewee	Supply Chain Stage
A	Fresh fruit	1	Owner	Grower
B	Fresh fruit and vegetables	2100	President	Grower, Processor, Wholesaler
C	Fresh vegetables	32	Director	Grower, Processor, Wholesaler
D	Fresh fruit and vegetables	230	President	Grower, Processor, Wholesaler
E	Fresh fruit	34	Vice-president	Grower, Processor, Wholesaler
F	Juices and canned vegetables	400	Sales manager Italy	Processor
G	Dried fruit and juices	110	Managing director	Processor
H	Frozen vegetables	1684*	Strategic buyer	Processor
			Business manager (FF&V category)	
			Plant manager (FF&V category)	
I	Fresh fruit	14	Director	Wholesaler
J	All	12,400	Sustainability and values innovation manager	Retailer
K	All	200	Purchasing manager	Wholesaler, Retailer
L	All	1000	Coordinator of fresh goods purchasing and production	Retailer
			Category buyers (Fruits and vegetables)	

Note: *value corresponding to the overall business group, not only FF&V category.

Therefore, the first objective of this study is to understand how different stages in the FF&V supply chain address sustainability assessment. Hence, we first need to describe the type of sustainability practices implemented, and then identify if they are assessed or monitored in any way. The first research question in this study is:

Research Question 1. How are sustainability practices assessed in the FF&V supply chain?

On the other hand, not all companies develop a sustainability assessment strategy or even apply indicators because, as Bourne et al. (2002) explain, they do not know what to measure and how. Moreover, bearing in mind the arguments of Gualandris et al. (2015) regarding how different stakeholder pressures and company's capabilities shape a firm's sustainability performance assessment strategy, the second objective of the study is to further characterize the elements that motivate sustainability assessment in the FF&V supply chain. Thus, the second research question in this study is:

Research Question 2. What are the factors that contribute to the application of sustainability assessment in the FF&V supply chain?

We applied a case-based methodology: the study involves multiple cases with the objective of collecting evidence that can compare behaviours (Eisenhardt & Graebner, 2007) regarding the sustainability approach in different companies of the Italian FF&V supply chain. Twelve cases operating in four stages of the FF&V supply chain in Italy were studied (see Table 15.1). The set of cases comprises companies of different sizes, in different geographical locations in Italy and with different levels of vertical integration, that is, different business units are integrated in one legal entity (Trienekens et al., 2012) and thus operate in more than one stage of the chain (Gualandris et al., 2015; Arena & Azzone, 2012; León-Bravo et al., 2019).

Data Collection and Analysis

Data were collected from several sources such as semi-structured interviews, company websites, online publications and, when available, the company's annual sustainability report. In addition, some of the companies provided internal documentation reporting sustainability projects and results. The use of multiple sources for data triangulation was helpful to ensure construct validity as well (Eisenhardt & Graebner, 2007; Yin, 2009).

The interviews followed a semi-structured approach: researchers followed a pre-defined protocol (see Appendix 15.1) while allowing the interviewee to develop his/her ideas, and in this way the researchers were able to take advantage of emergent themes and unique case features (Eisenhardt, 1989). Three researchers developed the interview protocol, which was based on the literature review and then validated and updated as interviews went on. Two or three researchers conducted the interviews and transcribed the data. Data analyses were revised and updated as new data were collected for each case. Researchers worked on identifying variables and recognizing patterns, first individually to avoid bias, then in groups for validation and agreement.

For the data analysis, the variables of the study were first analysed within each case to identify the sustainability practices implemented and assessment applied, if existing, in each company. Second, a cross-case analysis compared company behaviour in terms of practice implementation and assessment for pattern identification in cases in the same supply chain stage. Finally, a cross-stage analysis compared sustainability practices and assessment applied across the different supply chain stages studied.

Stakeholder theory and RBV theory provide the basis to analyse and interpret the findings. Stakeholder theory suggests that companies implement sustainability practices with the expectation of gaining or keeping competitive advantage (developing certain capabilities that are valuable and inimitable, as RBV explains). Moreover, such implementation is considered essential because of various stakeholder pressures (Sarkis et al., 2011).

FINDINGS AND DISCUSSION

Findings for each research question are described, first identifying the sustainability practices and assessment implemented in different stages of the supply chain, and then the elements identified as motivators for sustainability assessment.

Sustainability Practices in the FF&V Supply Chain

We observed a high variety of sustainability practices implemented in the FF&V supply chain, and noticed that attention to sustainability is not equally distributed among the sustainability areas: approximately 65% of the practices fall in the areas of "Emissions reduction and resource preservation", "Waste reduction and packaging" and "Health and safety" (see Figure 15.1).

Looking at the supply chain stage, in the *Processor* and *Retail* stages, practices are mostly focused on the three main areas mentioned before: "Emissions reduction and resource preservation", "Waste reduction and packaging" and "Health and safety". Regarding the *Growers*, their sustainability behaviour is almost entirely dedicated to the practices for crop protection and pesticides reduction. Companies recognize that even if the cost of production may be higher, they intend to develop products that are safer and healthier for consumers who are willing to pay a premium price. All companies in this stage are committed to this practice. Lastly, *Wholesalers* were found as the stage that implements the lowest number of sustainability practices.

Interviewees explained that companies consider these practices (i.e., practices in the three categories mentioned above) to be easier to implement than others, and they could perceive the benefits sooner, for instance, reducing emissions in transportation and production, or reducing waste. On the other hand, practices in other categories were case-specific where the company culture drove sustainability actions such as community involvement or reinsertion of displaced or disadvantaged people, as in Case J and Case K. This approach has been identified in the literature and in international organizations that increasingly propose social sustainability practices as part of the overall sustainability strategy (Maloni & Brown, 2006; Pullman et al., 2009; ISEAL, 2014; FAO, 2014). Findings in our study also support the expansive implementation of environmental and social sustainability practices in the food supply chain as companies intend to grab the attention of new consumers that value a wider range of sustainability initiatives, from philanthropic initiatives to the ones oriented to safer and healthier food.

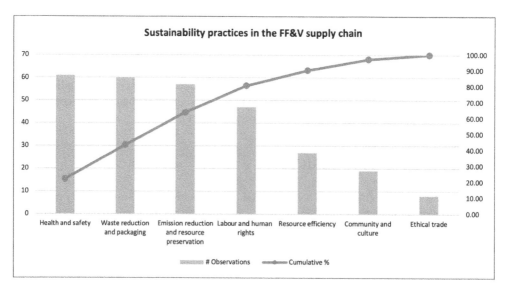

Figure 15.1   *Sustainability practices implementation in the FF&V supply chain*

Sustainability Assessment in the FF&V Supply Chain

To complete the answer to Research Question 1, we needed to identify which practices are assessed, if any, and how. Figure 15.2 shows that approximately half of the practices are either not assessed or assessed in a non-structured way, which means that even if companies are in fact evaluating their sustainability practices, there is not a standard or unique way of doing so in this supply chain. The level of formalization, i.e., definition of measurement criteria, frequency, cost of the measurement, obligations/responsibilities for each measurement and integration, i.e., if it is isolated or inputs are shared with other organizations (De Toni & Tonchia, 2001), varies among the practices implemented and among types of companies. Thus, the assessment method in this supply chain is highly heterogeneous and this behaviour is rather uniform across stages, that is, there is not a direct dependence between stages and type of assessment applied.

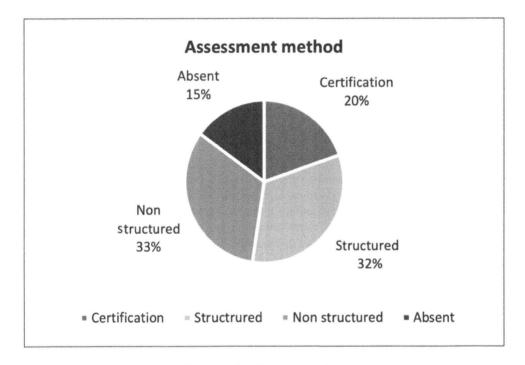

Figure 15.2   Assessment methods used in the cases studied

Furthermore, such heterogeneous sustainability assessment shows a variety of methods applied depending on the type of practices implemented (see Figure 15.3). For instance, "Health and safety" practices are mostly assessed with a certification or in a structured way, allegedly because these practices are regulated, whereas in the "Emissions reduction and resource preservation" and "Labour and human rights" areas, all kinds of assessment methods are present. This indicates that even if companies are in fact assessing their sustainability practices, there is not a standard or unique way of doing so in this supply chain. Such heterogeneity in the sustainability assessment is consistent with previous literature as well. Authors have mentioned that when the number of sustainability issues covered increases, the complexity of evaluation and verification tends to increase as well (Gualandris et al., 2015).

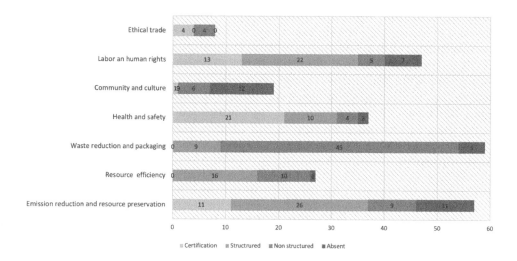

Figure 15.3   *Sustainability practices and assessment mechanisms in the FF&V supply chain*

According to the stakeholder theory and as summarized by Freeman et al. (2010), this variety of actions (i.e., assessment mechanisms applied) explains how companies respond to varied stakeholder pressures. Moreover, given the high complexity in the Italian fruit and vegetables supply chain (i.e., different sizes, locations, products, strategies), the assessment cannot be taken for granted. Thus, the potential competitive advantages generated, according to the RBV theory (Barney, 1991), are difficult to communicate. Companies in this food supply chain apply a more structured (or certification) kind of assessment when the practices are regulated or when a particular product is to be promoted (Marshall et al., 2015; Schmitt et al., 2017; Varsei et al., 2014), therefore responding to regulators' expectations. Therefore, in line with Clarkson (1995), we observed that companies in the FF&V supply chain generating assessment data demonstrate more attention to issues considered more important, e.g., regulations. Hence, this kind of stakeholder pressure justifies being managed and therefore, evaluated. Otherwise, the assessment is highly varied.

Furthermore, it was observed that practices in particular stages respond to specific objectives not necessarily related to sustainability performance but to achieving competitiveness and efficiency, increasing revenues or safeguarding reputation as suggested in Sarkis et al. (2011) Pullman et al. (2009), León-Bravo et al. (2019) and Varsei et al. (2014), and thus responding to different stakeholder pressures such as consumer expectations and developing competitive advantages in terms of quality or price, for example. Table 15.2 shows some examples of interviewees' statements in this regard.

Table 15.2   Examples of quotes supporting the findings of the study

Quote	Type of company	Topic
"Resource efficiency for us means also to respect what the soil needs when we reduce water waste [with the new irrigation system]; with this system we don't pour more liquid than what the plants need." (Case A)	Grower, Non-integrated	Sustainability practices implementation
"Regarding resources efficiency, we do not have only policies, we have photovoltaic systems, water re use for cleaning purposes, controlled re use of waste residuals that can become animal feed." (Case B)	Processor, Integrated	Sustainability practices implementation
"[as part of fair-trade] we help small producers with vulnerable conditions. For example, small farmers affected by violence, mafia, etc. We support also small cooperatives of prison workers." (Case I)	Wholesaler, Non-integrated	Sustainability practices implementation
"Water consumption is something we now, [...] new irrigation systems that are more efficient and report the number of litres per hour that are being used." (Case A)	Grower, Non-integrated	Sustainability assessment
"among others, we monitor waste generated and reduced each year in terms of CO2 emissions…" "maybe this [monitoring] will not represent much in costs, but we are certain of the importance of reducing CO2 in favour of the environment we work in and with." (Case K)	Wholesaler, Integrated	Sustainability assessment
"Fruit and vegetables are considered products with low added value. Product quality is perceived in products with higher prices because of the extra characteristics as environmental respect, attention to worker safety. Hence certifications are needed to show this." (Case B)	Processor, Integrated	Characteristics motivating sustainability assessment Sustainability assessment
[about work health and safety] "there are rigid codes of conduct that all our suppliers must adhere to." "Our clients (retailer) also require compliance with this type of certifications. We audit our supplier every 2 years to ensure everyone is aligned with those principles." (Case G)	Processor, Non-integrated	Sustainability assessment
"We don't measure plenty of practices, it would be certainly overwhelming! [...] we should not bear all the responsibility and costs, hopefully someone will also take care of us, the processors." (Case B)	Processor, Integrated	Sustainability assessment Characteristics motivating sustainability assessment
"[...], we found the right approach with vertical integration. From production to the distribution through different channels we can obtain better income levels, reach economies of scale. Another benefit was increasing product diversification and control while containing the infrastructure costs, therefore we can be more competitive." (Case D)	Processor, Integrated	Characteristics motivating sustainability assessment
[about transportation optimization] "we are a small company, for us, more than sustainability it is a matter of costs. Logistics efficiency is the priority in terms of costs, of course there is a double benefit (economic sustainability), but it is not the primary reason for doing this." (Case G)	Processor, Non-integrated	Characteristics motivating sustainability assessment

Characteristics Motivating Sustainability Assessment

Regarding the second research question, the main elements influencing the use of sustainability assessment are identified: company size, complexity of the measurements and the level of vertical integration.

In line with Arena and Azzone (2012), our study illustrates that smaller companies face more challenges implementing sustainability reporting or a more structured assessment due to lack of capabilities, resources and/or instruments to support them. For example, Case C and Case I implement several environmental practices but focus only on counting the amount of the material consumption for inventory refill, that is, a non-structured assessment, whereas for larger companies, evaluating or monitoring sustainability practices is not different than evaluating other activities, especially since they already have structured assessment systems or certification schemes implemented. For instance, Case J assesses almost all its practices with a structured method via its own yearly sustainability report or by adhering to certifications for animal welfare, traceability and transparency.

On the other hand, consistently with previous studies, the complexity of the measures or mechanisms also influences the assessment in the FF&V supply chain. The identification and selection of measures demand efforts that could be overloading the people involved with overly sophisticated or redundant information (Bourne et al., 2002; Genovese et al., 2017). Therefore, companies prefer to focus the evaluation on already existing systems that do not alter daily operations, and thus, sustainability assessment remains unstructured or even absent. Moreover, when the issue is not considered crucial, i.e., stakeholder pressure is not as important as others, as Clarkson (1995) argued, the company would not generate evaluation data at all.

The third feature identified in our case studies, vertical integration, is also in line with Trienekens et al. (2012) and Gualandris et al. (2015), who explained that in vertical organizations the use of standards could be spread, traceability facilitated and the scope of sustainability evaluation increased. Structured assessment (or certification) was observed more frequently in the companies with a higher level of vertical integration as they expand data collection and processing for different practices more efficiently along their operations. For instance, Case E evaluates its "Resource efficiency" practices through its own measurement system in a structured manner and adhered to the BRC and IFS certifications for their "Health and Safety" practices. Similarly, Case B certified its "Labour and human rights" practices and has its own structured performance measurement system for most of the practices implemented.

Nonetheless, these factors alone might not be the only ones fostering sustainability assessment and might not influence companies simultaneously. Sustainability assessment expectations from customers (wholesalers, retailers), regulators and other stakeholders have triggered the search for support in order to better manage those pressures considered more important than others, or that could be in conflict with others (Sarkis et al., 2011; Freeman et al., 2010; Clarkson, 1995). The way companies deal with different stakeholder pressures for sustainability and sustainability assessment could be also promoted by external actors. For instance, the role of cooperatives in the FF&V supply chain is determinant for sustainability assessment purposes, especially for *Growers*. Cooperatives usually group a high number of members and product volumes and facilitate collective investments to implement and assess sustainability. *Growers* in our cases are associated in cooperatives and have been able to implement European food safety sustainability certifications such as BRC Global Standards and IFS Food (previously known as International Food Standard). These international certifications have become mandatory for *Growers* in order to be able to work with the major retailers. Therefore, in order to access the mainstream market, *Growers* are compelled to get those certifications, and cooperatives play a key role for these companies to comply with the expectations and/or regulations. Actually, horizontal integration through cooperatives has allowed these *Growers* to obtain the production scale to meet the main customer requirements. Contrarily, Case A, which is not a member of any cooperative, does not have these certifications since it does not have the financial means to invest in them.

For better dealing with stakeholder pressures, companies should generate evaluation data (Clarkson, 1995) that help them to attain benefits expected from their sustainability efforts. Accordingly, companies in the FF&V supply chain need to set up sustainability practices and assessment mechanisms that allow them to gain competitive advantages and that are in line with their size, capabilities and with their own complexity determined by the level of vertical integration. External actors as cooperatives could assist to develop capabilities and improve such sustainability assessment objectives.

CONCLUSION

The first objective in this chapter was to identify if there is any kind of assessment used in different kinds of companies and in different stages in the FF&V supply chain, and what kind. We analysed 12 companies with operations in four different supply chain stages: *Growers*, *Processors*, *Wholesalers* and *Retailers*. Findings are in line with Clarkson (1995), as we saw that companies in the FF&V supply chain are generating assessment data that demonstrate more attention to issues considered more important, e.g., regulations. Hence, this kind of pressure justifies being managed and therefore, evaluated (León-Bravo et al., 2019). Otherwise, the assessment is highly varied.

The second objective in this study was to describe company characteristics that influence the adoption of sustainability along the FF&V supply chain. Findings outlined that sustainability assessment benefits depend on main company features such as size and level of vertical integration, and also on the degree of complexity of the intended measurement. The stakeholder theory and the RBV theory help to describe and interpret the findings considering how companies deal with pressures to act and evaluate sustainability, and how they generate or keep competitive advantages thanks to the implementation of sustainability.

In terms of theoretical implications, studies that consider the evaluation of sustainability beyond the performance metrics definition are lacking. As Bourne et al. (2000), Genovese et al. (2017) and Gualandris et al. (2015) argued, companies struggle with metrics implementation and information use, especially when multiple objectives are considered and multiple stakeholders are involved. Trade-offs need to be managed when conflicting stakeholder pressures exist (Freeman et al, 2010). In this regard, and in line with Clarkson (1995) and Freeman et al. (2010), sustainability assessment would provide the data reflecting the management of stakeholder pressures. Moreover, according to the RBV theory (Sarkis et al. 2011; Barney, 1991), if such sustainability data is collected and analysed, then companies would be able to determine if their sustainability efforts are worthwhile and can develop competitive advantages. However, not all companies are capable of deploying such assessment for different reasons or are partially doing it in response to what they consider to be the most *important* pressures. Sustainability assessment is found to be varied in the cases under study, evidencing that no standard or unique system is applied in this supply chain. Moreover, these findings support the perception that assessment is dependent on the type of company (i.e., size and vertical integration) and on the complexity of the assessment mechanisms. A wider supply chain view is also a novelty in this study (Fritz et al., 2017; Schöggl et al., 2016; Tachizawa & Wong, 2014) by comparing behaviour among different stages, highlighting the varied objectives and heterogeneity in the assessment along the chain.

This study could be also of practitioners' interest by identifying the assessment mechanisms implemented for different kinds of sustainability practices, and the factors that foster sustainability assessment. These could be useful for setting up better sustainability assessments along the FF&V supply chain according to companies' individual capabilities and objectives, supporting a more effective sustainability strategy and stakeholder management along the chain.

Future research opportunities could emerge from the findings in this study. The analysis here was concentrated on a specific type of food supply chain in a particular geography, and it could thus be interesting to validate the results in a supply chain dealing with products with longer shelf-life or with products that are exported/imported to/from other countries. In addition, future studies could investigate how to design ad-hoc sustainability assessment systems that address multiple dimensions simultaneously and are also practical for managers to apply.

NOTE

1. https://www.beverfood.com/industria-alimentare-italiana-2018-cresce-produzione-export-stagnati -consumi-interni-wd140787/

REFERENCES

Aramyan, L. H., Oude Lansink, A. G., van der Vorst, J. G., & Van Kooten, O. (2007). Performance measurement in agri-food supply chains: A case study. *Supply Chain Management: An International Journal*, 12(4), 304–315.

Arena, M., & Azzone, G. (2012). A process-based operational framework for sustainability reporting in SMEs. *Journal of Small Business and Enterprise Development*, 19(4), 669–686.

Banterle, A., Cereda, E., & Fritz, M. (2013). Labelling and sustainability in food supply networks: A comparison between the German and Italian markets. *British Food Journal*, 115(5), 769–783.

Barney, J. (1991). Firm resources and sustained competitive advantage. *Journal of Management*, 17(1), 99–120.

Beamon, B. M. (1999). Measuring supply chain performance. *International Journal of Operations & Production Management*, 19(3), 275–292.

Beske, P., Land, A., & Seuring, S. (2014). Sustainable supply chain management practices and dynamic capabilities in the food industry: A critical analysis of the literature. *International Journal of Production Economics*, 152, 131–143.

Bloemhof, J. M., van der Vorst, J. G., Bastl, M., & Allaoui, H. (2015). Sustainability assessment of food chain logistics. *International Journal of Logistics Research and Applications*, 18(2), 101–117.

Bourlakis, M., Maglaras, G., Gallear, D., & Fotopoulos, C. (2014). Examining sustainability performance in the supply chain: The case of the Greek dairy sector. *Industrial Marketing Management*, 43(1), 56–66.

Bourne, M., Mills, J., Wilcox, M., Neely, A., & Platts, K. (2000). Designing, implementing and updating performance measurement systems. *International Journal of Operations & Production Management*, 20(7), 754–771.

Bourne, M., Neely, A., Platts, K., & Mills, J. (2002). The success and failure of performance measurement initiatives: Perceptions of participating managers. *International Journal of Operations & Production Management*, 22(11), 1288–1310.

Clarkson, M. E. (1995). A stakeholder framework for analyzing and evaluating corporate social performance. *Academy of Management Review*, 20(1), 92–117.

De Toni, A., & Tonchia, S. (2001). Performance measurement systems-models, characteristics and measures. *International Journal of Operations & Production Management*, 21(1/2), 46–71.

Eisenhardt, K. M. (1989). Building theories from case study research. *Academy of Management Review*, 14(4), 532–550.

Eisenhardt, K. M., & Graebner, M. E., (2007). Theory building from cases: Opportunities and challenges. *Academy of Management Journal*, 50(1), 25–32.

European Commission (EU), Agricultural and Rural Development. (2014). The EU's common agricultural policy (CAP): For our food, for our countryside, for our environment. Accessed 29 January 2020: http://ec.europa.eu/agriculture/cap-overview/2014_en.pdf

Eurostat, (2019). The fruit and vegetable sector in the EU – a statistical overview. Accessed 27 February 2020: http://ec.europa.eu/eurostat/statistics-explained/index.php/The_fruit_and_vegetable_sector_in_the_EU_-_a_statistical_overview

FAO (Food and Agricultural Organization of the United Nations). (2014). The state of food and agriculture 2014. Accessed 29 January 2020: http://www.fao.org/publications/sofa/2014/en/?%DC%19-%07 =

FoodDrink Europe. (2018). Data & Trends EU food and drink industry 2018. Accessed 27 February 2020: https://www.fooddrinkeurope.eu/uploads/publications_documents/FoodDrinkEurope_Data_and_Trends_2018_FINAL.pdf

Freeman, R. E., Harrison, J. S., Wicks, A. C., Parmar, B. L., & De Colle, S. (2010). *Stakeholder Theory: The State of the Art*. Cambridge, UK: Cambridge University Press.

Fritz, M., & Matopoulos, A. (2008). *Sustainability in the agri-food industry: A literature review and overview of current trends*. In Eighth International Conference on Management in Agrifood Chains and Networks, Ede, Holland (pp. 28–30).

Fritz, M. M., Schöggl, J. P., & Baumgartner, R. J. (2017). Selected sustainability aspects for supply chain data exchange: Towards a supply chain-wide sustainability assessment. *Journal of Cleaner Production*, 141, 587–607.

Genovese, A., Morris, J., Piccolo, C., & Koh, S. L. (2017). Assessing redundancies in environmental performance measures for supply chains. *Journal of Cleaner Production*, 167, 1290–1302.

Grosvold, J., U. Hoejmose, S., & K. Roehrich, J. (2014). Squaring the circle: Management, measurement and performance of sustainability in supply chains. *Supply Chain Management: An International Journal*, 19(3), 292–305.

Gualandris, J., Klassen, R. D., Vachon, S., & Kalchschmidt, M. (2015). Sustainable evaluation and verification in supply chains: Aligning and leveraging accountability to stakeholders. *Journal of Operations Management*, 38, 1–13.

IFOAM - Organics International, (2005). Principles of organic agriculture. Accessed 29 January 2020: http://www.ifoam.bio/sites/default/files/poa_english_web.pdf.

Ilbery, B., & Maye, D. (2005). Food supply chains and sustainability: Evidence from specialist food producers in the Scottish/English borders. *Land Use Policy*, 22(4), 331–344.

ISEAL Alliance. (2014). ISEAL Code of good practice. Version 6.0 December 2014. Accessed 29 January 2020: http://www.isealalliance.org/sites/default/files/resource/2017-11/ISEAL_Standard_Setting_Code_v6_Dec_2014.pdf

Kaipia, R., Dukovska-Popovska, I., & Loikkanen, L. (2013). Creating sustainable fresh food supply chains through waste reduction. *International Journal of Physical Distribution and Logistics Management*, 43(3), 262–276.

León-Bravo, V., Caniato, F., & Caridi, M. (2019). Sustainability in multiple stages of the food supply chain in Italy: Practices, performance and reputation. *Operations Management Research*, 1–22.

Maloni, M. J., & Brown, M. E. (2006). Corporate social responsibility in the supply chain: An application in the food industry. *Journal of Business Ethics*, 68(1), 35–52.

Marshall, D., McCarthy, L., Heavey, C., & McGrath, P. (2015). Environmental and social supply chain management sustainability practices: Construct development and measurement. *Production Planning & Control*, 26(8), 673–690.

Pullman, M. E., Maloni, M. J., & Carter, C. R. (2009). Food for thought: Social versus environmental sustainability practices and performance outcomes. *Journal of Supply Chain Management*, 45(4), 38–54.

Sarkis, J., Zhu, Q., & Lai, K. H. (2011). An organizational theoretic review of green supply chain management literature. *International Journal of Production Economics*, 130(1), 1–15.

Schaltegger, S., & Burritt, R. (2014). Measuring and managing sustainability performance of supply chains: Review and sustainability supply chain management framework. *Supply Chain Management: An International Journal*, 19(3), 232–241.

Schmitt, E., Galli, F., Menozzi, D., Maye, D., Touzard, J. M., Marescotti, A., ... & Brunori, G. (2017). Comparing the sustainability of local and global food products in Europe. *Journal of Cleaner Production*, 165, 346–359.

Schöggl, J. P., Fritz, M. M., & Baumgartner, R. J. (2016). Toward supply chain-wide sustainability assessment: A conceptual framework and an aggregation method to assess supply chain performance. *Journal of Cleaner Production*, 131, 822–835.

Tachizawa, E. M., & Wong, C. Y. (2014). Towards a theory of multi-tier sustainable supply chains: A systematic literature review. *Supply Chain Management: An International Journal*, 19(5/6), 643–663. https://doi.org/10.1108/SCM-02-2014-0070

Trienekens, J. H., Wognum, P. M., Beulens, A. J. M., & van Der Vorst, J. G. A. J. (2012). Transparency in complex dynamic food supply chains. *Advanced Engineering Informatics*, 26, 55–65.

UN Global Compact (2012). Scaling up global food security and sustainable agriculture. Accessed January 2020: https://d306pr3pise04h.cloudfront.net/docs/issues_doc%2Fagriculture_and_food%2FScaling_Up_Food_Ag.pdf

Varsei, M., Soosay, C., Fahimnia, B., & Sarkis, J. (2014). Framing sustainability performance of supply chains with multidimensional indicators. *Supply Chain Management: An International Journal*, 19(3), 242–257

Yakovleva, N. (2007). Measuring the sustainability of the food supply chain: A case study of the UK. *Journal of Environmental Policy & Planning*, 9(1), 75–100.

Yin, R. K. (2009). *Case Study Research: Design and Methods* (4th ed.). Thousand Oaks, CA: Sage Publications.

APPENDIX 15.1   INTERVIEW PROTOCOL

Interview guidelines

Company profile

- What is the company's core business?
- How is the supply chain structured? Who are the suppliers and customers?
- Which and how many stages in the supply chain does the company work on?
- What are the main product categories? Are there any differences in terms of supply?
- Does the company have a specific sustainability corporate strategy?

Drivers for sustainability

- Why is the company investing to improve sustainability?
- What are the main reasons that motivate the implementation of sustainability in the company?

Sustainability practices

Considering the following areas: *Emissions reduction and resource preservation*, *Resource efficiency*, *Waste and packaging*, *Health and safety*, *Labour and human rights*, *Community*, *Ethical trade*

- What are the practices regarding {…} implemented?
- Are these practices implemented in collaboration with other companies?
- Has the company obtained any certification related to these practices?

Sustainability practices assessment

Considering the following areas: *Emissions reduction and resource preservation*, *Resource efficiency*, *Waste and packaging*, *Health and safety*, *Labour and human rights*, *Community*, *Ethical trade*

- Is the company able to measure the benefits from these practices?
- How do you measure these benefits?
- Is this assessment or measurement integrated within the systems already existing in the company?
- Does the company develop a sustainability report to communicate and disseminate your achievements to the customers?

16. Sustainable data management

Sreyaa Guha and Polina Landgraf

INTRODUCTION

Within the last decade, data have transformed from being a by-product of transactions to being the bedrock of innovation, competitive advantage, cost efficiency, and growth (Côrte-Real et al., 2020; McAfee et al., 2012). While the value of data for business goes without question today, managing data is far from trivial (Tabesh et al., 2019). For example, while 95% of C-level executives see data as an integral part of their business strategy, 91% are concerned that data management expends resources and sacrifices efficiency (Experian, 2018). Furthermore, over 50% of IT managers believe their organizations are not prepared to address even routine data management tasks (Commvault, 2018), let alone achieving *sustainable* data management. This chapter aspires to start bridging this gap between the growing importance of data and the lack of understanding on how to manage it in a sustainable way. Specifically, this chapter aims to provide insights into why achieving sustainability in data management is important, to outline basic components and common pitfalls to achieving sustainable data management, and to provide practical guidelines into sustainability-driven strategies for data management.

The chapter is organized as follows. The next section presents and defines the core concepts in the field of data management and sustainable data management. The third section identifies and discusses the key components and sources of sustainability in the context of data management. The fourth section builds on the proposed sources of (un)sustainability and examines common perils to achieving sustainable data management. Here, a Constraints, Utility, Risks, Liability, and Span framework (CURLS) is introduced to capture five critical factors in developing a sustainable data management strategy. The fifth section provides a deeper insight into devising a sustainable data management strategy through a data analytics case study. Finally, the chapter concludes with contributions and guidelines for sustainable data management in practice.

DATA MANAGEMENT AND SUSTAINABLE DATA MANAGEMENT: CORE CONCEPTS

As organizations increasingly rely on data as a source of value creation and even the backbone of a business model, data management becomes paramount (Vassakis et al., 2018). Despite the unanimous appreciation of the role of data management in creating value for business, theoretical understanding of the core concepts and principles of data management is still underway and the field is yet to converge on a well-accepted, uniform definition of what constitutes data management. For the purposes of this chapter, data management is formally defined as *all the practices and processes that enable organizations to acquire, utilize, store, and dispose of data across their entire lifecycle.* As this definition highlights, data management does not stop at the stages of data acquisition or utilization; in contrast, data management permeates the entire data lifecycle, that is, from acquisition to utilization to storage to destruction (Marshall, 2007; Williams et al., 2009). At every stage of data management process, it is critical that organizations introduce and adhere to appropriate, value-enhancing practices and processes of data management. Table 16.1 summarizes each stage in the data management process, highlighting exemplar best practices for implementation.

Although data management encompasses the entire data lifecycle, currently organizations tend to focus on data acquisition and utilization (Ashrafi et al., 2019), as these stages are imbued with the greatest value-creating potential. The prevailing focus on data acquisition (as opposed to data discarding) can be also explained by individuals' psychology, as people tend to accumulate (rather than get rid of) possessions. Acquiring new assets brings pleasure and parting with belongings inflicts pain (Kahneman & Tversky, 1979), and this principle can be applied to digital possessions – data. Moreover, in the case of data management, such natural tendencies to accumulate possessions are frequently exacerbated by seemingly costless data storage (Marshall, 2007). As a result, the balance in data lifecycle shifts toward acquiring at the expense of disposing, which creates an inclination for businesses to chase value maximizing practices and disregard later stages in data lifecycle (i.e., storing and disposing). Yet, limitless data proliferation makes it costly to manage organizational data (more servers are needed), increases burden on the environment (more energy to power servers), opens more possibilities for malicious attacks (the more data an organization has, the more difficult it is to protect it), permits unforeseen accidents and enables potential repercussions to data users (the more data an organization has, the more difficult it is to control it). In other words, organizations practising a short-sighted approach to data management, centred on a limited segment of the data lifecycle, are yet to arrive at a *sustainable* data management. Sustainable data management unconditionally addresses all stages of data lifecycle and requires mindful storage of data along with its timely disposal. For example, recognizing behavioural patterns that can lead to heedless data accumulation and balancing efforts for storing and disposing of data can serve as a discernible marker of sustainable data management.

Along with managing data throughout its full lifecycle, a critical characteristic of a sustainable approach to data management is consideration of risks. Sustainable data management not only involves cost-effective practices that maximize the value of data, but also entails practices and processes that minimize risks of data (mis)use to different users. Depending on the current beneficiary of the value extracted from data, the total composition of users can be divided into "core" and "peripheral". Core data users include those who are currently, directly benefiting from the data (e.g., a social media marketer who analyses Twitter sentiment to promote their organization). Peripheral data users comprise those who are not currently benefiting from the data in a direct way (e.g., future users of the same data, parties who provided data but are not directly benefiting from them or other groups who might be affected by the use of the data). (At the end of the chapter, a reader can find a glossary of the core concepts utilized in the chapter.) To illustrate potential repercussions to peripheral users of data, consider the controversial case of Cambridge Analytica's unauthorized work with Facebook users' data (for a counterfactual, a sustainable data management practice would be working with only respondent-authorized data).

Table 16.1   *Key stages of data management*

Stage	Definition and summary
Acquisition	The initial data management stage, which comprises practices and processes aimed at obtaining data that is novel for an organization. The most common processes (and associated practices) at the data acquisition stage include: • *Data creation*: Creation of novel data within an organization. For example, generating a report on quality tests. • *Data capture*: Capture of novel data generated by devices. For example, reading scanner data. • *Data receiving*: Obtaining previously existing data from outside of an organization. For example, purchasing industry reports.
Exemplar best practice	Data management Validating the veracity and accuracy of the incoming data. *Sustainable data management* Acquiring data from sources that explicitly granted an organization permission to use their data.
Utilization	The data management stage, which comprises practices and processes aimed at extracting value from data. The most common processes (and associated practices) at the data utilization stage include: • *Data preparation*: Bringing raw data into a state amenable for further processing and analysis, including data quality checks. For example, aligning different data formats. • *Data manipulation*: Transforming data to achieve an appropriate and desirable input. For example, reducing dimensionality of data or creating a composite variable of interest. • *Data processing and analysis*: Subjecting data to analytical procedures associated with extracting value from data. For example, visualizing data or conducting statistical analysis.
Exemplar best practice	Data management Implementing a clear data management policy that allows, for example, tracing all manipulations on the original datum. *Sustainable data management* Assessing the impact of generated insights beyond that of value for an organization.

Stage	Definition and summary
Storage	The data management stage, which comprises practices and processes aimed at preserving valuable data.
	The most common processes (and associated practices) at the data storage stage include:
	• *Data back-up and recovery*: Protecting data in short-term storage (i.e., data utilized currently) from accidental loss, corruption, or breach. For example, automating critical data back-ups.
	• *Maintenance of databases and repositories*: Sending valuable data to a centralized storage that allows for structured and rapid data search and retrieval. For example, creating an organizational knowledge repository.
	• *Long-term data storage and archiving*: Supporting availability of data over time. For example, keeping data related to a project for historical records.
Exemplar best practice	Data management
	Creating an actionable data recovery strategy in case of a blackout.
	Sustainable data management
	Encrypting sensitive data when utilizing third-party services for data archiving.
Disposal	The concluding data management stage, which comprises practices and processes aimed at discarding value-free data.
	The most common processes (and associated practices) at the data disposal stage include:
	• *Re-purposing*: Utilizing the datum, which was previously used for a specific purpose, for a completely different purpose. For example, releasing organizational data.
	• *Discarding*: Disposing of all copies of data. For example, discarding value-free information that exceeded retention period required legally.
Exemplar best practice	Data management
	Creating a data succession plan, specifying transfer of responsibility over repurposed data.
	Sustainable data management
	Establishing a regular data revision to ensure servers are operating efficiently and in a "green" way.

Summarizing the above theoretical insights and drawing on the United Nations perspective on sustainable development (Brundtland, 1987), this chapter formally defines sustainable data management as follows:

Sustainable data management is the collection of practices and processes of acquiring, utilizing, storing and disposing of data in such a way that no hazard or liability accrues for the core, peripheral or future users in addition to serving the requirements of the core, peripheral and current users.

This chapter advocates the view that data management practices and processes are only appropriate and valuable if they are sustainable. Unsustainable data management may not only compromise organizational performance and survival in the long run, but it can also pose serious risks to the economy, society, and environment at large. In contrast, achieving sustainable data management can help leverage an organization's data into a lasting strategic asset and an enduring competitive advantage, while preserving the ability of core and peripheral, current and future users to keep drawing benefits from the data.

SUSTAINABLE DATA MANAGEMENT: COMPONENTS AND SOURCES

Current thinking on sustainability stresses three critical, interconnected sustainability components – social, economic, and environmental (Brown et al., 1987; Du Pisani, 2006; Hansmann et al., 2012; Porter & Kramer, 2019). This section explicates how the three sustainability components translate into sustainable data management. Figure 16.1 provides an illustration of the core sustainability components, along with their accompanying sources from which sustainable data management emerges: Social data management sustainability ("Behaviour"), Economic data management sustainability ("Cost" and "Risk"), and Environmental data management sustainability ("Production & Operations").

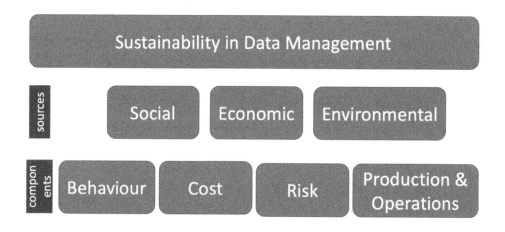

Figure 16.1　　*Components and sources of sustainable data management*

Social Sustainability in Data Management

The social component of sustainability captures an organization's efforts in identifying, assessing, and managing an organization's impact on different stakeholders, for example on employees via introducing employee wellbeing policies, on local and global communities via engaging in targeted help programmes, and on partners via creating responsible supply chains. Accordingly, *social sustainability in data management* entails recognizing, evaluating, and managing the impact of an organization's data management on core and peripheral, current and future data users (Lobschat et al., 2021).

This sustainability component has enjoyed considerable attention, following widely publicized cases of data misuse and privacy breaches (Anderson & Agarwal, 2011; Wadmann &

Hoeyer, 2018). Aside from the apparent abuse of private data (as, for example, claimed in the recent \$5 billion lawsuit against Google for tracking users' activities in the "incognito" [i.e., private] setting of the web browser; Mihalcik, 2020), oftentimes, the root cause of socially unsustainable data management practices can be found in behavioural patterns at the storing and disposing stages of the data lifecycle. The fifth section in this chapter utilizes a data analytics case study to illustrate some implementable practices to regulate such behavioural patterns.

Currently, industries, governments, and non-profits are battling the problem of socially unsustainable data management. Considerable resources and energy are put into developing sustainable frameworks and policies. For example, the European Union introduced the General Data Protection Regulation (GDPR) that aims to empower peripheral data users, redistribute control from organizations to different stakeholders, and widen individuals' authority over their private data (Regulation 2016/679). GDPR also emphasizes the disposal stage in data lifecycle and prescribes that organizations should not keep data for longer than needed. That is, companies should discard unnecessary data in a timely manner. Although to date such initiatives are in the early development stages, it is likely that approaches toward the social component of data sustainability will be actively developing over the next years and will mature rapidly.

Economic Sustainability in Data Management

The economic component of sustainability focuses on maintaining performance outcomes at a level that accommodates both shareholder and stakeholder interests. In other words, economic sustainability promotes healthy profit figures, while creating affordances for environmental and social components of sustainability. In line with this perspective, *economic sustainability in data management* aims to optimize value creation and efficiency in order to satisfy current users' needs and arises from two sources – "*Cost*" and "*Risk*".

At the surface, the *cost* source of data management sustainability may appear trivial; yet, a deeper look quickly disproves such hasty judgement. As the concepts of big data and data analytics were hyped a lot and became the "business rock-stars" (McAfee et al., 2012), some organizations rushed to make significant investments in the hopes of catching up with the competition. Yet, when data management is implemented without a clear set of goals and objectives, the costs of acquiring, managing, and storing data can very quickly become operationally incommensurate to the benefits that are derived from it. Implementation of data management in an organization can be associated with costly data acquisition (purchasing databases and equipment such as barcode scanners and RFID tags (radio frequency identification tags)), data utilization (hiring "fashionable" specialists, restructuring businesses, buying hardware, and even re-educating managers), and data storage (establishing data centres and storehouses, and powering their operations). When the value that an organization is able to extract from data does not exceed these costs, data management implementation may erode an organization's competitive posture and divert resources away from other value-creating functions.

Further, being a rather recent business function, data management creates unanticipated *risks* that organizations have only recently begun to realize. A common group of risks is associated with the ability to utilize data in a meaningful manner (Sivarajah et al., 2017). To illustrate, a wide variety of data sources may make different data points incomparable (for example, due to differences in formatting); technological compatibility and obsolescence may make some data inaccessible (for example, due to inability to migrate data from one platform to another);

and data loss may render data unattainable (for example, due to a blackout or human errors). These incidents can impede organizations from optimally utilizing data and they pose a risk of data inaccessibility. Another group of risks arises from the way organizations manipulate data. For example, flawed analysis may hamper an organization's ability to derive value from its data. Analytical approaches used on smaller samples may not be applicable to bigger datasets, which are frequently utilized in data management. In addition, challenges such as data heterogeneity, spurious correlations, noisy measurements, and incidental endogeneity can compromise the validity of insights extracted from data (Gandomi & Haider, 2015), offsetting its value for an organization. Importantly, incorrect analysis is not limited to risks to the current users, as it can also affect peripheral data users (for example, suppliers in the value chain who adjust their operations based on an organization's data management outcomes; Dubey et al., 2018). Finally, the risk of data breach cuts across economic and social sustainability, as data breach can damage an organization's reputation and erode its position on the market, while also impacting many different stakeholders. The more an organization places data at the heart of its competitive advantage, the more attractive these data may be for malicious attacks. For example, a scandalous controversy around the Ashley Madison data breach affected the dating service provider, millions of its customers, and these customers' partners, who may not have been clients of Ashley Madison. Together, risks of data inaccessibility, flawed analysis, and data breach map potential hazards and exemplify some of the challenges to economic data management sustainability.

Environmental Sustainability in Data Management

Finally, the environmental component of sustainability includes all efforts that organizations put into reducing their impact on the environment, such as reducing carbon footprints, decreasing production waste, and increasing resource utilization efficiency. Similarly, *environmental sustainability in data management* is primarily concerned with minimizing the influence that data acquisition, utilization, and storage can have on the environment. This component of sustainability can be particularly tricky, as people tend to think about data as something immaterial, and thus as not having an impact on the environment. Yet, "invisible" data management can have dramatic environmental consequences.

For example, one of the most pressing problems relates to the amount of carbon emissions produced from generating, consuming, and storing data. Carbon emissions can arise from several activities: manufacturing and shipping of hardware; enabling functioning of hardware (i.e., powering and cooling devices); and storing data (i.e., maintaining servers and data centres). As of 2018, the digital industry accounted for 3.7% of carbon emissions, making it "dirtier" than the airline industry (2.5%; The Shift Project Report, 2019). Every 60 seconds, about 150 million emails are sent across the world, releasing about 600,000 kg of carbon dioxide. This is equivalent to burning 232,258 kg of coal every minute (Viessmann, 2020). Most alarmingly, the contribution of data-related activities to carbon emissions is growing, and it is unlikely to reduce in the future unless organizations adopt sustainable data management practices. On a more positive note, insights from big data can inform general sustainability practices, such as production process optimization and adoption of green processes (Gaertner & Wong, 2019).

The three sustainable data management components – social, economic, and environmental – and their underlying sources are interconnected and influence each other. For example, unsustainable data management practices may be associated with storing an excess amount of data. According to some estimates, only 14% of data in organizations are considered critical, while 86% are redundant, obsolete, trivial (ROT) or not utilized data. Maintaining such massive amounts of data with undetermined value can generate up to $891 billion worth of additional storage and management costs (Veritas, 2015). These clearly avoidable expenditures not only have the potential to harm an organization's economic position but can also drive significant consumption of natural resources. Importantly, the impact of data management on the environment is not limited to energy; for instance, in 2014, 626 billion litres of water were consumed by the US data centres (Corbett, 2018). On the bright side, many organizations are already taking big steps in embracing environmental data management sustainability. To illustrate, production and operations of Apple are 100% based on renewable energy (Apple, 2018) and Facebook is catching up with 86% of operations based on renewable energy (Facebook, 2020). Research suggests that such investments in the environmental component of data management sustainability can carry over to the economic performance, contributing to an organization's sustainable economic development (Khuntia et al., 2018). Finally, maintaining ample amounts of data may be associated with increased risks to the privacy of an organization's stakeholders. In 2019, a significant number of data breaches were associated with unsecured organizational databases or sloppy data management, exposing about 7.9 billion private records (Hodge, 2019). Such incidents demonstrate the potentially adversarial impact of data management and highlight the importance of the social component of data management sustainability.

Overall, in developing and implementing sustainable data management strategies, organizations should consider each of the components and sources separately, as well as potential interactions among the components.

COMMON PITFALLS TO ACHIEVING SUSTAINABLE DATA MANAGEMENT

When organizations try to move toward sustainable data management, they often encounter a number of pitfalls that can undermine their efforts. These pitfalls typically arise from the nature of data – data are immaterial, frequently derive utility from the context, and generate costs and risks that often remain obscure (Marshall, 2007). This section integrates common traps on the way toward sustainable data management into a novel framework comprising five key factors: Constraints, Utility, Risk, Liability, and Span (CURLS). Each factor in the framework emerges from a typical pitfall in achieving sustainable data management. For each factor, directions on how managers can address the associated pitfall are discussed.

Constraints. Pitfall: "Constraints Do Not Exist"

Data are abundant and acquiring data is often easy and inexpensive. The costs of storing data are usually trivial compared with the costs of other value-generating functions, and the available data management tools are commonly user-friendly. These factors combine to breed a prevalent misconception that data management is virtually constraints-free. In fact, data management presents several important constraints; however, these constraints are often obscure. First, the economic costs of data management tend to scale up very quickly and have sharply risen since data analytics became mainstream (Raghavendra et al., 2008). This trend of increasing costs of data manipulation and maintenance is likely to continue and cost reduction emerges as a new challenge in data management (Irani, 2010). Second, lots of data consume lots of attention (Ocasio, 1997). A wealth of data is invariably constraining and creates a need for allocating a decision-maker's attention in a more efficient way (Jones, 2010). Moreover, too much data can not only be mentally taxing, but also detrimental for managerial decision-making, as irrelevant data tends to mask information that is actually important for the task (Whittaker, 2011).

When assessing constraints, it is useful to think about a datum as if it was a material production input, which has its costs, associated human labour (in terms of attention and motivation), and time frame before it starts generating value. Careful consideration of potential constraints can help identify scenarios in which data management can be economically unsustainable.

Utility. Pitfall: "Data Have an Identifiable and Constant Utility"

The major obstacle to sustainable data management is that the utility of data is dynamic (i.e., changes over time) and context-dependent (i.e., some data become meaningful when applied to a context, for example, references to email attachments). Thus, it is hard to determine whether a certain piece of datum will have meaning and value in the future or outside of a specific context. Conversely, the time-varying utility of data creates future affordances; that is, data may enable business opportunities, because the utility of the same piece of data in the future can be redefined (Huvila et al., 2014). Importantly, the dynamic utility of data can favour unsustainable data management practices. For example, potentially valuable data can be discarded, resulting in foregone value, or data of undetermined value can be retained, increasing constraints on overall data management.

In addressing this factor, organizations can apply the principles of cost-benefit analysis. When making a data-related decision, an analyst can approximate the potential future utility of data and calibrate it against the economic and attentional constraints of managing this data (Whittaker, 2011). Rulebooks with specific guidelines for data retention can be of help when forecasting data utility (e.g., dispose of a datum if not used for three years and retain otherwise). Of note, some guidelines for data management are already proposed by legislators. For instance, in order to comply with KYC (Know Your Customer) regulations, financial institutions are obliged to keep identifying information on their customers for five years after their accounts are terminated.

Risk. Pitfall: "Risks Can Be Managed by Data Duplication"

Data can be easily copied and replicated, which brings forth the risks associated with protection of intellectual property and sensitive information. A common reaction to these hazards is to duplicate the important information across different platforms and storages (e.g., a manager can save an important financial projection on a shared drive, a hard drive, and a private USB drive). Ironically, however, duplicating valuable data increases the likelihood that these data are lost or compromised (e.g., through a password loss, theft of hard drives, malware attacks, or proprietary lock-in by third parties). This pitfall can be especially difficult to grasp, as judgemental biases can conceal the associated risks of data duplication. For example, the base rate fallacy (Kahneman & Tversky, 1973) can lead decision-makers to underestimate the probability of data breach and evaluate the chances of its occurrence as low. Accordingly, decision-makers can be much more inclined toward duplicating data rather than using alternative data protection strategies (e.g., stronger passwords). These data management decisions are critical to efficiency and sustainability; yet, they are often overlooked or made hectically (Barreau, 1995).

In addressing this pitfall, an organization can scan the data-related environment for potential risks. Some key directions to consider include: How does an organization assess the risk of data loss (e.g., due to malicious attack, accidental loss, technical damage)? Where does business value come from – the output or the process?

Liability. Pitfall: "An Organization is Only Liable for its Profit-generating Use of Data"

Organizations that adopt a narrow, opportunistic approach to data-related responsibility risk being left behind the competition. As the use of technology is becoming more commonplace, stakeholders are getting more comfortable with the notion of their private data being a valuable resource. As a result, different groups of stakeholders start putting more and more pressure on organizations with regard to how data are used. In the coming years, organizations that embrace corporate digital responsibility (Lobschat et al., 2021) are likely to meet these rising calls of the public by holding themselves accountable to a wider group of stakeholders. Oftentimes, this means exploiting the time-varying utility of data and redefining its core users. For example, in the aftermath of the devastating Gorkha earthquake in Nepal in April 2015, the local mobile operator shared anonymized customer data with a non-profit organization, which created live maps of the population movements. The live maps allowed the government of Nepal and humanitarian missions to maximize their efforts in targeting the affected communities (Verhulst, 2017).

Accepting greater liability for data management is the primary pathway toward data management sustainability. At the moment, organizations may find it challenging to keep track of different legal requirements and to align data management practices with other business functions, as legal initiatives in this area are expanding and evolving. One way forward could be to promote an organizational culture that recognizes data-related responsibility as an indispensable aspect of any organizational activity (Lobschat et al., 2021).

Span. Pitfall: "Span of the Data Can Be Controlled"

Recent advances in computer science have led to the proliferation of data handling tools (e.g., Jovic et al., 2014), which discourages standardized data management processes. This contributes to the ever-expanding span of data (i.e., different formats, sources, and technologies) and brings about coordination and integration problems. For example, sharing data between different organizations in a value chain can be challenging (Al Nuaimi et al., 2015). Typically, each organization (and sometimes even departments within the organization) develops a unique data management process by using different data platforms, vendors, and formats, which makes it difficult to align with practices utilized by other organizations or functions.

This pitfall can be pre-empted by encouraging a culture of transparency and vigilance. Several simple steps can help promote this culture, for example, standardizing procedures for keeping meta-data, documenting best practices of data management, and developing a set of skills that help align different data setups with the dominant data arrangement in an organization. Assessing this factor can help assure sustainability of the data management strategy in the long run and secure accessibility of the data in the future.

The five factors – Constraints, Utility, Risk, Liability, and Span – comprise the CURLS framework and capture the critical aspects in developing a comprehensive sustainable data management strategy. The framework can also be used as a template for strategic analysis, in which a decision-maker critically assesses the current organizational environment with the goal of implementing or maintaining sustainability-driven data management strategies (see Figure 16.2). Specifically, the five aspects of the framework can guide organizations in identifying primary risks and opportunities and elaborating on the appropriate data management strategy. Importantly, the CURLS analysis directs a decision-maker's attention to sustainability aspects, thus encouraging adoption of sustainable data management strategies. The next section illustrates the applicability of the CURLS analysis to a real managerial problem with a case study. The section further illustrates how data analytics can be applied to devising sustainable data management strategies in practice.

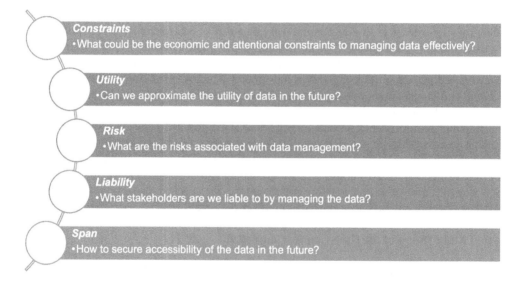

Figure 16.2   CURLS framework – template for analysis

DEVISING SUSTAINABLE DATA MANAGEMENT STRATEGIES: A CASE OF *BUENAS COMPRAS*

This section illustrates how decision analysis may be utilized to choose among potential strategies that lead to sustainable data management. The following case study (see Box 16.1) describes a common decision scenario, in which an organization optimizes data management practices by considering data costs, utility, and risks across the entire lifecycle of the data. Two decision-makers – Sylvia, the Data Management Activities Director, and Mark, the Digital Marketing Team Leader – develop a sustainable data management strategy for a struggling retailer. By using figures inspired by real practice, this case illustrates how organizations can develop sustainability-driven data management strategies.

BOX 16.1 THE *BUENAS COMPRAS* CASE STUDY

BUENAS COMPRAS

Sylvia Rosenthal, the Data Management Activities Director at *Buenas Compras*, a popular retailer, picked up a phone call. It was Andrew Tonk, the Chief Technology Officer. Like many other businesses, *Buenas Compras* was undergoing turbulent times because of the economic disruptions from the COVID-19 pandemic. As Sylvia expected, Andrew was worried about the company's bottom line given the decline in sales during the last two months. He asked Sylvia for a videoconference to discuss what initiatives in data management can help the company to stay afloat.

Buenas Compras is a B2C retailer established in 2015 in Spain. Despite being a small-sized company, *Buenas Compras* rapidly won consumers' hearts and became the leader in the local market. However, when the COVID-19 pandemic hit, the company faced supply chain disruptions and a decline in sales, as customers were cutting their regular shopping habits. Andrew, the Chief Technology Officer, felt that revising the company's data management strategies could facilitate cutting costs and increase efficiency, helping *Buenas Compras* survive the difficult times. "The tough times are the times for optimizing our strategies. We cannot afford sacrificing the well-being of our employees or the excellent service we provide our customers. To maintain *Buenas Compras*'s leadership, we need to make sure that all our data are used in a value-generating, cost-efficient way", Andrew said. His eyes were fixed on Sylvia Rosenthal, the Data Management Activities Director. Sylvia knew that a lot depended on her and her team.

SYLVIA ROSENTHAL'S DECISION PROBLEM

Although initially worried, Sylvia was eager to take up the challenge. Some time ago, she came across a data management framework that helps devise sustainable data management strategies – the CURLS framework. "This seems like a perfect opportunity to use CURLS", thought Sylvia. She called up her team for a brainstorming session and brought the CURLS template. Following a rather heated discussion, the team discovered that, although *Buenas Compras* did very well in terms of *Liability* and *Span*, the confluence of C-U-R (*Constraints*, *Utility*, and *Risk*) was a problematic area. Armed with these insights, Sylvia tasked herself with reviewing approaches to data risk management.

Sylvia found that about 1000 Terabytes of sales data were being held under the Digital Marketing vertical. Clearly, *Buenas Compras* could cut some costs by retaining only high-utility masses of data under this vertical and getting rid of redundant data servers and cloud environments. Sylvia called in the Digital Marketing Team Lead, Mark, and asked him to review and assess which data is to be (a) Retained, (b) Duplicated, or (c) Discarded. She laid down three guiding principles in making a decision:

(a) If the utility of the data today has remained the same as the utility of the data at the time of last use, the decision will be to *Retain*.
(b) If the utility of the data today has increased since the time of last use, the decision will be to *Duplicate*.
(c) If the utility of the data today has decreased since the time of last use, the decision will be to *Discard*.

COST AND UTILITY

Having decided on the guiding principles, Sylvia turned to working out specific levels for utilities and constraints:

- Cost if retained. The cost of retaining data was estimated at $0.004 per GB per month.
- Cost if duplicated. For simplicity, Sylvia instructed the team to assume that the cost of duplication will be twice as much as retention.
- Utility if retained. Sylvia asked Mark to estimate the utility of the datum based off the cost of storing this datum. Thus, Mark could choose the utility-to-cost ratio based on his own experience with this type of data and the business that it was able to generate per month. For example, if consumer purchase history data occupied 100 Terabytes (100,000 GB) of storage and was able to generate sales worth $400 per month through targeted advertising, the utility of consumer purchase history data was estimated to be the same as the cost of storing it (100,000 GB × $0.004).
- Utility if duplicated. A similar approach was used for estimating utility of duplicated datum. For example, for duplicating the same consumer purchase history data, since *Buenas Compras* would incur an additional cost of $400, *Buenas Compras* should be able to generate an additional $400 sales to keep the utility-to-cost ratio at 1 (i.e., utility from data is same as cost of data, if duplicated).
- Cost and Utility if discarded. If a datum was discarded, its potential utility is foregone; however, the cost of retention is freed.

RISKS

Just as Sylvia was about to finish giving her guidelines, she realised that the risks of data loss, breach, misuse, or inaccessibility had to be accounted for. These risks could potentially affect *Buenas Compras*'s stakeholders and the CURLS analysis revealed that liability was an important concern for the company. She benchmarked some industry figures to estimate the risks:

- Risk if datum is retained. Thales Data Threat Report on Data Security from 2019 estimated that 36% of the American and 30% of the world companies have experienced a data breach. Sylvia asked Mark to adopt a conservative estimate of 36% for any complication related to retained datum. She also noted that these numbers may serve as benchmarks, but in reality there could be a lot of uncertainty surrounding them.

- Risk if datum is duplicated. It is plausible to assume that both original copy of data and the duplicated copy of the data are exposed to the same risk. In that case, total risk if data is duplicated is equal to the sum of probabilities that either copy is compromised and the probability that both copies are compromised simultaneously. The probability that any one copy is compromised is given by $2 * (1 - p) * p$ and the probability that both copies are compromised is given by By summing these two probabilities, the total probability of risk when data is duplicated is given by $1 - (1 - p)^2$.

Sylvia also remarked, "Mark, we cannot get any utility from this data once it is compromised".

SOURCES AND LINKS
1. The archival storage rates of Google Cloud start from $0.004 per GB per month: https://cloud.google.com/storage/pricing.
2. Data generated and used by companies can range from 1 Terabyte per day (e.g., New York Stock Exchange) to more than 500 Terabytes per day (e.g., Facebook): https://www.guru99.com/what-is-big-data.html.
3. Thales Data Threat Report: https://www.thalesesecurity.com/sites/default/files/2020-02/2019-thales-data-threat-report-global-edition-slide-deck.pdf.

The characters and the company are fictitious.
Any resemblance to real-life persons and companies is coincidental.

The Decision Analysis

There were 500 Terabytes of consumer purchase data that had not been reviewed since last quarter. Mark decides to examine these data by performing a decision analysis using a decision tree. First, to implement a decision tree, Mark draws the event timeline (Figure 16.3). The first "decision" event pertains to the choices "Retain", "Duplicate" or "Discard" data. The second "chance" event pertains to a chance that the data are compromised. In a decision tree, each event is represented through a node: a decision node is indicated by a green square and a chance node is indicated by a red circle. The possibilities for each event are denoted by branches.

Figure 16.3   Data event chronology

Accordingly, Mark develops three branches from the *Data-Decision node*, where each branch pertains to a choice (see Figure 16.4). Each of the choices is accompanied by the cost that is incurred if that choice is implemented. For example, the choice to *Retain* will be associated with a cost of $2000 (500 Terabytes × 0.004 $ per GB) denoted by –$2,000 under the branch. The second event for the *Retain* branch is indicated by a chance node named as *Risk*. This chance node indicates that the stored data may either be compromised (which is indicated by the *Yes* branch) or not compromised (indicated by the *No* branch), and that either event will incur a cost with a given probability. The probabilities that the retained data are compromised (36%) or not compromised (64% = 100%–36%) are entered into the respective branches. Since no utility can be drawn from the data if it is compromised (*Yes* branch), Mark indicated $0 for the *Yes* branch. The total payoff (cost + utility) for this outcome is then –$2000 + $0 = –$2000 (indicated at the end of the branch). Utility will be derived when data is not compromised (*No* branch). Mark decides to proceed with a utility-to-cost ratio of 1, i.e., utility is same as cost, i.e., $2000. The total payoff for this outcome is –$2000 + $2000 = $0. Since these outcomes are uncertain with the *Yes* branch having a probability of 36% and the *No* branch having a probability of 64%, none of the outcomes are guaranteed. Therefore, the expected value or the weighted average of these possible payoffs for the chance node *Risk* must be calculated, which is given as 36% × (–$2000) + 64% × $0 = –$720 (shown at the *Risk* node).

Mark performs the same exercise for the *Duplicate* branch with cost as $4000 (2 × 500 Terabytes × 0.004 $ per GB), and utility as $4000. After duplicating the data, the probability that either set of data is compromised increases. Therefore, the risk probabilities are now 59.04% $(1 - (1 - 36\%)^2)$ and 40.96% (100 – 59.04%) for the *Yes* and the *No* branches, respectively. The expected value for the *Risk* node pertaining to the *Duplicate* branch is given as 59.04% × (–$4000) + 40.96% × $0 = –$2361.60.

For the *Discard* branch, the payoff is $0, which is the difference between the foregone utility (–$2000) and saved cost ($2000). This branch has no uncertainties and only one outcome, and therefore the only payoff available from this branch is $0.

The ultimate goal of analysing a decision tree is to arrive at an optimal decision, i.e., to determine which choice among Retain, Duplicate, and Discard is an optimal strategy. (Note that this analysis assumes risk-neutral decision-makers.) Thus, Mark derives the optimal decision among the Retain, Duplicate, and Discard choices by simply selecting the branch with the highest (least negative) expected value. Based on the decision tree, the optimal decision is to *Discard* since the expected value of the decision is highest ($0.00) from this choice and which is why this branch shows up as the TRUE while the branches pertaining to Retain (expected value: –$720) and Duplicate (expected value: –$2361.6) show up as FALSE. Figure 16.5 shows the optimal branch/decision.

However, Mark is not satisfied with the results. He reckons that with the current costs, utilities, and risk probabilities, the strategy would always be to discard data every time. However, he knew that was not feasible. He goes to consult with Sylvia.

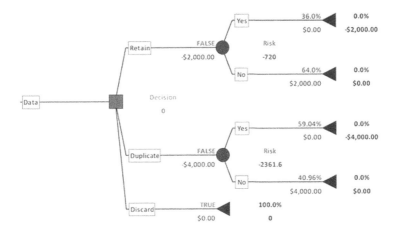

	Data Retained	Data Duplicated
Cost	-$2,000.00	-$4,000.00
Utility	$2,000.00	$4,000.00
Risk	36.00%	59.04%

Figure 16.4   *Decision tree – retain, duplicate, or discard?*

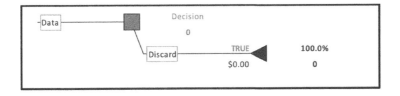

Figure 16.5   *Optimal decision*

BOX 16.2 THE *DECISION-MAKERS* CASE STUDY (CONTINUED)

By looking at the optimal results from the decision tree, it became clear to Sylvia that the decisions needed to be analysed for the uncertainties. Sylvia pointed out to Mark that there were two uncertainties in the decision problem.

- Utility-to-cost ratio – The current optimal decision from Mark's decision tree was subject to a utility-to-cost ratio of 1 both in case of choice to Retain and choice to

Duplicate. However, this ratio could vary for different data. The utility derived from the data can be very low compared with the cost or very high compared with the cost. For example, if consumer purchase history data occupied 100 Terabytes of storage and was able to generate sales worth $200 per month through targeted advertising, the utility of consumer purchase history data would be half of the cost of storing it (100,000 GB × $0.004). Or, if the generated sales from the same data was $10,000, the utility would be 2.5 times the cost of storing it. Sylvia suggested that it was practical to look at the optimal decisions across a range of utility-to-cost ratios both for the choice of retaining and duplicating.

- Risk – The current optimal decision was also subject to 36% probability of risk for the choice of retaining and 59.04% probability of risk for the choice of duplicating. Sylvia suggested a range of probabilities must be looked into for the choice of retaining and choice of duplicating in order to have a strategy structure.

Sensitivity Analysis for Utility-to-cost Ratios

Mark knew what he had to do. He took Sylvia's suggestions and performed a sensitivity analysis on utilities.

Sensitivity analysis shows how sensitive an output is to various realizations of an uncertain input. In the case of Mark's decision tree, the output was the payoff given by the Retain, Duplicate and Discard scenarios. The first uncertainty that Mark analyses for is the utility-to-cost ratio. Therefore, the sensitivity analysis would show how the optimal choice changes as the utility-to-cost ratios vary.

The decision tree in Figure 16.4 assumes *two different utility-to-cost ratios*: one arising from the cost and utility from *retention*, and one arising from the cost and utility from *duplication*. As such, sensitivity analysis will vary both ratios and determine the optimal strategy for each combination of utility-to-cost ratios. In Mark's decision tree, the utility-to-cost ratio arising from the cost and utility from retention was 1, and the utility-to-cost ratio arising from the cost and utility from duplication was also 1. This combination yielded an optimal decision to Discard, which intuitively makes sense for the said combination of utility-to-cost ratios. A utility-to-cost ratio of unity assumes that the data are only as valuable as the cost of storing them. Since the data are also exposed to a risk of breach, then the expected utility from the data will always be less than the utility if there were no risk. A reduced utility from the data makes their value decrease below the cost, thus making the overall value from Retain and Duplicate decisions negative. Compared with this negative value, a $0 value is preferable and hence appears as the optimal decision assuming risk neutrality.

To carry out the sensitivity analysis, Mark varies the utility-to-cost ratios for the Retain and Duplicate decisions between 0.5 (indicating that utility is half of cost) and 3 (indicating utility is 3 times of cost).[1] For every combination of utility-to-cost ratios, he plots the optimal decision to obtain a strategy region in the form of a sensitivity matrix. Figure 16.6 demonstrates the strategy region for varying utility-to-cost ratios. There are several important insights from this analysis.

1. When the utility-to-cost ratio for data duplication is no more than 2, the optimal decision is to either:

(a) Discard, if the utility-to-cost ratio for data retention is less than or equal to 1, which means utility is less than or equal to cost for retention. (Note that the optimal decision for the decision tree shown in Figure 16.4 is obtained as a result of this combination of utility-to-cost ratios.)

(b) Retain, if the utility-to-cost ratio for data retention is greater than 1, which means utility is less than or equal to cost for retention.

The interpretation of this insight suggests that if the utility from retaining the data does not exceed the cost of storing the data, it is best to discard the data. Retention is a better decision only when the utility is more than the cost.

1. When the utility-to-cost for data duplication is greater than 2, the optimal decision is more nuanced. In that case, the optimal decision is to:

(a) Discard, if the utility-to-cost ratio for data duplication is between 2.25 and 2.5 and the utility-to-cost ratio for data retention is between 0.5 and 0.75.

(b) Duplicate, if the utility-to-cost ratio for data duplication is between 2.5 and 3 and the utility-to-cost ratio for data retention is between 1 and 1.5.

(c) Retain, if the utility-to-cost ratio for data duplication is between 2.25 and 2.75 and the utility/cost for data retention is between 2 and 3.

The intuition behind this finding is that as long as the utility from data retention is less than the cost of retention, the best strategy always remains to discard. When the utility exceeds the cost, the choice toggles between duplication and retention. If the utility from duplication is very high compared with the cost, but utility from retention is high yet not too high compared with the cost, the optimal decision is to duplicate. To illustrate, imagine a situation when Mark can give a duplicate copy of the consumer purchase data to one of the stakeholders, for example, the suppliers. The sales from the same data can be increased by implementing product bundling strategies suggested by the suppliers. In that case, it is best to duplicate the data. However, if the utility from data retention is very high, but utility from duplication is not too high, it is better just to retain the data. For example, by doing better marketing analytics from the retained data Mark can increase the sales from the retained data.

Sensitivity Analysis for Risk Probabilities

Next, Mark performs a sensitivity analysis by varying the risk probabilities when data are retained or duplicated. Here, the utility-to-cost ratios when data are retained and when data are duplicated are held at 1.25 and 2.25, respectively. Mark specifically chooses these values because in the previous sensitivity analysis he finds that the optimal decisions are most sensitive around these values for the utility-to-cost ratios. The risk probability when data are retained is varied between 36±6%, whereas the risk probability when data are duplicated is varied between 51% and 66% (lower and upper bounds are calculated based on the formula 1 $- (1 - p)^2$, where p between 36±6%). Figure 16.7 demonstrates the strategy region for varying risks. This analysis generates the following insights.

1. The optimal decision is to:

(a) Discard, if the probability of risk from data retention is greater than 40% and the probability of risk from data duplication is greater than 60%.

(b) Retain, if the probability of risk from data retention is less than 40% and the probability of risk from data duplication is greater than 60%.
(c) Duplicate, as long as the probability of risk from data duplication is less than 58%.

The interpretation of these results is that when probability of risk is very high for both data retention and data duplication, the best decision is to discard the data. For example, Mark may be contemplating duplicating the data to share with his suppliers. If neither the data security system of *Buenas Compras* nor the security system of the suppliers is robust, then it will be a good decision for Mark to discard the data. However, if Mark is considerably confident about robustness of the data security system at *Buenas Compras* but has serious doubts about that of the suppliers, the best decision for him is to just retain the data. Finally, if Mark assesses both security systems as robust enough then he might want to duplicate the data. In addition to these three clear scenarios, there is one less straightforward scenario for a 58–60% range of probability of risk from data duplication. Here, the optimal decision toggles between Duplicate and Retain, depending on which risk is comparatively lower.

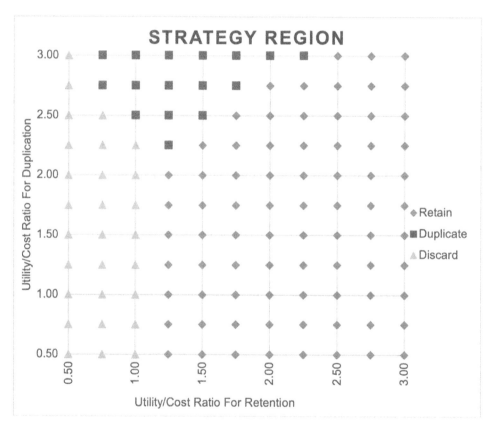

Figure 16.6   Sensitivity analysis for utility-to-cost ratio – a strategy region

As Mark and Sylvia discussed the results that came through the additional sensitivity analyses, Sylvia felt optimistic. With these strategy regions of optimal decisions, she could devise an actionable, sustainability-driven data management strategy. *Buenas Compras* could finally use the strategy to free up storage space from some data that they currently held and could apply the strategies for data that would be acquired in the future.

This case illustrates how sustainable data management strategies can be implemented in practice. This section reviewed three analytical mechanisms – decision tree analysis, sensitivity analysis of the optimal decision with respect to utility-to-cost ratios, and sensitivity analysis of the optimal decision with respect to risks. Moreover, the decision scenario tackled all three components of sustainability – social, economic, and environmental – simultaneously. While social sustainability was addressed by incorporating the potential risks from the decision to the organization and stakeholders, economic sustainability was addressed by optimizing the cost-to-utility ratios. Finally, the nature of the decision itself implied a direct impact on environmental sustainability by reviewing whether the data must be stored or discarded, suggesting a higher or lower resulting carbon digital footprint.

Figure 16.7   Sensitivity analysis for data-related risk probabilities – a strategy region

GUIDELINES FOR SUSTAINABLE DATA MANAGEMENT AND CONCLUDING REMARKS

This chapter advocates that an appropriate and valuable strategy for data management is necessarily sustainability-driven, and conceptualizes sustainable data management as the one addressing all three sustainability components – social, economic, and environmental. By considering data management-related implications to society, economy, and environment, organizations can support their performance and survival in the long run, as well as make a bigger, positive change for everyone in the now and in the future (Newman, 2017). Moreover, this chapter offers several theoretical insights on what defines sustainable data management and outlines its key components and sources. Finally, this chapter adds to the theory on data management sustainability by establishing the CURLS framework that offers a template for strategic analysis of sustainable data management practices for managers.

Data management is an emerging area, and organizations may find it challenging to pursue an effective data management strategy, let alone to pursue a *sustainable* data management strategy. As this field of management matures and industry practices evolve, more guidelines will become available, some of them potentially in the form of laws, regulations, and government policies. In anticipation, this chapter offers an implementable framework and practical insights that can readily be used to inform sustainability-driven data management strategies. The following paragraphs detail these guidelines, derived from the critical analysis of typical pitfalls to achieving sustainable data management strategy (presented in the fourth section) and from the decision strategy analysis that organizations face in data management practice (presented in the fifth section).

Think Big: Ascertain the CURLS (Constraints, Utility, Risks, Lability, and Span)

Organizations operate in a complex environment, where many different stakeholders affect or can be affected by the implications of an organization's data management practices. Pragmatically, organizations can adopt a wider perspective on data management in order to minimize economic and reputational costs. In terms of sustainability however, it is imperative that an organization, when planning and executing a data management strategy, accounts for the possible "ripple" effect that data-related decisions can have on different groups of stakeholders (i.e., "core", "peripheral", "current", and "future" users). "Thinking big" about (big) data is a fundamental requirement in order to achieve sustainable data management.

To facilitate such an approach, this chapter outlined five critical factors that can compromise data management sustainability. These factors are summarized in the CURLS framework (Constraints, Utility, Risks, Liability, and Span), and cover the indispensable aspects of any sustainable data management strategy. Considering and incorporating these factors into decision-making when devising a data management strategy can guide organizations toward embracing sustainable data management.

Watch the Cost: Ascertain the Utility-to-Cost Ratio

As demonstrated in the fifth section, utility-to-cost ratios can and should affect data management decisions. Careful consideration of potential utility of the data (i.e., not keeping everything "just-in-case") and weighing this utility against the costs can increase efficiency and reduce the carbon digital footprint of organizations. To accomplish this, organizations can identify the ROT (redundant, obsolete, and trivial) data and reduce its amount (as illustrated by the case in Box 16.1). Further, to make these efforts sustainable and ensure their implementation in the long-term, the principles of balancing data utility and data cost should be woven into the fabrics of an organizational culture. In other words, organizations can promote a mindful approach to data management among their employees, ensuring that data-related decisions (retain, duplicate, or discard) are always on the table.

Practically, the utility-to-cost ratio can be quantified as the ratio of the sales (donations, value-generating units, etc.) produced by the datum per unit of time, and the storage cost of the datum for the same unit of time. This ratio is likely to be conservative, given that the attentional and motivational costs are not included into the storage costs. That is, potential constraints to employees' productivity while navigating the data are not considered. Alternatively, the attentional costs can be quantified in terms of man-hours and therefore money-hours, decreasing the utility-to-cost ratio. Furthermore, if the utility is yet to be realized (e.g., the potential sales pertain to a future period), then the utility in the current period can be adjusted accordingly.

Look 360°: Ascertain the Risk

Data management entails numerous risks, both to the organization that manages the data and to its stakeholders. Such risks can include data inaccessibility (i.e., inability to utilize potentially value-generating data), flawed analysis (i.e., erroneous implications from incorrect analysis), and data breach (i.e., privacy hazard). Moreover, some organizations may face more risks than other organizations, owing to the nature of their business. For example, healthcare, finance, retail, accommodation and the public sectors are the top industries when it comes to being at risk of data breach (Ekran, 2019).

To address data management-related risks appropriately, organizations should account for the probability of occurrence of risky events when developing a data management strategy. For example, fostering risk considerations in data-related decision-making can promote optimal decisions in the long run. Furthermore, careful consideration of risks and the probability of their occurrence can reveal impactful yet improbable scenarios. Such "black swans", although rare, can have unprecedented impact, and should be taken as an input in organizational strategic thought experiments. Decision-makers can consider scenarios and potential responses to situations such as whether the organization is ready for remote functioning. For example, operational disruption caused by COVID-19 required many businesses across different industries to quickly re-wire to online services in no time, demanding superior data management capabilities and posing additional data-related risks.

Data is becoming "the new oil" (Bhageshpur, 2019). In line with this metaphor, data management was previously discussed from a perspective of an industrial, resource-based economy. Data management was seen as an idiosyncratic, tool-centred, locked in-house, and organization-specific technology (e.g., Customer Relationship Management (CRM) packages) that organizations desired in order to achieve competitive advantage (Kettinger et al., 1994). In contrast, in today's digital economy, the concept of data management is evolving. An organization's data are viewed as an asset, and the value of this asset depends on organization's ability to manage it. Simultaneously, organizations are expected to be more and more accountable of the use of data, given the astounding opportunities data management provides.

Indeed, data hands organizations great power. This chapter argues that such power comes with great responsibility.

NOTE

1. For this analysis, the probability values for risk when data are retained and when data are duplicated are held at 36% and 59.04%, respectively.

GLOSSARY

Core data users – users who are currently, directly benefiting from the data. For example, a warehouse manager who optimizes his/her inventory by analysing real-time consumer purchase data.

CURLS (Constraints, Utility, Risks, Liability, and Span) – a strategic framework summarizing five core factors in achieving sustainable data management. Helps to analyse the current state of datum, brainstorm what-if scenarios, identify opportunities and threats, and derive a sustainability-driven data management strategy.

Data management – all the practices and processes that enable organizations to acquire, utilize, store, and dispose of data across their entire lifecycle.

Peripheral data users – users who are not currently benefiting from the data in a direct way. This may include future users of the same data (e.g., sales managers examining demand curves based on the data from previous year); parties who provided data but are not directly benefiting from them (e.g., participants in online surveys, who get compensated for their time but are not provided the insights from their data); other groups who might be affected by the use of the data (e.g., users of navigation applications, who get diverted from path A to path B because of the increased predicted probability of traffic jams in path A), etc.

Sustainable data management – the collection of practices and processes of acquiring, utilizing, storing, and disposing of data in such a way that no hazard or liability accrues for the core, peripheral, or future users in addition to serving the requirements of the core, peripheral, and current users.

REFERENCES

Al Nuaimi, E., Al Neyadi, H., Mohamed, N., & Al-Jaroodi, J. (2015). Applications of big data to smart cities. *Journal of Internet Services and Applications, 6*(1), 6–25.

Anderson, C. L., & Agarwal, R. (2011). The digitization of healthcare: Boundary risks, emotion, and consumer willingness to disclose personal health information. *Information Systems Research, 22*(3), 469–490.

Apple (2018, April 9). *Apple now globally powered by 100 percent renewable energy*. Retrieved from: https://www.apple.com/newsroom/2018/04/apple-now-globally-powered-by-100-percent-renewable-energy/.

Ashrafi, A., Ravasan, A. Z., Trkman, P., & Afshari, S. (2019). The role of business analytics capabilities in bolstering firms' agility and performance. *International Journal of Information Management, 47*, 1–15.

Barreau, D. K. (1995). Context as a factor in personal information management systems. *Journal of the American Society for Information Science, 46*(5), 327–339.

Bhageshpur, K. (2019). *Data is the new oil – and that's a good thing*. Retrieved from: https://www.forbes.com/sites/forbestechcouncil/2019/11/15/data-is-the-new-oil-and-thats-a-good-thing/#431ed0c87304.

Brown, B. J., Hanson, M. E., Liverman, D. M., & Merideth, R. W. (1987). Global sustainability: Toward definition. *Environmental Management, 11*(6), 713–719.

Brundtland, G. H. (1987). *Our common future: Report of the 1987 World Commission on Environment and Development*. United Nations, Oslo.

Commvault (2018). *The definitive report on today's IT transformation crisis*. Retrieved from: https://info.veristor.com/commvault-todays-it-transformation/.

Corbett, C. J. (2018). How sustainable is big data? *Production and Operations Management*, *27*(9), 1685–1695.

Côrte-Real, N., Ruivo, P., & Oliveira, T. (2020). Leveraging internet of things and big data analytics initiatives in European and American firms: Is data quality a way to extract business value? *Information & Management*, *57*(1), 1–16.

Du Pisani, J. A. (2006). Sustainable development–historical roots of the concept. *Environmental Sciences*, *3*(2), 83–96.

Dubey, R., Gunasekaran, A., Childe, S. J., Luo, Z., Wamba, S. F., Roubaud, D., & Foropon, C. (2018). Examining the role of big data and predictive analytics on collaborative performance in context to sustainable consumption and production behaviour. *Journal of Cleaner Production*, *196*, 1508–1521.

Ekran (2019, June 27). *Five industries most at risk of data breaches*. Retrieved from: https://www.ekransystem.com/en/blog/5-industries-most-risk-of-data-breaches.

Experian (2018). *Global data management benchmark report*. Retrieved from: https://www.edq.com/resources/data-management-whitepapers/2018-global-data-management-benchmark-report/.

Facebook (2020). *Facebook sustainability*. Retrieved from: https://sustainability.fb.com/.

Gaertner, K., & Wong, B. (2019, November 14). *Data-led sustainability drives innovation*. Retrieved from: https://industrytoday.com/data-led-sustainability-drives-innovation/.

Gandomi, A., & Haider, M. (2015). Beyond the hype: Big data concepts, methods, and analytics. *International Journal of Information Management*, *35*(2), 137–144.

Hansmann, R., Mieg, H. A., & Frischknecht, P. (2012). Principal sustainability components: Empirical analysis of synergies between the three pillars of sustainability. *International Journal of Sustainable Development & World Ecology*, *19*(5), 451–459.

Hodge, R. (2019, December 27). *2019 data breach hall of shame: These were the biggest data breaches of the year*. Retrieved from: https://www.cnet.com/news/2019-data-breach-hall-of-shame-these-were-the-biggest-data-breaches-of-the-year/.

Huvila, I., Eriksen, J., Häusner, E. M., & Jansson, I. M. (2014). Continuum thinking and the contexts of personal information management. *Information Research: An International Electronic Journal*, *19*(1), n1.

Irani, Z. (2010). Investment evaluation within project management: An information systems perspective. *Journal of the Operational Research Society*, *61*(6), 917–928.

Jones, W. (2010). *Keeping Found Things Found: The Study and Practice of Personal Information Management*. Morgan Kaufmann.

Jovic, A., Brkic, K., & Bogunovic, N. (2014, May). An overview of free software tools for general data mining. In *2014 37th International Convention on Information and Communication Technology, Electronics and Microelectronics (MIPRO)* (pp. 1112–1117).

Kahneman, D., & Tversky, A. (1973). On the psychology of prediction. *Psychological Review*, *80*(4), 237–251.

Kahneman, D., & Tversky, A. (1979). On the interpretation of intuitive probability: A reply to Jonathan Cohen. *Cognition*, *7*(4), 409–411.

Kettinger, W. J., Grover, V., Guha, S., & Segars, A. H. (1994). Strategic information systems revisited: A study in sustainability and performance. *MIS Quarterly*, *18*(1), 31–58.

Khuntia, J., Saldanha, T. J., Mithas, S., & Sambamurthy, V. (2018). Information technology and sustainability: Evidence from an emerging economy. *Production and Operations Management*, *27*(4), 756–773.

Lobschat, L., Mueller, B., Eggers, F., Brandimarte, L., Diefenbach, S., Kroschke, M., & Wirtz, J. (2021). Corporate digital responsibility. *Journal of Business Research*, *122*, 875–888.

Marshall, C. C. (2007). How people manage personal information over a lifetime. In *Personal Information Management* (pp. 57–75). Seattle, WA: University of Washington Press.

McAfee, A., Brynjolfsson, E., Davenport, T. H., Patil, D. J., & Barton, D. (2012). Big data: The management revolution. *Harvard Business Review*, *90*(10), 60–68.

Mihalcik, C. (2020, June 3). *Google faces $5 billion lawsuit for tracking people in incognito mode.* Retrieved from: https://www.cnet.com/news/google-faces-5-billion-lawsuit-for-tracking-people-in -incognito-mode/.

Newman, D. (2017, November 21). *How digital transformation aligns with corporate social responsibility.* Retrieved from: https://www.forbes.com/sites/danielnewman/2017/11/21/how-digital -transformation-aligns-with-corporate-social-responsibility/#47c1dfe458bf.

Ocasio, W. (1997). Towards an attention-based view of the firm. *Strategic Management Journal, 18*(S1), 187–206.

Porter, M. E., & Kramer, M. R. (2019). Creating shared value. In *Managing Sustainable Business* (pp. 323–346). Dordrecht: Springer.

Raghavendra, R., Ranganathan, P., Talwar, V., Wang, Z., & Zhu, X. (2008, March). No "power" struggles: Coordinated multi-level power management for the data center. In *Proceedings of the 13th International Conference on Architectural Support for Programming Languages and Operating Systems* (pp. 48–59).

Regulation (EU) (2016). 2016/679 of the European Parliament and of the Council. *REGULATION (EU), 679*, 2016.

Sivarajah, U., Kamal, M. M., Irani, Z., & Weerakkody, V. (2017). Critical analysis of Big Data challenges and analytical methods. *Journal of Business Research, 70*, 263–286.

Tabesh, P., Mousavidin, E., & Hasani, S. (2019). Implementing big data strategies: A managerial perspective. *Business Horizons, 62*(3), 347–358.

The Shift Project Report (2019, July). *Climate crisis: The unsustainable use of online video.* Retrieved from: https://theshiftproject.org/wp-content/uploads/2019/07/2019-02.pdf.

Vassakis, K., Petrakis, E., & Kopanakis, I. (2018). Big data analytics: Applications, prospects and challenges. In *Mobile Big Data* (pp. 3–20). Cham: Springer.

Verhulst, S.G. (2017, February 15). *Corporate social responsibility for a data age.* Retrieved from: https://ssir.org/articles/entry/corporate_social_responsibility_for_a_data_age.

Veritas (2015). *The data hoarding report: The data employees save puts businesses at risk.* Retrieved from: https://www.veritas.com/content/dam/Veritas/docs/reports/Veritas-Data-Hoarders-Report-US .pdf.

Viessmann (2020). *Why does the world need to get serious about combating carbon emissions now?* Retrieved from: https://www.viessmann.co.uk/heating-advice/the-worlds-digital-carbon-footprint.

Wadmann, S., & Hoeyer, K. (2018). Dangers of the digital fit: Rethinking seamlessness and social sustainability in data-intensive healthcare. *Big Data & Society, 5*(1), 1–13.

Whittaker, S. (2011). Personal information management: From information consumption to curation. *Annual Review of Information Science and Technology, 45*(1), 1–62.

Williams, P., John, J. L., & Rowland, I. (2009, July). The personal curation of digital objects. In *Aslib Proceedings* (pp. 340–363). Bingley, UK: Emerald Group Publishing.

PART 5

SUSTAINABILITY-DRIVEN BUSINESS STRATEGIES IN FINANCE AND ACCOUNTING

17. Do CSR reports impact firms' stock returns? A pilot study analysis

Andreas Dutzi, Julian Schröter and Eshari Withanage

INTRODUCTION

With the dynamic and competitive market environment there is a strong need for firms to disclose their Corporate Social Responsibility (CSR) activities to their stakeholders. It can be seen that there is a gradual increase in firms engaging in and conducting CSR activities, while considering such activities as a business strategy. This leads to the creation of an interaction between firms and society at large. While engaging in CSR activities, firms have the possibility of creating a sustainable impact on society and creating a favourable impact on business in a larger context (Monsuru and Abdulazeez 2014). However, mismanagement of this connection between society and business can be penalised by negative effects on the reputation of firms, while creating adverse impact on financials. Hence, it is advisable for firms to treat this relationship with great care by taking necessary actions to ensure that they communicate their CSR activities promptly and appropriately. It can be seen that there is an increase in the usage of non-financial reporting by firms to embrace the social, environmental and economic impact on a firm's business operations, while engaging it more as a business strategy than considering it only as an accountability tool.

Researchers found that even for firms involved in significant CSR activities, the availability of disclosures seems to be very limited (Solomon and Lewis 2002). Similar studies stated that even though some firms consider themselves as CSR reporting firms, their behaviour cannot be treated as sustainable (Moneva et al. 2006). This shows that firms fail to communicate their sustainability activities successfully to the general public. However, with the emergence of the reporting standards and guidelines, firms are guided to disclose their sustainability activities clearly. The introduction of these standards not only allowed firms to report their sustainability activities in a structured and precise manner but also to offer their readers transparency. Another aspect on which firms need to focus their attention is identifying necessary communication channels, apart from traditional communication methods, such as annual reports (Branco and Rodrigues 2006) or corporate websites (Capriotti and Moreno 2007; Chaudhri and Wang 2007) to disclose their CSR activities. Empirical studies show that most firms communicate their CSR activities with the use of sustainability reports (Idowu and Towler 2004; Sweeney and Coughlan 2008).

Friedman (1970) stated that business has a solitary responsibility of maximising stockholders' wealth by upholding the fundamental rules of the society, both legal and ethical. This argument forces firms to consider whether they can gain economic value by communicating their CSR activities. It is the case that the value of CSR cannot be achieved immediately, as any gain will only be recognised in the long term. Hence, for firms to continue with their business operations for the next generation of consumers it is vital for them to promote their sustainability activities. However, do companies communicate their sustainability activities altruistically or do they engage with their stakeholders (O'Donovan 2002)? It is vital for firms to serve and maintain their mutual relationships with their stakeholders. With the emergence of stakeholder theory, it is said that stakeholders have a legitimate interest in firms. As opposed to the latter in shareholder theory, managers focus their attention only towards the interest of the shareholders and ensure that this interest is met (Donaldson and Preston 1995). In the current context, environmental concerns have become detrimental factors for the sustainability of firms, as their institutional investors are more concerned with non-financial factors of the firms when making investment decisions.

With the linkage of CSR reporting and share prices, firms have the possibility of showing investors that CSR will insure the long-term performance of the firm, as the current share prices will help create good perceived performance. However, investors still question the correct choice between CSR and financial performance, as the costs involved in conducting CSR activities are considerable and could erode a firm's profitability. This will raise the question of whether managers wish to compromise long-term sustainability in order to achieve a short-term result and vice versa. While Cramer (2003) has stated that by implementing CSR firms can generate wide opportunities, including value addition, Holmes (1976) has further stated that the most likely benefits that firms can generate via CSR are improved reputation and enriching the societal community, although there will be a decline of short-term financial performances of the firms and the creation of conflict of interest between social and financial motives of the managers. These variations have caused scholars to examine such a relationship between CSR reporting and share prices (Griffin and Mahon 1997; Ullmann 1985).

Although, in a general context, it can be seen that CSR and firm stock prices should be linked, empirical studies have found mixed results (Saeidi et al. 2015), with positive (Alexander and Buchholz 1978; Orlitzky et al. 2003; Pava and Krausz 1996; Preston and O'Bannon 1997; Ruf et al. 2001), negative (Brammer et al. 2006; Waddock and Graves 1997; Wood and Jones 2005) as well as neutral (Anderson and Frankle 1980; Aupperle et al. 1985; Elsayed and Paton 2005; Fauzi 2009; Fiori et al. 2007; Freedman and Jaggi 1986; McWilliams and Siegel 2001; van Dijken 2007) impact. Nevertheless, as such results do not provide a clear justification for the cause and effects, it is vital to proceed with additional examination (Preston and O'Bannon 1997; Waddock and Graves 1997). Hence, this study intends to fill this research gap with a diverse overlook on how the CSR report creation date has an impact on stock volatility.

The aim of this chapter is to comprehend whether there is any link between CSR reports and firms' stock performances. Such a study has the probability of influencing the investment decisions of the investors, leading to volatility in the share prices of the firms. Further, the shareholders might elect not to invest in such firms that will not share and disclose sufficient information on CSR. Share prices are selected as a proxy for firm performances. This is due to the findings of Bowman (1973) which depicted that the market's perception of CSR can affect stock prices, the cost of capital of the firm and, ultimately, the returns of the investors. The study examines whether and how shareholders are sensitive towards the stock performance of firms upon releasing CSR reports. It is found that in the context of a competent market, the market would promptly adjust to the new information within a shorter period of time after a formal announcement of information (Fama et al. 1969). By observing share price movements it can be seen how effectively the market will respond to the immediate release of CSR reports.

The study was conducted by analysing the CSR reports' creation dates of the top 50 companies in the Fortune 500 company list for 2015 and these companies' share prices. However, due to the non-availability of the CSR reports' creation dates, 11 firms have been eliminated from the study and only 39 firms have been selected for the final analysis. The share prices are then collected for ten trading days before the CSR report creation date and ten trading days after the CSR report creation date, for the selected firms. The results generated from the 39 firms show that the share prices of 26 firms were significantly influenced, amounting to a 67% overall change from before to after the CSR report creation date.

This chapter is organised as follows: the literature review section illustrates the concepts of CSR and CSR reports, and the development of the hypothesis is based on the empirical findings on the link between CSR and share prices. In the theoretical domain, legitimacy theory and stakeholder theory are elaborated upon in the latter part of the literature review. The methodology, results and discussion sections follow. The final remarks, future research and limitations are discussed in the conclusion section.

LITERATURE REVIEW

Corporate Social Responsibility (CSR)

As CSR is a multifaceted concept it has been elaborated upon in many studies over the past few years. The definition of the term has varied from time to time, according to the needs of the society. It is crucial for the going concern of the business to be sustainable and to generate economic growth. It is the duty and the obligation of businesspeople to ensure that they follow the policies of action that are desirable for the values of their society (Carroll 1979). The concept of CSR has continued to propagate over the decades. CSR has become a mainstream focus, rising to a corporate priority in management (Etter and Fieseler 2010; Gomez and Chalmeta 2011). Carroll (1979) defined CSR as "the social responsibility of business encompasses the economic, legal, ethical, and discretionary expectations that society has of organizations at a given point in time". On the other hand, McWilliams and Siegel (2000) argued that firms need to have a vast obligation towards the society more than focusing on exploiting their earnings.

In the era of the 1950s, CSR was considered by firms as an obligation towards society (Balmer et al. 2007). However, in the past, the ultimate objective of business was to maximise shareholder wealth (Friedman 1970). This thinking, which was generated by considering only economic aspects, has changed over time. Hence, currently, CSR is the factor that progresses businesses towards sustainability. (D'Amato et al. 2009). When a firm conducts activities which will enhance the society consisting of humans and the environment it will have an effect on a firm's CSR, corporate ability as well as its reputation (Piriyakul and Wingwon 2013). CSR is considered a concept that concerns the vitality of the relationship between firms and society. It is the act of a business to integrate responsible business practices and policies into its business model to enhance the well-being of the society while maintaining profits (Hopkins 2007).

Similar arguments have been raised when claiming the business has its own responsibility in generating profits and satisfying its shareholders while ensuring that the necessary laws and regulations are followed while also being ethical and a good corporate citizen. With this thought, Carroll (1979) identified four responsibilities in CSR – namely, economic, legal, ethical and philanthropic. It is a concept where firms assimilate both environmental as well as social concerns of the business processes and their stakeholders (European Commission 2011). It engages in societal philanthropy, environmental friendliness, being ethical and business practices regarding concerns of sustainability, product safety, ending poverty, eliminating pollution, maintaining human rights and growth of the economy (Rindova et al. 2005). CSR is an umbrella term that classifies sustainability development, corporate citizenship, corporate philanthropy and compliance (Verboven 2011). In contrast, it is argued that firms needs to have an enormous commitment towards the society in which they operate, rather than focusing only on expanding their earnings (McWilliams and Siegel 2000).

The European Commission (2011) defines CSR as "the responsibility of enterprises for their impacts on society". It further states,

> To fully meet their CSR, enterprises should have in place a process to integrate social, environmental, ethical, human rights and consumer concerns into their business operations and core strategy in close collaboration with their stakeholders, with the aim of, maximizing the creation of shared value for their owners/shareholders and for their other stakeholders and society at large; and identifying, preventing and mitigating their possible adverse impacts […].

However, the findings of Schwartz and Carroll (2003) state that the definitions of CSR can be broadly identified as the minimalist view and the contemporary view. The minimalist view considers that the sole objective of business is to maximise profits while maintaining law and ethics (Friedman 1970); on the other hand, the contemporary view considers that business has a due responsibility towards the society in which it operates. Hence, irrespective of the various definitions by the researchers, there is still no accepted definition that can be found to illustrate CSR (Carroll 1979, 2008).

CSR and CSR Reporting

It is challenging to understand whether CSR is used in business communication as a promotional tool or as a responsibility tool to reveal to society that the business conducts sustainable business operations. One reason for this is due to the case of Nike, which used annual reports to inform the public on the sustainability activities that it conducted (DeTienne and Lewis 2005). Similarly, by communicating CSR activities some firms tend to disguise their unethical activities, which can be seen as using CSR for 'greenwashing'. Scholars also found that though the firms used websites to communicate their CSR activities, the implications are less effective due to their inability to carry out two-way communication (Capriotti and Moreno 2007; Gomez and Chalmeta 2011). Moreover, the most common readers of such CSR activities belong to the potential and existing employees of the firm and not to other stakeholders.

Further arguments can be raised that, to enhance a firm's reputation, it is vital to disclose its CSR activities (Neu et al. 1998). Similarly, reporting CSR activities effectively enables firms to continue with their operations while maintaining their legitimacy (Neu et al. 1998) as well their brand image. As some of the green brands are focused purely on gaining sustainability, it is vital for firms to be an environmentally healthy brand in order to increase and maintain higher returns (Hartmann et al. 2005). Accordingly, CSR and reputation can be seen as two sides of a coin. Where the current CSR activities will have a tremendous effect in the future, which in return will have an effect on the overall reputation of the firm. Neu et al. (1998) further stated that firm size also has an effect on reporting CSR activities.

Reporting of CSR has emerged in recent years. Initially, firms did not follow any standard or regulations when reporting such non-financial activities. Consequently, in the late 1980s and 1990s, the reporting of CSR activities emerged by following some standardised approaches. At the same time, various governments and non-government organisations began introducing specific guidelines to firms about reporting their CSR activities, with varying goals, such as diminishing corruption and pollution as well as improving the well-being of humans and maintaining the rights of the general public. These guidelines are very similar to the demand raised by the stakeholders to inform a firm's sustainability (O'Rourke 2004). According to the survey conducted by KPMG, over the years from 1993 to 2015, the N100[1] companies CSR reporting rate is currently at 73%, while the G250[2] companies CSR reporting rate was at 92%, as of year 2015 (KPMG 2015). Scholars have found that the most preferred method of publishing CSR activities is by using annual reports, purely due the reliability of information that is stated in the annual reports with respect to financial as well as non-financial perspectives (Neu et al. 1998).

Scholars have depicted that firm performance on social activities has a positive link with respect to discretionary environmental disclosures (Clarkson et al. 2008). In the current context, there is an evolution of investor behaviour to adopt CSR reporting as a screening tool to differentiate 'good' as opposed to 'bad' firms (Friedman and Miles 2001). The contents of the CSR reports are dependent on the information that the firms want to share with their stakeholders. Accordingly, a CSR report can be prepared as a means of following the trend without having any intention to deceive stakeholders, or it can be to reflect the transparency of a firm and to enhance firm values (Cai et al. 2012). Moreover, it can be to deceive their stakeholders and as a means of legitimisation (Cai et al. 2012).

Firms have the choice of disclosing their information to the general public by either using the mandatory approach or the voluntary approach. Mandatory discloses are based on the laws and regulations which are enforced by International Financial Reporting Standards (IFRS) or Generally Accepted Accounting Principles (GAAP), which will vary based on geography, industry or country specific laws and regulations, whereas voluntary discloses are provided separately without being bounded by any laws and regulations. Scholars have found that when firms disclose information voluntarily they have benefited from increasing their stock performances (Healy et al. 1999). This reveals that the institutional investors are keener in investing in firms that focus on more transparency when disclosing their information. In contrast, the findings of Fishman and Hagerty (2003) have stated that mandatory disclosures may aid informed investors while the benefit is neutral to the uninformed investors. However, it is also found that, irrespective of whether they are mandatory or voluntary discloses, both complement the investors' information   (Ball et al. 2012).

It can be identified that the most common and acceptable standards and guidelines when initiating CSR reporting are the Global Reporting Initiative (GRI), the UN Global Compact (UN Global Compact) and ISO 14001:2004. The UN Global Compact (2015) states that by incorporating the principles of human rights, labour, environment and anti-corruption in the firm's policy, procedure and strategies, firms have the possibility to enhance their responsibility towards people and wildlife while developing strategies for long-term success. As these are general principles, it does not allow firms to understand how they should report their CSR activities. Unlike the UN Global Compact (2015), GRI (2013) introduces a set of guidelines to firms for presenting disclosures in various report formats, such as standalone reports, integrated reports, annual reports, online reporting or reports in particular international norms

(Lim and Tsutsui 2012). Hence, the GRI reporting framework overlooks the triple bottom line of economic and environmental as well as social aspects. This is due to the fact that GRI offers a set of metrics where the firms have the possibility of assessing the effects of their activities on the triple bottom line (Stenzel 2010). On the other hand ISO 14001:2004 (ISO 2013) introduces specific guidelines to firms who wish to initiate and implement an environmental management system. This framework focuses only on those environmental aspects that the firms have a possibility of controlling and influencing. Hence, by having a functional environmental management system, firms have the possibility of expanding their environmental protection as well as improving their communication of their performance to their stakeholders. However, the framework does not indicate any environmental performance criteria.

CSR and Share Performance

Due to the correlation between costs incurred in conducting CSR activities and the return, many empirical studies have focused their attention on finding out the impact of CSR on firm financial performance (Bagnoli and Watts 2003; Dowell et al. 2000; Griffin and Mahon 1997; McWilliams and Siegel 2000). The link between CSR and economic state has been seen by scholars either as modest or consistent (Godfrey and Hatch 2007; Margolis and Walsh 2003). Friedman (1970) has supported the latter view of this opinion by stating that the sole responsibility of the firms is to maximise profits, whereas for a firm to take responsibility for its activities it is essential to be accountable. Nevertheless, other scholars have found that by investing in CSR firms have the possibility of enhancing corporate image and overall financial performances and the end return is higher than the costs incurred in such CSR activities (Pava and Krausz 1996; Preston and O'Bannon 1997).

The empirical studies that have been conducted to verify the link between CSR and financial performances have generated mixed results (Saeidi et al. 2015). While some have stated that there is no relationship between CSR and financial performances (Anderson and Frankle 1980; Aupperle et al. 1985; Elsayed and Paton 2005; Fauzi 2009; Fiori et al. 2007; Freedman and Jaggi 1986; McWilliams and Siegel 2001; van Dijken 2007), others have found that there is a positive link between CSR and financial performances (Alexander and Buchholz 1978; Orlitzky et al. 2003; Pava and Krausz 1996; Preston and O'Bannon 1997; Ruf et al. 2001). Moreover, researchers have also found negative relationship between CSR and financial performances (Brammer et al. 2006; Waddock and Graves 1997;Wood and Jones 2005). Empirical studies have depicted that negative stock performances are due to the inefficient use of resources and due to the economic disadvantages caused by CSR investments (Cho and Patten 2007; Ullmann 1985), whereas the positive link is due to the fact that return and the benefits related to CSR activities are greater than the costs involved in implementing such activities (Fombrun et al. 2000). Alternatively, a missing relationship might indicate that it is not possible for the existing market models to effectively measure the effect of CSR on firm financial and portfolio performances (Derwall et al. 2005).

Ruf et al. (2001) conducted a study by examining sales, and defined the period of years that will positively be affected by the changes in CSR. Good CSR behaviour can lead to enhancing the relationship between the stakeholders in general (Stanwick and Stanwick, 1998; Verschoor 1998). In contrast, the findings of McWilliams and Siegel (2000) stated that by controlling investments in research and development, CSR has a neutral impact on stock performances. They concluded these outcomes by comparing econometric studies. Hence, such contradictory results can be due to flawed empirical analysis. Firms disclose CSR information in a truthful manner as they are concerned about the assessment of the financial market towards such reporting (Darrough 1993).

Accordingly, the empirical studies can be summarised with the argument that, although investing in CSR-driven activities is costly, there is the potential of gaining benefits in the distinct future (Henderson 2002). It is also argued that the firms will get engaged in CSR activities only when the benefits can be seen as maximising profits, irrespective of whether a firm has a responsibility that goes beyond legal requirements to fulfil the needs of stakeholders (Davis et al. 2006). Contradictory arguments were raised by Waddock and Graves (1997) indicating that CSR will increase financial performances due to the enhancement of the corporate image and reputation. However, in conducting CSR activities firms have the potential of enlisting in the stock market, as this will lead to boosting their stock prices while generating positive returns to their investors (Robins 2015).

Stock volatility is often linked to the risk of owning stock, as the higher the stock volatility the higher the risk investment (Fama and French 1992). Studies can be found to prove the fact of how corporate social performance has the possibility of enhancing shareholder wealth by reducing stock volatility (Luo and Bhattacharya 2009). Accordingly, this depicts the fact that firms that disclose their CSR activities towards their shareholders have the potential to reduce the investment risks of their investors. By disclosing more information on CSR, firms become more transparent and their investors have ample information with respect to firms in which they are investing. The availability of this vital and ample information can lead to influencing the investment decisions of the investors, which ultimately leads to creating an impact on the volatility of the share prices. When the market has more information available, it will enrich the more informed investors and the stock prices will provide the necessary information, as the stock prices are now more informative and the need for the investors to gather additional information will be reduced (Vlastakis and Markellos 2012).

Additionally, most of the studies that have been conducted to analyse whether CSR reports have an impact on share prices are country specific (Fiori et al. 2007; Wang and Li 2016; Guidry and Patten 2010). Fiori et al. (2007) conducted their study based on Italian listed firms during 2002–2007 and implied that CSR does not have an impact on firms' stock prices. Similarly, Wang and Li (2016) conducted a study based on Chinese firms listed in the Shanghai Stock Exchange during the period 2007–2012, while Guidry and Patten (2010) conducted their study based on the US market. Moreover, many empirical studies have adopted regression analysis to find the link between CSR and share prices (Fiori et al. 2007; Guidry and Patten 2010; Wang and Li 2016). Henceforth, in contrast to empirical studies, this study has been conducted to analyse the link between CSR reports and stock prices with the adoption of global firms listed in the Fortune 500 irrespective of country.

Although the above-stated empirical studies have been conducted and generated controversial results, by testing the link between CSR activities and firm performance less prominence has been given in the empirical studies depicting the link between CSR reports and share prices of the firms. Hence, this study fills this gap by examining the link between CSR reports and firms' share price movements and testing whether the link is positive, negative or neutral.

Accordingly, the below hypotheses are generated in this study:

H_0: $P(X>Y) = P(Y>X)$, where the distributions of both populations, firm's share prices/stock volume before/after CSR-report publication are equal.

H_i: $P(X>Y) \neq P(Y>X)$, where the distributions are not equal.

Legitimacy Theory and Stakeholder Theory

The theory of legitimacy relies on the social contract where it states that the firm will comply with the societal actions and expectations of the general public (Deegan 2002). Perceptions or the expectations of the actions of the stakeholders are considered to be desired. However, due to the rapid and dynamic changes in society it is vital for firms to establish the fact that they conduct their business operations legitimately and that they behave as good corporate citizens. According to Suchman (1995), legitimacy is the perception or assumption of the firm's activities. The generalised aspect of legitimacy shows that the actions of a firm should be seen as an umbrella of events and that society needs to take all activities together and should not look at actions individually (Suchman 1995). On the contrary, perception or assumption-based legitimacy states that society will view the activities of firms differently and that the reaction towards the firm will depend on such assumptions (Suchman 1995). Finally, social construct legitimacy implies that the legitimacy of a firm is dependent on how society views it and, as such, people might have a different view on the firm (Suchman 1995).

To ensure this fact, most corporations disclose their social activities via corporate social reporting. In contrast, there is doubt about the quality and the reliability of the information contained in these reports. Similarly, CSR communication intends to provide information that legitimises firm's behaviour by taking actions to influence its image among stakeholders as well as the public. Irrespective of the method of communication, it is advisable for the firm to be cautious in not sharing any negative information, which will lead to damaging the reputation of the firm. Corporations who fail to communicate such social activities will tend to create a threat to the firm's legitimacy. When the information is not properly communicated it will not be possible for the stakeholders to understand the CSR activities that the firm has conducted.

If a firm has a higher level of legitimacy it would mean that the firm is regarded as a good corporate citizen, which shows that the firm acts responsibly towards society and that society has a favourable perception of the firm (O'Donovan 2002). In contrast, when a firm has a low level of legitimacy it indicates that the firm is not highly dependent on society, such that the firm is not accountable towards society (O'Donovan 2002). The level of legitimacy that a firm wishes to achieve and maintain will depend on how much the firm wants to work towards it. Hence, if a firm considers that it wishes to maintain only a low level of legitimacy, then it acts mainly in response to institutional rules and expectations, but if it wishes to maintain a higher level of legitimacy then it will take an extra step to achieve the aims of society and the environment at large (O'Donovan 2002).

As legitimacy is where firms interact with society and how society views the firm, it is vital to take into account the voluntary versus mandatory discloses that firms produce to share their information with the general public, where the stakeholders – especially the investors – are included. Hence, with CSR disclosures, investors can obtain further information with respect to the social and environmental aspects in which the firm has conducted itself and it will further enable them to make the necessary investment decisions (O'Donovan 2002). In the current context, standalone CSR reports and environmental reports are considered as becoming more common for firms to disclose information to investors (Brown and Deegan

1998; O'Donovan 2002). Similarly, there are situations where firms use annual reports with a crossreference to a section in a standalone CSR, and environmental reports, to ensure thorough presentation of information (O'Donovan 2002). All in all, it can be determined that for firms who wish to maintain and gain legitimacy in society, they are in need of disclosing their environmental and CSR activities either in standalone CSR and environment reports or in annual reports (O'Donovan 2002).

As opposed to legitimacy theory, which focuses on society as a whole, stakeholder theory focuses on a particular group. Stakeholder theory stated that the managers have a moral obligation towards their stakeholders (Freeman, 1994). Firms are obliged to disclose financial as well as non-financial information, such as social and environmental information, to their stakeholders. The theory has also been elaborated in a descriptive manner, by indicating how the various parties of the stakeholders should be defined. The categorisation of the stakeholders is made based on their power, legitimacy as well as urgency (Mitchell et al. 1997). The information that the firm shares among its stakeholders plays a vital role in obtaining their support and approval or their disapproval.

Scholars have categorised the stakeholders in various forms. Some of these categories would be internal and external stakeholders (Chan et al. 2014) or primary and secondary stakeholders (Clarkson 1995). External stakeholders provide firms with various resources and in return they expect firms to provide various actions (Chan et al. 2014), whereas the internal stakeholders will influence the managers within the firm. On the other hand, firms cannot survive without their primary stakeholders (investors, employees, customers and suppliers) as they depend heavily on these stakeholders (Clarkson 1995). However, firms can survive without their secondary stakeholders but it is vital for firms to take them into consideration as they can cause damage to the firm (Clarkson 1995). Hence, it can be seen that firms and stakeholders are influenced by each other. By disclosing CSR activities firms can be more transparent with their information, which is vital for the stakeholders (Dubbink et al. 2008). This will open the windows of information to all stakeholders and not only to the investors. Nevertheless, the consequences of transparency would be that sometimes it will lead to oversharing a firm's information with its stakeholders.

By conducting good CSR practices, firms have the potential to enhance their relationships with their stakeholders (Stanwick and Stanwick 1998; Verschoor 1998). Studies have revealed that the investors actually utilise CSR information when making investment decisions (Cho et al. 2013). Although not all investors have the same information institutional investors and analysts usually have access to higher degree of information. Moreover, both negative as well as positive CSR performance of firms provide the relevant information that reduces asymmetry of information between investors (Cho et al. 2013). Similarly, with respect to the stakeholder approach, firms needs to take CSR into consideration to ensure the development of both firms as well as society. It will further enable firms to enhance market share, organisational learning, committed employees and to build positive investor relations (Morrison and Siegel 2006; Heslin and Ochoa 2008). Although, in the current context, most of the multinational firms have strengthened their commitment towards CSR activities (Davis et al. 2006; Fiori et al. 2007), conflicts of interest have arisen as the managers need to make a choice between satisfying all their stakeholders on one hand while satisfying all their shareholders on the other (Reich 2008).

Scholars stated that both legitimacy and stakeholder theories are political economic theories as they both focus on social, economic and political frameworks (Gray et al. 1995). Although both these theories differ conceptually, they have the same focus on firms and their operations. Similarly, both theories cover the external pressure which has an effect on firms, and suggest approaches that can be taken to eliminate or minimise such adverse consequences. Firms need to conduct their business operations legitimately and in a socially acceptable manner while ensuring that they strike a balance between the interests of the stakeholders.

METHODOLOGY

To falsify hypothesis H0, this study considers the top 50 companies listed in the Fortune 500 company list in the year 2015 (Fortune 500 2015). The publicly available CSR reports for the year 2014 and 2015 for each selected company were downloaded from each company's websites as a PDF file. The PDF file creation data were then identified for each firm from the property function in the edit tab of Adobe Acrobat Reader. As this is a pilot study it is assumed that the creation date of the CSR report is the same as the publishing date of the report. However, due to non-availability of the CSR report creation dates, 11 firms were removed from the analysis and only 39 firms were considered for the final analysis. The share prices are then collected for ten trading days before the CSR report creation date and ten trading days after the CSR report creation date along with the share volumes from the respective share markets for all 39 selected firms. The study has been conducted using the two-sided Wilcoxon-Mann-Whitney-Test (WMW) (Siegel 1957; Wilcoxon 1945). This is a non-parametric statistical method to "detect the difference between the medians of two samples from independent populations" (Deep 2006). It is used instead of the t-test, which, although the variables have a metrical scale level, cannot be applied due to non-normal distribution.

The test statistics is

$$W = \sum_{i=1}^{m} \sum_{j=1}^{n} S(X_i, Y_j)$$

where X_i refers to the stock prices/stock volume ten trading days *before* the CSR report creation date and Y_j refers to stock prices/stock volume ten trading days *after* the CSR report creation date.

RESULTS

The detailed results of the selected 39 firms and their changes in stock prices/volume ten trading days before the CSR report creation dates and ten trading days after the CSR report creation dates are depicted in Table 17.1, whereas in Table 17.2 the percentage results of the changes in stock prices as well as stock volume are illustrated. Accordingly, the results reflected that 67% of the firm's stock prices might be influenced by the CSR reports and 33% of the firm's share volumes might also be influenced. These results show that the investors are cautious about CSR activities that are conducted by the respective firms and have a higher consideration towards CSR reports which force them to make necessary investment adjustments.

Table 17.1   Stock prices

Rank	Company Name	Symbol	*CSR Report Creation Date	*Opening Stock Price	*Highest Stock Price	*Lowest Stock Price	*Closing Stock Price	Stock Volume	Significance of Closing Share Price	Significance of Share Price	Significance of Share Volume
5	Apple	AAPL	21/05/2015	0.01	0	0	0.02	0.436	1		0
34	Archer Daniels Midland	ADM	06/05/2015	0	0	0	0	0.481	1		0
49	Aetna	AET	10/03/2016	0	0	0	0	0.218	1	0	0
46	AIG	AIG	07/08/2015	0.123	0.315	0.436	0.684	0.481	0	0	0
27	Boeing	BA	08/07/2015	0	0	0	0.001	0.739	1	1	0
23	Bank of America Corp	BAC	22/06/2015	0	0	0	0	0.684	1		0
28	Citigroup	C	15/06/2015	0.11	0.075	0.029	0.105	0.123	0	0	0
26	Cardinal Health	CAH	04/08/2015	0.247	0.796	0.19	0.28	0.029	1	1	1
43	Comcast	CMCSA	05/08/2015	0	0	0	0	0.05	1	1	1
18	Costco	COST	26/03/2015	0.19	0.165	0.218	0.739	0.023	0	0	1
10	CVS Health	CVS	05/05/2015	0.029	0.165	0.529	0.436	0.005	0	0	1
3	Chevron	CVX	11/05/2015	0	0	0.02	0.01	0.739	1	1	0
48	Dow Chemical	DOW	31/07/2015	0.023	0.005	0.052	0.009	0.007	1	1	1
9	Ford Motor	F	15/06/2015	0.529	0.353	0.28	0.28	0.353	0	0	0
8	General Electric	GE	24/08/2015	0.631	0.853	0.971	0.529	0.007	0	0	1
6	General Motors	GM	19/05/2015	0.001	0	0.002	0	0.28	1	1	0
33	Home Depot	HD	30/10/2015	0.035	0.004	0.002	0.009	0.579	1	1	0
19	HP	HPQ	29/05/2015	0.143	0.218	0.19	0.143	0.684	0	0	0
24	IBM	IBM	22/07/2015	0	0	0	0	0.912	1	1	0
37	Johnson & Johnson	JNJ	18/08/2015	0.017	0.028	0.035	0.01	0	1	1	1
21	JP Morgan Chase	JPM	14/05/2015	0	0	0	0	0.11	1	1	1
20	Kroger	KR	21/07/2015	0.481	0.353	0.28	0.28	0.247	0	0	0
50	Lowe's	LOW	25/05/2015	0.123	0.023	0.063	0.019	0.218	1	1	1
11	McKesson	MCK	25/01/2016	0.075	0.123	0.075	0.052	0.315	1	1	0
39	MetLife	MET	14/09/2015	0.029	0.023	0.019	0.015	0.481	1	1	0
25	Marathon Petroleum	MPC	11/06/2015	0	0	0	0	0.143	1	1	0
31	Microsoft	MSFT	12/11/2015	0.631	0.28	0.579	0.739	0.075	0	0	0

Rank	Company Name	Symbol	*CSR Report Creation Date	*Opening Stock Price	*Highest Stock Price	*Lowest Stock Price	*Closing Stock Price	*Stock Volume	Significance of Closing Share Price	Significance of Share Volume
44	PepsiCo	PEP	23/09/2015	0.063	0.029	0.011	0.011	0.105	1	0
32	Procter & Gamble	PG	03/02/2016	0	0.002	0.001	0.003	0.684	1	0
12	AT&T	T	10/06/2015	0.481	0.853	0.063	0.165	0.739	0	0
36	Target	TGT	12/06/2015	0	0	0	0	0.089	1	0
14	United Health Group	UNH	24/07/2015	0.019	0.035	0.019	0.063	0.123	1	0
47	UPS	UPS	14/08/2015	0.004	0.002	0.004	0.023	0.218	1	0
13	Valero Energy	VLO	14/03/2016	0.001	0	0	0.001	0.035	1	1
15	Verizon	VZ	20/03/2015	0.052	0.052	0.052	0.19	0.043	0	1
35	Walgreens	WBA	03/02/2016	0	0	0	0	0.063	1	0
30	Wells Fargo	WFC	10/03/2015	0.143	0.023	0.218	0.052	0.002	0	1
1	Walmart	WMT	22/04/2015	0.015	0.023	0.063	0.105	0.684	0	0
2	Exxon Mobil	XOM	15/05/2015	0.002	0	0.011	0.011	0.043	1	1

Note: *Significance level of 5% is considered

Table 17.2   *Percentage outcome of stock price and stock volume*

Change in stock volume and price	Number of firms	Percentage (%)
Total firms	39	100
Change in closing share price 10 days before/after CSR report creation date	26	67
Change in volume10 days before/after CSR report creation date	13	33

DISCUSSION

When evaluating the results it can be observed that there might be an influence between share price/stock volumes ten days before/after CSR-report publication (report creation date). With the generated results, from 39 firms, the share prices of 26 firms have significantly changed, amounting to a 67% overall change before and after the CSR report creation date. Hence, the findings are in line with the empirical studies which depicted that there is a significant link between CSR and firm financial performances (Alexander and Buchholz 1978; Orlitzky et al. 2003; Pava and Krausz 1996; Preston and O'Bannon 1997; Ruf et al. 2001). Hence, it implies that the investors are keen on obtaining information on CSR via CSR reports before making their investments decisions, and if the firms have been transparent in sharing their social and environmental information there is a potential that they can enhance their share prices. However, this significance can also be due to the fact of causality, which needs further analysis to conclude.

As illustrated in the stakeholder theory, this study focuses mainly on the investors, who are the primary stakeholders of the firm (Clarkson 1995), and their impact on the firm. The results of the study have shown that the investors are more considered and cautious on the firms' CSR reports when making necessary investment decisions. Similar to the empirical studies, this study has revealed that the investors do give attention to firms' CSR activities when deciding on their investments (Cho et al. 2013). Additionally, it reflects the importance of CSR reports as a means of communicating a firm's social and environmental activities towards its stakeholders, mainly with respect to its investors. This, in turn, reveals the importance of firms engaging in CSR activities, which will lead to generating long-term strategic investments.

It is vital for firms not only to conduct various CSR activities but also to communicate these activities via CSR disclosures. This will enable the firms to inform their stakeholders, mainly their investors, about the social and environmental activities in which they are engaged. This additional information that the investors have can have an impact on them making their investment decisions with regard to a socially and environmentally friendly firm compared with a firm that is not considered to be a good corporate citizen. Additionally, socially responsible firms are likely to have a good reputation in the market, which will enable them to retain business for a longer period and to be less threatened in their survival. The reason for this is simply that these firms have built a superior commitment and loyalty from their stakeholders.

As information is considered to be a vital asset in the financial market context (Vlastakis and Markellos 2012) it is necessary to consider the type of CSR information that the firms should share with their stakeholders. On the other hand, this can be depicted as whether the firms should focus on maximising their profits or whether they should focus on social responsibility. However, as illustrated before, empirical studies state that firms needs to strike a balance between maximising profits while maintaining their societal activities towards society (Brown and Deegan 1998; O'Donovan 2002). As the findings of this study show a significant difference between CSR reports and share prices, this in turn shows that investors do concern themselves with such CSR activities that the firm conducts when making their investment decisions. Consequently, the link between stakeholder theory and CSR activities of the firm is dependent on what the managers show to their various stakeholders regarding the activities that they conduct, giving insights into their skills as managers (McGuire et al. 1988). Accordingly, the increased level of information that is disclosed will show the investors and other stakeholders what the managers of the respective firms are doing at present and their plans for the future (McGuire et al. 1988). Hence, this supports the theoretical domain of the stakeholder theory as well as legitimacy theory.

These findings will be of value to firms and managers when considering disclosing their CSR information, investors when making investment decisions, analysts when making the necessary investment advice, regulators when considering regulation on CSR disclosure practices and to all the other stakeholders who are interested in a firm's accountability with respect to social and environmental aspects. Moreover, the findings will also be beneficial for the firms who currently do not disclose their CSR information. As the results have shown a significance between CSR reports and share prices, this will direct the focus of the managers to disclose their CSR activities and create a volatility in their share prices and thereby consume the benefits.

For a firm to consume the maximum benefits of CSR it is vital for the firms to successfully implement sustainability into their business strategy. It is also implicit that CSR is a vital component of a firm's strategy as it leads to the creation of corporate changes to aid development and assimilation of a firm's activities as well as processes (Donaldson and Preston 1995). With the successful implementation of CSR strategy, firms have the possibility to enhance corporate reputation, reduce cost and, through transparency of reporting, also improve legitimacy. Apart from casually implementing sustainability into the business strategy it is necessary for the firms to properly understand and recognise the importance of sustainability towards the firm (Cramer 2005; Maignan et al. 2005). As the board of directors (BODs) of a firm ensures the continuation of a business and its direction, involvement of the BODs – not only for the strategic decisions but also for the development of sustainable strategies – will enable the firms to implement CSR successfully (Krechovska and Prochazkova 2014).

Subsequently, the firms also need to get their stakeholders to engage when developing a sustainability strategy (Cramer 2005). With the involvement of both internal and external stakeholders, firms have the possibility of enhancing various benefits towards the firm as well as the stakeholders, which then can be transferred to generate more sustainable activities (Maignan et al. 2005).

CONCLUSION

The study was conducted to fill the research gap due to the various results that were generated empirically to discover whether there is a difference between ten days before and after releasing CSR reports in financial performances. This study used share price and stock volume as proxies to measure financial performance. The results have shown a significant difference between CSR reports before/after creation dates and share prices as opposed to prior research where, in general, a relationship analysis is conducted. Therefore, this study has an event-based character.

One of the limitations of this pilot study is the assumptions made that the CSR reports' creation dates and the released dates are the same. This limitation could have an impact on the share prices if the firms have taken a considerable time period to publish these reports. Further, there can be other factors (investor sentiments, firm's financial performance, industry level performances and also economic factors, such as inflation, interest rates, etc.) that can cause volatility of the share prices apart from CSR reports. Hence, it is advisable to have some control variable in the analysis. However, for future research these limitations can be avoided by contacting each of the selected firms and obtaining the data with respect to the exact published dates of their CSR reports. Moreover, the study can be extended by incorporating other financial performance analysis, developing a theoretical framework and expanding the data collection.

NOTES

1. These are the largest 100 companies in 45 different countries across the world. The selection was based on the criterion of revenue.
2. These are the world's largest 250 companies as listed in the Fortune Global 500 ranking for the year 2014.

REFERENCES

Alexander, G. J., & Buchholz, R. A. (1978). Corporate social performance and stock market performance. *Academy of Management Journal, 21*, 479–486.

Anderson. J., & Frankle, A. (1980). Voluntary social report: An iso-beta portfolio analysis. *Accounting Review, 55*, 468–479.

Aupperle, K. E., Carroll, A. B., & Hatfield, J. B. (1985). An empirical examination of the relationship between corporate social responsibility and profitability. *Academy of Management Journal, 28*, 446–463.

Bagnoli, M., & Watts, S. (2003). Selling to socially responsible consumers: competition and the private provision of public goods. *Journal of Economics and Management Strategy, 12*, 419–445.

Ball, R., Jayaraman, S., & Shivakumar, L. (2012). Audited financial reporting and voluntary disclosure as complements: A test of the confirmation hypothesis. *Journal of Accounting and Economics, 53*, 136–166.

Balmer, J. M. T., Fukukawa, K., & Gray, E. R. (2007). The nature and management of ethical corporate identity: A commentary on corporate identity, corporate social responsibility and ethics. *Journal of Business Ethics, 76*, 7–15.

Bowman, E. H. (1973). Corporate social responsibility and the investor. Working paper 641-673.

Brammer, S., Brooks, C., & Pavelin, S. (2006). Corporate social performance and stock returns: UK evidence from disaggregate measures. *Financial Management, 35*(3), 97–116.

Branco, M. C., & Rodrigues, L. L. (2006). Communication of corporate social responsibility by Portuguese banks: A legitimacy theory perspective. *Corporate Communications: An International Journal, 11*(3), 232–248.

Brown, N., & Deegan, C. (1998). The public disclosure of environmental performance information – a dual test of media agenda setting theory and legitimacy theory. *Accounting and Business Research, 29*(1), 21–41.

Cai, Y., Jo, H., & Pan, C. (2012). Doing well while doing bad? CSR in controversial industry sectors. *Journal of Business Ethics, 108*(4), 467–480.

Capriotti, P., & Moreno, A. (2007). Corporate citizenship and public relations: The importance and interactivity of social responsibility issues on corporate websites. *Public Relations Review, 33*(1), 84–91.

Carroll, A. B. (1979). A three-dimensional conceptual model of corporate performance. *Academy of Management Review, 4*(4), 497–505.

Carroll, A. B. (2008). A History of corporate social responsibility: Concepts and Practices. In A. Crane, A. McWilliams, D. Matten, J. Moon, & D. Siegel (Eds.), *The Oxford Handbook of Corporate Social Responsibility* (pp. 83– 112). Oxford: Oxford University Press.

Chan, M. C., Watson, J., & Woodliff, D. (2014). Corporate governance quality and CSR disclosures. *Journal of Business Ethics, 125*, 59–73.

Chaudhri, V., & Wang, J. (2007). Communicating corporate social responsibility on the internet. A case study of the top 100 information technology companies in India. *Management Communication Quarterly, 21*(2), 232–247.

Cho, C. H., & Patten, D. M. (2007). The role of environmental disclosures as tools of legitimacy: A research note. *Accounting, Organizations and Society, 32*(7-8), 639–647.

Cho, S. Y., Lee, C., & Pfeiffer, R. J. (2013). Corporate social responsibility performance and information asymmetry. *Journal of Accounting and Public Policy, 32*, 71–83.

Clarkson, M. B. E. (1995). A stakeholder framework for analysing and evaluating corporate social performance. *Academy of Management Review, 20*(1), 92–117.

Clarkson, P. M., Li, Y., Richardson, G. D., & Vasvari, F. P. (2008) Revisiting the relation between environmental performance and environmental disclosure: An empirical analysis. *Accounting, Organizations and Society, 33*(4/5), 303–327.

Cramer, J. (2003). Corporate social responsibility: Lessons learned. *Environmental Quality Management, 13*(2), 59–66.

Cramer, J. M. (2005). Experiences with structuring corporate social responsibility in Dutch industry. *Journal of Cleaner Production, 13*(6), 583–592.

D'Amato, A., Henderson, S., & Florence, S. (2009). *Corporate Social Responsibility and Sustainable Business; A Guide to Leadership Task and Function*. Centre for Creative Leadership. North Carolina: CCL Press. https://www.ccl.org/wp-content/uploads/2015/04/CorporateSocialResponsibility.pdf

Darrough, M. N. (1993). Disclosure policy and competition: Cournot vs. Bertrand. *The Accounting Review, 68*(3), 534–561.

Davis, G. F., Whitman, M. V. N., & Zald, M. N. (2006, April). The Responsibility Paradox: multinational firms and global corporate social responsibility. Ross School of Business Working Paper Series, Working Paper No. 1031.

Deegan, C. (2002). The legitimising effect of social and environmental disclosures – a theoretical foundation. *Accounting, Auditing & Accountability Journal, 15*(3), 282–311.

Deep, R. (2006). *Probability and Statistics: With Integrated Software Routines*. Cambridge, MA: Academic Press.

Derwall, J., Guenster, N., Bauer, R., & Koedijk, K. (2005). The eco-efficiency premium puzzle. *Financial Analysts Journal, 61*(2), 51–63.

DeTienne, K. B., & Lewis, L. W. (2005). The pragmatic and ethical barriers to corporate social responsibility disclosure: The Nike case. *Journal of Business Ethics, 60*, 359–376.

Donaldson, T., & Preston, L. E. (1995). The stakeholder theory of the corporation: Concepts, evidence and implication. *Academy of Management Review, 20*(1), 65–91.

Dowell, G., Hart, S., & Yeung, B. (2000). Do corporate global environmental standards create or destroy market value? *Management Science, 46*, 1059–1074.

Dubbink, W., Graafland, J., & Liedekerke, L. V. (2008). CSR, transparency and the role of intermediate organisations. *Journal of Business Ethics, 82*(2), 391–406.

Elsayed, K., & Paton, D. (2005). The impact of environmental performance on firm performance: static and dynamic panel data evidence. *Structural Change and Economic Dynamics, 16*, 395–412.

Etter, M., & Fieseler, C. (2010). Studies in communication sciences. *Journal of the Swiss Association of Communication and Media Research, 10*(2), 167–189.

European Commission (2011, October 5). *Communication from the commission to the European Parliament, the Council, the European Economic and Social Committee and the Committee of the Regions*. A renewed EU strategy 2011–14 for Corporate Social Responsibility, Brussels.

Fama, E. F., Fisher, L., Jensen, M. C., & Roll, R. (1969). The adjustment of stock prices to new information. *International Economic Review, 10*(1), 1–21.

Fama, E. F., & French, K. R. (1992). The cross-section of expected stock returns. *The Journal of Finance, 47*(2), 427–465.

Fauzi, H. (2009). Corporate social and financial performance: Empirical evidence from American companies. *Globsyn Management Journal*, Forthcoming. https://ssrn.com/abstract=1489494

Fiori, G., Di Donato, F., & Izzo, M. F. (2007). Corporate social responsibility and firm's performance. An analysis on Italian listed companies. https://ssrn.com/abstract=1032851

Fishman, M. J., & Hagerty, K. M. (2003). Mandatory versus voluntary disclosure in markets with informed and uninformed customers. *Journal of Law, Economics, & Organization 19*(1), 45–63.

Fombrun, C. J., Gardberg, N. A., & Barnett, M. L. (2000). Opportunity platforms and safety nets: Corporate citizenship and reputational risk. *Business and Society Review, 105*(1), 85–106.

Fortune 500 (2015). Fortune 500 company list. http://fortune.com/fortune500/

Freedman, M., & Jaggi, B. (1986). An analysis of the impact of corporate pollution disclosure and economic performance. *Pollution Disclosure and Economic Performance, 1*(2), 43–58.

Freeman, E. R. (1994). The politics of stakeholder theory: Some future directions. *Business Ethics Quarterly, 4*(4), 409–421.

Friedman, A. L., & Miles, S. (2001). Socially responsible investment and corporate social and environmental reporting in the UK: An exploratory study. *The British Accounting Review 33*(4), 523–548.

Friedman, M. (1970). The social responsibility of business is to increase its profits. In W. Ch. Walther Zimmerli, K. Richter, & M. Holzinger (Eds), *Corporate Ethics and Corporate Governance*. Berlin, Heidelberg: Springer-Verlag. https://link.springer.com/chapter/10.1007/978-3-540-70818-6_14

Godfrey, P., & Hatch, N. (2007). Researching corporate social responsibility: An agenda for the 21st century. *Journal of Business Ethics, 70*(1), 87–98.

Gomez, L. M., & Chalmeta, R. (2011). Corporate responsibility in U.S. corporate websites: A pilot study. *Public Relations Review, 37*, 93–99.

Gray, R., Kouhy, R., & Lavers, S. (1995). Corporate social and environmental reporting. *Accounting, Auditing & Accountability Journal, 8*(2), 47–77.

GRI (2013). Sustainability Reporting Guidelines. https://www.globalreporting.org/resourcelibrary/GRIG4-Part1-Reporting-Principles-and-Standard-Disclosures.pdf.

Griffin, J., & Mahon, J. (1997). The corporate social performance and corporate financial performance debate. Twenty-five years of incomparable research. *Business and Society 36*(1), 5–31.

Guidry, R. P., & Patten, D. M. (2010). Market reactions to the first-time issuance of corporate sustainability reports: Evidence that quality matters. *Sustainability Accounting, Management and Policy Journal, 1*(1), 33–50.

Hartmann, P., Ibáñez, V., & Sainz, F. J. (2005). Green branding effects on attitude: Functional versus emotional positioning strategies. *Marketing Intelligence and Planning, 23*(1), 9–29.

Healy, P. M., Hutton, P. A., & Palepu, K. G. (1999). Stock performance and intermediation changes surrounding sustained increases in disclosure. *Contemporary Accounting Research, 16*(3), 485–520.

Henderson, D. (2002). *Misguided Virtue: False Notions of Corporate Social Responsibility*. London: Institute of Economic Affairs.

Heslin, P. A., & Ochoa, J. D. (2008). Understanding and developing strategic corporate social responsibility. *Organizational Dynamics, 37*(2), 125–144.

Holmes, S. L. (1976). Executive perceptions of corporate social responsibility. *Business Horizons, 19*(3), 34–40.

Hopkins, M. (2007). *Corporate Social Responsibility and International Development: Is Business the Solution?* London; Sterling, VA: Earthscan

Idowu, S. O., & Towler, B. A. (2004). A comparative study of the contents of corporate social responsibility reports of UK companies. *Management of Environmental Quality: An International Journal, 15*(4), 420–437.

ISO (2013). ISO 14001:2004. http://www.iso.org/iso/catalogue_detail?csnumber=31807. Accessed on 20 April 2016.

KPMG (2015). Survey on Corporate Responsibility Reporting 2015. https://www.kpmg.com/CN/en/IssuesAndInsights/ArticlesPublications/Documents/kpmg-survey-of-corporate-responsibility-reporting-2015-O-201511.pdf.

Krechovska, M., & Prochazkova, P. T. (2014). Sustainability and its integration into corporate governance focusing on corporate performance management and reporting. *Procedia Engineering, 69,* 1144–1151.

Lim, A., & Tsutsui, K. (2012). Globalization and commitment in corporate social responsibility: Cross-national analyses of institutional and political-economy effects. *American Sociological Review, 77*(1), 69–98.

Luo, X., & Bhattacharya, C. B. (2009). The debate over doing good: Corporate social performance, strategic marketing levers and firm idiosyncratic risk. *Journal of Marketing, 73,* 198–213.

Maignan, I., Ferrell, O. C., & Ferrell, L. (2005). A stakeholder model for implementing social responsibility in marketing. *European Journal of Marketing, 39*(9/10), 956–977.

Margolis, J. D., & Walsh, J. P. (2003). Misery loves companies: Rethinking social initiatives by business. *Administrative Science Quarterly, 48,* 268–305.

McGuire, B. J., Sundgren, A., & Schneeweis, T. (1988). Corporate social responsibility and firm financial performance. *Academy of Management Journal, 31*(4), 854–872.

McWilliams, A., & Siegel, D. (2000). Corporate social responsibility and financial performance: Correlation or misspecification? *Strategic Management Journal, 21*(5), 603–609.

McWilliams, A., & Siegel, D. (2001). Corporate social responsibility: A theory of the firm perspective. *Academy of Management Review, 26,* 117–127.

Mitchell, R. K., Agle, B. R., & Wood, D. J. (1997). Toward a theory of stakeholder identification and salience: Defining the principle of who and what really counts. *Academy of Management Review, 22*(4), 853–886.

Moneva, J. M., Archelb, P., & Correa, C. (2006). GRI and the camouflaging of corporate unsustainability. *Accounting Forum, 30,* 121–137.

Monsuru, A. F., & Abdulazeez, A. A. (2014). The effects of corporate social responsibility activity disclosure on corporate profitability: Empirical evidence from Nigerian commercial banks. *IOSR Journal of Economics and Finance (IOSR-JEF), 2*(6), 17–25.

Morrison, P. J. C., & Siegel, D. S. (2006). Corporate social responsibility and economic performance. *Journal of Productivity Analysis, 26*(3), 207–211.

Neu, D., Warsame, H., & Pedwell, K. (1998). Managing public impressions: Environmental disclosures in annual reports. *Accounting, Organizations and Society, 23*(3), 265–282.

O'Donovan, G. (2002). Environmental disclosures in the annual report: Extending the applicability and predictive power of legitimacy theory. *Accounting, Auditing & Accountability Journal, 15*(3), 344–371.

Orlitzky, M., Schmidt, F. L., & Rynes, S. L. (2003). Corporate social and financial performance: A meta-analysis. *Organization Studies, 24*(3), 403–441.

O'Rourke, D. (2004). *Opportunities and Obstacles for Corporate Social Responsibility Reporting in Developing Countries.* Washington, DC: The World Bank. http://nature.berkeley.edu/orourke/PDF/CSR-Reporting.pdf

Pava, L., & Krausz, J. (1996). The association between corporate social responsibility and financial performance. *Journal of Business Ethics, 15,* 321–357.

Piriyakul, M., & Wingwon, B. (2013). Effect of corporate ability and reputation on organizations performance and CSR. *African Journal of Business Management, 7*(9), 738–749.

Preston, L., & O'Bannon, D. (1997). The corporate social-financial performance relationship. *Business and Society, 36*(1), 5–31.

Reich, R. B. (2008, August 1). *The Case against Corporate Social Responsibility.* Goldman School Working Paper Series.

Rindova, V. P., Williamson, I. O., Petkova, A. P., & Sever, J. M. (2005). Being good or being known: An empirical examination of the dimensions, antecedents, and consequences of organizational reputation. *Academy of Management Journal, 48*(6), 1033–1049.

Robins, R. (2015, May 5). Does corporate social responsibility increase profits? *Business Ethics – the magazine of corporate social responsibility.* http://business-ethics.com/2015/05/05/does-corporate-social-responsibility-increase-profits/

Ruf, B. M., Muralidhar, K., Brown, R. M., Janney, J. J., & Paul, K. (2001). An empirical investigation of the relationship between change in corporate social performance and financial performance: A stakeholder theory perspective. *Journal of Business Ethics, 32*(2), 143–156.

Saeidi, S. P., Sofian, S, Saeidi P., Saeidi, S. P., & Saeidi, A. S. (2015). How does corporate social responsibility contribute to firm financial performance? The mediating role of competitive advantage, reputation, and customer satisfaction. *Journal of Business Research, 68*, 341–350

Schwartz, M. S., & Carroll, A. B. (2003). Corporate social responsibility: A three-domain approach. *Business Ethics Quarterly, 13*(4), 503–530.

Siegel, S. (1957). Non-parametric statistics. *The American Statistician, 11*(3), 13–19.

Solomon, A., & Lewis, L. (2002). Incentives and disincentives for corporate environmental disclosure. *Business Strategy and the Environment, 11*, 154–169.

Stanwick, P. A., & Stanwick, S. D. (1998). The relationship between corporate social performance, and organizational size, financial performance, and environmental performance: An empirical examination. *Journal of Business Ethics, 17*, 195–204.

Stenzel, P. A. (2010). Sustainability, the triple bottom line, and the global reporting initiative. *Global Edge Business Review, 4*(6), 1–2.

Suchman, M. C. (1995). Managing legitimacy: Strategic and institutional approaches. *Academy of Management Review, 20*(3), 571–610.

Sweeney, L., & Coughlan, J. (2008). Do different industries report corporate social responsibility differently? An investigation though the lens of stakeholder theory. *Journal of Marketing Communications, 14*(2), 113–124.

Ullmann, A. (1985). Data in search of a theory: A critical examination of the relationship among social performance, social disclosure, and economic performance. *Academy of Management Review, 10*, 450–477.

UN Global Compact (2015) Guide to Global Sustainability – Shaping a sustainable future. https://www .unglobalcompact.org/library/1151

van Dijken, F. (2007). Corporate social responsibility: Market regulation and the evidence. *Managerial Law, 49*(4), 141–184.

Verboven, H. (2011). Communicating CSR and business identity in the chemical industry through mission slogans. *Business Communication Quarterly, 74*(4), 415–431.

Verschoor, C. C. (1998). A study of the link between a corporation's financial performance and its commitment to ethics. *Journal of Business Ethics, 17*, 1509–1516.

Vlastakis, N., & Markellos, R. N. (2012). Information demand and stock market volatility. *Journal of Banking & Finance, 36*, 1808–1821.

Waddock, S. A., & Graves, S. B. (1997). The corporate social performance-financial performance link. *Strategic Management Journal, 18*(4), 303–319.

Wang, K. T., & Li, D. (2016). Market reactions to the first-time disclosure of corporate social responsibility reports: Evidence from China. *Journal of Business Ethics, 138*(4), 661–682.

Wilcoxon, F. (1945). Individual comparison by ranking methods. *Biometrics Bulletin, 1*(6), 80–83.

Wood, D. J., & Jones, R. E. (2005). Stakeholder mismatching: A theoretical problem in empirical research on corporate social performance. *The International Journal of Organizational Analysis, 3*(3), 229–267.

18. An analysis of business actions in private social reporting

Natalia Semenova

INTRODUCTION

Private social reporting has evolved into a sophisticated disclosure channel and a potentially powerful corporate governance mechanism to enhance company accountability into the social domain. This takes place in response to the growing recognition of social risks for institutional investment and business value (Solomon and Solomon 2006). Private reporting refers to private engagement and dialogue where one-on-one communications are held between institutional investors and their investee companies in relation to companies' strategic management of social risks (Thomsen and Conyon 2012; Logsdon and Van Buren 2009; Goranova and Ryan 2014; Solomon and Solomon 2006). Social risks are associated with company practices that violate the fundamental principles of human and labor rights. Private social reporting refers to forms of private disclosure such as specialized case reports used by institutional investors to summarize the details applied to the dialogue with the investee company and specialized questionnaires distributed to investee companies by institutional investors (Semenova 2020; Solomon and Solomon 2006). Institutional investors employ private reporting to maintain and pursue social actions in the investee companies and supplement the perceived market failure in public social disclosure (Solomon and Solomon 2006). In private reporting, a discourse of social actions can deal with risk management and crisis avoidance but can also present potential business opportunities for the investee companies to exploit. The actions of target companies can facilitate the renewal of sustainability-driven strategies and business processes. Academic scholars claim that companies frequently engage in private dialogue with their institutional investors (Logston and Van Buren 2009; Gond et al. 2018; Rehbein et al. 2013). Institutional investors can cultivate close relationships and strong private communication with their investee companies in order to add value to their stock selection decisions and supplement public disclosure (Solomon and Solomon 2006). The dialogic nature of such interactions contributes to the successful process of private reporting in which both parties can address mutually meaningful social risks, which results in strategic changes to company activities and practices. The dialogic process can entail accountability relationships, where the roles of principal and agent are fluid, and active negotiating, mutual learning, and flexibility in working together are present (Rehbein et al. 2013; Ferraro and Beunza 2018; Bebbington et al. 2007). Despite a significant rise in the sustainable and responsible engagement of institutional investors, a scant but emerging descriptive and empirical literature on private social reporting and business actions has been published (Rehbein et al. 2013; Ferraro and Beunza 2018; Solomon and Solomon 2006).

A small body of academic research has investigated private social reporting from different perspectives. Few studies have reviewed the academic literature on non-financial engagement and developed theoretical underpinnings to explain the process of private engagement and reporting in the areas of social accounting and corporate governance (Bebbington et al. 2007; Cundill et al. 2018; Goranova and Ryan 2014). A small body of broad-scale empirical research has analyzed the influence of private successful dialogues on the social performance of investee companies and their public social disclosures (Dimson et al. 2015; Barko et al. 2018; Bauer et al. 2015; Hoepner et al. 2018). It has further examined the reasons for different company responses to the strategic social actions demanded by institutional investors (Rehbein et al. 2013; Rehbein et al. 2004; Sikavica et al. 2018). The findings of large-scale empirical studies provide evidence to conclude that both companies and institutional investors can benefit from private dialogue. Successful dialogues can positively affect market value, sales growth, accounting performance, sustainability ratings, and institutional ownership. However, a few studies are skeptical and suggest that private social reporting can be employed as a relationship-building and cosmetic exercise and as a means of creating and disseminating a dual myth of social accountability by both investors and investee companies (Solomon et al. 2013; Solomon and Darby 2005). This chapter attempts to understand the specific social actions of companies that provide satisfactory outcomes of a private dialogue process to institutional investors. The discourse of business-related social actions within the context of private reporting is the subject of examination in this chapter.

This chapter aims to examine the content of private reporting with a focus on the social actions communicated by target companies to institutional investors. The social actions reveal how companies manage human and labor rights risks within their sustainability-driven business strategies. Examples of social risks include strikes, injuries, child labor, low salaries, and illness. There is currently little literature that investigates the content of private social reporting (Solomon and Solomon 2006; Solomon et al. 2013; Solomon et al. 2011). Indeed, studies normally employ semi-structured interviews with UK institutional investors holding one-on-one meetings with their primarily domestic investee companies in order to support and supplement public reports. Evidence is provided on the nature, character, and process of private reporting, the dominant forces at play, and the theoretical framing of the emerging discourse. This chapter introduces the following extensions to the previous studies on private climate change reports. It explores the discourse of social actions in actual private reports for complete, successful dialogues. This chapter proposes that these social actions achieve the agreement of both institutional investors and investee companies. The companies' actions are perceived by institutional investors to reduce social risk in the investee companies by improving their social preparedness in the form of policies and management systems. Furthermore, private social reporting is related to unexpected social incidents. Social incidents occur when the investee company's practices violate social norms, for example, UN Global Compact principles. The companies ultimately responsible for the incident bear certain costs (Deegan et al. 2000). The primary objective of private reporting is to provide comprehensive information on the reactive dialogue process aimed at the long-term reduction of the negative effects that may flow from unexpected incidents. The content of private reports includes the incident, the engagement goal, the milestones, the quality and quantity of interactions, and risk management in the form of social actions undertaken by target companies. Private social reports are collected from a professional agent who led negotiations with global companies in collaboration with Nordic institutional investors. Nordic institutional investors and their agent are guided by the Nordic stakeholder-oriented corporate governance model (Lekvall 2014; Thomsen and Conyon 2012). The Nordic model supports institutional investors in building a business case for private social reporting and facilitates a consensus-seeking dialogue resulting in changes to the companies' actions embedded in the company strategy. This chapter adopts a perspective of long-term sustainable and responsible investors who aim at supporting strategic social actions of investee companies in response to social incident.

In the next section, this chapter provides a theoretical framework and reviews prior research on private social reporting. In the third section, the chapter discusses the research method and data. The fourth section presents the empirical evidence and discusses the social actions arising from private reports. Finally, the fifth section concludes.

THEORY AND PRIOR RESEARCH

Theory

Cundill et al. (2018) identified the main theoretical approaches that deal with engagement in social risks. These are agency theory, stakeholder theory, institutional theory, and social movement theory. This chapter focuses on the social actions triggered by unexpected incidents. To explore the social actions of target companies in private reporting, this chapter will adopt the fine-grained framework of the dialogic theory and legitimacy theory. The dialogic theory is employed to present the case for a dialogic-informed engagement that extends beyond notions of communication. The reading of the dialogic theory literature suggests that private dialogue refers to the iterative mutual learning process designed to promote transformative social action (Bebbington et al. 2007). Furthermore, this chapter uses legitimacy theory to explain that companies can use private communication channels to alleviate the potentially adverse effects caused by unexpected incidents (Deegan et al. 2000). Where the legitimacy of the company is in question, any corrective social actions and inadequacies of public information are accompanied and compensated for by private disclosures of these actions to maintain legitimacy.

Applying dialogic thinking to social accounting, Bebbington et al. (2007), Thomson and Bebbington (2005), and Solomon et al. (2011) argue that private reporting displays dialogic characteristics. Dialogic private reporting is characterized by a "two-way dialogue; sharing of power rather than domination of a hegemonic group; demythologizing reality; breaking down existing hegemonic discourse; and transformation of behaviour" (Solomon et al. 2011 p. 1123). In line with dialogic theory, private reporting has the potential to engender the social actions of investee companies and contribute to their emancipatory social transformations (Bebbington et al. 2007). Ferraro and Beunza (2018) claim that the combination of reputation threat, such as public social incidents, and dialogue can produce a common ground between investor activists and companies and subsequent changes in the social practices of companies.

Legitimacy theory has concluded that the social reporting discourse is dominated by incidents and companies' attempts to respond rhetorically to social incidents triggered by companies' activities (Deegan and Unerman, 2011). Legitimacy theory argues that unexpected incidents threaten the legitimacy of companies. Companies maintain their legitimacy through social disclosure. Solomon et al. (2011) explain the social reporting discourse by companies' concern with social-related risks triggered by an incident or crisis. O'Dwyer (2003) suggests that a lack of trust is a feature of the emergence of social reporting as responsive postures to reduce the anxiety of society. Social reporting can dispel social fears by creating greater dialogue and restoring confidence and trust. Legitimacy theory has a perception that the content of public social reports is potentially inadequate and of insufficient quality (Deegan and Unerman, 2011). It is therefore likely that private disclosure channels can supplement and support public social disclosure. This chapter will explore the use of private reporting as a mechanism to maintain the legitimacy of the relationships between institutional investors and companies hit by unexpected incidents. Private reporting serves as a vehicle to communicate the social actions undertaken by companies during the hidden dialogue with institutional investors.

Prior Research

There is scant evidence relating to private social reporting. The dialogue between institutional investors and their investee companies in the area of social risks has, however, become a central aspect of corporate governance and social accounting. Using a series of interviews with members of the institutional investment community, Solomon and Solomon (2006) find that private social disclosure supplements public social disclosure. The interviews provide support to the dialogic theory with both the investors and the companies initiating the dialogue. It is not surprising that institutional investors initiate and dominate the dialogue process with companies. However, the study indicates that companies start to request information on the social disclosure required by institutional investors. Solomon et al. (2011) reveal that private climate change reporting is dominated by a discourse of risk and risk management. They also found that institutional investors use the private reporting process to compensate for inadequacies of public climate change reporting. The authors provide evidence of a discourse of opportunity in private climate change reporting. For example, the amount of revenue derived from products with environmental benefits. Furthermore, Atkins et al. (2015) present evidence that private social reporting is beginning to merge with private financial reporting. In previous studies, private reporting takes place in one-on-one meetings between institutional investors and investees on social and environmental issues. However, Solomon et al. (2013) provide contradictory evidence on private social reporting. Based on the perception of 20 UK institutional investors, the study shows that the frontstage, ritualistic impression management is present in private social reporting. The institutional investors perceive that their investee companies manage impressions in private social reporting and create a dual myth of social accountability. The empirical evidence informs the literature that both investors and investees manage impressions in meetings. However, the study suggests that private social reporting has the potential to act as an effective and powerful mechanism of social accountability. This chapter is based on actual private reports, not interviews with institutional investors which provide conflicting evidence.

There is a small body of the broad-scale empirical literature that analyses the outcomes of private dialogues. Focusing on a sole institutional investor who has extended its traditional governance concerns into thematic environmental, social, and governance (ESG) engagements, Hoepner et al. (2018) provide evidence that private dialogue on ESG topics reduces the downside risk of portfolio companies. Dimson et al. (2015) show that companies improve their accounting performance and governance and increase institutional ownership after successful private dialogues. Barko et al. (2018) identify that companies with poor ex ante ESG performance ratings obtain higher ESG scores after the dialogue. Dimson et al. (2018) demonstrate that successful dialogues are followed by improved profitability, increased sales growth, and enlarged ownership. In this chapter, we show that dialogic reporting enhances the accountability of companies and institutional investors by providing information on the social actions taken by target companies.

DATA AND METHODOLOGY

Private Social Reports

Private social reports are obtained from a professional agent specializing in sustainable and responsible investments (SRI). In 2005, the agent launched the Engagement Forum service, which is a collaborative platform on which a coalition of Nordic institutional investors is involved in an active ownership process led by the agent. The process of private reporting includes several steps. In the first step, the private social report defines the incident. In the second step, the private report summarizes the findings of the incident analysis and the risk analysis of the company. In the third step, the private social report presents a full dialogue case profile, including the goal of the dialogue, a possible action plan on how to achieve the goal, milestones to establish the progress and response of the company towards achieving the goal, and a recommendation on how to proceed with the dialogue. In the final step, the private report concludes if the goal is achieved and the dialogue case is resolved. The agent represents Nordic institutional investors in interactions with companies using private channels of communication. These include letters, conference calls, face-to-face meetings, and collaborative activities. When private dialogue is unsuccessful, the agent uses the public mechanism to impose pressure on the investee companies, including Principle for Responsible Investment Clearinghouse actions, proxy voting, statements and questions at annual general meetings, and filling and co-filling shareholder resolutions.

The Engagement Forum database of the agent has provided access for this study to data records on the private reports of dialogue cases. Data records are Excel files with specific information in relation to each dialogue case. In the data record, the information includes a unique key for the case, the name of the case, the current recommendation for the case, the location where the case took place, articles that serve as the start/base of the case, the summary of the case, text describing changes to the summary, new details applicable to the summary, summary of the dialogue, investor recommendations, an action plan, and so on. Private reports provide rich, structured evidence on the communication between Nordic institutional investors and target companies. The private reports reveal an emerging discourse of reactive company actions in relation to material risks triggered by unexpected incidents.

The sample of private reports is based on a point-in-time record of dialogue cases. The sample obtained from the Engagement Forum database contains 355 data records that address environment, human, and labor rights, corruption, and inhuman weapons risks between 2005 and 2013. The area of human rights risk comprises 36.9% of the records (131 cases), the area of labor rights 29.01% of the records (103 cases), the area of environment 19.15% of the records (68 cases), the area of inhumane weapons 8.18% of the records (29 cases), and the area of corruption 6.76% of the records (nine cases). Private dialogues on environmental, corruption, and labor rights risks have the highest success rates of 38.2%, 37.5%, and 35.9%, respectively. Private dialogues on human rights and inhuman weapons risks have success rates of 19.08% and 8.17%, respectively. This chapter examines ten private social reports, including four private reports on human rights risks and six private reports on labor rights risks. These reports relate to successful dialogue cases completed in the same time period. This chapter selects private social reports by limiting the date of recording the case to be successful (complete). The success of these cases is recorded in January–February 2013 when the goal of the dialogue is achieved and the case is resolved. As such, these ten records are the latest complete cases in the point-in-time record provided by the agent. The assumption is that the companies' social actions aimed at mitigating external risks have been competed under relatively similar general macro-economic conditions and business cycles in which companies operate.

Table 18.1 presents the sample of the private social reports. Private social reports relate to companies in different industries and countries. The industries include financials (one case), telecommunications (one case), consumer goods (two cases), utilities (one case), consumer services (four cases), and technology (one case). The countries consist of Portugal (one case), France (three cases), the US (four cases), Hong Kong (one case), and the UK (one case).

Methodology

This chapter draws on the methodological tool used in prior research on private reporting (Solomon et al. 2011; Atkins et al. 2015). In particular, it applies the discourse analytic approach to derive a picture of the discourse of social actions in private reporting. The discourse analytic method is used to analyze the text in private and public social reports (Tregidga and Milne 2006; Solomon et al. 2011). The method allows the "enactment of the reality organizations (members) wish to portray", rather than the content per se (Tregidga and Milne 2006 p. 224). The method focuses on the way in which the social reporting discourse is used as a means of creating and disseminating a "reality" about business actions. Discourse is defined as a system of text that brings an object into being (Tregidga and Milne 2006 p. 224); it aims to carry a view of the world to life and create a reality (Fairclough 2005). The discourse analytical approach thus provides a methodological tool for exploring the content of private reports at a particular point in time. For example, Solomon et al. (2011) use evidence from interviews with institutional investors as a means of gathering data on private reporting to interpret the evolving discourse of private climate change reporting. In the same way as Solomon et al. (2011), this chapter uses the database of dialogue cases as a lens through which to view and interpret the discourse of social actions in the private reports of dialogue cases. A microanalysis of the private reports results in the detection of two interrelated themes, such as social risks/incidents and social actions. At each stage of the analysis, memos are written in order to catalogue the impressions that are gleaned from the data.

RESULTS AND DISCUSSION

The Discourse of Social Risks in Private Reports

In Table 18.1, this chapter describes the themes used to interpret the discourse of social risks in a private report. The themes include the name of the incident, norm area, international conventions, reported party, and the number of companies involved in the incident. Next, we present the comparative content analysis of private social reports in relation to social risks.

Table 18.1   *Summary of private social reports*

Private report	Incident	Norm area	Norms	Industry	Country	Reported party	Involvement
A	Association to financing controversial project	Human rights	UN CG Principle 2; Guideline IV OECD Guidelines for Multinational Enterprises	Financials	Portugal	NGO	Multiple
B	Association to psychological harassments	Labor rights	UN CG Principle 1; Guideline V OECD Guidelines for Multinational Enterprises	Telecom.	France	Court	Single
C	Association to worker rights violations and safety negligence	Labor rights	UN CG Principle 1; Guideline V OECD Guidelines for Multinational Enterprises	Consumer goods	US	Institute for Global Labor and Human Rights	Multiple
D	Association to violation of international law	Human rights	UN CG Principles 1 and 2; Guideline IV OECD Guidelines for Multinational Enterprises	Utilities	France	Not available	Single
E	Association to labor rights violation in supply chain	Labor rights	UN CG Principle 4; Guideline V OECD Guidelines for Multinational Enterprises	Consumer service	US	Local Labor watch organization	Multiple
F	Association to violation of international labor standards in supply chain	Labor rights	UN CG Principle 1; Guideline IV OECD Guidelines for Multinational Enterprises	Consumer services	US	Institute for Global Labor and Human Rights	Multiple
G	Association to violation of international labor standards	Labor rights	UN CG Principle 3; Guideline V OECD Guidelines for Multinational Enterprises	Consumer services	UK	Human Rights Watch	Single
H	Association to sale of contaminated infant formula	Human rights	UN CG Principle 1, 2; Guideline IV, VIII OECD Guidelines for Multinational Enterprises	Consumer goods	Hong Kong	Local officials	Multiple

Private report	Incident	Norm area	Norms	Industry	Country	Reported party	Involvement
I	Association to child labor	Labor rights	UN CG Principle 5; Guideline V OECD Guidelines for Multinational Enterprises	Consumer services	US	Bloomberg	Single
J	Association to providing censorship and surveillance systems	Human rights	UN CG Principles 1 and 2; Guideline IV OECD Guidelines for Multinational Enterprises	Technology	France	TV	Single

Note: UN CG is the United Nations Global Compact; OECD is the Organization for Economic Co-operation and Development; NGO is non-governmental organization.

Private social report A relates to the contribution of the investee company to financing the project with social concerns. The project fails to protect human rights during the relocation process from their homes and to consult isolated indigenous groups. The reported practices are associated with a violation of the UN Global Compact Principle 2 on human rights and the corresponding Guideline IV of the OECD Guidelines for Multinational Enterprises.

Private social report B connects the investee company to a number of suicides in several years. Employees of the investee company point to a poor working environment, extreme pressure, inappropriate management methods, and low employee morale. The reported practices are associated with a violation of the UN Global Compact Principle 1 addressing human rights and correspondingly Guideline V of the OECD Guidelines for Multinational Enterprises.

Private social report C is associated with a reported violation of labor rights by a supplier of the investee company. The international organization finds that employees have long work hours, no days off, and extreme pressure from management's expectations. Employees have suffered several serious injuries in recent years and have not received training to work with dangerous machinery. The reported practices are associated with a violation of the UN Global Compact Principle 1 on human rights and the corresponding Guideline V of the OECD Guidelines for Multinational Enterprises.

Private social report D focuses on a joint venture of the investee company that is involved in a project associated with human rights abuses. The investee company's activities can also be associated with violating people's right to self-determination. The reported practices are associated with a violation of the UN Global Compact Principles 1 and 2 on human rights and the corresponding Guideline IV of the OECD Guidelines for Multinational Enterprises.

Private social report E relates to the connection of the investee company to a supplier that engages in illegal activities and violations of international labor standards, such as employing underage workers, paying significantly lower than the legal minimum wage, and providing a harsh working environment. The reported practices are associated with a violation of the UN Global Compact Principle 4 on labor standards and the corresponding Guideline V of the OECD Guidelines for Multinational Enterprises.

Private social report F deals with the subsidiaries of the investee company. The subsidiaries violate international labor rights, including abusive treatment, forced overtime, low wages, denial of freedom of association, failing to pay social security payments, employing underage workers, and a harsh working environment. The reported practices are associated with a violation of the UN Global Compact Principle 1 on human rights and the corresponding Guideline IV of the OECD Guidelines for Multinational Enterprises.

Private social report G points out that the investee company had the practice of preventing employees from exercising their right to form a union and threatening to permanently replace workers that join unions. The reported practices are associated with a violation of the UN Global Compact Principle 3 on labor standards and the corresponding Guideline V of the OECD Guidelines for Multinational Enterprises.

Private social report H focuses on the investee company, a company that produced infant milk powder that was contaminated. The contamination led to the deaths and illness of approximately 300,000 people. The reported incident is associated with a violation of the UN Global Compact Principles 1 and 2 on human rights and corresponding Guidelines IV and VIII of the OECD Guidelines for Multinational Enterprises.

Private social report I relates to the investee company linked to the use of child labor. The violations referred to many children working under poor conditions for many hours without payment and access to education. The reported practices are associated with a violation of the UN Global Compact Principle 5 addressing child labor and the corresponding Guideline V of the OECD Guidelines for Multinational Enterprises.

Private social report J considers the investee company that supplied the system used by the state regime to monitor and censor citizens' communication traffic in Burma. The company was accused of delivering and installing telecommunications equipment and facilitating censorship or surveillance. The reported practices are associated with a violation of the UN Global Compact Principles 1 and 2 on human rights and the corresponding Guideline IV of the OECD Guidelines for Multinational Enterprises.

To summarize, the social risks of investee companies deal with their internal social practices such as investment projects with social concerns, poor relations with employees, and products that cause health risks. The social risks also relate to external relations of investee companies with their suppliers who violate social norms and engage in irresponsible business practices. In the private reports, social risks refer to the specific social incident covered by external organizations and the media which potentially constitutes a non-financial risk for the portfolios of institutional investors and a strategic business risk for companies. The social incident reveals a contradiction between the sustainability-driven strategy of a company and global principles of human and labor rights, such as the UN Global Compact Principles and the OECD Guidelines for Multinational Enterprises.

The Discourse of Social Actions in Private Reports

Table 18.2 shows the summary of the process of private social reporting. The process of private social reporting takes place between 2008 and 2013. The period of dialogue is between 195 and 1522 days. Institutional investors request information via emails, calls, and meetings. Furthermore, institutional investors are found to dominate the dialogue. Investee companies can take the initiative by responding to the requests of investors and providing the information they demand.

Table 18.3 reports that the information on social risks comprises between 111 and 249 words in private social reports, with information on social actions spanning between 138 and

443 words. The following results present the comparative analysis of private social reports in relation to social actions.

Table 18.2   The process of private social reporting

Private report	Period	Horizon, days	Dialogue						
			email	call	meeting	fax	conference call	investor	target
A	2011–2013	602	10	1				8	3
B	2012–2013	230	21				1	10	12
C	2011–2013	714	15					11	4
D	2012–2013	195	8	1			2	4	7
E	2011–2013	421	6					4	2
F	2010–2013	804	19					13	6
G	2010–2013	846	34				1	18	17
H	2008–2013	1533	38	3	1			31	11
I	2011–2013	322	14	1				10	5
J	2010–2013	705	11					7	4

Table 18.3   The discourse of social risks and actions

Private report	Social risks, words	Social actions, words
A	135	138
B	249	286
C	142	170
D	243	162
E	146	138
F	149	210
G	176	443
H	111	301
I	115	208
J	143	496

In private social report A, the investee company reveals the action of being a member of the Equator principles. Based on the principles the company has developed the monitoring system applied to its clients with regard to their compliance with social and environmental norms. The company classifies the project as high risk. It appoints independent consultants to review the possible risks and adopts an action plan to cover them. The company's total financing of the project is approximately 1% of its total funding.

In private social report B, the investee company introduces a framework for relationships between the company and its employees. The company aims to create close relationships and increase cooperation. The policy is the foundation for the change of company management in relation to addressing the needs and problems of employees. The company has established employee representative bodies at different levels and listening and support areas. It trains managers in the management of sensitive situations and recruited additional doctors. The company commissions an independent institute to conduct regular surveys which show how the employees view the company's management, quality of life in the workplace, career development, and other indicators.

In private social report C, the investee company establishes a corrective action plan with a supplier. Its safety system and functions are examined. As a result, the investee company is no longer in a business relationship with the supplier.

In private social report D, the investee company provides the approach to human rights management and relations with stakeholders. The company presents evidence that the project does not relate to the sensitive territory. If the project is to be expanded it would be assessed based on the company's sustainability criteria, including human rights risks assessment.

In private social report E, the investee company implements a remediation plan. The company requires compliance from all suppliers with "Standards of Vendor Agreements" which address poor labor issues identified for the supplier.

In private social report F, the investee company performs an audit and regulates unpaid wages and benefits with all employees. The company will actively proceed further with remediation to ensure compliance with international labor standards within supply chains.

In private social report G, the investee company makes public its human rights policy which describes its commitment to the UN Declaration of Human Rights and ILO Core Conventions, including the right to freedom of association. The company maintains its compliance with all US legislation relating to labor practices and trade unions. The company trains managers on how to handle the union issue and to ensure that they do not breach employees' rights relating to unionization.

In private social report H, the investee company improves product safety and quality control by shifting from buying from small firms to buying from large firms with high quality control standards. This can reduce the risk of contamination. The product quality is checked twice; the first takes place at the dairy center and the second is performed at the retail shops. The company improves product quality by reducing human intervention. The company implements the tracking system to trace incidents back to the responsible people in the process chain. The company verifies its product safety standards using an external party. The company obtains certifications from ISO9001, ISO14000, OHSAS18001, and food and safety control systems GMP and HACCP.

In private social report I, the investee company uses Fairtrade-certified materials which prohibit forced and child labor. The suppliers have been investigated by Fairtrade International and the violations have not been confirmed. The company has the policy of direct contact with suppliers who are systematically audited for compliance with Fairtrade and other organizations. Fairtrade has formed partnerships with NGOs that focus on the well-being of children in this area to safeguard against inappropriate practices such as child labor.

In private social report J, the investee company updates its human rights policy according to the UN Guiding Principles on Business and Human Rights and the requirements of the Global Reporting Initiative, the Dow Jones Sustainability Index, and the UN Global Compact advanced level. The company includes business partners as part of the company Enterprise Risk Management Process and Supply Chain program. Based on these programs, the company screens significant suppliers for human rights risks. The company also monitors the evolution of government policy in the local area and supports the dialogue between the government administration and international stakeholders, such as the European Union, the US, Japan, the World Bank, and the International Telecommunication Union.

The private social reports of dialogue cases show that the investee companies respond to the requests of institutional investors by taking specific strategic actions to improve their social policies, relations with employees, the assessments of social risks, and product safety, and take social considerations in their investment projects. The social policy highlights the importance of investing in companies whose managers act responsibly considering social matters, in particular labor rights. The investee companies discontinue their agreements with irresponsible suppliers and develop verified policies and programs on human rights and supply chains. The private social reports do not particularly focus on short-term reactive actions of companies such as compensation, dismissal, and penalties.

Discussion

Based on the analysis of social risks and actions, the chapter identifies the conditions of the Nordic model that can be related to the use of private social reporting as an effective corporate governance mechanism. These contextual factors can serve as enablers to a successful private dialogue with a company resulting in business actions. The conditions include the risk aspects such as labor practices (working conditions, wages, child labor, and injuries); product safety and local community; the location of risks such as a whole company, joint venture, subsidiary, or supplier; a material incident that has received attention in the media; the social norms that are widely recognized by society; and a coalition that brings together active investors with shared interests and solid experience.

The data indicate that target companies tend to manage social risks that mainly address working practices. In Nordic countries, the interests of employees are typically taken into account because labor unions are an important force in encouraging companies to adopt progressive social policies and practices. The Nordic model can support universal owners and their agents in developing recommendations and negotiating solutions for labor-related risk management in target companies. Further, social risks that can be relevant for business actions can occur within and outside of the company where the typical entities are subsidiaries and suppliers. Another enabling condition of social action is the context of social risks that are material incidents revealed by the media. The media often threaten companies' reputation and public standing. Social incidents revealed by the media act as an incitement and base for a private dialogue. The next factor enabling effective private social reporting is the presence of specific international conventions and standards. Specifying voluntary global principles in relation to social risk establishes a boundary system that restricts business conduct and stands as a potential threat to a company's legitimacy. Finally, a coalition of social activists provides an infrastructure by facilitating collaboration and knowledge exchange between institutional investors and mobilizing their resources of influence on investee companies. Overall, these conditions are likely to drive the strategic actions of companies to manage social risk exposure.

This chapter develops a framework that connects the conditions of private social dialogues with social actions (Figure 18.1). The framework reflects the relationships between social risk, private social reporting, and the outcomes of social actions. It starts with the aspect and location of social risks that need to be managed. It then moves to the conditions that can drive successful interactions between institutional investors and company managers in order to reach the agreement on social actions. Lastly, the outcomes of social actions are categorized as management systems, policy, and transparency. This chapter proposes that private social reporting tends to contribute to a renewal of social policies, development of management systems in the form of risk assessments and quality standards, and the improvement of disclosure on social issues.

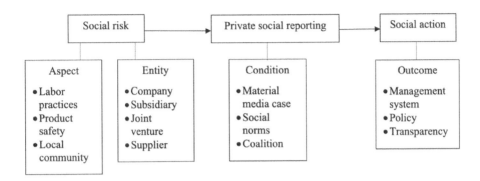

Figure 18.1   The model of social actions in private social reporting

CONCLUSION

This chapter has summarized the content of ten private social reports, focusing on the discourse of social risks and actions. Private social reporting takes place in dialogues between Nordic institutional investors and their investee companies. The findings support the dialogic theory and legitimacy theory. Consistent with dialogic theory, the reputation threat triggered by the incident establishes a common ground in private dialogue which prompts companies to take action. The dialogic nature of private reporting enables parties to reach an agreement and represents social transformation to change investees' behavior and reduce their social risks. In this way, this chapter interprets private social reporting as a discourse of risk avoidance, especially as it causes the social actions of investee companies. In accordance with legitimacy theory, target companies tend to respond to investors' requests and inform about the companies' actions that bring the activities and performance more in line with society's values and expectations.

This chapter documents that social incidents are viewed by the institutional investors as a significant material risk. Institutional investors consider human and labor rights to be vital social factors in institutional investments. They are especially concerned about social risks relating to relations with employees and suppliers, product safety, and child labor. In terms of the information required, the investee companies provide information about their social policy, assessment of social risks, and incorporation of social risks in production processes, investment projects, and relations with suppliers.

From the managerial perspective, companies can utilize the dialogic process of private social reporting to discover how they can deal with the unexpected incident in order to retain a leadership reputation in the area of social responsibility and good relations with institutional investors. The results of the discourse analysis reveal that company managers can use private reporting strategically to improve their long-term social policies, identify efficient social targets and performance measures, manage business risks, build better management control systems, and facilitate employee satisfaction. The findings also suggest that a company's sustainable reporting can be enhanced beyond the substantial attention given to climate change risks to inform individuals about the social preparedness of a company. Sustainability reporting can be extended to include value-relevant data on social policies in the areas of health and safety, diversity, freedom of association, wages, supply chain, working hours and child/forced labor, global human and labor rights-related principles, such as UN Global Compact and Equator principles, the devices of management control systems, assurance mechanisms, models of relations with employees and trade unions, and supply chain assessments. In addition, the chapter could be of interest to professional organizations in the area of sustainability. Accounting standard-setters can develop guidelines on how companies' public disclosures can reflect unexpected incidents and be extended to provide information concerning companies' preparedness to meet future social risks. Proponents of responsible investments could also be interested in the evidence on the efficiency of the SRI strategy of active ownership. Despite the growth in engagement on sustainability issues, what actions target companies undertake are poorly understood.

Furthermore, the findings contribute to earlier research which detected elements of a risk-driven discourse within private climate change reporting (Solomon et al 2011) and the academic literature examining public social disclosures with a focus on company performance (Semenova et al. 2010). The study extends the large-scale literature on the antecedents and outcomes of shareholder activism, in particular the form of private behind-the-scenes engagement with regard to sustainability risks (Dimson et al 2015; Barko et al. 2018; Bauer et al. 2015; Hoepner et al. 2018).

The study has limitations and may be extended in several ways. The conclusions are relevant for the Nordic model of private social reporting, which is based on the Engagement Forum in a collaboration led by the agent with institutional investors to engage with companies in connection to social incidents and controversies. However, this incident-based approach could be offered by other commercial parties and asset managers, particularly in Europe. The data are based on ten private social reports during the period of 2008–2013. The results of this chapter cannot be extended beyond this type of dialogue case or to other time periods. This is a qualitative study and has limited focus on control for the nature and qualities of the individual dialogues, including the characteristics of target companies and institutional investors. Further research can extend the chapter by focusing on other countries' models of corporate governance and approaches of private reporting. Little is also known about the inner progress of private dialogues between active investors and investee companies.

REFERENCES

Atkins, J., Solomon, A., Joseph, N., & Norton, S. (2015). The emergence of integrated private reporting. *Meditari Accountancy Research*, 23(1), 28–61.

Barko, T., Cremers, M., & Renneboog, L. (2018). Shareholder engagement on Environmental, Social and Governance Performance. Discussion Paper. Tilburg, Center for Economic Research.

Bauer, R., Moers F., & Viehs, M. (2015). Who withdraws shareholder proposal and does it matter? An analysis of sponsor identity and pay practices. *Corporate Governance: An International Review*, 23(6), 472–488.

Bebbington, J., Brown, J., Frame, B., & Thomson, I. (2007). Theorizing engagement: The potential of a critical dialogic approach. *Accounting, Auditing and Accountability Journal*, 20(3), 356–381.

Cundill, G., Smart, P., & Wilson, H. (2018). Non-financial shareholder activism: A process model for influencing corporate environmental and social performance. *International Journal of Management Reviews*, 20, 606–626.

Deegan, C. (2000). Firm's disclosure reactions to major social incidents: Australian evidence. *Accounting Forum*, 24(1), 101–130.

Deegan, C., & Unerman, J. (2011). *Financial Accounting Theory*. London: McGraw-Hill Higher Education.

Dimson, E., Karakas, O., & Li, X. (2015). Active ownership. *The Review of Financial Studies*, 28(12), 3225–3268.

Dimson, E., Karakas, O., & Li, X. (2018). Coordinated engagements. Available at: https://papers.ssrn .com/sol3/papers.cfm?abstract_id=3209072.

Fairclough, N. (2005). Peripheral vision: Discourse analysis in organization studies: The case for critical realism. *Organization Studies*, 26(6), 915–939.

Ferraro, F., & Beunza, D. (2018). Creating common ground: A communicative action model of dialogue in shareholder engagement. *Organizational Science*, 29(6), 1187–1207.

Gond, J-P., O'Sullivan, N., Slager, R., Homanen, M., Viehs, M., & Mosony, S. (2018). How ESG engagement creates value for investors and companies. *Principles for Responsible Investment*, 31 pp.

Goranova, M., & Ryan, L. (2014). Shareholder activism: A multidisciplinary review. *Journal of Management*, 40(5), 1230–1268.

Hoepner, A., Oikonomou, I., Sautner, Z., Starks, L. T., & Zhou, X. Y. (2018). ESG shareholder engagement and downside risk. *SSRN Working Paper*, the Smurfit Graduate Business School & Quinn School of Business, University College Dublin, Dublin, January.

Lekvall, P. (2014). *The Nordic Corporate Governance Model*. Stockholm: TMG Sthlm.

Logsdon, J., & Van Buren, H. (2009). Beyond the proxy vote: Dialogues between shareholder activists and corporations. *Journal of Business Ethics*, 87(1), 353–365.

O'Dwyer, B. (2003). Conceptions of corporate social responsibility: The nature of managerial capture. *Accounting, Auditing and Accountability Journal*, 16, 523–557.

Rehbein, K., Waddock, S., & Graves, S. (2004). Understanding shareholder activism: Which corporations are targeted? *Business & Society*, 43(3), 239–269.

Rehbein K., Logsdon J., & Van Buren H. (2013). Corporate responses to shareholder activists: Considering the dialogue alternative. *Journal of Business Ethics*, 112, 137–154.

Sikavica, K., Perrault, E., & Rehbein, K. (2018). Who do they think they are? Identity as an antecedent of social activism by institutional shareholders. *Business & Society*, published online (accessed 14 September 2018).

Semenova, N. (2020). Company receptivity in private dialogue on sustainability risks. *Sustainability*, 12, 532.

Semenova, N., Hassel, L., & Nilsson, H. (2010) The value relevance of environmental and social performance: Evidence from Swedish SIX 300 companies. *Nordic Journal of Business*, 3, 265–292.

Solomon, J., & Darby, L. (2005). Is private social, ethical and environmental disclosure mythicizing or demythologizing reality? *Accounting Forum*, 29, 27–47.

Solomon, J., & Solomon, A. (2006). Private social, ethical and environmental disclosure. *Accounting, Auditing and Accountability Journal*, 19(4), 564–591.

Solomon, J., Solomon, A., Joseph, N., & Norton, S. (2011). Private climate change reporting: An emerging discourse of risk and opportunity? *Accounting, Auditing and Accountability Journal*, 24(8), 1119–1148.

Solomon, J., Solomon, A., Joseph, N., & Norton, S. (2013). Impression management, myth creation and fabrication in private social and environmental reporting: Insights from Erving Goffman. *Accounting, Organizations and Society*, 38, 195–213.

Thomsen, S., & Conyon M. (2012). *Corporate Governance: Mechanisms and Systems*. London: McGraw-Hill Higher Education.

Thomson, I., & Bebbington, J. (2005). It doesn't matter what you teach. *Critical Perspectives on Accounting*, 15, 609–628.

Tregidga, H., & Milne, M. (2006). From sustainable management to sustainable development: a longitudinal analysis of a leading New Zealand environmental reporter. *Business Strategy and the Environment*, 15, 219–241.

19. How environment, social and governance scores impact company financial performance indicators: evidence from Denmark

Slobodan Kacanski

INTRODUCTION

Since the latest recession, which took place in 2008/2009, the European Commission has pursued a range of reforms to improve reporting processes in corporations, with the aim of enforcing the achievement of long-term goals at corporate level. The motivation behind the reforms changed from a short-term shareholder value policy to a more sustainable management strategy, which will take into account the interest of other internal and external stakeholders, for instance customers, employees and suppliers (Velte, 2017). Furthermore, the purpose of these reforms was to encourage boards of directors and management (both levels in a two-tier corporate governance system) to recognize the relevance for integration of social, environmental and governance considerations into their primarily profit-driven business strategies, which will arguably have a positive impact on their financial performance (Kaur & Lodhia, 2018; Schaltegger & Csutora, 2012; Unerman & O'Dwyer, 2007). Ultimately, the companies will also disclose the reports on these aspects in their annual statements.

Recognizing the importance of these reforms, different countries have started proposing and accepting various national and international initiatives and regulations according to which the companies complying with certain requirements become obligated to publicly disclose information on their sustainability efforts. There are different forms of reporting that companies might use, for instance separate environmental, social and governance (ESG) reports within their annual reports, integrated reports, etc. Depending on the country, there are different initiatives for disclosure of ESG reports, according to which companies are either intrinsically motivated or legally required to report on these issues (Schaltegger, 2012; Shell, 1998). Regardless of the type of initiative, implementing sustainable practices should not, at the other extreme, compromise corporate financial objectives. However, considering the expenses related to the conduct of sustainable practices, the problem that emerges is how much ethical behavior can be merged into a modern business context when the profit maximization logic is taken as a point of departure of almost any business strategy (Hellsten & Mallin, 2006; Ittner et al., 2003).

The relationship between sustainability and profitability has become of interest to a considerable body of research. Studies have particularly investigated the link between the alteration of profit-oriented business practices towards more sustainable processes and its effect on profitability. Findings indicated both positive (Griffin & Mahon, 1997; Margolis & Walsh, 2003; Orlitzky et al., 2003) and negative (and/or insignificant) relations between these two variables (Margolis & Walsh, 2003; Orlitzky et al., 2003). According to Wu (2006), the ambivalence in findings could be attributed to a combination of variables implemented to measure the direction and the presence of significant links between the ESG score and company financial performance indicators (Velte, 2017). In a few recent studies, researchers used ESG scores as the proxy for a company's corporate social responsibility (CSR) rating, while the financial performance indicator was divided into two separate parameters, namely, return on assets (ROA), which is an accounting-based variable, and Tobin's Q, as a market-based item in the aggregate financial performance measure.

The aim of this study is to measure the effects of the ESG scores on company financial performance. Using multiple panel data regression analysis (Scholtens, 2008), this study estimates the impact of ESG score both as an aggregated measure and as the separate effects of its three main components, i.e. ESG pillar scores. The financial performance indicators that are integrated into the models are considered with a one-year lag in relation to the year for which the rest of the variables were collected, as ESG scores would not be expected to make a significant impact on financial performance indicators in the same year. This is also because the announcements and the disclosure of the ESG reports appear in the same annual statement for which the effect could not be expected. Those four effects are separately measured by both ROA and Tobin's Q. In this way, this study builds on and contributes to an ongoing discussion on the direction and the strength of the link between ESG scores and financial performance indicators. Furthermore, decomposition of the measure strengthens the analysis further by intensifying the findings through the estimates of the strengths of the links between particular pillars and the overall financial performance. This study thus extends the prevailing emphasis on aggregate measures (e.g. Fischer & Sawczyn, 2013). Lastly, this study builds on Velte (2017) as it integrates both financial performance indicators (ROA and Tobin's Q) and measures the parameters in the Danish context.

The study uses Danish public company data for a number of reasons. First, during the last decade, a considerable number of Danish companies (start-up, private and public) were building and revising their strategies and models towards a greener business routine. These incentives were not primarily driven by the regulations established by the national government and the European Commission; they were also strongly ingrained as social values in this regard. Besides the incentives, Danish companies are also particularly active in providing public disclosures on their CSR efforts, both as a differentiation strategy and as disclosures within their annual statements.

For the empirical part of the study, panel data on 216 company-level observations was collected for the period 2010–2018. Regarding the measures of financial performance indicators, these were collected for the period of 2011–2019 with a one-year lag, due to the argument that the effects of a particular year's ESG scores could be not measured on a company's financial performance for at least a year after the scores are reported (Scholtens, 2008; Velte, 2017). The company sample covers public business entities listed on the Danish stock exchange (Nasdaq OMX Copenhagen) whose ESG scores on sustainability performance are available for the entire period of observation. The effects of the measures were controlled for a few company-level variables, e.g. company size, risk levels, industry, and research and development expenses. The findings demonstrate that the ESG score has only a partial impact on company financial performance, as it only has a positive impact on Tobin's Q. On the other hand, the social pillar score has the strongest influence on both financial performance indicators, whereas the environmental pillar positively impacts only Tobin's Q and the governance pillar negatively impacts ROA only.

This chapter is structured as follows. First, the theoretical foundation behind the study is established, according to which the hypothesis statement is defined. Second, the data collection process is explained together with the analytical method used to estimate parameters. The chapter ends with the presentation of empirical findings and includes theoretical reflections on the results for both theories and recommendations for future research. Lastly, concluding remarks are outlined together with the limitations of the study.

THEORETICAL FOUNDATION AND HYPOTHESIS DEVELOPMENT

A steady increase in the number of companies that report on their sustainability efforts demonstrates the relevance of communicating the information on actions taken to support society, environment and governance. These reports serve as a tool for the articulation of environmental and social sustainability efforts and objectives with the public, and aim to effectively link employees' actions to corporate strategies from both financial and non-financial perspectives (Epstein & Buhovac, 2014; Hubbard, 2009; Moller & Schaltegger, 2005; Searcy, 2012; Wisner et al., 2006).

In general, the impetus for disclosing ESG scores is either intrinsic or is incentivized by regulations – though an international standardization has not been attained yet (Schaltegger, 2012; Shell, 1998). There are a number of local, regional and international initiatives which aim to guide the preparation of the sustainability disclosures, e.g. GRI, AA1000, UN Global Compact and ISO26000. These predominantly self-contained initiatives are primarily localized around those regions and industries where the expectations of becoming green are of paramount importance relative to the others. They encompass different scopes ranging across environment, labor rights, human rights, society, anti-corruption, social responsibility and carbon-related facets at industry, national, supranational and international levels (Lodhia, 2012). Their goal is to raise awareness among companies of the problems to which profit-driven logics contribute (Lodhia, 2012). It is ironic that, despite the pivotal character of social and environmental problems, ESG disclosures remained voluntary in some countries (Lodhia, 2012) even though a number of countries made disclosures compulsory for corporations only.

The baseline proposition from which this chapter develops the argument is underpinned by Schumacher's (1973) meta-economical assumption that *economics* is a system that contains a set of relations between the elements constructing the social, economic and environmental setting rather than having solely a profit element. While accepting the assertion that profit is a natural driver of any economic activity, he also holds that a traditional economic metasystem should expand the content of what the economics is (see more: Schumacher, 1973), as it should also take into account environmental (ecological) and human elements, given their complementarity and interconnectedness.

Earlier studies on this topic substantiated the link between sustainability and profitability from two different theoretical standpoints: stakeholder theory and classical principal agent theory. Stakeholder theory assumes that satisfying the interests of different coalition partners with which the company is associated through a network of various joint ventures will ultimately determine the success of products and services (Freeman, 1984). However, according to the classical principal agent theory, a company constitutes a subset of society, which means that generating value is measured by the fulfillment of specific societal expectations, that should align in order to enable achieving corporate goals. So, in order to achieve those goals, it is crucial that management succeeds in reconciling a multitude of interests, so the corporate goals can be prioritized over the individuals' interests (Jensen & Meckling, 1976; Ross, 1973).

From a research perspective, there is still an ongoing (emotionally, normatively and ideologically loaded) debate about CSR on whether it is financially worthwhile for organizations to pay attention to societal demands (van Beurden & Gössling, 2008). This debate arises not only because of the need to understand how sustainability efforts impact financial performance in different industries and localities, but also because the usage of different methods for measuring the effects raises the question of the validity of previous findings (van Beurden & Gössling, 2008; Velte, 2017). It seems that this debate will prevail in the future, given the increasing pressure to establish corporate accountability (Waddock, 2004). It is still unclear in what manner and to what extent ESG scores impact company financial performance indicators, and whether there are any unobserved externalities that future studies should take into account.

A growing body of literature is still trying to give an answer on whether it pays off financially "to be good for society and environment". At first glance it is apparent that there is a clear ambivalence in findings on this relationship in the literature. Studies indicate that the link between the ESG performance and the financial performance of companies is still equivocal due to the lack of sustainability reporting standards and the lack of consent among definitions of the CSR concept. As a result, a body of knowledge has been assembled from a number of studies that found evidence of both a positive relationship (e.g. Cramer, 2003; Griffin, 2000; Maron, 2006; Orlitzky et al., 2003; Wu, 2006) and a negative relationship (e.g. Griffin & Mahon, 1997) between these two performance indicators. The first group assumed that the implementation of CSR improves the position of those firms relative to other firms that do not implement any CSR strategy. This means that pursuing sustainability-driven reforms may lead to a societal recognition of those efforts, which further increases employee productivity and market demand for outputs (Hou, 2019). Moreover, this further establishes a pre-condition for better financial performance (Callan & Thomas, 2009; Marti et al., 2015). For instance, Margolis and Walsh (2003) demonstrated that companies that invest more into their sustainable businesses, in fact, report lower financial performance indicators, which signifies that the adoption of environmental sustainability policies often leads to short-term decreases in profits, even though long-term profit may increase. In this regard, McWilliams & Siegel (2000) argued that the problem with the ambivalence of the results is concealed behind the fact that the limitations under which the studies were conducted are insufficiently disclosed, and that is why there is a relatively high number of studies that found a negative relationship between the two performance measures (van Beurden & Gössling, 2008). More concretely, the fact that firms acting in a socially irresponsible or illegal way decreases wealth for shareholders (Roman et al. 1999) should not lead to the conclusion that the relationship is negative (Frooman, 1997). This negative effect should be also seen as positive relations, as the direction of the effects is, in fact, the same. This argument was afterwards used as a guiding logic for most meta-analytical studies, which hypothesized and identified that the extent of ESG efforts is positively related to their financial performance (Allouche & Laroche, 2005; Orlitzky et al., 2003; Wu, 2006). In other studies, regardless of whether the sustainability indicators accounted for social and environmental elements as isolated indicators, or environmental, social and governance pillars were taken as the aggregate measures, findings are still polarized (van Beurden & Gössling, 2008).

Notwithstanding the existing ambivalence across the literature, an overall argument that is in line with the shareholder theory suggests that a positive link between sustainability and financial performance is rather more apparent than the negative one (Godfrey et al., 2009; Velte, 2017). Taking this into account, the following hypothesis statement is defined:

H1: ESG score has a positive impact on financial performance indicators.

Since only recently have studies started breaking down the aggregate indicator of the ESG score (e.g. Velte, 2017), this study will test the individual impacts of each of the components integrated into the overall score, since individual pillars might have a stronger impact on the company's financial performance relative to the others.

DATA AND METHODOLOGY

Sample Selection

The companies selected for the empirical part of the study include public business entities listed on the Copenhagen Stock Exchange (Nasdaq OMX Copenhagen). The aim of this study is to measure the effects of the ESG scores on company financial performance on the sample of Danish public companies after the fall of trust in the corporate world regarding the exploitation of natural and social resources following the period of crisis in 2008/2009. This research covers the empirical data for business years in the period 2010–2018. This period was chosen because the post-crisis period in Denmark was particularly characterized by the exponential increase in efforts related to improving companies' ESG performance. Due to the fact that the sampled companies face strict regulation in terms of information transparency in this regard, adequate CSR communication was expected. The sample size was consistent over the 9-year period as only the companies that were listed during the entire period and that also provided the ESG scores were selected for the study. Table 19.1 provides an overview of the final sample of 216 company-level observations.

Table 19.1   Sample selection procedure

Sample	2010–2018
Listed companies consistently present during the entire period on Nasdaq OMX Copenhagen	166
Missing company data	142
Final sample	24

Main Variables

Company data including financial and ESG indicators was primarily collected from Thomson Eikon Reuters Datastream for each company sampled. Missing data was hand-collected either from sustainability reports, integrated reports, status reports and annual reports or in direct contact with accounting/financial departments and investor relations departments. Companies' ESG scores, together with the measures of their integral components, were gathered from the database for each year in the period 2010–2018. Data on which the analysis was later performed was collected in June 2020. For the purpose of this study, a main independent variable is ESG score defined as an aggregated value of a company's CSR performance covering three elements: environmental, social and governance. Each of these is quantified based on the weights of their integral items in the final scores, which are finally aggregated in the overall ESG score. These items include the following: resource use, emissions, innovation, management, shareholders, CSR strategy, workforce, human rights, community and product responsibility. The weights of each of the items vary according to the item's relevance in its respective pillar and are not equally distributed. Based on the main model, this study aims to test the impact of the ESG score on a company's financial performance. Moreover, the impacts of each of the three components of the ESG score were also analyzed separately. EPS (environmental pillar score) indicates environmental performance, SPS (social pillar score) indicates social performance and GPS (governance pillar score) indicates governance performance. All the scores are obtained from the Eikon Reuters database. The measure of the impact of ESG controversies on financial performance, as an additional sub-category of ESG measures, was left out of the study because the score itself does not represent an integral element of the final ESG score, according to the methodology for the score calculation. The forthcoming table of results presents both the aggregated and the disaggregated impact of the ESG score on financial performance.

Instead of measuring the effect on the traditionally used dependent variable of ROA, following the suggestions of Choi & Wang (2009) and Velte (2017), besides the accounting measure this study also integrated a market-based measure (Tobin's Q) as an additional indicator of a company's financial performance. ROA is the most widely used accounting-based variable for measuring financial performance, which calculates it as a ratio of net income to total assets. On the other hand, Tobin's Q is the ratio between the physical assets' market value and their replacement value (Velte, 2017). It has become common practice in the accounting literature to measure the ratio by comparing the market value and the firm's equity and liabilities with its corresponding book values – this is because the replacement values of a company's assets are hard to evaluate (Choi & Wang, 2009). This study makes an important contribution to the existing body of knowledge as, on one hand, it extends the number of dependent variables on which the ESG score impacts are measured, and on the other hand, it enables the comparison of the outcomes with the existing literature.

Besides the variables mentioned above, a number of control variables were also integrated into the model. These were selected based on the list of commonly used variables in this research area (Choi & Wang, 2009; Fischer & Sawczyn, 2013; Velte, 2017), which includes the following: research and development expenses, beta, debt to assets, natural logarithm of total assets, and branch of industry a company belongs to. Research and development expenses represent the extent of companies' intensity of investment in their future developments. This data was collected from the statement of profit and loss and other comprehensive income provided within the annual financial statements. Following the arguments from the previous studies (Kogut & Zander, 1992), it could be expected that heavier investments lead to better financial performance. Also, company's systematic risk (beta) was also integrated into the model as a proxy measure for systematic risk and the ratio of total debt to total assets as a proxy for unsystematic risk (Fischer & Sawczyn, 2013; Velte, 2017). Earlier research argues that shareholders' relations and financial performance indicators are associated with the level of company risk (Waddock & Graves, 1997), as companies with better ESG scores are perceived as less risky and are thus connected to lower costs of debt (Godfrey et al., 2009).

Table 19.2   Variables used in the study

Variables	Explanation
Dependent variables	
ROA	The item represents the return on assets before taxes. It is calculated as *income before tax* for the fiscal year divided by the *average total assets* for the same period expressed as a percentage.
Tobin's Q	A ratio between market and book value of a company's equity and liability.
Independent variables	
ESG score	The environmental, social and governance score collected from the Thomson Reuters database.
EPS	The environmental pillar score measures a company's impact on resources used, emissions and innovation.
SPS	The social pillar score measures a company's capacity, beyond its product responsibility, for responsibility towards the workforce, the community and human rights.
GPS	The governance pillar score measures a company's internal systems and processes related to management, shareholders and CSR strategies.
Control variables	
R&D expenses	Research and development expenses reported in the annual statements.
Beta	The level of a company's systematic risk (beta factor).
Debt to assets	Debt/asset ratio – total debt/total assets as a measure of unsystematic risk.
Log total assets	Company size – natural logarithm of total assets used to improve data normality.
Industry	Industry branch – binary variable indicates (0) services and (1) manufacturing.

In addition, the natural logarithm of total assets is used as a measure of company size because prior studies demonstrated that this measure can be related to the extent of stakeholders' interest in the CSR activities of the company (Velte, 2017). The natural logarithm is used here in order to normalize the data, as large size can bring economies of scale and scope (Roberts & Dowling, 2002). This control variable can have both a positive and a negative impact. Lastly, the industry branch was integrated as a control variable in a binary form (manufacture/service) because the extent of stakeholder management and performance may be different across industries (Velte, 2017).

As previously mentioned, this study uses one-year lag data for the ROA and Tobin's Q variables in order to measure the impact of ESG score on a company's financial performance, which is in line with the arguments given in the literature that ESG scores do not immediately lead to any impact on financial performance indicators (Choi & Wang, 2009). Therefore, the models regress the independent and control variables for the period 2010–2018 with ROA and Tobin's Q for the period 2011–2019, which results in the collection of company-level data for a ten-year period from 2010 to 2019. Table 19.2 describes the variables used in the model.

Regression Model

In order to test the hypothesis, this study uses panel data regression with fixed effects, as the impact of ESG score on financial performance indicators is measured over the period of time in which the relationship between independent and dependent variables is measured within a particular entity – in this case, a company. The study is of a longitudinal character, which in its panel nature is characterized by both spatial and temporal dimensions. The spatial dimension pertains to a set of cross-sectional units of observation (in this case companies), and the temporal dimension pertains to periodic observations of a set of variables characterizing these cross-sectional units over a particular span of time (Yaffee, 2003). A fixed-effect regression is used here to estimate the model parameters for balanced data. Fixed-effect models are a class of statistical models that are used when it is of interest to analyze the impact of variables that vary over time but only within the entity for which the predictor may have an influence on a particular dependent variable.

This study tests whether, and in what matter, ESG performance indicators impact a company's financial performance. The indicator of company's financial performance is separated into two sub-indicators –ROA and Tobin's Q, previously defined as independent variables. Measures of the effects of ESG performance indicators are separately tested on each financial performance indicator. In accordance with the approach by Hair et al. (2009), the assumptions of regression regarding the linearity, homoscedasticity of residuals, normal distribution of error terms and multicollinearity were tested. Regression statistics are applied in RStudio. The following regression model equation refers to the total ESG performance indicator as a factor potentially impacting a company's financial performance. Additionally, the results below provide statistical estimates of the effects that each of the components of the ESG indicator might have on both financial performance indicators. The regression equation is defined as follows:

$$FinPerf\left(ROA, Tobin'sQ\right) = +_1 ESGscore +_2 RD_{expenses} +_3 Beta +_4 DebtToAssets$$
$$+_5 LogTotalAssets +_6 Industry + \varepsilon$$

RESULTS

Descriptive Statistics

Table 19.3 provides an outline of panel data descriptive statistics for each variable belonging to each of the three categories – ESG performance (i.e. independent variables), financial performance (i.e. dependent variables) and control variables. Measures of mean, median, standard deviation, minimum and maximum values are provided for each variable.

Values for ESG scores and their integral pillars range from 0 to 1. The ESG scores' mean (median) in this sample is 0.517 (0.524), while the score for the environmental pillar is 0.458 (0.518), for the social pillar the score is 0.527 (0.536) and for the governance pillar the score is 0.484 (0.504). According to this, the social pillar has the highest score compared with the environmental and governance pillars, respectively. Financial performance indicators have a mean (median) of 7.957 (5.280) for return of assets and 2.711 (1.455) for Tobin's Q. Control variables have the following descriptive statistics: R&D expenses 1.123 (0.143), systematic risk 1.047 (1.125), unsystematic risk 18.131 (15.680), company size 17.210 (16.730) and industry category 0.063 (1.000).

Table 19.3   Descriptive statistics

Variable	Mean	Median	SD	Minimum	Maximum
ESG performance					
ESG score	0.517	0.524	0.157	0.278	0.812
EPS	0.458	0.518	0.251	0.000	0.897
SPS	0.527	0.536	0.203	0.227	0.946
GPS	0.484	0.504	0.215	0.260	0.934
Financial performance					
ROA	7.957	5.280	12.705	−39.270	53.040
Tobin's Q	2.711	1.455	2.704	0.560	14.120
Control variables					
R&D expenses (in million dkk)	1.123	0.143	3.911	0.000	33.000
Beta	1.047	1.125	0.394	0.100	1.700
Debt to assets	18.131	15.680	13.609	0.000	60.500
Log total assets	17.210	16.730	1.704	13.760	22.000
Industry	0.063	1.000	0.500	0.000	1.000

Correlation Matrix

Table 19.4 provides the results of correlation indices given in the Pearson correlation matrix between each pair of variables integrated into the regression model, together with the indication of a pairwise significance between the variables. All integral parts of the overall ESG score are positively and significantly correlated (EPS, SPS, GPS), which would be expected as those elements, in summary, make up the final ESG score. The ESG scores are positively and significantly correlated with both dependent variables, while in their breakdown, only the social pillar score has a similar correlation with the dependent variables. In regard to the control variables, a positive and significant correlation is present between the research and development expenses and industry categorization, while a negative and significant correlation exists between both financial performance indicators and the level of unsystematic risk (debt to assets). On the other hand, there is no significant correlation identified for beta and assets relative to financial performance.

Regression Results

The results of multiple regression from fixed effects applied to panel data are provided in Table 19.5. ROA does not have any significant effect related to the overall ESG score. However, further analysis indicated that the social pillar score, in fact, has a positive and significant impact on ROA, while the governance pillar score has the opposite but also significant effect on ROA. The insignificant overall effect of ESG score on ROA could possibly be a result of the insignificant environmental pillar score effect, and also the opposite directions of the effects that the social and governance pillar scores have on ROA. With regard to Tobin's Q, the results showed that ESG score has a positive and significant relation with the Tobin's Q. That result can be possibly attributed to the positive and significant impact of both the environmental pillar and the social pillar on Tobin's Q, while the governance pillar does not have any particular influence on the same financial indicator.

Table 19.4   *Correlation coefficients table*

Variable	ROA	Tobin's Q	ESG score	EPS	SPS	GPS	R&D expenses	Beta	Debt to assets	Log total assets	Industry
ROA	1										
Tobin's Q	0.676*	1									
ESG score	0.274*	0.297*	1								
EPS	0.174	0.206	0.779*	1							
SPS	0.469*	0.455*	0.796*	0,627*	1						
GPS	-0.036	0.030	0.615*	0.388*	0.334*	1					
R&D expenses	0.268*	0.254*	0.118	0.037	0.193	0.019	1				
Beta	0.008	-0.063	0.127	0.161	-0.036	0.139*	-0.209	1			
Debt to assets	-0.189*	-0.314*	-0.011	-0.035	-0.009	0.057	-0.275*	0.038	1		
Log total assets	-0.063	-0.245	0.319*	0.205	0.177	0.139	0.086	0.127	0.409*	1	
Industry	0.394*	0.439*	0.312*	0.285*	0.336*	0.256	0.061	0.236	-0.269*	-0.475*	1

Note: * indicates significance at the 5% level ($p < 0.05$).

Table 19.5   *Results from fixed-effect regression of the ESG scores on ROA and Tobin's Q measures for panel data for the period 2010–2018*

Variables	ESG Score		Environmental Pillar Score		Social Pillar Score		Governance Pillar Score	
	ROA	Tobin's Q	ROA	Tobin's Q	ROA	Tobin's Q	ROA	Tobin's Q
Financial performance indicators	0.100 (0.062)	0.047*** (0.013)	0.029 (0.035)	0.018* (0.007)	0.211*** (0.045)	0.050*** (0.009)	-0.125** (0.037)	-0.009 (0.008)
Research and development expenses	0.006** (0.002)	0.001* (0.0004)	0.006* (0.002)	0.001* (0.0004)	0.005* (0.002)	0.001* (0.0004)	0.005* (0.002)	0.001* (0.0004)
Beta	-2.486 (2.206)	-0.981* (0.461)	-2.875 (2.161)	-1.154* (0.439)	-0.094 (2.143)	-0.515 (0.460)	-3.019 (2.111)	-1.201* (0.449)
Debt to assets	-0.111* (0.056)	-0.034* (0.013)	-0.119* (0.058)	-0.036* (0.014)	-0.083 (0.063)	-0.031* (0.013)	-0.121* (0.060)	-0.040** (0.014)
Log total assets	0.986 (0.705)	-0.242 (0.149)	1.406* (0.641)	-0.079 (0.137)	0.151 (0.639)	-0.293* (0.138)	2.142** (0.594)	0.099 (0.132)
Industry	11.197*** (2.313)	1.591*** (0.491)	12.509*** (2.138)	2.078*** (0.459)	7.342** (2.229)	1.146* (0.479)	15.58*** (2.021)	2.747*** (0.449)
R²	0.279	0.344	0.272	0.314	0.340	0.376	0.305	0.298
Adjusted R²	0.258	0.315	0.251	0.294	0.321	0.358	0.285	0.278
Observations	216	216	216	216	216	216	216	216

Note: The *p* values are two-tailed. The symbols *, ** and *** indicate significances at 10%, 5% and 1%, respectively.

In regard to the control variables, research and development expenses have a positive and significant influence on both financial performance indicators, while both systematic and unsystematic risks have a negative and significant impact on Tobin's Q. Unsystematic risk is the only factor in the group that has negative and significant impact on ROA. Lastly, the industry variable has a strong positive effect on financial performance indicators. Based on the results, we can conclude that the alternative hypothesis is only partially accepted.

SUMMARY AND CONCLUSION

This study investigated a one-way impact of ESG score and its components on one-year lagged financial performance indicators (ROA and Tobin's Q) on balanced Danish company-level data sampled from companies listed on the Danish stock exchange (Nasdaq OMX Copenhagen). To the author's knowledge, this is the first empirical analysis of its kind conducted on Danish public company data with the analysis of financial performance indicators and ESG scores. The analysis comprised a total of 216 observations collected from 24 companies over the 9-year period from 2010 to 2018 (and for dependent variables, from 2011 to 2019). The results demonstrate that ESG scores have an impact only on Tobin's Q but not on ROA, though a positive tendency has been identified, which could be due to a random occurrence. Observed separately, the component parts of the ESG scores affect financial performance indicators differently. For instance, both ROA and Tobin's Q are positively impacted by the social pillar score, while the environmental pillar score positively impacts only Tobin's Q. In contrast, the environmental pillar score has negative indications for both variables, but only significantly affects ROA. As a result of the joint effects of positive SPS and negative GPS, the overall impact of ESG score on ROA is insignificant, while both positive EPS and SPS produce the overall positive and significant impact on Tobin's Q.

The findings of this study are relevant for researchers, regulators and practitioners in regard to establishing stronger regulatory requirements for companies to integrate and comply with initiatives for integrated reporting practices, and also for enhancing the efforts towards conversion of current practices into sustainability-driven business processes. This research enriches our understanding of ongoing practices and the effects of those practices on another geographical region, which provides a building block for understanding the effects of sustainability practices across countries. Given the increasing relevance of this topic, further research on this issue is expected due to the growing importance of CSR awareness not only among companies, but also among investors and the public companies. Such research would also enable practitioners to address those areas that do not contribute to better financial performance indicators and to further examine the issues related to them. Practitioners are invited to boost reporting on ESG pillars in order to enable further investigation on this issue. It is also expected that the relevance of ESG reports will lead to improved standardization and compliance with international regulations, with the reports no longer seen as a marketing greenwashing tool but a reliable source of information (Velte, 2017).

The study is not without limitations. Even though it does not cover a short period of time, one main limitation in this study is the sample size and its lack of proportion to the number of public companies on the Danish market. Another important aspect to be reconsidered in future research is the methodology used for measuring the scores, which may potentially be a subject of subjective influences, and therefore lead to reduced validity of the results. Thus, it is suggested that future research should consider using some alternative measures of ESG pillar scores as broken down elements of the aggregate ESG score.

REFERENCES

Allouche, J., & Laroche, P. (2005). A meta-analytical investigation of the relationship between corporate social and financial performance. *Revue de Gestion des Ressources Humaines*, Eska, pp. 18. hal-00923906

Callan, S. J., & Thomas, J. M. (2009). Corporate financial performance and corporate social performance: An update and reinvestigation. *Corporate Social Responsibility and Environmental Management, 16*, 61–78.

Choi, J., & Wang, H. (2009). Stakeholder relations and the persistence of corporate financial performance. *Strategic Management Journal, 30*(8), 895–907.

Cramer, J. (2003). Corporate social responsibility: Lessons learned. *Environmental Quality Management, 13*(2), 59–66.

Epstein, M. J., & Buhovac, A. R. (2014). *Making Sustainability Work: Best Practices in Managing and Measuring Corporate Social, Environmental, and Economic Impacts.* San Francisco, CA: Berrett-Koehler.

Fischer, T. M., & Sawczyn, A. A. (2013). The relationship between corporate social performance and corporate financial performance and the role of innovation. Evidence from German listed firms. *Journal of Management Control, 24*(2), 27–52.

Freeman, R. E. (1984). *Strategic Management: A Stakeholder Approach.* Boston, MA: Pitman.

Frooman J. (1997). Socially irresponsible and illegal behavior and shareholder wealth: A meta-analysis of event studies. *Business and Society, 36*(3), 221–249.

Godfrey, P. C., Merrill, C. B., & Hansen, J. M. (2009). The relationship between corporate social responsibility and shareholder value: An empirical test of the risk management hypothesis. *Strategic Management Journal, 30*(4), 425–455.

Griffin, J. J. (2000). Corporate social performance: Research directions for the 21st century. *Business and Society, 39*(4), 479–491.

Griffin, J. J., & Mahon, J. F. (1997). The corporate social performance and corporate financial performance debate: Twenty-five years of incomparable research. *Business and Society, 36*(5), 5–31.

Hair, J. F., Black, W. C., Babin, B. J. & Anderson, R. E. (2009). *Multivariate Data Analysis*, 7th Ed. Prentice Hall, NJ: Pearson.

Hellsten, S., & Mallin, C. (2006). Are 'ethical' or 'socially responsible' investments socially responsible? *Journal of Business Ethics, 66*, 393–406.

Hou, T. C-T. (2019). The relationship between corporate social responsibility and sustainable financial performance: Firm-level evidence from Taiwan. *Corporate Social Responsibility and Environmental Management, 26*(1), 19-28.

Hubbard, G. (2009). Measuring organizational performance: Beyond the triple bottom line. *Business Strategy and the Environment, 18*(3), 177–191.

Ittner, C., Larcker, D., & Meyer, M. (2003). Subjectivity and the weighting of performance measures: Evidence from a balanced scorecard. *The Accounting Review, 78*(3), 725–758.

Jensen, M. C., & Meckling, W. H. (1976). Theory of the firm. *Journal of Financial Economics, 3*(4), 305–360.

Kaur, A., & Lodhia, S. (2018). Stakeholder engagement in sustainability accounting and reporting: A study of Australian local councils. *Accounting, Auditing & Accountability Journal, 31*(1), 338–368.

Kogut, B., & Zander, U. (1992). Knowledge of the firm, combinative capabilities and the replication of technology. *Organization Science, 3*(3), 383–397.

Lodhia, S. K. (2012). The need for effective corporate social responsibility/sustainability regulation. In: *Contemporary Issues in Sustainability, Accounting, Assurance and Reporting* (pp. 139 – 152). Bingley, UK: Emerald Group Publishing Ltd.

Margolis, J. D., & Walsh, J. P. (2003). Misery loves companies: Rethinking social initiatives by business. *Administrative Science Quarterly, 48*(2), 268–305.

Maron, I. Y. (2006). Toward a unified theory of the CSP– CFP link. *Journal of Business Ethics 67*(2), 191–200.

Marti, C. P., Rovira-Val, M. R., & Drescher, L. G. J. (2015). Are firms that contribute to sustainable development better financially? *Corporate Social Responsibility and Environmental Management, 22*, 305–319.

McWilliams, A., & Siegel, D. (2000). Corporate social responsibility and financial performance: Correlation or misspecification? *Strategic Management Journal, 21*(5), 603–609.

Moller, A., & Schaltegger, S. (2005). The sustainability balanced scorecard as a framework for eco-efficiency analysis. *Journal of Industrial Ecology, 9*(4), 73–83.

Orlitzky, M., Schmidt, F. L., & Rynes, S. L. (2003). Corporate social and financial performance: A meta-analysis. *Organization Studies, 24*(3), 403–441.

Roberts, P. W., & Dowling, G. R. (2002). Corporate reputation and sustained superior financial performance. *Strategic Management Journal, 23*(12), 1077–1093.

Roman R. M., Hayibor S., & Agle B. R. (1999). The relationship between social and financial performance: Repainting a portrait. *Business and Society, 38*(1), 109–125.

Ross, S. A. (1973). The economic theory of agency. *The American Economic Review, 63*(2), 134–139.

Schaltegger, S. (2012). Sustainability reporting beyond rhetoric: Linking strategy, accounting and communication. In Jones, S. & Ratnatunga, J. (eds) *Contemporary Issues in Sustainability, Accounting, Assurance and Reporting* (pp. 183–195). Bingley, UK: Emerald Group Publishing Ltd.

Schaltegger, S., & Csutora, M. (2012). Carbon accounting for sustainability and management. Status quo and challenges. *Journal of Cleaner Production, 36*, 1–16.

Scholtens, B. (2008). A note on the interaction between corporate social responsibility and financial performance. *Ecological Economics, 68*(1), 46–55.

Schumacher, E. F. (1973). *Small is Beautiful*. London: Blond & Briggs.

Searcy, C. (2012). Corporate sustainability performance measurement systems: A review and research agenda. *Journal of Business Ethics, 107*, 239–253.

Shell. (1998). *People, Planet, Profits*. Rotterdam: Shell.

Unerman, J., & O'Dwyer, B. (2007). The business case for regulation of corporate social responsibility and accountability. *Accounting Forum, 31*, 332–353.

Van Beurden, P., & Gössling, T. (2008). The worth of values – a literature review on the relation between corporate social and financial performance, *Journal of Business Ethics, 82*(2), 407–424.

Velte, P. (2017). Does ESG performance have an impact on financial performance? Evidence from Germany. *Journal of Global Responsibility, 80*(2), 169–178.

Waddock, S. A. (2004). Creating corporate accountability: Foundational principles to make corporate citizenship real. *Journal of Business Ethics, 50*(4), 1–15.

Waddock, S. A., & Graves, S. B. (1997). The corporate social performance–financial performance link. *Strategic Management Journal, 18*(4), 303–319.

Wisner, P., Epstein, M., & Bagozzi, R. (2006). Organizational antecedents and consequences of environmental performance. In M. Freedman & B. Jaggi (Eds.), *Advances in Environmental Accounting and Management* (*3*, 146–167). Bingley: Emerald.

Wu, M. (2006). Corporate social performance, corporate financial performance, and firm size: A meta-analysis. *Journal of American Academy of Business, 8*(1), 163–171.

Yaffee, R. (2003). A primer for panel data analysis. *Connect: Information Technology at NYU*, pp. 1–11.

20. The role of the internal audit function in fostering sustainability reporting

Mara Del Baldo, Selena Aureli and Rosa Lombardi

INTRODUCTION

In the latest decades large corporations have started to voluntarily disclose social, environmental and governance (ESG) information through different channels, i.e., reports, corporate websites, media releases, and CSR (corporate social responsibility), advertising (Cho et al., 2009; Perks et al., 2013). However, the primary communication tools adopted by corporations to respond to stakeholders' information needs and gain legitimacy (Deegan, 2002; Cho et al., 2012; Camilleri, 2015) are CSR reports, sustainability reports and, more recently, integrated reports (IIRC, 2013; Dumay et al., 2016; Mervelskemper & Streit, 2017; de Villiers & Maroun, 2017; de Villiers et al., 2017; Del Baldo, 2017), which integrate financial and non-financial information. These types of reports follow specific standards and guidelines that provide companies with a method to absorb sustainability principles and improve an organization's commitment to sustainable development. Therefore, when a company starts to communicate its social and environmental performance following established frameworks (Cohen et al., 2004; Frias-Aceituno et al., 2014; Mio & Fasan, 2014; Elving et al., 2015; Stacchezzini et al., 2016; Needles et al., 2016; de Villiers & Sharma, 2018), an internal shift toward sustainability behaviour is expected to advance.

Aiming to favour more responsible behaviour among companies and increase corporate transparency, the European Parliament recently issued the EU Directive 2014/95 on non-financial and diversity information (the so-called Non-Financial Directive, NFD) obliging certain companies ("public interest entities") to provide non-financial information and key indicators in their management report. The report will divulge "information on sustainability, such as social and environmental factors, with the view of identifying sustainability risks and increasing investor and consumer trust" (EU, 2014, p. 2).

All Member States have completed the process of transposing the NFD into their own local laws (La Torre et al., 2018). However, the impact of the shift from voluntary to mandatory non-financial reporting is not clear yet (Luque-Vilchez & Larrinaga, 2016; Doni et al., 2019) and its relationship with corporate governance (CG) practices need to be investigated (Michelon & Parbonetti, 2012; Allegrini & Greco, 2013; Baret & Helfrich, 2018).

CG is strongly linked to CSR and to sustainability-oriented strategies (Kolk, 2008; Lombardi et al., 2019). Letza et al. (2004) emphasize that CG does not merely regulate the relations between managers (agents) and shareholders (principals), but encompasses all stakeholders' relations and interests, as CG is about the way in which corporations are directed, administered and controlled that ensures that managers run the firm toward its goals and for the benefit of all stakeholders. Control practices of CG include the notions of compliance, accountability, fairness and transparency, which are the same principles of CSR and sustainability (Jamali et al., 2008). Hence, it is undeniable that, on one hand, sustainability contributes to the goal of

CG and company's success in the long term (Paape et al, 2003; Mihret, 2014; Garcia-Torea et al., 2016), while, on the other hand, the introduction of adequate systems and structures of CG facilitates the achievement of sustainability (Kolk & Pinske, 2010; Blackburn, 2012; Brinkmann & Garren, 2018; Bell & Morse, 2018).

In this scenario, one of the key elements of CG that can help companies to achieve sustainability is the Internal Audit (IA), as its goal is to perform "independent, objective, assurance and consulting activity designed to add value and help an organization accomplish its objectives by bringing a systematic, disciplined approach to evaluate and improve the effectiveness of risk management, control and governance processes" (definition of the Institute of Internal Auditors). The Internal Audit function (IAF) can help identify sustainability risks and assist the board of directors to accomplish corporate objectives related to sustainability (Mihret, 2014).

Nevertheless, there is a lack of studies on the role of the IAF in supporting a company's path toward sustainability. The Chartered Institute of Internal Auditors (2015) states that in the new context of non-financial reporting, IA needs to assume "a broad view across the organisation's systems and processes and it should have a role in providing assurance over the quality of information contained in the strategic and integrated reports". According to the study of Engelbrecht et al. (2018), the IAF may improve integrated reporting by providing assurance on data integrity, reviewing risks and opportunities, evaluating the adequacy of governance and risk management controls and giving assurance on the integrated report itself. Other authors argue that the increase of CSR reporting will enhance the need for consulting services from internal auditors and for independent assurance from external auditors (Holt, 2012; Soh & Martinov-Bennie, 2015). However, these studies mainly report theoretical argumentations or perceptions expressed by internal auditors in interviews, without relating to direct observations. At the same time, experts warn that the IAF should not be involved in the setting of materiality levels, taking decisions on integrated reporting strategy or imposing reporting processes (IIAEC, 2013) as this may cause internal auditors to lose their professional qualities of objectivity and neutrality and make IAF's assurance less credible. Accordingly, the main purpose of this chapter is to investigate the role of the IAF in relation to sustainability reporting and examine whether this department or figure may eventually be involved in the definition of sustainability-oriented strategies.

Since the introduction of the NFD also created the momentum for the implementation of corporate reporting on ESG aspects among companies that never disclosed their approach toward sustainability, this circumstance seemed the most appropriate for when to study the influence of the IAF in guiding, stimulating or dampening the shift toward sustainability. Among Italian listed companies that started reporting on non-financial information after 2017 for the first time, we found a case study that provides interesting insights to elucidate the activities performed by the IAF during and just after the preparation of the first sustainability report.

This case study helps answer the following questions: how does the IAF support ESG/sustainability reporting and does the IAF trigger sustainability-oriented strategies?

The remainder of the chapter is organized as follows. The next section is the literature review recognizing the main streams of research addressing CSR and non-financial disclosure in relation to CG and IA. The third section describes the case study method and the theoretical framework adopted. The fourth section presents our findings, while the fifth section defines conclusions and future research.

LITERATURE REVIEW

The Shift from Voluntary to Mandatory Disclosure of ESG Aspects

In the academic literature we find a great debate on the effectiveness of regulation on sustainability or ESG reporting compared with voluntary reporting (Gunningham, 2007; Perrault Crawford & Williams, 2010; Stubbs & Higgins, 2018). Critics such as Johansen (2016) state that regulation may be dangerous because it increases the risk of "window dressing" (i.e., the misuse of reporting as a public-relations exercise driven by opportunistic and marketing goals). According to Stubbs and Higgins (2018), there is little appetite for regulatory reform among stakeholders other than investors, especially when governments mandate complex reporting frameworks, which are difficult to understand. La Torre et al. (2018) state that the NFD may contribute to fill, but also risk increasing, the gap between non-financial reporting talk and real CSR performance.

On the contrary, researchers in favour of mandatory rules state that regulation makes reporting credible enough to be taken into account by investors. Similarly, several governments and the EU (UNEP, 2010; UN, 2013) assumed regulation on ESG reporting is necessary because of the inefficacy of voluntary reporting, which results in unbalanced, inaccurate, inconsistent and incomparable information (EC, 2013). One of the latest legislative interventions is represented by the European NFD, transposed in Italy with the enactment law 254/2016. The latter obliges large interest entities to prepare a non-financial statement and to obtain external assurance from auditing companies.

The intent of the EU was to use regulation to increase transparency, comparability of information and respond to accountability demands from non-financial stakeholders (Ernst & Young, 2014; Cohen et al., 2015). Regulation was seen as a means to avoid the gaps of voluntary reporting (Adams, 2004; Okoye, 2009; Saleh, 2009; Lock & Seele, 2016). In addition, the NFD was designed to "favour social change, i.e. to encourage companies to manage their social and environmental performance" (from the Preamble of the EU NFD), urging companies to change their behaviour and begin to monitor and manage their social and environmental performance (Aureli et al., 2018). Actually, a similar institutional reform is potentially able to foster multi-stakeholders dialogue and new structures of CG (Ioannou & Serafeim, 2017; Miras-Rodrìguez & Di Pietra, 2018; Höglund et., 2018). As highlighted by Owen et al. (1997) and Larrinaga et al. (2002), regulations (institutional reforms) are capable of increasing companies' accountability more than technical arrangements (administrative reforms), it then follows that the new provisions introduced with the NFD will move corporate behaviour toward a greater attention to stakeholders' needs.

The Contribution of Corporate Governance to Sustainability

CG defines principles, rules and regulations affecting the way a corporation (or company) is directed, administered or controlled by managers in the interests of current and potential investors (Paape et al., 2003; Botez, 2012). Its traditional assumption is that managers depend on their capability to create value for shareholders and the latter ask for several control mechanisms onto managers' actions. However, the scope of CG has recently broadened (especially in Europe and Asia) to consider all stakeholders, including workers, suppliers, customers and the community (Letza et al., 2004).

The 'stakeholder perspective' of CG is strongly linked to CSR (Jamali et al., 2008; Kolk, 2008; Kolk & Pinske, 2010). Both CG and CSR aim to create value for stakeholders. Moreover, studies (Contrafatto, 2011) indicate that CG systems, procedures and organs influence the adoption of CSR strategies and the integration of ESG aspects in annual reports (Adams & McNicholas, 2007; Bebbington et al., 2009) that end up providing a more well-informed picture of corporate performance and better transparency to society (Needles et al., 2018).

Owing to different histories and national regulations, there are currently different types or models of CG that companies can adopt (Mallin, 2004). The one-tier board of directors (also known as a unitary board of directors or monistic system) is a model in which the board of directors functions as a collectively appointed corporate body, including both executive and non-executive directors who work together to achieve a company's long-term sustainable value. This model is widespread in several countries and is the most diffused in Italy, as per the case study analysed in this chapter. By contrast, the two-tier board model (dualistic system) is based on two boards, consisting of high-profile directors, with distinctive tasks. On one hand, there is the management board and on the other hand, the supervisory board, which includes non-executive directors only and monitors the former (Aluchna, 2013).

In both models, CG is highly relevant for company success (Khan et al., 2013). CG has the ultimate objective of realising long-term shareholder value, while taking into account the interests of stakeholders (Johl et al. 2013; Mihret, 2014). As stated by Paape et al. (2003) and Mihret (2014), the quality of CG has a great impact on the efficiency of the assets used, the overall performance and fulfilment of shareholders' and stakeholders' expectations.

The Internal Audit Function

The role of the IAF has been traditionally limited to that of a "watchdog", a key element of the internal control system, and not a key player in supporting the achievement of corporate objectives (Spira & Page, 2003). Its key activity has been to focus on internal information flows and compliance with laws and regulations ensuring the auditability of internal processes and information (Jones & Solomon, 2010). In particular, its primary role has been to monitor the integrity of the financial statements produced by management. However, in the new scenario of CG as a system contributing to the achievement of organizational objectives and value creation for stakeholders, the IAF has expanded its role.

Today, the IAF represents an integral part of the CG structure and one of the mandatory committees of the board of directors that contributes to the achievement of an organization's objectives (Stewart & Subramaniam, 2010; Lenz et al., 2014; Lenz & Hahn, 2015) by providing consultation on issues concerning risks and helping in the definition of control governance mechanisms (Mahzana & Yan, 2014). The IAF is a control mechanism itself, which assists management and the board of directors to accomplish corporate objectives (Mihret, 2014; Dobija, 2015). Moreover, it facilitates the monitoring process of external auditors (serving as a liaison between the external auditor and the board of directors), by reducing information asymmetry and providing internal assurance on financial statements (Magrane & Malthus, 2010).

The expansion of the IAF's role is related to regulation and increased organizational complexity (Allegrini et al., 2006). With the passage of the Sarbanes Oxley Act (SOX), the work of IAF shifted its focus away from traditional assurance services related to compliance and financial audits to move toward risk assessment and more consulting services (Cohen et al., 2010;

Holt, 2012; Jones et al., 2017). In Belgium, the introduction of risk management transformed internal auditors into "teachers" vis-à-vis the different management levels to make them aware of their responsibilities in risk assessment (Sarens & De Beelde, 2006). Two Italian surveys found that the IAF of some large companies was focusing on consulting activities on CG and risk management, despite the fact that the internal auditor is still perceived as an inspector in many other companies (Allegrini & D'Onza, 2003; Allegrini et al., 2006). As a consultant, the IAF attempts to add value through more active support, to management processes, and in some countries is highly geared toward contributing to strategic management (Melville, 2003; Ernst & Young, 2016).

With the diffusion of non-financial reporting, IAF is expected to assure the quality of information contained in sustainability and integrated reports and provide a wide range of guarantees in the production process of information reported, which refers to the following elements (Chartered Institute of Internal Auditors, 2015; Page & Spira, 2016):

- the preparation of non-financial reports;
- identification of risks, especially those concerning reputation, compliance, operational aspects and relations with external stakeholders;
- materiality of non-financial information;
- balance between conciseness and transparency;
- accuracy of the organization's business model reported in the integrated report.

In the current scenario, companies are interested in avoiding reputation damages and destruction of shareholder value due to a failure in handling their non-financial aspects (Kakabadse & Kakabadse, 2007). Therefore, managers may ask the IAF to better account for non-financial performance (Aras & Crowther, 2008) and increase the credibility of company non-financial reports providing assurance (Holt, 2012).

We know that assurance may be provided in many ways, i.e., through external independent audits, stakeholder reviews and the IAF. Independent third-party assurance is preferred by the market, which may not value internal assurance because of a supposed lack of independence. Assurance provided by the IAF is primarily intended for internal stakeholders (e.g., managers and the board of directors) to help them improve the quality of non-financial reporting (Ackers, 2016). Thus, it is presumed that the increase of CSR and non-financial reporting practices will enhance the need for both assurance and consulting services from internal auditors as well as for external assurance (Soh & Martinov-Bennie, 2015).

Nevertheless, changes in the role of the IAF are not so clear cut (Kapoor & Brozzetti, 2012). Engelbrecht et al. (2018) found only a limited number of internal auditors providing any form of assurance on integrated reporting. These authors state that it depends on the stage of maturity of the reporting process (follower, maturity or leader stage). Activities of the IAF may remain confined to checking and reviews of the information reported to create CSR accounts that justify corporate action (Zadek et al., 2004). On the contrary, the IAF may be so pervasive that it participates in the definition of a report's design, goals, scope of content and main recipients. The present empirical research aims to investigate this topic.

RESEARCH METHODOLOGY AND THEORETICAL FRAMEWORK FOR DATA ANALYSIS

Our methodology is based on the case study research, which is useful to describe events in their real-life context (Yin, 2014) and answer "how" or "why" questions about contemporary events (Dumay & Dai, 2016). Starting from our research question, we proposed a single explorative and descriptive case study (Eisenhardt & Graebner, 2007) having the purpose of understanding which aspects of reporting, CG and the company's approach toward sustainability were modified after the new provision. We focused on role of the IAF in supporting the implementation of the sustainability reporting process and the consequent preparation of the first company report.

The case study analysed is relative to an Italian family firm listed on the Milan Stock Exchange, whose board of directors is composed of five executive directors (four of them bound by family ties and representing 51% of the share capital) and three independent members (entitled to independent directors). As previously mentioned, this model (one-tier system) is characterized by a unitary board charged with directing and controlling the company. Since 2003, in Italy, both models coexist but the former is the most widespread among Italian companies.

Despite the large size, the company mission rests on a set of values tied to the family and the local community of origin, such as fairness to all stakeholders, mutual trust and transparency. As described by the literature, family firms may appear less transparent in social reporting compared with firms whose shareholders are not directors (Nekhili et al., 2017; Garcia-Torea et al., 2016), but they often act in a socially responsible manner because they have a relational approach that involves a strong presence and significant roots in the community, greater respect for employees and trusting relationships with partners and suppliers (McGuire et al., 2012; Zellweger et al., 2012; Cennamo et al., 2012). The case study under investigation is an example of this type of family firm.

The company was chosen for two reasons. First, it never communicated ESG information before the law that enacted the NFD in Italy. Second, its board of directors decided to entrust the design and preparation of the first sustainability report to the IAF, and not to the marketing or communication department, nor to the finance function or the investor relator office. This is how the change took off as declared by the President and CEO in the 2017 sustainability report:

> Starting from requirements of the new regulation, we have taken the opportunity to do more. We started an internal and external process of reflection on the themes of sustainability with the aim to guarantee transparency towards all stakeholders while taking a current photo of our company and beginning to delineate new sustainability paths to take in the short and long term. In this way, the first sustainability report was born.

Although particular types of evidence are not required in the case study methodology, we defined a research protocol to ensure research reliability (Yin, 2014) and identify key informants to interview, and the questions. Semi-structured interviews (Qu & Dumay, 2011) were addressed to three selected members of the board of directors, namely two independent members (also sometimes known as outside directors, who sit at the board of directors but do not have a material or pecuniary relationship with the company or related persons, except sitting fees) and one executive director, and to two members of IA function. The aim of the interview was to understand the following aspects: (i) the activities and procedures started by the company when the legislation came into force; (ii) the role that CG was expected to play; and (iii) the activities planned and implemented by the IAF. Additionally, we accessed the first sustainability report regarding year 2017, the 2018 sustainability report and the latest annual report.

Information collected from interviews and official documents, such as the sustainability report and the annual report, were analysed using content analysis. All results were discussed among the authors to guarantee investigator triangulation and with the people interviewed achieving the results validation (Yin, 2014). Triangulation of data stemming from the different interviewees and documentary sources enhances trustworthiness (Lincoln & Guba, 1985) and contextualizes the data (Van Bommel, 2014).

The changes put in place in the analysed company are described through the institutional theory (DiMaggio & Powell, 1983; Scott, 1995; Dacin et al., 2002) understanding why the IAF was chosen by the board of directors as the "actor of change" and what influenced the implementation of the sustainability report. Institutional theory is extensively adopted in the accounting research stream (Hoque, 2018; Brammer & Pavelin, 2006) and is useful to explain CG (Aguilera, 2005; Adegbite, 2015), sustainability reporting (Bebbington et al., 2009; Baldarelli et al., 2014; Del Brado, 2012) and the IAF role (as performed by Jones et al., 2017, who analysed the impact of SOX legislation on the IA function).

Institutional theory explains organizational change as driven by legitimacy, i.e., the need to conform to expectations, recommendations or pressures of the social environment. These pressures are classified into three types (see Figure 20.1), corresponding to the concepts of organizations' changes: (i) coercive, (ii) mimetic and (iii) normative (Di Maggio & Powell, 1983; Scott, 1995). First, coercive change justifies organizational changes depending on external factors' influences, such as regulation and government. Therefore, legitimacy is a consequence of obedience to non-legal and legal obligations. Second, mimetic change identifies the organization's imitation of procedures and/or structures from other closer organizations. Third, the normative change determines the company's adoption of procedures and/or structures assumed by main professional organizations and dominant professions. In other words, legitimacy occurs via the adaptation of a commonly accepted framework.

FINDINGS AND DISCUSSION

Documents and interviews indicate that before the NFD was enacted, the company never reflected on how much its actions could impact on society and the environment. However, it has always been concerned about social and environmental effects deriving from its investment projects ("the company cannot disregard the territory in which it operates") and used to support several local charities and associations. In addition, the board of directors has always taken care of relations with employees and trade unions. As one director said: "our people are important, and even during the worldwide financial crisis of 2008/2009, we retained the entire workforce". Therefore, the new provision was conceived by the board as "an opportunity to enhance company's social-environmental sensitivity and its attention to the local community that has historically characterised the group". In other words, it was "an opportunity to put things that already existed in place", marking a shift from walking (CSR and sustainability) to talking.

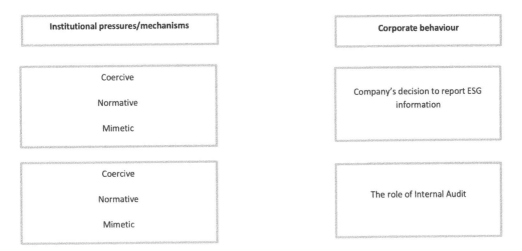

Figure 20.1   Institutional pressures and corporate behaviour dimensions

In this context, the board of directors decided to entrust the IAF to guide the company in the process of change required by the preparation of the mandatory non-financial statement. The IA of the company felt the "duty to trigger the evolution of the organisational culture toward sustainability" and elicit the process of internal change required by the preparation of the non-financial statement. In other words, regulation has "pushed the sustainability issue into the boardroom" and then the board endorsed the IAF to implement the reporting process, because the IAF was held as the unique function capable of helping the board and senior management in this challenge. The IA function was chosen because its personnel "has great knowledge of the company's processes and structure, and is able to interact with people of different functions and branches". Moreover, the board engaged the IAF "to get comfort over data" as the "IAF is held to work with objectivity" and grant data integrity. Finally, "the internal auditor had sufficient standing and authority within the organization that could enable it to accomplish this activity".

Adopting an institutional lens to understand what happened in the case study, we may state that the reporting of ESG aspects was driven by the new legislation (coercive pressure) reinforced by the sensitivity of the board of directors toward the local territory and the pre-existing informal-based sustainability orientation of the business model of family firms (Nekhili et al., 2017). The company never felt the need to prepare a social or sustainability report due to normative pressures because "it never had problems or received criticism raised from stakeholders". In addition, no need for imitation or mimetic behaviour emerged. Looking at its two most direct competitors, "none of them ever prepared a CSR or sustainability report".

On the contrary, the choice of delegating the IAF to design the reporting process is not related to the legislation, which actually defines managers and directors as key responsible subjects. Nor is the choice similar to what other companies do: the survey of EY (2013) indicates that the responsibility for designing and releasing the sustainability report usually lies in a specialized CSR department or alternatively rests on other departments, such as marketing, investor relations or the finance department. The IAF was identified as the "internal key agent", who started and managed the internal process driving toward sustainability reporting, because both the sensitivity and the competences of the Chief Internal Auditor made him serve as a "facilitator", someone who "may have played a technical and very supportive role in helping the company to prepare its sustainability report" (as reported by an independent board member).

The choice of how to report non-financial information and which reporting standard or framework to adopt was taken by the board based on suggestions provided by the IAF. After going for dedicated CSR training promoted by auditing firms in Milan and supported by an external consulting company, the Chief Internal Auditor proposed the preparation of a sustainability report according to the GRI guidelines instead of preparing a simpler non-financial statement as allowed by the legislation. "We looked at what listed and unlisted companies that manufacture similar goods report and we had some explorative meetings with accountancy and auditing firms. In the end, we perceived that the GRI standard was the best one."

Preference for GRI guidelines, among the different national, European and international standards that Italian companies are allowed to choose, reveals that the board was somehow influenced by what was suggested by professional auditing firms (normative rule) and by mimetic pressures (what other companies used to report on ESG aspects). More importantly, the use of GRI guidelines, whose application requires a great investment, indicates that the company was not trying to make the minimum effort to obey regulation. According to the Chief Internal Auditor "the choice of following the GRI framework was fundamental because it helped the company understand what to do and which steps to take" and helped him to plan the necessary activities that compelled a change in some internal processes.

Although a sustainability report is addressed to all stakeholders by definition, the content of the company's sustainability report analysed here reveals that the preferred interlocutors are investors, customers and employees. This is also confirmed in the interviews. "Today sustainability issues 'count'; both traditional investors and socially responsible investment funds increasingly ask for this type of information." In addition, there are some "very important customers attentive to the issues of sustainability, so having a formalised sustainability strategy and communicating it through a report can make a difference with our competitors." Finally, the CEO argues that the report has also become a key tool of corporate communication addressed to other stakeholders. "Our report is useful to provide a more comprehensive picture of the group to employees and attract young talents". These findings indicate that the company is conforming to the widespread idea, emphasized by both academic literature and professionals, that investors are the salient addressees of sustainability reports (normative pressure), while the transposition law does not make any difference or prioritization among stakeholders.

From a practical point of view, the implementation process for sustainability reporting guided by the IAF included the key following activities:

- the identification of company stakeholders and the creation of a materiality matrix through the organization of several internal meetings;
- the creation of a map of company risks related to sustainability (strategic, operational, financial & reporting, and compliance risks), which were included in the Enterprise Risk Management process if they were not already considered;
- supervision of processes devoted to collect non-financial data;
- changes in CG structures and processes.

Most of the ideas related to how to implement the new reporting tool were triggered by the Chief Internal Auditor, who emerged as the key actor of the process of change because reporting brought a reflection on company's strategy related to sustainability, as he argues:

Sustainability in business relates to two key aspects: strategy and reporting. In our company reporting was viewed as the first critical step to possibly define a sustainability strategy because reporting was necessary to help the whole organisation to understand the impact on the economy, society and environment. In other terms, a sustainability strategy can become meaningful only if based on reliable data.

This perspective is confirmed by the executive board member:

With our first sustainability report we responded to a legal obligation, but more importantly, we have triggered an internal and external process of active reflection on the issues of sustainability. This first step allowed us to define a new sustainability journey and objectives related to the short and long term.

The first and most time-consuming activity guided by the IAF was the organization of internal meetings to create the materiality matrix. The IAF invited top managers of every company department to collect data on the processes they govern, identify who is impacted by their actions and estimate the related impacts. During meetings with managers, he sometimes felt the need to be (and serve as) a teacher for those that did not fully understand the relevance of sustainability matters.

Almost all functions participated in the drafting of the materiality matrix and we jointly decided what to put in the sustainability report. The aim was to mirror what the company really does in the document and not to draw up a report that merely advertises the company. The attempt of some people of the marketing area to transform the report into a communication tool on company products and innovation was stopped shortly thereafter.

The second demanding activity governed by the IAF was the mapping of the most significant risks linked to sustainability. In detail, the IAF gathered company managers to reflect on and identify possible sustainability risks. "Although the company already adopted an ERM [Enterprise Risk Management] model, the monitoring of risks linked to sustainability required additional work and became an integral part of the company's business strategy".

Another important activity, among the duties attributed to the IAF, refers to the supervision of the reliability of data disclosed in the sustainability report. This was a very demanding activity that required new procedures to supervise the company's internal processes established to collect, elaborate and visualize data. This is not a proper process of internal assurance, but it reinforces data reliability. Non-financial information reported is scrutinized by the board of statutory auditors and is audited by an external accounting firm as required by the Italian law ("The document has been submitted to limited assurance engagement performed by an auditing firm according to the criteria indicated by the ISAE 3000 Revised principle").

Finally, the IAF discussed and revised the anti-corruption code of conduct with the Control and Risk Committee (created within the board of directors). In 2017, the company adopted a new anti-corruption code of conduct (in addition to the previous one introduced in 2010) to strengthen the group's commitment to the principles that all employees and collaborators must observe to ensure compliance with anti-corruption regulations in force. Both active and passive corruption are key aspects to disclose according to the Italian law on non-financial reporting. It is important to notice that the IAF informs the Control and Risk Committee for all aspects of compliance and supervision required by the preparation of the sustainability report.

In addition, the IAF periodically meets the Control and Risk Committee to submit technical proposals, which are discussed and approved by the board.

Results indicate that the IAF did not act as an inspector (Allegrini & D'Onza, 2003), but he acted as a consultant and had a key supporting role. It served as educator within the organization, providing technical advice and favouring meetings and discussions within the company on sustainability topics (Sarens & De Beelde, 2006). To carry out all activities, the structure of the IA function was strengthened. A new office within the IAF with dedicated personnel was created to manage all procedures related to the preparation of the sustainability report. This office is in charge of entrusting the supervision of sustainability issues to the Control and Risk committee, in the absence of a sustainability committee within the board. The IA periodically met the Control and Risk committee to submit technical proposals, to be approved by the board.

Therefore, the IAF highly contributed to triggering a change in the organizational culture by spreading knowledge about sustainability and thus "contaminating" the strategic management of the company (Melville, 2003).

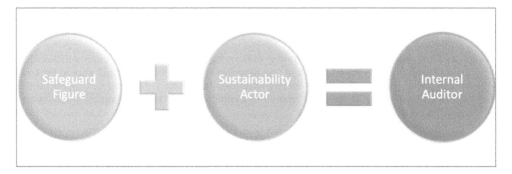

Figure 20.2   The role of IA function

The IAF represented the main actor in the preparation of the first sustainability report by making more certain the data collected and disclosed (safeguarding figure) and by suggesting how to identify and report relevant non-financial information (sustainability actor) (Figure 20.2). As one member of the board of directors states, most of the ideas concerning how to implement the new reporting tool were triggered by the IAF. "Decisions were not planned by the board but were proposed by the IAF and/or the CFO following a bottom-up approach." A synthesis of the nature of changes occurred and the key role of the IAF is provided by another member of the board:

> The regulation itself did not impose operational changes. The impact of the regulation was cultural because it forced us to introduce new concepts and address sustainability issues within the company to better communicate with stakeholders … The key actor in the changes put in place was the IAF.

Thanks to the activities associated with the drafting of the sustainability report, the IAF made directors and managers realize that many aspects related to CSR were not treated so far, and more environmental-friendly investments and initiatives had to be planned for the future. As one interviewed says, the company is now aware of the relevant change introduced by the regulation and knows that the increasing debate on CSR inside and outside the organization will never stop. Thus, the company is called to continue to reflect on these issues.

CONCLUSION

This work investigates the changes that occurred in an Italian listed company that never disclosed sustainability information before the transposition of the NFD in Italy. We found that the new reporting obligation greatly involved the IAF, which had a key role in designing the reporting framework, implementing the new processes associated with the collection of non-financial information, and also in disseminating the culture of sustainability within the organization.

The main changes are described through the lenses of institutional theory (DiMaggio & Powell, 1983; Scott, 1995; Clemens & Douglas, 2005), which helped us understand why the company opted for a specific type of reporting and why the IAF achieved such a pivotal role (Table 20.1).

The provisions introduced with the NFD elicited a change in corporate behaviour that in only six months has gone from nothing to the preparation of a full sustainability report according to GRI guidelines. However, legal obligations are not strict and leave room for manoeuvring to companies. Therefore, normative and mimetic pressures were more influencing than coercive pressures in defining the reporting process.

Findings show that preference for a sustainability report prepared according to GRI principles is mainly due to normative pressures stemming from the professional culture, while mimetic pressures i.e., mimicking what other organizations do, had a minor influence. Normative pressures are informed by standards of appropriate behaviours communicated to those within a particular profession through their involvement with professional training institutions and universities (i.e., workshops, seminars, professional magazines) (Galaskiewicz & Wasserman, 1989). In this case, normative pressures are revealed because the company and its IAF decided to draw upon a specific professional resource pool such as the auditing community.

Findings also show that the engine of this project of change was the IAF. Since the legislation does not list the internal auditor among the people responsible for the preparation of the non-financial statement, our findings suggest that companies do not always conform their behaviour to what is required by rules or widespread practices (isomorphism is not the only possible answer to external pressures), but they may provide different responses (Deloitte, 2013).

In this case study, the Chief Internal Auditor guided the company in the process of internal reflection and change based on the mandatory non-financial statement adoption, while trying to act as an independent safeguard figure (Mahzana & Yan, 2014) capable of taking care of the preparation of the sustainability report and the managing of sustainability issues through the definition of governance processes and practices (Cohen et al., 2010; Holt, 2012; Jones et al., 2017).

Different from what is anticipated by the literature, the IAF does not only monitor the reporting process and contribute to data reliability offering internal assurance (Chartered Institute of Internal Auditors, 2015); in our case study the IAF was a facilitator, had a more active role in the project of change required by the law and acted as a point of reference for managers offering knowledge and orientation toward sustainability issues and objectives.

Table 20.1   Types of pressures and corporate behaviour dimensions

	Coercive	Normative	Mimetic
Company's decision to report ESG information	The company had to start reporting non-financial information as required by the Italian law enacting the NFD.	The company was influenced by normative rules stemming from specialized consultants and the professional audit culture, which led the company to opt for the use of GRI guidelines. Key interlocutors of the sustainability report are investors, customers and employees; this is partially influenced by the common culture of increasing the provision of non-financial information to investors.	The company was influenced by the widespread use of GRI guidelines among listed and unlisted Italian companies.
The role of IAF	According to the law, the board of directors is responsible for the non-financial statement, while responsibilities of control are attributed to the board of statutory auditors and the auditing firm. Therefore, no coercive pressure led to the choice of the IAF as key actor of change	The IAF acts as a "guarantor" of non-financial data reliability, in line with the institutional goal of "contributing to the improvement of internal procedures and internal efficiency" typical of the professional audit culture. The IAF offers "consultancy" by providing technical advices to the board, in line with its contributing role to CG. The IAF also submits technical proposals to the Control and Risk Committee contributing to strategic management. The IAF also had a supportive role, acting as "facilitator" of the whole reporting process (favouring meetings and discussions within the company and triggering a sustainability-driven culture within the organization) and affecting the strategic management process by enhancing the board's orientation toward sustainability issues.	

While one may raise doubts about the independence of the IAF and reliability of non-financial data, drawing from the case study we may see the proactive role of the IAF as extremely valuable because based on profound knowledge of the company, laws and regulations, it also acted as a "defence" against possible attempts to transform the sustainability report as a marketing tool that does not correspond to real practices. This role is in line with an "enriched" institutional goal of the IAF and reinforces the contribution of the IAF to the goals of CG: the reporting process contributes to reflecting and achieving the company's objectives on sustainability. Despite acting as a mere "promoter-facilitator" of ESG activities by legislation, the IAF contributes to the strategic management, playing a pivotal role in providing technical advice, favouring meetings and discussions within the company about sustainability issues, supporting top managers to collect, disclose and communicate data on the ESG process they govern, and entrusting the supervision of sustainability issues to the Control and Risk committee.

The limitations of this chapter derive from the analysis of one case study, although we propose to refer to an analytic generalization of results (Yin, 2014). Future research might extend the analysis to other Italian and international companies. Additionally, future research should be directed to understanding whether other changes in CG practices are associated with the regulation on non-financial reporting.

ACKNOWLEDGEMENT

All authors have contributed equally.

REFERENCES

Ackers, B. (2016). An exploration of internal audit's corporate social responsibility role – Insights from South Africa. *Social Responsibility Journal, 12*(4), 719–739.

Adams, C. (2004). The ethical, social and environmental reporting-performance portrayal gap. *Accounting, Auditing, Accountability Journal, 17*(5), 731–757.

Adams, C. A., & McNicholas, P. (2007). Making a difference; sustainability reporting, accountability and organisational change. *Accounting, Auditing and Accountability Journal, 20*(3), 382–402.

Adegbite, E. (2015). Good corporate governance in Nigeria: Antecedents, propositions and peculiarities. *International Business Research, 24*, 319–30.

Aguilera, R. (2005). Corporate governance and director accountability: An institutional comparative perspective. *British Journal of Management, 16*(1), S39–S53.

Allegrini, M., & D'Onza, G. (2003). Internal auditing and risk assessment in large Italian companies: An empirical survey. *International Journal of Auditing, 7*(3), 191–208.

Allegrini, M., D'Onza, G., Paape, L., Melville, R., & Sarens, G. (2006). The European literature review on internal auditing. *Managerial Auditing Journal, 21*(8), 845–853.

Allegrini, M., & Greco, G. (2013). Corporate boards, audit committees and voluntary disclosure: Evidence from Italian listed companies. *Journal of Management and Governance, 17*(1), 187–216.

Aluchna, M. (2013). "Two-tier board". In: S. O. Idowu, N. Capaldi, L. Zu, & A. D. Gupta (Eds.), *Encyclopedia of Corporate Social Responsibility*. Berlin, Heidelberg: Springer, 2575–2587.

Aras, G., & Crowther, D. (2008). Corporate sustainability reporting: A study in disingenuity? *Journal of Business Ethics, 87*(1), 279–288.

Aureli S., Magnaghi E., & Salvatori F. (2018). The transposition of the non-financial reporting directive in UK, France and Italy, *Symphonia Emerging Issues in Management*, 1, 48–67. http://dx.doi.org/10.4468/2018.1.04aureli.magnaghi.salvatori

Baldarelli, M. G., Del Baldo, M., & Nesheva-Kiosseva, N. (2014). Implementing sustainability reporting: (Neo)institutional theory insights in the analysis of SGR Group Italy and CityGas Bulgaria. *Journal of Modern Accounting and Auditing, 10/11*(114), 1067–1104.

Baret, P., & Helfrich, V. (2018). The "trilemma" of non-financial reporting and its pitfalls. *Journal of Management and Governance, 23*(2), 485–511.

Bebbington, J., Higgins, C., & Frame, B. (2009). Initiating sustainable development reporting: Evidence from New Zealand. *Accounting, Auditing, and Accountability Journal, 22*(4), 588–625.

Bell, S., & Morse, S. (2018). *Routledge Handbook of Sustainability Indicators.* London: Routledge, 1539–1552.

Blackburn, W.R. (2012). *The Sustainability Handbook: The Complete Management Guide to Achieving Social, Economic and Environmental Responsibility.* London: Routledge.

Brinkmann, R., & Garren, S. J. (2018). *The Palgrave Handbook of Sustainability: Case Studies*: London: Palgrave, 58.

Botez, D. (2012). Internal audit and management entity. *Procedia Economics and Finance, 3*, 1156–1160.

Brammer, S., & Pavelin, S. (2006). Voluntary environmental disclosures by large UK companies. *Journal of Business Finance & Accounting, 33*(7-8), 1168–1188.

Camilleri, M. A. (2015). Environmental, social and governance disclosures in Europe. *Sustainability Accounting, Management and Policy Journal, 6*(2), 224–242.

Cennamo, C., Berrone, P., Cruz, C., & Gomez-Mejia, L. (2012). Socioemotional wealth and proactive stakeholder engagement: Why family controlled firms care more about their stakeholders. *Entrepreneurship Theory and Practice, 36*(6), 1153–1173.

Chartered Institute of Internal Auditors (2015). The role of internal audit in non-financial and integrated reporting. Definition necessary? *Journal of Business Ethics, 89*(4), 613–627.

Cho, C. H., Phillips, J. R., Hageman, A. M., & Patten, D. (2009). Media richness, user trust, and perceptions of corporate social responsibility: An experimental investigation of visual website disclosures. *Accounting, Auditing and Accountability Journal, 22*(6), 933–952.

Cho, C. H., Freedman, M., & Patten, D. M. (2012). Corporate disclosure of environmental capital expenditures. *Accounting, Auditing and Accountability Journal, 25*(3), 486–507.

Clemens, B. W., & Douglas, T. (2005). Understanding strategic responses to institutional pressures. *Journal of Business Research, 58*(9), 1205–1213.

Cohen, J., Krishnamoorthy, G., & Wright, A. (2004). The corporate governance mosaic and financial reporting quality. *Journal of Accounting Literature, 23*, 87–152.

Cohen, J., Krishnamoorthy, G., & Wright, A. (2010). Corporate governance in the post-Sarbanes-Oxley era: Auditors' experiences. *Contemporary Accounting Research, 27*(3), 751–786.

Cohen, R., Holder-Webb, L., & Zamora, V.L. (2015). Nonfinancial information preferences of professional investors. *Behavioral Research in Accounting, 27*(2), 127–153.

Contrafatto, M. (2011). Social & environmental accounting and engagement research: Reflections on the state of the art & new research avenues. *Economia Aziendale. Online, 2*(3), 273–289.

Dacin, M. T., Goodstein, J., & Scott, W. R. (2002). Institutional theory and institutional change: Introduction to the special research forum. *Academy of Management Journal, 45*(1), 45–56.

Deegan, C. (2002). Introduction: The legitimising effect of social and environmental disclosures. A theoretical foundation. *Accounting, Auditing and Accountability Journal, 15*(3), 282–311.

de Villiers, C., & Maroun, W. (2017). Introduction to sustainability accounting and integrated reporting. In: C. de Villiers, & W. Maroun (Eds.), *Sustainability Accounting and Integrated Reporting.* Oxford: Routledge, 13–24.

de Villiers, C., & Sharma, U. (2018). A critical reflection on the future of financial, intellectual capital, sustainability and integrated reporting. *Critical Perspectives on Accounting.* Accessed on 11/07/ 2017 from https://doi.org/10.1016/j.cpa.2017.05.003.

de Villiers, C., Venter, E. R., & Hsiao, P. C. K. (2017). Integrated reporting: Background, measurement issues, approaches and an agenda for future research. *Accounting and Finance, 57*(4), 937–959.

Del Baldo, M. (2012). Corporate social responsibility and corporate governance in Italian SMEs: The experience of some "spirited businesses". *Journal of Management and Governance, 16*(1), 1–36.

Del Baldo, M. (2017). The implementation of integrating reporting in SMEs. Insights from a pioneering experience in Italy. *Meditari Accountancy Research, 25*(4), 505–532.

Deloitte (2013). *CFO Insights Sustainability: Why CFOs Are Driving Savings and Strategy.* London, UK: Deloitte University Press.

DiMaggio, P., & Powell, W. (1983). The Iron Cage revisited: Institutional isomorphism and collective rationality in organizational fields. *American Sociological Review, 48*(2), 147–160.

Dobija, D. (2015). Exploring audit committee practices: Oversight of financial reporting and external auditors in Poland. *Journal of Management and Governance, 19*, 113–143.

Doni, F., Bianchi Martini, S., Corvino, A., & Mazzoni, M. (2019). Voluntary versus mandatory non-financial disclosure: EU Directive 95/2014 and sustainability reporting practices based on empirical evidence from Italy. *Meditari Accountancy Research, 28*(5), 781–802. https://doi.org/10.1108/MEDAR-12-2018-0423

Dumay, J., & Dai, T. (2016). Integrated thinking as a cultural control? *Meditari Accountancy Research, 25*(4), 574–604.

Dumay, J., Bernardi, C., Guthrie, J., & Demartini, P. (2016). Integrated reporting: A structured literature review. *Accounting Forum, 40*(3), 166–185.

Eisenhardt, K. M., & Graebner, M. E. (2007). Theory building from cases: Opportunities and challenges. *Academy of Management Journal, 50*(1), 25–32.

Elving, W. J., Golob, U., Podnar, K., Ellerup-Nielsen, A., & Thomson, C. (2015). The bad, the ugly and the good: New challenges for CSR communication. *Corporate Communications: An International Journal, 20*(2), 118–127.

Engelbrecht, L., Yasseen, Y., & Omarjee, I. (2018). The role of the internal audit function in integrated reporting: A developing economy perspective. *Meditari Accountancy Research, 26*(4), 657–674.

Ernst & Young (2014). *Sustainability reporting – the time is now.* Accessed on 05/02/2018 from http://www.ey.com/Publication/vwLUAssets/EY_Sustainability_reporting_ _the_time_is_now/$FILE/EY-Sustainability-reporting-the-time-is-now.pdf.

Ernst & Young (2016). *Top Priorities for US Boards in 2017.* EY Center for Board Matters Accessed on 16/07/2019 from https://www.ey.com/Publication/vwLUAssets/ey-top-priorities-for-us-boards-in-2017/$FILE/ey-top-priorities-for-us-boards-in-2017.pdf

European Commission (2013). *Impact Assessment.* Accessed on 06/04/2018 from https://eur-lex.europa.eu/legal-content/EN/TXT/?uri=CELEX%3A52013SC0127

European Union Directive (2014). *2014/95/EU of the European Parliament and of the Council of 22 October 2014 amending Directive 2013/34/EU as regards disclosure of non-financial and diversity information by certain large undertakings and groups,* available at https://eur-lex.europa.eu/legal-content/EN/TXT/?uri=CELEX%3A32014L0095

EY Report (2013). Sustainability reporting – the time is now. Ernst & Young.

Frìas-Aceituno, J. V., Rodrìguez-Ariza, L., & Garcìa-Sànchez, I. M. (2014). Explanatory factors of integrated sustainability and financial reporting. *Business Strategy and the Environment, 23*(1), 56–72.

Galaskiewicz, J., & Wasserman, S. (1989). Mimetic processes within an interorganizational field: An empirical test. *Administrative Science Quarterly, 34*(3), 454–479.

Garcia-Torea, N., Fernandez-Feijoo, B., & de la Cuesta, M. (2016). Board of director's effectiveness and the stakeholder perspective of corporate governance: Do effective boards promote the interests of shareholders and stakeholders? *Business Research Quarterly, 19*, 246–260.

Gunningham, N. (2007). Corporate environmental responsibility: Law and the limits of voluntarism. In: D. McBarnet, A. Voiculescu, & T. Campbell (Eds.), *The New Corporate Accountability: Corporate Social Responsibility and the Law.* Cambridge: Cambridge University Press, 476–500.

Höglund, L., Mårtensson, M., & Safari, A. (2018). Expectations and the performance of governance functions between a board, management and other stakeholders: The case of Robotdalen. *Journal of Management and Governance, 22*, 805–827.

Holt, T. P. (2012). The effects of internal audit role and reporting relationships on investor perceptions of disclosure credibility. *Managerial Auditing Journal, 27*(9), 878–898.

Hoque, Z. (2018). *Methodological Issues in Accounting Research.* London: Spiramus Press.

IIAEC (2013). *The Role of IA in Nonfinancial and IR.* The Institute of Internal Auditors Audit Executive Centre.

IIRC (2013). *The International Framework,* December, International Integrated Reporting Council Accessed on 05/07/2019 from http://integratedreporting.org/wp-content/uploads/2013/12/13-12-08-THE-INTERNATIONAL-IR-FRAMEWORK-2-1.pdf

Ioannou, I., & Serafeim, G. (2017). The consequences of mandatory corporate sustainability reporting. *Harvard Business School Research,* Working Paper No. 11-100, 156–171.

Jamali, D., Safieddine, A. M., & Rabbath, M. (2008). Corporate governance and corporate social responsibility synergies and interrelationships. *Corporate Governance: An International Review, 16*(5), 443–459.

Johansen, T. R. (2016). EU regulation of corporate social and environmental reporting. *Social and Environmental Accountability Journal, 36*(1), 1–9.

Johl, S. K., Johl, S. K., Subramaniam, N., & Cooper, B. (2013). Internal audit function, board quality and financial reporting quality: Evidence from Malaysia. *Managerial Auditing Journal, 28*(9), 780–814.

Jones, K., Baskerville, R. L., Sriram, R. S., & Balasubramaniam, Ramesh (2017). The impact of legislation on the internal audit function. *Journal of Accounting & Organizational Change, 13*(4), 450–470.

Jones, M. J., & Solomon, J. F. (2010). Social and environmental report assurance: Some interview evidence. *Accounting Forum, 34*(1), 20–31.

Kakabadse, A., & Kakabadse, N. (2007). *CSR in Practice: Delving Deep.* New York: Palgrave Macmillan.

Kapoor, G., & Brozzetti, M. (2012). The transformation of internal auditing. *Critical Perspective of Accounting Journal, 82*(8), 32–35.

Khan, A., Muttakin, M. B., & Siddiqui, J. (2013). Corporate governance and corporate social responsibility disclosures: Evidence from an emerging economy. *Journal of Business Ethics, 114*, 207–223.

Kolk, A. (2008). Sustainability, accountability, and corporate governance: Exploring multinationals' reporting practices. *Business Strategy and the Environment, 17*(1), 1–15.

Kolk, A., & Pinkse, J. (2010). The integration of corporate governance in corporate social disclosures. *Corporate Social Responsibility and Environmental Management, 17*(1), 15–26.

La Torre, M., Sabelfeld, S., Blomkvist, M., Tarquinio, L., & Dumay, J. (2018). Harmonising non-financial reporting regulation in Europe: Practical forces and projections for future research. *Meditari Accountancy Research*, https://doi.org/10.1108/MEDAR-02-2018-0290.

Larrinaga, C., Carrasco, F., Correa, C., Llena, F., & Moneva, J. (2002). Accountability and accounting regulation: The case of the Spanish environmental disclosure standard. *European Accounting Review, 11*(4), 723–740.

Lenz, R., & Hahn, U. (2015). A synthesis of empirical internal audit effectiveness literature pointing to new research opportunities. *Managerial Auditing Journal, 30*(1), 5–33.

Lenz, R., Sarens, G., & D'Silva, K. (2014). Probing the discriminatory power of characteristics of internal audit functions: Sorting the wheat from the chaff. *International Journal of Auditing, 18*(2), 126–138.

Letza, S., Sun, X., & Kirkbride, J. (2004). Shareholding versus stake-holding: A critical review of corporate governance. *Corporate Governance: An International Review, 12*(3), 242–263.

Lincoln, Y. S., & Guba, E. G. (1985). *Naturalistic Inquiry*, Vol. 75. Thousand Oaks, CA: Sage.

Lock, I., & Seele, P. (2016). The credibility of CSR reports in Europe. Evidence from a quantitative content analysis in 11 countries. *Journal of Cleaner Production, 122*, 186–200.

Lombardi, R., Trequattrini, R., Cuozzo, B., & Cano Rubio, M. (2019). Corporate corruption prevention, sustainable governance and legislation: First exploratory evidence from the Italian scenario. *Journal of Cleaner Production, 217*, 666–675.

Luque-Vilchez, M., & Larrinaga, C. (2016). Reporting models do not translate well: Failing to regulate CSR reporting in Spain. *Social and Environmental Accountability Journal, 36*(1), 56–75.

Magrane, J., & Malthus, S. (2010). Audit committee effectiveness: A public sector case study. *Managerial Auditing Journal, 25*(June), 427–443. DOI: 10.1108/02686901011041821

Mahzana, N., & Yan, C. M. (2014). Harnessing the benefits of corporate governance and internal audit: Advice to SME. *Procedia – Social and Behavioral Sciences, 115*, 156–165.

Mallin, C. A. (2004). *Corporate Governance.* Oxford: Oxford University Press.

McGuire, J., Dow, S., & Ibrahim, B. (2012). All in the family? Social performance and corporate governance in the family firm. *Journal of Business Research, 65*(11), 1643–1650.

Mervelskemper, L., & Streit, D. (2017). Enhancing market valuation of ESG performance: Is integrated reporting keeping its promise? *Business Strategy and the Environment, 26*(4), 536–549.

Mihret, G. M. (2014). How can we explain internal auditing? The inadequacy of agency theory and a labor process alternative, *Critical Perspectives on Accounting, 25*, 771–782.

Melville, R. (2003). The contribution internal auditors make to strategic management. *International Journal of Auditing, 7*(3), 209–222.

Michelon, G., & Parbonetti, A. (2012). The effect of corporate governance on sustainability disclosure. *Journal of Management and Governance, 16*(3), 477–509.

Mio, C., & Fasan, M. (2014). Beyond financial reporting: A journey from sustainability towards integrated reporting. *Journal of Environmental Accounting and Management, 2*(3), 1–14.

Miras-Rodrìguez, M., & Di Pietra, R. (2018). Corporate governance mechanisms as drivers that enhance the credibility and usefulness of CSR disclosure. *Journal of Management and Governance*, *22*(3), 565–588.

Needles Jr., B. E., Frigo, M. L., Powers, M., & Shigaev, A. (2016). *Integrated Reporting and Sustainability Reporting: An Exploratory Study of High Performance Companies*. In: M. J. Epstein, F. Verbeeten, & S. K. Widener (Eds.), *Performance Measurement and Management Control: Contemporary Issues. Studies in Managerial and Financial Accounting*, Vol. 31. Bingley: Emerald Group Publishing, 41–81.

Nekhili, M., Nagati, H., Chtioui, T., & Rebolledo, C. (2017). Corporate social responsibility disclosure and market value: Family versus nonfamily firms. *Journal of Business Research*, *77*, 41–52.

Okoye, A. (2009). Theorising corporate social responsibility as an essentially contested concept: Is a definition necessary? *Journal of Business Ethics*, *89*(4), 613–627.

Owen, D., Gray, R., & Bebbington, J. (1997). Green accounting: Cosmetic irrelevance of radical agenda for change. *Asia-Pacific Journal of Accounting*, *4*(2), 175–198.

Paape, L., Scheffe, J., & Snoep, P. (2003). The relationship between the internal audit function and corporate governance in the EU – a survey. *International Journal of Auditing*, *7*(3), 247–262.

Page, N., & Spira, L. F. (2016). Corporate governance as custodianship of the business model. *Journal Management Governance*, *20*, 213–228.

Perks, K., Farache, F., Shukla, P., & Berry, A. (2013). Communicating responsibility practicing irresponsibility in CSR advertisements. *Journal of Business Research*, *66*(10), 1881–1888.

Perrault Crawford, E., & Williams, C. (2010). Should corporate social reporting be voluntary or mandatory? Evidence from the banking sector in France and the United States. *Corporate Governance: The International Journal of Business in Society*, *10*(4), 512–526.

Qu, S. Q., & Dumay, J. (2011). The qualitative research interview. *Qualitative Research in Accounting & Management*, *8*(3), 238–264.

Saleh, M. (2009). Corporate social responsibility disclosure in an emerging market: A longitudinal analysis approach. *International Business Research*, *2*(1), 134–141.

Sarens, G., & De Beelde, I. (2006). Internal auditors' perception about their role in risk management: A comparison between US and Belgian companies. *Managerial Auditing Journal*, *21*(1), 63–80.

Scott, W. R. (1995). *Institutions and Organizations*. Thousand Oaks, CA: Sage.

Soh, D. S. B., & Martinov-Bennie, N. (2015). Internal auditors' perceptions of their role in environmental, social and governance assurance and consulting. *Managerial Auditing Journal*, *30*(1), 80–111.

Stacchezzini, R., Melloni, G., & Lai, A. (2016). Sustainability management and reporting: The role of integrated reporting for communicating corporate sustainability. *Journal of Cleaner Production*, *136*, 102–110.

Stewart, J., & Subramaniam, N. (2010). Internal audit independence and objectivity: Emerging research opportunities. *Managerial Auditing Journal*, *25*(4), 328–360.

Spira, L. F., & Page, M. (2003). Risk management: The reinvention of internal control and the changing role of internal audit. *Accounting, Auditing and Accountability Journal*, *16*(4), 640–661.

Stubbs, W., & Higgins, C. (2018). Stakeholders' perspectives on the role of regulatory reform in integrated reporting. *Journal of Business Ethics*, *147*(3), 489–508.

UN (2013). *The UN Global Compact-Accenture CEO Study on Sustainability 2013*. Accessed on 27/12/2017 from https://www.unglobalcompact.org/docs/news_events/8.1/UNGC_Accenture_CEO _Study_2013.pdf

UNEP (2010). *Carrots and Sticks – promoting transparency and sustainability*. Accessed on 05/02/2018 from https://www.globalreporting.org/resourcelibrary/Carrots-And-Sticks-Promoting-Transparency -And-Sustainbability.pdf

Van Bommel, W. (2014). *Road Lighting: Fundamentals, Technology and Application*. Cham: Springer.

Yin, R. K. (2014). *Case Study Research: Design and Methods*. Thousand Oaks, CA: Sage Publications.

Zadek, S., Raynard, P., Foster, M., & Oelschlaegel, J. (2004). The future of sustainability assurance. In: *Accountability, the Council of the Association of Chartered Certified Accountants [ACCA], Working with Accountability*. London: ACCA.

Zellweger, T. M., Kekkermanns, F. W., Chrisman, J. J., & Chua, J. H. (2012). Family control and family firm valuation by family CEOs: The importance of intentions for transgenerational control. *Organization Science*, *23*(3), 1–18.

PART 6

SUSTAINABILITY-DRIVEN BUSINESS STRATEGIES IN HUMAN RESOURCES

21. Sustainability-driven HRM: the WHAT, the WHAT FOR and the HOW

Rosalía Cascón-Pereira, Tahereh Maghsoudi and Ana Beatriz Hernández-Lara

INTRODUCTION

In the last few years, the concept of sustainability has gained a strong degree of acceptance throughout the field of organization and management studies (Gladwin et al., 1995). However, despite an increasing body of research and interest on the need for sustainable businesses, there is still a lack of knowledge regarding relevant strategies, policies, or practices (Buller & McEvoy, 2016). In this context, the concept of sustainable-oriented human resource management (sustHRM) has emerged as a key business strategy. Likewise, human resource departments are now seen as playing a crucial role in developing sustainable practices within an organization (Ehnert et al., 2016; Podgorodnichenko et al., 2019).

In this new field, it is essential to design a research roadmap based on the accumulating research findings; this allows us to construct new, and develop existing, knowledge related to social and environmental impacts. This chapter aims to do this by conducting a critical and integrative literature review on sustainability-driven HRM to set a firm basis for future research and to prevent this new concept from becoming a new "void" managerial fad.

The chapter is structured into three further sections. At the end of each section, a brief critical discussion and some recommendations for further research are made. In the following section, we critically explore the WHAT of sustHRM, its ontological nature. To do so, we delineate its boundaries with related concepts such as corporate social responsibility (CSR), strategic human resource management (SHRM), and Green HRM. As Podgorodnichenko et al. (2019) recently highlighted, to allow future research progress in this young field, there is an urgent need for clarity. We also discuss its links with business strategy, showing it to be a new alternative paradigm to strategic HRM (Kramar, 2014), and a strategic necessity rather than a trendy fad (Bombiak, 2019).

The third section explores the WHAT FOR of sustainability-oriented HRM. Starik and Rands (1995) redefined the concept of performance to include people, societal and ecological performance in addition to the traditional financial performance. These have typically been referred to as the Triple Bottom Line (TBL) which consists of the "Three Ps" (PPP) principles (Elkington, 1994, 1998) – "People" (social equity), "Planet" (ecological performance), and "Profit" (economic prosperity), which are considered the hallmark of sustHRM. However, the majority of sustHRM research has focused either on studying HRM practices for the economic sustainability of the company (Jiang et al., 2012), or the environmental aspect of sustainability (e.g. Mishra, 2017; Saeed et al., 2019). The impact of HRM practices on the social component of the TBL is less explored (Ybema et al., 2020). This might be because of the inherent challenges and contradictions of simultaneously attaining PPP (Podgorodnichenko et al., 2019). Additionally, given the inherent difficulties of measuring intangible features of social sustainability, such as equality, diversity, democracy, and interconnectedness (Borgonovi & Compagni, 2013; McKenzie, 2004), the meaning of being "socially sustainable" has not yet been completely clarified. For this reason, the current chapter focuses on the social dimension of sustainability, the "forgotten" component of the TBL, and proposes a list of dependent variables to measure it with a view to paving the way forward for future research in this new field.

Finally, in the fourth section, we address the HOW of sustainability-oriented HRM and its contribution to sustainability. HRM practices play a crucial role in both the practical application of sustainable polices (Renwick et al., 2013) and the expansion of a sustainable development culture (Liebowitz, 2010). Sustainable HRM not only involves the conventional HRM practices of attracting and retaining employees, but other sustainable and environmental policies that result in a healthy work environment (these, for example, include work–family balance policies (WFB), and health and safety policies). Likewise, the novel and under-researched area (Sheehan et al., 2014) of sustainable Human Resource Development (HRD) practices becomes not only a tool to allow human resources to attain sustainability goals, but also an indicator of social sustainability in itself (Ehnert et al., 2016; Ybema et al., 2020). Hence, HRM and HRD practices constitute the primary contributors to developing sustainability-driven business strategies for the following reasons; first, human resources are the main channel for implementing the strategies, polices, and objectives within organizations; second, human resources are motivated, controlled, and conducted according to a set of polices, rules, and practices which are defined by HRM policies (Manzoor et al., 2019). As such, HRM and HRD practices are the best way, and human resources are the main actors, in arriving at a sustainable-driven business. However, there is a lack of agreement and, consequently, a need for research on which specific HRM and HRD practices are linked to sustainable outcomes (Lee, 2019; Manzoor et al., 2019). To respond to this research gap, this section reviews the empirical evidence in the literature on the relationship of certain HR practices with sustainable outcomes. For the purpose of this chapter, we adopt a capabilities perspective (Garavan et al., 1999; Cascón-Pereira & Valverde, 2006), according to which HRD is seen as a subset of the broader set of HRM practices that use adult development to increase the value of human resources in the drive to be competitive or attain organizational goals. Accordingly, in the category of "sustainability-driven HR", we include all HRM and HRD practices aimed at attaining sustainable organizational outcomes.

WHAT IS SUSTAINABILITY-DRIVEN HUMAN RESOURCE MANAGEMENT (SUSTHRM)?

sustHRM is defined as "the adaptation of HRM practices and strategies that enable (the organization) to achieve the financial, ecological and social goals of the organization over a long term horizon, while controlling for negative feedback and unintended side effects" (Kramar, 2014, p.1070). It plays a crucial role in contributing to a firm's corporate sustainability (CS) and CSR. In particular, it may help to make the challenge for the corporation of integrating the CS/CSR combination into their strategies, business models, and operating processes a reality.

CS and CSR have an external as well as an internal element. The former refers to meeting the expectations of external stakeholders while the latter refers to the way people within the organization are treated and, hence, implies HRM. So, CS/CSR and HRM are mutually interdependent (Gond et al., 2011). On the one hand, HRM practises impact CS/CSR through the creation of employee commitment and engagement with CS/CSR (as we will describe in the final section). But, on the other hand, CS/CSR contributes to HRM by helping to create a strong employer brand to attract and retain talent, informing selection procedures on issues of inclusion and equal opportunity, introducing decent work standards, and defining principles to reward employees (Stahl et al., 2019).

Another related concept is "Green HRM" which is the ecological domain of sustHRM and is defined as "the HRM activities which enhance positive environmental outcomes" (Kramar, 2014, p.1075). According to Renwick et al. (2013), Green HRM practices help organizations mitigate the effects of global climate change through reduced workplace-driven pollution and waste and better energy use.

Finally, we clarify the concept of sustHRM in relation to SHRM. SustHRM has been conceived in the last two decades as an alternative and new approach to SHRM (Kramar, 2014). SustHRM goes beyond SHRM by considering organizational outcomes which are broader than financial outcomes. In particular, it includes human, social, and environmental outcomes, and also the positive and negative effects of HRM on a variety of stakeholders (and not only on shareholders as in SHRM). Nonetheless, both approaches share a strategic dimension that is a vertical link with corporate strategy. Since human resources are seen as the key assets and source of competitiveness (Bombiak, 2019), any business strategy depends on them and so HRM practices are seen as key to achieving the sustainable strategic aims. However, there are different alternatives to strategic commitment to sustainability. In the conceptual framework proposed by Lopez-Cabrales and Valle-Cabrera (2019), there are four different strategic approaches to sustainability and their links with HRM strategies. These are, first, being reactive or lacking a sustainability strategy. These firms do not consider any standards or regulations in terms of their environmental or social sustainability. They are characterized by high levels of labour conflict, turnover, and absenteeism. The investment in HRM practices is minimal and the underinvestment in staff has a negative impact on sustainability outcomes. Employees are offered precarious working conditions, low salaries, a lack of incentives, and no investment in their development.

The second strategic approach is adopting a compliance sustainability strategy. These firms are concerned only with meeting the legal requirements at minimum cost and their prevailing concern is to seek maximum returns for their shareholders. For them, HRM practices are only symbolic, short-term, and for compliance with legal requirements. For instance, investment in training will be minimal and merely to guarantee compliance with environmental legislation.

The third strategic approach is to adopt an analyser sustainability strategy. In terms of impact on the TBL, analyser sustainability is positioned between the compliance and proactive strategies. These companies go beyond the requirements established by legislation when pressure from different stakeholders requires the organization to react so as not to lose its market position. HRM practices are long-term oriented and substantive, generating a supportive culture for sustainability which leads the company to internalize sustainability principles over the long term, in order to compete.

The fourth, and final, strategic approach is adopting a proactive and innovative sustainability strategy. These companies genuinely attempt to outperform competitors in terms of green impact, social effects, and long-term effectiveness. The HRM practices of Employer Branding are used to attract the best qualified employees for achieving the TBL and, in line with that, non-monetary remunerations are linked to employee sustainability contributions.

All in all, the first two CS/CSR strategies are effectively symbolic or a mere charade, whereas the third and the fourth, regardless of their final purpose (to compete or to outperform sustainably due to their core values), can be regarded as substantive (Stahl et al., 2019).

Hence, these strategic choices determine the HRM practices described in the final section. In line with them, we can distinguish different degrees of involvement of the HRM function in attaining sustainable outcomes, depending on the true engagement of the company with sustainability. In particular, it is proposed that the extent to which a firm's CS/CSR activities are substantive (tangible, measurable, and impactful), as opposed to symbolic (just ceremonial or defensive), will determine the degree of HRM involvement (Stahl et al., 2019). Therefore, if the sustainable strategic approach adopted by the company is (1) or (2) according to the Lopez-Cabrales and Valle-Cabrera (2019) classification, the link of HRM with sustainability and its role is minimal, symbolic, and superficial. This may explain why, despite the vital role of HRM in attaining sustainable outcomes, HRM specialists and departments in some companies are not currently accepted as partners in influencing CS/CSR strategies, nor is HRM a key implementer of CS/CSR initiatives and programmes (Cohen et al., 2012). This might be because, for most organizations, CS/CSR is purely symbolic, serving as a compliance function largely decoupled from core business process, so the HRM function is not involved in the design and implementation of CS/CSR strategies. The final section in this chapter describes how to overcome this lack of recognition by detailing the ways in which HR can practically contribute to the CS and CSR goals through policies and practices and therefore, contribute to substantive, rather than symbolic, CS/CSR. In doing so, it allows clarification of the link between HRM and CS as one of the most frequent calls for future research. Future research should also distinguish not only conceptually, but also empirically, between the different roles adopted by the HRM function in attaining sustainability outcomes as a key mediator/moderator for understanding the different outcomes of social, ecological, and financial organizational performance.

WHAT ARE SUSTAINABILITY-DRIVEN HRM PRACTICES FOR: SOCIAL SUSTAINABILITY INDICATORS

For the last two decades, including the social and ecological dimensions of organizational performance alongside the traditional financial/economic dimension has been seen as crucial (Starik & Rands, 1995). These three dimensions of organizational performance constitute the TBL, which Elkington (1994, 1998) described as (i) social equity for the aspects referring to *People*, societal welfare, and individual wellbeing; (ii) environmental integrity for the aspects referring to the *Planet* and the efficient use and conservation of its natural resources; and (iii) economic prosperity for the aspects relating to the long-term effectiveness and *Profitability* of companies. These three dimensions (PPP) of the TBL are considered to define sustHRM. Until recently, however, research has been mostly focused either on HR practices for the economic sustainability of the company (Jiang et al., 2012), or for environmental aspects of sustainability (Mishra, 2017; Saeed et al., 2019), neglecting the social component despite the need to involve all three dimensions in guaranteeing sustainability-driven business (Ybema et al., 2020).

So, without neglecting either the "planet" HR practices to reduce companies' impact on natural resources and improve conservation, or the "profit" HR measures to improve financial and economic performance and shareholder value, they also need a stronger commitment to "people" HR practices which nurture other agents and stakeholders, including employees, their families, and their communities. Short-term, cost-driven HR practices that harm these should be avoided, and long-term sustainable HR practices, which integrate the societal perspective, encouraged (Ehnert et al., 2016).

Within the social domain of sustHRM, the global reporting initiative (GRI), now aligned to the UN's 2030 Sustainable Development Agenda, is considered the standard for sustainability reporting (Hahn & Lülfs, 2014). It provides reporting guidelines on six indicator categories in the three PPP dimensions and is used by both researchers and leading companies (Hahn & Lülfs, 2014). The Profit and Planet dimensions each contain a single indicator category (EC – Economic) and (EN – Environmental) respectively. The People dimension, however, consists of four categories (LA – Labour Practices and Decent Work); (HR – Human Rights); (SO – Society), and finally (PR – Product Responsibility). The first two of these are related to sustHRM and we will now consider them in some detail.

Labour Practices and Decent Work

This category tries to reflect the quality of work and the working environment, extracted from the International Labour Organization (ILO) "ILO Decent Work Agenda" and its four strategic goals of employment, dialogue, rights, and protection (with gender as a cross-cutting theme – see GRI, 2011, 2014).

The performance indicators highlighted in terms of employment seek to guarantee proper levels of workforce by employment type, contract, and region; as well as proper levels of employee turnover by age, gender, and region (Ehnert et al., 2016). The recommended sustHRM practices seek to promote dialogue, communication, and employee involvement, commitment and engagement with CS and in particular with social sustainability issues (Guerci & Carollo, 2016), seeking an improvement in organizational identification by workers, and organizational citizenship behaviour (OCB) aligned with the social domain of sustHRM (Shen & Benson, 2016; Newman et al., 2016). Beside the issues related to employment, the literature recognizes the relevance of employability (Ybema et al., 2017) when referring to the extent to which workers are able and willing to remain in and maintain their jobs.

In terms of labour and management relations, the core performance indicators are related to the need for guaranteeing the employees who are covered by collective bargaining agreements; and minimum notice periods prior to significant operational changes (Ehnert et al., 2016). To also guarantee the wellbeing of workers, their families, and communities, HRM practices should reduce or eliminate burnout and precarious work and ensure good working conditions that foster fairness and equality (Bidwell et al. 2013; Mariappanadar, 2012).

Regarding occupational health and safety, the core performance indicators are established with the objectives of reducing the rates of injury, occupational diseases, lost days, and absenteeism, as well as the number of work-related fatalities by region. The purpose is also to improve education, training, counselling, prevention, and risk-control programmes to assist workforce members, their families and communities in issues related to occupational health and safety (Ehnert et al., 2016).

In the more general training and education domain, some core performance indicators are the observation of the average hours of training per year per employee and category, trying to guarantee access for the majority of workers to this training and education, and to reduce asymmetries among different worker types and categories.

Within the diversity and equal opportunity topics, the main indicators underline the composition of governance bodies and the breakdown of employees per category according to gender, age group, minority group membership, and other diversity indicators; as well as the ratio of the basic salaries of men and women by employee category, with the objective of reducing discrimination and improving equality in the composition of the workforce and the governing bodies.

All in all, we propose that these indicators (organizational identification, OCB, turnover, workforce composition, collective bargaining agreements, burnout, precarious work, absenteeism, sick leaves, hours of training per year per employee, etc.) be used in future research as dependent variables that are proxies for social sustainability. Hence, future research should explore what particular HR practices as independent variables lead to specific social sustainability outcomes measured through the suggested dependent variables.

Human Rights

The GRI also includes the "Human Rights" category, within the social domain of sustHRM, driven by the 1998 "ILO Declaration of Fundamental Principles and Rights at Work" (Hassel, 2008). It includes six core performance indicators focused on non-discrimination or the avoidance of forced and compulsory labour (Parsa et al., 2018). The "Human Rights" category highlights investment and procurement practices, such as vigilance over investment agreements that include human right clauses or that have undergone human rights screening, and the percentage of significant suppliers and contractors that have undergone screening on human rights and actions taken. Among its indicators, this category also includes freedom of association and collective bargaining, identifying operations in which the right to exercise freedom of association and collective bargaining may be at significant risk and the actions taken to support these rights. In terms of child labour, the indicators considered include identifying operations with significant risk for incidents of child labour and measures taken to contribute to their elimination. Finally, to control forced and compulsory labour, it is recommended that operations of significant risk for incidents of forced or compulsory labour be identified and measures conducive to their elimination be put in place (Ehnert et al., 2016). The objective of all these measures is to avoid the violation of human rights in the domain of workforce and labour market relationships.

As in the case of labour practices and decent work indicators, we propose these human rights indicators as dependent variables that are proxies for social sustainability. In particular, future research might explore which particular HR practices (e.g. recruitment and selection practices) as independent variables lead to specific social sustainability outcomes measured through the suggested dependent variables (e.g. discrimination legal complaints).

Despite recent efforts to establish and define social indicators of sustHRM, there remains a need for further work to propose social indicators more adapted to the characteristics, features, and aims of each organization. Additional research is necessary to solve the dilemma related to the integration of indicators that belong to the three dimensions of sustHRM. There are inherent tensions and trade-offs among the economic, ecological, and social objectives of sustHRM (Bansal & Song, 2017), provoked by the challenges and contradictions of simultaneously attaining the different dimensions of the TBL (Podgorodnichenko et al., 2019). The balance between environmental integrity, social equity, and economic prosperity constitutes a challenge for sustHRM (Bansal, 2005), given the difficulties of increasing companies' profit and profitability while at the same time allocating resources to preserve the environment, protect its natural resources, and improve the economic and social conditions of their workers and the community where they operate.

HOW DO SUSTAINABILITY-DRIVEN HR PRACTICES CONTRIBUTE TO SOCIAL SUSTAINABILITY?

This section reviews the empirical evidence in the literature on the relationship of certain HR practices with sustainable outcomes in order to provide practical recommendations to companies. In particular, it reviews the evidence in relation to the less explored dimension of the TBL, which is the social dimension (Alcaraz et al., 2019). Increasingly, organizations are looking to establish and develop the social sustainability dimension of TBL, and this demands a contribution from all management practices, particularly HR practices (Pellegrini et al., 2018). Table 21.1 summarizes the main evidence found. Next, we describe the main findings grouped by HRM policies, and discuss them in relation to future research and practical recommendations for companies.

Recruitment, Selection, and Socialization

Recruitment and selection are key in increasing the effectiveness of the HRM function (Sorenson et al., 2010), as they contribute to attracting the most suited candidates, not only to the organization's job positions (person–job fit) but also to the organizations' objectives (person–organization fit). In addition, recruitment plays a crucial role in enriching candidates' information about the organization's values, priorities, and objectives so that candidates can prepare for the selection and also self-exclude if they feel their values are not in accordance with the organizational objectives. Thus, to improve social sustainability, it appears critical to define value-based recruitment and selection policies in line with the social sustainability objectives of the organization. In this regard, socially responsible recruitment and selection policies should be developed based on "the principles of adequacy of training and the potential for growth and promotion of the new candidates as a first step in the process of attraction and retention" (Barrena-Martínez et al., 2019, p. 2557).

Socially responsible companies, as compared with companies with poor social performance, employ and retain better employees (Sharma & Henriques, 2005). Increasingly, employees wish to work for companies that are committed to positive social and environmental impacts (Turner et al., 2019). This employee preference is not only based on the alignment of the individuals' social sustainability values with the companies' culture, but also because sustainable companies are more likely to be perceived as better employers (Turner et al., 2019; Sharma et al., 2009). Therefore, individuals' perceptions of the social sustainability of the company can be indicated as contingent factors between HR practices, namely recruitment, and social sustainability. A significant number of corporate CSR and HRM professionals (more than 700) surveyed in the USA (SHRM, 2011) found that including social responsibility practices can result in attracting top talent (89%) and improving employee retention (85%).

Table 21.1   *Social sustainability HR Practices*

HRM Policies	Social sustainability HRM Practices	Literature sources
Recruitment, selection and socialization (see pages 375–378)	Define social sustainability value-based recruitment and selection policies.	Santana & Lopez-Cabrales (2019), Diaz-Carrion et al.(2018), Lam & Khare (2010), Barrena-Martínez et al. (2019), App et al. (2012)
	Include social sustainability responsibilities in job descriptions.	
	Select candidates who have knowledge, skills, and experience in the context of social sustainability.	
	Select candidates committed to social sustainability objectives.	
	Select transformational and transactional leaders with social sustainability experience.	
	Prioritize internal recruitment.	
	Provide new employees with information regarding the social sustainability objectives of the organization and the relevant behaviours in accordance with social sustainability.	
	Create a socially responsible organizational image to attract socially responsible employees (Social Employer Branding).	
	Ensure equal and transparent opportunities in selection and promotion processes.	
	Generate a diverse workforce, especially in terms of gender, ethnic origin, and age.	
Training and development (HRD practices) (see pages 378–380)	Promote a culture of social sustainability and continuous learning (the learning organization).	Barrena-Martínez et al. (2019), Perron et al. (2006), Pellegrini et al. (2018), Santana & Lopez-Cabrales (2019), Diaz-Carrion et al. (2018), Lu et al. (2019), Linnenluecke & Griffiths I2010), Ybema et al., (2017), Frangieh & Yaacoub (2019), Voegtlin & Greenwood (2016).
	Ensure training programmes to increase social awareness among employees.	
	Ensure training for vulnerable groups to qualify for a job	
	Ensure competency-based development programmes	
	Ensure equal opportunity training	
	Support individuals' employability and career development through continuous learning activities and internal promotion.	
	Implement fair, transparent, and objective assessment procedures to determine career development.	
	Integrate social sustainability activities/objectives into career management policies.	
	Provide periodic feedback regarding employee development.	
Pay and reward (see pages 380–381)	Offer variable pay, incentives and rewards based on social sustainability behaviours and achievements.	Berrone & Gomez-Mejia (2009), Chanda & Goyal (2020), Diaz-Carrion et al. (2018), Barrena-Martínez et al.(2019), Farndale et al. (2011), Santana & Lopez-Cabrales (2019), Frangieh & Yaacoub (2019)
	Ensure a fair and transparent reward system.	
	Ensure a reward and compensation system	
	Reward those who express their ideas on social sustainability.	
	Provide social benefits to employees (childcare, life insurance, etc.).	
	Define a competency-based remuneration system.	

HRM Policies	Social sustainability HRM Practices	Literature sources
Performance evaluation and management (see pages 381–382)	Develop a fair, objective, and transparent evaluation system. Include social sustainability indicators in performance evaluation system. Ensure promotion based on employee competency Define a flexible evaluation system based on the different employee groups. Provide periodic feedback regarding employee development. Delegate authority to employees to decide on their career. Consider the dis-benefits of not achieving social targets in the evaluation system. Develop fair and transparent career plans for all employees.	Diaz-Carrion et al. (2018), Jamali et al. (2015), Santana & Lopez-Cabrales (2019), Barrena-Martinez et al. (2019)
Work–family balance (see page 382–383)	Ensure a flexible working schedule Ensure breast-feeding permissions and rooms for nursing mothers. Ensure different leave types. Transfer employees to other centres/branches. Ensure vouchers for childcare.	Barrena-Martinez et al.(2019), Diaz-Carrion et al. (2018), Oh et al. (2019), Santana & Lopez-Cabrales (2019), Celma et al. (2014)
Well-being, health, and safety (see page 383)	Minimize psychological and physical work risks. Develop sport activities and healthy practices inside and outside the organization. Train and share information regarding health and safety laws and preventive measures. Credit an appropriate level of health and safety with standards and certifications. Define formal health and safety committees. Record job-related accidents with the objective of improvement.	Barrena-Martinez et al. (2019), Diaz-Carrion et al. (2018), Renwick et al. (2013), De Stefano et al. (2018)
Communication and employee involvement (see pages 383–384)	Develop trust-based and open communication with employees. Translate the social sustainability objectives of the organization into teams. Facilitate information and knowledge exchange regarding sustainability issues. Apply social media for communication among employees regardless their professional status. Use tools such as suggestion systems and quality circles to exchange ideas and knowledge. Provide advice and guidelines. Empower employees regarding social sustainability issues.	Pellegrini et al. (2018), Boiral et al. (2015), Cantor et al. (2012), Diaz-Carrion et al. (2018), Bhattacharya et al. (2008), Barrena-Martinez et al. (2019), Santana & Lopez-Cabrales (2019)

The ethical and social images of such companies influence their attractiveness and foster the motivation and retention of employees, which in turn can lead companies to win the "War of Talent" (Bhattacharya et al., 2008). That is why Social Employer Branding is indicated as a driver to enhance employer attractiveness and consequently retain and attract high quality employees (Santana & Lopez-Cabrales, 2019). The sustainability message should be integrated into the employer brand. This, in turn, enhances the commitment of employees, and, as a result, they are more likely to be involved in volunteerism and citizenship behaviours (Shen & Benson, 2016). In this regard, companies can expand their socially responsible image by providing grants related to social initiatives. For instance, Google offers several grants for social initiatives such as the Equal Justice Initiative, Goodwill Industries International, and

Pratham Book's StoryWeaver platform (Classy, 2020). Similarly, making donations helps develop a socially responsible image. For instance, Warby Parker distributes prescription eyewear to people in developing countries through their non-profit partners (Classy, 2020). Also, describing sustainability objectives and related responsibilities or tasks as criteria for recruitment and selection can help candidates to perceive the organization as a socially responsible company and attract the best talent (Santana & Lopez-Cabrales, 2019).

Notwithstanding the recognized importance of recruitment and selection in achieving the company's sustainable objectives (Subramanian et al., 2016), it often seems to be superficially implemented in companies (Alcaraz et al., 2019). A number of studies exist to support recruitment and selection significance and to explore how it can contribute to developing organizations that have social sustainability (see Table 21.1). For instance, the selection process can focus on screening the candidates who have the knowledge, skills, and commitment to the social responsibility objectives of the organization (Santana & Lopez-Cabrales, 2019). In addition, the selection of both transformational and transactional leaders with social responsibility experience has been identified as a key practice in the development of social responsible policies in the organization (Lam & Khare, 2010), since they can inspire followers to adopt social sustainability behaviours. Unbiased and transparent selection processes can also guarantee that all employees are provided with equal opportunities (Diaz-Carrion et al., 2018). Along the same lines, internal versus external recruitment can contribute to social sustainability (Diaz-Carrion et al., 2018), as, first, staffing from the available employees can result in improvement of employee motivation (Snape & Redman, 2010) and, second, senior employees are more aware of, and compatible with, the sustainable values of the company (Lam & Khare, 2010). Also, generating a diverse workforce through recruitment and selection practices can lead to social sustainability outcomes. For instance, the involvement of women in executive management and on boards is indicated as a criterion for ranking sustainable companies (Forbes, 2019a). The percentages of women included on boards in the top three sustainable companies are 29% (Chr. Hansen Holding A/S), 64% (Kering SA), and 38% (Neste Corporation) (see Forbes, 2019b). Similarly, the recruitment of refugees or veterans is considered a socially responsible HR practice. For instance, Starbucks planned employing 10,000 refugees across 75 countries and 25,000 veterans by 2025 (SmartRecruiters, 2017).

Finally, socialization can play a critical role in the development of social sustainability behaviours since it helps employees to adapt their goals and values in alignment with the objectives and values of the organization (Santana and Lopez-Cabrales, 2019). In this regard, when social sustainability objectives are integrated into the companies' policies and strategies, socialization can guide employees to engage in and adjust their daily operations toward sustainability development. Accordingly, new employees should be provided with initial training or socialization in regard to the organization's socially sustainability objectives and values and the appropriate social sustainability behaviours.

Training and Development

Training and development are regarded as sustainability-driven HRD practices when they are aimed at attaining sustainable goals (Sheehan et al., 2014). Such HRD practices create and expand a sustainability culture through training (Forbes, 2020a). Training can expand an employee's attitudes, skills, and knowledge to appreciate sustainability values and attain sustainability goals (Govindarajulu & Daily, 2004). Sustainability training enables employees to perceive the complexity of sustainability in daily work tasks (Perron et al., 2006). Pellegrini et al. (2018) found that such training programmes should primarily aim to stimulate employee awareness, while also emphasizing the key importance of their own understanding and attitudes in achieving sustainability. This bolsters employee decision-making capabilities in relation to sustainability issues (Sarkis et al., 2010), as they can align their daily operations based on sustainability principles. For the HRM function to facilitate institutional change, HR professionals increasingly require training in social sustainability behaviours (Voegtlin & Greenwood, 2016).

Training is a key contributor to the social responsibility of companies, particularly in the case of vulnerable people. For instance, according to Kwan (2020), the main reason for disabled individuals to be out of the labour market is the lack of vocational skills that link to the available jobs. Hence, training addressed to this group is a social sustainability-driven HR practice. Likewise, some companies, such as LinkedIn, work with several organizations aiming for youth training, veterans' career services, and refugee resource networks (SmartRecruiters, 2017).

There are at least six different learning methods which can be used individually, or in combination, in educating for social sustainability behaviours. First, sustainable-oriented culture plays an important role in training; it can be a crucial factor in shaping the behaviour of employees as well as in transferring and acquiring the relevant knowledge (Linnenluecke & Griffiths, 2010). In this regard, first, the development of social values and principles in the work environment may educate employees to adjust their daily operations toward social sustainability behaviours. Second, face-to-face or classroom training tools, such as lectures or role-playing and case studies, and using either internal or external trainers, can provide employees with closer communication for exchanging information and ideas on social sustainability (Barrena-Martínez et al., 2019). Third, online training can be an effective alternative to enrich the perception of employees about the concept and value of social sustainability. Fourth, blended training combining face-to-face training with online training also can be used for training social sustainability (Forbes, 2020b). Fifth, socially sustainable behaviours can be generated and shared by internal promotion. The exchange of positions between employees can result, not only in learning social sustainability behaviours from new tasks and responsibilities, but also in developing new social sustainability ideas. Sixth, coaching and mentoring methods can be also effective methods to guide and support employees to learn social sustainability behaviours and appreciate their value through role modelling and close communication. Finally, Virtual Reality (VR) is increasingly used in corporate training. Strivr and Mursion, leaders in the market, are introducing VR solutions for a range of training, including safety and customer services, to accelerate behaviour change in building up new skills in the organization, as it enables employees to practice before encountering a situation (Forbes, 2020b). This technology is well adapted to the development of employee social sustainability behaviours.

Notwithstanding the agreement in the literature on the contribution of training to social sustainability outcomes, there are contradictory results about the contribution of training in the development of sustainable behaviours, either directly or through mediator, moderator, or contingent variables such as commitment (e.g. Barrena-Martínez et al., 2019; Ybema et al. 2017; Pellegrini et al., 2018). The first two of these studies found that training and continuous development was a socially oriented HR practice that increases an employee's sustainable employability, and also, since employees are provided with the skills, knowledge, and competencies needed for effective social performance, enhances ESB (employees' sustainable behaviours). The third study found, however, that training does not directly affect ESB but may indirectly result in ESB through the mediating role of commitment. The authors showed that training can enhance the commitment of employees to adopting in-role and extra-role social sustainability behaviours.

Career development is also a driver for social sustainability development. Lack of continuous career development can cause dissatisfaction and turnover, while continuous career development programmes can enhance the commitment of employees (Davis, 2015) and retain valuable employees (Malik et al., 2017). Thus, developing rigorous, fair, transparent, and objective assessment procedures to determine career development plans can contribute to social sustainability improvement (Diaz-Carrion et al., 2018; Santana & Lopez-Cabrales, 2019). In this regard, social sustainability behaviours can be integrated into career management policies which, in turn, can be evidence for the importance of social sustainability objectives at a business level and can guide employees to become involved in social sustainability activities in order to meet their career objectives. Continuous training plays a key role in career development; it offers opportunities for employees to develop their skills and enable them to have flexibility in choosing their future career (Frangieh & Yaacoub, 2019). In this regard, the Open Talent Market is applied as an initiative to provide employees with career development and growth options (Forbes, 2020b). For instance, Schneider Electric uses the Open Talent Market as a one-stop career development and mobility platform; if they create a profile, employees are able to search the range of jobs of interest or new career vacancies, and even to make contact with a mentor to prepare for a future role. In addition, periodic feedback surrounding employee development is indicated as a sustainability HR practice (Diaz-Carrion et al., 2018). This can, first, help employees by putting them on the right track and, second, enhance their engagement in social sustainability activities as they receive organizational support with periodic feedback. In addition, regarding employability, continuous training activities enable employees to face a fast-changing labour market, which results in sustainable career development (Diaz-Carrion et al., 2018; Lu et al., 2019; Ybema et al., 2017). Finally, providing competency-based development training contributes to employability through maintaining or promoting functional learning and the career competencies of employees (Lu et al., 2019).

Pay and Reward

Paying and rewarding for sustainability reflect the integration of sustainability principles in business activities, which in turn represent the genuine commitment of the organization to sustainability objectives (Daily & Huang, 2001; Pellegrini et al., 2018; Berrone & Gomez-Mejia, 2009). However, things are not so clear with regard to the impact of monetary or non-monetary rewards as contingent factors on ESB. For instance, Berrone and Gomez-Mejia (2009) recognized that monetary rewards help employees to perceive the importance and value of sustainability. In contrast, Longoni (2016) found that non-monetary incentives, such as acknowledgements, rather than monetary incentives, also contribute to ESB. Similarly, Lam and Khare (2010) pointed out that non-monetary rewards, including social sustainability training and introducing opportunities to develop employee skills related to social sustainability, and expanding more challenging and meaningful sustainable work may develop ESB. There is also contradictory evidence about the contribution of reward, monetary or non-monetary, in the development of ESB (e.g. Chanda & Goyal, 2020; Pellegrini et al., 2018). The former found that a fair reward system, one that incentivizes social sustainability behaviours, can result in social performance enhancement. The latter, however, found that rewards do not affect ESB, because ESB develops through intrinsic, and not extrinsic, motivation. Hence, more research based on evidence is needed to investigate the effect of monetary and non-monetary rewards on ESB.

Despite these contradictions, different practices have been identified to support the motivation of employees in regard to social sustainability behaviours (see Table 21.1), such as setting incentives that enhance social goals (Jamali et al., 2015), a fair and transparent reward system based on performance and competency rather than gender, age, and ethnicity (Chanda & Goyal, 2020; Diaz-Carrion et al., 2018), offering variable pay and incentives (company's shares, bonuses) as a reward for social sustainability behaviours, rewarding employees who share their ideas about sustainability improvement (Diaz-Carrion et al., 2018), implementing a competitive reward and compensation system (Frangieh & Yaacoub, 2019), rewarding social volunteering activities (Jamali et al., 2015), a socially responsible package benefit system that provides employees with a variety of benefits, such as life/accident insurance, medical service, retirement plans, free education, and employee discounts (Buller & McEvoy, 2012). Such benefits, as social assistance to employees, exhibit the continuous welfare and ethical climate of the organization. This, in turn, may encourage employees to commit to the organization in return for the social responsibility of the organization toward employees (Barrena-Martínez et al., 2019; Farndale et al., 2011). Providing a competitive reward system for employee participation in sustainability activities is a driver to enhance employee interest (Frangieh & Yaacoub, 2019). In addition, Chanda and Goyal (2020) indicated that, if organizations invest in a fair compensation policy, this investment will return due to the satisfaction and commitment of employees. Ensuring a fair remuneration system and adding value in social benefits which is free from any discrimination and also setting up a competency-based remuneration system can result in shaping the positive perception among employees that their effort will be fairly rewarded. According to the ranking conducted by Corporate Knights, "CEO–Average Employee Pay" is one of the elements to grade the social sustainability of companies (Forbes, 2019a). It is calculated as total CEO compensation divided by average employee compensation. Lower ratios rank higher in the list of sustainable companies. In Chr. Hansen Holding A/S (the first ranked company in the list of sustainable companies), the CEO salary is only 24 times that of an average employee.

Finally, the active involvement of all managers and employees is key in developing social sustainability behaviours within an organization (Berrone & Gomez-Mejia, 2009). In particular, rewarding social performance can be a driver for stimulating managers to deploy resources and endeavours toward social responsibility initiatives (Berrone & Gomez-Mejia, 2009). Managers thus encouraged might in turn encourage their subordinates to apply social sustainability behaviours in their daily operations. In this regard, Corporate Knights offered "Sustainability Pay Link" as another element for ranking sustainable companies (Forbes, 2019a). This element gives higher weights to senior executives who achieve sustainability goals through mechanisms such as reducing health and safety accidents and improving energy efficiency.

Performance Evaluation and Management

Performance management can be a key driver in enhancing organizational social sustainability by involving both economic and social objectives in performance assessment systems (Jamali et al., 2015). In this regard, employees need prior information on what factors are included in their social performance assessment. Employees are more likely to commit to social objectives when they perceive them as a part of their performance assessment. For instance, including service to community and contribution to social initiatives in their performance assessment can motivate employees. Additionally, the evaluation of the social performance of employees in a formal assessment system highlights the social responsibility of the organization, which in turn develops employee perception of organizational fairness and justice (Aguilera et al., 2007). This may result in the reduction of turnover intention as a social sustainability indicator because employees perceive wider and meaningful objectives (Guerci et al., 2019). Employees may even feel more satisfaction, commitment or OCB due to such social-oriented assessment system, and they may take a step further by becoming involved in social volunteering activities (Newman et al., 2016). Furthermore, ongoing performance feedback and support may improve employee perception of organizational social sustainability objectives (Lam & Khare, 2010) which, in turn, results in the development of their social performance.

The HR practices identified in the literature to develop a performance assessment and management plan that promote social sustainability behaviours in employees are (see Table 21.1): developing a fair, objective, and transparent evaluation system, including social sustainability indicators in the evaluation of employees, , promotion based on employee competencies, a flexible evaluation system based on different employee groups (considering age, gender and other sources of diversity), providing periodic feedback regarding employee development, delegating authority to employees to decide on their career, considering dis-benefits in the evaluation system for not achieving well-defined and determined social targets, and developing fair and transparent career plans for all employees (Santana & Lopez-Cabrales, 2019; Barrena-Martínez et al., 2019; Jamali et al., 2015; Diaz-Carrion et al., 2018).

Work–Family Balance

The lack of WFB can lead to various problems in terms of social sustainability indicators, such as an increased number of sick leaves and higher rates of turnover work (Oh et al., 2019). WFB policies in themselves constitute social sustainability because their aim is to increase the wellbeing of employees. Organizational investment in the development of a balance between the personal and professional lives of employees would be recouped as it promotes employees' satisfaction and motivation and commitment (Chanda & Goyal, 2020). Such employees are more likely to be involved in work beyond their regular responsibilities (Chanda & Goyal, 2020). As such, WFB can incite employees to feel more committed to social sustainability objectives in an organization, adapt social sustainability behaviours in their daily activities, and involve themselves in community activities.

However, measures to balance the personal and professional life of employees, compared with other HR policies such as discrimination, have not been extensively applied and have even been reduced (Celma et al., 2014). The WFB measures on offer are mainly related to flexible working hours and different types of leaves. In this regard, different social responsible practices, such as breast-feeding, maternity/pregnancy leave, parenthood, flexible work schedules, shifting, unpaid leave for family reasons, vouchers for childcare, considering rooms for nursing mothers, and transferring employees to other centres/branches (Barrena-Martínez et al., 2019; Celma et al., 2014; Diaz-Carrion et al., 2018; Oh et al., 2019; Santana & Lopez-Cabrales, 2019) have been explored to develop WFB (see Table 21.1).

Wellbeing, Health, and Safety

Social sustainability HRM promotes the wellbeing of employees and ensures good health and safety conditions. In return, employees may increase their motivation, satisfaction, and performance (Waring & Edwards, 2008). A lack of consideration of employee wellbeing, health and safety can lead to high rates of turnover, sick leave, and even suicides motivated by labour conditions, such as in the case of France Telecom (24 suicides in 2008/2009) and Foxconn China (nine suicides in 2010) (Cohen et al., 2012). Poor working conditions, such as long shifts, military-style discipline, and work overload, were indicated as the main reason for these. In this regard, existing studies suggest different social sustainability HR practices for improving the health and safety conditions of employees (see Table 21.1), such as minimizing psychological and physical work risks, developing sport activities and healthy practices inside and outside of the organization, training and sharing information regarding health and safety laws and preventive measures, crediting an appropriate level of health and safety with standards and certifications such as OSHAS, ISOS, having formal health and safety committees to monitor, educate, and guide occupational health and safety programmes, and recording job-related accidents and workers at risk of occupational diseases to minimize physical and emotional risks from work (Barrena-Martínez et al., 2019; Diaz-Carrion et al., 2018).

Nonetheless, to develop substantive CS/CSR activities as opposed to symbolic (just ceremonial or defensive) activities, companies should not only ensure compliance with legal requirements on health and safety, but also foster and develop preventive measures among employees (Cooke & He, 2010), such as offering training or sharing information to improve health among employees through enriching their knowledge regarding relevant rules and preventive measures (Barrena-Martínez et al., 2019; Diaz-Carrion et al., 2018).

Communication and Employee Involvement

Communication is deemed essential to convey social sustainability objectives and to involve employees in their attainment (Cantor et al., 2012). Employees feel more engaged and committed to organizational objectives when they perceive social and ethical, in addition to economic, development (Ziek, 2009). In this regard, HR professionals can serve as a channel for effectively communicating CSR activities to employees and the public (Inyang et al., 2011). Bhattacharya et al. (2008) suggested open, direct, formal, and informal communication mechanisms among supervisors and employees, group meetings, and social networking chats as effective tools to facilitate dialogue among employees and between them and their managers. In this regard, Barrena-Martínez et al. (2019) suggested the following practices to improve communication: implementation of social media as a free environment to interact and share ideas among employees regardless of their professional status, applying tools such as a suggestion system, discussion, and a quality circle to exchange ideas among employees both vertically and horizontally, and the enhancement of transparency to employees concerning the results, not only of economic outcomes, but also of social objectives and activities. Communicating the results of social sustainability activities might result in an expansion of a set of norms, values, and expectations (Lam & Khare, 2010) which encourage more engagement with sustainability objectives among employees. Communicating the high performance of certain employees also improves social sustainability. Marks and Spencer, for instance, has sustainability "champions" in every store while Unilever has "ambassadors" across all levels of the organization (Shaughnessy, 2018). This Unilever approach results in the satisfaction of 76% of employees from delivering the sustainability agenda, and about 50% of new employees joined the company due to its ethical and sustainability policies. Moreover, Santana and Lopez-Cabrales (2019) indicated internal rotation, group meetings and brainstorming as alternatives to expanding communication, and knowledge sharing on social sustainability issues. Nonetheless, the quantity and quality of communication within the organization can moderate the relationship between HR practices of communication and social responsibility initiatives (Turner et al., 2019).

Finally, beyond communication, supervisory support can also contribute to the involvement of employees in social sustainability behaviours (e.g. Cantor et al., 2012; Ramus & Steger, 2000). Social sustainability-oriented supervisory support refers to resources and feedback provided for employees to embed sustainability principles and policies in their daily tasks (Cantor et al., 2012). This can facilitate employee involvement in specific community activities, such as fund-raising for denotations or contributing in voluntary community services, the management of time and resources and assistance of their junior colleagues by monitoring, coaching, and sharing their experience and knowledge. Additionally, supervisor support plays a key role in guiding and encouraging employees to involve themselves in sustainable behaviour because, first, supervisors are accountable for transmitting organizational-level sustainable policies and objectives to teams or subordinates (Pellegrini et al., 2018). Second, supervisory support can improve the perception of organizational support (Cantor et al., 2012) and this can motivate employees to follow sustainable goals in return for the perceived organizational support (Aselage & Eisenberger, 2003). Third, supervisors can expand trust-based and open communication with employees and facilitate information and knowledge sharing and idea exchange around the importance of sustainability issues. This can enrich employee understanding and sense-making of social concerns (Pellegrini et al., 2018) and enable employees to develop their creativity and innovation about social sustainability behaviours. Finally, supervisors can stimulate employees to engage in sustainable behaviours by empowering them (Boiral et al., 2015; Cantor et al., 2012).

In conclusion, in this section on how sustainability-driven HR practices can contribute to social sustainability, we argue that future empirical research is needed on employee perception of these practices as contingent factors that influence their social sustainability impact. Until now, research effort has been focused on identifying the HR practices but, future research work should explore the effects of these practices on individual employees.

CONCLUSION

This chapter has provided a synthesis on what sustainability-driven HRM is, how the social dimension of sustainability can be measured, and how it can be attained through the implementation of HRM and HRD practices. The foundations of the strategic level of HRM are made explicit through the set of HRM and HRD practices outlined and exemplified. Hence, this chapter aims to contribute to turn sustHRM into practice and, therefore, contribute to substantive, rather than symbolic CSR, by offering a useful roadmap and starting point for HR practitioners and researchers. In doing so, it clarifies the link between HRM and CS as one of the most frequent calls for future research.

Nonetheless, this chapter has also identified some research gaps if sustHRM is to become a new HRM paradigm, not only in theory but also in practice. First, future research should explore which particular HR practices as independent variables lead to specific social sustainability outcomes as dependent variables. However, to do that, measures for both types of variables should be refined and improved since measurement in this area is a controversial subject if self-reporting is used or if public reporting is employed. Second, future empirical research is needed on employee perception of these practices as contingent factors that influence their social sustainability impact. Employees' perceptions about HR practices play an important intermediary role that has been neglected in sustainability research. Hence, future research work should explore the effects of these practices on individuals' perceptions as mediators or moderators on social sustainability outcomes. The challenge is now to empirically study all these suggested relationships for sustainability to generate HR evidence-based practice.

REFERENCES

Aguilera, R. V., Rupp, D. E., Williams, C. A., & Ganathati, J. (2007). Putting the "S" back into CSR: A multi-level theory of social change in organisations. *Academy of Management Review, 32*(3), 836–863. https://doi.org/10.2307/20159338

Alcaraz, J. M., Susaeta, L., Suarez, E., Colón, C., Gutiérrez-Martínez, I., Cunha, R., & Pin, J. R. (2019). The human resources management contribution to social responsibility and environmental sustainability: Explorations from Ibero-America. *International Journal of Human Resource Management, 30*(22), 3166–3189. https://doi.org/10.1080/09585192.2017.1350732

App, S., Merk, J., & Büttgen, M. (2012). Employer branding: Sustainable HRM as a competitive advantage in the market for high-quality employees. *Management Revue, 23*(3), 262–278. https://doi.org/10.2307/41783721

Aselage, J., & Eisenberger, R. (2003). Perceived organizational support and psychological contracts: A theoretical integration. *Journal of Organizational Behavior, 24*(5), 491–509. https://doi.org/10.1002/job.211

Bansal, P. (2005) Evolving sustainably: A longitudinal study of corporate sustainable development. *Strategic Management Journal, 26*, 197-218.

Bansal, P., & Song, H-C. (2017). Similar but not the same: Differentiating corporate sustainability from corporate responsibility. *Academy of Management Annals, 11*(1), 105–149. http://doi.org/10.5465/annals.2015.0095

Barrena-Martínez, J., López-Fernández, M., & Romero-Fernández, P. M. (2019). Towards a configuration of socially responsible human resource management policies and practices: Findings from an academic consensus. *International Journal of Human Resource Management, 30*(17), 2544–2580. https://doi.org/10.1080/09585192.2017.1332669

Berrone, P., & Gomez-Mejia, L. R. (2009). The pros and cons of rewarding social responsibility at the top. *Human Resource Management, 48*(6), 959–971. https://doi.org/10.1002/hrm.20324

Bhattacharya, C., Sen, S., & Korschun, D. (2008). Using corporate social responsibility to win the war for talent. *MIT Sloan Management Review, 49*, 37–44.

Bidwell, M., Briscoe, F., Fernandez-Mateo, I., & Sterling, A. (2013). The employment relationship and inequality: How and why changes in employment practices are reshaping rewards in organizations. *Academy of Management Annals, 7*(1), 61-121. http://doi.org/10.1080/19416520.2013.761403

Boiral, O., Talbot, D., & Paillé, P. (2015). Leading by example: A model of organizational citizenship behavior for the environment. *Business Strategy and the Environment, 24*(6), 532–550. https://doi.org/10.1002/bse.1835

Bombiak, E. (2019). Green human resource management – the latest trend or strategic necessity? *Entrepreneurship and Sustainability Issues, 6*(4), 1647–1662. https://doi.org/10.9770/jesi.2019.6.4(7)

Borgonovi, E., & Compagni, A. (2013). Sustaining universal health coverage: The interaction of social, political, and economic sustainability. *Value in Health, 16* (1), S34–S38. https://doi.org/10.1016/j.jval .2012.10.006

Buller, P. F., & McEvoy, G. M. (2012). Strategy, human resource management and performance: Sharpening line of sight. *Human Resource Management Review* https://doi.org/10.1016/j.hrmr.2011 .11.002

Buller, P. F., & McEvoy, G. M. (2016). A model for implementing a sustainability strategy through HRM practices. *Business and Society Review, 121*(4), 465–495. https://doi.org/10.1111/basr.12099

Cantor, D. E., Morrow, P. C., & Montabon, F. (2012). Engagement in environmental behaviors among supply chain management employees: An organizational support theoretical perspective. *Journal of Supply Chain Management, 48*(3), 33–51. https://doi.org/10.1111/j.1745-493X.2011.03257.x

Cascón-Pereira, R., & Valverde, M. (2006). "Variety is the spice of life"...but is it so in HRD? A discussion on the convenience of defining the discipline. *International Journal of Learning and Intellectual Capital, 3*(1), 14–28.

Celma, D., Martínez-Garcia, E., & Coenders, G. (2014). Corporate social responsibility in human resource management: An analysis of common practices and their determinants in Spain. *Corporate Social Responsibility and Environmental Management, 21*(2), 82–99. https://doi.org/10.1002/csr.1301

Chanda, U., & Goyal, P. (2020). A Bayesian network model on the interlinkage between socially responsible HRM, employee satisfaction, employee commitment and organizational performance. *Journal of Management Analytics, 7*(1), 105–138. https://doi.org/10.1080/23270012.2019.1650670

Classy. (2020). 6 socially responsible companies to applaud | Classy. Retrieved May 31, 2020, from https://www.classy.org/blog/6-socially-responsible-companies-applaud/

Cohen, E., Taylor, S., & Muller-Camen, M. (2012) HR's role in corporate social responsibility and sustainability. Alexandria, VA: SHR; Foundation Executive Briefing.

Cooke, F. L., & He, Q. (2010). Corporate social responsibility and HRM in China: A study of textile and apparel enterprises. *Asia Pacific Business Review, 16*(3), 355–376. https://doi.org/10.1080/ 13602380902965558

Daily, B. F., & Huang, S. C. (2001). Achieving sustainability through attention to human resource factors in environmental management. *International Journal of Operations and Production Management, 21*(12), 1539–1552. https://doi.org/10.1108/01443570110410892

Davis, P. J. (2015). Implementing an employee career-development strategy: How to build commitment and retain employees. *Human Resource Management International Digest.* Ltd. https://doi.org/10 .1108/HRMID-05-2015-0066

De Stefano, F., Bagdadli, S., & Camuffo, A. (2018). The HR role in corporate social responsibility and sustainability: A boundary-shifting literature review. *Human Resource Management, 57*(2), 549–566.

Diaz-Carrion, R., López-Fernández, M., & Romero-Fernandez, P. M. (2018). Developing a sustainable HRM system from a contextual perspective. *Corporate Social Responsibility and Environmental Management, 25*(6), 1143–1153. https://doi.org/10.1002/csr.1528

Ehnert, I., Parsa, S., Roper, I., Wagner, M., & Muller-Camen, M. (2016). Reporting on sustainability and HRM: a comparative study of sustainability reporting practices by the world's largest companies. *International Journal of Human Resource Management, 27*(1), 88–108.

Elkington, J. (1994). Towards the sustainable corporation: Win-win-win business strategies for sustainable development. *California Management Review, 36*(2), 90–100.

Elkington, J. (1998). Accounting for the triple bottom line. *Measuring Business Excellence, 2*(3), 18–22. https://doi.org/10.1108/eb025539

Farndale, E., Hope-Hailey, V., & Kelliher, C. (2011). High commitment performance management: The roles of justice and trust. *Personnel Review, 40*(1), 5–23. https://doi.org/10.1108/00483481111095492

Forbes. (2019a). *The 2019 Global 100: Overview of Corporate Knights Rating Methodology.* Retrieved from www.global100.org

Forbes. (2019b). *The Most Sustainable Companies in 2019.* Retrieved May 31, 2020, from https:// www.forbes.com/sites/karstenstrauss/2019/01/22/the-most-sustainable-companies-in-2019/ #2d08d51d6d7d

Forbes. (2020a). *Council Post: 15 Effective Ways HR Can Help Create a Sustainable Company Culture.* Retrieved June 3, 2020, from https://www.forbes.com/sites/forbeshumanresourcescouncil/2018/09/ 25/15-effective-ways-hr-can-help-create-a-sustainable-company-culture/#67122ae778fd

Forbes. (2020b). *Top 10 HR Trends that Matter Most in the 2020 Workplace*. Retrieved June 5, 2020, from https://www.forbes.com/sites/jeannemeister/2020/01/15/top-10-hr-trends-that-matter-most-in -the-2020-workplace/#48ab00837dfc

Frangieh, C. G., & Yaacoub, H. K. (2019). Socially responsible human resource practices: Disclosures of the world's best multinational workplaces. *Social Responsibility Journal*, *15*(3), 277–295. https:// doi.org/10.1108/SRJ-11-2017-0226

Garavan, T., Heraty, N. and Barnicle, B. (1999). Human resource development literature: Current issues, priorities and dilemmas. *Journal of European Industrial Training*, *23*(4–5), 169–179.

Gladwin, T. N., Kennelly, J. J., & Krause, T.-S. (1995). Shifting paradigms for sustainable development: implications for management theory and research. *Academy of Management Review*, *2*(4), 874–907. https://doi.org/10.2307/258959

Gond, J. P., Igalens, J., Swaen, V., & El Akremi, A. (2011) The human resources contribution to responsible leadership: An exploration of the CSR-HR interface. *Responsible Leadership* (pp.115-132). Dordrecht: Springer.

Govindarajulu, N., & Daily, B. F. (2004). Motivating employees for environmental improvement. *Industrial Management and Data Systems*, *104*(3), 364–372. https://doi.org/10.1108/02635570410530775

GRI. (2011). Indicators protocol set LA. Retrieved from http://www.globalreporting.org/NR/rdonlyres/ B52921DA-D802-406B-B067-4EA11CFED835/3880/G3_IP_Labor_Practices_Decent_Work.pdf

GRI. (2014). About GRI. Retrieved from https://www.globalreporting.org/information/about-gri/Pages/ default.aspx

Guerci, M., & Carollo, L. (2016). A paradox view on green human resource management: Insights from the Italian context. *International Journal of Human Resource Management*, *27*(2), 212–238. http://doi .org/10.1080/09585192.2015.1033641

Guerci, M., Decramer, A., Van Waeyenberg, T., & Aust, I. (2019). Moving beyond the link between HRM and economic performance: A study on the individual reactions of HR managers and professionals to sustainable HRM. *Journal of Business Ethics*, *160*(3), 783–800. https://doi.org/10.1007/ s10551-018-3879-1

Hahn, R., & Lülfs, R. (2014). Legitimizing negative aspects in GRI-oriented sustainability reporting: A qualitative analysis of corporate disclosure strategies. *Journal of Business Ethics*, *123*, 401–420. http://doi:10.1007/s10551-013-1801-4

Hassel, A. (2008). The evolution of a global labor governance regime. *Governance*, *21*, 231–251. http:// doi:10.1111/j.1468-0491.2008.00397.x

Inyang, B. J., Awa, H. O., & Enuoh, R. O. (2011). CSR-HRM nexus: Defining the role engagement of the human resources professionals. *Special Issue on Contemporary Issues in Business and Economics*, *2*, 118–126.

Jamali, D. R., El Dirani, A. M., & Harwood, I. A. (2015). Exploring human resource management roles in corporate social responsibility: The CSR-HRM co-creation model. *Business Ethics*, *24*(2), 125–143. https://doi.org/10.1111/beer.12085

Jiang, K., Lepak, D. P., Hu, J., & Baer, J. (2012). How does human resource management influence organizational outcomes? A meta-analytic investigation of the mediating mechanism. *Academy of Management Journal*, *55*, 1264–1294.

Kramar, R. (2014). Beyond strategic human resource management: Is sustainable human resource management the next approach?. *International Journal of Human Resource Management*, *25*(8), 1069–1089.

Kwan, C. K. (2020). Socially responsible human resource practices to improve the employability of people with disabilities. *Corporate Social Responsibility and Environmental Management*, *27*(1), 1–8.

Lam, H., & Khare, A. (2010). HR's crucial role for successful CSR. *Journal of International Business Ethics*, *3*(2), 2–4.

Lee, H.-W. (2019). How does sustainability-oriented human resource management work?: Examining mediators on organizational performance. *International Journal of Public Administration*, *42*(11), 974–984.

Liebowitz, J. (2010). The role of HR in achieving a sustainability culture. *Journal of Sustainable Development*, *3*(4), 50. https://doi.org/10.5539/jsd.v3n4p50

Linnenluecke, M. K., & Griffiths, A. (2010). Corporate sustainability and organizational culture. *Journal of World Business*, *45*(4), 357–366. https://doi.org/10.1016/j.jwb.2009.08.006

Longoni, A. (2016). Sustainable operations strategies. *European Journal of Operational Research*, 1–22. https://doi.org/10.1007/978-3-319-06352-2

Lopez-Cabrales, A., & Valle-Cabrera, R. (2019). Sustainable HRM strategies and employment relationships as drivers of the triple bottom-line. *Human Resource Management Review* https://doi.org/10.1016/j.hrmr.2019.100689

Lu, X., Zhu, W., & Tsai, F. S. (2019). Social responsibility toward the employees and career development sustainability during manufacturing transformation in China. *Sustainability (Switzerland)*, *11*(17). https://doi.org/10.3390/su11174778

Malik, A. R., Singh, P., & Chan, C. (2017). High potential programs and employee outcomes: The roles of organizational trust and employee attributions. *Career Development International*, *22*(7), 772–796. https://doi.org/10.1108/CDI-06-2017-0095

Manzoor, F., Wei, L., Bányai, T., Nurunnabi, M., & Subhan, Q. A. (2019). An examination of sustainable HRM practices on job performance: An application of training as a moderator. *Sustainability*, *11*(8), 2263. https://doi.org/10.3390/su11082263

Mariappanadar, S. (2012). Harm of efficiency oriented HRM practices on stakeholders: An ethical issue for sustainability. *Society and Business Review*, *7*, 168–184. http://doi:10.1108/17465681211237628

McKenzie, S. (2004). Social sustainability: Towards some definitions. *Working Paper Series No.27.* Magill, South Australia: Hawke Research Institute.

Mishra, P. (2017). Green human resource management. *International Journal of Organizational Analysis*, *25*(5), 762–788. https://doi.org/10.1108/IJOA-11-2016-1079

Newman, A., Miao, Q., Hofman, P. S., & Zhu, C. J. (2016). The impact of socially responsible human resource management on employees' organizational citizenship behaviour: The mediating role of organizational identification. *International Journal of Human Resource Management*, *27*(4), 440–455. https://doi.org/10.1080/09585192.2015.1042895

Oh, I., Hwang, W. S., & Yoon, H. J. (2019). The role of work-family balance policy for enhancing social sustainability: A choice experiment analysis of Koreans in their twenties and thirties. *International Journal of Environmental Research and Public Health*, *16*(14), 1–15. https://doi.org/10.3390/ijerph16142553

Parsa, S., Roper, I., Muller-Camen, M., & Szigetvari, E. (2018). Have labour practices and human rights disclosures enhanced corporate accountability? The case of the GRI framework. *Accounting Forum*, *41*(2), 47–64. https://doi.org/10.1016/j.accfor.2018.01.001

Pellegrini, C., Rizzi, F., & Frey, M. (2018). The role of sustainable human resource practices in influencing employee behavior for corporate sustainability. *Business Strategy and the Environment*, *27*(8), 1221–1232. https://doi.org/10.1002/bse.2064

Perron, G. M., Côté, R. P., & Duffy, J. F. (2006). Improving environmental awareness training in business. *Journal of Cleaner Production*, *14*(6–7), 551–562. https://doi.org/10.1016/j.jclepro.2005.07.006

Podgorodnichenko, N., Edgar, F., & McAndrew, I. (2019). The role of HRM in developing sustainable organizations: contemporary challenges and contradictions. *Human Resource Management Review*, https://doi.org/10.1016/j.hrmr.2019.04.001

Ramus, C. A., & Steger, U. (2000). The roles of supervisory support behaviors and environmental policy in employee "ecoinitiatives" at leading-edge European companies. *Academy of Management Journal*, *43*(4), 605–626. https://doi.org/10.2307/1556357

Renwick, D. W. S., Redman, T., & Maguire, S. (2013). Green human resource management: A review and research agenda. *International Journal of Management Reviews*, *15*(1), 1–14. https://doi.org/10.1111/j.1468-2370.2011.00328.x

Saeed, B. Bin, Afsar, B., Hafeez, S., Khan, I., Tahir, M., & Afridi, M. A. (2019). Promoting employee's proenvironmental behavior through green human resource management practices. *Corporate Social Responsibility and Environmental Management*, *26*(2), 424–438. https://doi.org/10.1002/csr.1694

Santana, M., & Lopez-Cabrales, A. (2019). Sustainable development and human resource management: A science mapping approach. *Corporate Social Responsibility and Environmental Management*, *26*(6), 1171–1183. https://doi.org/10.1002/csr.1765

Sarkis, J., Gonzalez-Torre, P., & Adenso-Diaz, B. (2010). Stakeholder pressure and the adoption of environmental practices: The mediating effect of training. *Journal of Operations Management*, *28*(2), 163–176. https://doi.org/10.1016/j.jom.2009.10.001

Sharma, S., & Henriques, I. (2005). Stakeholder influences on sustainability practices in the Canadian forest products industry. *Strategic Management Journal, 26*(2), 159–180. https://doi.org/10.1002/smj .439

Sharma, S., Sharma, J., & Devi, A. (2009). Corporate social responsibility: The key role of human resource management. *Business Intelligence Journal, 21,* 205–215.

Shaughnessy, G. (2018). 9 ways that HR and People teams can drive sustainability | Sage Business Cloud People. Retrieved June 2, 2020, from https://www.sagepeople.com/about-us/news-hub/hr -sustainability-tips/#

Sheehan, M., Garavan, T. & Carbery, R. (2014). Sustainability, corporate social responsibility and HRD. *European Journal of Training and Development, 38*(5), 370-386.

Shen, J., & Benson, J. (2016). When CSR is a social norm: How socially responsible human resource management affects employee work behavior. *Journal of Management, 42*(6), 1723–1746. http://doi .org/ 10.1177/0149206314522300

SHRM. (2011). Employee job satisfaction and engagement – the road to economic recovery: A research report by the Society for Human Resource Management. Alexandria, VA: SHRM.

SmartRecruiters. (2017). Top 20 socially responsible companies 2017 | SmartRecruiters. Retrieved May 31, 2020, from https://www.smartrecruiters.com/blog/top-20-corporate-social-responsibility -initiatives-for-2017/

Snape, E., & Redman, T. (2010). HRM practices, organizational citizenship behaviour, and performance: A multi-level analysis. *Journal of Management Studies, 47*(7), 1219–1247. https://doi.org/10.1111/j .1467-6486.2009.00911.x

Sorenson, S., Mattingly, J. E., & Lee, F. K. (2010). Decoding the signal effects of job candidate attraction to corporate social practices. *Business and Society Review, 115*(2), 173–204. https://doi.org/10.1111/ j.1467-8594.2010.00361.x

Stahl, G. K., Brewster, C. J., Collings, D. G., & Hajro, A. (2019). Enhancing the role of human resource management in corporate sustainability and social responsibility: A multi-stakeholder, multidimensional approach to HRM. *Human Resource Management Review,* 100708. https://doi.org/10.1016/J .HRMR.2019.100708

Starik, M., & Rands, G. P. (1995). Weaving an integrated web: Multilevel and multisystem perspectives of ecologically sustainable organizations. *Academy of Management Review,* 20(4), 908–935.

Subramanian, N., Abdulrahman, M. D., Wu, L., & Nath, P. (2016). Green competence framework: Evidence from China. *International Journal of Human Resource Management, 27*(2), 151–172. https://doi.org/10.1080/09585192.2015.1047394

Turner, M. R., Mcintosh, T., Reid, S. W., & Buckley, M. R. (2019). Corporate implementation of socially controversial CSR initiatives: Implications for human resource management. *Human Resource Management Review, 29*(1), 125–136. https://doi.org/10.1016/j.hrmr.2018.02.001

Voegtlin, C., & Greenwood, M. (2016). Corporate social responsibility and human resource management: A systematic review and conceptual analysis. *Human Resource Management Review, 26*(3), 181–197. https://doi.org/10.1016/J.HRMR.2015.12.003

Waring, P., & Edwards, T. (2008). Socially responsible investment: Explaining its uneven development and human resource management consequences. *Corporate Governance: An International Review, 16*(3), 135–145. https://doi.org/10.1111/j.1467-8683.2008.00676.x

Ybema, J. F., Vuuren, T. V., & Dam, K. V. (2017). HR practices for enhancing sustainable employability: Implementation, use, and outcomes. *The International Journal of Human Resource Management, 28*(October), 1–22

Ybema, J. F., Vuuren, T. V., & Dam, K. V. (2020). HR practices for enhancing sustainable employability: Implementation, use, and outcomes. *The International Journal of Human Resource Management, 31*(7), 886–907. https://doi.org/10.1080/09585192.2017.1387865

Ziek, P. (2009). Making sense of CSR communication. *Corporate Social Responsibility and Environmental Management, 16*(3), 137–145. https://doi.org/10.1002/csr.183

22. The role of human resource management function in the institutionalization of sustainability: the case study of the Dutch hotel industry

Andrew Ngawenja Mzembe

INTRODUCTION

The notion of sustainability has attracted the attention of scholars as well as practitioners. For the sake of this chapter and drawing on Podgorodnichenko et al. (2020) and Stahl et al. (2020), the term 'sustainability' is used interchangeably with Corporate Social Responsibility (CSR). These terms are considered to be closely related. For many years, sustainability has been embraced by some businesses for several reasons. Sustainability is considered by some businesses in order to enhance their image and ultimately achieve competitive advantage; other businesses considered adoption of sustainability as 'the right thing to do' (Dubois and Dubois, 2012; Ronnenberg et al., 2011; Qi et al., 2012). Implementation of a sustainability agenda therefore can help a business meet the needs and interests of internal and external stakeholders (Jamali et al., 2015). Furthermore, the recent attention accorded to the United Nations Sustainable Development Goals (SDGs) means that sustainability is no longer an optional issue, but it is integral to business operations (Scheyvens et al., 2016).

For many businesses, it has been noted that the development and implementation of a sustainability agenda can be a fundamental organizational change that requires adaptation of the prevalent organization systems and structures (Ronnenberg et al., 2011). Thus, for a sustainability agenda to be effectively institutionalized within an organization, it is fundamental that various organizational functions take an active role in its development and implementation. The fundamental problem however is that some businesses lack the capacity in terms of structures and systems or will to effectively formulate and translate their sustainability agenda into practices (Qi et al., 2012). The Human Resource Management (HRM) function can arguably play a fundamental role in the integration of a sustainability agenda into organizations (Gond et al., 2011; Sarvaiya et al., 2018; Smith et al., 2018; Voegtlin and Greenwood, 2016). Nascent literature suggests that the HRM function can serve as a 'wheel' that propels the sustainability agenda within organizations (Sarvaiya et al. 2018).

While a limited stream of studies have begun to consider the relationship between sustainability or CSR and HRM (Alcaraz et al., 2017; Chiappetta Jabbour and Lopes de Sousa Jabbour, 2016; Dubois and Dubois, 2012; Ehnert et al., 2016; Gond et al., 2011; Jamali et al., 2015; Richards, 2020; Roscoe et al., 2019; Saeed et al., 2019; Sarvaiya et al., 2019; Wirtenberg et al., 2007; Zibarras and Coan, 2015), studies on the actual and potential roles that human resource (HR) professionals can perform in advancing the sustainability agenda within their organizations are scant (Jamali et al., 2015; Sarvaiya et al., 2018, 2019). In addition, literature that explores conditions under which the HRM functions within an organization can be effective (or not) in advancing the sustainability agenda, is acutely scarce (Sarvaiya et al., 2019).

This chapter therefore builds on previous scholarly work by integrating sustainability literature with HRM literature – specifically Ulrich and Beatty's (2001) model of HRM – to understand the roles of the HRM function (or HR professionals) in advancing the sustainability agenda within an organization. Furthermore, it builds upon Sarvaiya et al. (2019) to unravel organizational contextual embeddedness of the HRM–sustainability interface within an organization. This chapter highlights the need for organizations and HRM functions to develop and implement strategies that can institutionalize the sustainability agenda within an organization. This chapter therefore seeks to answer the following questions:

● What roles do HR professionals perform in the institutionalization of the sustainability agenda within their hotels?
● What are the organizational contextual factors that influence the effectiveness of the HRM functions in the institutionalization of the sustainability agenda within hotels?

LITERATURE

Extant Studies on the Relationship between HRM and Sustainability

Literature on the relationship between sustainability and HRM is dominated by two dominant strands. The first strand considers HRM practices to be a fundamental part of the internal social sustainability agenda. Proponents of this perspective, sometimes known as sustainable HRM or responsible HRM, principally focus on advancing the people dimension of the triple bottom line of sustainability (Richards, 2020). Thus, the design of HRM practices that consider the wellbeing of employees in the workplace, and rewards and benefits and diversity management, is viewed as the crucial component of an organization's sustainability agenda (Ehnert et al., 2016; Kramar, 2014; Richards, 2020; Saeed et al., 2019). This perspective is considered the most inward-looking with a primary emphasis on satisfying the needs of internal stakeholders (Yong et al., 2020; Kramar, 2014). Such an orientation can lead to better organizational outcomes such as enhanced employee commitment and retention, enhanced attractiveness to potential employees and staving off stringent regulations and external stakeholder activisms (Jamali et al., 2015; Voegtlin and Greenwood, 2016).

The second strand posits that HRM can play a fundamental role in the achievement of the firm's overall sustainability agenda (Dubois and Dubois, 2012; Jamali et al., 2015; Sarvaiya et al., 2018, 2019). This is a broader and an inside-outside perspective, which is manifested through what Voegtlin and Greenwood (2016) term as the social integrative CSR (sustainability) – HRM interface. The relationship between HRM and sustainability (CSR) is considered socially integrative when the HRM function can stimulate the wider organization to engage in actions that help address the broad sustainability challenges that modern society currently faces (Ehnert et al., 2016; Saeed et al., 2019; Voegtlin and Greenwood, 2016). This perspective may be normatively and instrumentally laden at the same time. It implies that the HR function's noble task is to garner the involvement of internal organizational stakeholders to undertake actions that can benefit them as well as the wider stakeholders of the organization (Jamali et al., 2015; Dubois and Dubois, 2012; Sarvaiya et al., 2019; Wirtenberg et al., 2007). Jamali et al. (2015) precisely address such a sustainability–HRM interface in their co-creation model. In this model, they draw extensively on Ulrich's (1997) strategic partnership model to identify four roles that the HR function can play in the CSR agenda. These roles are strategic partner, change agent, administrative expert and employee champion. The HRM and CSR (sustainability) interface therefore provides a fertile ground on which shared sustainability-oriented outcomes can be achieved with stakeholders when HR professionals take on the four roles as proposed by Ulrich (1997).

While the emergent conceptual research and recent empirical studies suggest that there could be a mutual relationship between HRM and sustainability agenda, the effectiveness of such relationships in practice remains limited (Sarvaiya et al., 2019; Wirtenberg et al., 2007). It has been argued that the HR function plays a limited role in the key strategic issues relevant to the advancement of the organization's sustainability and CSR agenda. For example, Wirtenberg et al. (2007) found that the HR function's role was noticeable in areas such as leadership development, training, talent management, employee engagement, promotion of diversity and inclusion and development of ethical values, but less effective in areas such as health and safety, organizational culture and change management and stakeholder relationship management. These studies, however, highlight an unbalanced and unintegrated approach in the HRM function's involvement in the CSR/sustainability agenda; its role in externally facing sustainability actions appears somewhat piecemeal. Such an unbalanced scope and depth of the HRM function's engagement with sustainability underscores the fundamental influence of a number of contextual factors (Chiappetta Jabbour and Lopes de Sousa Jabbour, 2016; Collier and Esteban, 2007; Garavan and McGuire, 2010; Islam et al., 2019; Jamali et al., 2015; Sarvaiya et al., 2019; Wirtenberg et al., 2007). These factors are fundamentally internal organizational attributes, and include: the organization's ability to have HR professionals that possess knowledge and skills in sustainability, the organizational culture and values, the degree to which an organization undertakes stakeholder integration, the level of inter-function collaboration, size and stage of development of the organization (Roscoe et al., 2019; Zibarras and Coan, 2015).

The extent to which the HR function essentially may be able to take part in the sustainability agenda is conditioned on the place the HR leader occupies in the wider organization's decision-making structure (Sarvaiya et al., 2019; Wirtenberg et al., 2007). Wirtenberg et al. (2007) found that HR managers with strategic positions were more likely to have a much broader involvement in the wider sustainability agenda than the HR function's leaders that were based at operational level. In many organizations, however, the HRM function's sphere of influence in relation to the sustainability agenda is limited because the HR function is not considered as a partner in the development and implementation of such an agenda (Stahl et al., 2020). Similarly, although the HR function has a potential to develop both internally and externally facing strategic and operational actions for CSR (sustainability), Sarvaiya et al. (2019) contend that its involvement in external facing CSR/sustainability actions, regardless of the level being strategic or operational, was somewhat limited. Just like Wirtenberg et al. (2007), they concluded that organizational factors – in particular those that are functional-oriented, and resource-based – may perhaps influence the scope and depth of the HR function's involvement in such agendas. For many organizations, the inherent tensions between line management, the specialist CSR managers and the HR functions with respect to which function champions the organization's sustainability agenda can limit the scope with which the HR function can perform actions aimed at the wider sustainability agenda (Podgorodnichenko et al., 2020; Sarvaiya et al., 2018). Further to this, Podgorodnichenko et al. (2020) suggest that striking a healthy balance between the traditional HRM actions and the new and additional sustainability roles the HRM professionals are expected to play can be daunting.

How can the Human Resources Function Contribute to a Firm's Sustainability Agenda? An HR Player's Perspective

Ulrich and Beatty (2001) propose that the HRM function should play a central role in the strategic direction of organizations. For these scholars, the HRM function needs to move beyond the traditional HRM agenda of ensuring employees are compliant with organizational standards to becoming a major player in the development and implementation of the wider organization agenda. They cite the emerging strategic challenges and complexities – involving disruptive innovations, an increasingly competitive and uncertain business environment – as drivers of a shift from just being a strategic partner to line managers – as previously proposed by Ulrich (1997) – to being a player. Such a shift means that the HRM function is expected to be at the core of the business and deliver results for the wider organization rather than being at the peripheral while providing support to line management (Ulrich and Beatty, 2001).

To this end, Ulrich and Beatty's (2001) framework – from partners to players: extending the HR playing field – is reviewed in order to draw insights for understanding the roles the HR professionals can play in advancing the sustainability agenda within their organizations. Ulrich and Beatty suggest that the metaphoric HR player needs to perform six roles to make a significant contribution to the organization: (a) coach; (b) architect; (c) builder; (d) facilitator; (e) leader; (f) conscience. These roles are, in the succeeding section, examined in relation to how sustainability can be advanced with an organization.

HR professionals as coaches

Institutionalization of the sustainability agenda requires a big shift in attitudes and behaviour of internal stakeholders such as employees and managers with respect to sustainability issues (Gond et al., 2011). Ulrich and Beatty (2001) suggest that coaching can make a significant contribution towards effecting employee behavioural change within organizations. Coaching employees in sustainability issues involves HR professionals observing, providing directions and feedback and rewarding employees who can demonstrate positive changes in attitude and behaviour towards sustainability issues within and outside the organization. HR coaches therefore need to analyse an organization's stakeholders in order to develop a better understanding of the organization's approach to the management of its relationship with its stakeholders. Such an analysis can allow HR professionals to identify gaps in top management's and employees' performance with respect to sustainability issues. It can further help HR professionals in developing appropriate materials for regularly coaching top management in the development and implementation of sustainability policies. Equipped with a greater understanding of employees' levels of understanding and implementation of the sustainability agenda, regular coaching that centres on imparting knowledge and skills related to sustainability can promote professional growth and development of employees. For top management, coaching can provide them with a clear focus to realize their maximum potential in directing the organization's sustainability agenda.

HR professionals as architects

Organizational architects are strategists who develop the strategic framework that provides organizational direction towards superior performance. Ulrich and Beatty (2001) argue that, by virtue of their influence over employees and the direct relationship with top management, HR professionals have a deeper understanding of the internal organizational political realities. Being at the focal position effectively allows HR professionals to assume the role of organizational architects. In relation to sustainability, being sustainability architects requires HR professionals to demonstrate that they understand the features of an ideal sustainable organization, and that they are able to apply such features to their organization.

Organizational culture and values are important aspects of the organization's architecture that are required in the institutionalization of the sustainability agenda (Maon et al., 2010). HR professionals can inculcate these elements and develop them further into the unique capabilities required to deliver superior sustainability outcomes. HR professionals can ensure that the sustainability agenda advanced by the organization is closely aligned with the overall strategic framework, organizational culture and values and structures (Roscoe et al., 2019). Thus, having sustainability-oriented organizational culture and values can help top management turn the sustainability agenda into a unique capability that can ultimately differentiate their organizations from their rivals in the eyes of stakeholders. In addition, as organization architects, HR professionals can ensure that the organizational actions are well aligned with regulations as well as the various industry-based codes of conduct (Richards, 2020).

HR professionals as builders

Ulrich and Beatty (2001) consider the role of HR professionals as builders of an organization's strategies. In relation to sustainability, HR professionals can create a strategic blueprint for the organization's pursuit of a sustainability agenda. To contribute towards building a sustainability-oriented organization, HR professionals can devise processes for the implementation of a sustainability agenda that creates value for organizations as well as their stakeholders (Jamali et al., 2015).

More importantly, HR professionals have a role to mobilize resources – including employees – to act on sustainability actions emanating from the strategic sustainability blueprint. In order to garner support for the implementation of sustainability practices, HR professionals can develop HR policies that can induce and promote sustainability-oriented culture within the organization over an extended time period (Roscoe et al., 2019; Saeed et al., 2019). They can also take an active role in the sharing of employee best practices in sustainability with employees to demonstrate to them the fact that sustainability matters to the organization.

Apart from sharing of best practices, HR professionals have a role of aligning recruitment and selection policies, performance management and rewards systems with the organization's sustainability agenda (Islam et al., 2019). HR professionals can build and align the structures required for the implementation of a sustainability agenda with the prevailing organization structures. Furthermore, given that the adoption and implementation of sustainability in an organization is a fundamental organizational change which demands behavioural and attitudinal change across the different strata and that knowledge management is crucial, continuous organizational learning becomes imperative. Therefore, HR professionals can build a conducive environment in which learning and innovation related to sustainability take centre stage (Jamali et al., 2015).

HR professionals as facilitators

HR professionals can play a fundamental role in facilitating sustainability-oriented change within their organizations. Drawing on Ulrich and Beatty (2001), the role of HR professionals can be performed in three main realms of influence. First, they can facilitate the proper functioning of teams that are tasked with the institutionalization of a sustainability agenda. Considering that integration of sustainability within the organization requires concerted efforts, HR professionals can facilitate identification and leveraging of team members' talents to achieve superior sustainability performance of their organizations. Furthermore, given that teams often face problems in getting organized, HR professionals can facilitate team efforts in defining and making the requisite tasks for promotion of the sustainability agenda within the organization. Second, HR professionals can facilitate sustainability-oriented change to proceed at a much faster and sustainable pace. They can facilitate the acquisition and development of competences for the implementation of the sustainability-oriented change. Third, HR professionals can signal an organization's top management to form alliances with other organizations in order to institutionalize the broad sustainability agenda. Thus, as the organization embarks on formation of alliances, HR professionals can help managers and their organizations navigate and effectively respond to changes that can be brought about by accommodating values of different alliance partners.

HR professionals as leaders

Ulrich and Beatty (2001) theorize that committed leadership can be a strategic capability in bringing out organizational change. In a similar manner, it has been argued that adoption and implementation of a sustainability agenda requires committed leadership (Gond et al., 2011). It has also been suggested that the effective implementation of a sustainability agenda can be determined by the overall governance structures and the position where the axis of power rests with an organization (Sarvaiya et al., 2018, 2019). Given the central position the HRM function occupies within some organizations, HR professionals may be better placed to assume leadership in embedding the sustainability agenda within their organizations (Jamali et al., 2015).

Through the leadership role, HR professionals are expected to coordinate not only the implementation of internally focused sustainability initiatives but also the implementation of external sustainability initiatives. Furthermore, HR professionals can vigorously advocate for increased investment in all sustainability actions undertaken within the organizations (Saeed et al., 2019). Finally, as sustainability leaders, HR professionals are equally required to determine the level of sustainability performance individuals and organizational functions can achieve and be held accountable for during periodic performance measurements.

HR professionals as custodians of conscience

Despite the position the HR function occupies in an organization as well as its potential role in ensuring compliance with HR-related regulations, evidence suggests that the HR function is often less involved in ensuring business integrity and promotion of sustainability initiatives that are specifically outward-facing (cf. Sarvaiya et al., 2019). In many organizational settings however, it is common to find the responsibility of implementation of ethical and sustainability issues to be organized around finance, legal and marketing departments. However, without an internal adjudicator or referee, implementation of sustainability can often be a subject of intense contention. In most cases, the function or department that has been charged to lead the implementation of the agenda often favours the implementation of sustainability (ethical) issues that it considers relevant to its core activities. The HR function can thus play an active role in ensuring that the implemented sustainability actions reflect and serve the interest of the wider organization and its stakeholders. In such a role, the HR function can ensure that the executive leadership and employees are held to account for the implementation of plans and actions related to the sustainability agenda. For organizations that possess codes of conduct, the HRM function can also ensure that those who fail to play by the moral and sustainability standards are motivated to comply and sanctioned accordingly when non-compliance persists. Thus, in organizations where different functions may either be preoccupied with ethical/sustainability issues that are only relevant to their function or are not at all paying attention to sustainability issues, HR professionals can help their organization avert some organizational-wide business risks and ultimately help their organization create value for all stakeholders.

METHODOLOGY

The Dutch hotel industry is highly diversified in terms of the ownership structures and operating models. Recent figures suggest that there are 5300 registered hotels in the Netherlands – with most of them based in the metropolitan Amsterdam.[1] The Dutch hotel industry is dominated by hotels, mostly medium and large sized, which are affiliated to large multinational chains through various arrangements such as management agreements, franchising, leasing and direct ownership. Apart from the multinational chain affiliated hotels, there are several small and independent hotels that are owned and operated by local investors. As revealed elsewhere in this chapter, the ownership structures and operating models can have an influence on the hotel's orientation towards sustainability and the sophistication of the HRM function.

The chapter draws on a qualitative and interpretative-based study. The study utilized a case study research strategy (Saunders et al., 2016). Although the case study strategy is criticized for lack of generalization of the study findings (Flyvberg, 2011), in this study it was the most appropriate strategy to employ considering that it allowed an in-depth understanding of the often complex phenomenon – the relationship between HRM and sustainability within organizational settings (Yin, 2018). We adopted purposive sampling of hotels that participated in this study. Saunders et al. (2016) suggest that purposive sampling can be used in phenomenological studies in which individuals' participation requires them to have adequate knowledge about the issue under investigation. Hence, this study focused on 12 large and medium-sized hotels in the Netherlands. These hotels have some form of sustainability agenda that is based upon the Green Key certification scheme[2] and an HRM department – the parameters that made them better positioned to provide adequate information about the issue under investigation. However, the stage and maturity of these hotels markedly differed, and often reflected the extent to which the HRM function is perceived vital to the institutionalization of the sustainability agenda (see Table 22.1). Eighteen semi-structured interviews were used to gather data from top managers, HR managers (specialists) and an employee from one of the hotels[3] (see Table 22.2). Semi-structured interviews are suited for this study because they can potentially allow participants to freely provide insights into the role of HRM function in the development and implementation of a sustainability agenda. It has to be noted that prior to the interviews, participants were asked to describe (a) the level of their hotel's engagement with sustainability; (b) the HRM function's place within the hotel's decision-making structure.

Table 22.1   Hotel's HRM profile and stage of the hotel's sustainability agenda

Hotel's code	Responsibility for HRM	Position of HRM within the hotel	Number of employees[4]	Number of HR professionals	Nature of hotel	Stage of hotel's sustainability agenda
H1	Human Resource Coordinator	Central	139	2 plus 1 intern	Large chain affiliated multinational hotel	Mature
H2	Human Resources Manager	Peripheral	90	1	Large independent hotel	Nascent
H3	Human Resource Coordinator	Central	53	2	Medium-sized independent hotel	Mature
H4	Human Resources Manager	Central	155	3	Large chain affiliated multinational hotel chain	Mature
H5	Human Resources Manager	Peripheral	39	1	Medium-sized independent hotel	Nascent
H6	Human Resources Advisor	Peripheral	61	1	Medium-sized independent hotel	Nascent
H7	Human Resources Advisor	Peripheral	76	1	Medium-sized independent hotel	Nascent
H8	Human Resources Manager	Central	154	1	Large multinational hotel	Mature
H9	Human Resources Coordinator	Peripheral	57	1	Medium-sized independent hotel	Nascent
H10	Human Resources Director	Central	196	4	Large independent hotel	Mature
HR11	Human Resource Manager	Peripheral	71	1	Medium-sized hotel	Nascent
H12	Human Resource Manager	Central	79	1	Medium-sized hotel	Nascent

Thematic analysis was adopted in which data contained in the interview transcripts were be broken into fragments. Drawing on Miles and Huberman (1994), we particularly searched for similarities and differences in the transcribed data by subjecting them to open and axial coding. This was initially conducted by reading the data and tentatively assigning labels to chunks of data. This process proceeded until we could no longer identify new codes. Next, we iteratively reviewed the research questions and further deductively identified five principal *a priori* themes from the literature review such as: (a) HR professionals as architects, (b) HR professionals as coaches, (c) HR professionals as leaders, (d) HR professionals as facilitators, (e) HR professionals as custodians of conscience. These themes provided a basis for developing the primary list of codes. The primary list of codes included, for example, various items related to actions HR professionals undertake to institutionalize sustainability and contextual (enabling and limiting) factors relevant to the various roles HR can perform in pursuing a sustainability agenda. Patterns and recurrent themes and divergent and similar themes across the different cases were iteratively searched and arrived at.

Table 22.2   *Profiles of respondents and the hotels they represent*

Respondent's code	Respondent's position	Interview duration (minutes)	Nature of hotel	Stage of hotel's sustainability agenda
R1	Assistant General Manager	41	Large multinational hotel	Mature
R2	Human Resource Coordinator	32		
R3	Human Resources Manager	24	Large independent hotel	Nascent
R4	Owner/General Manager	40	Medium-sized independent hotel	Mature
R5	Human Resource Coordinator	39		
R6	Human Resources Manager	43	Large Multinational hotel chain	Mature
R7	Waitress	10		
R8	Human Resources Manager	22	Medium-sized independent hotel	Nascent
R10	Human Resources Advisor	23	Medium-sized independent hotel	Nascent
R11	Human Resources Advisor	25	Medium-sized independent hotel	Nascent
R12	Human Resources Manager	42	Large multinational hotel	Mature
R13	Financial Controller	11	Medium-sized independent hotel	Nascent
R14	Human Resources Coordinator	17	Medium-sized independent hotel	
R15	Human Resources Director	28	Large independent hotel	Mature
R16	Hotel Manager	31	Medium-sized hotel	Nascent
R18	Human Resource Manager	20	Medium-sized hotel	Nascent

FINDINGS

This section presents qualitative findings of this study based on interviews with managers, HR professionals and employees of hotels in the Netherlands. These findings are organized along the five HR roles based on Ulrich and Beatty's (2001) model, focusing on the role of HR professionals as coaches, architects, facilitators, leaders and conscience custodians. The HR professional role as builders did not come out explicitly in our study. Organizational contextual factors that influence the extent to which HR professionals performed each of the roles and the choice between the development and implementation of internally facing and externally facing sustainability actions are also presented.

The Role of HR Professionals as Coaches

Our study reveals that in a number of hotels HR professionals contributed to the hotels' sustainability agenda by coaching employees as well as managers. Their coaching targeted employees and managers who had little or no prior exposure to sustainability initiatives. Such on-the-job training provided HR professionals with an opportunity to effect behavioural change that can be instrumental to the institutionalization of the sustainability agenda. To effect behavioural change in sustainability issues, regular coaching served two purposes. First, HR respondents argued that coaching was important because it offered employees the necessary support as they embarked on a new journey to embrace sustainability:

> We also provide regular training for all employees. We have our own academy where we coach them and give them support. Some trainings are done by external companies and some trainings we do ourselves. So, I made a training for Green Key as well because in the beginning I visited all the locations and later I developed training and coaching sessions. So, they could just come to one place where

I can help them with what they are working on. There is also a training for shift leaders or managers, and the theme is sustainable leadership. (Interview R2)

It is important to note that regular coaching sessions were instrumental in inculcating the sustainability-oriented organizational values and culture in such employees. Second, it was also revealed that for some managers for hotels who had no prior experience of implementing a sustainability agenda and who were not fully convinced yet of the business case of engaging in sustainability, coaching helped to motivate and reassure them to take major steps towards integration of sustainability issues. Indeed, transitioning from being an unsustainable hotel towards becoming a sustainable hotel can be challenging for many managers and employees without prior experience of sustainability. As such, HR professionals undertook regular communication and provided feedback to employees and managers in order to reinforce the skills and knowledge imparted through coaching; the actions of which were instrumental in embedding sustainability actions into the organization's routines:

> But of course, we have to communicate to them our sustainability strategies. Everyone gets our policy/strategy in the first month of working here. We also have a green employee questionnaire in which we check the knowledge of our staff about sustainability. It's an annual assessment. We offer feedback and support when they are not doing what is in our strategy or plan. (Interview R5)

The propensity of HR professionals to assume the role of a coach is influenced by several contextual factors. First, the stage at which the hotel is, in terms of a sustainability agenda, determines the degree of coaching HR professionals undertake. For instance, for hotels that are at the beginning of their sustainability journey, HR professionals spent a great deal of time coaching employees as well as managers to deal with new ways of working that incorporate sustainability. However, interestingly for such hotels, HR professionals largely focused their coaching on the internal implementation of sustainability initiatives as opposed to coaching staff on the implementation of broad-based sustainability actions. Second, the specific value orientation of the hotel had an influence over the degree to which coaching was undertaken. For example, it was consistently observed that the HRM functions of hotels that adopted the sustainability agenda for instrumental purposes as opposed to the HRM functions of hotels which implemented sustainability initiatives because it is 'the ethically right thing to do', profoundly showed enthusiasm in coaching employees and managers in sustainability actions. In most cases, coaching was done in a piecemeal manner to meet the requirements of external certification schemes:

> In my opinion I am not really engaged, you only receive the information at the start of your employ-ment and during the first coaching or training sessions, and that's it unfortunately. I was told it's a condition from the Green Key people. (Interview R7)

The Role of HR Professionals as Architects

HR professionals can play the role of architects in the HR–sustainability interface through the development of sustainability policy and strategies. In our study we found that the degree to which HR professionals took part in the sustainability strategies varied considerably. The manifestation of HR professionals' role as architects puts these HR professionals into three categories. The first category of HR professionals, which were found in most hotels, made limited or no contribution to the development of sustainability strategies. However, the second category of HR professionals, who were found in a limited number of hotels, only took a leading role in the development of internally focused sustainability strategies which were mostly related to HRM practices:

> We are responsible for working on sustainability initiatives within our hotel as a part of the project team, but we are also seen as advisers on sustainability to the whole team when we develop projects. (Interview R12)

They were involved in the development of strategies and initiatives that were aimed at enhancing the welfare of employees. In addition, their contribution was fundamental in the development of recruitment and selection, training and development, performance measurement and reward systems that put a primacy on the integration of the sustainability agenda. One of the respondents had this to say:

> Of course, we have a recruitment policy that we check the candidate for knowledge in sustainability. The potential employee has to be able to show support for our concepts and preferably love it as well. But that's an important thing. (Interview R4)

Integrating sustainability into HRM practices can be considered as a remarkable contribution for such professionals given that these issues are rarely prioritized in the hospitality industry because of the industry's preoccupation with undertaking sustainability initiatives that are more visible to external stakeholders (Bagri et al., 2010).

Nevertheless, it has to be noted that the final category of HR professionals in a limited number of hotels that have mature sustainability agendas were thought to be undertaking a leadership role in the development of broad-based sustainability strategies:

> I think it might be in some hotels that HRM takes a more administrative role, and then they let other functions actually do sustainability initiatives, but in this case, our HR director, continental Europe, is really involved in the strategies that are implemented within all the hotels. The HR director is really there to give a focus on how employees should take part in sustainability action within the hotel. (Interview R1)

Overall, the limited contribution of HR professionals to the development of the wider sustainability strategies, as noted in this study, highlights the influence of a number of organizational contextual factors. For most of the hotels, the HRM function is largely perceived as a peripheral and mere support function that exists to ensure hotels' compliance with HR related regulations and to manage the reward systems. Furthermore, the general preference in the hospitality industry for environmental sustainability means that when sustainability strategies are developed, the contribution by the HRM professionals tends to be overlooked since the contribution made by the technical or operations functions may often be prioritized. In a similar way, the values that drive the hotel's engagement in a sustainability agenda have also been noted to play a fundamental role regarding the HRM function involvement in, and the emphasis accorded to, the development of broad-based sustainability strategies. Thus, we observed that hotels that consistently linked their adoption of sustainability agenda to market benefits, notwithstanding the stage of their sustainability agenda, rarely involved HR professionals in the development of externally facing sustainability strategies (cf. Sarvaiya et al., 2018). These hotels oftentimes gave the marketing function the leading role to the development of such strategies and their subsequent implementation.

HR Professionals as Facilitators

Ulrich and Beatty (2001) suggest that HR professionals' role has been evolving towards the creation of a conducive and facilitating environment in which strategies can be translated into actions that ultimately lead to good organizational outcomes. In our study, we found some variations in the way HR professionals facilitated the creation of structures and routines for implementation of sustainability initiatives within their respective hotels. In some hotels with advanced stages of a sustainability agenda, it was revealed that HR professionals facilitated the formation of cross-functional teams to spearhead the implementation of a sustainability agenda, although they were not fully involved in the development and implementation of the wider sustainability agenda:

> We are seen by other departments as a unifying department. So, naturally when there is a need for a lot of colleagues from different departments to work together. We take that opportunity; we led in the establishment of the Green Key team that has members from the technical department, from food and beverage and housekeeping. (Interview R6)

Clearly, the fundamental role HR professionals play in the establishment of cross-functional teams reflects the widely held perception that HR professionals possess strong soft skills that can be used effectively in the facilitation of collaboration between different functions within the organization. It also underscores the HR function's perceived competences in the organizational design that considers changes that an organization may be going through.

Given that teams often face problems in getting organized, HR professionals were instrumental in facilitating team efforts in defining the teams' sustainability tasks. Additionally, although not ubiquitous in the sampled hotels, it was learnt that HR professionals played a facilitating role in the development of new sustainability-focused routines and processes and spearheaded their alignment with the pre-existing organizational-wide processes:

> You know we started taking part in sustainability not long ago; we started after joining the Green Key. So, the Green Key people asked us to do certain new things to prove that we are sustainable. Some of the things we [HRM] have started in this hotel is the internal communication system of sustainability to our employees. We have made sustainability communication to be part of the regular staff communication. In every meeting and staff update we include what we are doing in sustainability. We want every employee to know what is being done in the area of sustainability. (Interview R8)

Developing a conducive environment to facilitate organizational learning and sharing of best practices from within and outside their hotels was identified as another role of the HR professionals in the institutionalization of the sustainability agenda in their hotels. Respondents from a limited number of hotels particularly stated that the HR departments were responsible for collecting the information about best sustainability-oriented practices from employees and other hotels and certification organizations and sharing them internally to enhance learning:

> Our HR manager participates in regular meetings that are organised by the Green Key where new sustainability practices are discussed with the Green Key owners and other hotels that are also certi-

fied. The HR manager passes this information to all employees via the Green Key team and meetings. (Interview R16)

However, respondents from the majority of hotels, as the quote below shows, felt that the HR professionals should have done more to propagate best practices regarding implementation of sustainability:

> I think that they [HRM] should share more information about the best practices of the Green Key implementations in the hotel. How much water do we save per month or year for instance? (Interview R7)

Nevertheless, since embedding sustainability into the organizational fabrics involves continuous improvements and innovation, HR professionals' pursuit of organizational learning associated with sustainability may have helped them to inculcate sustainability-oriented values among hotels' employees and managers. This may have also helped them facilitate the development of capabilities for hotels to be effective in creating sustainable value for all stakeholders.

Finally, we found that a limited number of HR professionals facilitated their hotels' move to develop alliances with external organizations to implement sustainability initiatives. This role was particularly enacted in hotels that had a mature sustainability agenda but also in those hotels that consider the HR function to be of strategic importance rather than a supporting one. Respondents from such hotels stated that they facilitated such initiatives by helping their colleagues – whose responsibility was to form and manage alliances – to navigate the challenges that are associated with working in alliances including accommodating the different values partners bring into alliances:

> Our work with the local municipality and the prison service to provide work placements for the unemployed people and ex-prisoners was made less problematic thanks to the HR advisors who worked with us when we were forming partnerships with these organisations. We did not have a clue as to how working with public servants was going to be. (Interview R1)

Overall, HR professionals' facilitating role in the development of structures and routines, their increased role in organizational learning and capabilities development and facilitation of alliance formation, suggests that the role of HRM function is increasingly being considered as strategic to the achievement of better sustainability performance outcomes. This, apparently, is the departure from the widely held perception in the hospitality industry that the traditional position of the HR function should be at the periphery and only playing a supporting role (cf. Ulrich, 1997). Such a new position allows the HR professionals to play a fundamental role in the implementation of internally and externally focused sustainability actions.

HR Professionals as Leaders

Institutionalization of sustainability within an organization requires strong and committed leadership because it involves changes in the organizational values and culture and reconfiguration of structures and systems (Blok et al., 2015; Collier and Esteban, 2007). In our study, a few respondents stated that HR professionals played a strategic leadership role in the development and implementation of the sustainability agenda. These respondents worked for hotels that have a mature sustainability agenda. In part, this is because the HR function was regarded as an integral part of the hotels' decision-making structure. In such hotels, the HRM function assumed both joint leadership with the hotels' sustainability (CSR) coordinators in developing and implementing a sustainability agenda that included actions beyond the internal sustainability actions:

> Yes, I lead most of the development of strategy just by talking with our colleagues. We have regular meetings with our other managers where we just talk to them and give them updates on sustainability things that are going on and things that are in the planning, and they do it for their side as well. So, we can talk about where we see opportunities for sustainable choices, or they come to us with the question. (Interview R12)

The central position the HRM function occupied in the decision-making structures of such hotels and the leadership role it played allowed it to assume greater power for advocating for increased investment in the wider sustainability agenda. This ultimately places the HR function at the axis of influence over the direction the hotels take in their sustainability journey.

In contrast, in the majority of the hotels, especially those that have a nascent sustainability agenda, respondents framed the only leadership role HR professionals played in the sustainability agenda was the setting of objectives and development of sustainability actions that had a strong alignment with their HRM practices:

> We always know that the HR department is there to make a connection between human resource practices and sustainability. They lead in formulating objectives, actions, although I think they can do a better job than just being pushed by the sustainability organisations which we have recently joined. (Interview R18)

The HR function partaking in the leadership role in the development and implementation of employee-focused sustainability agenda reflects the current thinking that an employee-focused sustainability agenda is an integral part of the contemporary responsible HRM (Ehnert et al., 2016; Richards, 2020; Saeed et al., 2019; Sarvaiya et al., 2019; Voegtlin and Greenwood, 2016). By virtue of its strategic position in such hotels, the HRM function can hold line managers accountable for internally focused sustainability outcomes that are associated with employee wellbeing.

An interesting element we came across, regarding the leadership role of the HRM function in advancing the sustainability agenda, was how the small nature of the HR departments in some small to medium hotels with nascent sustainability agendas, affected their ability to take on sustainability leadership roles. Their small size and limited access to resources compelled the HR department and its professionals to be parsimonious in so far as spreading out their efforts and resources in leading the development and implementation of a sustainability agenda within their hotels and beyond was concerned:

> We are a very small HR department; so, in our view, adding sustainability would be stretching our resources. We would rather see the sustainability specialists lead us. (Interview R10)

Indeed, with their small size and the peripheral positions they occupy within the hotels' decision-making structures, it may be possible that HR professionals may not only lack prior experience in developing and implementing sustainability, but may also have a limited understanding of the organizational context in which the nexus between sustainability and HRM exists.

HR Professionals as Custodians of Sustainability Conscience

Effectively embedding sustainability within an organization requires organizational actors to generally accept norms that guide the organization's behaviour when interacting with internal and external stakeholders. These norms are often manifested as codes of ethical conduct (Schwab, 1996). Although codes of ethical conduct in strictest form are not prevalent in many of the hotels that we studied, some hotels embed a clause in employment contracts that is supposed to compel employees to act in an ethical and sustainable manner:

> New employees undergo training in sustainability organised by the HR department, and then the person who goes through is required to sign the contract. The contract will also have a form with all the information about sustainability and what we are doing. The employee has to sign that s/he will stick to what they have signed for. (Interview R15)

However, the effectiveness of such clauses in employees' contracts in terms of ethical (sustainability-related) behaviour varies across hotels that participated in this study. In some hotels – in particular those that had a nascent sustainability agenda – it was revealed that the HRM function paid lukewarm or no attention to the employees' and managers' compliance with the sustainability terms of their employment contracts:

> Our new employment contracts demand employees to do sustainability because the Green Key people want us to have it. But in this hotel, checking regularly whether employees and managers do sustainability actions has never been part of our [HR department] job description. We are just a small unit with two people and two interns. Doing that will be taking things too far and also opening ourselves to conflicts with managers of different departments. I don't see management supporting us when those conflicts arise. (Interview R11)

For some hotels, a lukewarm approach to performing such a role may perhaps be reflective of the pressure to demonstrate to certification organizations that the entire hotel is aware of their sustainability obligations (Mzembe et al., 2020). Some HR professionals were concerned about the lack of support from top management and line managers to enforce compliance. Furthermore, some respondents felt that top management, line managers and the HRM department were mainly concerned about employees' productivity to such an extent that they turned a blind eye to employees' compliance with sustainability guidelines that are embedded in their contracts:

> I think it can be misleading that we are a green certified hotel, and everyone thinks that sustainability for us is doing the right things for the sake of it. Everyone at the top is just interested in room occupancy and profits at the end of the year. So, the last thing for us as HR professionals is to hassle employees and their managers with sustainability metrics and asking them how they are actually doing. We know that we will just be wasting our time if I may say so. (Interview 11)

The stage at which the hotel's sustainability agenda is observed to influence the extent to which HR professionals and top management prioritized the enforcement of compliance. In a large majority of hotels that pursue nascent sustainability agenda, both the HRM function and top management did not particularly consider employees' compliance with the hotel's sustainability standards as a serious issue that needed HR professionals' attention. For these hotels, it is also particularly important to note that the HR departments were poorly resourced. HR professionals were only left to attend to purely HRM issues and eventually became 'toothless lions' regarding ensuring employee and management's compliance with the sustainability guidelines. In contrast, the HRM functions of hotels that have elaborate and mature sustainability agendas were empowered to set standards and targets and received support from top management to ensure that there was adequate compliance with the sustainability-related terms in their employment contracts. Indeed, in hotels where HRM managers were influential top management team members, their ability to monitor and sanction non-compliance was much stronger than in the hotels where the HRM function was seen to be at the periphery of the decision-making structure.

The centrality of the HRM function within the hotel can be fundamental to HR professionals playing such a role. The respondents reiterated that by virtue of working with employees across different functions, the HRM function may be better positioned to serve as an enforcer of ethical conduct and employees' compliance with the sustainability terms of their contracts:

> I think the centrality of the HR department and also because they are like the 'police men or women of the hotel', the job of seeing to it that everyone takes part in sustainability to fulfil their contractual obligations fits them well if you compare with any other department in a hotel. They deal with everyone whether is from finance department, marketing, F&B etc. (Interview R1)

DISCUSSION

This chapter demonstrates that the HRM function can fundamentally contribute to the sustainability agenda of hotels. First, in part conformity with Ulrich and Beatty's (2001) conceptualization, our study reveals that the HRM functional roles can take the form of sustainability coaching, leadership, facilitation, sustainability architecture and conscience policing. In our sampled hotels, we found that HR professionals' roles in advancing the sustainability agenda were to a greater degree variable, and that only HR professionals from a limited number of hotels performed all five roles. The roles HR professionals performed to institutionalize the sustainability agenda in order of frequency are coaching, facilitation, architecture building, conscience policing and leadership. The frequency such roles were performed depended on the main organizational contextual factors, which are discussed in the succeeding section.

In this chapter, the various roles HR professionals perform to institutionalize a sustainability agenda are also examined in relation to Voegtlin and Greenwood's (2016) conceptualization of the three domains associated with the sustainability (CSR)–HRM interface. The first domain involves considering HRM as an integral part of sustainability. In our study, none of the roles HR professionals play in the institutionalization of sustainability suggested that HRM is largely viewed in terms of it being a crucial part of the sustainability agenda. HR professionals in a limited number of hotels with mature sustainability agendas regarded sustainability as a strong component of HRM and to be in line with Voegtlin and Greenwood (2016). Thus, within this domain, sustainability is considered as an important instrument for achieving responsible HRM (Ehnert et al., 2016; Kramar, 2014; Richards, 2020; Saeed et al., 2019). For our study, HR professionals who favoured such a perspective also performed the roles of architects and leaders in the development and implementation of organizational strategies that strongly linked HR practices with sustainability. However, the downside of the HR professionals' preference for the internal sustainability agenda and, in particular, being responsible for HRM practices can inadvertently limit other organizational functions from active involvement in such a kind of HRM–sustainability interface.

Our study conforms with Voegtlin and Greenwood's (2016) last proposition and reveals that the link between sustainability and HRM can either be mutually dependent or independent. On the one hand, we came across HR professionals, from a limited number of hotels with a mature sustainability agenda, who favour the symbiotic relationship between sustainability and HRM. For such professionals, they identify themselves with all five roles as examined in this study. As such, these roles may have enabled the HRM function to get actively involved not only in the building of hotels that are internally sustainable but also in the contribution towards the public good (Jamali et al., 2015; Sarvaiya et al., 2018). On the other hand, in most studied hotels, especially those that have nascent sustainability agendas, there was a strong perception that sustainability and HRM were mutually exclusive. For such hotels, it was unsurprising that the HRM function's role was largely performed by facilitating the establishment of sustainability teams.

The nature of the roles and the extent to which HR professionals can perform them in pursuit of the sustainability agenda were influenced by organizational contextual factors (Sarvaiya et al., 2019; Wirtenberg et al., 2007). These factors include (a) the internal stakeholders' perception and the position of the HRM function in the hotel's decision-making structure; (b) the level of the maturity of the hotel's sustainability agenda. First, we noted that in hotels where the HRM functions were highly regarded and their heads were core to the decision-making process, HR professionals were more likely to assume all five roles than in hotels where the HRM functions were regarded to be at the periphery of the organization but also whose heads were not part of the hotel's management team. In line with Stahl et al. (2020), the low level of perception about the HRM function in some hotels meant that HR professionals were only allowed to perform limited roles such as coaching and facilitation, which were mostly done in a piecemeal manner.

While HR professionals in hotels that considered the HRM function to be strategic were given adequate support to perform different roles that were central to the embeddedness of sustainability, their counterparts in hotels where the HRM function was merely seen as a supporting function were not fully supported by management and other internal actors to take on pro-active roles such as sustainability leadership, architects and conscience custodians. Relatedly, for some hotels, we found that such a lack of support to the HRM function to pro-actively embed a sustainability agenda meant that the HRM functions' resources were largely strained and limited (Stahl et al., 2020). Even when some HR professionals were willing to take an active role in the institutionalization of sustainability, a lack of resources compelled them to only engage in actions that were traditionally closer to their function.

Second, our study reveals that the level of maturity of the hotel's sustainability agenda influenced the propensity of the HRM function to assume and perform certain roles and leave out others (Stahl et al., 2020). Related to the influence of the maturity level of the hotel's sustainability agenda is the value orientation of the hotels. We established that, in hotels with the advanced sustainability agenda and those that had strong ethical value orientation, HR professionals were more likely to take a pro-active stance towards performing multiple roles in the promotion of sustainability. HR professionals in such hotels received more top managerial and other line management functions' support. As such, HR professionals considered institutionalization of the sustainability agenda to be one of their core responsibilities. Given that pro-active involvement in the hotels' sustainability agenda was taken as an integral part of their job, HR professionals assumed and performed different roles that enabled them to provide leadership in the development and implementation of a broad sustainability agenda that even involved wider stakeholders (Jamali et al., 2015; Sarvaiya et al., 2019; Voegtlin and Greenwood, 2016).

This however was not the case with the HRM functions in hotels that had a nascent sustainability agenda and especially those that had an overly instrumental value orientation. HR professionals in such hotels assumed reactive, more supportive and more operational and internally focused roles, such as coaching and, to a very limited degree, facilitation (Stahl et al., 2020). Overall, we specifically found that the level of maturity of the hotel's sustainability agenda was the overarching factor, to an extent that even the degree to which other organizational contextual factors shaped the sustainability–HRM relationship was largely reflective of its influence (Sarvaiya et al., 2019).

CONCLUSION

This chapter has examined the relationship between sustainability and HRM and the roles HR professionals can perform in institutionalization of the sustainability agenda within the selected hotels in the Dutch hospitality industry, by drawing on Ulrich and Beatty's (2001) framework. This chapter has also explored the internal organizational factors that influence the sustainability–HRM relationship as well as the propensity of HR professionals to assume the various roles as proposed by Ulrich and Beatty (2001). It is important to note that while Ulrich and Beatty's (2001) framework identifies six roles that HR professionals can perform in an organization (coach, facilitator, architect, builder, leader, custodian of conscience), this chapter reveals that HR professionals can assume five roles (coach, architect, leader, facilitator and custodian of sustainability conscience) in embedding the sustainability agenda within their hotels. By broadening the HR role from a strategic partner (Ulrich, 1997) to a player (Ulrich and Beatty, 2001), closely related roles such as 'builders' and architects' tended to overlap, rendering one obsolete and non-consequential. The chapter further provides insights into how the contextual embeddedness of the HR professionals' roles influences the institutionalization of the sustainability agenda within an organization (cf. Jamali et al., 2015; Sarvaiya et al., 2019).

This chapter has the following implications for practice. First, it highlights the potential roles that HR professionals can perform in order to enhance the effectiveness of their organization's sustainability agenda. However, as this chapter shows, attention will need to be paid to some of the internal organizational issues (and areas of support) that management and other actors may require in order to strengthen the sustainability–HRM nexus. For many hotels, the HRM function will need to be perceived as a strategic part of the business rather than a supporting function that only performs recruitment and selection. Top management can not only enhance the HRM function by establishing a well-resourced HRM department, but can also ensure that different functions within a hotel provide adequate support to the HR professionals as they perform their different roles in the institutionalization of the sustainability agenda. Central to this would be pursuit of an elaborate awareness programme about sustainability and the fundamental roles the HRM function can play in such an agenda.

Furthermore, the notion that an HR professional can be a 'player', as evidenced in this study, is at best paradoxical given the inherent tensions in many organizations regarding the need to contribute to superior financial performance as well as meeting the expectations arising from the performance of emerging roles in the institutionalization of the sustainability agenda within the organization (Hahn et al., 2010; Podgorodnichenko et al., 2020). Such tensions highlight the fact that, while Ulrich and Beatty (2001) advance the notion of the HRM function being an active player in the organizational field, the framework does not make a prescription of the rules of the game that all players are expected to follow. Hence, when HR professionals assume various roles as players in the institutionalization of a sustainability agenda, such an orientation has been fraught with tensions and misunderstandings between various functions within an organization and HRM function. It is therefore suggested that in order to address these tensions, coordination across different functions with the HRM function can help HR professionals develop genuine relationships with different stakeholders. Taking a multi-stakeholder approach in their involvement in the sustainability agenda can allow HR professionals to make a contribution towards meeting the interests of multiple stakeholders, and eventually address the tensions that may exist between the economic, social and environmental objectives of the firm.

This study on which this chapter is based has several limitations that provide avenues for further research. First, this study involved a limited number of hotels in the Dutch hotel industry context. As such, the findings generated from this study may have limited generalization beyond such a context. Second, it is based on a limited number of interviews, primarily from HR professionals and a limited number of line managers and one employee. Considering that different internal stakeholders such as employees and line managers can play a fundamental role in the institutionalization of the sustainability agenda within an organization, it is suggested that special consideration for the inclusion of employees and line managers in future studies should be made. Third, the aim of this study was to examine HR professional roles in the institutionalization of a sustainability agenda within their hotels. However, in pursuing such roles, tensions between various organizational goals exist, requiring HR professionals to strike a delicate balance (Podgorodnichenko et al., 2020). Given the scope of our study, it is recommended that further studies be conducted to examine how HR professionals in their new and emerging roles can resolve such tensions while taking a multi-dimensional approach to fully bring to light the complexities associated with the HRM–sustainability nexus.

NOTES

1. https://www.statista.com/statistics/624424/revenue-index-of-the-hospitality-industry-in-the-netherlands/
2. For detailed information about the Green Key scheme in the Netherlands, please visit www.greenkey.nl
3. For many hotels, employees were not allowed by their employers to participate in the study. However, getting employees' insights would have allowed triangulation of information from different managers.
3. It has to be noted the numbers presented here are for the regular employees. Most of the studied hotels depend on sub-contracted or agency workers especially in the house-keeping departments, and for a few hotels, they use also use agency workers for the Food and Beverage Departments.

REFERENCES

Alcaraz, J. M., Susaeta, L., Suarez, E., Colón, C., Gutiérrez-Martínez, I., Cunha, R., … & Pin, J. R. (2017). The human resources management contribution to social responsibility and environmental sustainability: Explorations from Ibero-America. *International Journal of Human Resource Management, 30*(22), 3166–3189.

Bagri, S. C., Babu, S., & Kukreti, M. (2010). Human resource practices in hotels: A study from the tourist state of Uttrakhand, India. *Journal of Human Resources in Hospitality & Tourism, 9*(3), 286–299.

Blok, V., Wesselink, R., Studynka, O., & Kemp, R. (2015). Encouraging sustainability in the workplace: A survey on the pro-environmental behaviour of university employees. *Journal of Cleaner Production, 106*, 55–67.

Chiappetta Jabbour, C. J. C., & Lopes de Sousa Jabbour, A. B. (2016). Green human resource management and green supply chain management: Linking two emerging agendas. *Journal of Cleaner Production, 112*, 1824–1833.

Collier, J., & Esteban, R. (2007). Corporate social responsibility and employee commitment. *Business Ethics: A European Review, 16*(1), 19–33.

DuBois, C. L. Z. and Dubois, D. A. (2012). Strategic HRM as social design for environmental sustainability in organization. *Human Resource Management, 51*, 799–826.

Ehnert, I. Parsa, S., Roper, I., Wagner, M., & Muller-Camen, M. (2016). Reporting on sustainability and HRM: A comparative study of sustainability reporting practices by the world's largest companies. *International Journal of Human Resource Management, 27*(1), 88–108.

Flyvberg, B. (2011). Case study. In N. K. Denzin and Y. S. Lincoln (Eds.), *The Sage Handbook of Qualitative Research* (4th ed.). London: Sage, pp. 301–316.

Garavan, T. N., & McGuire, D. (2010). Human resource development and society: Human resource development's role in embedding corporate social responsibility, sustainability, and ethics in organizations. *Advances in Developing Human Resources, 12*(5), 487–507.

Gond, J., Igalens, J. Swaen, V., & El Akremi, A. (2011). The human resources contribution to responsible leadership: An exploration of the CSR–HR interface. *Journal of Business Ethics, 98*, 115–132.

Hahn, T., Figge, F., Pinkse, J., & Preuss, L. (2010). Trade-offs in corporate sustainability: You can't have your cake and eat it. *Business Strategy and the Environment, 19*(4), 217–229.

Islam, M. A., Hunt, A., Jantan, A. H., Hashim, H., & Chong, C. W. (2019). Exploring challenges and solutions in applying green human resource management practices for the sustainable workplace in the ready-made garment industry in Bangladesh. *Business Strategy and Development, 3*(3), 1–12.

Jamali, D. R., El Dirani, A. M., & Harwood, I. A. (2015). Exploring human resource management roles in corporate social responsibility: The CSR-HRM co-creation model. *Business Ethics: A European Review, 24*(2), 125–143.

Kramar, R. (2014). Beyond strategic human resource management: Is sustainable human resource management the next approach? *International Journal of Human Resource Management, 25*(8), 1069–1089.

Maon, F., Lindgreen, A., & Swaen, V. (2010). Organizational stages and cultural phases: A critical review and a consolidative model of corporate social responsibility development. *International Journal of Management Reviews, 12*(1), 20–38.

Miles, M. B., & Huberman, A. M. (1994). *Qualitative Data Analysis: An Expanded Sourcebook* (2nd ed.). Thousand Oaks, CA: Sage Publications.

Mzembe, A. N., Lindgreen, A., Idemudia, U., & Melissen, F. (2020). A club perspective of sustainability certification schemes in the tourism and hospitality industry. *Journal of Sustainable Tourism, 28*(9), 1332–1350.

Podgorodnichenko, N., Edgar, F., & McAndrew, I. (2020). The role of HRM in developing sustainable organizations: Contemporary challenges and contradictions. *Human Resource Management Review, 30*(1), 100685, https://doi.org/10.1016/j.hrmr.2019.04.001

Qi, G., Zeng, S., Li, X., & Tam, C. (2012). Role of internalization process in defining the relationship between ISO 14001 certification and corporate environmental performance. *Corporate Social Responsibility and Environmental Management, 19*(3), 129–140.

Richards, J. (2020). Putting employees at the centre of sustainable HRM: a review, map and research agenda. *Employee Relations*, forthcoming, https://doi.org/10.1108/ER-01-2019-0037

Ronnenberg, S. K., Graham, M. E., & Mahmoodi, F. (2011). The important role of change management in environmental management system implementation. *International Journal of Operations and Production Management*, *31*(6), 631–647.

Roscoe, S., Subramanian, N., Jabbour, C. J. C., & Chong, T. (2019). Green human resource management and the enablers of green organisational culture: Enhancing a firm's environmental performance for sustainable development. *Business Strategy and the Environment*, *28*(5), 737–749.

Saeed, B. B., Afsar, B., Hafeez, S., Khan, I., Tahir, M., & Afridi, M. A. (2019). Promoting employee's proenvironmental behavior through green human resource management practices. *Corporate Social Responsibility and Environmental Management*, *26*(2), 424–438.

Sarvaiya, H., Arrowsmith, J., & Eweje, G. (2019). Exploring HRM involvement in CSR: Variation of Ulrich's HR roles by organisational context. *International Journal of Human Resource Management*, DOI: 10.1080/09585192.2019.1660698

Sarvaiya, H., Eweje, G., & Arrowsmith, J. (2018). The role of HRM in CSR: Strategic partnership or operational support? *Journal of Business Ethics*, *153*(3), 825–837.

Saunders, M. N. K., Lewis, P., & Thornhill, A. (2016). *Research Methods for Business Students*. London: Prentice Hall.

Scheyvens, R., Banks, G., & Hughes, E. (2016). The private sector and the SDGs: The need to move beyond 'Business as Usual'. *Sustainable Development*, *24*(6), 371–382.

Schwab, B. (1996). A note on ethics and strategy: Do good ethics always make for good business? *Strategic Management Journal*, *17*(6), 499–500.

Smith, S., Rohr, S., & Panton, R. (2018). Human resource management and ethical challenges: Building a culture for organization success. *International Journal of Public Leadership*, *14*(2), 66–79.

Stahl, G. K., Brewster, C. J., Collings, D. G., & Hajro, A. (2020). Enhancing the role of human resource management in corporate sustainability and social responsibility: A multi-stakeholder, multidimensional approach to HRM. *Human Resource Management Review*, 100708. https://doi.org/10.1016/j.hrmr.2019.100708

Ulrich, D. (1997). *Human Resource Champions: The Next Agenda for Adding Value and Delivering Results*. Boston, MA: Harvard Business School Press.

Ulrich, D., & Beatty, D. (2001). From partners to players: Extending the HR playing field. *Human Resource Management*, *40*(4), 293–307.

Voegtlin, C., & Greenwood, M. (2016). Corporate social responsibility and human resource management: A systematic review and conceptual analysis. *Human Resource Management Review*, *26*, 181–197.

Wirtenberg, J., Harmon, J., Russell, W., & Fairfield, K. (2007). HR's role in building a sustainable enterprise: Insights from some of the world's best companies. *Human Resource Planning*, *30*(1), 10–20.

Yin, R.K. (2018). *Case Study Research and Application: Design and Methods* (6th ed.). Los Angeles: Sage

Yong, J. Y., Yusliza, M. Y., Ramayah, T., Chiappetta Jabbour, C. J., Sehnem, S., & Venkatesh, M. (2020). Pathways towards sustainability in manufacturing organizations: Empirical evidence on the role of green human resource management. *Business Strategy and the Environment*, *29*(1), 212–228.

Zibarras, L. D., & Coan, P. (2015). HRM practices used to promote proenvironmental behavior: A UK survey. *International Journal of Human Resource Management*, *26*(16), 2121–2142.

23. Profits with purpose: corporate and entrepreneurial toxic leadership and threats to organizational sustainability

David Coldwell and Robert Venter

INTRODUCTION

In a recent article in the *Financial Times*, Kaplan and Owen (2019: 11) state that:

> It would be a serious mistake to assume that the contribution that business makes directly to the welfare of society is largely independent of its profitability. It is equally wrong to conclude that society has conferred on business certain privileges in return for which they must do good works that are not related to profitability.

Business Roundtable, an institution comprising leading US chief executives, stated recently (Kaplan and Owen, 2019: 11) that the interests of stockholders as well as stakeholders, must be considered by business leaders. By this they meant that there must be interest balanced leadership that advocates both profitability and purpose in the functioning of their organizations.

The fourth industrial revolution has created a rapidity of change that has bewildered business leaders and entrepreneurs in the appropriateness of specific responses. Threats to profitability from increasing competition wrought by new technologies on the one hand, and the constant sustainability refrain of modern stakeholders on the other (Coldwell, 2019), has confronted business leaders in a values' pincer movement making it difficult for them to decide on what the organizational balance of *profits* with *purpose* should be. Sometimes the response of corporate leaders has been extreme and generated different types of *toxic leadership.*

Toxic leadership is a concept that has been defined in different ways according to the context in which it has been adopted. Reed (2004: 67), for example, in the military context defines it as a syndrome recognizable as: an apparent lack of concern for the well-being of subordinates, an interpersonal technique that negatively affects organizational climate, and a conviction by subordinates that the leader is mostly motivated by self-interest.

Lipman-Blumel (2005) defines toxic leadership in the business and political contexts as destructive behaviour and dysfunctional personal characteristics. Heppell (2011) defines toxic leadership in the political context as being bad or destructive leadership. The basic emphasis of these definitions is on the *personal characteristics* of the leaders, their destructiveness, self-interest, lack of concern for others rather than leadership that becomes toxic through an unbalanced and extreme focus on strategies of *profit* or *purpose*. This type of toxic leadership is not driven by deliberate personal destructiveness, nor is it necessarily driven through a lack of concern for employee well-being (although this may be an unintended consequence), it may even be seen as a bona fide (but ultimately misguided) attempt by the leader to maintain organizational objectives and the sustainability of the firm. Few studies within the last decade have dealt with toxic leadership in business organizations, and, in line with Coldwell and Callaghan (2014) and Coldwell's (2016, 2019) recent research, the current study defines toxic leadership as an overriding, but not purposively destructive drive, by business leaders of large (macro) established organizations and entrepreneurs of smaller (micro), more recently established businesses, to maintain or initiate organizational competitiveness through extreme strategic processes. These extreme and usually personally-driven strategies are maximally focused on either environmental sustainability (purpose) or economic sustainability (profits). Trickle downs of extreme forms of toxic leadership can generate toxic employee work behaviour responses. In such cases, organizational entropy begins to emerge and threaten company survival.

Organizational entropy is defined by DeMarco and Lister (1999) as disorder in energy utilization leading to energy wastage and entropy. They point out that entropy arising from such sources can be counteracted by managerial interventions. Toxic leadership also must be distinguished from destructive leadership, defined by Einersen et al. (2007) as behaviour by a leader to deliberately undermine the organization's objectives and employee well-being. Toxic leadership, however, is not deliberately destructive and is usually implemented with the intention of attaining organizational goals, albeit through the adoption of either extreme *profits* or *purpose* strategic focus.

Examples of extreme *purpose*-oriented toxic leadership in macro established organizations are seen in Anne Roddick's Body Shop (Roddick, 1991) and Ben & Jerry's (Murray, 2014). These are examples of leadership strategic fixations on driving through environmental policies (purpose) to the detriment of the economic viability which threatened their sustainability.

Examples of toxic leadership in macro, established organizations arising from toxic leadership fixation on *profits* are illustrated in the chapter by the VW 'Dieselgate' scandal (Swartz and Bryan, 2018) and the recent Boeing crisis (Pontefract, 2019). In both cases, leadership's toxic fixation on maintaining economic competitiveness (profitability) and neglect of their social responsibilities threatened the sustainability of both organizations.

Micro organizational examples of the same toxic leadership effects can be seen in relatively recently established entrepreneurial projects, some of which have proved stillborn, as the values embodied by the leadership have proven inimical to their survival. Examples of a balanced approach of *profits* with *purpose* in micro organizational leadership, have, on the other hand, tended to be associated with the success and sustainability of entrepreneurial projects.

It is common cause that the values of founder entrepreneurs become the 'de facto' values for organizations as they grow and may determine whether they survive as micro, newly established organizations and grow into macro established ones. It is these entrepreneurial values that determine the culture of the organization and its short and long-term sustainability. Some newly established micro-entrepreneurial organizations fall on stony ground through too great an exclusive fixation on *profits* or *purpose*. Others are initially successful with unbalanced profits and purpose strategies and may even grow into established macro organizations, but become choked by a toxic leadership fixation on *profit* or *purpose*. Still other macro long-term established organizations, whose entrepreneurial founders no longer lead the firm, become unsustainable through toxic leadership introduced to run it. Prioritizing values and culture at the outset further serves as an important signalling device to investors and customers alike through the legitimization of the start-up and its initial survival propensity. The inculcation of wrong values at the outset might necessarily be something of concern. A potential negative effect of such adverse values is the propensity for toxic leadership to emerge, and the development of an entrepreneurial micro organization into a macro established organization is therefore snuffed out at an early stage.

The chapter focuses on how management and Human Resources Management (HRM) can help in identifying toxic leadership fixations on either *profits* or *purpose* aspects of strategy and take pre-emptive remedial steps to act on 'unbalanced' strategic emphases before they take root in the organization, and contaminate employees and their work environment, as the resultant entropic energy wastages can threaten organizational sustainability.

The research objectives of the chapter are:

- To contribute to the extant literature discussing the concepts of toxic leadership and entrepreneurship in micro and macro business organizations.
- To develop an exploratory model of the interrelationship between organizational toxicity emanating from toxic leadership and entrepreneurship in macro and micro business organizations and its effects on organizational entropy and sustainability.
- To discuss practical management and HRM interventions to identify and act pre-emptively on toxic leadership.

The study incorporates a secondary case study data that utilizes *directed* content analysis (Hsieh and Shannon, 2005) as an appropriate methodology to build the exploratory model of organizational sustainability.

The chapter takes the following form. After the introduction and outline of the methodology used in the study, the chapter is divided into three basic parts. The first part deals with aspects of toxic leadership in established large-scale organizations referred to in the chapter as 'macro' toxic leadership effects. The second part deals with smaller organizations which have not established themselves fully in the market. The first part presents an eclectic, *directed* content analysis (Hsieh and Shannon, 2005) of recent secondary data reported in the extant literature highlighting effects of toxic leadership on organization sustainability. The second part focuses on secondary data analysis of micro aspects of toxic leadership as evidenced in toxic forms of entrepreneurship in small-scale organizations. The third part deals with the development of an exploratory model of 'balanced leadership' incorporating a sustainable mix of *profits* with *purpose*. This is followed by a discussion of the importance of Strategic Human Resource Management (SHRM) and HRM in ensuring leadership in micro and macro organizations is strategically driven towards attaining objectives balancing *profits* with *purpose* that help ensure its sustainability. The discussion also suggests that in established macro organizations, HRM must also behave as a management 'watchdog' to counteract tendencies towards toxic leadership in its senior leadership team.

The conclusion follows and briefly discusses the limitations of the study, its practical implications, and recommendations for further research.

METHODOLOGY: SECONDARY DATA ANALYSIS

The chapter adopts a secondary data methodological approach that incorporates analysis of extant literature to develop an exploratory model of balanced leadership and organizational sustainability.

Secondary data analysis can be broadly defined as, "an analysis of data collected by someone else" (Boslaugh, 2007). Data analysis using this method involves material collected from secondary data sources. The methodological approach "… can include any data that are examined to answer a research question other than the question(s) for which the data were initially collected" (Vartanian, 2011: 43) as in the case of the current study. Although formal testing of hypotheses using primary data sources are excluded, exploratory conceptual models can be built from secondary data analysis and subjected to less rigorous forms of falsification than that possible through the use of primary data. Comparing consistency and uniformity of specific outcomes from secondary data analyses from different sources can aid in the validation process. Although, as Popper (1972) indicates, even in the case of primary data analysis, the strength of any hypothesis depends on its degree of corroboration and is always open and subject to falsification. In principle, the same applies to secondary data with the degree of corroboration of a specific data analysis being open to further confirmation or contradiction. Despite the recent explosion of secondary data made possible by computer technology and its general availability, it is still largely an underutilized scientific data resource, largely because of problems in establishing its validity and reliability in experimental and statistical research designs. However, secondary data can be checked for its validity by the fidelity and reputability of the data origins (i.e. the scientific status of its source) and the consistency with which the same data is reported by independent secondary sources. Nonetheless, secondary data always remains more difficult to formally corroborate because of eclectic and personal biases, and because, as in the case of the current study, objectives are different from those of the original researchers (Boslaugh, 2007). Secondary data analysis is often necessarily eclectic because, as in the case of the current study, it extracts specific observations from a wide and diverse range of sources to explore the utility of proposed theories and models. Eclectic qualitative secondary data is interpreted as evidence supporting specific theoretical conjectures by illustrating specific themes. Like analytical eclecticism, secondary data analysis is broadly inclusive and can generate widely varied research outputs including: formal models, statistical causal inferences, historical narratives, and ethnographies (Sil and Katzenstein, 2010). The current study uses eclectic secondary data analysis to support an exploratory theoretical model developed from interpretations of reported historical narratives .

Hsieh and Shannon (2005) indicate three distinct ways of conducting content analysis: the conventional, directed, and summative approaches. All three of these methods interpret meaning from the content of textual data. Conventional content analysis proceeds by obtaining codes derived directly from the textual data. *Directed* content analysis starts with a theory or conjecture (Popper 2002) and uses this conjecture to drive the search for textual data using preconceived codes in the form of keywords for interpretive guidance. The *directed* content approach adopted in the current study uses the keywords and themes of: *toxic leadership, toxic entrepreneurship, macro/micro organizations, profits, purpose, entropy,* and *sustainability* for interpretation of the eclectic historical narratives.

The third approach to content analysis, the summative approach, involves counting and comparisons of content and its interpretation. Directive keywords/concepts derived from the conjectural theoretical model (Popper, 2002) in the current study are extracted from the various selected historical narratives

The strategy for the *directed* content analysis used in the current study essentially conforms to that suggested by Hsieh and Shannon (2005), to begin coding and interpreting the data with predetermined codes. However, as Hsieh and Shannon (2005) point out, using theory as a guide for eclectic secondary data analysis is limited in that researchers approach the data with strong eclectic data biases, which might be more prone to finding supportive rather than non-supportive evidence for a theory.

Also, overemphasis on theory causes a researcher to overlook differing contextual factors that may have a bearing on specific outcomes.

Despite these obvious shortcomings, *directed* content analysis provides a useful preliminary first step in building exploratory theoretical models that can subsequently be tested using primary data.

Part 1 of the chapter, below, uses *directed* content analysis with eclectic narratives of examples of toxic leadership in established macro organizations emanating from extreme strategic fixations on either *profits* or *purpose*. Each aspect is discussed sequentially in separate sub-sections.

PART 1: TOXIC LEADERSHIP AND SUSTAINABILITY IN MACRO ORGANIZATIONS

When Profits Count More than Purpose

The recent Volkswagen crisis offers an example of an established macro organization that nearly became unstuck through the relentless drive of senior leadership in pursuing and upholding company profitability no matter what. Under pressure from above in the rigid hierarchy that characterizes the Volkswagen company structure, a group of company engineers found a way to manipulate diesel emissions tests on Volkswagen cars because they were unable to find a technical solution to the problem in the time made available to achieve this objective and that was financially feasible and within the company's stipulated budget. Analysis of the Volkswagen crisis shows clearly that the pressure on the engineers to find a solution to the problem of excessive diesel emissions emanated from senior leadership in the company, which gave subordinate management no alternative other than maintaining profits by *whatever means necessary* or of being held accountable for the failure to do so. Toxic leadership should be distinguished from 'destructive leadership', the systematic, repeated behaviour by a leader to undermine the organization's objectives, well-being, and job satisfaction of its employees (Einersen et al., 2007). Toxic leadership, as indicated earlier, is behaviour that is not deliberately destructive, and which is often implemented with the intention of meeting the organization's goals. However, because it is severely unbalanced leadership, aimed towards the singular fulfilment of either *profits* or *purpose*, it generates counterproductive tendencies capable of undermining organizational sustainability.

In the case of Volkswagen, it was toxic leadership that led to toxic employee behaviour that severely dented Volkswagen's 'purpose' reputation and threatened its long-term sustainability. Driven by the company's fixated determination to become the world's top-selling car maker, senior leadership created a toxic organizational values scenario that generated a 'stop at nothing' organizational climate aimed at attaining this goal. Volkswagen, run by a highly centralized authoritarian hierarchy in Wolfsburg, expected employees to 'deliver the goods no matter what', which put enormous pressure on the employees to achieve organizational goals by working 24/7 until a solution had been found to the excessive diesel emissions from its manufactured cars. This 'profits above all' value emphasis emanating from senior Volkswagen leadership generated toxic employee behaviour that became embedded in the organization and led to the deliberate mis-recording of emission tests on its diesel cars so as not to impede their sales to the public (Schwartz and Bryan, 2017).

Although VW survived the 'Dieselgate' crisis, it cost the company in the region of 30 billion US dollars to resolve (Trefis Team, 2018). Also, the potential of VW leaders' toxic behaviour spreading to other German business organizations and affecting their production and the manufacturing output of the German economy as a whole, is clearly described in an article at the time (Goodman, 2018: 4) which states:

> recent emissions scandal is most likely to have far-reaching consequences. Rigging pollution results will not only cost the automaker dearly in terms of legal fines, investor and customer backlash, class action suits, possible criminal investigation, and loss of future sales, but the ill-effects of this scandal could spill over to other automakers, particularly Germans who make cars that run on diesel, and have a broader impact on the automotive industry. In fact, given how this scandal has everybody raising their eyebrows at the previously trusted and respected German engineering, the blow to the country's largest automotive company could, in turn, hurt the country's economic growth.

The Volkswagen example shows in general terms how toxic leadership behaviour encouraged and abetted an organizational climate that drove employees to behave illicitly to maintain the company's profitability above any other consideration. This extreme '*profits* before *purpose*' organizational climate emphasized by Volkswagen leaders impacted on the automotive industry in Germany as a whole and undermined other sections of German industry that depended on the automotive industry for their economic sustainability.

A second, more recent, example of a '*profits* before *purpose*'-instigated crisis is that endured by Boeing, largely initiated by a past and ongoing toxic leadership focus on profits. The recent catastrophic crashes of the 737 Max aircraft that killed all passengers and crew in both cases, presents a further example where the leadership of a macro organization with a highly reputable history, turned toxic due to the pressures by senior leadership, which were themselves brought about by rapid advancements in aeronautical engineering and inter-firm competition. In this instance, pressure from competition came from Airbus. The problem confronting Boeing was to produce an aircraft that was 15% more fuel efficient than the current 737 models in time to successfully compete with Airbus. Boeing leadership was under intense pressure to find a solution with a very short time frame in which to do so. Pushed downwards by senior leadership and filtered through to the engineers and computer personnel who were beset with the task 'to do whatever was necessary' to meet the target on time and keep Boeing competitive and profitable (Pontefract, 2019), the company became responsible for two avoidable catastrophic airline accidents. As in the case of the VW crisis, toxic leadership pressure generated an organizational climate that induced employees 'to go the extra mile' to find – in a very short space of time and above any other company purpose – a solution that would maintain Boeing's competitiveness in the market. Boeing's toxic leadership pressure soon spread to the Federal Aviation Administration (FAA) whose job it is to license aircraft only once they have met their strict safety standards and requirements. The FAA did in fact give its safety approval for the 737 Max, but only after inordinate pressure from Boeing's leadership. As Pontefract (2019: 3) puts it,

> The FAA with its reduced staff and growing lists of actions to take care of might have simply been fine with it. Maybe it even freed up time to get other actions completed on their lists. Boeing – in a herculean race to keep pace with Airbus – were likely keen to ensure that the plane made it to the

market as soon as possible, and with the least amount of disruption and cost overruns (let alone pilot training cost concerns from the airlines).

As it transpired, the rushed-out solution was the Manoeuvring Characteristics Augmentation System (MCAS), a computer automated stall-control system that was designed to override the pilot's control of the 'angle of attack' when it computed from electronic sensors that a stall was imminent. In fact, and what the subsequent investigations showed clearly, was that once locked in to a particular (and in both cases wrong) 'line of attack' computer intervention, it became very difficult for pilots to disengage the system to stabilize the aircraft before it became locked into an irretrievable stall.

Whether this serious crisis will lead to a complete entropy of Boeing through wasting energy in attempts to salvage an automated system to make an aircraft designed more than 50 years ago safe and competitively fuel efficient, remains to be seen, but the threat to Boeing's long-term sustainability is clearly severe.

When Purpose Counts More than Profits

Anita Roddick's Body Shop (Roddick, 1991) was a pioneering example of leadership that put more emphasis on social purpose than profits, which led to it becoming a macro organizational leader in the manufacturing and retailing of eco-friendly cosmetics. This resulted in the company becoming enormously profitable. However, the fixation of the leadership on social purpose developed into becoming progressively toxic, ultimately undermining its economic viability and long-term sustainability.

The Body Shop was founded on social activism and advocated in its leadership the principles of social and environmental change. Anita Roddick (1991) saw business as more than the unwavering pursuit of profit and also regarded it as a vehicle for influencing social change and making the world a better place to live. Her focus and leadership values emphasized human rights and environmental preservation and she attracted and recruited employees who had been carefully selected to embrace these values in their business behaviour. Over time, however, the fixation of company leadership on social purpose became toxic and created a toxic climate where the drive and emphasis on people and community welfare engendered social activism in employees that undermined the economic sustainability of the organization itself. Ultimately, and largely as a result of this toxic leadership fixation on *purpose* embraced by its employees, the company became the object of a number of ethical controversies regarding its adoption of specific social activist causes, which damaged its profitability and economic sustainability. Although its origins in social activism and emphasis on social and environmental change were the main reasons for the Body Shop's initial success, the company lost sight of its responsibility to maintain economic sustainability. It is now owned by Brazilian Cosmetics Company "Natura Cosméticos" who bought the company from L'Oréal in 2017.

Murray's (2014) account of Ben and Jerry's and CPI's (Community Products Inc.) struggles with an over-indulgent and ultimately toxic leadership focus on purpose and social responsibility provides a more recent example. Ben Cohen, the co-founder of Ben and Jerry's, which is today a large and established macro organization, embarked on a partnership venture with CPI to produce a new ice cream after attending a concert promoting the protection of the Brazilian rainforest. The new product 'Rainforest Crunch' was made with Brazilian nuts and cashews. Ben Cohen, who was also president of CPI, contracted the company to distribute

40% of its profits from the sale of 'Rainforest Crunch' to rainforest preservation groups and other selected international environmental projects. A further 20% would go to '1% for Peace' and 10% would be shared among employees. However, the veracity of CPI's social and environmental claims eventually came under public scrutiny. As it transpired, the original small cooperative nut farmers were unable to meet the increasing demand for their product and, at the same time, comply with US health standards. It was discovered that shipments of nuts arrived with broken shells, cigarette butts, rocks, and coliform bacteria from these cooperative small-scale farms. It was also discovered that 95% of the nuts for 'Rainforest Crunch' were in fact supplied by large corporate suppliers, which included notorious anti-union agribusinesses. Only 5% of the nuts came from local co-operatives. As a result, Ben and Jerry's were forced to reconsider their '*purpose*' social responsibility orientation, which proved to be a façade and an honest balanced profitability and purpose needed to be instilled if the company were to survive. However, this proved to be too late for 'Rainforest Crunch', which was no longer manufactured. CPI went bankrupt.

The organizational leadership had become so fixated on its *purpose* function and its drive to solve community social and environmental problems, that leadership lost sight of the company's economic viability, which ultimately led to bankruptcy.

The following section develops the concept of toxic entrepreneurship and entrepreneurial leadership in small newly established business organizations. The section indicates with *directed* content analysis of eclectic secondary data narratives, the use of both unbalanced and balanced *profits/purpose* entrepreneurial strategies and effects on sustainability.

Micro, newly established entrepreneurial organizations are more emphatically influenced by their founder, and toxic entrepreneurs may be more interested in pursuing either *purpose* or *profit* strategies out of short-term self-interest rather than long-term sustainability.

PART 2: TOXIC ENTREPRENEURSHIP, LEADERSHIP, AND SUSTAINABILITY IN MICRO ORGANIZATIONS

Toxic Entrepreneurship

Toxic entrepreneurship is proposed as an extension to the notion of toxic leadership. Toxic leadership is a relatively well-documented phenomenon, given its propensity to result in detrimental outcomes for organizations, and its deleterious impact on followers. Yet scant attention has been paid to the potential for toxic entrepreneurship to cause toxic leadership behaviour. In keeping with Shepherd's (2019) call for research into the 'dark side' of entrepreneurial behaviour, we believe that this chapter, in addressing micro-organizational effects of toxic leadership, provides insights into a novel concept, namely 'toxic entrepreneurship'.

What, then, is 'toxic entrepreneurship'? While little exists by way of a formal definition in scholarly literature, it is possible to draw inferences as to what toxic entrepreneurship might entail based on extant explanations of toxic leadership. Here, Heppell's (2011: 243) definition is particularly informative such that it incorporates

> … those individuals whose leadership generates a serious and enduring negative, even poisonous, effect upon the individuals, families, organisations, communities, and societies exposed to their methods.

This broad definition moves toxic leadership beyond a narrow focus on 'leader–follower' relationships within organizations to include broader societal effects. At the same time, toxic leaders often display narcissistic, unethical, destructive, selfish, collusive, and manipulative tendencies in the pursuit of self-interest (cf. Padilla et al., 2007; Reed, 2004; Schmidt, 2008). To this end, and in applying these considerations of toxic leadership to Shane and Venkataraman's (2000) seminal opportunity-centric definition of entrepreneurship, toxic entrepreneurship might be:

> the demonstration of malfeasant behaviour by entrepreneurs in the discovery, evaluation, and exploitation of opportunities in the pursuit of self-interest, with detrimental effects on the overall sustainability of the new venture.

Several key determinants might be seen to underpin this conceptualization of toxic entrepreneurship. These potentially include the application of values by the founder-entrepreneur to the inception of the new venture, as well as associated extended considerations of entrepreneurial ethics and legitimacy. These determinants will be considered in turn before a consideration of two different examples of toxic entrepreneurship is provided.

Founder Values and Orientation

If values are seen as so-called guiding principles which ultimately inform the overall desirability of a particularly course of action (cf. Hofstede, 2001; Morris and Schindehutte, 2005; Morris, Schindehutte and Lesser, 2002; Schwarz et al., 2001), it stands to reason that these become important determinants of the overall sustainability of the start-up. It is common cause that the values of founder-entrepreneurs become the de facto values for organizations as they grow. Indeed, values are often touted as the foundation for effective judgement and decision making, and, as such, might be seen to imbue policies, structures, and culture of an organization, thus setting the tone for governance and leadership even after the founding entrepreneur exits the business (Berson et al., 2008; Tomczyk et al., 2013).

The inculcation of the 'wrong' values intuitively leads to morally suspect decisions being made. Indeed, the inextricable interplay between values and ethics is most apparent when reflecting on ethics and the entrepreneur. Entrepreneurial decision making is often considered to take place under conditions of ethical complexity (Venter, 2016), with ethical challenges occurring at the micro-, meso- and macro-levels (Brenkert, 2002). Realistically, entrepreneurs are concerned in the first instance with the dilemmas that they confront when starting a new venture. Decisions are often limited by the fact that "… the entrepreneurial context poses a number of unique ethical challenges" (Morris, Schindehutte, Walton, and Allen, 2002: 331). Thus, nascent entrepreneurs of micro organizations in particular might likely be confronted with uncomfortable choices, particularly in the face of 'cut-throat' competition, resulting in potential breaking of rules through unethical and illegal behaviour, including corruption, misrepresentation of product and service offerings and the like (Brenkert, 2002; Morris, Schindehutte, and Lesser, 2002). Here, an 'at all costs' approach to survival might be adopted to justify ethically compromised decisions (De Clerq and Dakhli, 2009; Morris and Zahra, 2000). At the meso- and macro-levels, decisions are no less ethically mired. As values are considered to be a central tenet of organizational culture, ensuing 'negative' organizational culture that is premised on the wrong values will encourage employees to similarly adopt ethically poor judgement. At the same time, at a societal level, entrepreneurs will need to navigate the broader complexities of legislative compliance, particularly under conditions where inflexible legislative frameworks stifle entrepreneurial activity, while simultaneously paying close attention to the needs of different stakeholders beyond just the shareholder (Venter, 2016).

Beyond contexuality of entrepreneurial ethics, close attention should also necessarily be paid to the agency of the individual entrepreneur. Critically, in this regard, the notion of the ethical entrepreneur has often been considered something of an oxymoron (Venter, 2016). Entrepreneurs have long been seen to be guided by egoism and self-interest, given their desire for independence (DeLeon, 1996; Longenecker et al., 1988). Similarly, the notion of an entrepreneur as deviant is useful to consider. In this regard, Merton's (1938) Strain Theory of Deviance is particularly informative to the extent that it provides a basis for the understanding of deleterious behaviour as arising through the 'strain' that occurs between goals as valued by society and the means of achieving these 'legitimately' (also called Anomie). While it is true to say that Merton's Theory was originally intended to postulate reasons for criminal activity amongst the lower classes, its application to the field of entrepreneurship is relatively self-evident. For instance, when entrepreneurs are compelled to achieve their success (ordinarily deemed to be what society would value of entrepreneurs) 'at all costs', they might then experience this strain. This is particularly true when entrepreneurs lack the necessary financial means to become successful (De Clercq and Dakhli, 2009). To this end, and with reference to Merton's Theory, entrepreneurs might typically be categorized as 'innovative' (that is accepting societal goals to the extent that they see entrepreneurial success as desirable, but pushing against constriction and limitations, which they perceive prevents them from achieving such means). Indeed, for Goss (2005), deviance within the context of entrepreneurship is framed as innovation to the extent that entrepreneurs go against the grain through a potential rejection of normative constraints (Venter, 2016).

Values and Entrepreneurial Legitimacy

The attainment of entrepreneurial legitimacy is an important consideration when reflecting on the notion of toxic entrepreneurship. There has been a recent resurgence in attention being paid by various researchers to the intersection between entrepreneurial behaviour and the attainment of legitimacy (cf. De Clerq and Voronov, 2009; Fisher, 2020; Fisher et al., 2017; Fisher et al., 2016; Nagy et al., 2017; Überbacher, 2014; Webb et al., 2009). Critically, nascent entrepreneurs of micro organizations suffer from what has been termed a 'liability of newness' (Stinchcombe, 1965: 148), which is overcome through the attainment of legitimacy (Fisher, 2020). Such entrepreneurial legitimacy is best understood as "a generalised perception or assumption that the actions of an entity are desirable proper or appropriate within some socially constructed system of norms, values, beliefs, and definitions" Suchman (1995: 571). For entrepreneurs, the attainment of such legitimacy is a necessary precursor to obtaining critical resources, yet, they invariably face a 'legitimacy threshold' below which they lack the necessary legitimacy to obtain resources, which generally then flow into the organization once transcended (Fisher et al., 2016; Nagy et al., 2017; Zimmerman and Zeitz, 2002). Importantly, however, the attainment of legitimacy is largely dependent on the nature of the audience (Fisher et al., 2017). Here, in particular, the pressure that is placed on an entrepreneur to conform to normative expectations of different audiences forces him/her "…to adapt and change so as to effectively compete for the resources provided by [these] audiences" (Fisher et al., 2016: 394). One particular example of this is how hybrid values are potentially leveraged as a form of cultural capital. For instance, there is a simultaneous coexistence and embodiment of 'western' and 'indigenous' values within informal African entrepreneurs (cf. Venter, 2012). Through this coexistence, there is propensity for hybrid values to emerge. Chabal and Daloz (1999: 147) suggest it thus: "…on the [African] continent it is both legitimate and advantageous to operate according to different logics of modernity and tradition in all areas of life and work." This reframing of values, which is often purposive), allows for effective switching between spaces (the modern and traditional, or potentially the formal and informal) as it were in order to achieve different resources (Venter, 2014). Thus, while informal activities are seen to fall outside formal institutional boundaries and are thus deemed 'illegal', they nonetheless fall within in societal expectations of informal social purpose to the extent that society regards this as acceptable, and hence institutional boundaries are thus perceived to be 'legitimate' (Venter, 2014; Webb et al., 2009). This said, such frame-switching might simultaneously be perceived to increase the propensity for deviant behaviour. By straddling different spaces of social purpose, pressures to conform might result in concomitant potentially unethical behaviours in order to acquire legitimacy, particularly where informal entrepreneurs are vulnerable and fall below the 'legitimacy' threshold. Here, for instance, there might be a propensity to engage in bribery to obtain lower cost resources (Ufere et al., 2012; Li et al., 2015).

'Detoxifying' the Entrepreneurial Space – Balancing Profits with Purpose in Entrepreneurial Micro organizations

Thus far, a case has been made for the understanding of toxic entrepreneurship and its determinants. In particular, given both the agency of individual founder-entrepreneurs as well as expectations of different audiences, the propensity for deleterious behaviour arises. This is particularly evident when considering the slew of scandals that has rocked the corporate world for the past two decades. Although a large and established macro organization at the time of the crisis, Enron is an example of a culture that developed from a relatively small foundation characterized by excess, greed, deception, extreme risk-taking and general malfeasance, which remained with it as it grew (Burkus, 2011; Ferrell and Ferrell, 2011; Johnson, 2003). Ensuing deviance through 'innovative behaviour' was driven in part through societal norms which focused on short-term gains as well the 'cult' of the business leader and success at all costs (Johnson, 2003, Moncarz et al., 2006).

A counter position to such behaviour is potentially found in the form of so-called social enterprises, where the focus is on satisfying a double-, or even, triple-bottom line in favour of renewed demands from different audiences who require different commitments. Such enterprises are arguably afforded with a 'moral legitimacy' to the extent that they exhibit a preferred form of organization, such that they balance both profit and purpose (Dart, 2004). Two examples are pertinent in this regard by way of illustration. The first, Reel Gardening, is a social enterprise that is based in Johannesburg, South Africa. Reel Gardening, a for-profit, adopts a hybrid enterprise structure, and in conjunction with Reel Life (its associated not-for-profit organization) seeks to achieve the twin goals of profit and purpose through a focus on food and water security (https://reelgardening.co.za/social-impact/). This is primarily achieved through its underlying social innovation in the form of a biodegradable seed-strip that is planted directly into the ground, which contains chemically treated seed that are placed in the strip at the correct 'growing' distance. Once planted, the strip uses up to 80% less water (https://

reelgardening.co.za/how-it-works-2/). Both Reel Gardening and Reel Life achieve purpose through the growing of school- and community-based vegetable gardens throughout South Africa. This is achieved through the attraction of sponsorship and donor funding. At the same time, Reel Gardening encourages a 'buy one – give one' philosophy, such that for every seed strip bought, one is donated. Corporate clients, in particular are able to leverage this through social impact, and cause-related marketing campaigns as well as concomitant reporting (https://reelgardening.co.za/custom-branding/). A further aspect of the organization to note, which satisfices 'purpose', is the fact that seed-strips are manufactured using hand-powered machines which are operated by unemployed mothers (https://reelgardening.co.za/about-us/how-it-all-began/). Overall profitability is maintained through selling of products directly to the public through an online store, as well as through various distributors. Moreover, Reel Gardening enjoys a presence in the US market through the Girl Scout of the USA (GSUSA). Finally, Reel Gardening further engages in custom branding of corporate gifts and the like.

The second example of social enterprise that manages to satisfy both profit and purpose is that of The Awethu Project. Also operating out of Johannesburg, South Africa, The Awethu Project seeks to directly target South Africa's burgeoning unemployment rate through the identification and support of entrepreneurial talent. Its South African born, Harvard- and Oxford-educated founder identified the structural imbalances largely introduced under Apartheid that excluded (and still largely exclude) the majority of South Africans from accessing necessary resources to grow and sustain businesses (Venter, 2016). To this end, The Awethu Project provides incubation of businesses founded and run by Black South Africans. Funding is attracted through two particular sources. The first is through Enterprise and Supplier Development spend as part the Black Economic Empowerment score card. Here, in particular, participating large (or so-called 'generic') enterprises contribute 3% of Net Profits After Tax to the development of emerging black enterprises as well as suppliers (1% and 2% respectively). Through its transformation fund, The Awethu Project manages such contributions on behalf of participating enterprises through the investment in high-potential entrepreneurs (http://www.awethuproject.co.za/b-bbee-solutions). Such enterprises further take equity positions in different businesses that are incubated by The Awethu Project. Further investments are encouraged through ESD spend in their virtual and in-person incubators (Awethu Project, 2019). Finally, The Awethu Project also seeks to attract impact investment into its Small and Medium-sized Enterprise (SME) Equity Fund, with a targeted of Internal Rate of Return (IRR) of some 20% and concomitant social returns in terms of job creation, skills development and the like (http://www.awethuproject.co.za/products/sme-equity-fund).

While, therefore, the aforementioned examples of social enterprises illustrate how toxic entrepreneurship might be countered through a dual profit/purpose focus, there is an important caveat to this. Social enterprises in their own right do seek, in turn, to become legitimate according to audience-type, to the extent that such legitimacy is deemed pragmatic (Dart, 2004). In particular, Nicholls (2010a: 77–78), using a Weberian typology, distinguishes between different investor logics such that "means-ends calculations (zweckrational) underscoring capital investors are distinguished from 'values-driven purposes' (wertrational) underscoring philanthropists with 'systemic rationality' focussing on a balance between the two, through blended returns". Conformance to these different logics is thus incumbent on entrepreneurs wanting to attract different levels of investment. This is further underscored by logics and narratives that underscore legitimation of social ventures to the extent that these relate to the process of securing resources (Nicholls, 2010b). Here, 'hero-entrepreneur' narratives are most directly associated with 'cooperative, communitarian' traditions which are disassociated from the market, whereas 'ideal-type' logics in contrast are most strongly attached to market-driven, commercial business models that drive social impact (Nicholls, 2010b: 620–621).

The next part of this chapter develops an exploratory model of balanced *profits* with a *purpose* strategy built from the eclectic *directed* content analysis of the secondary data discussed in Parts 1 and 2. Directed content analysis of eclectic secondary data narratives of macro and micro organizations suggests that unbalanced, toxic leadership drives for *profit* or *purpose* promote entropy, while leadership that promotes a balanced, *profits*-with-*purpose* strategy, enhances the prospect of organizational sustainability.

PART 3: THE DEVELOPMENT OF A BALANCED 'PROFITS WITH PURPOSE' MODEL

Secondary data analyses of toxic leadership values/orientation and employee behaviour in macro and micro organizations emanating from imbalances and resulting in the fixated, overriding pursuit of *profits* or *purpose*, have suggested that such imbalances threaten organizational sustainability and can promote entropy. Secondary data analysis has also shown that balanced *profits* with *purpose* entrepreneurial leadership orientation leads to sustainable business success.

Figure 23.1 depicts the exploratory model derived from the earlier analysis.

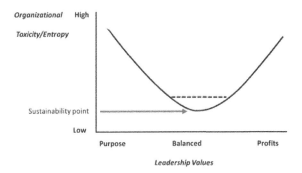

Figure 23.1　　*An exploratory model of leadership values/orientation, organizational toxicity and entropy interrelations*

Figure 23.1 indicates that as leadership *profits* or *purpose* values/orientation become increasingly unbalanced, i.e. when senior leadership increasingly drives the organization and its employees towards meeting either '*profit*' or '*social purpose*' objectives, the toxicity of the leadership and its employees increases and, with it, the overall toxicity of the organization. Furthermore, as Figure 23.1 suggests, the greater the level of organizational toxicity, the greater the threat to sustainability and risk of entropy. Figure 23.1 also indicates a 'sustainability point' with a boundary suggesting that imbalances in *profitability* and *purpose* are compatible with different phases of the organization's development. For example, in nascent entrepreneurial micro organizations, leadership emphasis will necessarily be on the economic viability of the project rather than its social purpose.

The *directed* content analysis of toxic leadership discussed earlier in the chapter, shows that leadership drives for *profits* or *purpose* above all else, are toxic forms that will undermine sustainability and potentially lead to the organization's ultimate fall. The analysis has also shown that balanced strategies of *profits* with *purpose* being developed in newly established, entrepreneurial micro organizations provide a solid foundation for their future growth and sustainability.

THE IMPORTANCE OF HRM AND SHRM IN MAINTAINING 'PROFITS AND PURPOSE' LEADERSHIP BALANCE AND ORGANIZATIONAL SUSTAINABILITY

HRM and SHRM are critical in ensuring that leadership and organizational values in micro and macro organizations are driven towards attaining objectives that balance *profits* with *purpose* to ensure their, HRM must also act as a management bloodhound and watchdog to counteract tendencies towards toxic leadership in senior leaders and employee behaviour that may ultimately undermine organizational sustainability.

Ulrich (1998: 2) describes the ongoing function of HRM in the following way: "In most companies HR is sanctioned mainly to play policy police and regulatory watchdog. It handles the paperwork involved in hiring and firing, manages bureaucratic aspects of benefits and administers compensation decisions made by others." Although writing more than 20 years ago, not much has changed for many HR departments. The watchdog aspect of HR alluded to by Ulrich (1998) however needs to be extended to monitoring excessive *profits* or *purpose* orientations by senior management and leadership to avoid toxic forms of behaviour taking root in the firm, undermining its sustainability and potentially leading to its entropic collapse. Narendian (2019), in an article entitled "Role of HR in corporate governance: A watchdog or bloodhound?" suggests how HR can be a positive force in fostering improvements in corporate governance by 'sniffing' out toxic forms of leadership and/or employee behaviour before they take root and undermine organizational sustainability.

Of course, it should be acknowledged that in start-ups (micro organizations), it is unlikely that formal HR departments exist (Dabić et al., 2011). Instead, this role of being the proverbial bloodhound would fall on the founder-entrepreneur. Indeed, it is well established that entrepreneurs play numerous roles during the early stages of the business (Mueller et al., 2012). Such roles might not only include the inculcation of values as alluded to earlier in this chapter, but also, the directing and managing of human resources, and the behaviour of employees.

Bratton and Gold (2017) maintain that strategic HRM is considered to be a continuous activity that requires constant adjustments in three major interdependent factors:

- The values of senior management and leadership;
- The environment in which the organization functions; and
- The material, financial and human resources available to the firm.

The constant adjustment in senior managers and leader's values and strategic orientations needs to be closely monitored and evaluated by HR. This is (or should be) a key aspect of HR's organizational competency. HR needs to act as the organizational 'bloodhound' to detect early leadership orientation imbalances in *profits* or *purpose* strategic drives that may pervade employees in the firm before they threaten the organization's survival.

The crises at Volkswagen and Boeing could both have been avoided if HR had pre-emptively acted on the toxic leadership drive downwards towards employees that focused organizational values on the pursuit of profits above all else. Early instance shifts in leadership orientations from a balanced approach should have been identified and acted on during the monitoring and evaluation of practical strategic implementation. Senior management and leaders should have been cautioned that radical imbalance in corporate values towards the singular pursuit of *profit* and the creation of an organizational climate reflecting this imbalance, threatened the firms' sustainability.

The same applies to the Body Shop and Ben and Jerry's where an increasing fixation by leaders and employees on social activism should have been identified by HR, and senior management cautioned in the monitoring and evaluation process of strategy implementation, and prescriptive remedial steps taken before it led as it did in both these examples, to organizational entropy.

CONCLUSION

The study has indicated through the use of secondary data and *directed* content analysis that *profit/purpose* imbalances emanating from the leadership of macro organizations and founding entrepreneurs of micro organizations, can cause serious threats to sustainability and risk entropy. *Directed* content analysis of secondary data narratives of entrepreneurial micro organizations has also suggested that balanced *profits* with *purpose* leadership can offer a strong foundation for the growth and development of sustainable organizations.

Limitations to the study include the fact that secondary data rather than primary data was used in the analysis and that *directed* content analysis was used in the study, which introduces threats of researcher bias. However, the study's underlying thrust is conjectural and the exploratory model open to primary data empirical investigation and this is recommended as a future research development.

The study also indicates the primary importance of HRM, particularly, strategic HRM, as performing the roles of both 'watchdog' when leadership is swayed towards *profits* or *purpose* above all else, and 'bloodhound' to proactively 'sniff out' potential problem areas and take prescriptive remedial steps for their early resolution. The monitoring and evaluation process of the practical implementation of strategic objectives, and in this case prevailing leadership values and orientation, should provide an adequate early warning system to root out toxic imbalances before they become serious organizational threats to sustainability.

REFERENCES

Awethu-Project (2019). Introduce your ambition to opportunity. Available online: http://www.awethuproject.co.za/products/sme-equity-fund (accessed 14 April 2019).

Berson, Y., Oreg, S., & Dvir, T. (2008). CEO values, organizational culture and firm outcomes. *The International Journal of Industrial, Occupational and Organizational Psychology and Behavior*, 29(5), 615–633.

Boslaugh, S. (2007). *Secondary Data Sources for Public Health: A Practical Guide*. New York: Guilford Press.

Bratton, J., & Gold, J. (2017). *Human Resources Management* (6th ed.). London, UK: Red Globe Press.

Brenkert, G. (2002). Entrepreneurship, ethics, and the good society. *The Ruffin Series of the Society for Business Ethics*, 3, 5–43.

Burkus, D. (2011). A tale of two cultures: Why culture trumps core values in building ethical organizations. *The Journal of Values Based Leadership*, 4(1), 1–8.

Chabal, P., & Daloz, J. (1999). *Africa Works: Disorder as Political Instrument*. Bloomington: Indiana University Press.

Coldwell, D. A. L. (2016). Entropic citizenship behaviour and sustainability in urban organizations: Towards a theoretical model. *Entropy*, 18(12), 453.

Coldwell, D. A. L. (2019). Negative influences of the 4th industrial revolution on the workplace: Towards a theoretical model of entropic citizen behaviour in toxic organizations. *International Journal of Environmental Research and Public Health*, 16(15), 2670.

Dabić, M., Ortiz-De-Urbina-Criado, M., & Romero-Martínez, A. M. (2011). Human resource Coldwell, D. A. L., & Callaghan, C. (2014). Specific organizational citizenship behaviour and organizational effectiveness: The development of a conceptual heuristic device. *Journal for the Theory of Social Behaviour*, 44, 347–367.

management in entrepreneurial firms: A literature review. *International Journal of Manpower*, 32(1) 14–33.

Dart, R. (2004). The legitimacy of social enterprise. *Non-Profit Management and Leadership*, 14(4), 411–424.

De Clercq, D., & Dakhli, M. (2009). Personal strain and ethical standards of the self-employed. *Journal of Business Venturing*, 24(5), 477–490.

De Clercq, D., & Voronov, M. (2009). Toward a practice perspective of entrepreneurship: Entrepreneurial legitimacy as habitus. *International Small Business Journal*, 27(4), 395–419.

DeLeon, L. (1996). Ethics and entrepreneurship. *Policy Studies Journal*, 24(3), 495–510.

DeMarco, T., & Lister, T. (1999). *Peopleware: Productive Projects and Teams* (2nd ed.). Dorset, UK: House Pub.

Einersen, S., Aasland, M. S. & Skogland, A. (2007). Destructive leadership behavior: A definition and conceptual model. *Leadership Quarterly*, 18(3), 207–221

Ferrell, O. C., & Ferrell, L. (2011). The responsibility and accountability of CEOs: The last interview with Ken Lay. *Journal of Business Ethics*, 100(2), 209–219.

Fisher, G. (2020). The complexities of new venture legitimacy. *Organization Theory*, 1(2), DOI: 10.1177/2631787720913881.

Fisher, G., Kotha, S., & Lahiri, A. (2016). Changing with the times: An integrated view of identity, legitimacy, and new venture life cycles. *Academy of Management Review*, 41(3), 383–409.

Fisher, G., Kuratko, D. F., Bloodgood, J. M., & Hornsby, J. S. (2017). Legitimate to whom? The challenge of audience diversity and new venture legitimacy. *Journal of Business Venturing*, 32(1), 52–71.

Goodman, L. M. (2018). Why VW cheated. *Newsweek*. Available online: https://www.newsweek.com/2015/12/25/why-volkswagen-cheated-404891.html (accessed 10 November 2018).

Goss, D. (2005). Schumpeter's legacy? Interaction and emotions in the sociology of entrepreneurship. *Entrepreneurship Theory and Practice*, 29(2), 205–218.

Heppell, T. (2011). Toxic leadership: Applying the Lipman-Blumen model to political leadership. *Representation*, 47(3), 241–249.

Hofstede, G. (2001). *Culture's Consequences: Comparing Values, Behaviors, Institutions, and Organizations across Nations*. Thousand Oaks, CA: Sage.

Johnson, C. E. (2003). Enron's ethical collapse: Lessons for leadership educators. *Journal of Leadership Education*, 2(1), 45–56.

Kaplan, S., & Owen, G. (2019). Are companies right to abandon the shareholder-first mantra? *Financial Times*, 27 August.

Hsieh, H. F., & Shannon, S. E. (2005) Three approaches to content analysis. *Qualitative Health Research*, 15, 1277–1288.

Li, Y., Yao, F. K., & Ahlstrom, D. (2015). The social dilemma of bribery in emerging economies: A dynamic model of emotion, social value, and institutional uncertainty. *Asia Pacific Journal of Management*, 32(2), 311–334.

Lipman-Blumen, J. (2005). *The Allure of Toxic Leaders: Why We Follow Destructive Bosses and Corrupt Politicians—And How to Survive Them*. New York: Oxford University Press.

Longenecker, J. G., McKinney, J. A., & Moore, C. W. (1988). Egoism and independence: Entrepreneurial ethics. *Organizational Dynamics*, 16(3), 64–72.

Merton, R. (1938). Social structure and anomie. *American Sociological Review*, 3(5), 672–682.

Moncarz, E. S., Moncarz, R., Cabello, A., & Moncarz, B. (2006). The rise and collapse of Enron: Financial innovation, errors and lessons. *Contaduría y Administración*, (218), 17–37.

Morris, M., and Schindehutte, M. (2005). Entrepreneurial values and the ethnic enterprise: An examination of six subcultures. *Journal of Small Business Management*, 43(4), 453–479.

Morris, M., Schindehutte, M., Walton, J., & Allen, J. (2002). The ethical context of entrepreneurship: Proposing and testing a developmental framework. *Journal of Business Ethics*, 40(4), 331–361.

Morris, M., Schindehutte, M., & Lesser, J. (2002). Ethnic entrepreneurship: do values matter? *New England Journal of Entrepreneurship*, 5(2), 35–46.

Morris, M., & Zahra, S. (2000). Adaptation of the business concept over time: The case of historically disadvantaged South African owner/managers. *Journal of Small Business Management*, 38(1), 92–100.

Mueller, S., Volery, T., & Von Siemens, B. (2012). What do entrepreneurs actually do? An observational study of entrepreneurs' everyday behavior in the start–up and growth stages. *Entrepreneurship Theory and Practice*, 36(5), 995–1017.

Murray, H. J. (2014). Ben & Jerry's Struggles with corporate social responsibility in an international context. Available online: https://ssrn.com/abstract=2443318 (accessed 25 April 2019).

Nagy, B. G., Rutherford, M. W., Truong, Y., & Pollack, J. M. (2017). Development of the legitimacy threshold scale. *Journal of Small Business Strategy*, 27(3), 50–58.

Narendian, R. (2019). Role of HR in corporate governance: A watchdog or bloodhound? *NHRD Network Journal*, 12(4), 344–350.

Nicholls, A. (2010a). The institutionalization of social investment: The interplay of investment logics and investor rationalities. *Journal of Social Entrepreneurship*, 1(1), 70–100.

Nicholls, A. (2010b). The legitimacy of social entrepreneurship: Reflexive isomorphism in a pre–paradigmatic field. *Entrepreneurship Theory and Practice*, 34(4), 611–633.

Padilla, A., Hogan, R., & Kaiser, R. B. (2007). The toxic triangle: Destructive leaders, susceptible followers, and conducive environments. *Leadership Quarterly*, 18(3), 176–194.

Pontefract, D. (2019). Boeing's 737 Max crisis is a leadership issue. Available online: https://www.forbes.com/sites/danpontefract/2019/03/18/boeings-737-max-crisis-is-a-leadership-issue/#127504c16a0a (accessed 14 April 2019).

Popper, K. R. (1972). *Objective Knowledge: An Evolutionary Approach*. Oxford, UK: Oxford University Press.

Popper, K. R (2002). *Conjectures and Refutations: The Growth of Scientific Knowledge*. London, UK: Routledge Classics.

Reed, G. (2004). Toxic leadership. *Military Review*, 84(4), 67–71.

Roddick, A. (1991). *Body and Soul: Profits with Principles, the Amazing Story of Anita Roddick & The Body Shop*. New York: Crown.

Schmidt, A. (2008). Development and validation of the toxic leadership scale. Unpublished master's thesis. University of Maryland.

Schwartz, J., & Bryan, V. (2017). VW's Dieselgate bill hits $ 30 billion after another charge. Reuters. Available online: https://www.reuters.com/article/legal-uk-volkswagen-emissions/vws-dieselgate-bill-hits-30-bln-after-another-charge-i (accessed on 20 April 2019).

Schwartz, S., Melech, G., Lehmann, A., Burgess, B., Harris, M., & Owens, V. (2001). Extending the cross-cultural validity of basic human values with a different method of measurement. *Journal of Cross-Cultural Psychology*, 32(5), 519–542.

Shane, S., & Venkataraman, S. (2000). The promise of entrepreneurship as a field of research. *Academy of Management Review*, 25(1), 217–226.

Shepherd, D. A. (2019). Researching the dark side, downside, and destructive side of entrepreneurship: It is the compassionate thing to do! *Academy of Management Discoveries*, 5(3), 217–220.

Sil, R., & Katzenstein, P. J. (2010) Analytic eclecticism in the study of world politics: Reconfiguring problems and mechanisms across research traditions. *Perspectives in Politics*, 8, 411–431.

Suchman, M. C. (1995). Managing legitimacy: Strategic and institutional approaches. *Academy of Management Review*, 20(3), 571–610.

Stinchcombe, A. (1965). Social structure and organizations. In J. G. March (Ed.), *Handbook of organizations*. Chicago: Rand McNally, 142–193.

Tomczyk, D., Lee, J., & Winslow, E. (2013). Entrepreneurs' personal values, compensation, and high growth firm performance. *Journal of Small Business Management*, 51(1), 66–82.

Trefis Team (2018). The domino effect of Volkswagen's emissions scandal. Forbes. Available online: https://www.forbes.com/sites/greatspeculations/2015/09/28/the-domino-effect-of-volkswagens-emissions-scandal (accessed 8 November 2018).

Überbacher, F. (2014). Legitimation of new ventures: A review and research programme. *Journal of Management Studies*, 51(4), 667–698.

Ufere, N., Perelli, S., Boland, R., & Carlsson, B. (2012). Merchants of corruption: How entrepreneurs manufacture and supply bribes. *World Development*, 40(12), 2440–2453.

Ulrich, D. (1998). A new mandate for human resources. *Harvard Business Review*. Available online: https://hrb.org (accessed 25 May 2020).

Vartanian, Y. P. (2011). *Secondary Data Analysis*. New York: Oxford University Press.

Venter, R. (2012). Entrepreneurial values, hybridity and entrepreneurial capital: Insights from Johannesburg's informal sector. *Development Southern Africa*, 29(2), 225–239.

Venter, R. (2014). Reflections on the informal economy: Beyond survivalism. In B. Urban (Ed.), *Entrepreneurship and Society* (pp. 115–139). Cape Town: Pearson.

Venter, R. (2016). Compliance and ethical issues. In R. Venter & B. Urban (Eds), *Entrepreneurship Theory in Practice* (3rd ed.) (pp. 376–426). Cape Town: Oxford University Press.

Webb, J. W., Tihanyi, L., Ireland, R. D., & Sirmon, D. G. (2009). You say illegal, I say legitimate: Entrepreneurship in the informal economy. *Academy of Management Review*, 34(3), 492–510.

Zimmerman, M. A., & Zeitz, G. J. (2002). Beyond survival: Achieving new venture growth by building legitimacy. *Academy of Management Review*, 27(3), 414–431.

PART 7

SUSTAINABILITY-DRIVEN BUSINESS STRATEGIES ACROSS FUNCTIONAL AREAS IN AN ORGANIZATION

24. Cross-functional integration in sustainability-driven business practice

Duane Windsor

INTRODUCTION

Cross-functional integration is key to systematic improvement of sustainability-driven business practice. Integration of functions can make a sustainability improvement contribution that is stronger than the sustainability contribution of improving each function separately. As an illustration, if one function improves by amount A and another function improves by amount A, integrating the two functions should result in a contribution that is greater than simply 2A. This vital aspect of sustainability is under-developed in available sources, particularly with reference to how integration can be successfully implemented.

The emphasis in this chapter, which has shaped the selection of the literature and business examples, is on the environmental pillar of sustainable business practice. The selection aims to illustrate and support the basic arguments rather than provide a fully developed literature review. Illustrations provide support rather than fully developed evidence based in analysis of operational data or respondent information. The language of the chapter refers to three pillars of sustainability (economic, environmental, and social) and to functions and dimensions within the firm. In Figure 24.1, a dimension can be either a standalone function (such as human relations) or a compound of two or more functions put together for the purposes of exposition (such as innovation and operations and supply chain management). The dimension is deliberately chosen to be a general-purpose term. A dimension is simply an aspect of an organization relevant to this investigation.

Purpose of the Chapter

The chapter examines the state of knowledge concerning cross-functional integration with respect to improving sustainability-driven business practice. The examination is a critique of the strengths and weaknesses of that knowledge. The general purpose of a critique is to assist with the development or improvement of the existing body of knowledge. A critique is partly critical in looking at weaknesses. However, that examination is intended to correct or improve on those weaknesses. In this sense, a critique should ideally lead to recommendations concerning theory and action. For instance, Purvis et al. (2019) provide an examination of the conceptualization and developmental history of understanding sustainability or sustainable development in terms of the three pillars or dimensions of economy, environment, and society. This "triple bottom line" orientation leads to a "win-win-win" framing in which all dimensions can improve. This conceptualization should lead to a practical assessment of effective integration of the economic, environmental, and social pillars of sustainability (Gibson, 2006; cited by Purvis et al., 2019).

The chapter is not concerned directly with the question of whether business can, either alone or with government assistance, address climate change (Oreskes & Schendler, 2015). The path forward from today may lead toward an impending environmental catastrophe or future resolution through institutional and technological innovations (Windsor, 2018). The issue for this chapter is what progress, either marked or minor, a business can achieve through cross-functional integration for environmental sustainability. The presumption that cross-functional integration is beneficial requires both testing of validity and of implementation planning knowledge.

Sustainability comprises economic, environmental, and social pillars. Ideally, a sustainable business contributes positively to economic, environmental, and social pillars while being sufficiently profitable to remain in operation. This chapter focuses on the environmental pillar, emphasizing environmental responsibility or stewardship. From an environmental perspective, sustainability involves balancing resource consumption against resource renewal over time to support intergenerational equity while maintaining nature's capacity to support resource renewal (Bansal & DesJardine, 2015).

There is some discussion of the social pillar to the extent that principles and lessons of corporate social responsibility (CSR) and corporate social performance (CSP) may provide insight into the environmental pillar and vice versa (Delmas & Montes-Sancho, 2011). CSR focuses on responsibility to people. CSR grounded in normative ethics may involve borrowing from the future to satisfy present stakeholder needs in a way that diminishes nature's capacity to support resource renewal (Bansal & DesJardine, 2015). Thus, environment and CSR may work against one another. For example, an improvement in living standards of the poor may involve increased environmental damages. Sustainable development suggests that economic development and environmental sustainability can occur together, but in specific situations the two goals might be opposed. To provide air conditioning for everyone in tropical locations may increase environmental deterioration. This difficulty deserves additional investigation.

Last (2012) identifies six differences between CSR and sustainability. In *vision*, the first looks backward to report social contributions and the latter looks forward to plan changes. In *target*, CSR focuses on opinion formers and sustainability focuses on the whole value chain. In *business*, CSR is becoming compliant, while sustainability focuses on enhancing the firm. In *management*, communications teams dominate CSR; operations and marketing should handle sustainability. In *reward*, CSR aims at politicians and sustainability aims at capital markets. In *drive*, CSR aims at reputations in developed markets and sustainability aims at opportunities in emerging markets.

There is parallel literature on cross-functional and organizational integration for CSR (Asif et al., 2013; Carlini et al., 2019). The chapter does not look at the economic pillar, which includes financial performance of businesses and economic performance of the market system (in terms of goods and services, employment, and compensation). Difficulties of an environmental focus arise when there is an unavoidable trade-off between environment and society, such that sustainable development is not feasible (Barnett, 2004), or when there is an unavoidable trade-off between environment and economy, such that businesses suffer rather than gain financially from environmental investments.

Research Question

The specific research question concerns the state of knowledge about sustainability integration among the dimensions of human resources, production, and operations and supply chain management. This narrow research question focuses on what we know about cross-functional integration. There is a significant research gap on cross-functional integration. Extant research efforts tend to focus above (at the strategic and environmental levels) or below (at the level of the individual functions considered separately) this cross-functional integration. The environmental level concerns the desirability of promoting sustainable practices in business and society. In the extant literature on business sustainability, the focus is on the strategic desirability of cross-functional integration at the level of top management or on the link in isolation of specific individual functions to sustainability. A limited amount focuses on the interaction of multiple functions within the organization.

Contribution

The intended contribution of this chapter is to identify the key issues raised by cross-functional integration of sustainability-driven business practices. These issues need more study to help managers understand how to implement those practices. The chapter focuses on human resources, internal operations and supply chain management, and innovation. Marketing and consumption involve special issues of greening and over-consumption. Accounting, finance, and information systems are more specialized functions.

Organization of the Chapter

The remainder of the chapter is organized as follows. The second section provides a literature review and conceptual background on the nature of the business case approach and the extant literature on cross-functional integration. The third section explains the research methodology. The subsequent section on findings provides a three-dimensional integration concept on the key dimensions at the core of a firm, including human resources (a function), innovation (combining two functions), and operations and supply chain management (also combining two functions). The fifth and sixth sections discuss theoretical contributions and management implications, respectively. The section on management implications discusses implementation issues, including board and management governance, investor reactions, stakeholder engagement, and two illustrative case studies for Walmart and REI. The chapter concludes with a discussion of limitations and future research. Sidebars throughout the chapter provide detailed information on relevant technical matters.

LITERATURE REVIEW/CONCEPTUAL BACKGROUND

Much of the extant literature looks at the strategic level (for specific sectors and industries) or environmental governance regimes. The strategic level emphasizes the rationales for why businesses should engage in sustainability practices. An example of a recent study of a specific sector or industry is the effort by Zhou et al. (2019) to apply a lifecycle perspective to a case study assessment of waste management systems in China. Baron and Lyon (2012) examine the nature and evolution of environmental governance regimes. From the perspective of levels of analysis, the regime level influences the strategic level, which influences, for instance, specific operations of waste management systems in a specific country. Other chapters in this publication investigate specific functions within the firm. Cross-functional integration for integrated sustainability management is, in contrast, a relatively understudied matter (Vitale et al., 2019). This chapter focuses on the state of knowledge about cross-functional integration and seeks to improve that knowledge.

The Business Case Approach

The literature relevant to this chapter emphasizes what is typically characterized as a business case for investing in sustainability as a strategy for the firm and for using cross-functional integration as a likely path for improving sustainability performance. The definition of a business case is that an investment or action should yield a reasonably immediate financial gain or a definite strategic gain to the firm. A strategic gain should yield a future financial gain. Ethical or environmental stewardship considerations may be independent of the business case or those considerations may reinforce a business case.

For instance, Whelan and Fink (2016) present a comprehensive business case for sustainability. This case explains the business advantages of investing in sustainability practices. The basic assumption of the business case approach is that the management of the firm should aim at increasing shareholder wealth (or market value) in the instance of a publicly traded corporation. Therefore, investments in sustainability practices will yield future positive financial return. There should be a tangible payoff to the business (Tonelli, 2011, citing Carroll & Shabana, 2010). Measurement of financial benefits of cross-functional integration can be an important influence on management decision making (Enz & Lambert, 2015).

Conceptually, the business case for any economic, environmental, or social investment is that the investment yields a financial return to the business. A business case typically involves measurement at the company level, demonstrating the relationship between benefits and costs to the business for a specific proposal or initiative or course of action (Weber, 2008). There are four basic problems with the business case approach when applied outside the economic pillar to environmental or social investments. One problem is that the approach emphasizes the tangible benefits and costs; the intangible is more difficult to define and measure. A second problem is that the approach tends to emphasize the short-term benefits and costs when the benefit effect may be longer term and, thus, in effect discounted. A third problem is that the path forward in social or environmental responsibility may be indirect rather than direct (Barnett, 2019). A final problem is that the business case approach tends to ignore ethical or environmental stewardship considerations unless captured in mandatory regulations. Such regulations alter the financial and strategic outcomes in a way that increases the business case for sustainability investments and actions.

The validity of the business case depends on empirical validation that there is a reliably positive relationship between the sustainability strategy and financial performance of the firm. In general, the empirical literature tends to find that sustainability investment can improve financial performance and the strategic advantage of the firm. The boxed material immediately below explains the nature of this empirical literature.

EMPIRICAL STUDY OF EFFECT OF ENVIRONMENTAL, SOCIAL, AND GOVERNANCE (ESG) PRACTICES ON FINANCIAL PERFORMANCE

There is an important difference between a statistical association (a correlation) and evidence of a definite causal relationship among any two or more variables. Association means that two or more variables are typically found together. Causality means that if a manager can change one or more variables, that manipulation results in some predictable change in other variables. While the volume in which this chapter appears is not a statistics book, cross-functional integration should rest on empirical evidence that provides a causal linkage between actions and outcomes. Much of the available empirical evidence in support of cross-functional integration is more in the nature of associational information and not causal information.

ESG is the environmental, social, and governance criteria for investors. A positive correlation between ESG criteria and firm financial performance supports a business case for sustainability. In the business case, an ESG investment will yield a positive financial return. There is also a separate ethical case for improved ESG performance. Ethical and business cases for ESG performance are mutually reinforcing.

The International Finance Corporation (IFC) conducted a study of 656 companies in its portfolio (IFC, 2012a, 2012b). The following information comes from that study's summary (IFC, 2012a). That study reports that companies with good performance on environmental and social pillars outperformed (on average) companies with worse performance on those two dimensions. The (average) difference was 210 basis points (2.1%) on return on equity (ROE) and 110 basis points (1.1%) on return on assets (ROA). The report found that the good performance companies also performed better than the MSCI Emerging Market Index (measuring equity market performance in emerging markets) by 130 basis points (1.3%). The report found further that companies with a strong reporting culture did better financially than companies with a weak reporting culture. This analysis of reporting cultures separated between businesses reporting on more than half of the Sustainability Accounting Standards Board (SASB) (https://www.sasb.org/) material sustainability indicators and businesses reporting on less than half of those indicators.

The IFC report links to similar information provided in a study by Khan et al. (2016). That study hand-mapped material sustainability investments by industry into sustainability ratings for specific businesses. Using regression procedures, the authors reported that businesses with good ratings on material sustainability issues performed significantly better than businesses with poor ratings. They also found that businesses with good ratings on immaterial sustainability issues did not perform significantly better than businesses with poor ratings. The authors linked these results to future changes in accounting measures of performance. Here, materiality has an accounting meaning. Relatively large amounts are material or significant; relatively small amounts are material or insignificant from an accounting perspective.

As the reader can see, ESG studies tend to rely on correlation analysis. Generally stronger ESG criteria tend to associate with better financial performance at the firm level. However, such correlation does not identify causal mechanisms. Correlation suggests, but does not isolate, how to develop ESG within a firm or how and why ESG criteria lead over time to better financial performance. Correlation analysis does not reject that there are causal relationships. In addition, it does not generate causal mechanisms. In relationship to the focus of this chapter, the empirical issue is what steps or actions promote cross-functional integration and how such integration contributes to the firm's financial performance. The requisite information should be causal and not simply associational in nature to be of practical use to management.

Extant Literature on Cross-Functional Integration

There is significant literature on the expected or desired benefits of cross-functional integration, including studies of new product development teams (Bai et al., 2017). This literature recognizes that the implementation effort is an important link between organizational integration and organizational performance. This link is poorly defined and poorly specified for action (Barki & Pinsonneault, 2005). A problem with the extant literature is that it is not particularly strong on detailed implementation guidance (Ferreira et al., 2019). This longstanding concern emphasizes the lack of practical guidance for managers in terms of critical success factors (Holland et al., 2000). One problem is the weakness of concept development and appropriate measurement scales (Pellathy et al., 2019). Another problem is the under-studied role of politics (Franke & Foerstl, 2020). Finally, there is a problem due to the poor understanding of the mechanics of leadership in cross-functional teams (Dyar, 2019). It does appear that knowledge transformation is an important aspect of cross-functional integration (Hirunyawipada et al., 2010).

Turkulainen and Ketokivi (2012) test the relationship between cross-functional integration and performance in a sample of 266 manufacturing plant entities across nine countries. They use six propositions for the testing process. The basic finding of the study is that the concept of performance must be disaggregated into components because the effects of integration on performance are contingent on performance dimension. The overall effect is positive. However, it is variable by dimension. An aggregate conception of the relationship is inadequate to assist management actions. Vitale et al. (2019) critique literature that focuses on adoption of a particular sustainability tool, such as a sustainable balance scorecard or how traditional management practices and sustainability management practices may overlap. These authors point out the "underinvestigation" related to aligning multiple sustainability management practices. (The study concerns "accounting, control, and reporting systems," whereas the current chapter has a different concern.) Vitale et al. (2019), which provides a case study of an Egyptian firm, use an alignment process on cultural and organizational dimensions. "Despite its complexity, such a process is fundamental to pursue medium- to long-term goals, ensuring sustainable firm growth and social wellbeing" (Vitale et al., 2019, p. 1244).

METHODOLOGY

A different kind of study might collect detailed data (from company sources and company respondents) about cross-functional integration. It may subject the data to analysis to develop stronger evidence about determinants, processes, and outcomes of cross-functional integration efforts. This study relies on narrative exposition of selected case studies of retailers.

The methodology and approach, therefore, involve three aspects: (1) identification of conceptual logic; (2) assessment of relevant literature; and (3) case illustrations. (Boxed material at the end of this section amplifies on the methodology.)

First, as illustrated in Figure 24.1, there is an effort to identify the conceptual logic of the problem. For example, what is involved in cross-functional integration? In principle, a business might optimize each function for sustainability. Does cross-functional integration need to occur? Is functional optimization both sufficient and better? If cross-functional integration must occur for functional optimization, what do we know about such integration? What do we know about any trade-offs across functions? To address these questions, the chapter proposes to isolate three functions for closer examination. Second is an effort to identify relevant literature. The chapter critiques the strengths and weaknesses of that literature. Third, the chapter draws on illustrations from published case studies. Two case studies, Walmart and REI, appear useful. Both retail companies are closely positioned to consumers with upstream supply chains, which, for Walmart, is global. Walmart and REI illustrate sustainability issues and initiatives in retailing (Shewmake et al., 2020).

A NOTE ON THIS CHAPTER'S METHODOLOGY

The term "methodology" has the general meaning of the theoretical logic providing the rationale or justification for the selection and use of specific research methods. The theoretical logic for this chapter concerns how to assess whether cross-functional integration facilitates and improves sustainability-driven business practices. If so, how can it be implemented in businesses? The chapter has both theoretical implications (on why to engage in cross-functional integration) and managerial implications (on how to practice cross-functional integration, including criteria for investment of resources). The basic approach of this chapter combines two research methods: conceptual development and descriptive illustrations for real companies. The methodology is, thus, partly conceptual, and partly descriptive. The chapter does not test hypotheses about effects of and methods for cross-functional integration. The intention is to help identify the strengths and weaknesses of cross-functional integration literature. Conceptual development involves formulating insights into the logic of cross-functional integration for sustainability-driven business practices. This chapter limits cross-functional integration to three dimensions: (1) human resources (people); (2) operations and supply chain management (other resources); and (3) innovation (product/service and operations improvements). The reason for the limitation is to increase tractability of analysis and improve readability. Additional functions or dimensions add complications to both analysis and explanation. The examples of real companies reported in the chapter illustrate points about the requirements for cross-functional integration and the effects of the absence or weakness of such integration. The chapter also limits conceptual development and descriptive illustrations to the environmental pillar of sustainability to focus attention on that pillar. The other pillars of sustainability are economic and social. These research methods rest ultimately on a reading of selected relevant readings from the available literature. References cited in this chapter do not constitute a full and exhaustive bibliography. The references support the conceptual development and identification of illustrative cases for real companies. This literature assessment approach is not a systematic literature review. The literature on cross-functional integration is under-developed.

FINDINGS

The literature assessment reaches two key results. First, extant literature tends to emphasize either the environmental and strategic justifications for sustainability practices or implementation of such practices in specific functions considered in isolation from one another. Second, the extant literature is weak on cross-functional integration (other than recognizing its desirability and expected benefits). We know relatively little about practical implementation of cross-functional integration.

A Three-Dimension Integration Conception

Studying the integration of all the functions in a business is arguably too big and broad a topic at this early stage of investigation into under-developed literature. Therefore, the chapter restricts its attention to three dimensions: (1) human resources (people); (2) operations and supply chain management (other resources); and (3) innovation (product/service and operations improvements). Human resources is a function (as is marketing). The other two dimensions combine two functions for simpler exposition. Internal operations constitute a function, as does supply chain management. The study combines the two functions as the dimension of other resources (neither people nor money). Innovation is a combination of research and development (product innovation) and engineering (service and operations improvements). This restriction is not to suggest that other functions (see Figure 24.1) are not important. Rather, attention is focused on three dimensions involving at least five functions (rather than fewer or more, for expositional tractability).

Three dimensions are sufficient for the current examination. That is, integration of internal operations and supply chain management is presumed to examine the three-way integration with human resources and innovation. Similarly, integration of research and development and engineering is presumed. A focus is placed on these three dimensions as the core of the integration problem within the firm: (1) people; (2) resources; and (3) improvements. Other functions are important. However, they are not the core of the integration problem.

Figure 24.1 shows the relationship between human resources (Hamilton et al., 2019), innovation (Beder, 1994; Mulder, 2007), and operations and supply chain management. The firm operates within the system of environmental changes and impacts (Anderies, 2015), occurring at a level of analysis above environmental governance arrangements (Baron & Lyon, 2012). Environmental changes affect the organization. Environmental impacts result from actions of the organization. Between the external dimensions of environmental changes and environmental governance arrangements and the internal functions of interest is the board and management governance of the firm (Eapin, 2017; Smith & Soonieus, 2020). The basic perspective to be developed is that innovation and operations/supply chain management depend on the people working for the business. Figure 24.1 separates these three functions from the accounting, finance, and information systems functions considered elsewhere in this volume.

Figure 24.1 also separates these three dimensions from marketing as a specialized relationship to consumers. As designed here, Figure 24.1 is a depiction of the demand (consumption) and supply (production) sides of the marketplace as operating at the level of the specific business. The firm (supply) supplies consumers (demand). In Figure 24.1, the three functions for study other than marketing comprise supply (production). Marketing can expand, as shown, to include the demand dimensions. Marketing involves specialized issues of green consumption beyond the scope of this inquiry. Anti-consumption activism, whether by academics or environmental activists, aims at reducing and reshaping demand (Black & Cherrier, 2010; Urry, 2010). One can also define and operationalize consumer social responsibility (CnSR), which is the idea that consumers bear some social responsibility for how they handle consumption and disposal of goods (Caruana & Chatzidakis, 2014).

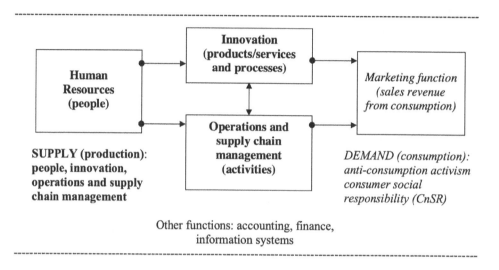

Figure 24.1   A depiction of the setting for cross-functional integration

Human Resources

The first dimension of Figure 24.1 is human resources. A question concerning human resources is whether people should have a "green" (environmental responsibility) orientation in addition to professional, management, or technical competence. Presumably, people should not be anti-green. Evidence on human resources in environmental stewardship is weak, although some systematic reviews of literature are available (Amrutha & Geetha, 2020; Hamilton et al., 2019). There is some evidence that social attributes can encourage or deter sustainability, at least in the instance of bottom-up management systems (Rivera et al., 2019). Dingra and Padmavathy (2019) provide case studies of three Indian automobile manufacturers (Tata Motor, Maruti Suzuki, and Mahindra) based on interviews of personnel (in comparison with Walmart). This research tells us that people are vital in "greening" innovation operations and supply chain management, as well as marketing effectiveness. The four companies studied have made varying degrees of "greening" progress, which can be traced to employees and managers. That is, implementation is highly dependent on the attitudes and actions of individuals. Cross-functional integration cannot neglect the human resources factor. Individuals who are strongly motivated and appropriately trained are vital to effect cross-functional integration. Such integration does not simply happen. People cause effective integration through sustainability-implementation best practices. Even if the practices are known, employees and managers must act to implement those practices.

Innovation

The second dimension of Figure 24.1 is green innovation in products (or services) and processes. Such innovation combines specialized human resources and technology (Beder, 1994). There is literature on sustainability innovation (Clinton & Whisnant, 2019; Mulder, 2007), as well as the mediating effect of cross-functional integration on the relationship between organizational structure and innovation (Su et al., 2019). One finding is that organizational context is a moderating factor that makes cross-functional innovation teams either effective or ineffective. In other words, the effectiveness of innovation teams depends on the organizational context (Blindenbach-Driessen, 2014). The Blindenbach-Driessen study of 142 projects in 95 firms found that effectiveness was highest in more functionally organized firms with a separate innovation unit and above-average interaction with other functions of the firm. Haas and Cummings (2020) report on team innovation cycles in which teams learn from experience and other teams. Some evidence indicates that cross-functional teams produce continuous improvement in operational performance by helping to align technology innovation effectiveness with operational effectiveness (Santa et al., 2011). That is, technology and operations interact to improve operational effectiveness. Cross-functional teams can complement each other in organizing innovation processes and outcomes (Love & Roper, 2009). There is also a study of how cross-functional teams helped encourage innovation in a Brazilian public organization (Stipp et al., 2018). In a study of two interactive media development teams, there appear to be identifiable cycles of creativity (Goh et al., 2013).

Operations and Supply Chain Management

The third dimension of Figure 24.1 combines operations and supply chain management. Again, this dimension combines specialized human resources and technology. ISO 14000 is the set of environmental management standards, guides, and technical materials and related topics that help inform how to improve operations and supply chain management. Consistent with Figure 24.1, a study examines how ISO 14000 standards can influence marketing success (D'Souza et al., 2019). Comparing two groups of firms, those preferring ISO 14000 standards and not preferring such standards, the study finds statistically that customer satisfaction is the best predictor of how well marketing efforts will work in terms of sales and profits. That is, consumer-driven green solutions for responsible consumption appear to work better. Investing in ISO 14000 standards, while not inexpensive, is beneficial for both the firm and the consumer because the firm profits and the consumer is better satisfied. A study of Japanese manufacturing firms reports a positive relationship between economic performance and the initial adoption of ISO 14001. This initial adoption resulted from a combination of stakeholders' environmental preferences and pressures on a firm and the firm's financial flexibility to undertake such investment (Nishitani, 2009). An earlier study of 55 United States certified firms (about 30% of such US firms in August 1998) found that stakeholders' involvement in ISO 14001 adoption was a competitive advantage due to difficulty of imitation (Delmas, 2001). Yet there is a "dark side" to ISO 14001, defined as a purely symbolic effort for reputational advantage with little practical effect on environmental impacts (Vílchez, 2017). The study used an international sample of 1961 manufacturing facilities (with over 50 employees). Symbolic environmental performance positively influenced the likelihood of ISO 14001 adoption by the facility. A study of 139 countries (over the period 1996–2006) concluded that regulation or coercion were more important early in the period while normative considerations (such as diffusion of other management standards) became more important later in the period (Delmas & Montes-Sancho, 2011). The explanation is that lack of consensus prevailed early. Thus, regulation or coercion were necessary to promote ISO 14011 adoption. Subsequently, normative considerations, including diffusion of other management standards, helped to increase diffusion more than could be achieved by more regulation or coercion.

THEORETICAL CONTRIBUTIONS

This chapter tries to reveal how little is known in detail about effective implementation of cross-functional integration in the environmental pillar of sustainability. The chapter also seeks to provide a more systematic means for the guidance of managers and scholars. Much of the chapter focuses on practical implications for managers.

The chapter concludes with two key theoretical implications coming from this inquiry into the environmental pillar of business sustainability. One implication is that there needs to be more attention to the prevention of irresponsible conduct and how cross-functional integration can contribute to such prevention. A second implication is that there needs to be more attention paid to the effects of national culture and corporate culture on cross-functional integration.

Both the business case for sustainability and an environmental responsibility and steward-ship commitment rule make corporate social irresponsibility unacceptable. Irresponsibility is defined as imposing harms on the environment, society, or stakeholders, whether intentionally or negligently (Windsor, 2013). Responsibility and stewardship focus on making positive improvements in environmental impacts. Thus, it is the exact opposite of irresponsibility: responsibility and stewardship. The emphasis in this chapter is on the role of cross-functional integration. The chapter draws management lessons and theoretical implications from the environmental pillar.

An illustration of irresponsibility is the reported environmental misconduct of DuPont (Shapira & Zingales, 2017). Basically, DuPont engaged in pollution. The discovery of that misconduct cost DuPont some $1 billion. Shapira and Zingales (2017) analyzed company doc-uments obtained through trial disclosure. Their analysis suggests that misconduct was not "due to ignorance, an unexpected realization, or a problem of bad governance" (Shapira & Zingales, 2017, p. 1). On the contrary, their analysis finds that given assumptions about "reasonable probabilities of detection," deliberate pollution was financially rational (Shapira & Zingales, 2017, p. 1). DuPont simply ignored the external costs of the health damages from pollution. In this instance, "different mechanisms of control – legal, liability, regulation, and reputation – all failed to deter" socially inefficient misconduct defined as the cost of pollution reduction being lower than the cost of resulting health damages (Shapira & Zingales, 2017, p. 1).

A theoretically important research question concerns whether, and if so how, national culture and corporate culture may influence cross-functional integration and its effects on various dimensions of performance (Holtbrügge & Dögl, 2012). A study (Engelen et al., 2012) analyzed 619 companies across six countries selected on a criterion of marked differences in national culture. The findings were that cross-functional integration functioned more strongly for an entity in "a national culture with strong collectivism" and that this relationship is reinforced by a strong corporate culture as the authors define the concepts (Engelen et al., 2012, p. 52).

MANAGERIAL IMPLICATIONS

The critical issue concerns what we know about how to implement cross-functional integration. Implementation, or action planning and execution, is the essential aspect of cross-functional integration (about which the least knowledge and empirical verification exists). Important contexts for implementation are board and management governance, investor reactions, and, more broadly, stakeholder engagement. Following a discussion of these contexts, the section examines implementation by management with an emphasis on case studies of retailers Walmart and REI.

Board and Management Governance

A view, one growing in importance, is that boards of directors are "key" to sustainability action (see Aliff, 2018; Crifo et al., 2019; Silk et al., 2018). In support of this view, Smith and Soonieus (2020) draw on "in-depth interviews with board directors" to evaluate the reality of board failure to deliver on this potential. The reason is limited board attention. While boards likely recognize that sustainability is a "strategic necessity," they often lack required resources ("people, knowledge, and tools") to implement this recognition. The study proposes five archetypes of board members with respect to sustainability: (1) Deniers; (2) Hard-Headed; (3) Well-Meaning; (4) Complacent; and (5) True Believers. These archetypes form a kind of continuum. At one end are resisters (Deniers and Hard-Headed), who are unlikely to undertake meaningful sustainability action. The mid-point of the continuum is Well-Meaning but Complacent. The more True Believers on a board, presumably, the better the situation for sustainability action. However, even True Believers will need resources for effective implementation.

Investing in environmental performance is arguably less risky and less controversial than investing in CSR initiatives. The difference is that environmental investment may reduce operating expenses and litigation risk while cultivating important stakeholders, including environmental regulators. Generally, poor financial performance will tend to result in the dismissal of the chief executive officer (CEO) (Hubbard et al., 2017). Hubbard et al. (2017) find that prior CSR investments increase the risk of CEO dismissal under conditions of poor financial performance. In other words, prior CSR investments significantly count against the CEO when financial performance declines. Prior CSR investments count for the CEO in conditions of good financial performance. In other words, prior CSR investments weakly reinforce the CEO's position. The question is whether environmental investments work the same with respect to CEO dismissal.

Investor Reactions

Boards and managers of publicly traded entities will pay attention to investor reactions. There is a difference among cash flows, accounting income, and stock market wealth in the sense that investors determine the latter and may not strictly link the latter to cash flows and accounting income for CSR and environmental investments (Mackey et al., 2007). That is, certain investments might result in positive shareholder reactions while not maximizing future cash flows or accounting income.

The definition of corporate sustainability is important. One view is that corporate sustainability is about creating long-term value at minimum environmental damage (Delmas et al., 2015). The key difficulty is the proper time horizon. Delmas et al. (2015) estimate the effect of greenhouse gas emissions on financial performance of 1095 US corporations for the period 2004–2008. They find that increasing environmental performance negatively affected ROA as a short-term financial performance indicator. They also find that increasing environmental performance positively affected Tobin's Q as a long-term financial performance indictor. Tobin's Q is a commonly used measure of fair market value: a simple version is the ratio of market value to asset replacement cost. At fair value, numerator and denominator should be the same. The measure can apply at the level of the whole stock market, a company, or a physical asset. The problem is that managers may pay more attention to short-term effects than long-term effects, resulting in a dampening of environmental performance investments relative to what investors would accept or endorse. A different study reports for US publicly traded entities (1980–2009) based on an event study of announcements of corporate environmental news. It reports how corporate environmental responsibility behavior results in a significant rise in stock prices. It also reports that corporate environmental irresponsibility results in significant stock price decline (Flammer, 2013). The study considers that, over the period 1980–2009, external pressure for environmental responsibility increased. As a result, punishment of irresponsibility increased longitudinally; reward for responsibility has correspondingly been reduced. Thus, negative stock market reaction increased and positive stock market reaction declined. In effect, the marginal return to environmental responsibility as a resource has declined. The higher the level of environmental responsibility exhibited by a firm, the lower the stock market reaction (whether negative or positive).

Stakeholder Engagement

Beyond the limits set by Figure 24.1 is a broader set of stakeholders defined as everyone who (individually, in groups, or as types) can affect the firm or be affected by the firm. Evidence supports the view that effective stakeholder engagement can be profitable for the firm. A study of gold mines reports findings in this direction (Henisz et al., 2014). The study uses 26 gold mines (held by 19 publicly traded entities) for the period 1993–2008. Based on more than 50,000 stakeholder events, the authors develop an index of stakeholder conflict versus cooperation for each mine. (Financial markets place a 72% discount on the net present value of the physical assets held by gold mines.) A more positive index reduces the financial market discount to 13–37% across the mines and entities. A different study of the S&P 500 reports that effective stakeholder management can increase shareholder wealth, while investing in social issues unrelated to a firm's primary stakeholders can decrease shareholder wealth (Hillman & Keim, 2001).

Implementation Examples

Cross-functional integration is a management task in the sense that managers and employees design and implement integration (Bower, 2017). This perspective informs the design of Figure 24.1, in which human resources are assigned to innovation activities on the one hand and to operations and supply chain management activities on the other hand. Other resources, such as funds, equipment, space, location, etc., are also assigned. Assignment of human resources and other resources involves a business resource allocation process. Bower (1986 [1970]) provides the classic study of the planning and investment process in businesses. Resource allocation in support of strategic management remains understudied. "Given its importance to strategic management, it is surprising to find that there is not a larger body of strategy research specifically about the allocation of financial, physical, technological, and human resources that support firm strategies" (Maritan & Lee, 2017, p. 2411). Resource allocation remains something of an organizational black box needing continued investigation (Busenbark et al., 2017). There may be underinvestment or overinvestment in an activity, organizational unit, or resource (Ahuja & Novelli, 2017).

Management processes, including resource allocation, can be political rather than technically neutral. The literature attests to this political reality, which likely varies by firm. Methodologically, the approach here is to set the political dimension aside in favor of a technically neutral analysis focused on what is required for cross-functional integration and how such integration can be achieved. Cross-functional integration involves two steps. The first step is technically neutral. The second step is to add the implications of organizational politics. The approach here is to recognize that reality but not develop it in detail, because organizational politics involves far too much variation across firms and their business units and functions for further analysis here. The chapter turns to the examples of Walmart and REI to illustrate the arguments.

Both Walmart and REI retailers work with large numbers of suppliers. Cross-functional integration is at work within each firm and through each firm's supply chain. Human resources, innovation, and operations and supply chain management must be at work for effective integration and sustainability outcomes. Large numbers of supplies do not automatically guarantee integration. However, Walmart and REI use a similar approach to supply chain management. A likely rationale is that the approach facilitates drawing multiple sources of innovation. The effect on cross-functional integration is likely indirect rather than direct.

Walmart's cross-functional integration approach

Walmart, founded in 1962 in Bentonville, Arkansas, has about 220,000 employees. It is one of the world's largest multinational retail corporations, with a global supply chain and retail presence in multiple countries. The company reports that it and the Walmart Foundation annually provide more than $1 billion in philanthropic support through cash and in-kind contributions. The summary in this chapter draws on several published cases reporting on Walmart's greening and sustainability initiatives launched in 2005. Henderson and Weber (2017) provide the main case study of Walmart's greening or sustainability initiative. In a general outline, the initiative was to reduce waste and move Walmart toward greater environmental and societal sensitivity. The main case study reports on progress through 2015. The main areas of environmental progress were energy efficiency in both facilities and the global supply chain, and reduced greenhouse gas emissions. Energy efficiency and renewability is an important consideration in both operating cost control and environmental impact reduction (Nguyen et al., 2019). Social sensitivity might be understood in terms of key stakeholders: customers, suppliers, and employees. Main areas of social progress were safer products (for both consumption and supply manufacturing) and improved worker treatment. The initiative included requiring suppliers to come into compliance with Walmart standards. Henderson and Weber (2017) indicate substantial, if uneven, progress and point out controversies such as whether Walmart makes enough progress or has proper motives. (The Henderson and Weber case study explores the motives or rationales for the initiative. Possibilities noted by those authors include public image, financial performance, and moral conviction.) The three objectives set for the sustainability initiative were to transition to 100% renewable energy, zero waste, and sustainable products (Denend & Plambeck, 2007, 2010). There is a 2017 update (Yoffie & Baldwin, 2017). Walmart launched a line of sustainable jewelry under the label "Love, Earth" (Smith & Crawford, 2019) and created a Sustainable Product Index to provide information to customers (Crawford & Smith, 2019). Amazon.com, a chief and growing competitor, has an increasing online competition impacting strategic implications for Walmart (Collis et al., 2020; Mark & Johnson, 2019). Walmart has been criticized on several grounds. A criticism here is whether sustainability is a form of corporate social irresponsibility (Lang & Klein, 2015).

In addition to case studies, company websites and blogs yield current information. For instance, the Walmart Careers Technology Website yields the following significant insight into cross-functional integration:

> Even the smallest projects at Walmart are often complex, require cross-functional collaboration, and rely on information that could change at any moment. Our Technology Project and Program Managers work across our technology teams and the business to keep everything on track. (Walmart Technology, n.d., para. 1)

The digital transformation being driven by competition with Amazon, as well as the 2020 COVID-19 pandemic, is reportedly having significant impacts at Walmart (Maras, 2019). Walmart has been increasing collaboration in its supply chain (Cremmins, 2014). Smithson (2017) identifies ten key sustainability improvement decisions from Walmart's operations management. In April 2019, Walmart announced a goal of having all US stores working only with Higg Index-qualified suppliers for textiles by 2022 (Baker, 2019). The 2012 goal of 70% of US stores was achieved in fiscal year 2017 (Walmart Sustainability Hub, n.d.). Walmart Advancing Sustainability (n.d.) and Walmart Textiles (n.d.) report updates on how Walmart works to advance sustainability, particularly in textiles.

Both Walmart and REI use the Higg Index to measure sustainability performance of companies and products. The Sustainable Apparel Coalition (SAC) developed the Higg Index tool suite in 2012 for sustainability measurement. SAC originated in 2009 as a partnership between Walmart and Patagonia. As of 2019, SAC had about 250 members. Over 10,000 suppliers use the index measurement procedure. REI is a SAC member, as are Disney and Target. Clothing and shoe suppliers include Adidas, Gap, and Nike (Feloni, 2019; REI, n.d.; Sustainable Apparel Coalition, n.d.).

REI's cross-functional integration approach

While Walmart is a large-scale, diversified retailer, REI is focused on outdoor sports equipment and apparel. REI was founded in 1938 in Seattle, Washington. The business began as a small consumers' cooperative to help in the acquisition of reasonably priced quality climbing gear. REI still operates as a member cooperative with about 150 locations and over 11,000 employees (full and part time). Unlike Walmart, the REI tradition always included environmental stewardship in some form (Hoyt & Reichelstein, 2011a). The REI sustainability initiative also began in 2005 under CEO Sally Jewell (2005–2013), who became US Secretary of the Interior (2013–17) in the Obama Administration and subsequently interim CEO of The Nature Conservancy (from September 2019). There are two main cases on REI (Hoyt & Reichelstein, 2011a; Larson & Meier, 2011). The 2005 initiative was to undertake (through the CSR group) "a systematic analysis of energy use, greenhouse gas emissions, and waste sent to landfills" to develop measures, specific goals (short and long term), and planning to add future dimensions including "water, toxics, and social impact" (Hoyt & Reichelstein, 2011a, p. 1). An interesting avoidance of tradeoff thinking was built into the REI initiative: to achieve both "financial and environmental goals without sacrificing either" through innovations for "a virtuous cycle of environmental sustainability and financial success" (Hoyt & Reichelstein, 2011a, p. 1). In practice, the problem was how to build consensus, within and without, about sustainability. The company sought to reduce the operations footprint, improve product stewardship, and reorient philanthropy toward REI sustainability goals (Larson & Meier, 2011). REI has been expanding into renewable energy sources, including solar electric systems and purchase of renewable energy certificates (RECs) (Hoyt & Reichelstein, 2011b; REI, 2014).

In April 2018, REI released its REI Product Sustainability Standards to its approximately 1000 brand partners (REI Staff, 2018). REI collected input during 2017 and planned for the standards to be fully effective after 2020. The October 2019 standards Version 1.1 highlights brand expectations and preferred attributes (REI, 2019). Gonzalez (2018, Paragraph 4) attributes the outcome to the combination of industrial innovation, sustainability dedication, and "sweat equity" occurring "behind-the-scenes." In relationship to consumers, the planned result is of constant (or better) outdoor performance at a lower "environmental footprint."

PRICING ENVIRONMENTAL AND SOCIAL SUSTAINABILITY

A faculty-supervised undergraduate (senior) thesis estimates value placed on environmental and social sustainability in the outdoor apparel industry (Lindahl, 2019). Valuation is, in effect, an estimation of consumer-revealed preference for product attributes. The hedonic pricing model finds that the type of material has a statistically significant effect on a product item. The model finds no such significant effect for level of brand sustainability. In effect, hedonic pricing breaks down a good into constituent parts, such as material and brand sustainability, while considering both internal product and external factors if possible. Rosen (1974) invented the approach in connection with prices for housing or real estate, which has multiple attributes for a buyer.

LIMITATIONS AND FUTURE RESEARCH

This study has some significant limitations. First, the study is exploratory. As noted, the findings section limits an initial cross-functional integration framework to the following dimensions: (1) human resources (people); (2) operations and supply chain management (other resources); and (3) innovation (product/service and operations improvements). The reason for the limitation is to increase tractability of analysis and improve readability. Additional functions and dimensions complicate both analysis and explanation. A future extension of this exploratory study would be to develop a full and comprehensive multiple-function integration framework. The current study sketches an approach for such an extension.

The chapter limits conceptual development and descriptive illustrations to the environmental pillar of sustainability. The other two pillars of sustainability are economic and social. Once a full multiple-function integration framework is available, that framework could be extended to include the other two pillars of sustainability.

Future research should take two further steps. One step concerns the literature. The current study is based on a selected literature assessment. Second, a future study would provide a systematic literature review and a meta-analysis of available empirical studies. However, a meta-analysis might need more than a few empirical studies with adequate sample sizes.

Future investigations should emphasize a true empirical study (if feasible). A significant barrier to such an empirical investigation is that firms do not necessarily provide either detailed operational data or systematic insights into how they address cross-functional integration in the environmental pillar. Therefore, future empirical investigation may prove difficult. Nevertheless, such empirical investigation would be superior to the limited approach in this chapter of summarizing illustrative cases and available empirical studies. A future study might collect detailed data (from company sources and company respondents) about cross-functional integration and subject the data to careful analysis to develop stronger evidence about determinants, processes, and outcomes of cross-functional integration efforts.

REFERENCES

Ahuja, G., & Novelli, E. (2017). Activity overinvestment: The case of R&D. *Journal of Management*, *43*(8), 2456–2468. https://doi.org/10.1177/0149206317695770

Aliff, G. (2018, June 13). *Sustainability and the board: A director's perspective.* [Interview with K. Sullivan]. https://deloitte.wsj.com/riskandcompliance/2018/06/13/sustainability-and-the-board-a-directors-perspective/

Amrutha, V. N., & Geetha, S. N. (2020). A systematic review on green human resource management: Implications for social sustainability. *Journal of Cleaner Production, 247*, Article 119131. https://doi.org/10.1016/j.jclepro.2019.119131

Anderies, J. M. (2015). Understanding the dynamics of sustainable social-ecological systems: Human behavior, institutions, and regulatory feedback networks. *Bulletin of Mathematical Biology, 77*, 259–280. https://doi.org/10.1007/s11538-014-0030-z

Asif, M., Searcy, C., Zutshi, A., & Fisscher, O. A. M. (2013). An integrated management systems approach to corporate social responsibility. *Journal of Cleaner Production, 56*(1), 7–17. https://doi.org/10.1016/j.jclepro.2011.10.034

Bai, W., Feng, Y., Yue, Y., & Feng, L. (2017). Organizational structure, cross-functional integration and performance of new product development team. *Procedia Engineering, 174*, 621–629. https://doi.org/10.1016/j.proeng.2017.01.198

Baker, D. (2019, April 10). *3 ways we're reducing the environmental impacts of your favorite textiles.* Retrieved from https://corporate.walmart.com/newsroom/2019/04/10/3-ways-were-reducing-the-environmental-impacts-of-your-favorite-textiles

Bansal, T., & DesJardine, M. (2015, January/February). *Don't confuse sustainability with CSR.* Retrieved from https://iveybusinessjournal.com/dont-confuse-sustainability-with-csr/

Barki, H., & Pinsonneault, A. (2005). A model of organizational integration, implementation effort, and performance. *Organization Science, 16*(2), 101–202. https://doi.org/10.1287/orsc.1050.0118

Barnett, M. L. (2004). Are globalization and sustainability compatible? A review of the debate between the World Business Council for Sustainable Development and the International Forum on Globalization. *Organization & Environment, 17*(4), 523–532. https://ssrn.com/abstract=624162

Barnett, M. L. (2019). The business case for corporate social responsibility: A critique and an indirect path forward. *Business & Society, 58*(1), 167–190. https://doi.org/10.1177/0007650316660044

Baron, D. P., & Lyon, T. P. (2012). Environmental governance. In P. Bansal & A. J. Hoffman (Eds.), *Business and the natural environment* (pp. 122–139). Oxford University Press. doi:10.1093/oxfordhb/9780199584451.003.0007

Beder, S. (1994). The role of technology in sustainable development. *IEEE Technology and Society Magazine, 13*(4), 14–19. doi:10.1109/44.334601

Black, I. R., & Cherrier, H. (2010). Anti-consumption as part of living a sustainable lifestyle: Daily practices, contextual motivations and subjective values. *Journal of Consumer Behavior, 9*(6), 437–453. https://doi.org/10.1002/cb.337

Blindenbach-Driessen, F. (2014). The (in) effectiveness of cross-functional innovation teams: The moderating role of organizational context. *IEEE Transactions on Engineering Management, 62*(1), 29–38. https://ieeexplore.ieee.org/abstract/document/6939710

Bower, J. L. (1986 [1970]). *Managing the resource allocation process: A study of corporate planning and investment.* Boston, MA: Harvard Business School Press, revised edn.

Bower, J. L. (2017). Managing resource allocation: Personal reflections from a managerial perspective. *Journal of Management, 43*(6), 2421–2429. https://doi.org/10.1177/0149206316675929

Busenbark, J. R., Wiseman, R. M., Arrfelt, M., & Woo, H-S. (2017). A review of the internal capital allocation literature: Piecing together the capital allocation puzzle. *Journal of Management, 43*(6), 2430–2455. https://doi.org/10.1177/0149206316671584

Carlini, J., Grace, D., France, C., & Lo Iacono, J. (2019). The corporate social responsibility (CSR) employer brand process: Integrative review and comprehensive model. *Journal of Marketing Management, 35*(1-2), 182–205. https://doi.org/10.1080/0267257X.2019.1569549

Carroll, A. B., & Shabana, K. M. (2010). The business case for corporate social responsibility: A review of concepts, research and practice. *International Journal of Management Reviews, 12*(1), 85–105. https://doi.org/10.1111/j.1468-2370.2009.00275.x

Caruana, R., & Chatzidakis, A. (2014). Consumer social responsibility (CnSR): Toward a multi-level, multi-agent conceptualization of the "other CSR." *Journal of Business Ethics, 121,* 577–592. https://doi.org/10.1007/s10551-013-1739-6

Clinton, L., & Whisnant, R. (2019). Business model innovations for sustainability. In G. Lenssen & N. Smith (Eds.), *Managing sustainable business* (pp. 463–503). Springer. https://doi.org/10.1007/978-94-024-1144-7_22

Collis, D., Wu, A., Koning, R., & Sun, H. C. (2020, revised January 31). *Walmart Inc. takes on Amazon.com.* Harvard Business School case 9-718-481.

Crawford, R. J., & Smith, N. C. (2019). Wal-Mart's sustainable product index. In G. Lenssen & N. Smith (Eds.), *Managing sustainable business* (pp. 35–62). Springer. https://doi.org/10.1007/978-94-024-1144-7_3

Cremmins, B. (2014, June 12). *The power of collaboration for supply chain sustainability.* Retrieved from https://corporate.walmart.com/newsroom/sustainability/20140612/the-power-of-collaboration-for-supply-chain-sustainability

Crifo, P., Escrig-Olmedo, E., & Mottis, N. (2019). Corporate governance as a key driver of corporate sustainability in France: The role of board members and investor relations. *Journal of Business Ethics, 159*(1), 1127–1146. doi:10.1007/s10551-018-3866-6

D'Souza, C., Marjoribanks, T., Young, S., Sullivan Mort, G., Nanere, M., & John, J. J. (2019). Environmental management systems: An alternative marketing strategy for sustainability. *Journal of Strategic Marketing, 27*(5), 417–434. https://doi.org/10.1080/0965254X.2018.1430054

Delmas, M. (2001). Stakeholders and competitive advantage: The case of ISO 14001. *Production and Operations Management, 10*(3), 343–358. https://doi.org/10.1111/j.1937-5956.2001.tb00379.x

Delmas, M. A., & Montes-Sancho, M. J. (2011). An institutional perspective on the diffusion of international management system standards: The case of the Environmental Management Standard ISO 14001. *Business Ethics Quarterly, 21*(1), 103–132. https://doi.org/10.5840/beq20112115

Delmas, M. A., Nairn-Birch, N., & Lim, J. (2015). Dynamics of environmental and financial performance: The case of greenhouse gas emissions. *Organization & Environment, 28*(4), 374–393. https://doi.org/10.1177/1086026615620238

Denend, L., & Plambeck, E. (2007, April 17). *Wal-Mart's sustainability strategy (A)*. Stanford Graduate School of Business case OIT-71A.

Denend, L., & Plambeck, E. (2010, October 15). *Walmart's sustainability strategy (B): 2010 update*. Stanford Graduate School of Business case OIT-71B.

Dingra, R., & Padmavathy, G. (2019). Green human resource management – A leap towards sustainability. *International Journal for Advance Research and Development, 4*(1), 50–57. http://www.ijarnd.com/manuscripts/v4i1/V4I1-1166.pdf

Dyar, C. (2019, April 9). *How to lead effective cross-functional teams: Focusing on three central tasks can help leaders foster better collaboration with cross-functional teams*. Retrieved from https://sloanreview.mit.edu/article/how-to-lead-effective-cross-functional-teams/

Eapin, S. (2017, August 2). *How to build effective sustainability governance structures*. BSR. Retrieved from https://www.bsr.org/en/our-insights/blog-view/how-to-build-effective-sustainability-governance-structures

Engelen, A., Brettel, M., & Wiest, G. (2012). Cross-functional integration and new product performance — The impact of national and corporate culture. *Journal of International Management, 18*(1), 52–65. https://doi.org/10.1016/j.intman.2011.07.001

Enz, M. G., & Lambert, D. M. (2015). Measuring the financial benefits of cross-functional integration influences management's behavior. *Journal of Business Logistics, 36*(1), 25–48. https://doi.org/10.1111/jbl.12068

Feloni, R. (2019, April 25). *Walmart and Patagonia were once the 'odd couple' of sustainability. Now, the world's biggest apparel brands are lining up to follow their example*. Retrieved from https://www.businessinsider.com/walmart-patagonia-sustainable-apparel-coalition-higg-index-2019-4

Ferreira, A. C., Pimenta, M. L., & Wlazlak, P. (2019). Antecedents of cross-functional integration level and their organizational impact. *Journal of Business & Industrial Marketing, 34*(8), 1706–1723. https://doi.org/10.1108/JBIM-01-2019-0052

Flammer, C. (2013). Corporate social responsibility and shareholder reaction: The environmental awareness of investors. *Academy of Management Journal, 56*(3), 758–781. https://doi.org/10.5465/amj.2011.0744

Franke, H., & Foerstl, K. (2020, in press). Understanding politics in PSM teams: A cross-disciplinary review and future research agenda. *Journal of Purchasing and Supply Management*. https://doi.org/10.1016/j.pursup.2020.100608

Gibson, R. B. (2006). Beyond the pillars: Sustainability assessment as a framework for effective integration of social, economic and ecological considerations in significant decision-making. *Journal of Environmental Assessment Policy and Management, 8*(3), 259–280. https://doi.org/10.1142/S1464333206002517

Goh, K. T., Goodman, P. S., & Weingart, L. R. (2013). Team innovation processes: An examination of activity cycles in creative project teams. *Small Group Research, 44*(2), 159–194. https://doi.org/10.1177/1046496413483326

Gonzalez, S. (2018, March 5). *Journey to sustainability: 3 products breaking new ground*. Retrieved from https://www.rei.com/blog/stewardship/journey-to-sustainability-3-products-breaking-new-ground

Haas, M. R., & Cummings, J. N. (2020). Team innovation cycles. In L. Argole & J. M. Levine (Eds.), *The Oxford handbook of group and organizational learning* (pp. 411–428). Oxford University Press. doi:10.1093/oxfordhb/9780190263362.013.8

Hamilton, C., Larcker, D. F., Miles, S. A., & Tayan, B. (2019). *Where does human resources sit at the strategy table?* Stanford University Graduate School of Business Research Paper No. 19–20.

Henderson, R., & Weber, J. (2017, February, revised). *Greening Walmart: Progress and controversy.* Harvard Business School case HBS 9-316-042. Retrieved from https://store.hbr.org/product/greening -walmart-progress-and-controversy/316042

Henisz, W. J., Dorobantu, S., & Nartey, L. J. (2014). Spinning gold: The financial returns to stakeholder engagement. *Strategic Management Journal, 35*(12), 1727–1748. https://doi.org/10.1002/smj.2180

Hillman, A. J., & Keim, G.D. (2001). Shareholder value, stakeholder management, and social issues: What's the bottom line? *Strategic Management Journal, 22*(2), 125–139. Retrieved from https://www .jstor.org/stable/3094310

Hirunyawipada, T., Beyerlein, M., & Blankson, C. (2010). Cross-functional integration as a knowledge transformation mechanism: Implications for new product development. *Industrial Marketing Management, 39*(4), 650–660. https://doi.org/10.1016/j.indmarman.2009.06.003

Holland, S., Gaston, K., & Gomes, J. F. S. (2000). Critical success factors for cross-functional teamwork in new product development. *International Journal of Management Reviews, 2*(3), 231–259. doi:10 .1111/1468-2370.00040

Holtbrügge, D., & Dögl, C. (2012). How international is corporate environmental responsibility? A literature review. *Journal of International Management, 18*(2), 180–195. https://doi.org/10.1016/j.intman .2012.02.001

Hoyt, D., & Reichelstein, S. (2011a, December 9). *Environmental sustainability at REI.* Stanford Graduate School of Business case SM-196.

Hoyt, D., & Reichelstein, S. (2011b, December 2). *REI's solar energy program.* Stanford Graduate School of Business case BE-17.

Hubbard, T. D., Christensen, D. M., & Graffin, S. D. (2017). Higher highs and lower lows: The role of corporate social responsibility in CEO dismissal. *Strategic Management Journal, 38*(11), 2255–2265. https://doi.org/10.1002/smj.2646

International Finance Corporation (IFC). (2012a, July). *The business case for sustainability* [press release]. Retrieved from https://www.ifc.org/wps/wcm/connect/topics_ext_content/ifc_external _corporate_site/sustainability-at-ifc/business-case

International Finance Corporation (IFC). (2012b, July). *The business case for sustainability* (brochure). Retrieved from https://www.ifc.org/wps/wcm/connect/topics_ext_content/ifc_external_corporate _site/sustainability-at-ifc/publications/publications_brochure_businesscaseforsustainability

Khan, M., Serafeim, G., & Yoon, A. (2016). Corporate sustainability: First evidence on materiality. *The Accounting Review, 91*(6), 1697–1724. https://doi.org/10.2308/accr-51383

Lang, S., & Klein, L. (2015). Walmart's sustainability initiative: Greening capitalism as a form of corporate irresponsibility. In G. Barak (Ed.), *The Routledge international handbook of the crimes of the powerful* (pp. 217–228). Routledge.

Larson, A., & Meier, M. (2011, June 29). *REI: Sustainability strategy and innovation in the outdoor gear and apparel industry.* Darden School, University of Virginia, case UV5324. Retrieved from https:// store.hbr.org/product/rei-sustainability-strategy-and-innovation-in-the-outdoor-gear-and-apparel -industry/UV5324 and http://store.darden.virginia.edu/rei-sustainability-strategy-and-innovation-in -the-outdoor-gear-and-apparel-industry

Last, A. (2012, October 29). *Six differences between CSR and sustainability: These two terms can seem interchangeable, but there are some subtle, and not so subtle, differences between them.* Retrieved from https://mullenlowesalt.com/blog/2012/10/differences/

Lindahl, E. (2019). *The outdoor apparel industry: Measuring the premium for sustainability with a hedonic pricing model.* Scripps Senior Theses, 1322. Retrieved from https://scholarship.claremont .edu/scripps_theses/1322

Love, J. H., & Roper, S. (2009). Organizing innovation: Complementarities between cross-functional teams. *Technovation, 29*(3), 192–203. https://doi.org/10.1016/j.technovation.2008.07.008

Mackey, A., Mackey, T. B., & Barney, J. B. (2007). Corporate social responsibility and firm performance: Investor preferences and corporate strategies. *Academy of Management Review, 32*(3), 817–835. Retrieved from https://www.jstor.org/stable/20159337

Maras, E. (2019, February 21). *An insider's view of Walmart's digital transformation.* Retrieved from https://www.retailcustomerexperience.com/articles/an-insiders-view-of-walmarts-digital -transformation/

Maritan, C. A., & Lee, G. K. (2017). Resource allocation and strategy. *Journal of Management, 43*(6), 2411–2320. https://doi.org/10.1177/0149206317729738

Mark, K., & Johnson, P. F. (2019, September 9). *Walmart: Supply chain management.* Ivey Publishing case W19317.

Mulder, K. F. (2007). Innovation for sustainable development: From environmental design to transition management. *Sustainability Science, 2*, 253–263. https://doi.org/10.1007/s11625-007-0036-7

Nguyen, J., Donohue, K., & Mehrotra, M. (2019). Closing a supplier's energy efficiency gap through assessment assistance and procurement commitment. *Management Science, 65*(1), 122–138. https:// doi.org/10.1287/mnsc.2017.2941

Nishitani, K. (2009). An empirical study of the initial adoption of ISO 14001 in Japanese manufacturing firms. *Ecological Economics, 68*(3), 669–679. https://doi.org/10.1016/j.ecolecon.2008.05.023

Oreskes, N., & Schendler, A. (2015, December 4). Corporations will never solve climate change. *Harvard Business Review.* Retrieved from https://hbr.org/2015/12/corporations-will-never-solve -climate-change

Pellathy, D. A., Mollenkopf, D. A., Stank, T. P., & Autry, C. W. (2019). Cross-functional integration: Concept clarification and scale development. *Journal of Business Logistics, 40*(2), 81–104. https://doi .org/10.1111/jbl.12206

Purvis, B., Mao, Y., & Robinson, D. (2019). Three pillars of sustainability: In search of conceptual origins. *Sustainability Science, 14*(3), 681–695. https://doi.org/10.1007/s11625-018-0627-5

REI. (2014, April 8). *REI now powered by renewable energy: National outdoor retailer broadens energy strategy to include renewable energy certificates.* Retrieved from https://newsroom.rei.com/news/rei -now-powered-by-renewable-energy.htm

REI. (2019, October). REI Product Sustainability Standards. https://www.rei.com/assets/stewardship/ sustainability/rei-product-sustainability-standards/live.pdf

REI. (n.d.). *Product sustainability.* Retrieved from https://www.rei.com/stewardship/sustainable-product -practices

REI Staff. (2018, April 9). *Raising the bar on product sustainability.* Retrieved from https://www.rei .com/blog/stewardship/raising-the-bar-on-product-sustainability

Rivera, A., Gelcich, S., García-Flórez, L., & Acuña, J. L. (2019). Social attributes can drive or deter the sustainability of bottom-up management systems. *Science of the Total Environment, 690*, 760–767. https://doi.org/10.1016/j.scitotenv.2019.06.323

Rosen, S. (1974). Hedonic prices and implicit markets: Product differentiation in pure competition. *Journal of Political Economy, 82*(1), 34–55. Retrieved from https://www.jstor.org/stable/ 1830899

Santa, R., Bretherton, P., Ferrer, M., Soosay, C., & Hyland, P. (2011). The role of cross-functional teams on the alignment between technology innovation effectiveness and operational effectiveness. *International Journal of Technology Management, 55*(1/2), 122–137. https://doi.org/10.1504/ IJTM.2011.041683

Shapira, R., & Zingales, L. (2017, September). Is pollution value-maximizing? The DuPont case. Retrieved from http://www.law.northwestern.edu/research-faculty/colloquium/law-economics/ documents/Spring18Zingales.pdf

Shewmake, T., Siegel, A., & Hiatt, E. (2020). The history and progression of sustainability programs in the retail industry. In S. Ray & S. Yin (Eds.), *Channel strategies and marketing mix in a connected world* (pp. 247–274). Springer. https://doi.org/10.1007/978-3-030-31733-1_10

Silk, D. M., Katz, D. A., & Niles, S. V. (2018, June 29). *ESG and sustainability: The board's role.* Retrieved from https://corpgov.law.harvard.edu/2018/06/29/esg-and-sustainability-the-boards-role/

Smith, N. C., & Crawford, R. J. (2019). Walmart: Love, Earth (A). In G. Lenssen & N. Smith (Eds.), *Managing sustainable business* (pp. 243–267). Springer. https://doi.org/10.1007/978-94-024-1144 -7_13

Smith, N. C., & Soonieus, R. (2020, February 11). *Turning board sustainability aspirations into action.* INSEAD Working Paper No. 2020/08/ATL. http://dx.doi.org/10.2139/ssrn.3536342

Smithson, N. (2017, January 28). *Walmart's Operations management: 10 decisions, productivity.*

http://panmore.com/walmart-operations-management-10-decisions-areas-productivity-case-study
-analysis

Stipp, D. M., Pimenta, M. L., & Jugend, D. (2018). Innovation and cross-functional teams: Analysis of innovative initiatives in a Brazilian public organization. *Team Performance Management*, *24*(1/2), 84–105. https://doi.org/10.1108/TPM-12-2016-0056

Su, Z., Chen, J., & Wang, D. (2019). Organisational structure and managerial innovation: The mediating effect of cross-functional integration. *Technology Analysis & Strategic Management*, *31*(3), 253–265. https://doi.org/10.1080/09537325.2018.1495324

Sustainable Apparel Coalition. (n.d.). *The Higg Index*. Retrieved from https://apparelcoalition.org/the
-higg-index/

Tonelli, M. (2011, June 26). *The business case for corporate social responsibility*. The Conference Board. Retrieved from https://corpgov.law.harvard.edu/2011/06/26/the-business-case-for-corporate
-social-responsibility/

Turkulainen, V., & Ketokivi, M. (2012). Cross-functional integration and performance: What are the real benefits? *International Journal of Operations & Production Management*, *32*(4), 447–467. https://doi
.org/10.1108/01443571211223095

Urry, J. (2010). Consuming the planet to excess. *Theory, Culture & Society*, *27*(2–3), 191–212. https://
doi.org/10.1177/0263276409355999

Vílchez, V. F. (2017). The dark side of ISO 14001: The symbolic environmental behavior. *European Research on Management and Business Economics*, *23*(1), 33–39. https://doi.org/10.1016/j.iedeen
.2016.09.002

Vitale, G., Cupertino, S., Rinaldi, L., & Riccaboni, A. (2019). Integrated management approach towards sustainability: An Egyptian business case study. *Sustainability*, *11*(5), 1244. https://doi.org/10.3390/
su11051244

Walmart Advancing Sustainability (n.d.). *Advancing sustainability*. Retrieved from https://walmart.org/
what-we-do/advancing-sustainability

Walmart Sustainability Hub (n.d.). *Walmart's sustainability index program*. Retrieved from https://www
.walmartsustainabilityhub.com/sustainability-index

Walmart Technology. (n.d.). Project and program management – Technology. Retrieved from https://
careers.walmart.com/technology/project-and-program-management-technology

Walmart Textiles. (n.d.). *Sustainable textiles*. Retrieved from https://www.walmartsustainabilityhub
.com/sustainable-textiles

Weber, M. (2008). The business case for corporate social responsibility: A company-level measurement approach for CSR. *European Management Journal*, *26*(4), 247–261. https://doi.org/10.1016/j.emj
.2008.01.006

Whelan, T., & Fink, C. (2016, October 21). The comprehensive business case for sustainability. *Harvard Business Review*. Retrieved from https://hbr.org/2016/10/the-comprehensive-business-case
-for-sustainability

Windsor, D. (2013). Corporate social responsibility and irresponsibility: A positive theory approach. *Journal of Business Research*, *66*(10), 1937–1944. http://dx.doi.org/10.1016/j.jbusres.2013.02.016.

Windsor, D. (2018). Environmental dystopia versus sustainable development utopia: Roles of businesses, consumers, institutions, and technologies. In M. I. Espina, P. H. Phan, & G. D. Markman (Eds.), *Social innovation and sustainable entrepreneurship* (pp. 9–24). Edward Elgar. https://doi.org/
10.4337/9781788116855.00007

Yoffie, D. B., & Baldwin, E. (2017, revised October 18). *Wal-Mart update, 2017*. Harvard Business School case 8-717-468.

Zhou, Z., Chi, Y., Dong, J., Tang, Y., & Ni, M. (2019). Model development of sustainability assessment from a life cycle perspective: A case study on waste management systems in China. *Journal of Cleaner Production*, *210*, 1005–1014. https://doi.org/10.1016/j.jclepro.2018.11.074

25. Strategic alignment of purchasing for sustainability: a multi-level framework

Melek Akın Ateş and Nüfer Yasin Ateş

INTRODUCTION

Sustainability has become a major issue in corporate agendas, prompting firms to consider the environmental and social impact of their strategies and practices beyond financial outcomes (Hahn et al., 2018; Luzzini et al., 2015; Seuring, 2008; Walker et al., 2014). However, achieving sustainability is difficult. It requires organisation-wide effort, and dedication from all organisational functions (Harms, 2011; Luzzini et al., 2015; Schneider & Wallenburg, 2012). Among these functions, purchasing plays a key role, as it is the immediate interface to the suppliers, and serves as a link between several other organisational functions, such as operations, logistics, R&D, marketing and finance (Du Preez & Folinas, 2019; Schneider & Wallenburg, 2012; Tate et al., 2012). The purchasing function can help improve suppliers' commitment to sustainability objectives, select the most sustainable suppliers, and engage in environmental supplier development practices (Foerstl et al., 2010; Tate et al., 2012). In addition to fostering collaboration with suppliers in the development of more sustainable products and services, the purchasing function can also enable the identification of sustainability-related supplier risks early on in the purchasing process (Foerstl et al., 2010; Tate et al., 2012). However, a precondition for achieving these benefits is the alignment of the purchasing function with corporate goals and other business functions (Luzzini et al., 2015; Luzzini & Ronchi, 2016; Schneider & Wallenburg, 2012; Tchokogué et al., 2018). Surprisingly, there has been limited research investigating purchasing alignment for sustainability.

Purchasing alignment, in general, refers to the congruence of the purchasing strategy with the business strategy (Baier et al., 2008; González-Benito, 2007; Watts et al., 1992). Previous studies illustrate that purchasing alignment results in better purchasing, operational, and business performance (Baier et al., 2008; González-Benito, 2007; Hochrein et al., 2017). Purchasing alignment is especially crucial in the sustainability context, because research shows that purchasing alignment is required for implementing advanced purchasing practices (Baier et al., 2008; González-Benito, 2007) such as sustainable purchasing, as opposed to more operational, day-to-day practices (Caniato et al., 2014; Luzzini et al., 2015; Schneider & Wallenburg, 2012).

Achieving a fit between business and purchasing strategies bestows the purchasing function a means to participate in strategic decision-making and increases its legitimacy within the organisation (Foerstl et al., 2013; Tchokogué et al., 2018). This increased recognition enables the purchasing function to obtain the necessary resources from the organisation for successful implementation of sustainability strategies and practices (Brandon-Jones & Knoppen, 2018; Luzzini et al., 2016). In contrast, lack of purchasing alignment for sustainability endangers organisation-wide sustainability efforts. For instance, in a firm that emphasises sustainability as part of its overall business strategy, a misaligned purchasing function might cause supplier sustainability compliance to deteriorate, and negatively affect the firm's sustainability performance. In order to implement sustainable supplier management practices in purchasing processes, the alignment of not only the purchasing managers, but also the purchasing employees is required.

Although the commonly held belief is that purchasing alignment for sustainability results in performance gains, the accumulated empirical evidence is limited (Schneider & Wallenburg, 2012; Tchokogué et al., 2018), and there are only a few studies investigating purchasing alignment specifically in the sustainability context (e.g. Dabhilkar et al., 2016; Schneider & Wallenburg, 2012; Tchokogué et al., 2018). Before scholars can properly examine the impact of purchasing alignment for sustainability on the implementation of sustainable practices and sustainability performance, there is a need for a comprehensive conceptualisation of purchasing alignment for sustainability.

In response to this gap in the literature, we discuss, first, the importance of purchasing alignment for sustainability, and provide an integrative review of the related literature by adopting a multi-level framework. Drawing on rich insights from the strategic alignment literature (Kellermanns, et al., 2005; Markoczy, 2001; Noble, 1999; Tarakci et al., 2014), we assert that purchasing alignment for sustainability needs to be examined at multiple organisational levels in order to achieve effective implementation of sustainable purchasing practices (Hesping & Schiele, 2015; Formentini et al., 2019). More specifically, we propose three levels of purchasing alignment for sustainability: (i) *vertical alignment* (i.e. between top management and the purchasing function); (ii) *horizontal alignment* (i.e. between the purchasing function and other functions); and (iii) *internal alignment* (i.e. between the individual members of the purchasing function). Next, we introduce a tool to assess and visualise purchasing alignment for sustainability at multiple levels (i.e. Strategic Consensus Mapping, Tarakci et al., 2014) and illustrate the use of this tool via a single case study.

We contribute to the sustainable purchasing literature by highlighting the importance of purchasing alignment for sustainability, and by offering a comprehensive conceptualisation. Our integrative review of the dispersed and scarce studies on purchasing alignment for sustainability, and our multi-level framework, offer a unifying perspective to the field. Further, we introduce a novel methodology from the strategy literature that successfully captures multiple levels of alignment. This method advances the research on purchasing alignment by providing reliable assessments for all levels of alignment, so that scholars can adopt this tool to build and test further theory about purchasing alignment for sustainability. The tool is also useful for purchasing practitioners since it enables visual exploration of their alignment within the function, and with other functions.

SUSTAINABLE PURCHASING

We live in times which are defined by the incompatibility between prolific consumption and the scarcity of natural resources. Consequently, achieving sustainability – 'meeting the needs of the present without compromising the ability of future generations to meet their own needs' (WCED, 1987) – has become a major focus of governments, consumers, NGOs, and firms. Increasingly, firms realise that, in order to achieve economic viability, they first need to ensure environmental and social continuity (Seuring, 2008; Walker et al., 2014). Therefore, a growing number of firms adopt corporate social responsibility strategies and practices (McGuire et al., 1988; Porter & Kramer, 2006).

In order to meet the increasing expectations of a variety of stakeholders, it is no longer sufficient for firms to strive for sustainability only in their internal operations. Firms also need to consider their extended supply chains, which are likely to include end consumers, B2B customers, retailers, distributors, and suppliers (Golicic & Smith, 2013; Krause et al., 2009). Firms increasingly engage in sustainable supply chain management practices, as they come to acknowledge that 'a company is no more sustainable than its supply chain' (Krause et al., 2009). A firm's reputation for sustainability can easily be damaged by environmentally unfriendly or unethical practices of its supply chain members (Hoejmose & Adrien-Kirby, 2012; Leppelt et al., 2013). Among these members, suppliers play a major role, as the final product or service performance highly depends not just on direct suppliers, but also on second- and third-tier suppliers (Tachizawa & Wong, 2014; Wilhelm et al., 2016). For instance, after the collapse of the Dhaka garment factory in 2011, several Western textile retailers came under the scrutiny of customers worldwide, who demanded more sustainable working conditions at their suppliers. Other firms have faced criticism regarding environmentally unfriendly supplier practices, such as destruction of rainforests or depletion of world's critical resources. In order to prevent these negative outcomes, and instead to improve sustainability performance through collaboration with suppliers, more and more firms engage in *sustainable purchasing* (Schneider & Wallenburg, 2012, Tate et al., 2012) as part of their overall sustainable supply chain management strategies and practices.

Sustainable purchasing is defined as the extent to which *environmental* and *social* sustainability objectives are reflected in purchasing strategies, processes, and practices (Giunipero et al., 2012, Schneider & Wallenburg, 2012; Tchokogué et al., 2018). Environmentally sustainable purchasing practices focus on reducing suppliers' environmental burden, for instance by encouraging recycling, reuse, and resource reduction (Schneider and Wallenburg, 2012, Tate et al., 2012). These considerations may be integrated into several parts of the purchasing processes, such as supplier selection (e.g. Reuter et al., 2012; Tate et al., 2012), supplier performance monitoring and evaluation (e.g. Foerstl et al., 2010; Vachon & Klassen, 2006; Zimmer et al., 2016) and supplier development (e.g. Ağan et al., 2016; Blome et al., 2014; Sancha et al., 2016). Socially sustainable purchasing practices aim to increase supplier compliance with health, safety, and ethical rules and guidelines (Schneider & Wallenburg, 2012; Zimmer et al., 2016). Similar to environmental purchasing practices, socially sustainable purchasing practices can also be implemented across several purchasing processes, such as the inclusion of social compliance in supplier selection and evaluation criteria (Bai et al., 2019; Sancha et al., 2016), and investment in improving suppliers' social sustainability capabilities (Sancha et al, 2015; Zimmer et al., 2016). Such practices aim for the establishment of supplier codes of conduct, improvement of working conditions at suppliers' premises (e.g. no child labour, minimum living wage, high worker-safety standards) and the cultivation of a diverse supply base (Ağan et al., 2016; Blome et al., 2014; Sancha et al., 2016).

Although the number of studies investigating sustainable purchasing practices has increased substantially in the past decade, the studies report mixed findings on the performance implications. Whereas some studies have found a positive effect, for instance on financial performance, competitive performance, and supplier performance (e.g. Ağan et al., 2016; Blome et al., 2014), other studies have reported mixed results, or no significant effect (e.g. Hollos et al., 2012; Luzzini & Ronchi, 2016; Mitra & Datta, 2014). Although there are a plethora of factors which might prevent effective implementation of sustainable purchasing practices, a strong determinant, which has not received much attention in the literature to date, is purchasing alignment (Du Preez & Folinas, 2019; Hartmann et al., 2012; Schneider & Wallenburg, 2012). This lack of attention is rather surprising, considering that sustainable purchasing practices tend to cut across several other functions, and therefore require alignment, coordination and communication between functions, as well as commitment from top management (Johnsen et al., 2017; Luzzini et al., 2015; Pullman & Wikof, 2017; Schneider et al., 2014). Without a shared understanding on the importance of sustainability throughout an organisation (Amason, 1996; Markoczy, 2001), the effective implementation of sustainability practices is unlikely. In view of this gap in the literature, we examine purchasing alignment for sustainability in this research.

STRATEGIC ALIGNMENT OF PURCHASING FOR SUSTAINABILITY

In this section, we propose a multi-level framework to assess the strategic alignment of purchasing for sustainability. We review, first, the existing research on purchasing alignment in general, in order to provide definitions and provide an overall context, and then we specifically examine the studies that have investigated purchasing alignment with respect to sustainability strategies and practices.

Purchasing Alignment: A Multi-level Assessment

The role of purchasing in contributing to the overall success of organisations has attracted increased attention from both scholars and practitioners, in line with its transformation from a tactical function into a strategic function (Nair et al., 2015; Paulraj, 2011; Schneider & Wallenburg, 2012). However, it has also been argued that the new value-adding contributions can only be achieved if the purchasing function acts coherently with the overall business goals and other functions' objectives (Baier et al., 2008; Du Preez & Folinas, 2019; Foerstl et al., 2013; González-Benito, 2007; Hochrein et al., 2017; Pagell & Krause, 2002).

Scholars have provided various definitions of purchasing alignment, focusing on alignment at *different levels* of the organisation. Some studies define purchasing alignment as the consistency of the purchasing strategy with the overall business strategy (e.g. Baier et al., 2008; González-Benito, 2007). Other studies highlight the alignment between purchasing strategy and other functional strategies, referring to cross-functional coordination and collaboration (e.g. Foerstl et al., 2013; Hochrein et al., 2017; Pagell & Krause, 2002). Several related terms have also been used in the literature to describe purchasing alignment, such as 'strategic purchasing' (e.g. Carr & Pearson, 2002; Nair et al., 2015), 'internal fit' (Pagell & Krause, 2002), or 'purchasing competence' (e.g. González-Benito, 2007; Das & Narasimhan, 2000). The multiplicity of the concepts and the divergence of their meanings tend to restrict the assimilation of knowledge in this field, and lead to incoherent research findings.

In this research, we adopt a holistic perspective and define *purchasing alignment* as 'the congruency of the purchasing strategy with business strategy, and functional strategies, and across purchasing function members' (González-Benito, 2007; Pagell & Krause, 2002; Pohl & Foerstl, 2011). We define congruence in terms of agreement across strategic objectives (Boyer

& McDermott, 1999; Colbert et al., 2008; Kellermanns et al., 2005; Pagell & Krause, 2002). More specifically, we conceptualise the alignment of the purchasing function for sustainability at three levels: the *horizontal alignment* between top management and purchasing function, the *vertical alignment* between purchasing function and other organisational functions, and the *internal alignment* between individual members of the purchasing function. With this conceptualisation, we aim to illustrate the importance of aligning purchasing at all three levels in order to successfully implement sustainable purchasing practices, and, ultimately, achieve high sustainability performance (see Figure 25.1).

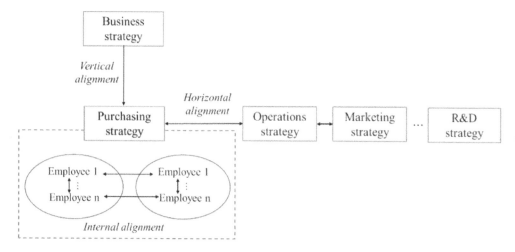

Figure 25.1   Multi-level purchasing alignment framework

The impact of purchasing alignment on the performance of firms has been examined to some extent, in relation to operational performance (e.g. Das & Narasimhan, 2000; Foerstl et al., 2013; Rodríguez-Escobar & González-Benito, 2017), innovation performance (e.g. Das & Narasimhan, 2000; Foerstl et al., 2013), and financial performance (e.g. Baier et al., 2008; González-Benito, 2007; Foerstl et al., 2013). However, there is a scarcity of research focusing on the importance of purchasing alignment for sustainability performance (Leppelt et al., 2013; Schneider & Wallenburg, 2012; Schneider et al., 2014; Tchokogué et al., 2018). Accordingly, our framework represents a first step towards examining this phenomenon in detail, by proposing a multi-level purchasing alignment conceptualisation, together with a tool to accurately assess the alignment at each level. The following subsections provide an overview of the extant studies about purchasing alignment, and review those studies with a particular focus on the sustainability context.

Vertical Alignment between Business Strategy and Purchasing Strategy

Vertical alignment is defined as 'the fit between business strategy and purchasing strategy' (Baier et al., 2008, p. 36), which requires that the purchasing function's strategic priorities are aligned with those of the business as a whole (Baier et al., 2008; González-Benito, 2007; Pagell & Krause, 2002). Strategy literature emphasises the importance of vertical alignment between business strategy and functional strategies in general (Kellermanns et al., 2005;

Kellermanns et al., 2011). Having a shared understanding of business competitive priorities (i.e. strategic alignment) fosters strategy implementation, prevents coordination issues, and increases collaboration within the organisation (Amason, 1996; Kellermanns et al, 2005). Strategic alignment helps employees within different functions to prioritise their daily tasks with reference to the organisational strategy as a whole, thereby coordinating their individual efforts (Ketokivi & Castaner, 2004). In the absence of such shared understanding, conflicts may arise between departments, preventing the coherent action throughout the organisation which is required to successfully put the strategy into practice (Markoczy, 2001). There are also some studies which note that too much alignment can be detrimental; for example, it might restrict the generation of innovative ideas (Priem, 1990). While we agree that conflict and dissent are useful in the strategy formulation phase, it is also widely acknowledged that alignment is necessary for effective strategy implementation (Kellermann et al, 2005).

Based on the upper echelon theory (Hambrick and Mason, 1984), vertical alignment is often operationalised as the alignment between the CEO (representing the business strategy) and an individual manager (e.g. purchasing manager) regarding the importance of strategic competitive priorities (e.g. Colbert et al., 2008; Ateş et al., 2020). Managers within each business function may have views of the business strategy which differ from those of the CEO/management, as these managers are often focused on their own daily operations (Walsh, 1995). When managers are not strategically aligned with the CEO, they might attempt to build consensus among their subordinates around other strategic priorities among their subordinates (Ateş et al., 2020). However, if the managers are strategically aligned with the CEO, they act as facilitators within their functions, and improve strategy implementation efforts within their teams (Ateş et al., 2020). Translating this into the sustainability context, one can argue that if firms emphasise sustainability in their business strategies, then purchasing strategies also need to reflect this emphasis. As a case in point, if an organisation's business strategy prioritises sustainable operations, then (echoing these priorities) its purchasing strategy is likely to integrate sustainability requirements into its supplier selection and development practices (Dabhilkar et al., 2016; Krause et al., 2009).

It has been widely suggested that purchasing vertical alignment leads to improved financial performance (e.g. Baier et al., 2008; González-Benito, 2007), yet there is a paucity of research focusing on its impact upon sustainability strategies and performance. Among the few relevant studies, Dabhilkar et al. (2016) find that strategic alignment of sustainability objectives between the corporate and supply functions results in better financial performance, but only for strategic purchase categories. Paulraj et al. (2011) examine vertical alignment as part of the broader 'strategic purchasing' concept, and argue that strategic purchasing can increase sustainability performance, both indirectly by supporting more supply management practices, and directly, by supporting internal sustainability practices. Similarly, Hollos et al. (2012) discuss the alignment between business and purchasing strategies as part of the 'strategic orientation' concept, and find that strategic purchasing orientation improves collaboration with suppliers, which, in turn, improves both environmental and social sustainability practices.

In summary, the number of studies investigating vertical alignment of purchasing in relation to sustainability strategies, practices and performance is limited. Furthermore, as there are often varying conceptualisations, and vertical alignment is usually operationalised as a subcategory of the broader strategic purchasing/purchasing integration concepts, making it difficult to assess its specific role. In this research, we operationalise vertical alignment as the alignment between the top management team (TMT) and the purchasing department (including the purchasing manager) in terms of their emphasis on strategic objectives, and more specifically investigate their alignment on the sustainability objective. Considering the actors beyond the CEO and the purchasing manager (Colbert et al., 2008; Ateş et al., 2020), this approach better captures the extent of vertical alignment between the purchasing function and the whole TMT.

Horizontal Alignment between Purchasing Function and Other Functions

Horizontal alignment of purchasing is defined as 'the congruence between purchasing strategy and other functional strategies such as operations strategy, marketing strategy, logistics strategy, R&D strategy, and so on' (Du Preez & Folinas, 2019; Hochrein et al., 2017; Foerstl et al., 2013). This congruence often refers to the level of agreement across a firm's functions regarding its strategic competitive priorities (Foerstl et al., 2013; Pagell & Krause, 2002). As a case in point, if a firm emphasises high quality and zero defects in its manufacturing processes, its purchasing function needs to reflect this strategic focus, for instance by selecting high quality suppliers, although these might come at a higher price. In order to establish a horizontal alignment of purchasing, there is also a need for information sharing and joint decision-making across different functions (Foerstl et al., 2013; Luzzini et al., 2015; Kang et al., 2018).

Strategy literature also recognises the importance of horizontal alignment (Porck et al., 2020; Noda & Bower, 1996). In order to transform strategies into practices, departmental functions should not only support the overall business strategy, but also one another (Lingle and Schiemann, 1996). When departments lack horizontal alignment, the organisation tends to suffer from 'silo thinking' (Balogun, 2006; Gulati, 2007), which hinders strategy implementation (Floyd & Wooldridge, 1992). Since implementation requires coherent action from all departments which are required to execute the strategy, these departments cannot operate in isolation when each function has a separate understanding of the strategic priorities (Porck et al., 2020). In that regard, horizontal alignment prevents interdepartmental communication problems, and enhances communication between departments (Cronin & Weingart, 2007), thereby serving the successful realisation of the envisioned strategic goals. Similarly, supply chain literature acknowledges the role of horizontal alignment, as it gives more legitimacy to the business functions, increases participation in strategic decision-making, and encourages information sharing and collaboration between the functions (Hartmann et al., 2012; Foerstl et al., 2013; Kang et al., 2018; Luzzini et al., 2015).

In the purchasing literature, several related terms have been used for horizontal alignment, such as *cross-functional integration and cooperation* (Hartmann et al., 2012; Foerstl et al., 2013) or *intra-firm collaborative capabilities* (e.g., Luzzini et al., 2015). Among the three purchasing alignment levels, horizontal alignment has attracted the most attention. Horizontal alignment is often discussed as an important dimension of purchasing maturity, or as a purchasing capability (e.g. Foo et al., 2019; Hartmann et al., 2012; Luzzini et al., 2015; Schneider & Wallenburg, 2012). For instance, Schulze and Bals (2017) suggest that scholars ought to investigate whether new purchasing capabilities such as cross-functional collaboration ability are needed to successfully implement sustainability strategies and practices.

Horizontal alignment is especially important for implementing sustainability strategies that inherently concern several business functions, and require collaborative efforts (Schneider & Wallenburg, 2012; Kang et al., 2018). While cross-functional integration – a likely enabler of horizontal alignment – is often accepted as an important precondition of successfully implementing sustainability strategies (Crittenden et al., 2011; Hart, 1995), little scholarly attention has been paid to the integration of purchasing per se with other functions (e.g., Gölgeci et al., 2019; Schneider et al., 2014). At best, cross-functional integration of purchasing with other functions is discussed briefly as a subsidiary element of green supply chain management. However, it is important to understand under which conditions a high level of purchasing horizontal alignment is needed, and in which cases there is no need for alignment at all (Schneider et al., 2014).

There has been a limited number of studies discussing purchasing horizontal alignment related to sustainability strategies, practices and performance. Some of these studies focus on the importance of horizontal purchasing alignment. For instance, Schneider and Wallenburg (2012) argue that organisations, which emphasise sustainability in their business strategies, need to adopt sustainable purchasing practices in order to achieve a high sustainability performance. Focusing on the means to achieve this high performance, Peters et al. (2011) propose that horizontal purchasing alignment enables internal acceptance and overall feasibility of sustainable purchasing practices. Yook et al. (2018) adopt a dynamic capability perspective and argue that cross-functional cooperation is a dimension of green purchasing capability; however, this item is subsequently dropped from their dynamic purchasing capability construct operationalisation.

Other studies on horizontal alignment provide insights on the distinction between sustainable purchasing practices and sustainability performance. For instance, Luzzini et al. (2015) hypothesise that intra-firm collaborative capabilities improve purchasing sustainability performance, but they do not find empirical evidence for this proposition. One possible explanation is that horizontal alignment of purchasing does not have a direct effect on performance, but, rather, an indirect effect via the implementation of more sustainable purchasing practices. Supporting this view, Foo et al. (2019) found that green intra-organisational capabilities – defined as the capability of an organisation to allocate, empower individuals, and coordinate its resources effectively and efficiently at all levels within the organisation – had a significant positive effect upon the adoption of green purchasing practices. Kang et al. (2018) found that internal integration of purchasing with other departments increased intra-organisational sustainable management practices, but not inter-organisational sustainability practices. Finally, a few studies emphasise the need for the purchasing function to collaborate with certain functions with which it has a more inherent link, such as the marketing function (e.g. Walker et al., 2014). For instance, Schneider et al. (2014) focus specifically on the integration of purchasing and marketing functions for sustainability implementation, and examine the coordination mechanisms (i.e. organic vs. mechanistic).

In summary, although the importance of purchasing horizontal alignment has been acknowledged in the literature, there is a dearth of research investigating purchasing horizontal alignment in the specific context of sustainability. Furthermore, the purchasing literature to date lacks a tool to operationalise purchasing horizontal alignment. This is important because, before we can further theorise and test the impact of purchasing horizontal alignment on sustainability practices and performance, we need consistent measures for the horizontal alignment.

Internal Alignment within the Purchasing Function

We define *internal alignment* as 'consensus on strategic objectives among the members of the purchasing function'. There is very little research in the purchasing literature which directly investigates purchasing teams and individuals' behaviours (e.g. Driedonks et al., 2010; Timmer & Kaufmann, 2019). Internal alignment within the purchasing function has often been examined in terms of coordination of purchasing activities across purchase categories, suppliers, and locations (e.g. Foerstl et al., 2013), rather than focusing on the individual members of the purchasing function.

Strategy literature suggests that internal alignment enables individuals to act independently 'but in a way that is consistent with the actions of others and consistent with the spirit of the decision' (Amason, 1996, p. 125). When unplanned situations arise, internal alignment ensures that they are solved coherently, in line with the understanding which lies behind the strategy (Ateş et al., 2020). In the event of a lack of internal alignment, intra-departmental conflicts may obstruct implementation of strategies (Markoczy, 2001).

Internal purchasing alignment has not received much attention in the purchasing literature. Foerstl et al. (2013) examine 'functional coordination'; however, this concept focuses on alignment across the worldwide locations of the purchasing function, rather than alignment across the individual members of the purchasing function. Meschnig and Kaufmann (2015) investigate the impact of strategic consensus on supplier performance, focusing on cross-functional purchase category teams. To the best of our knowledge, internal purchasing alignment in relation to sustainability strategies, practices, and performance has not been examined in the literature so far. We have noted a few studies in the operations management literature which investigate related concepts such as 'worker involvement'. For instance, Longoni and Cagliano (2015) argue that worker involvement improves alignment of lean practices with environmental and social sustainability practices in day-to-day operations. However, we have not found any exact conceptual matches.

In summary, although the strategy literature strongly emphasises the importance of strategic consensus within teams and functions for successful strategy implementation (Kellermanns et al., 2005; Kellermanns et al., 2011), internal alignment within the purchasing function has, interestingly, received very little attention, and none of the studies to date focus on the sustainability context.

Conclusion

In this section, we have elaborated on the three levels of purchasing alignment (vertical alignment, horizontal alignment, and internal alignment), and have discussed the state of research with respect to sustainability strategy and practices. Our review illustrates that, although the importance of purchasing alignment has been acknowledged in the literature, there has been only a limited number of studies, mostly focusing on business and operational performance, rather than sustainable purchasing practices and sustainability performance. Of the three purchasing alignment dimensions we have examined, it would seem that the majority of research concerned with sustainability has focused on horizontal alignment; for instance, between manufacturing and purchasing, and between marketing and purchasing. Internal alignment, on the other hand, has remained an unexamined research topic.

ASSESSING PURCHASING ALIGNMENT FOR SUSTAINABILITY USING STRATEGIC CONSENSUS MAPPING

In this section, we introduce a tool to assess and visualise purchasing alignment for sustainability, which fits with our multi-level conceptualisation. We then demonstrate the use of this tool in an illustrative case study.

Strategic Consensus Mapping

The limited material within the purchasing literature, which investigates alignment, has built upon more established concepts from the strategy literature (i.e. Baier et al., 2008; González-Benito, 2007). Similarly, we draw on the strategy literature in order to capture the multiple levels of purchasing alignment for sustainability.

Strategy literature defines alignment as congruence, in terms of agreement across strategic goals (Boyer and McDermott, 1999; Colbert et al., 2008; Kellermanns et al., 2005; Pagell & Krause, 2002). In line with this definition, *vertical alignment* concerns the degree of shared understanding about strategic priorities between the TMT and the purchasing function; the *horizontal alignment* stands for such alignment between other functions and the purchasing function; and the *internal alignment* refers to alignment between individuals within the purchasing function.

Tarakci and colleagues (2014) propose a method called 'Strategic Consensus Mapping' that is capable of quantifying and visualising these three levels of purchasing alignment. This method is particularly suitable for visualising and quantifying the multiple levels of purchasing alignment for sustainability. Successful execution of sustainability strategies requires a shared understanding among multiple business functions across organisational levels (Johnsen et al., 2017; Luzzini et al., 2015; Pullman & Wikof, 2017; Schneider et al., 2014), and Strategic Consensus Mapping captures the extent of this shared understanding within and between functions. Furthermore, the positioning of the sustainability goal among other, more conventional, strategic objectives (e.g. cost reduction, quality improvement, operational excellence, customer satisfaction) is essential, and needs to be explicitly studied. This is because alignment of conventional strategic priorities can be achieved much more smoothly and with less effort, since the importance of these issues in theory and practice has been debated for decades, and the role of the purchasing function in realising these objectives has been well established (Baier et al., 2008). Strategic Consensus Mapping is well-suited to considering multiple strategic goals at the same time. Accordingly, this method offers value to scholars seeking to advance the research on purchasing alignment for sustainability, as well as being a useful method for purchasing practitioners to visually explore their alignment within the purchasing function, and with other functions.

There are other techniques designed to visualise and assess alignment (and other types of cognitive structure in general) within the broader managerial and organisational cognition research (Hodgkinson & Healey, 2008). These include team mental models (Edwards et al., 2006; Mathieu et al., 2000), belief structures (Walsh et al., 1988), causal mapping (Carley, 1997; Markoczy, 2001), and strategic groups (DeSarbo et al., 2009). We acknowledge that some of these methods may have superior features for certain specific purposes, however none of them offers a multi-level and multi-dimensional assessment of alignment (Tarakci et al., 2014) that fits with the conceptual development in our previous section. We elaborate below on how the core features of the Strategic Consensus Mapping method match with our multi-level framework of purchasing alignment for sustainability.

Strategic Consensus Mapping combines a set of established statistical procedures in a unique way[1] in order to capture the multiple facets of consensus (Tarakci et al., 2014) in a manner consistent with the three levels of purchasing alignment we examined above. A comprehensive review of this method is beyond the scope of our research; we simply refer to the original article for the technical details. An online tool to apply Strategic Consensus Mapping is freely available online.[2] Nonetheless, it is important to mention the inputs and the outputs of the method, and to clarify how the outputs are useful in interpreting purchasing alignment at multiple levels.

The input for the Strategic Consensus Mapping is the data on how individuals evaluate the importance of organisational strategic goals. A rating or ranking of strategic goals (e.g. strategic priorities, objectives, initiatives, means, ends, thrusts, ambitions) collected by means of a survey is typically used in strategic management research (Kellermanns et al., 2011). There are two visual outputs: (i) a biplot for each unit, which demonstrates the *internal alignment* within that unit; and (ii) a bubble plot for the whole organisation, which illustrates the *vertical and horizontal alignments*. Based on these plots, the Strategic Consensus Mapping operationalises the *internal alignment* for each unit with an α_i measure, and the *horizontal alignment* between units with an $r_{i,j}$ measure, where the $r_{i,TMT}$ represents the *vertical alignment* with the TMT (*i* and *j* denotes the departments). While α takes values between 0 and 1, *r* ranges between –1 and 1 (as a correlation coefficient).

Figure 25.2 depicts a sample Strategic Consensus Mapping analysis. Panel (a) shows a bubble plot. In a bubble plot, each organisational unit is represented by a bubble, and the closeness between the bubbles represents the *horizontal alignment* between the units. The closer the bubbles of two departments *i* and *j*, the higher the $r_{i,j}$ value. The TMT is placed at the centre of the plot. Therefore, the closeness of the bubbles to the centre represents the *vertical alignment*. If department *i* is very distant from the centre, it would have a low $r_{i,TMT}$ value. The size of a bubble represents the *internal alignment* within the respective unit. The larger the bubble for department *i*, the higher the α_i value. Panels (b) and (c) show biplots. A biplot shows the details of the *internal alignment* within a unit. In a biplot, each member of the unit is represented by a vector, and each strategic priority by a point. An orthogonal projection of a point onto a vector indicates the rating of that particular strategic priority by that member, such that longer projections in the positive direction represent higher importance. The narrower the angle between two vectors, the more these members share a similar view. Accordingly, a wide spread of the vectors (like rays evenly distributed around a circle) represents the lack of *internal alignment* within a unit (i.e. a low α_i value). A tight bundle of vectors (when all members share similar prioritisations) represents high *internal alignment* (i.e. a high α_i value).

In Panel (a) of Figure 25.2, Unit A and Unit C are positioned far from each other. Therefore, the *horizontal alignment* between them is very low ($r_{A,C} = -0.20$). While Unit B is the closest to the TMT, Unit C is the farthest away. Accordingly, the *vertical alignment* of Unit B is the highest ($r_{B,TMT} = 0.95$), while that of Unit C is the lowest ($r_{C,TMT} = 0.35$). The largest bubble belongs to Unit A, while the smallest bubble belongs to Unit C. Hence, *the internal alignment* of Unit A is the highest ($\alpha_A = 0.87$), and that of Unit C is the lowest ($\alpha_C = 0.2$).

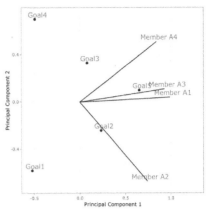

Panel (b): The *Internal Alignment* of Unit A

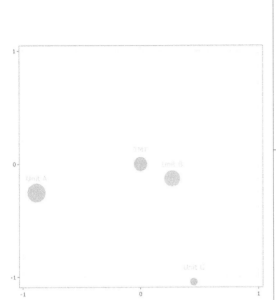

Panel (a): The *Vertical Alignment* of the units with the TMT and the *Horizontal Alignment* between units

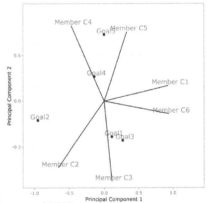

Panel (c): The *Internal Alignment* of Unit C

Note: Panel (a) shows a bubble plot. Bubbles represent organisational units. The closeness between the bubbles represents the *horizontal alignment* between units. Top Management Team is placed at the centre. The distance between bubbles and the centre indicates their *vertical alignment*. The size of a bubble represents the *internal alignment* within a unit (among members of the unit). Panels (b) and (c) show biplots. Vectors represent members of the unit, and points represent strategic priorities. An orthogonal projection of a point onto a vector indicates the rating of that particular strategic priority by that member, such that longer projections in a positive direction represent higher importance. If two vectors are close to each other, those two members share a similar view. The spread of all of the vectors represents the lack of *internal alignment* within a unit.

Figure 25.2   A sample Strategic Consensus Mapping analysis

In Panels (b) and (c) of Figure 25.2, the biplots for Units A and C, respectively, are shown. Unit A is composed of four team members and Unit C has six team members. Vector lengths are similar in both biplots (i.e. no disproportionately short vectors), which means that all members' preferences are satisfactorily represented in the plots. Orthogonal projections of the strategic goal points onto the vector of Member A2 indicate that this member prioritises Goal 1 and 2 the most and Goal 4 the least. The angle between Members A1 and A3 is very small, which means that both members have similar strategic goal prioritisations. The prototypical member of Unit A is shown through the orthogonal projections of strategic goal points on the *x*-axis. The average team member prioritises Goal 5 the most, and Goal 1 and 4 the least. The spread of all member vectors is quite narrow, indicating a high *internal alignment* within Unit A ($a_A = 0.87$). Conversely, the member vectors in Unit C are widely spread across the plot, which indicates a low *internal alignment* within Unit C ($a_C = 0.2$).

An Illustrative Case for Mapping Purchasing Alignment for Sustainability

In this section, we present a real-life case featuring an organisation which prioritises sustainability as a strategic goal. We conducted an organisational survey and asked the managers and employees to rate the importance they attached to each of the organisation's strategic goals. The strategic goals were determined prior to the survey at a strategy workshop with the top management team. The data presented here were collected in 2012 as part of a larger research project. Here, we present a selection of the core departments and employees from the organisation for illustrative purposes (Yin, 2013).

The case organization is a national transportation service provider in a European country. Apart from maintaining network infrastructure, the organisation purchases many types of service from numerous suppliers, which makes it one of the largest buyers of services in the country. The organisation strives for 'sustainable business operations'. With this strategic goal, the organisation expresses its ambition to fully integrate sustainability into its business operations. It wants to operate more sustainably by means of the circular use of materials, by lowering its CO_2 emissions, and by using less energy. Some examples of its initiatives include introducing new routes, reusing roadside waste and reaching step five on the five-step CO_2 performance ladder within the next five years. The company not only focuses on the environmental side of sustainability, but also emphasises the social side; both internally, within the business, and externally, with their suppliers and contractors.

Purchasing is a major business function within the organisation. It outsources large projects to contractors, who then order a variety of services from suppliers. These projects involve construction, maintenance, and purchase of materials and services. The company requires its suppliers to comply with certain environmental and social criteria. Furthermore, if they meet certain levels of environmental standards (e.g. low CO_2 emissions) and social standards (e.g. worker safety), potential suppliers are scored more highly, meaning that they are more likely to win tenders.

In this illustrative case, we examine whether the organisation's purchasing function is aligned with its recent decision to emphasise sustainability objectives in its organisational strategy. In order to do this, we use data collected from six business functions; namely, purchasing, marketing, operations, business development, finance, and HR, and from the TMT. Our data include 42 individual respondents. The average age of the respondents was 42.3 (SD = 7.21), 28.5% of the respondents were female, and the average tenure was 9.2 years (SD = 8.7). The purchasing manager has five staff reporting directly to them, while the TMT is composed of five members, including the CEO.

We investigate the three levels of purchasing alignment within this organisation, together with the emphasis it puts on its sustainability strategy. Figure 25.3 demonstrates the vertical, horizontal, and internal alignments within the organisation. After we apply a strategic consensus mapping analysis, we obtain the bubble plot and the biplot shown in Panels (a) and (b) of the figure, respectively. Table 25.1 shows the α and the r measures corresponding with the three levels of alignment.

In Panel (a) of Figure 25.3, we see a snapshot of the purchasing alignment within the organisation. The purchasing function is located far from the TMT, indicating low *vertical alignment* ($_{r\text{Purchasing,TMT}} = -0.04$). Its position is close to the Marketing and Operations, implying high *horizontal alignment* between these functions ($_{r\text{Purchasing,Marketing}} = 0.48$, $_{r\text{Purchasing, Operations}} = 0.64$). Finally, the size of the bubble for the purchasing function is relatively small, showing low *internal alignment* ($\alpha_{\text{Purchasing}} = 0.53$).

Table 25.1 *The vertical, horizontal, and internal alignment measures in the illustrative case*

	Internal alignment	Vertical alignment	Horizontal alignment r_{ij}					
	α	$r_{i,\text{TMT}}$	2	3	4	5	6	7
1 TMT	0.71							
2 HR	0.57	-0.69						
3 Purchasing	0.53	-0.04	0.35					
4 Finance	0.71	-0.41	-0.40	-0.09				
5 Operations	0.66	-0.41	0.63	0.64	-0.70			
6 Marketing	0.77	-0.05	0.24	0.48	-0.56	0.75		
7 IT	0.47	-0.29	-0.27	-0.17	0.76	-0.57	-0.46	
8 BD	0.77	-0.72	-0.50	0.30	0.32	-0.12	-0.08	0.04

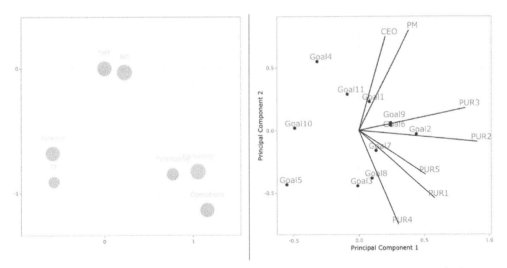

Note: Goal1: Sustainable Business Operations; Goal2: Safety; Goal3: Punctuality; Goal4: Pleasantness; Goal5: Speed; Goal6: Growth in Freight; Goal7: Growth in Passengers; Goal8: Efficiency; Goal9: Reliability; Goal10: Frequency; Goal11: Accessibility. BD: Business Development department; IT: Information Technologies department; PM: Purchasing Manager. CEO is positioned on the internal alignment plot of the purchasing function for interpretative purposes.

Figure 25.3 *Visualisation of the purchasing alignment in the illustrative case*

Panel (b) in Figure 25.3 illustrates in detail the internal alignment within the purchasing function. In addition to the individual members of the purchasing function, we also included the CEO's preferences on this plot. The purpose of this was to compare the department members' preferences to the CEO's, to allow inferences to be made about vertical alignment as well. Because the TMT has high internal alignment ($\alpha_{\text{Purchasing}}$ = 0.71), and the CEO's vector lies close to the first axis (i.e. the prototypical member), we can confidently regard him as representative of the TMT, and of the overall business strategy.

In 2011, the organisation went through a strategic renewal. From a strategic orientation towards 'operational excellence', the organisation shifted its focus to 'customer satisfaction'. The TMT was satisfied with the organisation's existing operational performance, and decided to shift focus to its customers. Since operational excellence manifested itself in the strategic priorities of *Punctuality* (Goal3), *Speed* (Goal5), and *Efficiency* (Goal8), these priorities were already highly regarded. However, the organisation's more recent strategic position revolves around its customers. The strategic priorities of *Sustainability* (Goal1), *Pleasantness* (Goal4) and *Accessibility* (Goal11) were proposed in a strategy workshop, and were given high importance by the top managers. The emphasis on *Safety* (Goal2), *Growth* (Goals 6 and 7) and *Reliability* (Goal9) has remained, as these are still considered to be among the most important strategic priorities. At the time of data collection, the TMT was still striving to disseminate the new strategy throughout organisational units, and secure 'buy-in' to this strategy.

The orthogonal projections of the strategy points on the CEO's vector in Panel (b) demonstrate the new preference set. The CEO prioritises *Pleasantness* (Goal4), *Accessibility* (Goal11), *Reliability* (Goal9), *Safety* (Goal2), and *Sustainability* (Goal1). Note that the purchasing manager (PM) is highly aligned with the CEO, as the angle between their vectors is very small. This means that the PM and the CEO share similar views on the relative importance of strategic priorities. This includes their views of the importance of 'Sustainable Business Operations' (Goal1). However, we note that the rest of the purchasing function members have a different opinion. They continue to favour the strategic priorities associated with the old strategy (operational excellence), particularly *Punctuality* (Goal3), *Speed* (Goal5), and *Efficiency* (Goal8). While they also acknowledge the importance of *Safety* (Goal2), *Reliability* (Goal9), and *Growth* (Goals 6 and 7), they do not find *Sustainability* (Goal1), *Pleasantness* (Goal4), and *Accessibility* (Goal11) as important. We therefore observe that, while the purchasing manager is individually aligned with the CEO (and thus with the TMT), he appears not to have convinced his team members. This shows the importance of the *internal alignment* dimension of our multi-level purchasing alignment conceptualisation. If one considers only the alignment between managers, and disregards the team members, the *vertical alignment* of the purchasing function would be falsely assessed as quite high. Since our approach places attention on what individual team members think, the method accurately captures the true *vertical alignment* with the TMT, as well as the *horizontal alignment* between business functions.

This situation gets more troubling, as we can observe from Panel (a) that the marketing and operation functions are positioned close to the purchasing function. This is worrying for the organisation, as it implies that the strategic renewal has not been successful. The TMT was able to create some buy-in for the business development department, since it is closely located to the TMT and thus has high vertical alignment ($r_{\text{BD,TMT}}$ = 0.77). However, the other departments fall far from the centre. For effective strategy execution, strategy process literature suggests that the departments being relied upon to put strategy into practice ought to be aligned (Ateş et al., 2020).

In summary, this illustrative case demonstrates the importance of assessing purchasing alignment for sustainability at multiple levels: vertically, horizontally, and internally. Although the organisation studied has shifted its business strategy towards sustainability, there is a lack of horizontal alignment. While there seems to be horizontal alignment between the key business functions of purchasing, operations, and marketing, they are aligned on objectives different from those which management prioritises. In particular, these core business functions do not see sustainability as a top priority. Thus, the vertical alignment is lacking. Our findings also illustrate that if vertical alignment had been assessed by taking into account only the CEO and purchasing manager's similar views, as has been done previously in the strategy literature (Colbert et al., 2008), there would have been a misconception that there was good vertical alignment. However, the Strategic Consensus Mapping adopts a holistic approach. Thus, when internal alignment of the purchasing team members is taken into account, the mapping captures the vertical alignment more accurately. Taking the internal alignment into account is important, because it is concerned with the shared understanding of individuals within a function, whose everyday operational and tactical decisions might either support or undermine the overall strategic goal of sustainability.

DISCUSSION AND CONCLUSION

Sustainability strategies are now well established among organisations' strategic priorities (Porter & Kramer, 2006; Pullman & Wikoff, 2017). Like other strategic priorities, successful implementation of sustainability strategies depends on the alignment of many actors within the organisation, throughout different levels, and across departments (Noble, 1999). In this research, we have proposed a multi-level purchasing alignment framework for sustainability, reviewed the related literature, highlighted potential future areas of research to address current gaps, and provided an illustration of a tool from the strategy literature which is useful in assessing and visualising purchasing alignment for sustainability.

Theoretical Implications

Our research contributes to the purchasing and supply management literature in several ways. First, we have illustrated the current state of research about purchasing alignment for sustainability (Schneider & Wallenburg, 2012; Tchokogué et al., 2018). We have found that there was little extant research investigating purchasing alignment within the sustainability context (e.g. Dabhilkar et al., 2016; Luzzini et al., 2015; Schneider & Wallenburg, 2012; Schneider et al., 2014). In the majority of studies, purchasing alignment was mentioned as an important factor for sustainability strategies (e.g. Schneider & Wallenburg, 2012; Tchokogué et al., 2018), but there have been few empirical studies. What studies there have been highlight that purchasing alignment has an impact on sustainable practices, but does not affect sustainability performance (e.g. Foo et al., 2019; Kang et al., 2018; Luzzini et al., 2015). Future studies might usefully investigate the factors behind this observation. Such studies might focus, in particular, on the effects of internal alignment, since our review shows that this is the least-frequently examined dimension.

Second, our research has answered the call for research that emphasises the importance of multi-level analysis in purchasing and supply management research (e.g. Carter et al.,

2015; Meschnig et al., 2018). By definition, purchasing and supply management deals with cross-functional and inter-organisational phenomena (Meschnig et al., 2018), yet there is a paucity of studies that adopt a multi-level approach. Our proposed framework allows scholars to investigate multiple levels of purchasing alignment for sustainability, which is considered a necessary factor for successful implementation of sustainable purchasing practices (Luzzini et al., 2015; Schneider & Wallenburg, 2012; Tchokogué et al., 2018). Studying purchasing alignment at multiple levels with the assistance of our framework will allow scholars to make meaningful contributions to the literature.

Third, we have introduced a novel methodology from the strategy literature that successfully captures multiple levels of purchasing alignment (Tarakci et al., 2014). This is an important contribution because there is a divergence of conceptualisations, and a variety of operationalisations of purchasing alignment in the literature (Baier et al., 2008; Carr & Pearson, 2002; Foerstl et al., 2013; González-Benito, 2007; Hochrein et al., 2017; Nair et al., 2015; Pagell & Krause, 2002), which prevents assimilation of knowledge in the field. Together with our conceptual distinctions about purchasing alignment, this method is capable of capturing the multiple levels of alignment accurately. Thus, it encourages further studies which focus on the preconditions and outcomes of purchasing alignment for sustainability. Furthermore, because this method quantifies all levels of alignment based on the same raw data, the distinctions between different types of alignment (i.e. vertical, horizontal, internal) are not obscured by differences in measurement (Tarakci et al., 2014).

Guidelines for Managers

Our research offers practical insights for purchasing managers and professionals as well. Practitioners can use our proposed mapping tool periodically to visualise and assess their organisations' strategic consensuses on sustainability objectives. This tool does not require extensive data collection, and is therefore easy to implement, yet it offers a quick snapshot of alignment. The bubble plot and biplot visualisations provide practitioners with intuitive and readily understandable illustrations to help map the three levels of alignment in relation to their organisations. In particular, the biplots demonstrate the substance of internal alignment within the functional units. Organisations can use this information to design effective interventions of bringing on board employees who have not adopted the desired objectives.

Our research also highlights that purchasing alignment is a multi-dimensional phenomenon, in which each dimension requires separate attention. In line with our conceptual model, top managers sometimes involve purchasing managers in strategic decision-making processes, which creates vertical alignment. Organisations often hold strategy workshops for strategy formulation where the heads and/or representatives from functional departments are invited (Hodgkinson et al., 2006). This may be instrumental in engendering horizontal alignment. Our model also suggests that internal alignment should not be neglected; it is important for individual employees to be directed towards realisation of shared strategic goals. For instance, although the purchasing manager might be aligned with the sustainability emphasis of business strategy, employees within the purchasing function also need to be so aligned, in order to successfully implement sustainability principles in their day-to-day purchasing activities.

Limitations and Future Research

This research is not without limitations. First, it focuses on reviewing the dispersed literature, developing a unifying conceptual model, and proposing a tool to assess and visualise alignment, but it does not test the impact of alignment on sustainable practices or sustainability performance. We argue that achieving alignment is a first step in implementing sustainability strategies; however, there might be other factors, such as lack of incentives, systems, procedures or resources, which affect whether a shared understanding on sustainability goals is actually put into practice. Furthermore, some studies suggest that purchasing alignment has either a direct or moderating effect on purchasing practices, but not a direct effect on performance (e.g. Rodríguez-Escobar & González-Benito, 2017). Hence, future research might investigate the impact of purchasing alignment for sustainability on purchasing practices and performance. Such research might also differentiate between environmental and social performance. Considering that the majority of firms assess purchasing performance in terms of traditional objectives such as cost, quality, and delivery (Caniato et al., 2014), assessing the impact of purchasing alignment on purchasing sustainability performance might be a challenging but fruitful research topic.

Second, we examined purchasing alignment for sustainability by focusing on the shared understanding of business objectives. An alternative approach might be to investigate alignment on intra-departmental goals (e.g. a purchasing department's formal objectives) and/or practices (e.g. sustainability in supplier selection criteria, conducting environmental audits). Our illustrative case study adopted a broader perspective (i.e. focusing on organisational strategies) which allowed us to capture horizontal and vertical alignment simultaneously with the same input (so the internal, vertical, and horizontal alignment measures are not obscured by differences in input material). However, we would also stress the value and importance of research endeavours which build and test theory about departmental goals and sustainability practices.

Third, we solely present a single case from the services sector for illustrative purposes. We acknowledge that different organisations in other sectors are likely to take different approaches towards purchasing alignment for sustainability. For instance, Hoejmose and Adrien-Kirby (2012) find that the link between business strategies and sustainable supply chain management practices is not so evident in business-to-business sectors as it is in business-to-consumer sectors. Future studies using our framework and methodology should take account of different expectations within different contexts.

Fourth, another potential future area for research might be to examine which specific capabilities are required to achieve purchasing alignment for sustainability. Schulze and Bals (2017) list networking skills, relationship management, communication, and the ability to cope with uncertain situations as competencies that purchasing managers and buyers require in order to implement sustainable purchasing practices. Scholars might usefully extend this line of research by focusing on additional competencies which might be required to achieve purchasing alignment at multiple levels.

Finally, although our research focused on purchasing alignment for sustainability, our proposed multi-level alignment framework and Strategic Consensus Mapping tool are capable of being used to assess alignment of objectives in other contexts. We believe that it would be especially useful in assessing alignment in relation to contemporary strategies such as sustainability and innovation, as opposed to more traditional competitive priorities such as cost reduction and quality improvement. Our methodology might also be used to compare different sustainability objectives within organisations, such as environmental sustainability versus economic sustainability.

In conclusion, our research paves the way for further research by providing a multi-level, illustrative tool that can be useful in empirically assessing purchasing alignment for sustainability, as well as its preconditions and consequences.

NOTES

1. The Strategic Consensus Mapping implements a vector model for unfolding on respondents' strategic priority ratings to operationalise the degree of consensus within a unit and to visualise the content of consensus on a biplot. The correlations between the orthogonal projections of the strategic priorities on the first axis for two units generates the degree of consensus between these units. Finally, a multi-dimensional scaling analysis of the between-unit consensus measures produces a map for alignment throughout the organisation.
2. https://mtarakci.shinyapps.io/consensus

REFERENCES

Ağan, Y., Kuzey, C., Acar, M. F., & Açıkgöz, A. (2016). The relationships between corporate social responsibility, environmental supplier development, and firm performance. *Journal of Cleaner Production, 112*(Part 3), 1872–1881.

Amason, A. C. (1996). Distinguishing the effects of functional and dysfunctional conflict on strategic decision making: Resolving a paradox for top management teams. *Academy of Management Journal, 39*(1), 123–148.

Ateş, N. Y., Tarakci, M., Porck, J. P., van Knippenberg, D., & Groenen, P. J. F. (2020). The dark side of visionary leadership in strategy implementation: Strategic alignment, strategic consensus, and commitment. *Journal of Management, 46*(5), 637–665.

Bai, C., Kusi-Sarpong, S., Ahmadi, H. B., & Sarkis, J. (2019). Social sustainable supplier evaluation and selection: A group decision support approach. *International Journal of Production Research, 57*(22), 7046–7067.

Baier, C., Hartmann, E., & Moser, R. (2008). Strategic alignment and purchasing efficacy: An exploratory analysis of their impact on financial performance. *Journal of Supply Chain Management, 44*(4), 36–52.

Balogun, J. (2006). Managing change: Steering a course between intended strategies and unanticipated outcomes. *Long Range Planning, 39*(1), 29–49.

Blome, C., Hollos, D., & Paulraj, A. (2014). Green procurement and green supplier development: Antecedents and effects on supplier performance. *International Journal of Production Research, 52*(1), 32–49.

Boyer, K. K., & McDermott, C. (1999). Strategic consensus in operations strategy. *Journal of Operations Management, 17*(3), 289–305.

Brandon-Jones, A., & Knoppen, D. (2018). The role of strategic purchasing in dynamic capability development and deployment: A contingency perspective. *International Journal of Operations and Production Management, 38*(2), 446–473.

Caniato, F., Luzzini, D., & Ronchi, S. (2014). Purchasing performance management systems: An empirical investigation. *Production Planning and Control, 25*(7), 616–635.

Carley, K. M. (1997). Extracting team mental models through textual analysis. *Journal of Organizational Behavior, 18*(S1), 533–558.

Carr, A. S., & Pearson, J. N. (2002). The impact of purchasing and supplier involvement on strategic purchasing and its impact on firm's performance. *International Journal of Operations and Production Management, 22*(9), 1032–1053.

Carter, C. R., Meschnig, G., & Kaufmann, L. (2015). Moving to the next level: Why our discipline needs more multilevel theorization. *Journal of Supply Chain Management, 51*(4), 94–102.

Colbert, A. E., Kristof-Brown, A. L., Bradley, B. H., & Barrick, M. R. (2008). CEO transformational leadership: The role of goal importance congruence in top management teams. *Academy of Management Journal, 51*(1), 81–96.

Crittenden, V. L., Crittenden, W. F., Ferrell, L. K., Ferrell, O. C., & Pinney, C. C. (2011). Market-oriented sustainability: A conceptual framework and propositions. *Journal of the Academy of Marketing Science, 39*, 71–85.

Cronin, M. A., & Weingart, L. R. (2007). Representational gaps, information processing, and conflict in functionally diverse teams. *Academy of Management Review, 32*(3), 761–773.

Dabhilkar, M., Bengtsson, L., & Lakemond, N. (2016). Sustainable supply management as a purchasing capability: A power and dependence perspective. *International Journal of Operations and Production Management, 36*(1), 2–22.

Das, A., & Narasimhan, R. (2000). Purchasing competence and its relationship with manufacturing performance. *Journal of Supply Chain Management, 36*(2), 17–28.

DeSarbo W. S., Grewal R., & Wang, R. (2009). Dynamic strategic groups: Deriving spatial evolutionary paths. *Strategic Management Journal, 30*(13), 1420–1439.

Driedonks, B. A., Gevers, J. M. P., & van Weele, A. J. (2010). Managing sourcing team effectiveness: The need for a team perspective in purchasing organizations. *Journal of Purchasing and Supply Management, 16*(2), 109–117.

Du Preez, H. C., & Folinas, D. (2019). Procurement's contribution to the strategic alignment of an organisation: Findings from an empirical research study. *Supply Chain Forum: An International Journal, 20*(3), 159–168.

Edwards, B.D., Day, E. A., Arthur, W. Jr., & Bell, S. T. (2006). Relationships among team ability composition, team mental models, and team performance. *Journal of Applied Psychology, 91*(3), 727–736.

Floyd, S. W., & Wooldridge, B. (1992). Middle management involvement in strategy and its association with strategic type: A research note. *Strategic Management Journal, 13* (S1), 153–167.

Foerstl, K., Hartmann, E., Wynstra, F., & Moser, R. (2013). Cross-functional integration and functional coordination in purchasing and supply management: Antecedents and effects on purchasing and firm performance. *International Journal of Operations and Production Management, 33*(6), 689–721.

Foerstl, K., Reuter, C., Hartmann, E., & Blome, C. (2010). Managing supplier sustainability risks in a dynamically changing environment – Sustainable supplier management in the chemical industry. *Journal of Purchasing and Supply Management, 16*(2), 118–130.

Foo, M. Y., Kanapathy, K., Zailani, S., & Shaharudin, M. R. (2019). Green purchasing capabilities, practices and institutional pressure. *Management of Environmental Quality: An International Journal, 30*(5), 1171–1189.

Formentini, M., Ellram, L. M., Boem, M., & Da Re, G. (2019). Finding true north: Design and implementation of a strategic sourcing framework. *Industrial Marketing Management, 77*(February), 182–197.

Giunipero, L. C., Hooker, R., & Denslow, D. (2012). Purchasing and supply management sustainability: Drivers and barriers. *Journal of Purchasing and Supply Management, 18*(4), 258–269.

Golicic, S. D., & Smith, C. D. (2013). A meta-analysis of environmentally sustainable supply chain management practices and firm performance. *Journal of Supply Chain Management, 49*(2), 78–95.

González-Benito, J. (2007). A theory of purchasing's contribution to business performance. *Journal of Operations Management, 25*(4), 901–917.

Gölgeci, İ., Gligor, D. M., Tatoglu, E., & Arda, O. A. (2019). A relational view of environmental performance: What role do environmental collaboration and cross-functional alignment play? *Journal of Business Research, 96*(March), 35–46.

Gulati, R. (2007). Silo busting: How to execute on the promise of customer focus. *Harvard Business Review, 85*(5), 98–108.

Hahn, T., Figge, F., & Pinkse, J. (2018). A paradox perspective on corporate sustainability: Descriptive, instrumental, and normative aspects. *Journal of Business Ethics, 148*, 235–248.

Hambrick, D. C., & Mason, P. A. (1984). Upper echelons: The organization as a reflection of its top managers. *Academy of Management Review, 9*(2), 193–206.

Harms, D. (2011). Environmental sustainability and supply chain management: A framework for cross-functional integration and knowledge transfer. *Journal of Environmental Sustainability*, *1*(1), 121–141.

Hart, S. L. (1995). A natural-resource-based view of the firm. *The Academy of Management Review*, *20*(4), 986–1014.

Hartmann, E., Kerkfeld, D., & Henke, M. (2012). Top and bottom line relevance of purchasing and supply management. *Journal of Purchasing and Supply Management*, *18*(1), 22–34.

Hesping, F. H., & Schiele, H. (2015). Purchasing strategy development: a multi-level review. *Journal of Purchasing and Supply Management*, *21*(2), 138–150.

Hochrein, S., Muther, M., & Glock, C. H. (2017). Strategy alignment in purchasing and supply management: A systematic literature review and research framework on the performance impact. *International Journal of Integrated Supply Management*, *11*(1), 44–86.

Hodgkinson, G. P., & Healey, M. P. (2008). Cognition in organizations. *Annual Review of Psychology*, *59*, 387–417.

Hodgkinson, G. P., Whittington, R., Johnson, G., & Schwarz, M. (2006). The role of strategy workshops in strategy development processes: Formality, communication, co-ordination and inclusion. *Long Range Planning*, *39*(5), 479–496.

Hoejmose, S. U., & Adrien-Kirby, A. J. (2012). Socially and environmentally responsible procurement: A literature review and future research agenda of a managerial issue in the 21st century. *Journal of Purchasing and Supply Management*, *18*(4), 232–242.

Hollos, D., Blome, C., & Foerstl, K. (2012). Does sustainable supplier co-operation affect performance? Examining implications for the triple bottom line. *International Journal of Production Research*, *50*(11), 2968–2986.

Johnsen, T. E., Miemczyk, J., & Howard, M. A. (2017). Systematic literature review of sustainable purchasing and supply research: Theoretical perspectives and opportunities for IMP-based research. *Industrial Marketing Management*, *61*(February), 130–143.

Kang, M., Yang, M. G., Park, Y., & Huo, B. (2018). Supply chain integration and its impact on sustainability. *Industrial Management and Data Systems*, *118*(9), 1749–1765.

Kellermanns, F. W., Walter, J., Floyd, S. W., Lechner, C., & Shaw, J. C. (2011). To agree or not to agree? A meta-analytical review of strategic consensus and organizational performance. *Journal of Business Research*, *64*(2), 126–133.

Kellermanns, F. W., Walter, J., Lechner, C., & Floyd, S. W. (2005). The lack of consensus about strategic consensus: Advancing theory and research. *Journal of Management*, *31*(5), 719–737.

Ketokivi, M., & Castaner, X. (2004). Strategic planning as an integrative device. *Administrative Science Quarterly*, *49*(3), 337–365.

Krause, D. R., Vachon, S., & Klassen, R. D. (2009). Special topic forum on sustainable supply chain management: Introduction and reflection on the role of purchasing management. *Journal of Supply Chain Management*, *45*(4), 18–25.

Leppelt, T., Foerstl, K., Reuter, C., & Hartmann, E. (2013). Sustainability management beyond organizational boundaries–sustainable supplier relationship management in the chemical industry. *Journal of Cleaner Production*, *56*(1), 94–102.

Lingle, J. H., & Schiemann, W. A. (1996). From balanced scorecard to strategic gauges: Is measurement worth it? *Management Review*, *85*(3), 56–61.

Longoni, A., & Cagliano, R. (2015). Cross-functional executive involvement and worker involvement in lean manufacturing and sustainability alignment. *International Journal of Operations and Production Management*, *35*(9), 1332–1358.

Luzzini, D., Brandon-Jones, E., Brandon-Jones, A., & Spina, G. (2015). From sustainability commitment to performance: The role of intra- and inter-firm collaborative capabilities in the upstream supply chain. *International Journal of Production Economics*, *165*(July), 51–63.

Luzzini, D., & Ronchi, S. (2016). Cinderella purchasing transformation: Linking purchasing status to purchasing practices and business performance. *Production Planning and Control*, *27*(10), 787–796.

Markoczy, L. (2001). Consensus formation during strategic change. *Strategic Management Journal*, *22*(11), 1013–1031.

Mathieu, J. E., Heffner, T. S., Goodwin, G. F., Salas, E., & Cannon-Bowers, J. A. (2000). The influence of shared mental models on team process and performance. *Journal of Applied Psychology*, *85*(2), 273–283.

McGuire, J. B., Sundgren, A., & Schneeweis, T. (1988). Corporate social responsibility and firm financial performance. *Academy of Management Journal*, *31*(4), 854–872.

Meschnig, G., & Kaufmann, L. (2015). Consensus on supplier selection objectives in cross-functional sourcing teams. *International Journal of Physical Distribution and Logistics Management*, *45*(8), 774–793.

Meschnig, G., Carter, C., & Kaufmann, L. (2018). Conducting multilevel studies in purchasing and supply management research. *Journal of Purchasing and Supply Management*, *24*(4), 338–342.

Mitra, S, & Datta, P. P. (2014). Adoption of green supply chain management practices and their impact on performance: An exploratory study of Indian manufacturing firms. *International Journal of Production Research*, *52*(7), 2085–2107.

Nair, A., Jayaram, J., & Das, A. (2015). Strategic purchasing participation, supplier selection, supplier evaluation and purchasing performance. *International Journal of Production Research*, *53*(20), 6263–6278.

Noble, C. H. (1999). The eclectic roots of strategy implementation research. *Journal of Business Research*, *45*(2), 119–134.

Noda, T., & Bower, J. L. (1996). Strategy making as iterated processes of resource allocation. *Strategic Management Journal*, *17*(S1), 159–192.

Pagell, M., & Krause, D. R. (2002). Strategic consensus in the internal supply chain: Exploring the manufacturing–purchasing link. *International Journal of Production Research*, *40*(13), 3075–3092.

Paulraj, A. (2011). Understanding the relationship between internal resources and capabilities, sustainable supply management, and organizational sustainability. *Journal of Supply Chain Management*, *47*(1), 19–37.

Peters, N. J., Hofstetter, J. S., & Hoffmann, V. H. (2011). Institutional entrepreneurship capabilities for interorganizational sustainable supply chain strategies. *International Journal of Logistics Management*, *22*(1), 52–86.

Pohl, M., & Foerstl, K. (2011). Achieving purchasing competence through purchasing performance measurement system design: A multiple-case study analysis. *Journal of Purchasing and Supply Management*, *17*(4), 231–245.

Porck, J. P., van Knippenberg, D., Tarakci, M., Ateş, N. Y., Groenen, P. J., & de Haas, M., (2020). Do group and organizational identification help or hurt intergroup strategic consensus? *Journal of Management*, *46*(2), 234–260.

Porter, M. E., & Kramer, M. R. (2006). Strategy and society: The link between competitive advantage and corporate social responsibility. *Harvard Business Review*, *84*(12), 78–92.

Priem, R. L. (1990). Top management team group factors, consensus, and firm performance. *Strategic Management Journal*, *11*(6), 469–478.

Pullman, M., & Wikoff, R. (2017). Institutional sustainable purchasing priorities: Stakeholder perceptions vs environmental reality. *International Journal of Operations and Production Management*, *37*(2), 162–181.

Reuter, C., Goebel, P., & Foerstl, K. (2012). The impact of stakeholder orientation on sustainability and cost prevalence in supplier selection decisions. *Journal of Purchasing and Supply Management*, *18*(4), 270–281.

Rodríguez-Escobar, J. A., & González-Benito, J. (2017). The effect of strategic alignment on purchasing management. *Management Research Review*, *40*(11), 1175–1200.

Sancha, C., Gimenez, C., & Sierra, V. (2016). Achieving a socially responsible supply chain through assessment and collaboration. *Journal of Cleaner Production*, *112*(3), 1934–1947.

Sancha, C., Longoni, A., & Gimenez, C. (2015). Sustainable supplier development practices: Drivers and enablers in a global context. *Journal of Purchasing and Supply Management*, *21*(2), 95–102.

Schneider, L., & Wallenburg, C. M. (2012). Implementing sustainable sourcing – Does purchasing need to change? *Journal of Purchasing and Supply Management*, *18*(4), 243–257.

Schneider, L., Wallenburg, C. M., & Fabel, S. (2014). Implementing sustainability on a corporate and a functional level: Key contingencies that influence the required coordination. *International Journal of Physical Distribution and Logistics Management*, *44*(6), 464–493.

Schulze, H., & Bals, L. (2017). Implementing sustainable supply chain management – A literature review on required purchasing and supply management competences. In: M. Brandenburg, G. Hahn, & T. Rebs (Eds), *Social and environmental dimensions of organizations and supply chains. Greening of industry networks studies* (Vol. 5, pp. 171–194). Springer.

Seuring, S. (2008). Sustainability and supply chain management – An introduction to the special issue. *Journal of Cleaner Production, 16*(15), 1545–1551.

Tachizawa, E. M., & Wong, C. Y. (2014). Towards a theory of multi-tier sustainable supply chains: a systematic literature review. *Supply Chain Management: An International Journal, 19*(5-6), 643–663.

Tarakci, M., Ates, N. Y., Porck, J. P., van Knippenberg, D., Groenen, P. J., & de Haas, M. (2014). Strategic consensus mapping: A new method for testing and visualizing strategic consensus within and between teams. *Strategic Management Journal, 35*(7), 1053–1069.

Tate, W., Ellram, L. M., & Dooley, K. (2012). Environmental purchasing and supplier management (EPSM): Theory and practice. *Journal of Purchasing and Supply Management, 18*(3), 173–188.

Tchokogué, A., Nollet, J., Merminod, N., Paché, G., & Goupil, V. (2018). Is supply's actual contribution to sustainable development strategic and operational? *Business Strategy and the Environment, 27*(3), 336–358.

Timmer, S., & Kaufmann, L. (2019). Do managers' dark personality traits help firms in coping with adverse supply chain events? *Journal of Supply Chain Management, 55*(4), 67–97.

Vachon, S., & Klassen, R. D. (2006). Extending green practices across the supply chain: The impact of upstream and downstream integration. *International Journal of Operations and Production Management, 26*(7), 795–821.

Walker, H., Seuring, S., Sarkis, J., & Klassen, R. (2014). Sustainable operations management: recent trends and future directions. *International Journal of Operations and Production Management, 34*(5), 1.

Walsh, J. P. (1995). Managerial and organizational cognition: Notes from a trip down memory lane. *Organization Science, 6*(3), 280–321.

Walsh, J. P, Henderson, C. M., & Deighton, J. (1988). Negotiated belief structures and decision performance: An empirical investigation. *Organizational Behavior and Human Decision Processes, 42*(2), 194–216.

Watts, C. A., Kim, K. Y., & Hahn, C. K. (1992). Linking purchasing to corporate competitive strategy. *International Journal of Purchasing and Materials Management, 28*(4), 2–8.

WCED (1987). *Our common future. The report of the World Commission on Environment and Development*. Oxford: Oxford University Press.

Wilhelm, M. M., Blome, C., Bhakoo, V., & Paulraj, A (2016). Sustainability in multi-tier supply chains: Understanding the double agency role of the first-tier supplier. *Journal of Operations Management, 41*(January), 42–60.

Yin, R. K. (2013). *Case study research: Design and methods.* Thousand Oaks, CA: Sage publications.

Yook, K. H., Choi, J. H., & Suresh, N. C. (2018). Linking green purchasing capabilities to environmental and economic performance: The moderating role of firm size. *Journal of Purchasing and Supply Management, 24*(4), 326–337.

Zimmer, K., Fröhling, M., & Schultmann, F. (2016). Sustainable supplier management – A review of models supporting sustainable supplier selection, monitoring and development. *International Journal of Production Research, 54*(5), 1412–1442.

26. Purchasing and marketing of social and environmental sustainability in high-tech medical equipment

Adam Lindgreen, Michael Antioco, David Harness and Remi van der Sloot

INTRODUCTION

This chapter examines a given product's (high-tech medical equipment) social and environmental sustainability and its potential to support a product purchasing process. Sustainability describes how an organization integrates social, environmental, and economic activities in pursuit of outcomes beyond generating profit (Amaral and La Rovere, 2003; Cowell et al., 1999). Historically, companies focused on the economic dimension, which is to utilize resources to maximize the company's profit (e.g., Friedman, 1970; Gauthier, 2005; Walker, 2002). In response to the view that "companies do not only serve shareholders, but are embedded in their economic, ecological and social environment, which they must take into consideration when doing business" (Seuring et al., 2003, p. 204), companies should pursue other aspects of sustainability, balancing economic prosperity with environmental protection and social equity to meet the principles of sustainable development (Isaksson and Garvare, 2003; Keeble et al., 2003). Customers' perception of a product's social and environmental sustainability influences their purchase choice, as they seek offerings compatible with their views of sustainable development (Isaksson and Garvare, 2003). Whilst this influence has been identified, its nature is yet to be defined making the use of environmental and social sustainability to support product purchasing and marketing problematic. For example, few offerings are labeled to highlight social sustainability credentials (Isaksson and Garvare, 2003) although when such credentials are perceived as relevant by customers this may provide marketing opportunities. Whilst economic and environmental dimensions of sustainability are reasonably well understood, social dimensions of sustainability remains novel and little explored (e.g., Amaral and La Rovere, 2003; Keeble et al., 2003).

An example of the rising importance of social sustainability can be found in the high-tech medical equipment industry. Philips Medical Systems introduced MRI scanning equipment in 1983, and currently commands 25% of the worldwide market, equating to 24.8% of the company's total sales. With annual growth levels of 6% plus, the European market for high-tech medical equipment is both attractive and strategically important for Philips and its competitors, including GE Healthcare and Siemens Medical Solutions. Increasingly, as the technological capabilities of MRI scanners converge, companies are using social and environmental responsibility standards to influence customers' purchasing decision making. Within the Netherlands, four types of institutions purchase MRI scanning equipment—academic, teaching, and community hospitals in addition to private imaging centers. Additionally, the purchasing decision-making process in each was broadly similar and was influenced by three types of stakeholder—clinicians, operators, and business managers (van Heesch, 2006). The influence that each stakeholder has during the different stages in purchasing MRI scanning equipment has been summarized into a customer purchasing framework (Figure 26.1).

Stages \ Decision-influencers	Clinical				Operational		Business			
	Radiologist	Referring physician A	Referring physician B	Clinical physician	Technical services	Operator	Board of directors	Supervisory board	Purchasing manager	Department manager
1. Identify benefits of and acquire budget for magnetic resonance imaging scanner	X						X	X		X
2. Identify specifications of magnetic resonance imaging scanner	X	X		X	X	X				X
3. Evaluate alternatives and select supplier of magnetic resonance imaging scanner	X	X		X			X		X	X

Figure 26.1　Stages and key decision-making stakeholders in the purchasing process

The study has three objectives. First, we provide clearer insights into what a product's environmental and social sustainability is. Second, we identify whether, and how, social and environmental sustainability influences the purchasing processes of high-tech medical equipment. Third, we consider how social and environmental sustainability can enhance the marketing of such products. To address these objectives, the remainder of the chapter is structured as follows. First, a literature review explores environmental and social dimensions of sustainability to conceptualize a theoretical framework. Second, findings are reported of an empirical study that qualitatively explores the influence of social and environmental sustainability within the purchasing of MRI scanning equipment. Third, an analysis and discussion of these empirical findings is presented. Finally, the study's theoretical and managerial contributions are identified, limitations addressed, and avenues for further research suggested.

THEORETICAL BACKGROUND

Dimensions of environmental and social sustainability are concerned with how these impact on society's future needs (e.g. Cowell et al., 1999; Fiksel et al., 1998; Seuring et al., 2003; Veleva and Ellenbecker, 2001). This means satisfying present needs without compromising the needs of future generations (e.g., Cowell et al., 1999; Ottman, 1997). A sustainable company is one "whose characteristics and actions are designed to lead to a 'desirable future state' for all stakeholders" (Funk, 2003: p. 65). Stakeholders are "those groups who can affect or are affected by a firm's objective" (Seuring et al., 2003, p. 205). These definitions provide a context to consider social and environmental sustainability.

Environmental sustainability relates to a company's use of natural resources and its ecological impact (Isaksson and Garvare, 2003; Veleva et al., 2000). Whilst environmental sustainability is reasonably well understood in the literature, social sustainability is not, thereby making the nature of 'social matters' unclear (Littig and Griessler, 2005). Because social sustainability is intangible and qualitative in nature, a consensus about what its dimensions are is difficult to reach, though it is related to how a company impacts on individuals' or society's well-being (von Geibler et al., 2006). As depicted in the framework in Appendix 26.1, however, by adapting a concept specification model to show different aspects and their sub elements (termed indicators) of social sustainability some clarification has been achieved (von Geibler et al., 2006).[1] This study explores the nature of sustainability indicators (second objective), then considers how these might be summarized into sustainability aspects to provide insights into what a product's social and environmental sustainability is (first objective), and finally examines how social and environmental sustainability can enhance product marketing (third objective).

Sustainability Indicators

Sustainability indicators are specific, measurable product attributes that characterize contribution to social and environmental sustainability (Fiksel et al., 1998). Such indicators should be relevant, understandable, robust, and limited in number; they should be easy to use, collect, and reproduce; they should complement existing legal follow-up programs; financially feasible; and, finally, they should be useful as a management tool and able to protect company data, as well as be adaptable to future developments (Amaral and La Rovere, 2003; Isaksson and Garvare, 2003). Indicators should take account of a product's resource consumption and value creation throughout the whole of its lifecycle (Fiksel et al., 1998; Gauthier, 2005; Seuring et al., 2003). The lifecycle in this respect includes extraction of raw materials, as well as manufacture, packaging, storage, distribution, recycle, and destruction of the product (Gauthier, 2005), which in turn requires that companies' social and environmental indicators relate to internal and external stakeholder needs throughout product production, consumption, and disposal (Amaral and La Rovere, 2003; Funk, 2003; Global Reporting Initiative, 2006; Seuring et al., 2003). The broad nature of sustainability (Fiksel et al., 1998) suggests companies risk generating too many indicators, obscuring those most relevant to the product (Isaksson and Garvare, 2003).

Environmental aspects

With environmental sustainability well understood, at Philips Medical Systems, the company's environmental credentials have been defined within five aspects: reducing products' energy consumption, packaging materials, hazardous substances, and weight; whilst increasing levels of recycling and safeguards during disposal of products (Philips Sustainability Report, 2006). Governments, companies, and other organizations adopt sustainable development to address concerns about climate change and depletion of natural resources though this is reinforced by consumers and activists pushing large companies to develop such practices (Cowell et al., 1999; Keeble et al., 2003). Companies failing in this often become the target of activist pressures (Gauthier, 2005).

Social aspects

As discussed, social sustainability is less well understood. Adding to the Brundtland Commission's (WCED, 1987) view on social sustainability, it has been suggested that this term relates to how companies contribute to the well-being and quality of life of society and individuals for current and future generations (Steurer et al., 2005). Product-related social aspects, therefore, summarize how production, use, and disposal satisfy such conditions. Social aspects conceptualized and derived predominantly from studies linked to the chemical industry can be identified in the literature. These aspects differ in level of focus. For example, some discuss "taking employees into consideration" to summarize how an organization supports employees (e.g., Gauthier, 2005), whilst others separate this into "working conditions," "education and training," and "equity" (Tanzil and Beloff, 2006; von Geibler et al., 2006). The differentiation in level of focus suggests that the nature of production, product characteristics, and product use influence level of focus.

Various social aspect themes can be identified in the literature. For example, one theme relates to health and safety (Gauthier, 2005; von Geibler et al., 2006); this theme is also referred to as safety and well-being (Tanzil and Beloff, 2006) or accident and injury reduction (Fiksel et al., 1998). All are based on the premise that the supplying company should minimize potential for a product to harm an individual throughout the product's lifecycle.

Another theme is product usage within the product's operating context. The quality of the working environment, for example issues of noise level and room temperature, is discussed in the literature as a factor that impinges on how individuals perform (Gauthier, 2005; Tanzil and Beloff, 2006; von Geibler et al., 2006). Such issues have been related to how user "peace of mind" is created (Fiksel et al., 1998). A product has to answer stakeholders' needs (Gauthier, 2005; Seuring et al., 2003), for example a MRI scanning equipment providing quality images of the internal workings of a body. The product generates employment or wealth in different social environments (Steurer et al., 2005). Ethical production relates to treating employees and those within the supply chain fairly (Gauthier, 2005; Seuring et al., 2003; von Geibler et al., 2006); ensuring production protects individuals and does not violate human rights or uses child labor (Fiksel et al., 1998; Gauthier, 2005: Steurer at al., 2005; Tanzil and Beloff, 2006). Social sustainability is seen as a force for good, including equity transfer, which refers to the fact that profit should be more evenly distributed between those involved in their manufacture within the organization and those within the supply chain (Seuring et al., 2003). For Philips Medical Systems, greater use of social sustainability in the marketing of products would require a more complete understanding of the social sustainability dimensions—hereunder aspects and indicators—that stakeholders of MRI scanning equipment view as important.

METHODOLOGY

Qualitative methods are appropriate when studying complex phenomena, and when there is a need to take into account numerous variables for studying the issue(s) at hand (Eisenhardt, 1989; Matthyssens and Vandenbempt, 2003; Yin, 1994). To enable a focus on social sustainability, this exploratory study adapts von Geibler et al.'s (2006) concept specification model. The adaptation of the model is based on social sustainability aspects and indicators identified in the literature; customer perception interviews with key decision-making stakeholders involved in purchasing of MRI scanning equipment; interviews with marketing and other functional managers in Philips Medical Systems; and secondary research of this company.

The study identified how decision-making stakeholders (both purchasers and users) perceive sustainability indicators; this identification is undertaken in two stages. The first stage involves a focus group with a range of marketing and other functional managers from Philips Medical Systems to evaluate potential sustainability aspects and indicators. The second stage employs customer perception interviews supported by a short questionnaire to enable theory to be built, tested, and validated (Newman and Benz, 1998; Onwuegbuzie and Leech, 2005).

Selection of Case Company

The study is based on Philips Medical Systems, which is considered an excellent vehicle to explore the idea of sustainability, in particular social sustainability. The company generally has a good reputation in undertaking sustainability projects, for example replacing the traditional lamp bulb (environmental sustainability), as well as purchasing costs, exploitation costs, etc. (economic sustainability). It is less clear, however, what the social sustainability aspects are, though, as a company, Philips Medical Systems appreciates that its product offerings have a social sustainability dimension. Apart from its sustainability reputation, the simplicity of the company's competitive scenario and strategic response relative to larger and more complex manufacturers of high-tech medical equipment makes Philips Medical Systems attractive. Finally, the company was chosen because its MRI scanning equipment is likely to have a number of identifiable social sustainability indicators potentially perceivable by customers.

The selection of the case study as a research methodology and the associated techniques of this method comply with Yin's (1994) principles. First, a comprehensive understanding of Philips Medical Systems' contextual setting is important, as analytical criteria are developed with respect to the company's industry sector, in this instance the high-tech medical equipment sector. Second, one of the authors works within the company, offering a unique opportunity to access otherwise unobtainable data.

The use of secondary data and multiple interviews are used to develop rich insights, and provide the basis for greater transferability of the study's findings to other contextual settings (Eisenhardt, 1989). Specifically, a stakeholder assessment (e.g., Seuring et al., 2003) is undertaken to clarify hospitals' and imaging scanning centers' view of social sustainability aspects and indicators, with key decision-making stakeholders plus a customer context person from the hospital or imaging center. The inclusion of a variety of stakeholders with different points of view enhances the overall validity of model development stage.

A literature review enables the conditions under which social sustainability indicators can be established and potential aspects identified. These are combined with company-specific data and information gained from marketing and other functional managers to help develop a framework to assess the perception of key decision-making stakeholders involved in the purchase and use of MRI scanning equipment. This approach is undertaken to develop an in-depth understanding of what social sustainability aspects and related indicators are, and to identify how these can be used to support the marketing of MRI scanning equipment (see Appendix 26.1 for the development of conceptualized social aspects and potential indicators).

Data Collection and Analysis

To build the case, data are collected using a number of methods. First, to increase the familiarity with the issues at hand, from Philips Medical Systems a variety of written documentation is available, including annual reports, research and development reports, promotional materials, benchmark studies, and business customer records. Also, financial and other data relating to the subject of the study are accessible. In addition, the study involves a widespread search for industry and consulting reports and academic papers. Over 90 documents are reviewed for the study. This data are comprehensive, particularly in outlining the company's social sustainability values and how these translate into activities, for example the ethical treatment of suppliers and the sustainability criteria used when sourcing inputs into the business.

Focus group research is used to gain a complete understanding of Philips Medical Systems' view of sustainable aspects and indicators. The focus group research consists of 24 representatives from marketing, sales, medical systems customer visitor center, X-ray total quality management, corporate sustainability office, and eco-facilitators from different functional areas within the company. Representatives also include individuals responsible for managing customers' purchasing to identify the type of social sustainability indicators used in the production and marketing of MRI scanning equipment. Discussion points in the focus group research focus on social sustainability aspects and indicators of MRI scanning equipment and how these are communicated to institutions (purchasers and users). Also, hospitals and imaging centers suitable for interviewing are identified during this stage.

Customer perception interviews are conducted to identify how different key decision-making stakeholders (purchases and users) value environmental and social sustainability indicators. The study took place in the Netherlands at two academic hospitals, three teaching hospitals, two community hospitals, and one imaging center. At each institution, interviews were conducted with key stakeholders involved with MRI scanning equipment—the responsibilities of these stakeholders are summarized as clinicians, operators, and business managers. In total, 22 interviews were conducted with these stakeholders in addition to a focus group with the institutions; the length of interviews and focus groups lasted between 60 and 90 minutes. The use of multiple data collection methods adds to the robustness of the study's findings; compensates for weaknesses of a specific data collection method, improves final interpretation quality, and helps ensure triangulation (Jick, 1979; Strauss and Corbin, 1998; Yin, 1994). The unit of analysis is the case company or each of the institutions and their decision-making unit. Finally, information from each set of interviews and the secondary sources are combined into one final case manuscript.

At the formulation of the study stage, data gathered from Philips Medical Systems is analyzed in order to confirm the research problem. This, together with data gathered by a literature review, is then analyzed to suggest additional areas to von Geibler et al.'s (2006) social sustainability dimensions model. In the confirmatory phase, data reduction is largely done by within-case analysis, supported by data from the customer perception tool. This approach allows insight into how different decision-making stakeholders view social sustainability aspects and indicators within their job role to be identified for subsequent use in data displays. The data are also compared with the adapted social sustainability model, which is used as the frame of reference (Yin, 1994). The hospital cases are then compared to analyze similarities and differences, and to gain greater understanding of the phenomenon. Theoretical categories are expanded during open and axial coding procedures (Strauss and Corbin, 1998).

Throughout the analysis, the authors' tack back and forth between literature on sustainability and the data. This integration leads to the development of a number of theoretical categories and sub-categories (Spiggle, 1994). Such practices are consistent with case studies in general, as well as studies on corporate social responsibility (e.g., Beverland and Lindgreen, 2006; Maon et al., 2009; Wood, 1996).

Throughout the study, a number of methods for improving the quality of the research have been adopted. Industry experts were used to help select the case company and, subsequently, institutional customers; four researchers provided independent interpretations of the findings; multiple interviews were conducted; and interviewees were given the opportunity to provide feedback on initial findings, all of which reinforces reliability. Interviews were conducted by the same interviewer, thereby reducing the role of bias (Lincoln and Guba, 1985; Strauss and Corbin, 1998).

FINDINGS

Customer Perception Analysis

The customer perception questionnaire contained 11 social and five environmental sustainability indicators derived from the literature and interviews with Philips Medical Systems' personnel. The interviewees were asked the following question: "When purchasing MRI scanning equipment, do you think 'X' is important, and why?" The results were recorded as "1" if important and "0" if unimportant, supported, where relevant, by quotes from interviewees who were asked to elaborate on their answers.

None of Philips Medical Systems' five "green focal areas" indicators were universally seen as important in influencing the purchasing decision of interviewees. Sixty-three percent of interviewees stated that "hazardous substances" should be minimized. The business managers felt this was their duty of care toward employees and patients, whilst operators' concern was for their personnel's welfare. Information minimizing "harm" to individuals outweighs the need for information on environmental impact. Weight was the second most important indicator with interviewees' concern for moving and installing heavy equipment considered above environmental factors associated with raw material consumption. Fifty percent of interviewees mentioned that weight determined the location within a hospital that scanning equipment could be sited and transported to safely.

> Weight places restrictions on the room an MRI scanner can be put in. On the one hand, it concerns floor pressure per square meter; on the other hand, it's whether there is a transport route through the hospital. (Operator, teaching hospital)

Environmental damage caused by inappropriate recycling and disposal was seen as important by 45% of interviewees, although increasing government legislation and taxation will make this more relevant. Packaging was not seen as important because the benefits of using the scanner far outweigh environmental concerns about the packaging used. Finally, energy was seen as important by 27% of the sample, although unexpectedly only by one business manager. Knowledge of energy usage was less relevant than scan quality, and was perceived as a minor cost compared with purchasing and running costs, which were subsumed into the hospitals' overall electricity costs. The business manager's view was moderated by the desire to apportion actual energy cost per patient.

Customer type	Customer	Responsible Type	Energy use	Weight	Packaging	Hazardous substances	Recycling and Disposal	Proactive safety regulation	Health complaints operators	Health complaints patients	Availability in different markets	Accessibility different patienttypes	Ethical production producer	Ethical production suppliers	Operator comfort	Patient comfort	Contribution to science	Increase level of living
Academic Hospital	AZM	Business responsible	0	1	0	1	0	1	1	1	0	1	1	1	1	1	1	0
Academic Hospital	AZM	Operational responsible	0	1	0	1	1	1	1	1	0	1	1	1	1	1	1	0
Academic Hospital	LUMC	Business responsible	0	1	0	1	0	1	1	1	0	1	0	0	1	1	1	0
Academic Hospital	LUMC	Clinical responsible	0	0	0	1	0	1	1	1	0	1	1	1	1	1	1	0
Academic Hospital	LUMC	Operational responsible	1	1	0	1	1	1	1	1	0	1	1	1	1	1	1	0
Teaching Hospital	CWZ	Clinical responsible	0	0	0	0	0	1	1	1	0	1	1	1	1	1	1	0
Teaching Hospital	CWZ	Operational responsible	1	0	0	1	1	1	1	1	0	1	1	1	1	1	1	0
Teaching Hospital	JBZ	Business responsible	0	1	0	0	1	1	1	0	0	1	0	0	1	1	1	0
Teaching Hospital	JBZ	Clinical responsible	1	1	0	0	0	1	1	1	1	1	1	1	1	1	1	0
Teaching Hospital	JBZ	Operational responsible	0	0	0	0	0	1	1	1	0	1	0	0	1	1	1	0
Teaching Hospital	Kennemer Gasthuis	Business responsible	0	1	0	1	0	1	1	1	0	1	0	0	1	1	0	0
Teaching Hospital	Kennemer Gasthuis	Clinical responsible	1	0	0	0	0	1	1	1	0	1	1	1	1	1	1	0
Teaching Hospital	Kennemer Gasthuis	Operational responsible	0	0	0	0	1	1	1	1	0	1	1	1	1	1	1	0
Community Hospital	Gelderse Vallei	Business responsible	0	0	0	1	1	1	1	1	0	1	1	1	1	1	1	0
Community Hospital	Gelderse Vallei	Clinical responsible	0	1	1	1	1	1	1	1	0	1	1	1	1	1	0	0
Community Hospital	Gelderse Vallei	Operational responsible	0	0	0	1	0	1	1	1	0	1	1	1	1	1	1	0
Community Hospital	St. Anna	Business responsible	0	1	0	1	1	1	1	1	0	1	0	0	1	1	1	0
Community Hospital	St. Anna	Clinical responsible	0	0	0	0	0	1	1	1	0	1	1	1	1	1	1	0
Community Hospital	St. Anna	Operational responsible	0	1	0	1	0	1	1	1	0	1	0	0	1	1	1	0
Imaging Centre	DiaSana	Business responsible	1	1	0	1	1	1	1	1	0	1	1	1	1	1	1	0
Imaging Centre	DiaSana	Clinical responsible	1	0	0	0	1	1	1	1	0	1	0	0	1	1	1	0
Imaging Centre	DiaSana	Operational responsible	0	0	0	1	0	1	1	1	0	1	1	1	1	1	1	0
		Total	6	11	1	14	10	22	22	21	1	22	15	15	22	22	20	0
		Percentage (%)	27.3	50	4.55	63.6	45.5	100	100	95.5	4.55	100	68.2	68.2	100	100	90.9	0

Figure 26.2   Summary of social and environmental sustainability indicators

Social Sustainability Aspects

Five social aspects were derived from the literature, as well as a company-based focus group combined with production and usage attributes of MRI scanning equipment: customer health and safety; customer comfort; ethical production; product accessibility; and contribution to society (see Figure 26.3).

Customer health and safety

"Health and safety" summarizes how product usage can harm individuals and producer initiatives to minimize such harm. All interviewees identified this as an important influence. Philips Medical Systems was perceived as proactively engaged in enhancing safety during usage and equipment maintenance based on the assumption of duty of care rather than tangible evidence.

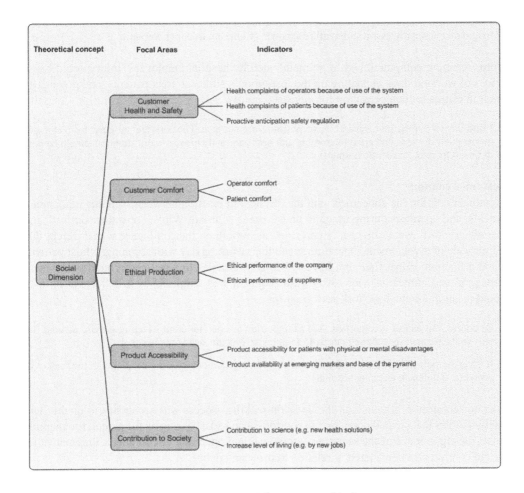

Figure 26.3   MRI scanning equipment social aspects and indicators

The complexity of MRI scanning equipment meant users were reliant on the company's expertise to guarantee safeness:

> I assume the producer pays attention to that so that it will be OK, I hardly can know if a system is safe or not; we don't have that level of knowledge. (Clinician, academic hospital)

In a similar vein, the indicators "health complaints operators" and "health complaints patients" influenced purchase in three ways. First, safety of use:

> You cannot allow it to do something medical which gets the patient hurt... I cannot imagine that a client would get a health complaint and not get a lawyer. (Operator, imaging center)

Second, continued exposure to the scanning equipment should not cause health problems. Concern exists that the long term impact on operators from continual use of scanning equipment was unknown:

Field strength health complaints, we still assume that it has no short term consequences, but the real long term consequences are still a little unknown. (Clinician, teaching hospital)

Third, scanning equipment had to be maintained by hospital employees. Injury could result in loss of working days impacting on the institution's ability to treat patients, and potentially result in claims for compensation for industrial injury:

I find this very important; several repair positions are not nice. The coils are not good from an ergonomic point of view, and are often too big and heavy to easily move—more attention should be paid to this. (Operator, academic hospital)

Customer comfort

"Customer comfort" is concerned with the physical interaction between scanning equipment, patients, and operators during usage to create peace of mind. Whilst "operator comfort" and "patient comfort" were universally perceived as important, their influence was different due to timescale of involvement. Operators spend their working day with scanning, whilst patients spend a fraction of that time, but have to be "comfortable" to ensure scan quality. Business managers' and clinicians' view of operator comfort was tempered by a belief that its lack would result in diminished work performance:

Of course, this aspect is important. Not as important as operator comfort because these patients are only in the scanner for half an hour to 45 minutes. (Clinician, academic hospital)

It is very important because if operators don't work very hard or well then the quality of the scans will decrease. (Clinician, teaching hospital)

Operator comfort's influence on the decision-making process was secondary to quality and safety. Factors that created operator "discomfort" also had a bearing on the patent, for example noise, the ergonomics of the scanning equipment, and operating environment. Pragmatically, patient comfort was considered in relation to the scan quality:

I find this important, but it still has to be practical. Patients don't come for a beauty session. Issues like less noise and a more comfortable table are very important, but we have to remain realistic. (Operator, community hospital)

Interestingly, these different views require a range of information to help address the concerns of the stakeholders, for example information about the task of maintenance, the level of noise created during operation, and the impact on the operator after a number of hours of usage. This suggests comfort indicators should be included within promotional material to create differential advantage.

Ethical production

"Ethical production" is relevant because an MRI scanner's production consumes raw materials sourced from global markets and requires the application of human capital. "Ethical production" and "ethical production at the producer's suppliers" were considered synonymous by the interviewees. Surprisingly, given that unethical production has high media impact, only 68% of interviewees found this indicator professionally important, although the majority considered it personally so. Interviewees believed Philips Medical Systems was an ethical producer and used ethical suppliers, eliminating the need to seek this information. If the company was shown producing unethically it would become an issue:

> We never really think about this aspect and assume that it is okay. But I think that if I found out and it's in the media, for example, child labor or forced labor, then I would not want to work with the scanner of that supplier. (Operator, imaging center)

The fact that 32% of interviewees did not see ethical production as important can perhaps be explained by a difference between personal and professional views. Professionally, the first priority was that the scanner had superior performance:

> As a person, of course I would totally disagree, even in my function this matters to me. But it is difficult, even if I knew, I don't know if it changes my perception of the scanner, because I know how good the system is. (Operator, imaging center)

Currently, the ethical standing of Philips Medical Systems and of other suppliers negates the need for such information. However, its inclusion during the purchase process could provide a base for comparisons between competitors.

Product accessibility

"Product accessibility" is concerned with answering the needs of different stakeholders and providing availability in different markets. Only one interviewee thought this indicator professionally important. The majority found the issue too distant to impact on them, and that their concern was closer to home:

> This is far beyond the scope of our organization, so from a functional perspective this is unimportant. Personally, I find this not important because in these markets other things, for example immunization programs and health education, are more important and have a much higher priority. (Clinician, teaching hospital)

Although not a direct influence on the purchase decisions, all the interviewees, due to conscience and job orientation, saw this issue as personally important. Indirect communication of how Philips Medical Systems improves developing countries' health care may enhance the company's reputation with health care professionals thereby providing subliminal differentiation between their products and those of competitors.

The notion of distance explains why all interviewees identified the indicator "accessibility for different types of patients" as important because it directly impacts on their ability to treat patients. Stakeholders wanted to identify at pre-purchase the scanner's dimensions and ability to cope with different types of patients, for example claustrophobic or extremely overweight:

> The people scanned here all have a certain physical problem; otherwise they would not be here… if these people that have a disability, walk with difficulty or are overweight, so that they cannot be scanned, then that's a problem. The gantry for each scanner differs. This can make a difference too if a patient can be scanned or not, even if it is only about a few centimeters. (Business manager, teaching hospital)

Contribution to society

"Contribution to society" describes the scanners' benefit to society through improved diagnosis techniques, illness reduction, knowledge development, and enhanced employment. Ninety percent of the interviewees believed the indicator "contribute to science" was important because they perceived it to mean that the scanner advances the science of diagnosis. Hospital type influenced how interviewees interpreted this dimension. Academic and teaching hospitals wanted information that helped them understand the potential for research, whilst community hospitals and the imaging center wanted reassurance that the innovation and contribution to science was an inherent quality of the scanner. The indicator "Increase level of living" was seen as irrelevant by the respondents.

Summary

The findings above have identified that defining the social and environmental aspects a product might have is worthwhile because the majority of these are seen to influence the purchasing process of MRI scanning equipment. The implications of this are considered in the following section.

DISCUSSION

The study identified that sufficient stakeholders view social and environmental sustainability aspects as influencing their perception of MRI scanning equipment. Additionally, considerable similarity between the customer institution and the three stakeholder groups in information sought and product requirements was identified. This suggests companies, which supply high-tech medical equipment, should incorporate social and environmental sustainability in their marketing effort. Whilst this finding is derived from a study conducted within a clearly defined and narrow context, the principle offers insights and possibilities for other businesses and product types.

The lack of a robust definition of social sustainability was identified within the literature. Building on the work of von Geibler et al. (2006), the study identified that the majority of social sustainability indicators were known and understood and seen to influence the purchasing decision. In light of this it is possible to tentatively suggest a definition of social sustainability:

> A product or system that meets the performance requirements and expectations of customer stakeholders without causing harm to the well-being of society and its members over different time periods.

In addition to this, the identified indicators add to our understanding of what social sustainability is by, first, linking them to actual product function, for example the scanner's ability to produce quality images; and, second, by taking account of the fact that customers' views of social and environmental dimensions and indicators are personal, but that these inform how they think professionally about social sustainability. The study also demonstrated that society is about the impact on an individual and groups connected to the production, use, and disposal of the MRI scanner. Finally, and directly related to technology, which contains hazardous substances and emits radiation, is the idea that stakeholders are concerned about the long-term potential for harm. This has applicability beyond the production of high-tech medical equipment.

The concept specification model was used to conceptualize the social sustainability aspects and their linked indicators. The five social sustainability aspects were validated and can be considered relevant to high-tech medical equipment. The majority of the social sustainability indicators were also validated, providing a basis for measuring both the extent to which customers see these aspects as important, and their awareness of the product's relationship to these aspects. The aspects and indicators also comply with the success criteria suggested in literature (Amaral and La Rovere, 2003; Fiksel et al., 1998; Isaksson and Garvare, 2003) in that they are relevant, understandable for the users, limited in number, and adaptable to future developments.

The findings highlighted that not all indicators can be used as constructs to measure performance. First, because interviewees could not differentiate between ethical production of the company and that of its suppliers, this suggests that measuring beyond the "headline" title would not provide meaningful results although ethical production is important in the customers' overall perception of the company and can be considered to influence at a holistic level as a brand attribute. Second, the indicators of "packaging," "accessibility in different markets," and "increase in living" were not seen as important in the context of purchasing MRI scanning equipment. This questions both these indicators' inclusion within the model and their value as input into measuring performance. The implication is that the framework suggested by von Geibler et al. (2006) has provided a useful way to conceptualize both sustainability aspects and linked indicators and as such will have applicability beyond its current focus.

The hierarchy of influence of the social aspects and indicators could be identified. Whilst it is not possible to rank actual indicators, it is possible to define these into three levels. The cost and performance of the scanning equipment form the first level and provide the business context upon which all other levels exist. This is not surprising; the actual cost of scanning equipment is likely to constitute a major element of capital expenditure for a hospital or imaging center. Performance is concerned with its ability to fulfill its core function, the higher the quality of the scan, the greater its use as a diagnosis tool. The second level comprises indicators, which were seen as professionally relevant because they had a direct or potentially direct impact on users of the scanning equipment, such as "hazardous substance," "health complaints of operators," and "patient comfort." The third level is factors that matter personally, but have little direct influence on the purchasing decision, for example "packaging," "accessibility to different markets," and "increase in level of living." Being able to see different levels of perceived importance of social and environmental sustainability dimensions enables companies to focus effort onto dimensions valued by their customers. This is in line with the view that too many indicators become hard to measure and organizations need to be selective when choosing social and environmental dimensions (Isaksson and Garvare, 2003).

Managerial Implications

Marketing guidelines for each of the 11 social and five environmental sustainability indicators can be suggested based on answers to three key questions. First, which stakeholder should be targeted? Second, when within the purchasing process should marketing communication occur? Third, how should it be communicated? In answering these questions, note is taken of the importance attached to each aspect by the interviewees, and the communication tools used by Philips Medical Systems (Figure 26.4).

	TO WHOM			WHEN		HOW				
	Business Responsibles	Clinical Responsibles	Operational Responsibles	Periodically in time	During the purchase process	Customer magazines	Purchaser meetings	Brochures	White papers	Sales conversations
Energy use	X	X	X		X			X	X	X
Weight	X	X	X		X			X	X	X
Packaging										
Hazardous substances	X	X	X		X			X	X	X
Recycling and disposal	X	X	X		X			X	X	X
Environmental Aspects	X	X	X	X	X	X	X	X		X
Proactive safety regulation	X	X	X	X	X	X	X	X		X
Health complaints operators	X	X	X		X			X	X	X
Health complaints patients	X	X	X		X			X	X	X
Availability in different markets										
Accessibility different patient types	X	X	X	X	X	X		X	X	X
Ethical performance producer	X	X	X	X		X	X			
Ethical performance suppliers	X	X	X	X		X	X			
Operator comfort	X	X	X	X	X	X	X	X	X	X
Patient comfort	X	X	X	X	X	X	X	X	X	X
Contribution to science	X	X	X	X	X	X		X	X	X
Increase level of living										
Social Aspects	X	X	X	X	X	X	X	X		X
Sustainability Aspects	X	X	X	X		X	X			

Figure 26.4   Summary of social and environmental sustainability related marketing opportunities

The similarity in the purchasing process of the institutions and their stakeholders groups provides common ground for a marketing effort. The stakeholders should have general awareness of the products' social and environmental sustainability credentials for all indicators with the exception of "packaging," "availability in different markets," and "increase level of living" because these were not seen as important or professionally relevant by the interviewees and therefore do not currently have a role to play in influencing the purchasing process. To ensure that stakeholders gain an appropriate and complete understanding of the MRI scanning equipment's sustainability credentials, marketing should be focused on a more generic view of environmentalisms.

The interviewees' own "ethical" standpoint on social and environmental sustainability tended to be greater than their employers' view, although for indicators related to the potential of the scanning equipment to do "harm" (socially or environmentally), views of importance were equal. Marketing of social and environmental indicators should focus on how the supplier minimizes potential for "harm" and reassures that scanning equipment is already safe and that adequate concern about the whole life safety is in place. However, the price of the scanning equipment and image quality were considered more influential in the purchasing decision than either social or environmental sustainability indicators. Reputation in these two areas might be used by stakeholders to differentiate between products and suppliers.

Getting the social and environmental sustainability credentials of the MRI scanning equipment known to the stakeholders requires a range of approaches and careful selection of media. The selection of media should be based on proximity to the purchasing decision combined with targeting of specific "concern" areas of stakeholders. For Philips Medical Systems this would be a function of its brand positioning used to reinforce at a holistic level that the company is concerned with sustainability. Opportunities to reinforce the company's general adoption of sustainability into its business practices could also be communicated through trade literature used by the stakeholders to keep abreast of developments in the field, and during meetings with customer stakeholders related to ongoing development and use of scanning equipment. The specific social and environmental sustainability indicators need to be communicated to support the sales process. Product brochures should address the key concerns related to the product's potential to harm and how the company minimizes this risk. This should also be incorporated into briefing sessions from the company.

Although the concept of companies' "doing the right thing" underpins corporate social responsibility, of which the environmental dimension is integral, its use to support marketing activities has two commercial advantages. First, it increases the sustainability of the company by supporting the sales of its products. Second, it embeds the policies into the company helping to create a virtuous circle of improvement thereby further strengthening the company's reputation and generating a positive halo for its product offerings. Overall, the study has provided an embryonic overview of how social and environmental indicators of sustainability can be used to strengthen the marketing of high-tech medical products and provide differentiation within the minds of key customer stakeholders.

Limitations and Further Research Directions

As in most research, this study has certain limitations that affect our interpretation of the results, while at the same time suggesting directions for further research. These limitations must therefore be considered. First, a limitation of the study arises from employing a single-case approach. Although the sample of customer institutions can be considered representative of Dutch hospitals that purchase MRI scanning equipment, a study which considered other European customers and North America ones where regulations and the customer institutions' operating environments are different would provide other insights. A second limitation was that the research focused on the purchasing stage despite the fact that the findings indicated that stakeholders formed personal opinions about social and environmental sustainability factors pre-purchase. This process needs to be better understood to enable ways in which to influence their development to support the purchase process stage to be determined. A third limitation is patients as customer stakeholders were excluded from the study. This limits understanding how their views on indicators such as safety and comfort can influence the opinions of the decision makers, making it unclear as to the desirability and practicability of targeting marketing effort at them. A fourth limitation was that the context of the medical systems may limit transferability of the findings. Further studies in other business contexts would broaden understanding of the role played by social and environmental sustainability in influencing corporate purchasing decisions. Finally, the study relied on historical information and interviewees' recall; real-time data collection could identify transitory influences on stakeholder's views, whilst a longitudinal research would distinguish how these impacted on company policy.

All of the limitations mentioned above should be kept in mind when considering our results. Despite the limitations, we believe that we have made a substantial step toward both understanding the social and environmental responsibilities that purchasers of high-tech medical equipment identify as important, as well as developing guidelines that can aid manufacturers to market such equipment.

ACKNOWLEDGMENTS

This chapter first appeared as Lindgreen, A., Antioco, M. D. J., Harness, D., and van der Sloot, R. (2009). Purchasing and marketing of social and environmental sustainability for high-tech medical equipment. *Journal of Business Ethics*, 85(Suppl. 2), pp. 445–462.

NOTE

1. It has been suggested that the term "aspect" be changed to "focal area" to reflect its use as a summarizing label of indicators (von Geibler et al., 2006). This is in line with Philips Medical Systems' incorporation of environmental sustainability in its marketing of high-tech medical equipment, which the company refers to as "green focal areas" (Philips Sustainability Report, 2006). In this chapter, however, we use the term aspect.

REFERENCES

Amaral, S. P. and La Rovere, E. L. (2003). Indicators to evaluate environmental, social, and economic sustainability: A proposal for the Brazilian oil industry. *Oil & Gas Journal*, 101(19), 30–35.
Beverland, M. and Lindgreen, A. (2006). Implementing market orientation in industrial firms: A multiple case study. *Industrial Marketing Management*, 36(4), 430–442.
Cowell, S. J., Wehrmeyer, W., Argust, P. W., Graham, J., and Robertson, S. (1999). Sustainability and the primary extraction industries: Theories and practice. *Resources Policy*, 25(4), 277–286.
Eisenhardt, K. M. (1989). Building theories from case study research. *Academy of Management Review*, 14(4), 532–550.
Fiksel, J., McDaniel, J., and Spitzley, D. (1998). Measuring product sustainability. *The Journal of Sustainable Product Design*, July (Volume not specified), 1–15.
Friedman, M. (1970). The social responsibility of business is to increase its profits. *The New York Times Magazine*, September 13.
Funk, K. (2003). Sustainability and performance. *MIT SLOAN Management Review*, 44(2), 65–70.

Gauthier, C. (2005). Measuring corporate social and environmental performance: The extended life-cycle assessment. *Journal of Business Ethics*, 59(2), 199–206.

Global Reporting Initiative (2006). RG; sustainability reporting guidelines. *Guidelines developed by GRI*, 19 September.

Isaksson, R., and Garvare, R. (2003). Measuring sustainable development using process models. *Managerial Auditing Journal*, 18(8), 649–656.

Jick, T. D. (1979). Mixing qualitative and quantitative methods: Triangulation in action. *Administrative Science Quarterly*, 24(4), 602–611.

Keeble, J. J., Topiol, S., and Berkeley, S. (2003). Using indicators to measure sustainability performance at a corporate and project level, *Journal of Business Ethics*, 44(2), 149–158.

Lincoln, Y. S. and Guba, E. (1985). *Naturalistic Inquiry*. Beverly Hills, CA: Sage.

Littig, B., and Griessler, E. (2005). Social sustainability: A catchword between political pragmatism and social theory. *International Journal of Sustainable Development*, 8(1–2), 65–79.

Matthyssens, P. and Vandenbempt, K. (2003). Cognition-in-context: Reorienting research in business market strategy. *Journal of Business and Industrial Marketing*, 18(6/7), 595–606.

Maon, F., Lindgreen, A., and Swaen, V. (2009). Designing and implementing corporate social responsibility: An integrative framework grounded in theory and practice. *Journal of Business Ethics*, 87(Suppl. 1), 71–89.

Newman, I. and Benz, C. R. (1998). *Qualitative-Quantitative Research Methodology: Exploring the Interactive Continuum*. Thousand Oaks, CA: Sage.

Onwuegbuzie, A. and Leech, N. L. (2005). Taking the 'Q' out of research: Teaching research methodology courses without the divide between quantitative and qualitative paradigms. *Quality and Quantity*, 39(3), 267–296.

Ottman, J. (1997). What sustainability means to marketers. *Marketing News*, July 21, 31, 15, p. 4.

Philips Sustainability Report (2006). Improving lives, delivering value.

Seuring, S. A., Koplin, J., Behrens, T., and Schenidewind, U. (2003). Sustainability assessment in the German detergent industry: From stakeholder involvement to sustainability indicators. *Sustainable Development*, 11(4), 199–212.

Sherwin, C. (2004). Design and sustainability: A discussion paper based on personal experience and observations. *The Journal of Sustainable Product Design*, 4(3), 21–31.

Spiggle, S. (1994). Analysis and interpretation of qualitative data in consumer research. *Journal of Consumer Research*, 21(3), 491–503.

Steurer, R., Langer, M. E., Konrad, A., and Martinuzzi, A. (2005). Corporations, stakeholders and sustainable development I: A theoretical exploration of business-society relations. *Journal of Business Ethics*, 61(3), 263–281.

Strauss, A. and Corbin, J. (1998). *Basics of Qualitative Research*, 2nd ed. Newbury Park, CT: Sage.

Tanzil, D. and Beloff, B. (2006). Assessing impacts: Overview on sustainability indicators and metrics: Tools for implementing sustainable development in the chemical industry, and elsewhere. *Environmental Quality Management*, 15(4), 41–56.

van Heesch, T. (2006). Customer value analysis at Philips Medical Systems magnetic resonance. What's the fun of selling just on price? Unpublished MA thesis, Eindhoven University of Technology, the Netherlands.

Veleva, V., and Ellenbecker, M. (2001). Indicators of sustainable production: Framework and methodology. *Journal of Cleaner production*, 9(6), 519–549.

Veleva, V., Hart, M., Greiner, T., and Crumbley, C. (2000). Indicators of sustainable production. *Journal of Cleaner Production*, 9(5), 447–452.

von Geibler, J., Liedtke, C., Wallbaum, H., and Schaller, S. (2006). Accounting for the social dimension of sustainability: Experiences from the biotechnology industry. *Business Strategy and the Environment*, 15(5), 334–346.

Walker, S. (2002). A journey in design: An exploration of perspectives for sustainability. *The Journal of Sustainable Product Design*, 2(1), 3–10.

WCED (1987). *Our Common Future*. Report of the World Commission of Environment and Development.

Website 8: SIGMA Project, last viewed April 15, 2007. http://projectsigma.co.uk

Wood, L. M. (1996). Added value: Marketing basics. *Journal of Marketing Management*, 12(November), 735–755.

Yin, R. K. (1994). *Case Study Research: Design and Methods*, 2nd ed. Thousand Oaks, CA: Sage.

APPENDIX 26.1 CONCEPTUALIZED SOCIAL ASPECTS WITH POTENTIAL SOCIAL INDICATORS

Social aspects	Heading	Potential social indicators
Customer health and safety	Health complaints of operators because of use of equipment	Health and safety[1,7]
		Health[2]
	Health complaints of patients because of use of equipment	Quality, health, and safety[3]
		Peace of mind[4]
	Proactive anticipation of safety regulations	Illness and disease reduction[4]
		Accident and injury reduction[4,8]
		Health and well-being[4]
		External social improvements[5]
		Products and service labeling[7,8]
Customer comfort	Operator comfort	Quality of working conditions[1]
	Patient comfort	Satisfaction of needs[2]
		Peace of mind[4]
		External social improvements[5]
		Noise and pollution[8]
Ethical production	Ethical performance of the company	Quality of working conditions[1,6]
	Ethical performance of the suppliers	Education and training[1,2]
		Health[2]
		Equity[2]
		Individual contentment[2]
		Taking employees into consideration[3]
		Quality, health, and safety at work[3]
		Quality of life[4]
		Illness and disease reduction[4]
		Equity within organization[5]
		Internal social improvements[5]
		Ethical production[8]
		Accidents or incidents[8]
		Supplier fairness[9]
Product accessibility	Product accessibility for patients with physical or mental disadvantages	Equity[2]
		Quality of life[4]
	Product availability at emerging markets and base of pyramid	International equity[5]
		External social improvements[5]
		Accessibility to key services[8]
		More equitable accessibility[9]
Contribution to society	Contribution to science (e.g., new health solutions)	Employment[1,9]
		Innovation potential[1]
	Increase level of living	Product acceptance and societal benefits[1]
		International equity[5]
		Social impact of operations[6]
		Quality of life in community[6]
		Community development[8]
		Regeneration and rebuilding of communities[8]
		Intellectual assets[9]

1: von Geibler et al. (2006)
2: Seuring et al. (2003)

3: Gauthier (2005)
4: Fiksel et al. (1998)
5: Steurer et al. (2005)
6: Tanzil and Beloff (2006)
7: Global Reporting Initiative (2006)
8: Website 8: Sigma project (2007)
9: Sherwin (2004)

PART 8

CASE STUDIES ON SUSTAINABILITY-DRIVEN BUSINESS STRATEGIES

27. Ecoalf: a brand with a conscience

Nicholas Ind

According to a study by McKinsey and Global Fashion Agenda, the fashion industry produced around 2.1 billion tonnes of greenhouse gas emissions in 2018 – equal to 4% of the global total (McKinsey/Global Fashion Agenda, 2020). Fashion has come to be a significant polluter, not least because of the rapid growth in demand with the average consumer buying 60% more clothes than they did 15 years ago and wearing them less – if indeed they wear them at all – before they dispose of them (UN Alliance for Sustainable Fashion 2019). The impacts of over-consumption are various. Producing clothes is resource intensive – according to the UN it takes 10,000 litres of water to make a pair of denim jeans and it causes environmental degradation both in the toxics used in manufacturing and in the disposal of discarded items. The way out of this impasse is for consumers to buy less and for fashion companies to improve their sustainability commitments.

Apart from Esprit, Patagonia and Vivienne Westwood, not many companies have challenged consumers to buy less. Indeed the idea of Green Demarketing (Soule and Reich, 2015; Reich and Soule, 2016), as it has been labelled, can seem contradictory when it is presented by commercial companies who need consumers to buy their products. The premise though of the green demarketers is to persuade consumers to purchase on the basis of quality and to keep their clothes for longer. The other approach, used by fashion brands, is to focus on their sustainability commitments through innovation in materials, improving supply chains, reducing waste through better inventory controls, developing new business models, offering repair services and encouraging recyclability. Again, Patagonia has been a pioneer in this regard, although the company has preferred to talk about responsibility rather than sustainability on the basis that producing clothes always has an impact in terms of energy, resources, carbon emissions and waste (Chouinard and Stanley, 2012). Following in Patagonia's wake, companies such as Stella McCartney, Mud (who lease jeans) and mainstream businesses such as adidas and H&M, have taken up the cause of making sustainability work.

Spanish, fashion brand, Ecoalf has combined both these approaches. It encourages its customers to 'buy less, but buy better' – better in this context meaning quality clothes made from recycled fabrics produced by companies that are transparent about their values and processes. It also urges its customers to repair the clothes they own rather than buying new and to wash them less and at lower temperatures to help ensure their longevity. Alongside this, the brand has also been a pioneer in co-creating new recycled fabrics and championing the cause of sustainability. For Ecoalf, the idea of sustainability draws on the Brundtland Commission's 1987 definition of sustainable development, by arguing that the focus is on meeting current needs without compromising those of future generations. Ecoalf describes sustainability as a project for "the future of our society (all humans), with social, economic and environmental pillars at its heart" (www.ecoalf.com).

THE CLARITY OF AN INSPIRING PURPOSE

Similar to such brands as Patagonia, Esprit and Stella McCartney, Ecoalf is the product of an inspired individual. Javier Goyeneche, who founded Ecoalf in Madrid in 2012, was motivated by the environmental challenges that the world faces and frustrated by the unsustainable practices of many fashion brands who pushed low-price, low-quality products and encouraged over-consumption through multiple collections, while paying little attention to the use or after-life of what people purchased. Goyeneche saw an opportunity to change fashion. However, he faced two challenges. First, while some companies had long been working with recycled and recyclable material, consumer perceptions were that recycled fabrics were generally of lower quality. Second, because sustainable brands were often niche, there was a limited number of manufacturers who could supply innovative materials. Goyeneche's solution was to work together with manufacturers to create a high quality fabric out of waste materials that would have a long lifecycle. The first such fabric was Ecoalf 1.0, a flexible fabric developed out of recycled PET (Polyethylene terephthalate) plastic bottles, which was used in the company's first products. This was the beginning of a journey that has led to the development of some 400 fabrics (2020) using a variety of materials, from discarded fishing nets to coffee grounds to used car tyres.

What has given Ecoalf unity and direction as it progressed from initial idea into a brand was its clarity of purpose, which provides the ultimate reason for why the brand exists. The purpose is rooted in a commitment to a circular economy approach that avoids using natural resources in a careless way and delivers recycled products that are of the same quality and design as the best non-recycled products. The purpose is then made explicit in the core message used by the company, "Because there is no planet B", which appears in communications and on products (Figure 27.1).

A purpose only has value if it is used and one of the criticisms of brands that espouse a sustainability message is the gap between promise and action (Vos 2009). However, Ecoalf refers to itself as a 'storydoing' organization, in that the narrative about its purpose is carried through into all manifestations of the brand in creating an overall experience. Head of Marketing and Communications, Carolina Alvarez-Ossorio Speith, notes "we consider the brand DNA of Ecoalf to be around the commitment we have for people and the planet ... we're concerned about the coherence between what we say and what we do". This 'doing' orientation is evident in the design and development of its clothing range and also in its work to Upcycle the Oceans, which involves partnering with fishermen to collect ocean waste and to recycle and upcycle it. The initiative started in Spain in 2015, when Goyeneche went out with fishermen who showed him the scale of the problem in the Mediterranean. Working together with them, Ecoalf arranged for the waste found on the sea bed to be collected and for the reusable plastics to be incorporated into Ecoalf products, while the rest is recycled by Ecoembes, a waste processor (Figure 27.2). By 2019, 2600 fisherman from 45 Spanish ports were collecting more than 500 tonnes of waste. The initiative has since been extended to Thailand and Greece.

Figure 27.1   Because there is no planet B

TRANSPARENCY AND TRUST

A challenge that consumers face in making choices when it comes to sustainability is knowing which brands are more sustainable than others (Vogel 2007). Partly this is a result of the wide diversity of environmental and social labels, especially within clothing (such as Fair Trade, Better Cotton Initiative, PETA and bluesign), which consumers find hard to decipher, and partly this is as a result of brands not communicating their sustainability commitments. The latter comes about both because brands are not always confident in their claims and because they are unsure as to the benefits of communication. The result of this reticence is consumers are confused as to who they should trust.

Ecoalf knows that its customers buy its products both because of the quality and the ethos of sustainability. To convey these attributes, Ecoalf has become an activist brand that campaigns through education and events and encourages its customers to do likewise. It also tries to be open about the impacts of its products and publishes a sustainability report that is based on independent verification by BCOME, which measures systemic sustainability management against three criteria across the value chain: Planet (environmental initiatives), People (social and ethical initiatives) and Transparency (traceability initiatives). This system shows, in a credible way, the positive effects of Ecoalf's commitment, and indicates where further progress can be made. In this regard, Ecoalf is a good illustration of humble leadership (Iglesias et al., 2013) and continually works to improve itself. In a letter to employees and partners, during the height of COVID-19, Goyeneche noted, "We are not afraid to show our weaknesses, frustrations and challenges. We are not perfect and do not claim to be so."

Figure 27.2   Telling the story: 235 grams of fishing nets = 1 metre of Ecoalf fabric

CO-CREATING

Ecoalf is a small brand with five retail stores and over 1500 points of sale worldwide. However, key to the company's relevance is the influence it has on suppliers and other brands, as well as consumers. The trove of fabrics developed by Ecoalf are co-created together with suppliers. This is a process of exploration to both find new ways to recycle waste materials and to reduce the use of resources, such as water in production processes. Ecoalf is demanding in that it asks its suppliers to commit to specific sustainability standards, but it is also keen to listen and learn together with its partners. Those partners come from within the industry, but also include companies outside it, such as Spanish waste tyre company, Signus, who worked with Ecoalf to develop a recycling process that would provide sufficiently clean rubber to develop a powder that could be used to create glue-free, flip-flops.

As well as supply chain organizations, Ecoalf communicates its ideals by working with hotel chains and consumer brands, such as Gwyneth Paltrow's Gloop, Barneys of New York and Swatch – for whom it produced uniforms out of recycled cotton – and involves customers through monthly Act Now events in its stores. Alvarez-Ossorio Speith, says,

> I think collaboration is very important in sustainability and it's the way forward to be able to share, the talent that everybody has, the expertise and the know-how of each partner, and to bring it together to be able to accomplish the sustainable standards that we want.

A CONSCIENTIOUS BRAND - STAKEHOLDER APPROACH

A conscientious brand is guided by a transformative purpose and a set of guiding principles. It uses its distinctive capabilities to make strategic decisions that are fair, open and responsible. This indicates that such a brand must be true to itself, be accountable to all its stakeholders, including investors, employees, partners, society and the planet (Iglesias and Ind, 2016; Iglesias et al., 2020) and be willing to subject its decisions to public scrutiny. Measuring

Ecoalf against these attributes, we can see that it is an apt example of a brand with a con-science. It quite deliberately judges itself in terms of its impact on people, planet and profit and is convinced that there is a relationship and a hierarchy in these elements. The brand is not interested in growth for its own sake (although it has been growing steadily), but rather in providing products that can deliver an environmental benefit and that can influence others through their messages. The underlying assumption here is that decisions that are good for the planet will be also be good for the business. The conscientious approach also integrates with Ecoalf's position as a B Corporation, which means that it is certified as an organization that meets high standards in terms of its social and environmental performance, transparency and accountability to balance profit and purpose.

CONCLUSION

Ecoalf has become a persuasive advocate for sustainability because it has kept to its purpose and principles as it has evolved and avoided the temptation to cut corners and be expedient. Goyeneche knows that the integrity of the brand is a key asset in its journey to become an exemplar for other fashion businesses and to make sustainability a standard for all. That feeling of integrity is also important to customers. Purchasing an Ecoalf product emblazoned with 'Because there is no planet B', becomes an identity statement; an expression of not simply a fashion choice, but one's fundamental beliefs. This helps to bring the brand close to customers and, in turn, creates the potential for customers to become advocates for Ecoalf. Beyond the specifics of materials innovation and fashion design, it is the company-wide com-mitment to a cause that makes Ecoalf an authentic and appealing brand.

REFERENCES

Chouinard, Y., & Stanley V. (2012). *The responsible company: What we've learned from Patagonia's first 40 years.* Patagonia Books.

Iglesias, O., Ind, N., & Alfaro, M. (2013). The organic view of the brand: A brand value cocreation model. *Journal of Brand Management, 20*(8), 670–688

Iglesias, O., & Ind, N. (2016). How to be a brand with a conscience. In N. Ind and S. Horlings (Eds), *Brands with a conscience: How to build a successful and responsible brand.* Kogan Page, pp. 203–211.

Iglesias, O., Markovic, S., Bagherzadeh, M., & Singh, J. J. (2020). Co-creation: A key link between corporate social responsibility, customer trust, and customer loyalty. *Journal of Business Ethics, 163*(1), 151–166.

McKinsey & Global Fashion Agenda (2020). Fashion on climate: How the fashion industry can urgently act to reduce its greenhouse gas emissions. https://www.mckinsey.com/~/media/mckinsey/industries/retail/our%20insights/fashion%20on%20climate/fashion-on-climate-full-report.pdf (accessed 6 October 2020).

Reich, B. J., & Soule, C. A. A. (2016). Green demarketing in advertisements: Comparing "buy green" and "buy less" appeals in product and institutional advertising context. *Journal of Advertising, 45*(4), 441–458.

Soule, C. A. A., & Reich, B. J. (2015). Less is more: Is a green demarketing strategy sustainable? *Journal of Marketing Management, 31*(13-14), 1403–1427.

UN Alliance for Sustainable Fashion (2019). https://www.unenvironment.org/news-and-stories/press-release/un-alliance-sustainable-fashion-addresses-damage-fast-fashion (accessed 14 March 2019).

Vogel, D. (2007). *The market for virtue: The potential and limits of corporate social responsibility.* Brookings Institution Press.

Vos, J. (2009). Actions speak louder than words: Greenwashing in corporate America. *Notre Dame Journal of Law, Ethics & Public Policy, 23*, 673–697.

28. Sustainability as strategy: the case of Comwell Hotels

Kristian J. Sund and Rasmus Downes-Rasmussen

THE COMWELL GROUP

Comwell Hotels is a Danish family-owned hotel chain established in 1969. The group currently operates 16 hotels in Denmark, and two in Sweden. In 2019, the group signed an international branding franchise agreement with Wyndham Hotels & Resorts, covering Comwell's Aarhus hotel and the newly built Comwell Copenhagen Portside hotel and conference facilities, under the sub-brand Dolce by Wyndham. This new hotel is set to become the largest in the group with almost 500 rooms. Comwell Hotels has over 1000 permanent employees, and in 2019 had a turnover of DKK 867.6 million. Comwell introduced its meeting concept in Denmark in 1969, then called Scanticon, and in 1992 opened its first spa hotel in Denmark. Conferences and meetings are core business areas today. Among others, the group has a key supplier agreement with the Danish state for conferencing.

THE SUSTAINABILITY STRATEGY

The group has for many years had a focus on its wider social responsibilities. The logic behind this focus was, on the one hand, to attract and maintain employees, for example by offering attractive staff training opportunities. This resulted in Comwell being elected fourth among large Danish employers by Great Place to Work in 2013. On the other hand, it was to deliver the brand's customer promise, which at the beginning of the decade could be summarized as "Intimacy, Precision, Harmony". The idea was to deliver a highly professional, yet personalized service. At the same time, there was a focus on the efficient use of resources, and of living up to environmental responsibilities. Comwell thus adopted the voluntary eco-label scheme Green Key for some of its hotels as early as 2009.

These early initiatives laid the foundation for what was to come, and in 2016 it was decided by group management to intensify the focus on sustainability. A first sustainability strategy was developed, and around the same time a sustainability steering group was formed, comprised of CEO, COO, CCO, HR Director, and a Food and Beverages (F&B) Manager. A new mission was defined as follows: "Our mission is for us to be the industry's preferred sustainable hotel chain for our guests, employees and business partners". The mission was deliberately formulated in terms of customer preference, not in terms of any absolute measure of sustainability. The logic behind this was that sustainability initiatives themselves can easily be copied by competitors, and in fact this would even be welcomed, as it would ultimately benefit the environment. It is instead by developing unique resources and capabilities around sustainability, and by orchestrating these, that the company can build an advantage (Wu et al., 2012; Sund et al., 2018). Once established, Comwell's position in the mind of the customer is something that is difficult to copy, as it is the result of the sum of all the individual initiatives and activities carried out across the hotel group, as well as the branding and service efforts accompanying these.

The conceptual model for the strategy was inspired from the original Brundtland idea of combining economic growth with both social and environmental responsibility, where these go hand-in-hand (Brundtland Commission, 1987). The original definition of sustainability was thus to contribute to a development of the hotel business without compromising the ability of future generations to meet their own needs. Rather than treating the three objectives of economic, social, and environmental sustainability as separate, the model was to make operational changes that would contribute to all three at once. The following basic principles were adopted as part of the sustainability strategy:

- "We take responsibility for our resource consumption and minimise and reuse as much as we can.
- We focus on creating a balance and taking people and the environment into consideration every single day.
- We acquire new knowledge and new skills to carry out a sustainable conversion without compromising our guests' good experience."

IMPLEMENTATION

It was important to the steering group that the basic principles adopted in the strategy would rapidly be turned into operational action. To do this, it was decided that every area of operations would contribute with ideas for more sustainable practices. For example, within the F&B area, a policy was defined, according to which the group would prioritize local, organic, and seasonal produce. For example, in the case of seafood, this would be sourced mainly from Danish waters, and endangered species would be avoided, following the Marine Stewardship Council guidelines. Beverages would be moved towards organic variants, so that hotel bars and restaurants would carry mainly organic beers, wines, and sodas. Implementing this F&B policy required communicating the intention to all suppliers, which was done during 2016. The effect was that some suppliers would, in the end, be dropped, some would transition themselves over time towards supplying sustainable ingredients, whilst new suppliers would be found for products not available in organic or local variants from existing suppliers. The objective was whenever possible to engage in co-creation with suppliers to develop more sustainable solutions. Suppliers were thus involved in answering the question: "How do we introduce more sustainable and organic raw materials, without increasing the cost for customers?" For those suppliers that could meet this challenge, the group offered some degree of exclusivity, so that any increased costs for suppliers in terms of providing local and organic variants would be offset by the economies of scale of becoming a lead supplier for the whole group. The move resulted in Comwell earning in 2017 its first so-called "Økologisk Spisemærke i Bronze", an organic label controlled by the Danish Food Administration, rewarding restaurants that source between 30% and 60% of their ingredients spending from organic sources. The same year Comwell was awarded the Organic food award ("Årets Økopris") by Organic Denmark, an association representing Danish organic farmers, food companies, and consumers.

Within the HR department, a particular focus was on staff development. A partnership was made with a Danish hotel and restaurant school, to design and deliver a specialized further education programme for all staff during 2017 and 2018. Staff received training focused on sustainable operations, whilst frontline staff, such as sales or reception teams, focused more on sustainability communication. In terms of performance indicators, these were adjusted across the organization to reflect a balanced scorecard approach measuring not just financial results, but also resource usage, such as water, electricity, and heating; food waste and re-use; and the meeting of external criteria for a variety of labels, such as the aforementioned organic food label. The thinking was extended over time to all areas of operations, with housekeeping reducing the use of chemicals, towels and sheets swapped for new ones made of organic cotton, and so forth. In several cases the close work with suppliers allowed these suppliers to introduce new sustainable products onto the market that would be available to competitors as well, thereby benefiting both the supplier and the wider environment.

Today, Comwell Hotels are renowned for their extensive work within sustainability. The group's hotels are Green Key labelled, in addition to the organic cuisine label. Furthermore, the group adheres to the REFOOD label, which focuses on limiting food waste. This has been achieved by, for example, switching food portions towards more vegetables, and reducing meat portion sizes, whilst increasing the quality of meat. Energy use has meanwhile been reduced by over 20%, and there is a target to continue reducing energy use by 2% per year. Thanks to its sustainability policy and labels, the group has been able to win more conference tenders since an increasing number of institutional customers demand such policies as part of their own sustainability and responsibility drives. Finally, in 2019, Comwell was labelled Denmark's most sustainable hotel chain, a position it kept in 2020.

LESSONS LEARNT

Valuable lessons were learnt during the process of implementing the sustainability strategy. From an environmental perspective, implementing the strategy required a change of mindset and behaviours from all actors involved. For example, in addition to reducing food waste, it was necessary to start viewing waste as a resource. When a kitchen has leftovers from buffets and production, instead of throwing this away as garbage, chefs need to rethink about how these could be used as a resource and upcycled for new meals. There was initially some resistance from chefs, who were afraid of the consequences of the new strategy for their usual routines, or even for their jobs. Suppliers also needed to change perspective, and some suppliers were not able or willing to do so. One issue faced was bottlenecks when suppliers initially moved towards organic produce and other supplies.

Furthermore, it was necessary to keep the focus. It is easy to celebrate initial wins and forget that sustainability is not a goal that is ever completely reached. Instead, it is a mindset that needs to be constantly pursued if the group is to remain the most sustainable hotel chain, as viewed by the customer. It was necessary to keep measuring sustainability, keep setting new targets, and to focus on sustainability during the induction of new employees, so they too could contribute to the process.

From a social perspective, sustainability became a surprisingly positive creator of meaning for employees and even their families. This was also the case for some suppliers. This could be seen in measures of job satisfaction, which rose as employees became proud of what the group was achieving in terms of sustainability. Quickly the group achieved some of the highest job satisfaction scores in the industry. Employee turnover dropped as employees became more loyal towards the brand. Many employees became more aware of sustainability in their own personal lives as well, changing behaviours in their own households. It was also noted that the sustainability focus made it easier to attract new young talent. It was helpful that the group had a flat management structure, in which line managers and employees could take some degree of ownership over problems, and present local solutions to these. Policies within the different operational areas were developed in collaboration with employees, helping them to feel empowered.

From an economic perspective the big lesson was that social and environmental sustainability could be achieved with a neutral economic effect. Changing behaviours led to a general reduction in waste, a reduction in the use of resources, and an increase in re-use, reducing costs. For example, smaller portion sizes and less food waste in hotel restaurants created cost savings that neutralized the higher cost of sourcing local and organic raw materials. Furthermore, local suppliers of organic eggs, beers, and other products were able to gain in scale thanks to their close supplier relationship with the Comwell Group. For some of these local farmers and producers, this has resulted in an ability to achieve lower cost levels, making them competitive with multinational traditional non-organic suppliers. These suppliers have gone on to increase their market shares in other hotels, restaurants, and even supermarkets, converting other actors in society towards more nature and climate friendly consumption. Customer satisfaction scores have been on the rise since the implementation of the sustainability strategy as well.

Finally, it is worth noting that the strategy could not have been developed and implemented without the commitment and support of group management, who invested in training initiatives and facilitated the sharing of best practice. Headquarters also facilitated communication about sustainability both inside and outside the group, ensuring that both employees and guests are constantly reminded of the importance of sustainability, and of what Comwell is doing to achieve its aim of being recognized as the most sustainable hotel group in Denmark.

REFERENCES

Brundtland Commission (1987). *Our Common Future*. Oxford: Oxford University Press.
Sund, K. J., Barnes, S., & Mattsson, J. (2018). The IPOET matrix: Measuring resource integration. *Organizational Analysis*, *26*(5), 953–971.
Wu, Q., He, Q., Duan, Y., & O'Regan, N. (2012). Implementing dynamic capabilities for corporate strategic change toward sustainability. *Strategic Change*, *21*(5-6), 231–247.

29. Boat trip adventure changing the lives of thousands: the story of Song Saa Private Island

Ilia Gugenishvili and Nikolina Koporcic

HOW IT ALL STARTED

The Song Saa Private Island is a resort built on the twin islands of Koh Rong Archipelago. Constructed by an Australian couple, Melita Koulmandas and Rory Hunter, the mission of the resort is to offer luxury accommodation to visitors by being the frontrunner of sustainable tourism in the region. Song Saa is not only built and furnished with recycled materials but it also projects a deep commitment to sustainability in its daily operation; it conserves the environment and recycles water and waste. At the same time, the resort sustainably produces its own products, while purchasing locally sourced, seasonal, and wildlife-friendly ingredients to cook the delicacies of the local cuisine. In addition, supporting the community is at the heart of the enterprise; it offers employment and education opportunities to locals and supplies local schools and hospitals (www.songsaacollective.com, 2020a).

The story of this eco-friendly establishment started in 2005. It was on their boat trip adventure in Cambodia when Melita and Rory discovered the pristine islands of Koh Rong Archipelago. On their last day of travel, they chatted with the family in a fishing village and decided to dine together. Before their dinner was over, the family asked Melita and Rory whether they wanted to buy the islands – a question that would turn their lives upside down. The couple was already in love with the white sand beaches, blue waters, and friendly locals and could vividly see the potential of these islands. Besides, its price was a bargain at USD 15,000! A week later, Melita and Rory signed the contract and became the owners of two small islands: Koh Ouen (meaning "woman") and Koh Bong (meaning "man") (www.songsaacollective.com, 2020a).

The active construction of the resort started in February 2009, when the couple first cleaned the islands up. They personally witnessed the destructive consequences of over-fishing and the hardships of local people, suffering from extreme poverty. Thus, Melita and Rory developed the vision of sustainable luxury tourism that would benefit locals and conserve the natural beauty of the islands. To bring their vision to life, they consulted the locals of the Koh Rong Archipelago, as well as experts from the James Cook University in Australia, and set out to create a commercially successful, ethnically led integrated resort, where luxury tourism blends with the conservation, restoration, and improvement of the local environment and community. With that in mind, the concept of Song Saa was born (www.songsaacollective.com, 2020a).

> As the first company to own islands in Cambodia, we felt a deep sense of responsibility to protect the environment and local communities and set a benchmark for the local tourism industry", writes the couple (www.songsaacollective.com, 2020a).

This benchmark for the tourism and hospitality industry that shows responsibility to the environment and local communities, as they describe it, is indeed needed. By representing a major contributor to CO_2 and greenhouse gas emissions (Lenzen et al., 2018), wasting a massive amount of energy and water supplies, and producing waste and pollutions, hotels drastically harm the environment (Nilashi et al., 2019) and negatively contribute to climate change and global warming (Koçak et al., 2020). Besides, the tourism and hospitality industry has negative economic and socio-cultural consequences by increasing the dependency of locals on unstable and seasonal employment. It also causes imitation of Western values, intergeneration conflict and social tension, and increases the burden to women (Rai, 2017). Being aware of these issues, Melita and Rory decided it was time for a change.

SUSTAINABILITY OF THE SONG SAA PRIVATE ISLAND

Opened in 2012, the Song Saa Private Island (Figure 29.1) features 24 villas, each with its own private pool, on-site restaurant and bars, gym, spa centre with a large infinity pool, private beach, and other luxury facilities. In addition to these luxurious offerings for guests to unwind in, the resort takes the 360-degree approach for addressing environmental, economic, and socio-cultural aspects of sustainability. Sustainable development "meets the needs of the present without compromising the ability of future generations to meet their own needs" (Brundtland, 1987, p. 37), thus corresponding to the Triple Bottom Line (TBL) theory (Elkington, 1998, 2013) which focuses on economic, environmental, and social values that each firm adds or destroys with its operation. Implementing and following sustainability practices ensures the maintenance of the environment and good life quality for all, now and in the future, on- and off-land (Kim et al., 2019). The Song Saa Private Island tackles all the aspects of sustainability by viewing its operation through the lens of the United Nations' Sustainable Development Goals (SDGs)[1] of protecting the planet, ending poverty, and providing an equal opportunity for everyone to attain peace and prosperity. By offering a perfect mix of eco-friendly leisure and volunteering activities, high-quality relaxation, and luxurious accommodation, the resort proves that luxury and sustainability are not mutually exclusive.

Next, we present specific activities that Song Saa implements to achieve the SDGs.

Conserving

Conservation is of utmost importance for this low impact, eco-friendly establishment.

Right from the construction stage, Melita and Rory made sure the resort respects the environment. For example, in the places where they had to build pipes, they replanted the coral, rather than simply destroying it. As a result, the local ecosystem on and around the islands thrives, and a year after launching the construction, tiny seahorses appeared in the waters.

In addition, since the first day the resort was opened, staff collect plastic and clean the islands and waters twice a day. Guests are more than welcome to participate, which is something many of them do. The resort also provides ecotourism activities, such as kayaking and sailing, where the visitors can not only see how coral is grown and experience the mangrove forests (www.ampersandtravel.com, 2012) but also collect the debris and waste encountered in the water using the reclamation bags made from recycled fishing lines (www.songsaa.com, 2018). On some of the conservation tours, tourists visit local villages to learn more about the ongoing projects, such as the establishment of sustainable farming or waste management practices (www.ampersandtravel.com, 2012).

Figure 29.1   Song Saa Private Island

This is not all, as the resort also protects tropical marine life throughout the Cambodian coast-line. It conserves the sea turtles, coral, mangroves, and rare seagrass species. To learn about these projects, guests can visit the resort's Life Centre (www.songsaa.com, 2018)

Recycling

The resort is mostly built from recycled or locally and responsibly produced materials. The buildings, the brainchildren of Melita Koulmandas, are built with recycled timber or local sandstone, thus minimizing the transportation carbon emission (www.songsaa.com, 2019). Melita and Rory handpicked and salvaged timber and driftwood from the beaches, local factories, and demolition yards, transforming discarded fishing boats into flooring, disposed construction materials into décor and furniture, and oil drums into lamps (www.songsaa.com, 2019; www.thehoteljournal.com, 2020).

In addition, the entire island is fitted with a sewage and irrigation system, ensuring that 100% of waste is recycled and absolutely nothing enters the water. The wastewater system cleans the used water, which is reused for the toilets and irrigation, while the organic waste is being used as a fertilizer (www.songsaa.com, 2019; www.thehoteljournal.com, 2020).

To reduce plastic waste, Song Saa Private Island also encourages its staff and visitors to refill water bottles rather than buy new ones (www.songsaa.com, 2018).

Producing and Purchasing Local Products and Services

We saw the hardships of the local villages, who had no source of livelihood and no way to break out of the poverty cycle. We saw the opportunity for us to bring something to the community and to do something that would protect the Koh Rong Archipelago. (Melita and Rory, www.songsaacollective .com, 2020a)

Sticking to its original plan, Song Saa Private Island purchases ceramics, as well as decorative and ornamental pieces inspired by Cambodian culture, from local artisans. Most of these decorations are made of bamboo roots and driftwood washed out on neighbouring beaches (www .thehoteljournal.com, 2020).

The food produced and served on the island is mostly Cambodian, produced by raw ingredients purchased from the locals, who have adopted sustainable fishing and farming practices. Song Saa Foundation also organizes educational programmes to support and encourage locals to embrace organic and sustainable farming (www.songsaa.com, 2019; www.thehoteljournal .com, 2020). In addition, the resort itself produces some of the herbs, spices, and vegetables in its own organic gardens (www.thehoteljournal.com, 2020).

In addition to buying local products, the resort is committed to providing employment opportunities to local people. To assure ethnic, racial, and gender diversity in its workplace, job openings are advertised in places inhabited by the minority population and deliver suitable and non-discriminatory working terms and conditions to all, including the people with disabilities. Moreover, the company has a pay scale equity policy, which ensures liveable and fair wages, as well as insurances, paid vacations, and leaves to its team (Thorne, 2019).

Supporting Community

Collaborating and helping the local community does not only revolve around the above-mentioned activities.

In 2013, Rory and Melita established an NGO – the Song Saa Foundation – which raises funds to support hundreds of local schools and hospitals around the archipelago (www.songsaa .com, 2018). By closely collaborating with International Medical Relief (IMR), the foundation also established several health clinics across the archipelago, which provide healthcare to more than 3000 local people annually (www.songsaacollective.com, 2020c).

The resort offers its guests tours to the Prek Svay village, where they can learn about, observe, and participate in activities that support locals. Moreover, using the Boat of Hope missions, the resort reached over 3000 people since 2013 (www.songsaa.com, 2018) and conducted the "distribution of 6,000 school stationery items, 200,000 vitamins, 600 toothbrushes, 450 clothing items, 200 sports items, 250 mosquito nets, and 50 solar lamps to local communities" (www.songsaacollective.com, 2020b).

The Boat of Hope is also used in a Song Saa sea turtle programme that provides local children and adolescents with educational workshops to improve their eco-literacy and raise their awareness of the importance of protecting the environment (www.songsaacollective .com, 2020c). Finally, all sustainable practices of the Song Saa Private Island are summarized in Table 29.1.

Table 29.1   Sustainable practices of the Song Saa Private Island

Environmental	Economic	Socio-cultural
Eco-friendly and low impact building and furnishing	Purchasing locally produced materials, such as food, ceramics, and decorative pieces	Providing educational opportunities for tourists, such as conservation tours and visits to the Life Centre
Cleaning the islands and waters twice a day	Sustainably producing herbs, spices, and vegetables	Providing education opportunities to locals
Providing ecotourism activities, such as kayaking and sailing	Providing fair and non-discriminatory employment opportunities to locals	Establishing sustainable farming and waste management practices
Protecting tropical marine life throughout Cambodian coastline	Attracting international visitors to local villages	Establishing health clinics across the archipelago
		Supporting local schools and hospitals
Recycling and reusing the water		Giving access to doctors to local people
Contributing to the minimization of carbon dioxide emissions	Attracting international investors	
Using organic fertilizers		Distributing water filters throughout the archipelago to provide safe drinking water to locals
Creating Cambodia's first marine reserve		Helping locals to adopt sustainable farming practices
Contributing to the minimization of carbon dioxide emotion		Raising the awareness of local culture
Recycling materials, such as fishing lines, oil drums, wood, sandstone, and bottles		Providing medications, vitamins, hygiene items, clothes, solar lamps, and other sustainable products to locals

LOOKING TOWARDS THE FUTURE

Today, the importance of sustainable practices is even more profound as we face new global challenges. Although the current Covid-19 crisis has had a devastating impact on the hospitality and tourism industries, it uncovered new opportunities for social change. Thus, the way Song Saa Private Island and other establishments respond to current challenges, by re-evaluating and further improving their sustainable practices, may offer a brighter future for many.

Shifting its focus from international visitors to expats and locals, and establishing the necessary measures, the Song Saa Private Island managed to stay open during the uncertain times of the Covid-19 crises. They offer "a sanctuary where people craving to be reunited with friends and family may gather freely and celebrate" (www.remotelands.com, 2020).

In 2019, Song Saa Private Island received the "JUST label" as an acknowledgment of their efforts for the achievement of the SDGs (Figure 29.2).

We're proud to say that with the help of our partners, collaborators and volunteers, the Song Saa Foundation has had a positive impact upon our communities and our environment. In 2019 we were awarded a prestigious "JUST label" by the International Living Future Institute to showcase how we champion social and environmental equality. (Song Saa Private Island, www.songsaacollective.com, 2020b)

Encouraged by the recognition of its efforts, the company plans to continue following the already-established sustainable practices while planning to adopt new ones in the future:

> We've seen first-hand the power of business to drive positive societal change – particularly in frontier markets – and we're proud of the brand we've built along the way. We're now embarking on a series of new adventures that are unapologetically ambitious and unique in their aims and approach. We believe our upcoming Song Saa Reserve project at Banteay Srey is the next step in achieving our vision for a better future. (www.songsaa-collective.com, 2021)

Over the next five years, Song Saa and its sister NGO will introduce water catchment systems, institute a long-term coral nursery and grow 5000 more mangrove plants (www.songsaa -collective.com, 2020). Investments in the protection of marine life will bring back fish reserves, which will ultimately restore the livelihood of villagers (www.songsaa-privateisland .com, 2020). In addition, the Song Saa Private Island understands the importance of collaboration with other actors in achieving the SDGs. Thus, it plans not only to maintain relationships with existing partners, such as the local community, NGOs, IMR, and medical centres but also to establish new cooperations with carefully chosen partners. By following the TBL theory and focusing on a wide range of environmental, economic, and social issues, Song Saa will ultimately benefit not only itself but also the planet and society in general.

Figure 29.2   *JUST label of Song Saa Foundation*

NOTE

1.   https://www.un.org/development/desa/disabilities/envision2030.html

REFERENCES

Brundtland. (1987). *Report of the World Commission on Environment and Development: Our Common Future* (A/42/427). https://bit.ly/3hm0rSu

Elkington, J. (1998). Partnerships from cannibals with forks: The triple bottom line of 21st-century business. *Environmental Quality Management, 8*(1), 37–51.

Elkington, J. (2013). Enter the triple bottom line. In *The Triple Bottom Line*. Routledge, pp. 23–38.

Kim, Y. H., Barber, N., & Kim, D.-K. (2019). Sustainability research in the hotel industry: Past, present, and future. *Journal of Hospitality Marketing & Management, 28*(5), 576–620.

Koçak, E., Ulucak, R., & Ulucak, Z. Ş. (2020). The impact of tourism developments on CO2 emissions: An advanced panel data estimation. *Tourism Management Perspectives, 33*, 100611.

Lenzen, M., Sun, Y.-Y., Faturay, F., Ting, Y.-P., Geschke, A., & Malik, A. (2018). The carbon footprint of global tourism. *Nature Climate Change, 8*(6), 522–528.

Nilashi, M., Rupani, P. F., Rupani, M. M., Kamyab, H., Shao, W., Ahmadi, H., Rashid, T. A., & Aljojo, N. (2019). Measuring sustainability through ecological sustainability and human sustainability: A machine learning approach. *Journal of Cleaner Production, 240*, 118162.

Rai, D. B. (2017). Tourism development and economic and socio-cultural consequences in Everest Region. *Geographical Journal of Nepal, 10*, 89–104.

Thorne, B. (2019). *Song Saa Foundation Policies*. https://songsaa-collective.com/files_press/SSF_Policies.pdf

www.ampersandtravel.com. (2012). *The Story behind Song Saa Cambodia's First Private Island Resort*. https://www.ampersandtravel.com/blog/2012/the-story-behind-song-saa-cambodias-first-private-island-resort/#:~:text=AT%2022%3A A12-,The%20story%20behind%20Song%20Saa%2C%20Cambodia's%20first%20private%20island%20resort,their%20adopted%20home%20of%20Cambodia

www.remotelands.com. (2020). *Donald Wong of Song Saa on the Future of Travel in Cambodia*. https://bit.ly/3i7raCK

www.songsaacollective.com. (2020a). *Our Story*. https://songsaacollective.com/our-story

www.songsaacollective.com. (2020b). *Small Steps. Big Changes*. https://songsaacollective.com/our-impact

www.songsaacollective.com. (2020c). *United Nations Sustainable Development Goals*. https://songsaacollective.com/goals

www.songsaa-collective.com. (2020). *What We Do*. https://songsaa-collective.com/what-we-do

www.songsaa-collective.com. (2021). *The World of Song Saa*. https://songsaa-collective.com/collective

www.songsaa.com. (2018). *Why Choose Song Saa as an Eco-Friendly Holiday Destination*. https://www.songsaa.com/en/blog/2018/07/11/why-choose-song-saa-as-an-eco-friendly-holiday-destination/73-6/

www.songsaa.com. (2019). *The Sustainable Design of Song Saa*. https://www.songsaa.com/en/blog/2019/06/17/design/the-sustainable-design-of-song-saa/73-16/

www.songsaa-privateisland.com. (2020). *Song Saa Foundation Building Futures*. https://www.songsaa-privateisland.com/en/blog/2020/07/22/song-saa-foundation-building-futures/73-21/

www.thehoteljournal.com. (2020). *The World's Most Sustainable Hotels: Stay in Eco-friendly Style*. https://thehoteljournal.com/worlds-most-sustainable-hotels/

30. Doing business the sustainable 'Novo Nordisk Way'

Marija Sarafinovska and Yuqian Qiu

This case study is about Novo Nordisk, a well-known Danish brand working on changing the world of diabetes, obesity and hemophilia care as well as hormone replacement and growth hormone therapy. In the following sections, we aim to introduce Novo Nordisk and its key sustainability initiatives by analyzing and presenting relevant data from its official website, annual reports, books, and news articles.

Founded in 1923, Novo Nordisk positions sustainability as a core aspect of its strategy and its business decisions (Morsing et al., 2019). According to the World Commission on Environment and Development (WCED), sustainability refers to "development that meets the needs of the present without compromising the ability of future generations to meet their own needs" (WCED, 1987, p. 8). In this regard, Novo Nordisk makes every single decision according to this "Novo Nordisk Way" (Novo Nordisk, 2020b) and translates this decision-making philosophy into the "Triple Bottom line" (Novo Nordisk, 2020c) – a combined balance of the three dimensions of sustainability: environmental, social, and economic considerations. In the environmental dimension, Novo Nordisk aims to minimize the footprint that company activities leave on the environment. In the social dimension, Novo Nordisk conducts beneficial and fair business practices to both its employees and extended communities. In the economic dimension, Novo Nordisk focuses on the growth of the company and provides economic value to support future generations.

This is in line with the "Novo Nordisk Way" – behaving responsibly towards all stakeholder groups, including customers, employees, communities, suppliers and investors (Novo Nordisk, 2020b). Novo Nordisk defines its success by the solutions it brings to society in benefiting the health and well-being of people. It aims to accelerate the prevention of chronic diseases and broaden access to affordable care for patients worldwide. In the letter, *Making good progress*, Helge Lund, Chair of the Board of Directors of Novo Nordisk, describes Novo Nordisk's responsibility to sustainable development (Novo Nordisk, 2019).

> As a large company, Novo Nordisk also has large responsibilities. Society is expecting more from business to help solve challenges such as bending the curve on diabetes, climate change and environmental degradation. I believe Novo Nordisk, with its purpose and commitment to pursuing a more sustainable development, is well placed to rise to the challenge.

CHALLENGES AND POTENTIAL SOLUTIONS – ENVIRONMENTAL ASPECTS

Since 2004, Novo Nordisk has published integrated annual reports, including its environmental performance, i.e., resource use, CO_2 emissions and waste handling. In these annual reports, the company always addresses the 17 universal Global Goals and 169 targets. Novo Nordisk puts a focus on an integrated approach implemented through partnerships and involvement of the public and private sectors, across the multiple goals. The company believes that this involvement is crucial in achieving its goals and targets. Novo Nordisk reviews its contribution to each of the 17 Global Goals whilst putting special emphasis on health and improving the well-being of people living with non-communicable diseases. Novo Nordisk's approach is based on three main principles of the sustainability development goals (SDGs): universality, integration and transformation. The first principle, universality, focuses on the fact that the Goals apply to every nation and sector. The second, integration, centers on the fact that all SDGs are inter-connected in a system and that success will not be achieved in the world until all the SDGs have been implemented. The third principle, transformation focuses on the fact that achieving the SDGs involves making big, fundamental changes in how people live on Earth.

The company concluded from its assessments that the main impact could be on SDG 3 (Good health and well-being) and SDG Goal 12 (Responsible consumption and production). According to United Nations Development Programme's (UNDP's) SDG Goal 3, most countries, especially poorer ones, have an insufficient amount of resources, including medical supplies and healthcare workers, to meet their health-related demands (*Sustainable development goals*, 2021a). Good health and well-being are essentially important to sustainable development. Accordingly, Goal 3 aims at improving life and well-being for people at all ages. Further, SDG Goal 12 aims to ensure economic growth and sustainable development. This requires a reduction of ecological footprint by changing the ways that goods and resources are produced and consumed (*Sustainable development goals*, 2021a, 2021b).

Moreover, in 2018, Novo Nordisk was awarded a performance score 'A' on the CDP Climate A list. As a not-for-profit charity that focuses on establishing a sustainable economy together with companies, cities and regions, CDP provides the world with a "gold standard" of environmental reporting on corporate initiatives on environmental protection (CDP, 2020).

However, the company's CO_2 emissions are still increasing, especially when we take into account transportation. A large amount of its products ends up in landfills after their use. This puts the pharmaceutical company in the frontline on the biggest environmental issues: climate change, water and resource scarcity, plastic waste, and pollution. In order to tackle these challenges, the company adopted a circular mindset – designing reusable/recyclable products, eliminating waste, and working with suppliers who share the same ambitions. Further, the company has a target of reaching zero environmental impact by 2030. Some of the major endeavors of Novo Nordisk are listed in Table 30.1.

Going 100% Renewable Power

With Novo Nordisk's investment in energy optimization and shift to renewable energy, they have cut carbon emissions from their production sites by circa 60% since 2004. In 2015, the company joined RE100, a global initiative of businesses, which is committed to using 100% renewable power and working towards increasing the demand and delivery of renewable energy (The Climate Group, 2020a, 2020b). The company's share of electricity from renewable sources was 78% in 2016, 79% in 2017, and 77% in 2018.

Table 30.1   *Sustainability endeavors – environmental aspects*

Endeavors	Effects or arrangements	Future visions
Going 100% renewable power	• Carbon emissions cut by circa 60% since 2004 • 100% renewable electricity across global production	"Circular for Zero"
Designing eco-friendly products	• Designing for sustainable materials, no waste in production, and recycling after use	50% of raw materials will be sustainable by 2030
Working with suppliers with the same ambitions	• Business partners encouraged to optimize use of all relevant resources (energy, water, chemicals, raw materials) and limit use of scarce resources. • Avoid use of hazardous materials where possible • Engage in reuse/recycle activities	Closer partnerships towards building sustainability
Water consumption and management	• Treat all wastewater in biological-chemical waste-water treatment plants • Local water innovation projects to i.e., increase water use and reuse efficiency	Further management on water consumption
CO_2 emission management	• A decrease of 54% in 2019	Further decrease in CO_2 emissions
Chemicals	• Finding non-hazardous alternatives • Supporting the use of safe chemicals	Further focus on EU REACH regulation and chemical management

In 2019, there was a decrease of 3% in the company's energy consumption for operations in comparison with 2018. Energy consumption for production decreased by 2% due to reduced energy use in order to produce diabetes products. Moreover, in 2019, 76% of the power used at its production sites was produced using renewable energy, a decline from 77% in 2018. This is mainly due to lower power consumption at Denmark's largest production site, which that operates on wind power. Further, in 2020, Novo Nordisk managed to achieve its goal of using 100% renewable electricity across its global production. Its production sites in Denmark use wind electricity, in China it operates on renewable wind energy, and in Brazil, hydropower. Moreover, in 2020, it switched to solar power in the US.

After the RE100 achievement, Novo Nordisk is now pursuing to reach zero CO_2 emissions from all transport and operations by 2030, which is part of its environmental strategy "Circular for Zero". When asked about targets, Kenneth Strømdahl, SVP for device R&D in 2019 stated (Kryl, 2019):

> We know, of course, the final target: zero.

Designing Eco-friendly Products

Novo Nordisk is redesigning products to reduce waste. From raw materials to the way they are put together, the company is working towards solving the end-of-life challenge so that materials can be reused and recycled. According to its Circular Design guidelines, Novo Nordisk is focusing on products that have the lowest environmental impact over their intended lifetime (Novo Nordisk, 2020a). Moreover, the company is improving products' lifetime impact by making a life-cycle assessment of the current products or comparable products and identifying the largest contributors to the environmental footprint.

Designing for sustainable materials

To leverage circular material flow, the target is that 50% of raw materials will be sustainable by 2030. This includes carbon footprint and sustainable origins in material selection. The company is also designing for sustainable materials to avoid the use of fossil-based materials and reduce its carbon footprint. Further, the company aims to understand which materials have the lowest carbon footprint; whether materials with bio-based or recycled content are available and whether they can be recycled after use.

Designing for no waste in production

The biggest impact on process selection and waste generation during production is made during the design phase. In its Circular Design guidelines, Novo Nordisk discusses circular production regarding both existing and future devices (Novo Nordisk, 2020a). Accordingly, the most value from recycling can be obtained through small recycling loops and through a short supply chain from waste to new product. In order to design for no waste in production, the company focuses on designing out waste by eliminating scrap from component manufacturing, ensuring a long shelf life of modules and optimizing volume utilization of packaging. Further, it focuses on selecting the processes with the lowest energy and material consumption per unit, designing for internal recycling by selecting recyclable materials and enabling an efficient separation of material types.

Designing for recycling after use

As many of the company's products end up in landfills, which is a waste of resources and a cause of pollution, it is key to take responsibility for the end-of-life of products. Hence, Novo Nordisk also focuses on designing products for recycling in target markets.

Working with Suppliers with the Same Ambitions

The company recognizes that many of its business partners operate in different legal and cultural environments. However, the company only engages with business partners that meet its standards, as it is through collaboration and partnerships that it can advance its ethical, social and environmental performance along the supply chain. Similarly, the collaboration aims to embed circular thinking across the value chain and switch to circular procurement and sourcing.

Moreover, Novo Nordisk's business partners are to comply with all of the environmental regulations applicable to them. All required environmental licenses, permits, registration of information and restrictions should be obtained and their reporting and operational requirements followed. The company's business partners are expected to have systems in place to ensure safe handling, storage, movement, disposal, reuse, recycling of raw materials, waste, emissions and wastewater discharges.

Novo Nordisk's partners are also expected to ensure an effective protection on the ground and that they have systems in place to prevent and mitigate accidental spills and releases in the environment. They should also disclose and document any use of conflict minerals from a country that has financed or benefited armed groups if such minerals are relevant to the functionality of the final product manufactured by Novo Nordisk. In order to achieve the above, the business partners are encouraged to optimize the use of all relevant resources, i.e. energy, water, chemicals and raw materials, and limit the use of scarce resources. More specifically, they should avoid use of hazardous materials, where possible, and engage in reuse/recycle activities.

Table 30.2   Sustainability endeavors – social aspects

Endeavors	Effects or arrangements	Future visions
Cities Changing Diabetes	• Established in over 30 cities globally: reaching more than 150 million people for type 2 diabetes prevention	Reduce rate of obesity by 25% by 2045
Working at Novo Nordisk	• Promoting work–life balance	Attracting talents towards a sustainable business
Access to care and affordability	• Lower human insulin price policy covering 76 countries, i.e., Least Developed Countries	Continuously providing access to care and affordability
World Diabetes Foundation	• Commitments of DKK 1.69 billion to Foundation for period until 2024	Continuous financial commitment
Children with type 1 diabetes	• In 208 clinics across 14 low- and middle-income countries, providing medical care, insulin and supplies to over 26,000 children	To reach 100,000 children by 2030
Preventing childhood obesity	• Partnership with UNICEF to address environments promoting obesity	Further change how the world perceives, prevents and treats obesity

CHALLENGES AND POTENTIAL SOLUTIONS – SOCIAL ASPECTS

Chronic diseases such as type 2 diabetes and obesity have disturbed people's lives for decades. Type 2 diabetes can cause symptoms such as excessive thirst, tiredness, unintentional weight loss, and blurred vision. People with type 2 diabetes tend to have higher risks of developing serious complications with their eyes, heart, and nerves (Diabetes UK, 2020). Likewise, obesity is often related to health problems such as type 2 diabetes, heart diseases, and certain types of cancer. Although some of the chronic diseases are due to inevitable factors such as individual genetics, Novo Nordisk believes that doing nothing to prevent the chronic diseases would eventually result in more people suffering. Therefore, preventing chronic diseases is not about improving the business, but helping the global healthcare systems have a sustainable approach and helping the world have a sustainable future (Novo Nordisk, 2020c). Some of the major endeavors of social sustainability activities are listed in Table 30.2.

Preventing Chronic Diseases

Cities Changing Diabetes
Since two-thirds of people with type 2 diabetes live in cities, how urban lives are structured largely influences people's lives, and considerably increases people's vulnerability to type 2 diabetes. In order to address the social and cultural factors that influence urban lives and type 2 diabetes vulnerability, in 2014 Novo Nordisk coined "urban diabetes" to describe this situation and launched the program "Cities Changing Diabetes" (Cities Changing Diabetes, 2020). In this program, together with University College London and Steno Diabetes Center Copenhagen, Novo Nordisk established more than 100 partnerships to support research and build policies to bring positive interventions and influences to urban lives and to prevent type 2 diabetes in the long run.

Currently, Novo Nordisk's Cities Changing Diabetes is partnered with over 30 cities around the world, reaching more than 150 million people for type 2 diabetes prevention. Accordingly, Novo Nordisk has launched various engagement tools, e.g., the Cities Changing Diabetes Briefing Books to provide practitioners in partner cities with prevalent challenges, common understandings, and practical actions on fighting diabetes. Currently, the program has established network across the globe, including North America (i.e., Houston), South America (i.e., Buenos Aires), Europe (i.e., Berlin, Copenhagen), Africa (Johannesburg), and Asia (i.e., Beirut, Beijing, Seoul). Houston, for example, has been a part of the program since 2014. As a city filled with concrete highways, only 1.5% of residents walk or bike to work, Houston is reported to have one of the highest obesity rates in the country. Statistics show that if the population's weight can remain within the distribution level in 2017, the rate of obesity can be reduced by 25% and nearly 150,000 cases of type 2 diabetes can be prevented by 2045. This can possibly save around 1.5 million US dollars in healthcare expenses. Accordingly, Novo Nordisk has focused on enhancing diabetes prevention awareness and has launched the Faith and Diabetes Initiative. Various organizations collaborated to work towards the common goal – preventing type 2 diabetes by enhancing general awareness and education on diabetes.

Driving a sustainable business

Apart from the great effort in preventing type 2 diabetes, Novo Nordisk also invested greatly in preventing childhood obesity (Novo Nordisk, 2020e). Currently, over 40 million children under five are obese and these children are at high risk of growing into obese adults and developing type 2 diabetes in later stages of their lives. Preventing childhood obesity has encountered many challenges, including the emotional difficulties of communicating with children, poor socialization, and stigmatization. In order to achieve the long-term goal of preventing childhood obesity and type 2 diabetes, Novo Nordisk has partnered with UNICEF to address environments that promote obesity (UNICEF, 2019).

Working at Novo Nordisk

With over 44,000 employees around the world, Novo Nordisk has the motto for all employees: "Together, we are life-changing" (Novo Nordisk, 2020d). The company has positioned sustainability at the core of its business and highlighted individual responsibilities on building sustainability. Internally, Novo Nordisk promotes work–life balance, as it believes that life is about balancing different stages of lives and careers. A broad variety of life situations are considered by Novo Nordisk and the company has strived to make sure that each employee is able to maintain a balance between work and life (Novo Nordisk, 2020d).

> We are inspired by life in all its forms and shapes, ups and downs, opportunities and challenges. From our colleagues in the lab, working to change lives through pioneering breakthrough treatments, to our colleagues putting sustainability at the core of our processes and working to prolong the life of our planet, this mission to improve lives is at the core of our every action.

Access to Care and Affordability

Millions of diabetes and rare blood disorders patients do not have access to medicine when in need. Possible reasons include the cost of medication or the cost of travelling to their GPs and/or pharmacies, which may cause time away from work and result in potential lost pay. In more extreme conditions, these patients have little or no access to doctors, healthcare clinics or access to insulin and related medicines. In reality, only a fraction of diabetic patients are able to receive treatment. It is, among other relevant stakeholders, in pharmaceutical companies' power, to close this gap so that patients have access to care and medications. Novo Nordisk has an ambition to provide access to the medicines available, for the largest number of people living with diabetes, rare blood diseases and rare endocrine disorders.

Children with type 1 diabetes

In many of the poorest countries, type 1 diabetes in children is a huge issue as many of these children die at a very young age. In 208 clinics across 14 low- and middle-income countries, Novo Nordisk ensures life-saving insulin and care for children with type 1 diabetes. Nowadays, the program is providing medical care, insulin and supplies to over 26,000 children. The company is planning to expand this program and reach 100,000 children by 2030.

In the poorest settings, the unfortunate reality is that when diabetes hits medicines are often not available or affordable. In low- and middle-income countries, Novo Nordisk focuses on the most vulnerable diabetes patients. In two-thirds of the countries where the company operates, it has established affordability and access programs to help patients in need. The company has made a commitment to provide low-cost insulin in its product portfolio, and to produce and make human insulin available for the upcoming years (Novo Nordisk, 2021).

Within its Defeat Diabetes strategy, Novo Nordisk is lowering the ceiling price for drugs in low- and middle-income countries. It is also expanding affordability programs in the United States and other parts of the world. In 2001, the company launched a policy to lower human insulin's cost in the most resource-constrained countries. Nowadays, the policy covers 76 countries. It is supplying human insulin to Least Developed Countries (LDCs) as defined by the United Nations, other low-income countries defined by the World Bank, middle-income countries in which large low-income populations lack sufficient health coverage, and specific humanitarian organizations.

The Access to Medicine Index, 2018, analyses how 20 of the world's largest pharmaceutical companies are addressing issues regarding access to medicine in 106 low- to middle-income countries for 77 diseases, conditions and pathogens. This index evaluates the world's largest research-based pharmaceutical companies on their actions to improve access to medicine, accounting for 70% of global pharmaceutical revenues. The companies are selected based on factors such as market capitalization and the importance of their products and pipelines. In 2018, Novo Nordisk was in sixth position, regarding its efforts in diabetes, a disease covered by the Index. According to this Index, Novo Nordisk is showing strong management structures for access and exhibits robust performance in applying good practice in donation programs as well as capacity building initiatives.

Novo Nordisk's contribution in promoting access to care is also illustrated by its continuous financial commitment (i.e., DKK 1.69 billion for the period until 2024) to the World Diabetes Foundation, which was established by Novo Nordisk in 2002 as an independent trust dedicated to prevention and treatment of diabetes in developing countries.

CHALLENGES AND POTENTIAL SOLUTIONS – ECONOMIC ASPECTS

Novo Nordisk has put the economic dimension of sustainability as a core of its business. It is incorporating climate-related disclosures, as per The Task Force on Climate-related Financial Disclosures (TCFD, 2020b) recommendations, into its Annual Reports. TCFD develops consistent, voluntary, climate-related economic risk disclosures for use by companies in providing information to investors, lenders, insurers, and other stakeholders. TCFD considers risks associated with climate change and what constitutes effective financial disclosures across the industries. This is in alignment with the company's strategy to conduct business in an environmentally, socially and economically responsible way. By incorporating TCFD recommendations, Novo Nordisk assures investors that it takes climate change seriously and works proactively in understanding the risks and opportunities relating to it (TCFD, 2020a).

CONCLUSION

As illustrated above, Novo Nordisk is an excellent example of an organization that positions sustainability as a core element of its strategy, and integrates it in all business decisions. In order to operationalize the sustainability concept, Novo Nordisk has adopted the "Novo Nordisk Way" (Novo Nordisk, 2020b) as a key operating tool and followed the philosophy of "Triple Bottom Line", which combines the three dimensions of sustainability: environmental, social, and economic (Novo Nordisk, 2020c).

First, the company is focusing on an ambitious target of 100% renewable electricity across global production, aiming for "Circular for Zero" by 2030, and another goal which will ensure that 50% of the company's raw materials are sustainable by 2030. Novo Nordisk also encourages business partners to optimize the use of all relevant and scarce resources as well to engage in recycling activities. The company's focus on greenhouse gas emissions has led to a performance score 'A' on the CDP Climate A list (CDP, 2020). Second, Novo Nordisk endeavors to prevent chronic diseases around the world and to help global healthcare systems have a sustainable approach. Internally, Novo Nordisk promotes a work environment that values work–life balance to attract the talents to establish a sustainable business. Third, Novo Nordisk always focuses on the economic growth of the organization to provide economic value to society.

REFERENCES

CDP (2020). *CDP: Disclosure, insight, action.* Retrieved from https://www.cdp.net/en (last accessed: January 1, 2021).

Cities Changing Diabetes (2020). *The Cities Changing Diabetes programme.* Retrieved from https://www.citieschangingdiabetes.com/about-us/programme.html (last accessed: November 16, 2020).

Diabetes UK (2020). What are the signs and symptoms of diabetes? Retrieved from https://www.diabetes.org.uk/diabetes-the-basics/diabetes-symptoms (last accessed: November 16, 2020).

Kryl, C. (2019). *The business case for sustainability in healthcare.* Retrieved from https://matter.health/posts/the-business-case-for-sustainability-in-healthcare/ (last accessed: September 8, 2020).

Morsing, M., Oswald, D., & Stormer, S. (2019). The ongoing dynamics of integrating sustainability into business practice: The case of Novo Nordisk A/S. In G. G. Lenssen & N. C. Smith (Eds.), *Managing Sustainable Business* (pp. 637–669). The Netherlands: Springer.

Novo Nordisk (2019). *Novo Nordisk annual report 2019*. Retrieved from https://www.novonordisk.com/content/dam/Denmark/HQ/investors/irmaterial/annual_report/2020/Novo-Nordisk-Annual-Report-2019.pdf (last accessed: September 8, 2020).

Novo Nordisk (2020a). *Circular design guideline*. Retrieved from https://novonordiskinnovationchallenge.com/docs/Circular%20design%20guideline_short%20version_02.pdf (last accessed: September 9, 2020).

Novo Nordisk (2020b). *Principles, positions and policies*. Retrieved from https://www.novonordisk.com/sustainable-business/Reporting-and-transparency/principles-positions-and-policies.html (last accessed: January 21, 2021).

Novo Nordisk (2020c). *Who we are*. Retrieved from https://www.novonordisk.com/about/who-we-are.html (last accessed: January 21, 2021).

Novo Nordisk (2020d). *Working at Novo Nordisk*. Retrieved from https://www.novonordisk.com/careers/working-at-novo-nordisk.html (last accessed: January 21, 2021).

Novo Nordisk (2020e). Retrieved from https://www.novonordisk.com/sustainable-business.html (last accessed: September 8, 2020).

Novo Nordisk (2021). *Access & affordability*. Retrieved from https://www.novonordisk.com/sustainable-business/access-and-affordability.html (last accessed: February 1, 2021).

Sustainable development goals. United Nations Development Programme (2021a). Retrieved from https://www.undp.org/sustainable-development-goals#good-health. (last accessed: August 19, 2021).

Sustainable development goals. United Nations Development Programme (2021b). Retrieved from https://www.undp.org/sustainable-development-goals#responsible-consumption-and-production. (last accessed: August 19, 2021).

TCFD (2020a). *Climate related financial disclosures*. Retrieved from www.novonordisk.com/sustainable-business/zero-environmental-impact/climate-related-financial-disclosures.html (last accessed: September 8, 2020).

TCFD (2020b). *Task Force on Climate-Related Financial Disclosures: TCFD – about*. Retrieved from www.fsb-tcfd.org/about/ (last accessed: September 8, 2020).

The Climate Group (2020a). *Novo Nordisk achieves RE100 target of 100% renewable power*. Retrieved from www.theclimategroup.org/news/novo-nordisk-achieves-re100-target-100-renewable-power (last accessed: September 8, 2020).

The Climate Group (2020b). *RE100 leadership awards shortlist: Companies going beyond on clean energy*. Retrieved from www.theclimategroup.org/news/re100leadership-awards-shortlist-companies-going-aboveand-beyond-clean-energy (last accessed: September 8, 2020).

UNICEF (2019). *The state of the world's children 2019*. Retrieved from https://www.unicef.org/reports/state-of-worlds-children-2019 (last accessed: November 16, 2020).

WCED, S. W. S. (1987). World commission on environment and development. *Our common future*, *17*(1), 1–91.

31. Sustainability in the chemical industry through an industrial spin-off: the case of Apricot

Miguel Saiz García

INTRODUCTION

Apricot is a new project currently under deployment, and born as a spin-off industrial business initiated by Marc Fargas, an executive with more than 30 years of experience at Ercros. This means that the project was originated by someone who has an in-depth knowledge of the target companies. It is not an external offering made by a third company, but a project originated from the inside out. Ercros is an industrial group headquartered in Barcelona (in the Spanish region of Catalonia), which has a hundred-year tradition and is diversified into three business areas: Chlorine Derivatives; Intermediate Chemicals; and Pharmaceuticals. It is currently the largest Spanish basic chemicals company.

Despite the fact that this case study will focus on the Apricot project, it is important to mention that Ercros's interest in becoming an environmentally friendly company did not happen overnight. As a recent example, in October 2018 the company was given an award[1] for its commitment to the environment, after ten years of uninterrupted presence in the European Eco-Management and Audit Scheme (EMAS). EMAS is a voluntary registration scheme driven by the European Union, and its mission is to guarantee corporations' commitment to the environment, and to certify their correct action, credibility, and transparency. Ercros has continuously engaged in social and environmental initiatives. As an example, one can mention the company's sharing of lessons learned about sustainable water management to the audience at the International Integrated Water Cycle Show held in November 2018.[2]

Company Mission and Benefits Realized

The mission of Apricot is the production and sale of thermal energy (in the form of steam) originating from an alternative fuel, and coming from non-fossil resources. The steam production will consist of a biomass boiler that is located inside the facilities of the customers. The raw material (wood chips) is processed by a strategic supplier at a separate plant, which will provide the chips to the different boilers located inside the customers' facilities.

The target customers of Apricot are the industries where there is a need for steam as an enabler for their processes. Within the chemical industry, steam is the main element of caloric contribution to industrial processes. Steam, like other utilities, is necessary but is not part of the core know-how of these companies, which are focused on the production of their portfolio (chlorine derivatives, such as ammonia, hydrochloric acid, potassium carbonate and others). Thus, steam production is not their focus, but an indispensable utility in their production process. For this reason, there is a widespread trend in outsourcing any service that does not correspond to the core business, in order to maintain the focus of the staff and their productive processes.

The global benefits originated by the Apricot business model are:

i. The application of circular economy principles implemented by recycling wasted wood. For example, it is estimated that, just in Catalonia, there are more than 200 kilotons of wood that could be recovered per year.[3] This means that a waste material that implies important disposal costs and would potentially become a contaminant is instead used as an energy source for steam creation.

ii. The subsequent saving (estimated by 25%) to the end customer (first, chemical industries) owing to a lower price per ton of steam, while remaining profitable for Apricot.

iii. The consideration of carbon neutrality compared with the use of fossil fuels. Due to Apricot's procurement method for steam production, it can currently be considered as carbon neutral according to the IPCC (Intergovernmental Panel on Climate Change), and therefore this generates an additional saving in CO_2 emission allowances.

iv. A lower exposure to potential cost fluctuations in energetic costs that are currently tied to petrol prices and the potential increases in the CO_2 allowance costs (which can, for example, be identified at the 2019 State of the EU ETS Report,[4] where a steady increase in EU ETS price can be seen from 2017 until 2019).

v. A decrease in the contribution to net CO_2 emissions, which is one of the most important strategic drivers at Apricot's target customers.

vi. An increase in community acceptance of the operational activities at the locations where Apricot and its customers are operating. This is achievable through a proper communication strategy and Green Deal environmental branding. That is, to communicate and promote environmental core values, in connection with Apricot and the customer's brands.

Market Assessment and Opportunity Verification

Apricot's value proposal is primarily aimed at the chemical industry, which in Europe reached a turnover of more than €710,000 million,[5] which is the total addressable market considered. However, the market in Spain is €42,000 million. The Spanish steam consumption estimate is short over 10 million tons per year, which would mean a current cost of potentially €200 million. This is considered the serviceable available market.

The project will start with the Chemical Industry based in Tarragona, which accounts for 50% of the whole production in Catalonia (which is 25% of the Spanish total). Current estimations of steam consumption at the chemical industry in Tarragona are almost 2 million tons per year, meaning a maximum cost of currently €40 million – being the serviceable obtainable market to which this project will be initially addressed.

To better evaluate the potential of this obtainable market, a survey was done of the Executives at the Chemical Industry Area of Tarragona (15 companies). From those, 86% stated that they would be interested in an alternative such as the one Apricot is offering.

Although the total potential could reach 2 million tons per year, a conservative scenario has been set, with an estimated initial production of 0.37 million tons per year during the first two years, 0.44 during the two following years, and 0.9 from year five onward.[6] Despite this conservative scenario, it is expected that the breakeven point will be reached in less than 12 months of operation.

Although this could have been an internal investment project inside an organization, it has been identified as a replicable and scalable business model that can take advantage of the economies of scale. Therefore, it is going to be independent from the beginning and is expected to be financed 30% by the investors and 70% by bank credits. It is expected to have a three-year payback period

Operational Model

There will be a steam producing plant inside the customer facilities. In some cases, depending on the skills of the existing staff, the employees could be shared or there is also the option that Apricot employees are the ones taking over the operation of the steam producing plant. In either case, it will imply one operator per shift, plus two multi-purpose operators (seven in total). Maintenance, logistics and health and safety support would be outsourced and be present at the customer plant. The customers are renting the land, as well as granting access to water, communications, electricity, and others.

The governance of Apricot can be handled by a Managing Director, who could be the Plant Director and who would report about the steam producing business to a Board from company property side. This business model is not new, and it replicates the governance model of many co-generation plants operating at the same sites. In addition, maintenance, logistics, HR and legal are to be outsourced. Some of these could also be shared with the customer organizations.

The availability of raw material is key to the continuity of operation. The primary source is planned through road transport and will be prioritized to establish a stable flow of materials from frequent suppliers. However, alternative transports are also being investigated to have potential spot buys in high volumes with even more competitive prices. It is not expected to have fluctuations in the steam consumption, and the estimate is 40 tons of steam per hour, which demands about ten wood chip tons per hour. It will be planned to have five days of stock (1000 tons) stored in a silo. This will imply a need for 13 trucks of supply per day.

There is also an advantage in that the wood chips are intended for exclusively industrial use. The reason is that domestic use is more sensitive to the wood quality, and the potential for recyclability is limited. However, industrial boilers are more tolerant and allow an extended use of recycled woods, leading to an even higher environmental benefit. This could potentially lead to the interest of several waste management companies in participating because the business models of waste management companies and Apricot are very similar.

One important complementary subsystem that must be connected to the boilers is the water treatment plant. Therefore, it is advantageous that this is currently available to the customers' companies, which can share this plant and therefore mitigate the initial need for investment.

CONCLUSION AND FUTURE EXPECTATIONS

This example shows how advancements in technology are enabling better industrial processes that are becoming profitable. Another conclusion is that well-established industrial companies are ready to venture into complementary businesses which, despite not being at the core of their technical know-how, are contributing to a greener society.

Although in the first years of operation, many resources and management can be shared, there is a high likelihood that some of the roles (such as an Account Manager, centered in the business) will become independent and serve all potential customers that are already expressing their interest in contracting Apricot's services.

ACKNOWLEDGEMENTS

I would like to thank Marc Fargas for sharing this interesting project with me and allowing me to write this summary, which I expect will be one of many examples we will all be seeing in the upcoming years in terms of contributing to the 17 Sustainable Development Goals in our everyday lives, businesses, and organizations.

NOTES

1. The Ercros factory in Tortosa won an award for its commitment to the environment: http://www.ercros.es/index.php?option=com_content&view=article&id=2303:he-ercros-factory-in-tortosa-awarded-for-its-commitment-to-the-environment&catid=54&lang=en&Itemid=1495
2. Conference on Ercros's sustainable water management: http://www.ercros.es/index.php?option=com_content&view=article&id=2344:ercros-model-of-sustainable-water-management&catid=54&lang=en&Itemid=1495
3. Precat20 - Programa general de prevención y gestión de residuos y recursos de Cataluña 2020: http://residus.gencat.cat/web/.content/home/ambits_dactuacio/planificacio/precat20_novembre15/PRECAT20_doc-principal_sigov-cast.pdf
4. 2019 State of the EU ETS Report: https://www.i4ce.org/wp-core/wp-content/uploads/2019/05/2019-State-of-the-EU-ETS-Report.pdf
5. The German Chemical Industry in Figures (includes worldwide numbers): https://www.vci.de/vci-online/die-branche/zahlen-berichte/chemical-industry-in-figures-online.jsp
6. The estimates given are intended to express a realistic order of magnitude in an initiative of this nature, although the exact quantification may differ due to the future project evolution.

Index

Printed and bound by CPI Group (UK) Ltd, Croydon, CR0 4YY

16/04/2025

14658390-0003